COMPUTERS, COMMUNICATIONS, AND INFORMATION

A USER'S INTRODUCTION

COMPREHENSIVE VERSION

SEVENTH EDITION

Sarah E. Hutchinson

Stacey C. Sawyer

Irwin
McGraw-Hill

Boston   Burr Ridge, IL   Dubuque, IA   Madison, WI
New York   San Francisco   St. Louis
Bangkok   Bogotá   Caracas   Lisbon   London   Madrid   Mexico City
Milan   New Delhi   Seoul   Singapore   Sydney   Taipei   Toronto

McGraw-Hill Higher Education

A Division of The **McGraw-Hill** *Companies*

COMPUTERS, COMMUNICATIONS, AND INFORMATION
A USER'S INTRODUCTION, COMPREHENSIVE VERSION

This book is printed on acid-free paper.

1 2 3 4 5 6 7 8 9 0 QPD/QPD 9 0 9 8 7 6 5 4 3 2 1 0 9

ISBN 0-07-229744-1

Publisher: *David Kendric Brake*
Senior sponsoring editor: *Jodie McPherson*
Development: *Cathy Crow & Burrston House*
Senior development editor: *Diane E. Beausoleil*
Senior marketing manager: *Jeff Parr*
Senior project editor: *Gladys True*
Senior production supervisor: *Heather Burbridge*
Senior designer: *Laurie Entringer*
Production and Quark makeup: *Stacey C. Sawyer*
Cover image: © *Jerry Burns/Workbook Co/Op Stock*
Senior supplement coordinator: *Carol Loreth*
Photo research coordinator: *Keri Johnson*
Photo research: *Roberta Spieckerman & Associates*
Compositor: *GTS Graphics*
Typeface: *10/12 Times/Roman*
Printer: *Quebecor Printing Book Group/Dubuque*

Library of Congress Cataloging-in-Publication Data

Hutchinson, Sarah E.
    Computers, communications, and information : a user's introduction : comprehensive version / b Sarah E. Hutchinson, Stacey C. Sawyer. — 7th ed.
        p.   cm.
    ISBN 0-07-229744-1
    1. Computers.   2. Telecommunication systems.   3. Information technology.   I. Sawyer, Stacey C.   II. Title.
QA76.5.H867   2000
004—dc21   99-047331

http://www.mhhe.com

At McGraw-Hill Higher Education, we publish instructional materials targeted at the higher education market. In an effort to expand the tools of higher learning, we offer texts, lab manuals, study guides, testing materials, software, and multimedia products.

At **Irwin/McGraw-Hill** (a division of McGraw-Hill Higher Education), we realize that technology has created and will continue to create new media for professors and students to use in managing resources and communicating information with one another. We strive to provide the most flexible and complete teaching and learning tools available, as well as offer solutions to the changing world of teaching and learning.

> **Irwin/McGraw-Hill is dedicated to providing the tools for today's instructors and students to successfully navigate the world of Information Technology.**

- **Seminar series**—Irwin/McGraw-Hill's Technology Connection seminar series offered across the country every year demonstrates the latest technology products and encourages collaboration among teaching professionals.

- **Osborne/McGraw-Hill**—This division of The McGraw-Hill Companies is known for its best-selling Internet titles *Harley Hahn's Internet & Web Yellow Pages* and the *Internet Complete Reference*. Osborne offers an additional resource for certification and has strategic publishing relationships with corporations such as Corel Corporation and America Online. For more information visit Osborne at **www.osborne.com**.

- **Digital solutions**—Irwin/McGraw-Hill is committed to publishing digital solutions. Taking your course online doesn't have to be a solitary venture, nor does it have to be a difficult one. We offer several solutions that will allow you to enjoy all the benefits of having course material online. For more information visit **www.mhhe.com/solutions/index.mhtml**.

- **Packaging options**—For more about our discount options, contact your local Irwin/McGraw-Hill Sales representative at 1-800-388-3987 or visit our website at **www.mhhe.com/it**.

Instructor's Guide to *Computers, Communications, and Information:* Goals/Philosophy

This book is written for future computer users—people who will use the computer as an everyday tool for working with reports, spreadsheets, databases, and, of course, telecommunications. It is not intended only for students who will eventually write programs or design computer systems.

We wrote this book to provide instructors and students with the most useful information possible in an introductory computer course. Specifically, we offer the following five important features:

1. Two versions—Core Version of 8 chapters, and Comprehensive Version of 14 chapters

2. Complete coverage, avoiding unnecessary detail

3. Practical orientation

4. Learning reinforcement

5. Complete course solutions: supplements that work

About the Book

Feature #1: Two Versions—Core Version and Comprehensive Version

We offer two versions:

■ *Core Version:* This version includes Chapters 1 to 8 and Episodes 1 to 4, with extensive coverage of hardware, software, the Internet, and the Web. This version works well in courses combined with applications.

■ *Comprehensive Version:* This version includes all the extensive coverage of the Core Version plus an additional six chapters, with detailed coverage on multimedia, information management, databases, systems development, and other advanced topics.

Feature #2: Complete Coverage, Avoiding Unnecessary Detail

This book offers complete coverage of core concepts of computers and information technology. We have tried to be neither too brief nor too encyclopedic, offering users just what they need to know to use a computer competently. Moreover, we have avoided the cluttered, over-illustrated look and style that many instructors tell us they find objectionable in other texts. Thus, you will not find icons, margin notes, cartoons, or similar distractions.

Feature #3: Practical Orientation

The text presents information on capabilities of microcomputers that users can apply at work, home, and school. For example, we provide up-to-date, practical discussion of . . .

■ Use of the Internet and the World Wide Web, including Amazon.com Episodes

■ Ethics, privacy, and security

■ Common features of applications software

■ The practical aspects of system software

■ Object-oriented programming, expert systems, virtual reality, and digital convergence

- PC and Macintosh hardware, addressing upgrading and compatibility issues
- Computer-related health and safety matters
- Career Boxes that show students how computers are used in the workplace and various professions

Feature #4: Learning Reinforcement

We have developed a variety of learning aids to provide learning reinforcement:

- ***Chapter key questions:*** Each chapter opens with a list of chapter *key questions* matched to each section in the chapter.

- ***What It Is / What It Does / Why It Is Important:*** At the end of each chapter is a summary that covers all the important terms in the chapter—and the page numbers where they appear. We also connect each summary item with its related key question from the beginning of the chapter.

- ***Self-tests, exercises, and critical-thinking questions:*** End-of-chapter "Self-Test" questions; "In Your Own Words" short-answer exercises; and "Knowledge in Action" critical-thinking questions enable students to test their comprehension and encourage them to learn more about microcomputers on their own. Some of these exercises are Web-related. The answers to the Self-Test questions are provided at the end of each chapter.

- ***Episodes:*** Several *Episodes* or case studies about *Amazon.com* appear throughout the text to provide students with practical insights into establishing a Web-based business.

Feature #5: Complete Course Solutions

The following is a list of supplemental material that can be used to help teach this course.

- ***Instructor's Resource Kit:*** Instructor's Resource Kits provide instructors with all the ancillary material needed to teach a course. Irwin/McGraw-Hill is committed to providing instructors with the most effective instructional resources. The supplements in the Instructor's Resource Kit have been developed as a fully integrated package. Each component supports a learning process that will facilitate students' understanding of facts and concepts and enable them to apply their knowledge. Many of these resources are available at our Information Technology Supersite, found at **www.mhhe.com/it**. Our Instructor's Resource Kits are available on CD-ROM and contain the following;

  —*Diploma by Brownstone:* Diploma is the most flexible, powerful, and easy-to-use computer-based testing system available in higher education. The Diploma system allows instructors to create an exam as a printed version, as a LAN-based online version, or as an Internet version. Diploma also includes grade book features, which automate the entire testing process.

  The question bank contains more than 1500 questions of various types, including multiple choice, true/false, matching, short answer, and essay. A test item table is included to illustrate which questions are included in each of three categories: definition, conceptual, and application. Answers are supplied, as well as page references to where answers appear in the textbook.

  —*Instructor's Manual:* The Instructor's Manual includes an introduction that clearly explains the features of the IM; learning objectives; chapter overviews; chapter outlines; key terms; answers to end-of-chapter exercises; and an index of key concepts.

  —*PowerPoint Slides:* The PowerPoint slides are designed to provide instructors with a comprehensive teaching aid and include key terms and definitions, concept overviews, art from the text, and discussion topics.

■ *Videos:* A broad selection of 20 video segments from the acclaimed PBS television series, *Computer Chronicles,* are available. Each video is 30 minutes long. The videos cover topics ranging from computers and politics, to online financial services, to the latest developments in PC technologies.

■ *Interactive Companion CD-ROM:* This free CD-ROM includes a collection of interactive tutorial labs on some of the most popular topics. By combining video, interactive exercises, animation, additional content, and actual "lab" tutorials, we expand the reach and scope of the textbook. The CD can be used in class, in the lab, or at home by students and instructors.

■ *Digital Solutions to Help You Manage Your Course*

—*PageOut:* PageOut is our Course Web Site Development Center that offers a syllabus page, URL, McGraw-Hill Online Learning Center content, online exercises and quizzes, gradebook, discussion board, and an area for student Web pages. For more information, visit the PageOut web site at **www.mhla.net/pageout**.

—*Online Learning Centers:* The Online Learning Center (OLC) that accompanies *Computers, Communications, and Information* is accessible through our Information Technology Supersite at **www.mhhe.com/it**. This site provides additional learning and instructional tools developed using the same three-level approach found in the text and supplements. This offers a consistent method for students to enhance their comprehension of the concepts presented in the text.

—*Online Courses Available:* **OLCs** are your perfect solutions for Internet-based content. Simply put, these Centers are "digital cartridges" that contain a book's pedagogy and supplements. As students read the book, they can go online and take self-grading quizzes or work through interactive exercises. These also provide students appropriate access to lecture materials and other key supplements.

Online Learning Centers can be delivered through any of these platforms:
McGraw-Hill Learning Architecture (TopClass)
Blackboard.com
eCollege.com (formerly Real Education)
WebCT (a product of Universal Learning Technology)

■ *Skills Assessment*

Irwin/McGraw-Hill offers two innovative systems to meet your skills assessment needs. These two products are available for use with any of our applications manual series.

—*ATLAS (Active Testing and Learning Assessment Software):* Atlas is one option to consider for an application skills assessment tool from McGraw-Hill. Atlas allows students to perform tasks while working live within the Microsoft applications environment. Atlas provides flexibility for you in your course by offering:

1. Pre-testing options
2. Post-testing options
3. Course placement testing
4. Diagnostic capabilities to reinforce skills
5. Proficiency testing to measure skills

ATLAS is Web-enabled, customizable, and is available for Microsoft Office 2000.

—*SimNet (Simulated Network Assessment Product)*: SimNet is another option for a skills assessment tool that permits you to test students' software skills in a simulated environment. SimNet is available for Microsoft Office 97 (deliverable via a network) and Microsoft Office 2000 (deliverable via a network and the Web). SimNet provides flexibility for you in your course by offering:

1. Pre-testing options
2. Post-testing options
3. Course placement testing
4. Diagnostic capabilities to reinforce skills
5. Proficiency testing to measure skills

■ ***Office 2000 Application Series:*** Available for discount packaging, our **Advantage Series** leads students through the features of Microsoft Office 2000 with a critical-thinking, "what, why, and how" orientation. Irwin McGraw-Hill also offers additional MS Office 2000 series to suit your teaching preference. Each MS Office 2000 series is Microsoft Office User Specialist (MOUS) certified.

Acknowledgments

Two names are on the front of the book, but a great many others are powerful contributors to its development.

First, we thank the many people at Irwin/McGraw-Hill: Jodi McPherson and Diane Beausoleil in Editorial, and Gladys True, Laurie Entringer, Heather Burbridge, and all others in the Production Department who helped us get this book out on time. Glenn Turner, Meg Turner, Cathy Crowe, and others at Burrston House provided invaluable assistance by analyzing manuscript reviews and establishing revision needs. Bernard Gilbert did an excellent copyediting job. Roberta Spieckerman was our invaluable photo researcher, and David Sweet took professional care of permissions fulfillment. And GTS Graphics in Los Angeles provided the best prepress services in the business (special thanks go to Kristina Vargas and Donna Machado). Last but not least, Brian Williams wrote the excellent Career Boxes.

Finally, we appreciate the helpful comments and suggestions provided by the following reviewers:

Robert Barrett, Indiana University—Purdue University, Fort Wayne
Rochelle Boehning, California State University, San Marcos
Joseph Braccia, Northern Virginia Community College, Annandale
Ronald Curtis, William Patterson University
Don Distler, Belleville Area Community College
Esther Frankel, Santa Barbara City College
Tom Gambill, University of Illinois
Thomas Gorecki, Charles County Community College
Nancy Grant, Community College of Allegheny County, North Campus
Robert Grazinski, Central Texas College
Ed Hoffman, Los Angeles Pierce College
James F. LaSalle, University of Arizona
Phil McCue, San Jacinto Community College
Lois Miller, Hampton University
Joseph Otto, California State University, Los Angeles
Edward G. Pekarek, Jr., Appalachian State University
Craig Pierce, Towson University
Joyce Stockinger, Portland Community College, Sylvania Campus

SEH
SCS

CONTENTS

CHAPTER 1

OVERVIEW

The Foundation for Your Future

This chapter starts you on your way to becoming computer literate and computer competent so that you can find that special job, the one that helps you realize what you want to do. Richard Bolles, author of the perennial best-selling job-hunting book *What Color Is Your Parachute?*, thinks he knows how to find that job. Luck, he says, favors people who are going after their dreams—the thing they really want to do most in the world—who work hardest at the job hunt, and who have told the most people what they're looking for. Luck also favors people who are prepared.[1]

You can prepare yourself to find your special job by working through this book. Taking this step could make a vast difference in your future. Among workers who were nonusers of computers, according to one survey, 70% reported they were struggling with serious employment problems—layoffs, low pay, dead-end jobs, and the like. By contrast, among those calling themselves "sophisticated" computer users, less than a third reported such problems.[2] Moreover, those who use a computer at work are estimated to make 20% higher wages than those who don't.[3]

This first chapter starts you on your way by presenting a brief overview of computers—hardware, software, and other concepts. Later chapters will cover these topics in detail.

1.1 Who Is the User? Mostly People Like You

KEY QUESTION What is the difference between a computer professional and a computer user?

First things first: Do you really know what a computer user is? Consider the following distinction:

- A **computer professional** is a person who has a certain amount of experience and/or at least a two-year degree in the technical aspects of using computers. For example, a *software engineer,* or *computer programmer,* designs, writes, tests, implements, and maintains the software programs that process the data. A *systems analyst* analyzes, designs, and develops entire information systems for businesses and other organizations. A *network administrator* may manage, maintain, and update networks.

Because of his conviction that the dead deserve a name, Russian forensic expert Alexander Panov has developed a sophisticated program that allows him to rapidly match unidentified skulls to lists of missing persons.

■ The **user** (or *end-user*) is a person perhaps like yourself—someone without much technical knowledge of computers but who uses or wants to use computers to perform work-related or personal tasks, enhance learning and productivity, or have fun. The user is not necessarily a computer expert and may never need to become one. Many companies, for example, prefer to train new employees in the specific computer uses applicable to their job—and these applications may never require the user to have a lot of technical knowledge.

Living in what is called the Information Age, you know by now that computers aren't just a passing fad. Many types of organizations depend on them, and you will use them not only in your career but also probably to pursue private interests. To use computers efficiently, however, you must become computer literate and computer competent.

1.2 The Importance of Becoming Computer Literate & Computer Competent

KEY QUESTION **What does it mean to become computer literate and computer competent?**

Computer literacy is having an understanding of what a computer is and how it can be used as a resource. Literacy, which refers to having knowledge and understanding, needs to be distinguished from competency, which refers to having a skill. **Computer competency** is applying your skill with computers to meet your information needs and improve your productivity. Computer competency also means being able to transfer basic skills to new systems and new software.

Pig farmers use computers to record pigs' weights, eating patterns, age, and so on.

It's increasingly difficult to find a professional field or area of work that does not require knowledge of computers. To help you become computer literate and computer competent, in this book and accompanying computer lab tutorials, we will help you learn the following:

- *Terms:* You will master the terminology used to describe computers and their operations.

- *Functions:* You will learn the functions of the parts of a computer system.

- *Uses:* You will learn how to use a computer to increase your productivity—to produce the information you need and perform the tasks required—and to meet future job requirements. You will also learn to be flexible—that is, knowledgeable about different kinds of computers and different types of software.

Besides becoming knowledgeable about and skilled in the use of computers, you should also learn to be "information literate"—to be able to find, analyze, and use information in your career.

A water inspector is using a laptop computer to record amounts of chemicals in water samples.

1.3 What Is a Computer-Based Information System?

KEY QUESTION **What are the six elements of a computer-based information system?**

The term **computer** describes a device made up of a combination of electronic and electromechanical (part electronic, part mechanical) components. By itself, a computer has no intelligence and is referred to as **hardware,** which means simply the physical equipment. The hardware can't be used until it is connected to other elements, all of which constitute the six parts of a **computer-based information system.** (*See Figure 1.1.*)

1. Hardware
2. Software
3. Data/information
4. People
5. Procedures
6. Communications

Software is the term used to describe the instructions that tell the hardware how to perform a task. Without software, the hardware is useless. (Hardware and software are covered in more detail shortly.)

The primary purpose of computer systems in most businesses today is to transform data into information that can be used by people to make decisions, sell products, and perform a variety of other activities. Data can be considered the raw material—whether in paper, electronic, or other form—that is processed by the computer. In other words, **data** consists of the raw facts and figures that are processed into information. **Information** is summarized data or otherwise manipulated (processed) data. For example, the raw data of employees' hours worked and wage rates is processed by a computer into the information of paychecks and payrolls.

Figure 1.1 A computer-based information system typically combines six elements: hardware, software, data/information, procedures, people, and communications (connectivity).

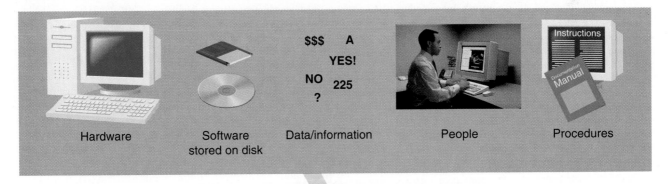

Hardware   Software stored on disk   Data/information   People   Procedures

Communications (connectivity)

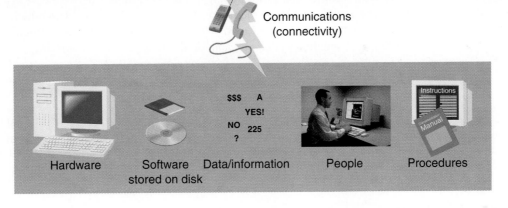

Hardware   Software stored on disk   Data/information   People   Procedures

(Left) Inuit man in northern Canada using a computer to record animal sightings. *(Right)* Class field trip; students are recording soil samples on a laptop computer.

Actually, in ordinary usage, the words *data* and *information* are often used synonymously. After all, one person's information may be another person's data. The information of paychecks and payrolls may become data that goes into someone's yearly financial projections or tax returns.

Note that information is not the same as knowledge. Whereas *information* is data that has been organized and communicated, *knowledge* requires the application of *reason.* Therefore, knowledge is the result of the reasoned analysis of information—a set of organized statements of facts or ideas, communicated in some systematic form.[4] I may receive the information that sales increased last month in the sportswear department, but that does not mean I necessarily have much knowledge about what makes sales go up or down.

People constitute the most important component of the computer system. People operate the computer hardware, they create and use the computer software, and they face ethical issues and decisions regarding the use of information technology. They enter the data and use the information the system generates. They also follow certain procedures when using the hardware and software. **Procedures** are descriptions of how things are done, steps for accomplishing a result. Procedures for computer systems appear in *documentation manuals,* also known as *reference manuals* and *user guides,* which contain instructions, rules, and guidelines to follow when using hardware and software.

When one computer system is set up to share data and information electronically with another computer system, **communications**—also called *connectivity*—becomes a sixth system element. In other words, the manner in which the various individual systems are connected—for example, by phone lines, microwave transmission, or satellite—is an element of the total computer system.

The Digital Basis of Computers

One of the main characteristics of a computer is its digital nature. No doubt you've heard this word often, but what does it really mean?

Computers may seem like incredibly complicated devices, but their underlying principle is simple. When you open up a microcomputer, what you see is mainly electronic circuitry. And what is the most basic statement that can be made about electricity? It is simply this: It can be either *turned on* or *turned off.*

In a two-state on/off arrangement, one state can represent a 1 digit, the other a 0 digit. People are most comfortable with the decimal number system, which has ten digits (0, 1, 2, 3, 4, 5, 6, 7, 8, 9). Because computers are based on on/off or other two-state conditions, they use the **binary number system,** which consists of only two digits—0 and 1.

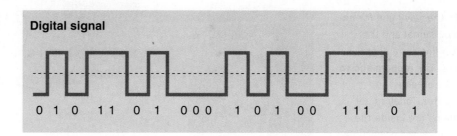

The word *digit* simply means "numeral." The word *digital* is derived from "digit," which refers to the fingers people used to count with. Today, however, **digital** is almost synonymous with "computer-based." More specifically, it refers to communications signals or information represented in a discrete (individually distinct) form—usually in a binary or two-state way.

In the binary system, each 0 and 1 is called a **bit**—short for *binary digit.* In turn, bits can be grouped in various combinations to represent characters of data—numbers, letters, punctuation marks, and so on. For example, the letter H could correspond to the electronic signal 01001000 (that is, off-on-off-off-on-off-off-off). In computing, a group of 8 bits is called a **byte,** and each character is represented by 1 byte.

Digital data, then, consists of data in discrete, discontinuous form—usually 0s and 1s. This is the method of data representation by which computers process and store data and communicate with one another.

The Analog Basis of Life

Most phenomena of the world are not digital: They are **analog,** having continuously variable values. Sound, light, temperature, and pressure values, for instance, can fall anywhere on a continuum or range. The highs, lows, and in-between states have historically been represented with analog devices rather than in digital form. Examples of analog devices are humidity recorders, mercury thermometers, and pressure sensors, which can measure continuous fluctuations. Thus, analog data is transmitted in a continuous form that closely resembles the information it represents. The electrical signals on a telephone line are analog-data representations of the original voices. Telephone, radio, broadcast television, and cable TV have traditionally transmitted analog data.

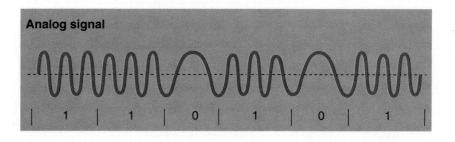

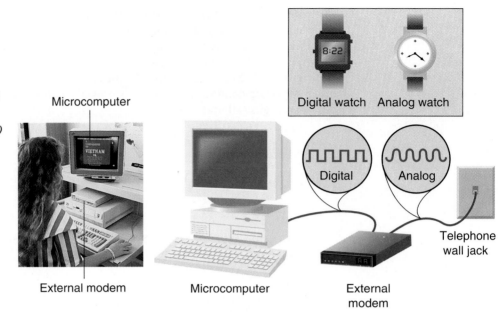

Figure 1.2 Analog versus digital signals, and the modem. *(Top)* On an analog watch, the hands move continuously around the watch face. On a digital watch, the display changes once each minute. *(Bottom)* Note the wavy line for an analog signal and the on/off line for a digital signal. The modem shown here is outside the computer. Today many modems are inside the computer and not visible.

The differences between analog and digital data transmission are apparent when you look at a drawing of a wavy analog signal, such as a voice message on a standard telephone line, and an on/off digital signal. (*See Figure 1.2.*)

Now, we'll focus on the *basics* of the first part of the typical computer-based information system—the hardware devices. You can use the following discussion to gain an overall perspective, or understanding, of computer hardware. We provide you with more specific hardware discussions in Chapters 2–4 and Chapter 7.

1.4 Computer Hardware

KEY QUESTION What are the five categories of computer hardware?

Hardware—what most people think of when they visualize a computer system—consists of, among other things, the keyboard, screen, printer, and the computer or processing device itself. In general, computer hardware is categorized according to which of the five computer operations it performs (*see Figure 1.3*):

- Input
- Processing and memory
- Output
- Storage
- Communications

Devices that are connected to the computer and controlled by the computer are referred to as **peripheral devices.** These devices can be external, such as keyboards, mice, monitors, and printers, or they can be internal (inside the computer cabinet), such as a floppy disk drive.

Input Hardware

The function of **input hardware** is to accept data and convert it into a form suitable for computer processing. In other words, input hardware allows people to put

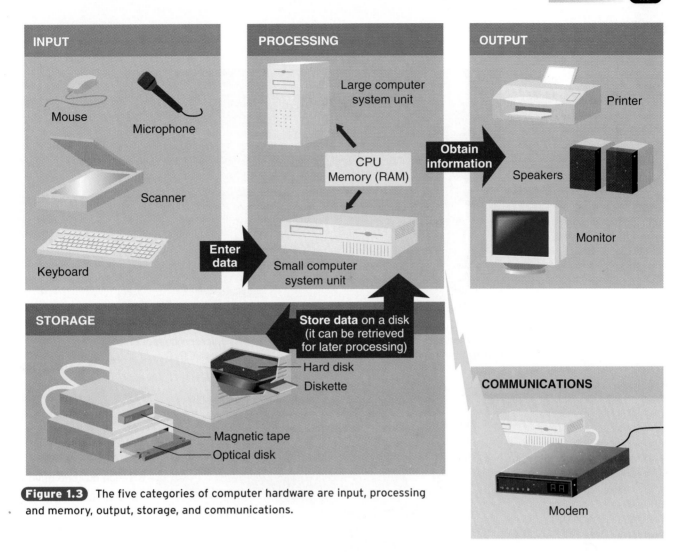

INPUT

Mouse

Microphone

Scanner

Keyboard

Enter data

PROCESSING

Large computer system unit

CPU Memory (RAM)

Small computer system unit

Obtain information

OUTPUT

Printer

Speakers

Monitor

STORAGE

Store data on a disk (it can be retrieved for later processing)

Hard disk

Diskette

Magnetic tape

Optical disk

COMMUNICATIONS

Modem

Figure 1.3 The five categories of computer hardware are input, processing and memory, output, storage, and communications.

data into the computer in a form that the computer can use. For example, input may be by means of a keyboard, mouse, or scanner.

■ *Keyboard:* A **keyboard** includes the standard typewriter keys plus a number of specialized keys. The standard keys are used mostly to enter words and numbers. Specialized keys are used to enter software-specific commands (covered in Chapter 6).

■ *Mouse:* A **mouse** is a device that is rolled about on a desktop to direct a pointer on the computer's display screen. The pointer is a symbol, usually an arrow, that is used to select items from lists (menus) on the screen or to position the cursor. The *cursor,* also called an *insertion point,* is the symbol on the screen that shows where data may be entered next, such as text in a document.

■ *Scanners:* **Scanners**—which are often used in desktop publishing—translate images of text, drawings, and photos into digital form. The digital images can then be processed by a computer, displayed on a monitor, inserted in documents, stored on a storage device, or transmitted to another computer.

Input devices are discussed in detail in the first half of Chapter 3.

Figure 1.4 The system unit. This cabinet houses the electronic processing circuitry and the memory that supports processing.

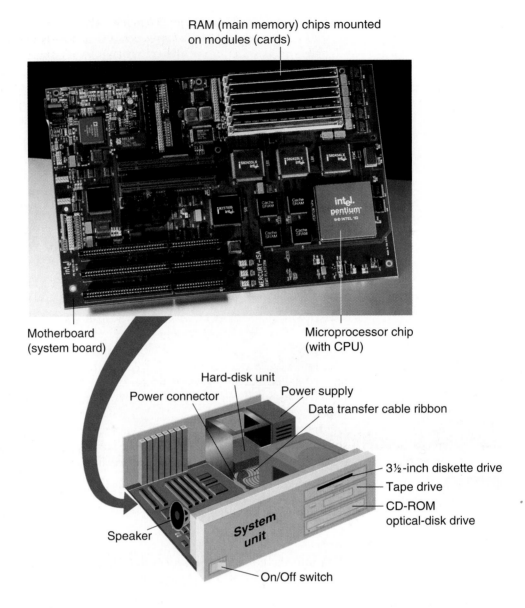

RAM (main memory) chips mounted on modules (cards)

Motherboard (system board)

Microprocessor chip (with CPU)

Hard-disk unit

Power connector

Power supply

Data transfer cable ribbon

3½-inch diskette drive

Tape drive

CD-ROM optical-disk drive

Speaker

System unit

On/Off switch

Processing and Memory (Primary Storage) Hardware

The computer's control center is made up of the processing and main memory devices, housed in the computer's system unit. The **system unit,** or system cabinet, houses that part of the electronic circuitry that does the actual processing and, except in large computers, the memory that supports processing. Together, these components are referred to as **processing hardware.** (*See Figure 1.4.*)

Microprocessor

■ *CPU—the processor:* The **CPU,** for **central processing unit,** is the processor, or computing part, of the computer. It controls and manipulates data to produce information. In a microcomputer the CPU is an approximately 1.5-inch (3.75-centimeter) square chip called a *microprocessor,* with electrical circuits printed on it. This microprocessor, and other components necessary to make it work, are mounted on a main circuit board called the *motherboard,* or *system board.*

■ *Memory—working storage:* **Memory**—also known as *primary storage, main memory,* and *RAM (random access memory)*—is temporary working storage. That means memory is the computer's "work space" or "desk area," where data and programs needed for immediate processing are held. Computer memory is contained on memory chips mounted on the motherboard. Memory capacity is important because it determines how much data can be processed at once and how big and complex the program used to process the data can be.

Despite its name, this kind of memory cannot "remember." Once the power is turned off, all the data and programs within memory simply vanish—that is, they are *volatile.* This is why data/information must also be stored in relatively permanent form on disks and tapes, which are called *secondary storage* devices to distinguish them from main memory's *primary storage.*

Processing and memory hardware are covered in detail in the next chapter.

Output Hardware

The function of **output hardware** is to provide the user with the means to view and use information produced by the computer system. For example, previously input but unorganized sales figures may be processed into meaningful form and displayed on a computer screen or printed out on paper.

Information is output in either hardcopy or softcopy form. *Hardcopy output* can be held in your hand—an example is paper with text (words or numbers) or graphics printed on it. *Softcopy output* is typically displayed on a *monitor,* a television-like screen on which you can read text and graphics. Another type of softcopy output is audio output, such as music.

Output hardware is discussed in the second half of Chapter 3.

Secondary Storage Hardware

As previously mentioned, the function of secondary **storage hardware** is to store software and data in a form that is relatively permanent, or *nonvolatile*—that is, the data is not lost when the power is turned off—and easy to retrieve when needed for processing. Secondary storage hard-

ware serves the same basic functions as do office filing systems except that it stores data as electromagnetic signals or laser-etched spots, commonly on magnetic disk, optical disk, or tape, rather than on paper.

Secondary storage hardware is discussed in Chapter 4.

Communications Hardware

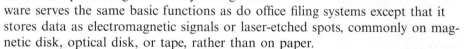

The function of **communications hardware** is to facilitate the connections between computers and between groups of connected computers called *networks.* Such connections allow the sharing of resources, both hardware and software, as well as data. Of course, computers can be "stand-alone" machines, meaning that they are not connected to anything else. However, the communications component of a computer system vastly extends the computer's range and utility. To transmit your computer's digital signals over telephone lines, you need to use a *modem* to translate them into analog signals. The modem provides a means for computers to communicate with one another while the old-fashioned copper-wire telephone network—an analog system built to transmit the human voice—still exists. We cover communications hardware and its uses in Chapters 7 and 8.

1.5 Computer Software

KEY QUESTION **What is software and what are two categories of software?**

A computer has no intelligence of its own and must be supplied with instructions that tell it what to do and how and when to do it. These instructions are called *software,* because you can't feel it or see it. It flows through the computer's circuits as coded pulses of electricity. The importance of software can't be overestimated. Without software to "breathe life" into the computer, to make it do what you want it to do, the computer will only take up space.

Software is made up of a group of related *programs* written in a specific code called a *programming language* and based on the computer's language of 0s and 1s. In turn, each program is made up of a group of related instructions that perform specific processing tasks. Software acquired to perform a general business function is often referred to as a *software package.* Software is usually created by professional software programmers and comes on disk, CD-ROM, or online, across the Internet.

Software can generally be divided into two categories:

1. System software

2. Applications software

System Software: The Computer's Boss

Software designed to allow the computer to manage its own resources and run the hardware and basic operations is called **system software.** This software runs the basic operations; it lets the CPU communicate with the keyboard, the screen, the printer, and the disk drive. However, it does not solve specific problems relating to a business or a profession. For example, system software will not help Silicon Valley entrepreneur Jerry Kaplan, self-styled "P.T. Barnum of cyberspace," process data about goods offered by his company ONSALE for online computer auction. It will, however, tell the computer where and how to store and retrieve data used during the processing.

Examples of system software are DOS, Windows, OS/2, Macintosh Operating System, Netware (Novell Operating System), Unix, and Linux. (We describe system software in detail in Chapter 5.)

Applications Software: Your Servant

Applications software allows you to increase your productivity and creativity in ways simply not possible without it. **Applications software** is software that performs tasks to directly benefit or assist the user. Examples are programs that do word processing, desktop publishing, payroll processing, or animation. (We cover applications software in Chapter 6.)

1.6 Types of Computer Systems: What's the Difference?

KEY QUESTION **What five categories can be used to describe computers?**

Computers have come a long way since the first operational computer in 1940. In 1969 the onboard guidance computer used by the Apollo 11 astronauts, who made the first moon landing, weighed 70 pounds (31 kilograms) and could hold the equivalent of a mere 2000 characters (bytes) of data in its main memory. The Mission Control computer on the ground had only 1 million characters of memory. "It cost $4 million and took up most of a room," says a space physicist who was there.[5]

Fast forward to the present: Today the shrinkage of computer components means that you can easily buy, for a couple of thousand dollars, a personal computer that sits on a desktop and has hundreds of times the processing power and about 32 to 64 times the memory of the 1969 Mission Control computer. You have more productivity at your fingertips than the American space program had a generation ago. And computer processing power is doubling at least every 18 months. In other words, that new computer that you just took out of the box may be only half as powerful as those introduced next year.

Although you may be familiar only with microcomputers, computers still come in a variety of sizes and with a variety of processing capabilities. We may categorize them as:

1. Supercomputers

2. Mainframe computers

3. Workstations

4. Microcomputers

5. Microcontrollers

It's hard to give a precise definition to each type because computer speeds and storage capacities change rapidly. Nevertheless, the following definitions will suffice:

- *Supercomputers:* First developed in the 1970s, **supercomputers** are the fastest and highest-capacity computers. Their cost ranges from several hundreds of thousands to millions of dollars. They may occupy special air-conditioned rooms and are often used for research. Among their uses are worldwide weather forecasting and analysis of weather phenomena, oil exploration, aircraft design, evaluation of aging nuclear weapons systems, predictions of spreads of epidemics, and mathematical research. Unlike microcomputers, which generally have only one central processing unit, supercomputers have hundreds to thousands of processors and can perform trillions of calculations per second.

  One supercomputer named Option Red fills 85 locker-size cabinets and 1600 square feet at Sandia National Laboratories in Albuquerque, New Mexico. At Los Alamos Laboratory in New Mexico, Blue Mountain (*left*), the fastest computer in the world, fills 11,000 square feet, cost $121.5 million, and looks like 48 refrigerator-high blue boxes.

■ *Mainframe computers:* The only type of computer available until the late 1960s, **mainframe computers** are less powerful than supercomputers, but they are still fast, mid- to large-size, large-capacity machines. Their size varies depending on how many concurrent users they are serving—from a few hundred to thousands of people. Mainframes are used by many banks, airlines, insurance companies, mail-order houses, universities, and the Internal Revenue Service. Mainframes also have many processors.

■ *Workstations:* **Workstations,** introduced in the early 1980s, are expensive, powerful desktop computers used mainly by engineers, scientists, and special-effects creators for sophisticated purposes. Providing many capabilities comparable to midsize mainframes, workstations are used for such tasks as designing airplane fuselages, prescription drugs, and movies' special effects. Workstations are often connected to a larger computer system to facilitate the transfer of data and information. The capabilities of low-end workstations overlap those of high-end microcomputers.

■ *Microcomputers:* **Microcomputers,** also called *personal computers (PCs),* are small computers that can fit next to a desk or on a desktop, or can be carried around. Some microcomputers, called *tower units,* are higher than they are wide and can be placed on the floor. Whether desktop, tower (floor-standing), notebook, palmtop, electronic organizer, or pen-based, personal computers are now found in most businesses (*see Figure 1.5*).They are either used as stand-alone machines or connected to a network, such as a local area network. A **local area network (LAN)** connects, usually by special cable, a group of desktop PCs and peripheral devices in an office or a building.

■ *Microcontrollers:* Also called *embedded, dedicated,* or *hidden computers,* **microcontrollers** are tiny computers installed in "smart" appliances like microwave ovens and pocket calculators. They are dedicated to performing a restricted number of tasks.

A wearable computer, from Japan. A mini-display screen is in front.

Types of Microcomputers

Desktop microcomputer

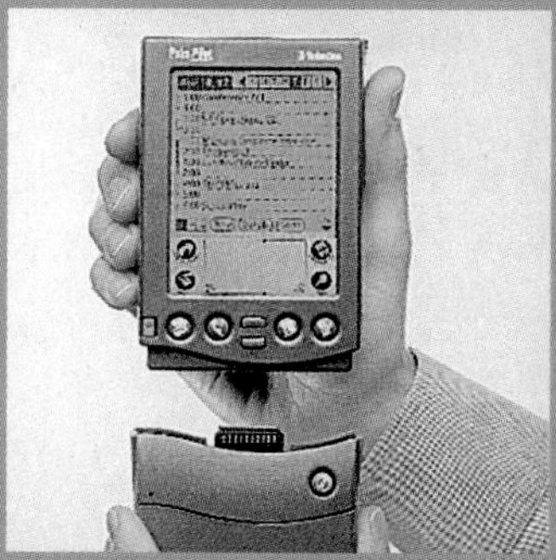

Handheld (palm top)

Tower microcomputer

Electronic organizer

Notebook

Pen computer

Figure 1.5

Microcomputers come in different sizes.

Some companies use a combination of computers, and, indeed, the predominant information system is now a hybrid model, whereby a variety of systems are connected, operated, and used by many people. For instance, an insurance company with branch offices around the country might use a mainframe computer to manage companywide customer data. To access information from the mainframe, a local claims adjuster might use a desktop microcomputer. That same microcomputer can also be used to perform specialized tasks such as generating invoices or drafting letters to customers. Because microcomputers are generally versatile, increasingly powerful, and more affordable than the other types of computers, they are practical tools for organizations wishing to improve their productivity.

■ *Server:* The word *server* does not actually describe a size of computer but rather a particular way in which a computer is used. However, because servers are important, they deserve mention here. (Servers are discussed in more detail in Chapter 8.)

A **server,** or *network server,* is a central computer that holds collections of data (databases) and programs for many PCs, workstations, and other computers, which are called *clients*. The entire network is called a *client/server network*. In small organizations, servers can store files and transmit electronic mail. In large organizations, servers can house enormous libraries of financial, sales, and product information. Servers also store the information available to users of the Internet and the World Wide Web.

Whatever their size, speed, and capacity, all computers operate according to similar principles. In the next section, we present a brief history of computer processing to show why these machines take the form they do today.

1.7 Milestones in Computer Development

KEY QUESTION **Through what generations have computers developed?**

Over the centuries, people have developed an amazing variety of data processing tools and techniques. Around 3000 B.C., the Sumerians used a box of stones as a device for representing numbers. About 2000 years later, the Chinese took the idea a step farther when they strung stones on threads in a wooden frame, the *abacus,* a device still in wide use in some parts of Asia. Other calculating tools were in use between the mid-1600s and the early 1900s, as described in Figure 1.6. However, the birth of the true electronic computer did not occur until the mid-1900s.

Figure 1.6 Which came first—computers or data processing? Many people think that we have been turning data into information only since computers came into use. The truth is that people have been processing data since prehistoric times. This illustration shows a few of the data processing methods used between the mid-1600s and the early 1900s. (a) Pascaline calculator (mid-1600s), the first automatic adding and subtracting machine. (b) Leibniz Wheel (early 1700s), the first general-purpose calculating machine. (c) Jacquard loom (1801), run by punched cards. (d) Thomas's arithnometer (1860), the first commercially successful adding and subtracting machine. (e) Hollerith's tabulating machine, used in the 1890 U.S. census. (f) Early IBM calculating machine (circa 1930).

Former German Chancellor Gerhard Schroeder tries out IBM's wearable PC mini-monitor with earphones during a computer fair in Hanover, northern Germany. This wearable PC is designed mainly for airplane mechanics and engineers for receiving data from a central database via a minicomputer attached to a belt.

The Evolution of Computers: March of the Generations

The first large-scale electronic computer, the grandparent of today's handheld machines, was the Electronic Numerical Integrator and Computer (ENIAC), which became operational in 1946. (*See Figure 1.7.*) ENIAC contained approximately 18,000 light-bulb-size electronic vacuum tubes that controlled the flow of electric current. It weighed 30 tons and occupied about 1800 square feet of floor space—a huge machine by today's standard. It was able to multiply four numbers in the then-remarkable time of 9 milliseconds (9/1000 of a second). From that start, computers have developed through four so-called *generations,* or stages, each one characterized by smaller size, more power, and less expense than its predecessor.

Figure 1.7 ENIAC, the first large-scale electronic computer. ENIAC weighed 30 tons, filled 1800 square feet, included 18,000 vacuum tubes—and it failed about every 7 minutes.

First Generation (1944–1958)

In the earliest general-purpose computers, most input and output media were punched cards and magnetic tape. Main memory was almost exclusively made up of hundreds of vacuum tubes—although one computer used a magnetic drum for main memory. These computers were somewhat unreliable because the vacuum tubes failed frequently. They were also slower than any microcomputer used today, produced a tremendous amount of heat, and were very large. They could run only one program at a time. ENIAC and UNIVAC I—the UNIVersal Automatic Computer, which was used by the U.S. Bureau of the Census from 1951 to 1963—are examples of first-generation computers. The UNIVAC was priced at $500,000 in 1950; today, you could purchase microcomputer chips with the same processing power for less than $100.

Second Generation (1959–1963)

By the early 1960s, transistors and some other solid-state devices that were much smaller than vacuum tubes were being used for much of the computer circuitry. (A transistor is an electronic switch that alternately allows or does not allow electronic signals to pass.) Magnetic cores, which looked like very small metal washers strung together by wires that carried electricity, became the most widely used type of main memory. Removable magnetic disk packs, stacks of disks connected by a common spindle (like a stack of records), were introduced as storage devices. Second-generation machines tended to be smaller, more reliable, and significantly faster than first-generation computers.

Third Generation (1964–1970)

In the third period, the **integrated circuit (IC)**—a complete electronic circuit that packages transistors (signal bridges) and other electronic components on a small silicon chip—replaced traditional transistorized circuitry. Integrated circuits are cost-effective because individual components don't need to be wired directly to the computer's system board.

The use of magnetic disks for secondary data storage became widespread, and computers began to support such capabilities as multiprogramming (processing several programs simultaneously) and timesharing (people using the same computer simultaneously). Minicomputers, priced around $18,000, were being widely used by the early 1970s and were taking some of the business away from the established mainframe market. Processing that formerly required the processing power of a mainframe could now be done on a minicomputer.

Computer Technology Timeline

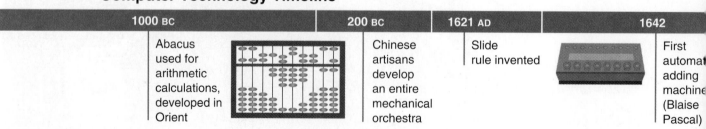

1000 BC	200 BC	1621 AD	1642
Abacus used for arithmetic calculations, developed in Orient	Chinese artisans develop an entire mechanical orchestra	Slide rule invented	First automatic adding machine (Blaise Pascal)

Tod Stabelfeldt, of Winslow, Washington, works on his computer at his job at Zortex Medical Management. Stabelfeldt, who was shot by a cousin when he was a boy, uses a program that helps the physically challenged succeed through technology. A University of Washington program helped outfit him with special computer equipment that enabled him to go to college and get a job.

Fourth Generation (1971–Now)

Large-scale integrated (LSI) and very-large-scale integrated (VLSI) circuits were developed that contained hundreds to millions of transistors on a tiny chip. In 1971 Ted Hoff of Intel developed the microprocessor, which packaged an entire CPU, complete with memory, logic, and control circuits, on a single chip. The microprocessor and VLSI circuit technology caused radical changes in computers—in their size, appearance, cost, availability, and capability—and they started the process of *miniaturization:* the development of smaller and smaller computers.

Also during this time, computers' main memory capacity increased, and its cost decreased, which directly affected the types and usefulness of software that could be used. Software applications like word processing, electronic spreadsheets, database management programs, painting and drawing programs, desktop publishing, and so forth became commercially available, giving more people reasons to use a computer.

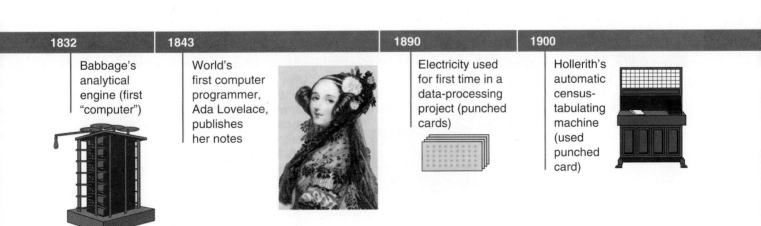

1832 Babbage's analytical engine (first "computer")

1843 World's first computer programmer, Ada Lovelace, publishes her notes

1890 Electricity used for first time in a data-processing project (punched cards)

1900 Hollerith's automatic census-tabulating machine (used punched card)

Japan's Seiko Instruments have produced what may be the world's first wristwatch personal computer, the Ruputer. It can download data including text and pictures from other PCs.

The Information Explosion: Data Overload or Knowledge?

The Clarion Auto PC, the first personal computer designed for a car.

What has been the effect of this tremendous increase in processing power? It has made data and information available to us not only more quickly but also in greater quantity.

Before the computer, most business transactions involved the use of paper—creating it, using it, sending it, storing it. One promise of the computer was that it would eliminate paper, but it seems now that there is more than ever. "By 2000," according to a forecast a few years ago, "U.S. businesses will still need a space equivalent to all of the office space in Pittsburgh to file the 120 billion sheets of new paper they will generate every year."[6]

The catch to information technology is that although it can generate information—mountains of information in both paper and electronic form—it does not always generate knowledge. Thus, we need to learn how to be selective about the information we get—to make sure that, in the classic definition of usefulness, it is *complete, accurate, relevant,* and *timely (CART)*. To avoid

1930	1944	1946	1952	1964	1967
General theory of electronic computers	First electro-mechanical computer (Mark I)	First operational electronic computer in United States (ENIAC)	UNIVAC computer correctly predicts election of Eisenhower as U.S. President	IBM introduces 360 line of computers	Handheld calculator

being buried in an avalanche of unnecessary data, we must be able to distinguish what we *really need* from what we *think we need.*

1.8 Connectivity Interactivity, & Digital Convergence

KEY QUESTION What are connectivity, interactivity, and digital convergence, and how do they affect the user?

The cause of the information explosion, the computer, allows us to reach out from our homes, desks, and offices to find information and share knowledge that was beyond the reach of the wealthiest person in the world just 100 years ago. Three computer-related concepts have enabled this process: connectivity, interactivity, and digital convergence.

Connectivity

Any communications network, such as a telephone system, can be connected to larger ones. This is one example of **connectivity,** the ability to connect computers, telephones, and other devices to other computers, devices, and sources of information. It is this connectivity that is the foundation of the Information Age.

Connectivity has made possible many kinds of activities. Although we cover these activities in more detail in Chapter 8, some examples follow.

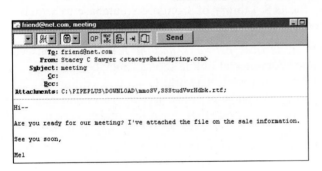

- *E-mail:* **E-mail**, or **electronic mail,** is a software-controlled system that allows computer users, through their keyboards, to send messages over a communications network and to receive responses. Whether the network is a company's small network or a worldwide network such as the Internet, e-mail allows users to send messages anywhere on the system.

- *Telecommuting:* In standard commuting, one takes transportation (car, bus, train) from home to work and back. In *telecommuting,* one works at home and communicates with ("commutes to") the office by phone, fax, and computer.

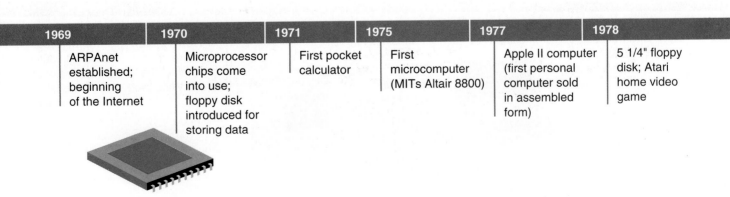

1969	1970	1971	1975	1977	1978
ARPAnet established; beginning of the Internet	Microprocessor chips come into use; floppy disk introduced for storing data	First pocket calculator	First microcomputer (MITs Altair 8800)	Apple II computer (first personal computer sold in assembled form)	5 1/4" floppy disk; Atari home video game

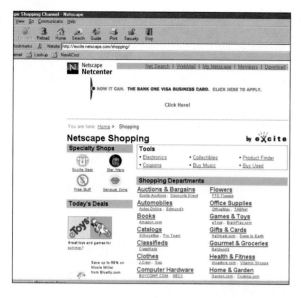

■ *Online shopping and e-commerce:* With *online shopping,* microcomputer users dial into a telephone-linked computer-based shopping service that lists prices and descriptions of products that may be ordered through the computer. You charge the purchase to a credit card. The shopping service sends the merchandise to you by mail or other delivery service. *E-commerce (electronic commerce)* goes beyond shopping and includes doing all sorts of business—between individuals, between individuals and companies, and between companies.

■ *Databases:* A database may be a large collection of data located on your own unconnected personal computer. Here, however, we are concerned with databases located elsewhere. These are libraries of information at the other end of a communications connection that are available to you through your microcomputer. A **database** is a collection of electronically stored data. The data is integrated, or cross-referenced, so that different people can access it for different purposes.

For example, suppose an unfamiliar company offered you a job. To find out about your prospective employer, you could go online to gain access to some helpful databases. Examples are Business Database Plus, Magazine Database Plus, and TRW Business Profiles. You could then study the company's prod-ucts, review financial data, identify major competitors, or learn about recent sales increases or layoffs. You might even get an idea of whether or not you would be happy with the "corporate culture." Also, if you are researching the use of photography during the U.S Civil War, you could access the U.S. Library of Congress's database to search for books, photos, and films on the topic.

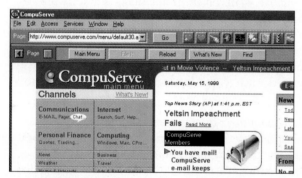

■ *Online services, networks, and the Internet:* Established major commercial online services include America Online, Microsoft Network, CompuServe, and Prodigy. **A computer online service** is a commercial information service that, for a fee, makes various services available to subscribers through their telephone-linked microcomputers. Sometimes online services are called *portals,* as we discuss in Chapter 8.

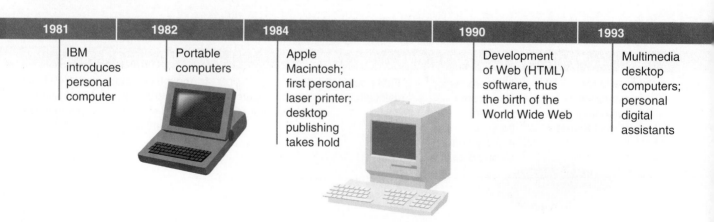

1981	1982	1984	1990	1993
IBM introduces personal computer	Portable computers	Apple Macintosh; first personal laser printer; desktop publishing takes hold	Development of Web (HTML) software, thus the birth of the World Wide Web	Multimedia desktop computers; personal digital assistants

Among other things, consumers can research information in databases, do online shopping, make airline reservations, and send e-mail.

Through an online service you may also gain access to the greatest network of all, the **Internet.** The Internet is an international network connecting approximately 400,000 smaller networks that link computers at academic, scientific, and commercial institutions. Millions of people are already on the Internet (estimates of the number change daily). The most well-known part of the Internet is the **World Wide Web,** which stores information in multimedia form—sounds, photos, and video, as well as text. The Web is covered in detail in Chapter 8.

Interactivity

Developed by ImagiNation Network, CyberPark is an online game service, a virtual (3-D) theme park where members can wander around, chat with other members, and play various games via computer. This is an example of interactivity. **Interactivity** means that the user is able to make an immediate response to what is going on and modify the processes. That is, there is a dialog—an exchange of input and output—between the user and the computer or communications device. Interactivity allows users to be active rather than passive participants in the technological process.

Among the types of interactive devices are multimedia computers and WebTV "Internet appliances."

- *Multimedia computers:* The word *multimedia,* one of the buzzwords of the '90s, has been defined in different ways. Essentially, however, **multimedia,** from "multiple media," refers to technology that presents information in more than one medium, including text, graphics, animation, video, music, and voice.

    Multimedia microcomputers (sometimes called *MPCs*) include sound and video capability, run CD-ROM disks, and allow you to play games and perform interactive tasks, such as taking a test online and getting feedback about wrong answers.

- *Internet appliances:* Already envisioning a world of crossbreeding among televisions, telephones, and computers, enterprising manufacturers have developed TV set-top control boxes, or *smart boxes* or *internet appliances.* With these devices, consumers presumably can listen to music CDs, watch movies, do computing, view multiple cable channels, and go online. Set-top boxes would provide two-way interactivity not only with video games but also with online entertainment, news, and educational programs. Video game consoles that can double as set-top boxes to access online offerings are being made by

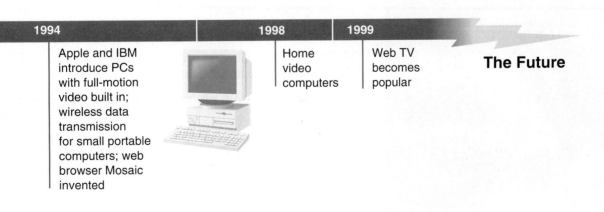

1994	1998	1999	
Apple and IBM introduce PCs with full-motion video built in; wireless data transmission for small portable computers; web browser Mosaic invented	Home video computers	Web TV becomes popular	**The Future**

various manufacturers, such as Philips, Sega, Sony, and Thomson. Microsoft's WebTV Plus sells a box a bit smaller than a VCR that you connect to your TV and a phone line. The hardware, which also includes a wireless keyboard, costs about $250, and Internet access costs about $15 per month. Once you subscribe to the WebTV service, you can explore the Web, send and receive e-mail, and watch regular TV, all at the same time. These set-top boxes, however, cannot make your TV set behave like a computer monitor. Because a TV screen has lower resolution than a computer monitor, Web pages can be difficult to read. You also cannot participate directly in the thousands of discussion groups (chat rooms) on the Internet, and you can't use computer software.

Digital Convergence

"We should all be concerned about the future," said engineer and inventor Charles Kettering, "because we will have to spend the rest of our lives there." *Convergence* is definitely part of our future. Basically, **digital convergence** is the technological merger of several industries through various devices that exchange information in the digital format used by computers. The industries are computers, communications, consumer electronics, entertainment, and mass media.

The direction in which digital convergence is going is illustrated by the PC/TV. In the recent past, it was not possible to use your television set as a computer or to use a personal computer to watch broadcast TV programs. Now, however, the technologies of television and computing are coming closer together.

Technological convergence has tremendous significance. It means that, from a common electronic base, information can be communicated in all the ways we are accustomed to receiving it. These include the familiar media of newspapers, photographs, films, recordings, radio, and television. However, it can also be communicated through newer technology—satellite, cable, cellular phone, fax machine, or compact disk, for example. More important, as time goes on, *the same information may be exchanged among many kinds of equipment, using the language of computers.* Understanding this shift from single, isolated technologies to a unified digital technology means understanding the effects of this convergence on your life, such as:

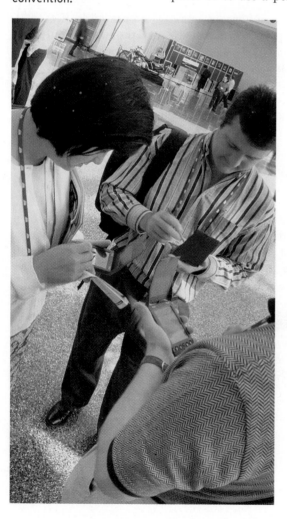

Users trying out pen-based computers at a convention.

■ The increased need for continuous learning

■ The necessity of adapting to less well-defined jobs as "information workers"

■ An increased pace of change

■ Exposure to relatively unregulated technical and social information from other cultures via global networks

This book will help you get ready.

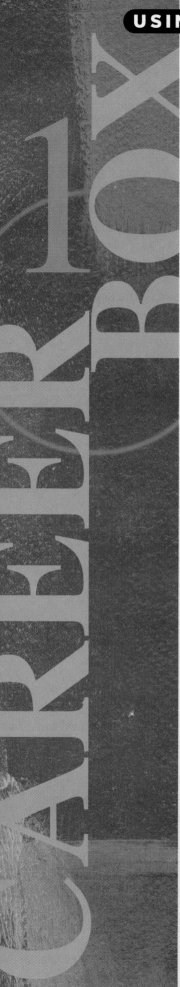

Real Estate

By the time Floridians Jim and Diane Levine got to Cape Cod, Massachusetts, to look for a summer home, they already had color pictures, maps, and information about prices in hand. And they hadn't even met their real estate agent.[a]

And thus has information technology—in particular, the World Wide Web—changed yet another industry. Realtors' Web sites "have become an invaluable source for sorting through information ranging from how to pick a neighborhood and a property to how to get the best mortgage," says one writer.[b] Whereas yesterday most of the control of information was in the hands of realtors, now it is under the control of consumers.

Some Web sites carry descriptions of homes, photographs, and even virtual walkthroughs so visitors can get a feel for the properties. Others list mortgage rates, details about neighborhoods and schools, and property tax rates. You can launch a search by specifying geographic location, number of bedrooms, price, and so on.

Want to know if a house you're interested in is overpriced for the neighborhood? You can go to an Internet site (*www.recomps.com*) established by Stewart Title of Orange County, California, and dial into a national database that allows you to compare recent sale prices of similar homes in the same neighborhood. Says Gregg Shuler, president of Stewart Title, "In addition to sales price data, detailed information is provided on square footage, lot size, number of bedrooms and bathrooms, taxes, and special amenities, such as a swimming pool, spa, and remodeling." The data search will cover as many as 30 comparable homes sold in a neighborhood during the past 12 months.[c] If you want to know where comparable properties are located, you can also go to the Web site for MapBlast (*www.mapblast.com*). MapBlast allows you to produce a detailed map from almost any street address in the United States.[d]

Normally it takes a month or more to arrange the financing and sign closing papers for a home purchase. But now there are ways to speed this up. St. Petersburg, Florida-based CREDCO offers one-stop-investigation shopping that provides residential mortgage credit reports, assesses a borrower's credit risk, and gives consumers a personal credit report.[e] And Alltel Information Systems and Data Track Systems formed a combined network that allows buyers to reduce the time for loan qualifying and closing from a month to a few days. With the real-estate agent, appraiser, bank, and insurer associated with the sale all on the same secure network, there is no need for the time-consuming process of printing, faxing, or express-mailing hard-copy forms and documents.

Finally, if you want to remodel your less-than-desirable new domicile or see how it might look with various kinds of floor, wall, and fabric coverings or furnishings and appliances, you can obtain three-dimensional models from a CD-ROM called Visual Home from the Palo Alto, California, company Books That Work. "Simply download these models and materials onto your PC," says one report, "and 'see' how a new appliance or cabinet will fit into your existing home—before it arrives on the delivery truck."[f]

Some popular real-estate-related Web sites are the following: *www.rent.net* advertises more than 2.5 million rental properties in the United States and Canada; *www.homepath.com* offers a starter kit for purchasing a home; *www.cyberhomes.com* includes homes from the multiple listing service.

Government and Politics

"In general, the Internet is being defined not by its civic or political content," says one writer, "but by merchandising and entertainment, much like television."[a] Even so, a Rutgers University study suggests that the Internet has great potential for civic betterment because it is free of government intrusion, is fast and cheap for users (once connected), and facilitates communication among citizens better than mass media such as radio and TV.[b]

The potential has been demonstrated since 1989 in Santa Monica, California, where the city has had an experiment in online democracy called the Public Electronic Network (PEN). In its first year, when the major topic on PEN was homelessness, Donald Paschal, himself homeless, logged on from a public terminal and said he would like to get a job but was dirty, had nowhere to wash, and nowhere to store his clothing. Out of the subsequent online discussions came a program called Swashlock, for "showers, washers, and lockers." Today 50% of Santa Monica's households have Internet access, and one in ten residents is a registered user of PEN.[c]

Similar strides have also been made elsewhere. Some cities have adopted Neighborhood Link, a free, easy-to-use system of neighborhood Web sites in which residents can communicate among themselves and with local governments. In Denver, for instance, the system serves 1186 neighborhoods.[d] In Austin, Texas, an entrepreneur formed E-The People, which describes itself as "America's Interactive Town Hall" and is designed to connect citizens with their government officials, local and national.[e] In Nevada, citizens visit the state legislature's hearings and floor voting sessions by accessing the legislators' Web site, either listening to Internet broadcasts or reading the text of legislation.[f]

If we can shop online, could we not vote online for political candidates? The U.S. Department of Defense is researching the matter of allowing voting via the Internet for some 6 million military and civilian Americans stationed overseas.[g] Ten states have also approved testing of online voting.[h] In early 1999, voters in the small city of Piedmont, California, were the first in the state to vote by "touch-screen" technology at their polling sites; the results were tallied in 29 minutes instead of the usual 3 hours.[i]

As you might expect, politicians and political candidates have found information technology to be of considerable use. They do online campaigning, even announcing their candidacies on the Internet. Every presidential candidate "has to have a Web site," says one research professor. "If you don't, it's like not having a telephone number."[j] Of course, the Net is not yet quite a mass medium, so it will be some time before we stop seeing political ads on television during election season.[k]

Government itself has been deeply involved with computers from the beginning. Some noteworthy examples: You can file tax returns online.[l] You can renew your passport online.[m] Eighteen-year-old males can register with the Selective Service online.[n] The U.S. Department of Housing and Urban Renewal has installed kiosks in public places in Camden, New Jersey, that direct people to emergency housing.[o]

Some interesting Web sites are as follows: Neighborhood Link, *www.neighborhoodlink.com*; E-The People, *www.e-the-people.com*. Information about Congress may be found at *thomas.loc.gov, www.capweb.net,* and *voter96.cqalert.com/Welcome.html.*

WHAT IT IS WHAT IT DOES

WHY IT IS IMPORTANT

analog (KQ 1.3,* p. 1.7)   Refers to nondigital (non-computer-based), continuously variable forms of data transmission, including voice and video. Most current telephone lines and radio, television, and cable-TV hookups are analog transmissions media.

An appreciation of the difference between analog and digital forms of communication is required to understand what is involved in connecting your computer to other computer systems and information services. As digital systems, computers cannot communicate over analog lines unless special measures are taken. Usually a modem and communications software are required to connect a microcomputer user to other computer systems and information services over (via) analog lines.

applications software (KQ 1.5, p. 1.12) Software that you can use to perform useful work on general-purpose tasks; compare with *system software*.

Applications software such as word processing, spreadsheet, database management, graphics, and communications packages provide tools for increasing your productivity.

binary digit (KQ 1.3, p. 1.5)   1 or 0 in the binary system of data representation in computer systems.

The binary digit is the fundamental element of all data and information stored in a computer system.

binary number system (KQ 1.3, p. 1.7)   A two-state system of numbers; contains *binary digits* 0 and 1.

Computer systems use a binary system for data representation; two digits, 0 and 1, refer to the presence or absence of electrical current or pulse of light.

bit (KQ 1.3, p. 1.7)   Short for *binary digit*; a 0 or a 1.

See *binary digit*.

byte (KQ 1.3, p. 1.7)   A group of 8 bits.

A byte holds the equivalent of a character—such as a letter or a number—in computer data-representation coding schemes.

communications (KQ 1.3, p. 1.6)   Also called *connectivity*; becomes an element of the computer-based information system when one computer system is set up to share data and information electronically with another computer system.

Communications technology vastly expands the opportunity for information sharing and increased productivity.

*KQ refers to the Key Question associated with the defined term.

communications hardware (KQ 1.4, p. 1.11)   Equipment that facilitates connections between computers and computer systems—for example, over phone lines using a modem.

Without communications hardware, users would not be able to transmit/receive data and information to/from other computer systems or share hardware and software resources

computer (KQ 1.3, p. 1.5)   Programmable, electromechanical machine that accepts raw data—facts and figures—and processes (manipulates) it into useful information, such as summaries and reports. The computer and all equipment attached to it are called *hardware;* the encoded instructions that tell the computer what to do are called *software.*

The computer greatly speeds up the process whereby people solve problems and perform repetitive tasks and thus increases their productivity. Computers also allow the electronic connections of people and businesses all over the world.

computer-based information system (KQ 1.3, p. 1.5)   Data processing system with six parts: (1) hardware; (2) software; (3) data/information; (4) procedures; (5) people; (6) communications.

The purpose of a computer-based information system is to transform raw data into useful information and quickly transmit it to the people who need it.

computer competency (KQ 1.2, p. 1.3)   The ability to apply computer skills in order to meet information needs and improve productivity; also the ability to transfer basic skills to new systems and new software.

It's becoming increasingly difficult to find a professional field or area of work that does not require knowledge of computers.

computer literacy (KQ 1.2, p. 1.3)   An understanding of what a computer is and how it can be used as a resource. Literacy, which refers to having knowledge and understanding, needs to be distinguished from competency, which refers to having a skill.

See *computer competency.*

computer online service (KQ 1.8, p. 1.22)   Company that provides access to all kinds of databases and electronic meeting places to subscribers equipped with telephone-linked microcomputers. Popular online services are CompuServe, America Online, and Microsoft Network.

Online information services offer a wealth of services—for example, electronic mail, home shopping, travel reservations, enormous research facilities, discussion groups, and special-interest bulletin boards.

computer professional (KQ 1.1, p. 1.2)   Person in a profession involving computers who has had formal education in the technical aspects of using computers; examples are computer programmer, systems analyst, and network administrator.

Computer professionals are to be distinguished from computer *users*—people who use computers to perform professional or personal tasks, enhance learning, or have fun.

connectivity (KQ 1.8, p. 1.21)   Refers to the connection of computer systems via phone lines and other communications channels.

Connectivity is the foundation of the latest advances in the Digital Age. It provides online access to countless types of information and services.

CPU (central processing unit) (KQ 1.4, p. 1.10)   The processor; it controls and manipulates data to produce information. In a microcomputer the CPU is usually contained on a single integrated circuit or chip called a *microprocessor.* This chip and other components that make it work are mounted on a circuit board called a *motherboard* (*system board*). More powerful computers have many processors.

The CPU is the "brain" of the computer; without it, there would be no computers.

data (KQ 1.3, p. 1.5)   Raw facts and figures that are processed into information; the third element in a computer-based information system.

Users need data to create useful information.

database (KQ 1.8, p. 1.22)   Collection of integrated, or cross-referenced, electronically stored data that different people may access for different purposes.

Users with online connections to database services have enormous research resources at their disposal. In addition, businesses and organizations build databases to help them keep track of and manage their activities.

digital (KQ 1.3, p. 1.7)   Refers to communications signals or information represented in a binary or two-state way.

With a two-state on/off, open/closed, present/absent, positive/negative, yes/no arrangement, the on state can be coded as the digit 1, the off state as the digit 0. Computers use digital signals— strings of on and off electrical pulses corresponding to codes of 1s and 0s—to represent software instructions and data.

digital convergence (KQ 1.8, p. 1.24)   Technological merger of several industries through various devices that exchange information in the electronic, or digital, format used by computers. The industries are computers, communications, consumer electronics, entertainment, and mass media.

From a common electronic base, the same information may be exchanged among many organizations and people.

e-mail (electronic mail) (KQ 1.8, p. 1.21)   Software-controlled system that allows computer users to send and receive messages over a communications network.

E-mail allows users, via their keyboards, to post messages and send files to people all over the world, and to read responses and receive files.

hardware (KQ 1.3, p. 1.5)   The electronic and the electromechanical parts—the first element—of the computer-based information system. Hardware is classified into five categories: input, processing and memory, output, secondary storage, and communications.

Basically, hardware *is* the computer; however, hardware runs under the control of software and is useless without it.

information (KQ 1.3, p. 1.5)   Summarized data or otherwise manipulated (processed) data. Technically, data comprises raw facts and figures that are processed into information. However, information can also be raw data for the next person or job. Thus, the terms are sometimes used interchangeably. Information/data is the third element in a computer-based information system.

The whole purpose of a computer (and communications) system is to produce (and transmit) useful information.

input hardware (KQ 1.4, p. 1.8)   Devices that allow people to put data into the computer in a form that the computer can use; that is, they perform *input operations.* The keyboard, mouse, and scanner are common input devices.

Useful information cannot be produced without input data.

integrated circuit (IC) (KQ 1.7, p. 1.18)   Collection of electrical circuits, or pathways, etched on tiny squares, or chips, of silicon about 1½ inches square.

The development of the IC enabled the manufacture of the small, powerful, and relatively inexpensive computers used today.

interactivity (KQ 1.8, p. 1.23)   Situation in which the user is able to make an immediate response to what is going on and modify processes; that is, there is a dialog between the user and the computer or communications device.

Interactive devices allow the user to participate actively in what is going on instead of just passively reacting.

Internet (KQ 1.8, p. 1.23)   International network connecting many thousands of smaller networks that link the computers of millions of users at educational, scientific, military, and commercial institutions and in homes.

The Internet allows millions of people around the world to share information and services.

keyboard (KQ 1.4, p. 1.9)   Input hardware device that uses standard typewriter keys plus a number of specialized keys to input data and issue commands.

Microcomputer users will probably use the keyboard more than any other input device.

local area network (LAN) (KQ 1.6, p. 1.14)   Communications network that connects users located near one another, as in the same building.

LANs have replaced mainframes and other large computers for many functions and are considerably less expensive. Local area networks enable users in the same office, building, or college to share data and information and some peripherals, such as printers.

mainframe computer (KQ 1.6, p. 1.14)   Second most powerful computer, after the supercomputer. There are small-, medium-, and large-scale mainframes serving from hundreds to several thousands of users. Small mainframes are often called *midsize computers,* which used to be called *minicomputers.*

Mainframes are used by large organizations—such as banks, airlines, insurance companies, and colleges—for processing millions of transactions.

memory (KQ 1.4, p. 1.11)   Also called *main memory, primary storage, RAM (random access memory);* the computer's "work space," where data and programs for immediate processing are held. Memory is electronically created by special memory chips mounted on the system board.

Memory size determines how much data can be processed at once and how big and complex a program may be used to process it.

microcomputer (KQ 1.6, p. 1.14)   Also called a *personal computer,* or *PC;* the computer used most by business professionals. Microcomputers range in size from small palmtops, notebooks, and laptops to powerful desktops and floor-standing (tower) models. The microcomputer has a small silicon chip, or microprocessor, as its CPU.

Microcomputers are used in virtually every area of modern life. People going into business or professional life today are often required to have basic knowledge of the microcomputer.

microcontroller (KQ 1.6, p. 1.14)   Also called an *embedded,* or *dedicated, computer;* the smallest category of computer.

Microcontrollers are built into "smart" electronic devices, such as microwave ovens and electronic calculators, as controlling agents.

mouse (KQ 1.4, p. 1.9)   Input hardware device that can be rolled about on a desktop to direct a pointer on the computer's display screen. The *pointer* is a symbol, usually an arrow, that is used to select items from lists (menus) on the screen or to position the cursor by clicking buttons on the mouse. The *cursor* is the symbol on the screen that shows where data may be entered next, such as text in a document.

With microcomputers, a mouse is needed to use most graphical user interface programs and to draw illustrations.

multimedia (KQ 1.8, p. 1.23)   Computer technology that presents information in more than one medium, including text, graphics, animation, video, music, and voice.

Increasingly, multimedia is used in business, the professions, and education to improve the way information is communicated.

output hardware (KQ 1.4, p. 1.11)   Devices that translate information processed by the computer into a form that humans can understand; that is, they perform *output operations.* Common output devices are monitors (softcopy output) and printers (hardcopy output). Sound is also a form of computer output.

Without output devices, computer users would not be able to view or use their work.

people (KQ 1.3, p. 1.6)   Most important part of the computer-based information system.

People design and develop computer systems, operate the computer hardware, create the software, and establish procedures for carrying out tasks.

peripheral device (KQ 1.4, p. 1.8)   Any hardware device that is connected to a computer. Examples are the keyboard, mouse, monitor, and printer (external peripherals) and disk drives (internal peripherals).

Most of a computer system's input and output functions are performed by peripheral devices.

procedures (KQ 1.3, p. 1.6)   Descriptions of how things are done, steps for accomplishing a result. Procedures for computer systems appear in *documentation manuals,* which contain the guidelines for using the hardware and software. Procedures for using a particular software package are also often available on disk.

Procedures are the fourth element in a computer-based information system. In the form of documentation, procedures help users learn to use hardware and software.

processing hardware (KQ 1.4, p. 1.10)   Hardware that retrieves and executes (interprets) instructions (software) provided to the computer. The main components of processing hardware are the central processing unit (CPU), which is the brain of the computer, and main memory, where all instructions and/or data ready for processing are held.

Processing hardware forms the essence of the computer; no other hardware would work without it.

scanner (KQ 1.4, p. 1.9)   Input device that translates images of text, drawings, and photos into digital form.

Scanners simplify the input of complex data. The images can be processed by the computer, manipulated, displayed on a monitor, stored on a storage device, and/or communicated to another computer.

server (KQ 1.6, p. 1.15)   Computer shared by several users in a network.

Servers enable users to share data and applications.

software (KQ 1.3, p. 1.5)   Also called *programs;* electronic instructions that tell the hardware how to perform a task. Software represents the second element of a computer-based information system.

Without software, hardware would be useless.

storage hardware (KQ 1.4, p. 1.11)   Hardware that provides a means of storing software and data in a form that is relatively permanent, or *nonvolatile.* This type of storage is referred to as *secondary.* (Data and information in main memory, *primary storage,* is volatile, meaning it is lost when the power is turned off.)

The storage phase enables people to save their work for later retrieval, manipulation, and output.

supercomputer (KQ 1.6, p. 1.13)   Largest, fastest, and most expensive computer available.

system software (KQ 1.5, p. 1.12)   Software that controls the computer and enables it to run the hardware and applications software. System software, which includes the operating system, allows the computer to manage its internal resources.

system unit (KQ 1.4, p. 1.10)   Also called the *system cabinet;* housing that includes the electronic circuitry (processor), which does the processing, and main memory, which supports processing.

user (KQ 1.1, p. 1.3)   Someone without much technical knowledge of computers but who uses computers to produce information for professional or personal tasks, to enhance learning, or to have fun.

workstation (KQ 1.6, p. 1.14)   Expensive, powerful desktop computers used mainly by engineers, scientists, and special-effects creators for sophisticated purposes.

World Wide Web (KQ 1.8, p. 1.23)   The best-known part of the Internet; connected servers store information in multimedia form—that is, in sound, photos, and video, as well as text.

Supercomputers are used for research, weather forecasting, oil exploration, airplane building, and complex mathematical operations, for example.

Applications software cannot run without system software.

The microcomputer was born when processing, memory, and power supply were made small enough to fit into a cabinet that would fit on a desktop.

See *computer professional.*

Providing many capabilities comparable to midsize mainframes, workstations are used for such tasks as designing airplane fuselages, prescription drugs, and movies' special effects. Workstations are often connected to a larger computer system to facilitate the transfer of data and information. The capabilities of low-end workstations overlap those of high-end microcomputers.

People and companies who maintain Web locations on the Internet do so in sites called *Web pages* that are stored on servers connected to the Internet. To view Web pages, users need special software called a *Web browser*—such as Netscape Navigator or Communicator, or Microsoft Explorer.

1. Fill in the following blanks:
   a. The primary purpose of a computer system is to transform

      _____ into _____ .

   b. Whereas most of the world is _____, computers deal with data

      in _____ form.

   c. Hardware devices that are connected to the computer are referred to as

      _____ devices.

   d. The category of hardware that can be compared to a filing cabinet is

      _____ hardware.

   e. _____ is the term used to describe instructions that tell the
      hardware how to perform a task.

2. Label each of the following statements as either true or false.

   _____ Computers are continually getting larger and more expensive.

   _____ Mainframe computers process faster than microcomputers.

   _____ Main memory is a software component.

   _____ System software tells the computer how to run the hardware.

   _____ The Internet is currently the largest network in the world.

3. Which of the following is a type of computer hardware?

   a. _____ printer

   b. _____ memory

   c. _____ monitor

   d. _____ programs

   e. _____ CPU

4. What are the six components of a computer-based information system?

   a. _____

   b. _____

   c. _____

   d. _____

   e. _____

   f. _____

5. Computer hardware is categorized according to the types of operations it performs. List these five operations.

   a. _____

   b. _____

   c. _____

   d. _____

   e. _____

6. List three common types of input hardware:

   a. _____

   b. _____

   c. _____

7. Which of the following items are commonly located in the system cabinet? (Check all that apply.)

   a. _____ CPU

   b. _____ mouse

   c. _____ memory

   d. _____ printer

   e. _____ input hardware

8. Computers come in a variety of sizes and with a variety of processing capabilities. Computers are often categorized as follows:

   a. _____

   b. _____

   c. _____

   d. _____

   e. _____

9. Which of the following terms describe fourth-generation computers?

   a. _____ large-scale integrated circuits

   b. _____ microprocessor

   c. _____ magnetic tape

   d. _____ vacuum tubes

   e. _____ miniaturization

10. Define these terms:
    a. Internet
    b. World Wide Web

IN YOUR OWN WORDS

1. Answer each of the Key Questions listed at the beginning of the chapter.

2. What is the purpose of a computer system?

3. What kind of number system does a computer use? Why is this system also called "digital"?

4. What is a microcomputer?

5. What is the difference between system software and applications software?

6. What is the importance of memory to a computer system?

7. What is the importance of the CPU to a computer system?

8. What is a server computer?

9. What role does communications hardware play in a computer system?

10. In terms of computer output, what is meant by the terms *hardcopy* and *softcopy*?

KNOWLEDGE IN ACTION

1. **Logging On to Your Network.** For this project, you need access to your school's network. Go to the computer lab and document the steps required to log on to and off of your school's computer network. Do you need to turn the computer on and/or type in a password? What other information do you need to provide? When you're finished with the current work session, are you supposed to turn off the computer or leave it on so that other students can use it?

2. **Improving Your Mouse Skills.** Solitaire is a computer version of the popular card game and provides an excellent practice ground for improving your mouse skills. If your computer uses the Windows 95 or 98 operating systems, you can load this game by clicking the Start button on the Windows desktop and then choosing Programs, Accessories, Games, Solitaire from the menus. The objective of the game is to place the deck of 52 cards in four suit stacks at the top of the playing board. To do so, you first arrange the cards in descending order, using alternating colors (hearts or diamonds and spades or clubs). You build upon each of the original seven piles using cards from the other piles and the deck. To score points, you place cards in the suit stacks at the top of the screen in ascending order, starting with an ace. When all cards appear in their respective suit stack, you have won the game.

   To flip through the cards, you click the mouse pointer on the top card in the deck. To place a card in the suit stack, you double-click the card on the playing board or drag it to the desired stack. To arrange cards below a card pile on the playing board, you drag the card using the mouse. To quit Solitaire, choose Game, Exit from the Menu bar.

3. **Practicing Your Keyboard Skills.** If your computer uses the Windows 95 or 98 operating sys-

tems, you can use the WordPad utility to practice your typing skills. WordPad is used for storing, retrieving, editing, formatting, and printing various types of documents. To load WordPad, click the Start button on the Windows desktop and then choose Programs, Accessories, WordPad from the menus.

After loading WordPad, you'll see the insertion point blinking in the upper-left corner of the window. The insertion point marks where your typed characters will be positioned. On your own, type in a few sentences. (Don't worry about making typing mistakes!) Then, press the Enter key twice and type in a few more sentences. Experiment with pressing the different keys on the keyboard. To quit WordPad, choose File, Exit from the Menu bar and then click the No command button when prompted to save your work. For additional practice, feel free to repeat this exercise.

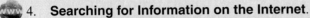

4. **Searching for Information on the Internet**. It's difficult to conceive how much information is available on the Internet and the Web. One method you can use to find information of interest among the millions of documents is to use a search engine. A *search engine* helps you find Web pages based on typed keywords or phrases. For this project, use your browser to visit the following search sites: *www.yahoo.com* and *www.infoseek.com*. Click in the Search text box and then type the phrase "personal computers" followed by the Enter key. When you locate a topic that you think would be of interest to your classmates, print it out by choosing File, Print from the Menu bar or clicking the Print button on the toolbar.

5. **Becoming Computer Literate and Computer Competent.** What do you think you still have to do to become computer literate and computer competent? Make a list, and then update it after you have finished the course.

Answers to Self-Test Exercises: 1a. data, information 1b. analog, digital 1c. peripheral 1d. secondary storage 1e. software 2. F, T, F, T, T 3. a, b, c, e 4. hardware, software, data/information, people, procedures, communications 5. input, processing and memory, output, storage, communications 6. keyboard, mouse, scanner 7. a, c 8. supercomputer, mainframe computer, workstation, microcomputer, microcontroller 9. a, b, e 10a. International network connecting many thousands of smaller networks that link the computers of millions of users at educational, scientific, military, and commercial institutions and in homes. b. The best-known part of the Internet; connected servers store information in multimedia form— that is, in sound, photos, and video, as well as text.

EPISODE 1

Whether you have a business or are planning to start a business, the World Wide Web provides numerous opportunities for reaching customers. It is accessed by millions of people in more than 200 countries and is growing at an astounding rate. Currently, commercial sites make up the fastest-growing segment of the World Wide Web. One reason is that in return for a minimal investment in creating a Web site, any business—large or small—can reach a worldwide audience.

For most businesses today, including business startups, the question isn't *whether* to create a Web site, but *when*. For you, the time is now. In this first of five Episodes, you assume the role of an entrepreneur who has decided to start a Web-based business. For inspiration and guidance as you work through each Episode, we profile Amazon.com Inc., a Web-based bookstore whose phenomenal success mirrors the expanding popularity of the Web.

Note: The Episodes are not "hands-on" tutorials, although they include some hands-on aspects; instead, they are meant to be thought provoking and to be the basis of discussions. You *can* complete the Episodes without access to the Web. However, you might not be able to answer all the questions at the end of each Episode.

In 1994, Jeffrey P. Bezos left a successful career on Wall Street to exploit the potential for electronic retailing on the World Wide Web. Soon thereafter, he founded Amazon.com, Inc. (www.amazon.com), an online bookstore that is today one of the leading commerce sites on the Web. For Jeff, success came quickly. Amazon.com sold its first book in July of 1995. By March 1999, Amazon.com had sales of more than $360 million and about 6 million customer accounts in more than 100 countries. When Amazon.com opened for business, it had 11 employees; now it has more than 1600. Amazon.com now also sells music and video CDs and some other items, and it also now owns Bookpage, one of the United Kingdom's largest online bookstores; Telebook, Germany's top-selling online bookstore; Internet Movie Database, a Web site for movie and TV information; and Sage Enterprises, a Web-based address-book/reminder service.

The Rationale Behind Amazon.com

For a number of reasons, Jeff felt that an opportunity existed for online book retailing. First, no traditional bookstore (that is, one confined by four walls) can possibly stock the more than 4.7 million titles offered by Amazon.com. Traditional bookstores must make substantial investments in real estate for retail stores and warehouses, and hire employees for each location. An online bookstore doesn't need retail locations or lots of warehouse space (Amazon.com orders books and CDs from the publisher *after* it takes an order), so can pass savings along to customers in the form of discounts. An online bookstore can obtain demographic information about its customers in order to offer personalized services, a difficult task for traditional bookstores. Amazon.com, for example, alerts customers via e-mail when books that are of interest to them are published.

Finally, Jeff saw opportunities for customer-customer and customer-author interaction. Today, customers post reviews of the books they read and share ideas with other customers interested in similar books and topics. For those customers interested in finding out more about their favorite authors, Amazon.com facilitates regular interviews with authors. Customers can also easily reach authors by e-mail to provide feedback.

Now let's preview some of the functions you might
perform at the Amazon.com site.

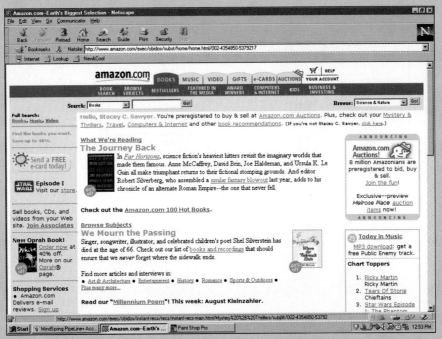

Navigate the site. After you enter the store, you click the underlined links
in the navigation bars (located on the left and right sides of each page) to
move around the site. Links also appear embedded on each page.

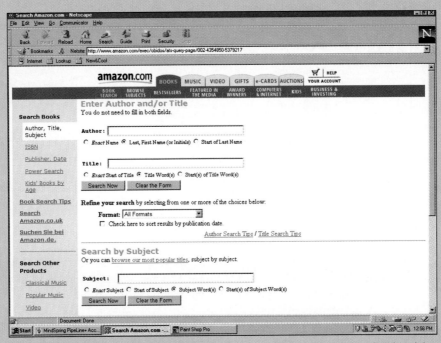

Perform targeted searches. If you click the Book Search button in the title
bar at the top of the page, the search page appears (*above*).

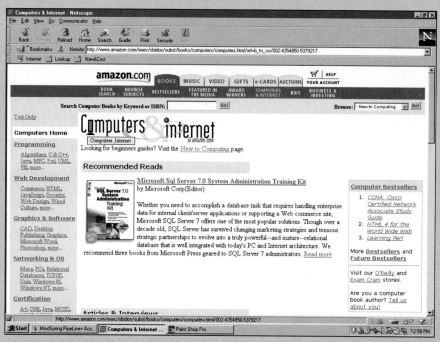

Browse a book category or featured list. For example, if you click the Computer & Internet link at the bottom of the opening page, the Home page for computer- and Internet-related books appears.

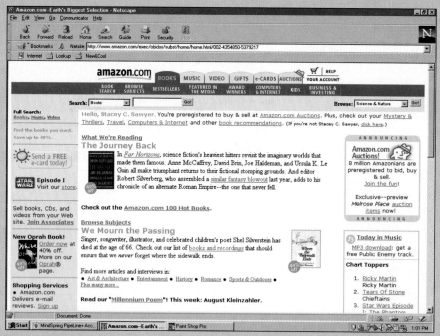

Participate in an Amazon.com auction. Click the Join the Fun! link in the navigation bar on the right side of the opening page to see what auctions you can participate in.

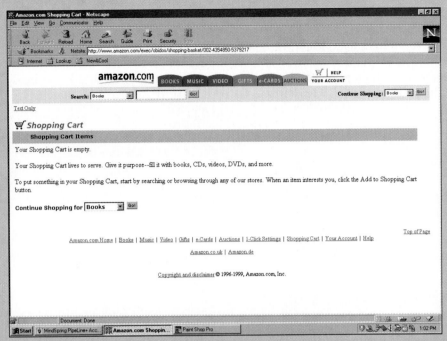

Make a purchase. At any point while shopping, you simply click a button or a shopping cart icon to proceed to the checkout stand to provide shipping and credit card details.

The Importance of Choosing a Name

So how did Mr. Bezos come up with the name *Amazon*? "Earth's biggest river, Earth's biggest bookstore. The Amazon River is 10 times as large as the next largest river, which is the Mississippi, in terms of volume of water. Twenty percent of the world's fresh water is in the Amazon River Basin, and we have six times as many titles as the world's largest physical bookstore," explained Amazon.com's founder in a 1996 interview.[1] Since that time, Amazon.com has vastly increased the amount of product that it offers.

Just as 1-800-FLOWERS is one of the world's largest florists because its name is so easy to remember, a memorable domain (address) name, such as *amazon.com, ibm.com,* or *television.com* can have a tremendous effect on the success of your Web business. (The suffix *.com* on the address means "commercial.") "In 1994, Mike O'Connor registered the Internet domain *television.com* as his own name. Domain names were free back then, and O'Connor had a hunch. He used to work in the radio business, where a station's call letters (like KOOL or WLIV) are one of its most valuable assets. O'Connor figured the same thing would happen to Internet domain names. His foresight paid off in May, 1996, when he sold his rights to *television.com* for more than $50,000," says Web author Vince Emery.[2]

For a couple of hundred dollars or less, your Internet access provider—or an address-registration service—will register your name for you. Your base charge per name is good for two years, plus you may have to pay an annual fee. Duplicate domain names can't exist on the Web. You can easily check to see if the name you choose already exists using the Internet Assigned Numbers Authority (iana) Web site at http://www.iana.org and click on Domain Name Services, then How to Get a Domain Name.

Introducing Yourname.com

Now it's your turn to come up with an idea for a small business that you would like to start on the Web. We emphasize the word *small* so that you can more easily identify the hardware, software, and communications requirements for the business in later Episodes. For simplicity, assume you will run your business from a single computer and that you will generate revenue from selling a product. It is highly possible that your business idea already exists on the Web. If so, feel free to use the existing business as a source of ideas for your new startup, but don't forget to come up with a memorable (and unique) name for your business.

Assume you will hire a Web consultant to take care of the technical aspects of designing your Web site and getting it to work online. Although you can purchase a software package that will lead you through this process, your role in these Episodes is to decide *what* you want to do, not *how* you're going to do it. Understanding all the technical details of the Web can be a full-time job in itself, so leave these technical details to your expert assistant.

What Do You Think?

1. Visit the Amazon.com Web site. What are the main features of the site? Is it easy to order a book? How are payment transactions performed? What features of the site do you find especially interesting? Would you consider buying your next book at Amazon.com rather than at your local bookstore? Why? Why not?

2. Visit the Amazon.com Web site and search for a book on a topic you're interested in. In a few paragraphs, describe the process of searching for a book, reading customer reviews, and learning more about the author.

3. Provide a general overview (1–2 paragraphs) of the business you would like to start on the Web. What product are you planning to sell? What advantages will the Web provide you in selling this product? Does a business like yours already exist on the Web? If so, how will your business compare/compete?

4. What kinds of tasks will you need a computer for in your new business? Will you need to keep track of inventory? Payroll? Monthly bills (accounts payable)? Receipts? Will you need a computer to keep tax records? What else?

5. Choose a name for your business. If you have Web access, check to see whether the name already exists by visiting iana's search page at http://www.iana.org. Describe the process of using the site and print out the results.

6. Some sites are dedicated to providing statistics about the Web. Visit Georgia University's site at www.cc.gatech.edu/gvu/user_surveys/ to find some interesting statistics.

PROCESSING HARDWARE

Turning Data into Something You Can Use

KEY QUESTIONS

You should be able to answer the following questions:

2.1 How Data & Programs Are Represented in the Computer *What is a binary coding scheme?*

2.2 The Processor, Main Memory, & Registers *What is a computer processor, and what does it consist of?*

2.3 Telling Computers Apart: RAM Capacity, Word Size, & Processor Speed *How are a computer's RAM, word size, and processing speed measured?*

2.4 Focus on the Microcomputer: What's Inside? *What factors should you consider before purchasing a microcomputer?*

2.5 Coming Attractions? *What processing technologies might we use in the future?*

Many types of computers are doing their jobs so unobtrusively that we hardly know they're there. "The best computer interface is my car's antilock braking system," says University of Virginia computer science professor Randy Pausch. "I jam on the pedal and a computer makes thousands of complex decisions for me and saves my life."[1]

The microprocessor, says Michael Malone, author of *The Microprocessor: A Biography,* "is the most important invention of the 20th century."[2] Quite a bold claim, considering the incredible products that have issued forth during the past 100 years. Part of the reason, Malone argues, is the pervasiveness of the microprocessor in the important machines in our lives, from computers to transportation. However, pervasiveness isn't the whole story. "The microprocessor is, intrinsically, something special," he says. "Just as [the human being] is an animal, yet transcends that state, so too the microprocessor is a silicon chip, but more." Why? The reason is that it can be programmed *to learn and adapt.* Malone writes:

> Implant [a microprocessor] into a traditional machine—say an automobile engine or refrigerator—and suddenly that machine for the first time can learn, it can adapt to its environment, respond to changing conditions, become more efficient, more responsive to the unique needs of its user. That machine now evolves, not from generation to generation but within itself.[3]

This ability to learn and adapt, Malone points out, "is something radically new in human history. The microprocessor constructs its own society; in the emptiness of its millions of transistors awaiting instruction lies a near-infinity of possibilities, from the Space Shuttle orbiting the earth to the toaster on your kitchen counter."

The development of the microprocessor enabled the development of the microcomputer. To understand the tremendous role microcomputers now play in

A northern California family shows how pervasive computer technology is in our lives. All these items have microprocessors.

This surgeon is using a computer application both to plan brain surgery and to train neurosurgeons. The area of the skull that must be cut to expose the appropriate part of the brain is shown in blue.

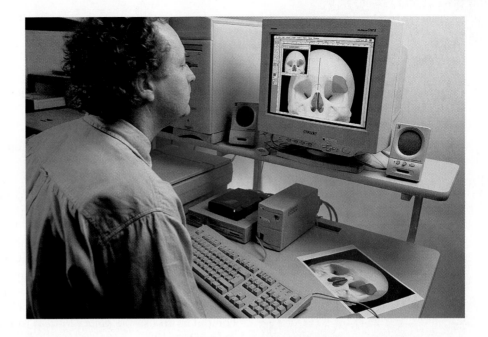

business and life in general, it's helpful to look at how that role has developed. With the introduction of the Apple II and the Radio Shack Model I and II systems in the late 1970s, the business community began to adopt microcomputers. Then a number of additional vendors, including Atari, Commodore, Osborne, and Kaypro, entered the marketplace with computers designed to be used in the office or in the home. The interest in microcomputers grew rather slowly at first for several reasons: (1) The starting costs (without peripherals) for some microcomputer systems was quite high, ranging up to $6000; (2) only a limited amount of applications software was commercially available; (3) the average person did not have sufficient background in computer-related subjects to use the computer without difficulty; and (4) there were no industry-wide standards to ensure the common usability of data and software on different brands of microcomputer systems.

However, when IBM introduced the IBM PC in 1981, along with DOS (disk operating system, developed in cooperation with Bill Gates of Microsoft), so many businesses adopted the product that an industry standard was set. Most vendors now design their products to be compatible with this standard, which is based on Intel processor design. The only relatively successful microcomputer product line today that uses a different microprocessor architecture (Motorola) is the Apple Macintosh.

There are now more than 15 billion microprocessors and microcontrollers (✔ p. 1.14) in use each day on earth. That is more than all the televisions, automobiles, and telephones combined. On those chips are more circuits than raindrops will fall in California this year. And the lines and structures on each of those chips now outnumber the streets and buildings of the largest cities ever built.

Were all these chips to disappear tomorrow, our civilization would be in deep trouble. The lights would go out, the Internet would go silent, TV screens and phone lines would be reduced to snow and static. Emergency rooms would malfunction, as would airplanes, trains, and cars. Commerce would halt.

This chapter covers this amazing device—the processor—and associated processing hardware. But before we examine the topic of processing, we need to discuss the language of computers.

2.1 How Data & Programs Are Represented in the Computer

KEY QUESTION What is a binary coding scheme?

Before we study the inner workings of the processor, we need to expand on Chapter 1's discussion of data representation in the computer—how the processor "understands" data. We started with a simple fact: Electricity can be either *on* or *off*.

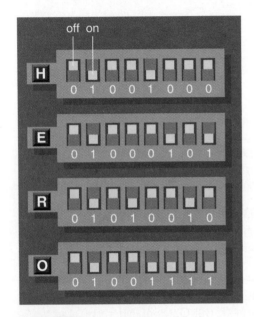

Other kinds of technology also use this two-state on/off arrangement. An electrical circuit may be open or closed. The magnetic pulses on a disk or tape may be present or absent. Current may be high voltage or low voltage. A punched card or tape may have a hole or not have a hole. This two-state situation allows computers to use the *binary system* to represent data and programs.

The decimal system that we are accustomed to has 10 digits (0, 1, 2, 3, 4, 5, 6, 7, 8, 9). By contrast, the **binary system** has only two digits: 0 and 1. (*Bi-* means "two.") Thus, in the computer the 0 can be represented by the electrical current being off (or at low voltage) and the 1 by the current being on (or at high voltage). All data and programs that go into the computer are represented in terms of these numbers. (*See Figure 2.1.*) For example, the letter H is a translation of the electronic signal 01001000, or off-on-off-off-on-off-off-off. When you press the key for H on the computer keyboard, the character is automatically converted into the series of electronic impulses that the computer recognizes.

Figure 2.1 Binary representation. How the letters H-E-R-O are represented in one type of off/on, 0/1 binary code.

Binary Coding Schemes

All the amazing things that computers do are based on binary numbers made up of 0s and 1s. Fortunately, we don't have to enter data into the computer using groups of 0s and 1s. Instead, we use natural-language characters such as those on the keyboard to input data. Then the computer system encodes the data by means of *binary,* or *digital, coding schemes* to represent letters, numbers, and special characters.

There are many coding schemes. Two common ones are EBCDIC and ASCII. Both commonly use 8 bits to form each character, or byte, providing up to 256 combinations with which to form letters, numbers, and special characters, such as math symbols and Greek letters. (*See Figure 2.2.*) One newer coding scheme uses 16 bits, enabling it to represent 65,536 unique characters.

- *EBCDIC:* Pronounced "*eb*-see-dick," **EBCDIC,** which stands for **Extended Binary Coded Decimal Interchange Code,** is commonly used in IBM mainframes. EBCDIC is an 8-bit coding scheme, meaning that it can represent 256 (2^8) characters.

- *ASCII:* Pronounced "*as*-key," **ASCII,** which stands for **American Standard Code for Information Interchange,** is the most widely used binary code with

Figure 2.2 Two common binary coding schemes: EBCDIC and ASCII. There are many more characters than those shown here. These include punctuation marks, Greek letters, math symbols, and foreign language symbols.

Character	ASCII-8	EBCDIC	Character	ASCII-8	EBCDIC
A	0100 0001	1100 0001	N	0100 1110	1101 0101
B	0100 0010	1100 0010	O	0100 1111	1101 0110
C	0100 0011	1100 0011	P	0101 0000	1101 0111
D	0100 0100	1100 0100	Q	0101 0001	1101 1000
E	0100 0101	1100 0101	R	0101 0010	1101 1001
F	0100 0110	1100 0110	S	0101 0011	1110 0010
G	0100 0111	1100 0111	T	0101 0100	1110 0011
H	0100 1000	1100 1000	U	0101 0101	1110 0100
I	0100 1001	1100 1001	V	0101 0110	1110 0101
J	0100 1010	1101 0001	W	0101 0111	1110 0110
K	0100 1011	1101 0010	X	0101 1000	1110 0111
L	0100 1100	1101 0011	Y	0101 1001	1110 1000
M	0100 1101	1101 0100	Z	0101 1010	1110 1001
0	0011 0000	1111 0000	5	0011 0101	1111 0101
1	0011 0001	1111 0001	6	0011 0110	1111 0110
2	0011 0010	1111 0010	7	0011 0111	1111 0111
3	0011 0011	1111 0011	8	0011 1000	1111 1000
4	0011 0100	1111 0100	9	0011 1001	1111 1001
!	0010 0001	0101 1010	;	0011 1011	0101 1110

non-IBM mainframes and virtually all microcomputers. Whereas *standard ASCII* originally used 7 bits for each character, limiting its character set to 128 (2^7), the more common *extended ASCII* uses 8 bits.

■ *Unicode:* Although ASCII can handle English and European languages well, it cannot handle all the characters of some other languages, such as Chinese and Japanese. **Unicode,** which was developed to deal with such languages, uses 2 bytes (16 bits) for each character, instead of 1 byte (8 bits), enabling it to handle 65,536 character combinations rather than just 256. Although each Unicode character takes up twice as much memory space and disk space as each ASCII character, conversion to the Unicode standard seems likely. However, because most existing software applications and databases use the 8-bit standard, the conversion will take time.

The Parity Bit: Checking for Errors

Dust, electrical disturbance, weather conditions, and other factors can cause interference in a circuit or communications line that is transmitting a byte. How does the computer know if an error has occurred? Detection is accomplished by use of a parity bit. A **parity bit,** also called a *check bit,* is an extra bit attached to the end of a byte for purposes of checking for accuracy.

Parity schemes may be *even parity* or *odd parity.* In an even-parity scheme, for example, the ASCII letter H (01001000) consists of two 1s. Thus, the ninth bit, the parity bit, would be 0 in order to make an even number of 1s. Likewise, with the letter O (01001111), which has five 1s, the ninth bit would be 1 to make an even number of 1s. *(See Figure 2.3, next page.)* The system software in the computer automatically and continually checks the parity scheme for accuracy.

Figure 2.3 Example of a parity bit. This example uses an even-parity scheme.

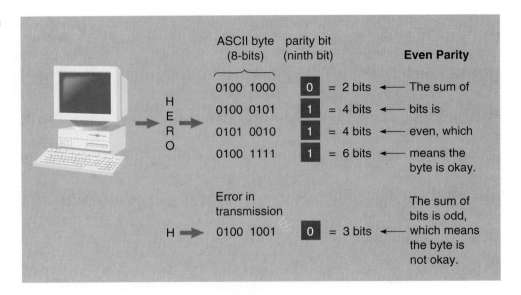

	ASCII byte (8-bits)	parity bit (ninth bit)	**Even Parity**
H	0100 1000	0 = 2 bits	← The sum of
E	0100 0101	1 = 4 bits	← bits is
R	0101 0010	1 = 4 bits	← even, which
O	0100 1111	1 = 6 bits	← means the byte is okay.

Error in transmission

			The sum of bits is odd,
H →	0100 1001	0 = 3 bits	← which means the byte is not okay.

Machine Language: Your Brand of Computer's Very Own Language

So far we have been discussing how *data* is represented in the computer—for example, via ASCII code in microcomputers. But if data is represented this way in all microcomputers, why won't word processing software that runs on an Apple Macintosh run (without special arrangements) on an IBM PC? In other words, why are these two microcomputer platforms incompatible? It's because each hardware platform, or processor model family, has a unique machine language for executing *programs*. **Machine language** is a binary programming language that the computer can run directly. To most people an instruction written in machine language is incomprehensible, consisting of long strings of 0s and 1s. However, it is what the computer itself can understand, and the 0s and 1s represent precise storage locations and operations. Following are only three examples of many different platforms:

- Intel processors, used in most IBM-type PCs
- Motorola processors, used in Macintoshes and other Apple computers
- S/370, used in IBM mainframes

Hong Kong vendor Matthew Chan creates custom-built computer systems—clients specify the amount of memory, disk-drive capacity, and the brand of CPU they want.

Many people are initially confused by the difference between the 0 and 1 ASCII code used for data representation and the 0 and 1 code used in machine language. What's the difference? ASCII is used for *data* files—that is, files containing only data in the form of ASCII code. Data files cannot be opened and worked on without *execution* programs, the software instructions that tell the computer what to do with the data files. These execution programs are run by the computer in the form of machine language.

But wouldn't it be horrendously difficult for programmers to write complex applications programs in seemingly endless series of machine-language groups of 0s and 1s? Indeed it would, so they don't. Instead, programmers write in special programming languages that more closely resemble human language. We discuss programming in Chapter 10.

How Computer Capacity Is Expressed: Bit by Bit

How many 0s and 1s will a computer's main memory or a storage device such as a hard disk hold? This is a very important matter. The following terms are used to denote capacity:

- *Bit:* In the binary system, the binary digit (bit)—0 or 1—is the smallest unit of measurement.

- *Byte:* To represent letters, numbers, or special characters (such as ! or *), bits are combined into groups. A group of 8 bits is called a **byte,** and a byte represents one character, digit, or other value. (For example, in one scheme, 01001000 represents the letter H.) The capacity of a computer's memory or a diskette is expressed in numbers of bytes or generally in multiples of bytes.

- *Kilobyte:* A **kilobyte (K, KB)** is about 1000 bytes. (Actually, it's precisely 1024 bytes, but the figure is commonly rounded.) The kilobyte was a common unit of measure for memory or secondary-storage capacity on older computers. The original IBM PC, for example, had 640 K (about 640,000 characters) of memory. An average printed page of text, such as in this book, would take up about 4100–4200 bytes, or 4.1–4.2 kilobytes of space.

- *Megabyte:* A **megabyte (M, MB)** is about 1 million bytes (1,048,576 bytes). Many measures of microcomputer capacity—such as for main memory and diskettes—are expressed in megabytes.

- *Gigabyte:* A **gigabyte (G, GB)** is about 1 billion bytes (1,073,741,824 bytes). A gigabyte measures the capacity of many microcomputer hard disks and the main memory capacity of mainframes and some supercomputers.

- *Terabyte:* A **terabyte (T, TB)** represents about 1 trillion bytes (1,009,511,627,776 bytes). This unit of measurement is used for some supercomputers' main memory capacity.

- *Petabyte:* A new measurement accommodates the huge storage capacities of modern databases—a **petabyte** represents about 1 million gigabytes!

A little later in the chapter we'll go into main memory capacity in more detail.

2.2 The Proc‑essor, Main Memory & Registers

KEY QUESTION **What is a computer processor, and what does it consist of?**

How is the information in "information processing" in fact processed? As we mentioned in Chapter 1, this is the job of the circuitry known as the **processor.** In large computers such as mainframes, this device, along with main memory and some other basic circuitry, is also called the **central processing unit (CPU)**; in microcomputers, it is often called the **microprocessor.** The processor works hand in hand with other circuits known as *main memory* and *registers* to carry out processing. Together these circuits form a closed world, which is opened only by connection to input/output devices, covered in Chapter 3.

The Processor: In Charge

The main processor follows the instructions of the software to manipulate data into information. The processor consists of two parts: (1) the control unit and (2) the arithmetic/logic unit. The two components are connected by a kind of electronic roadway called a **bus.** *(See Figure 2.4.)* (A bus also connects these components with other parts of the microcomputer, as we will discuss.)

■ *Control unit:* The **control unit** tells the rest of the computer system how to carry out a program's instructions. It directs the movement of electronic signals between main memory and the arithmetic/logic unit. It also directs these electronic signals between main memory and the input and output devices.

■ *Arithmetic/logic unit:* The **arithmetic/logic unit,** or **ALU,** performs arithmetic operations and logical operations and controls the speed of those operations.

   As you might guess, *arithmetic* operations are the fundamental math operations: addition, subtraction, multiplication, and division.

Figure 2.4 The control unit and the arithmetic/logic unit. The two components are connected by a kind of electronic roadway called a *bus*. A bus also connects to main memory. Temporary data storage holding/computation working areas called *registers* are located in the control unit and the arithmetic/logic unit.

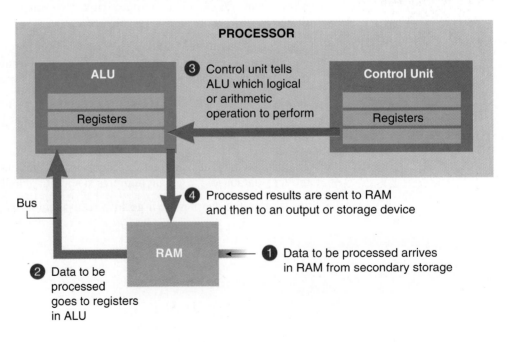

PROCESSOR

ALU

Registers

❸ Control unit tells ALU which logical or arithmetic operation to perform

Control Unit

Registers

Bus

❹ Processed results are sent to RAM and then to an output or storage device

RAM

❶ Data to be processed arrives in RAM from secondary storage

❷ Data to be processed goes to registers in ALU

Logical operations are comparisons. That is, the ALU compares two pieces of data to see whether one is "equal to" (=), "greater than" (>), or "less than" (<) the other. The comparisons can also be combined, as in "greater than or equal to" (>=) and "less than or equal to" (<=).

In the most powerful computers, the CPU is contained on several relatively large printed circuit boards. In the case of a microcomputer's microprocessor, the processor circuitry is etched on a thumbnail-size or slightly larger **chip** (or **microchip**) of silicon. The chip is mounted on a carrier with metal leads, or pins, on the bottom that plug into the computer's main circuit board, called the *system board.*

What is silicon, and why use it? *Silicon* is an element that is widely found in clay and sand. It is used not only because its abundance makes it cheap but also because it is a *semiconductor.* A *semiconductor* is material whose electrical properties are intermediate between a good conductor of electricity and a nonconductor of electricity. (An example of a good conductor of electricity is copper in household wiring; an example of a nonconductor is the plastic sheath around that wiring.) Because it is only a semiconductor, silicon has partial resistance to electricity. As a result, when good-conducting metals are overlaid on the silicon, the electronic circuitry of the integrated circuit can be created. *(See Figure 2.5, next page.)*

Specialized Processor Chips: Assistants to the CPU

Actually, modern computers may have a number of processors in addition to the main processor. Each of these **coprocessors** is dedicated to a special job. Two common examples are math and graphics coprocessor chips. A *math coprocessor chip* helps programs using lots of mathematical equations to run faster. A *graphics coprocessor chip* enhances the performance of programs with lots of graphics and helps create complex screen displays. Specialized chips significantly increase the speed of a computer system by offloading work from the main processor. These chips may be plugged directly into the motherboard; however, they are often included on "daughter cards," such as sound cards and graphics cards, used to expand a computer's capabilities.

In the next few years, we may see the phasing out of these specialized chips. National Semiconductor Corporation and Intel are both working on a "PC on a chip," one chip that would combine all the different chip functions found in current PCs.

Chips mounted on an IBM mainframe board

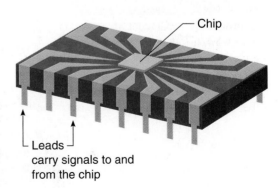

Chip

Leads carry signals to and from the chip

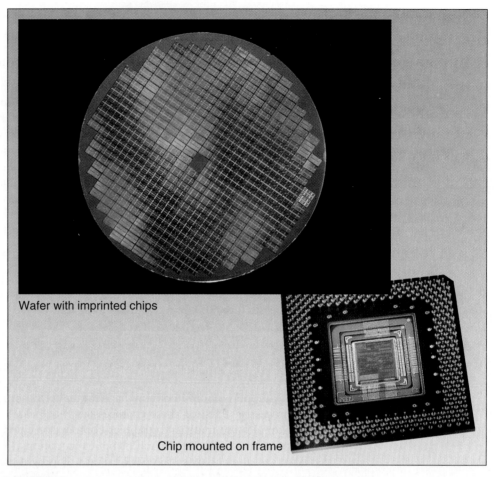

Wafer with imprinted chips

Chip mounted on frame

Chip designers checking out an enlarged drawing of chip circuits.

Figure 2.5 Manufacture of a chip. In brief, chips are created like this:

1. A large drawing of the electrical circuitry is made; it looks something like the map of a train yard (*see left*). The drawing is then photographically reduced hundreds of times so that it is of microscopic size.

2. That reduced photograph is duplicated many times to produce multiple copies of the same image or circuit, arranged like a sheet of postage stamps.

3. That sheet of multiple copies of the circuit is then printed (in a process called *photolithography*) and etched onto a 3-inch-diameter piece of silicon called a *wafer*.

4. Subsequent printings of layer after layer of additional circuits produce multilayered and interconnected electronic circuitry built above and below the original silicon surface.

5. Later, an automated die-cutting machine cuts the wafer into separate *chips*, which can be less than 1 centimeter square and about half a millimeter thick. A *chip*, or *microchip*, is a tiny piece of silicon that contains thousands of microminiature electronic circuit components, mainly transistors. (A transistor is like an electronic gate, or switch, that opens and closes to transmit or stop electrical current. It can alternate between on and off millions of times per second.)

6. After being tested, each chip is then mounted in a protective frame with extruding metallic pins that provide electrical connections, through wires, to a computer or other electronic device.

CISC, RISC, & MPP: Not All Processors Are Created Equal

Not all main processors are constructed exactly the same—a factor that also affects the speed of a computer system.

■ *CISC: CISC* (pronounced *sisk*) for *complex instruction set computer* refers to the processor architecture (chip design) found in most conventional mainframes and personal computers. CISC chips support many complex instructions. One argument against CISC technology is that this great number of instructions gets in the way of processing speed. These chips are also expensive to produce and use a lot of power.

■ *RISC: RISC* (pronounced *risk*), for *reduced instruction set computer,* refers to processors that support fewer instructions than do CISC chips. One advantage of RISC chips over CISC chips is that the reduced number of instructions enables them to execute instructions faster. RISC chips are also cheaper to produce, because they require fewer transistors.

   Still, experts debate about the ultimate value of RISC technology. RISC chips work by shifting the computational burden from hardware to software. Skeptics argue that adding burden to software isn't necessary because traditional CISC chips are getting faster and cheaper anyway. However, the entire argument may become unnecessary because CISC and RISC chips are getting more alike. Not only do many of today's RISC chips include as many instructions as CISC chips, but CISC chips are now incorporating features traditionally associated with RISC chips. Macintosh computers and many workstations use RISC technology.

■ *MPP:* Computers with a CISC or RISC processor execute instructions one at a time—that is, *serially.* However, a computer with more than one processor can execute more than one instruction at a time, which is called *parallel processing.* Although some powerful microcomputers and workstations are available with more than one main processor, the most powerful computers, such as supercomputers (✔ p. 1.13), often use *massively parallel processing (MPP),* which spreads calculations over hundreds or even thousands of standard, inexpensive microprocessors of the type used in microcomputers. (Option Red has 9072 processors!) Tasks are parceled out to a great many processors, which work simultaneously.

Main Memory (Primary Storage): Working Storage Area for the CPU

Mentioned briefly in Chapter 1, **main memory**—also known as *primary storage, internal memory, memory,* or *RAM (random access memory)*—is working storage (✔ p. 1.11). The term *random access* comes from the fact that data can be stored and retrieved at random—from anywhere in the electronic RAM chips—in approximately equal amounts of time, no matter what the specific data locations are. This circuitry has three tasks. (1) It holds data for processing. (2) It holds instructions (the programs) for processing the data. (3) It holds data that has been processed (become useful information) and is waiting to be sent to an output, secondary storage, or communications device.

   Main memory is in effect the computer's short-term storage capacity. It limits the total size of the programs and data files that the computer can work on at any given moment. There are two important facts to know about main memory:

■ *Its contents are temporary:* Once the power to the computer is turned off, all the data and programs within main memory simply vanish. This is why data must also be stored on disks and tapes—called secondary storage to distinguish them from main memory's primary storage.

Thus, main memory is said to be volatile. As mentioned earlier, *volatile storage* is temporary storage; the contents are lost when the power is turned off. Consequently, if your computer experiences a sudden power failure, whatever you are currently working on will immediately disappear. This impermanence is the reason why you should *frequently* save your work in progress to a secondary-storage medium such as a diskette or hard disk. By "frequently," we mean every 3–5 minutes.

■ *Its capacity varies in different computers:* The size of main memory is important. It determines how much data can be processed at once and how big and complex a program may be used to process the data.

Main memory is contained on chips called *RAM chips* that use CMOS (complementary metal-oxide semiconductor) technology. Common RAM technologies are dynamic RAM (DRAM) and static RAM (SRAM). Because SRAM chips are more expensive and use more power, DRAM chips are used in most personal computers. The drawback to DRAM chips is that their contents must be constantly refreshed, making them less reliable than SRAM chips.

Registers

The control unit and the ALU also contain registers, special high-speed circuitry areas that temporarily store data during processing and provide working areas for computation. *(Refer back to Figure 2.4.)* It could be said that main memory, which is outside the processor, holds material that will be used "a little bit later." Registers, which are contained in the processor, hold material that is to be processed immediately. The computer loads the program instructions and data from main memory into the registers just before processing. There are several types of registers, including an instruction register, which holds the instruction being executed; an address register, which holds the addresses (locations) of data to be processed; a program register, which holds status information; and an accumulator, which holds the results of the ALU's logic operations.

The Machine Cycle: How a Single Instruction Is Processed

How does the computer keep track of the characters of data or instructions in main memory? Like a system of post-office mailboxes, it uses addresses. An *address* is the location, designated by a unique number, in main memory in which a character of data or part of an instruction is stored during processing. To process each character, the processor's control unit retrieves that character from its address in main memory and places it into a register. This is the first step in what is called the *machine cycle.*

The **machine cycle** comprises a series of operations performed to execute a single program instruction. It is the shortest interval in which an elementary operation can take place within the processor. The machine cycle consists of two parts: an instruction cycle, which fetches and decodes; and an execution cycle, which executes and stores. *(See Figure 2.6.)*

■ *Instruction cycle:* In the **instruction cycle,** or **I-cycle,** the control unit (1) fetches (gets) an instruction from main memory and (2) decodes that instruction (determines what it means).

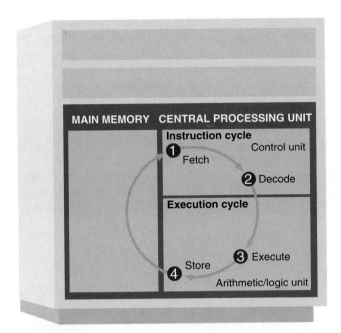
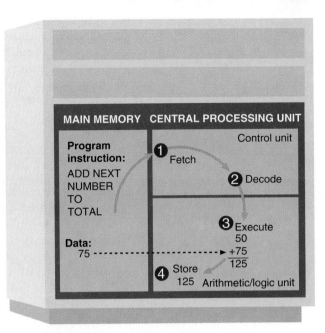

Figure 2.6 The machine cycle. *(Left)* The machine cycle executes instructions one at a time during the instruction cycle and the execution cycle, through four steps: fetch, decode, execute, store. *(Right)* Example of how the addition of two numbers, 50 and 75, is processed and stored in a single machine cycle.

■ *Execution cycle:* During the **execution cycle,** or **E-cycle,** the arithmetic/logic unit (3) executes the instruction (performs the operation on the data) and (4) stores the processed results in a register.

The details of the machine cycle are actually a bit more involved than this, but our description shows the general sequence. The machine cycle is important because a processor's speed is often measured by the time it takes to complete one cycle.

2.3 Telling Computers Apart: RAM Capacity, Word Size,& Processor Speed

KEY QUESTION **How are a computer's RAM, word size, and processing speed measured?**

An apocryphal tale says that, in 1949 the head of IBM, Thomas J. Watson, estimated that the demand for computers would never exceed more than about a dozen for the entire world.[4]

How far we have come! The world now has millions of computer users. Prices have fallen to the point that not only are computers not considered exotic, they are often considered as indispensable an appliance as a phone or television set. Watson's 12 computers have multiplied into millions. How to distinguish among the various types?

Recall from Chapter 1 that computers are classified according to how powerful they are—supercomputers, mainframes and midsize computers, workstations, microcomputers, and microcontrollers. Their power is measured according to three main units of measurement: RAM capacity, word size capability, and processor speed. Although there are other differentiating factors, these three are the most important.

RAM Capacity

The main memory capacity of most microcomputers is stated in megabytes (MB). If a microcomputer has less than 32 MB RAM, it will not be able to handle some of today's sophisticated software programs. Many software manufacturers recommend 32 MB or *more* of RAM for microcomputers. Fortunately, it's easy to increase RAM capacity if you find that you need more.

The RAM capacity of many mainframes and some supercomputers is measured in gigabytes (GB). Other supercomputers' RAM capacity is measured in terabytes (TB). (The Option Red supercomputer mentioned earlier has 600 gigabytes of memory.)

Word Size

Processor capacity is expressed in terms of *word size,* which refers to the number of bits it can hold in its registers, process at one time, and send through its internal (local) bus, the electronic pathway between the CPU, memory, and registers. Often the more bits in a word, the faster the computer. A 32-bit processor will work with data and instructions in 32-bit chunks. A 64-bit word processor is faster, working with data and instructions in 64-bit chunks. Other things being equal, a 64-bit computer processes 8 bytes in the time it takes a 32-bit machine to process 4 bytes.

Note that expansion bus capacity is also measured by word size. Expansion buses connect the processor, RAM, and registers to the computer's peripheral devices. In other words, you can characterize a processor by saying how many bits it can work with at a time *and* how many bits it can send or receive at a time. Thus you can have a microcomputer with a 32-bit local bus but a 16-bit expansion bus. In this case, certain input/output operations would slow down to the speed of 16-bit word size.

Thai Buddhist monks observe computer operations at Panthip Plaza, a Bangkok mall specializing in computer products. The monks use computers to learn about Buddha and his teachings.

Processing Speeds

Computers with a large word size can process more data in each instruction cycle. However, with transistors switching off and on at perhaps millions of times per second, the repetition of the machine cycle occurs at blinding speeds. Just how blinding? Every computer contains a system clock—an internal timing device that switches on when the power to the computer is turned on. The **system clock** controls how fast all the operations take place. The system clock uses fixed vibrations from a quartz crystal to deliver a steady stream of digital pulses to pace the processor. The faster the clock, the faster the processing, assuming the computer's internal circuits can handle the increased speed.

Microcomputer speeds are commonly measured in **megahertz (MHz),** with 1 MHz equal to 1 million beats (machine cycles) per second. Microcomputers purchased today commonly run at 200–400 MHz or more. Assuming that all the computer's other specifications are the same, the faster the megahertz rating, the faster the computer. The speeds of larger computers are sometimes measured in MIPS (*millions of instructions per second*) and FLOPS (*floating-point operations per second*), however, these ratings aren't commonly used anymore.

Now that we have covered some of the basics relating to computer processing in general, let's focus on the type of computer you will most likely have to work with: the microcomputer.

2.4 Focus on the Microcomputer: What's Inside?

KEY QUESTION **What factors should you consider before purchasing a microcomputer?**

As important as the microprocessor is to you, would you recognize it if you saw one? If someone opened up a microcomputer cabinet and let you look inside, could you identify it? And what else is inside the box that we call "the computer"? This section covers these issues.

The box or cabinet that contains the microcomputer's processing hardware and other components is called the **system unit.** *(See Figure 2.7, next page.)* The system unit does not include the keyboard or printer. Usually it also does not include the monitor (display screen). It usually does include a hard disk drive, one or two diskette drives, and a CD-ROM drive. We describe these secondary storage devices and other peripheral devices in the chapters on input/output devices and storage devices. Here we are concerned with the following parts of the system unit:

- Power supply
- Motherboard
- Microprocessor
- RAM chips
- ROM chips

- Other forms of memory—cache, VRAM, flash
- Ports
- Expansion slots and boards
- Bus lines and PC slots and cards

Figure 2.7 The system unit and its contents

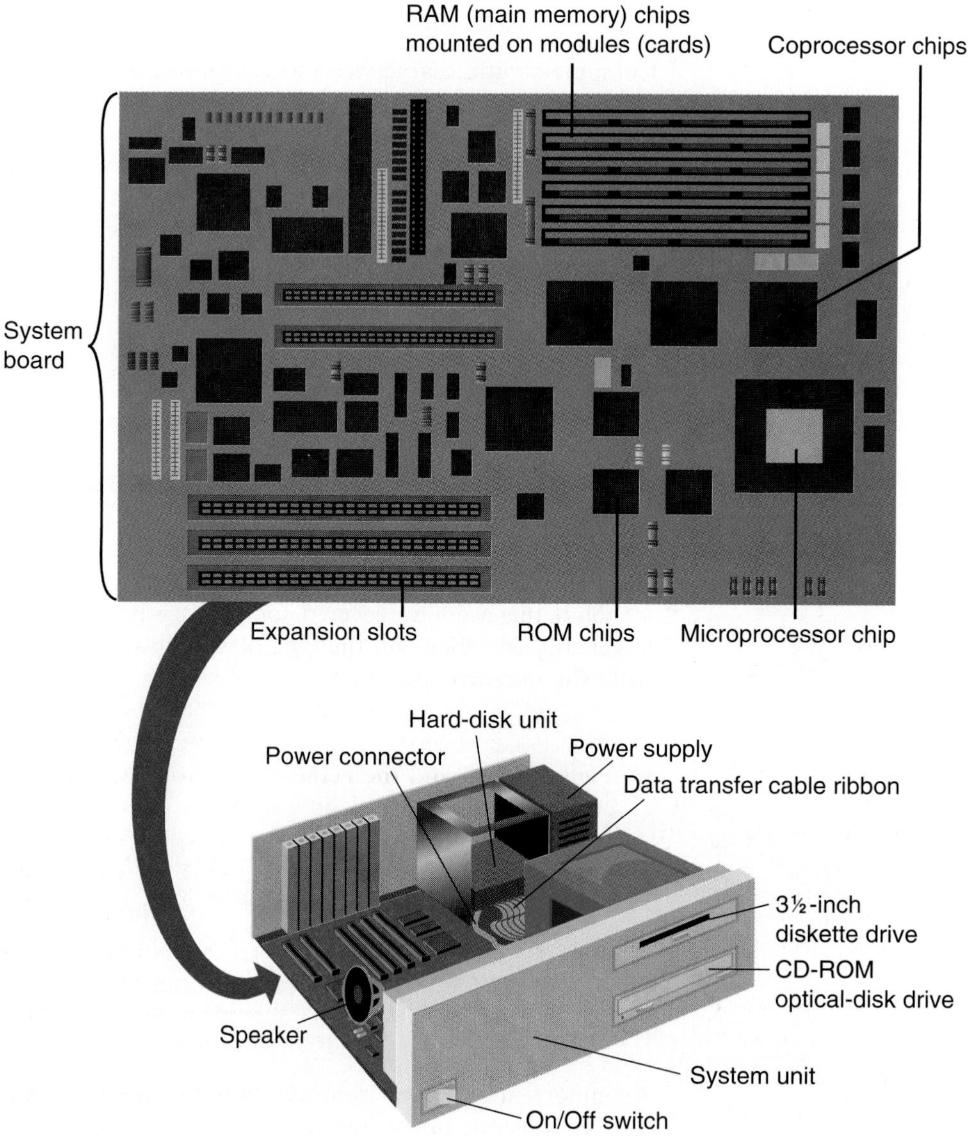

These terms appear frequently in advertisements for microcomputers. After reading this section, you should be able to understand what those ads are talking about.

The Power Supply

The electricity available from a standard wall outlet is AC (alternating current), but a microcomputer runs on DC (direct current). The **power supply** is the device that converts power from AC to DC to run the computer. The on/off switch in your computer turns on or shuts off the electricity to the power supply. Because electricity can generate a lot of heat, a fan inside the computer keeps the power supply and other components from becoming too hot.

Electrical power drawn from a standard AC outlet can be quite uneven. A sudden surge, or spike, in AC voltage can burn out the low-voltage DC circuitry in your computer ("fry the motherboard"). Instead of plugging your computer directly into the wall electrical outlet, it's a good idea to plug it into a power protection device, which is in turn plugged into the wall outlet. The two principal types are *surge protectors* and *UPS (uninterruptible power supply)* units.

The Motherboard

The **motherboard,** also called the *system board,* is the main circuit board in the system unit. *(See Figure 2.7.)* This board acts as a container for the different components in the system unit such as the microprocessor, any coprocessor chips, RAM chips, ROM chips, some other types of memory, and *expansion slots,* where additional circuit boards, called *expansion boards,* may be plugged in.

The Microprocessor

Most microcomputers today use microprocessors of two kinds—those made by Intel and those by Motorola—although that situation may be changing.

- *Intel chips:* Intel makes chips for personal computers such as Compaq, Dell, Gateway, Tandy, Toshiba, and Zenith. Variations of Intel chips are made by other companies, such as Advanced Micro Devices (AMD), Cyrix Inc., and Chips and Technologies.

  Intel used to identify its chips by numbers—8086, 8088, 80286, 80386, 80486: the "x86" series. Intel's successor to the x86 chips is the Pentium family of chips. Whereas microprocessors in the 1970s may have had about 2300 transistors, microprocessors today have more than 8 million transistors. In the 1970s a microprocessor may have run at only 1 MHz; now some microprocessors run faster than 450 MHz. Listed from slowest to fastest, the current chip models available from Intel are the Pentium, Pentium with MMX technology, Pentium Pro, and the Pentium II. (Note: MMX stands for *MultiMedia eXtension.* This technology is intended to speed up any application that uses multimedia, such as games and slide presentations.)

  About 90% of microcomputers use Intel-type microprocessors; thus, most applications software packages have been written for Intel platforms.

- *Motorola chips:* Motorola produces the family of chips for Apple Macintosh computers. These chips use RISC architecture. With some software and/or hardware add-ons, late-model Power PC and G3 Macintoshes can run applications software whether it's written for the Apple or the PC platform.

Most new chips are "downward compatible" with older chips. *Downward compatible,* or *backward compatible,* means that you can run the software written for computers with older chips on a computer with a newer chip. For example, the word processing program and all the data files that you used for your '486 machine will continue to run if you upgrade to a Pentium machine. Of course, new, sophisticated software programs have minimum processor requirements to run *efficiently.* These requirements are listed on the software box *(see left).*

Farallon

Timbuktu Pro

Remote Control Software for Macintosh

System Requirements:
- One license required per computer
- Macintosh II, LC (or other 68020), or higher required
- 5 MB RAM (8 MB recommended) for 68020 and higher
- 8 MB RAM (16 MB recommended) for PowerPCs
- Standard installation requires 9 MB of hard disk space
- System 7; some features require System 7.5

  For LAN connections:
  - A network using AppleTalk, TCP/IP (MacTCP or Open Transport required) and/or Novell/IPX network (MacIPX included), including LocalTalk, Ethernet, Token Ring

  For Dial Direct and remote dial-in connections:
  - A 14,400 bps Hayes compatible modem or faster or ISDN Terminal Adapter

  For dial-in server connections:
  - Apple Remote Access Client (included) requires System 7.1 or later
  - An ARA Personal Server or Multiport server (or any ARA-compatible server) is required.
  - For PPP dial-in connections, PPP software and a PPP server are required

Package Contents:
- A license to install software*
- Five 3.5" HD (1.44MB) disks or CD ROM included in 10-Pack
- Apple Guide 2.0 online help system
- User's Guide
- At-A-Glance Guide

At an Intel plant in Penang, Malaysia, after a battery of sophisticated tests, a technician visually inspects a tray of finished processors.

PC CHIPS

Year	Chip	Architecture	Speed	Word Size (Internal Bus)
1978	Intel 8086 (29 K transistors)	CISC	4.77 MHz	16 bits
1979	Intel 8088	CISC	4.77 MHz	16 bits
1982	Intel 80286 (134 K transistors)	CISC	8–20 MHz	16 bits
1985	Intel 80386 (275 K transistors)	CISC	16–66 MHz	32 bits
1989	Intel 80486 (1.18 M transistors)	CISC	33–100 MHz	32 bits
1993	Intel Pentium Classic	CISC	60–200 MHz	64 bits
1995	Intel Pentium Pro	CISC	133–200 MHz	64 bits
1997	Intel Pentium II (7.5 M transistors)	CISC	233–450 MHz	64 bits
1998	Intel Pentium Celeron	CISC	266–400 MHz	64 bits
1999	Intel Pentium II Katmai (icode name for the Pentium III)	CISC	450–500 MHz	64 bits
1999	Cyrix II/MXI/Jedi	CISC	350–500 MHz	64 bits
1999	Intel Pentium III	CISC	450–500 MHz	64 bits
2000	Intel Celeron	CISC	500 MHz	64 bits
2000	Intel Merced (10 M transistors)	RISC	800 MHz	64 bits

MAC CHIPS

Year	Chip	Architecture	Speed	Word Size (Internal Bus)
1982	Motorola 68000	CISC	8–12.5 MHz	32 bits
1984	Motorola 68020	CISC	16.7–33.3 MHz	32 bits
1987	Motorola 68030	CISC	20–50 MHz	32 bits
1989	Motorola 68040	CISC	25 MHz	32 bits
1993	Power PC* 601	RISC	50–80 MHz	32 bits
1994	Power PC 603	RISC	100–300 MHz	32/64 bits
1994	Power PC 604	RISC	180–360 MHz	32/64 bits
1996	Power PC 620	RISC	133+ MHz	64/128 bits
1997[†]	Power PC 750	RISC	200–400 MHz	64 bits

*Power PC chips were made by a joint effort of IBM and Apple.
[†]Predictions for 2000 include RISC chips operating at 450 MHz and 700 MHz.

RAM Chips

As we described earlier in the chapter, *main memory,* or *RAM (random access memory)*, is memory that temporarily holds data and instructions that will be needed shortly by the processor. RAM operates like a chalkboard that is constantly being written on, then erased, then written on again.

Single in-line memory module (SIMM)

Dual in-line memory module (DIMM)

Like the microprocessor, RAM is made up of circuit-inscribed silicon chips. Microcomputers come with different amounts of RAM. The more RAM you have, the faster the software can operate. If, for instance, you type such a long document in a word processing program that it will not all fit into your computer's RAM, the computer will put part of the document onto your disk (either hard disk or diskette). This means you have to wait while the computer swaps data back and forth between RAM and disk. Microcomputer users need 16–64 MB or more of RAM to run today's software.

Having enough RAM has become a critical matter! Before you buy any software package, look at the outside of the box to see how much RAM is required to run it by itself and to run it at the same time as other programs you commonly use. (If you're downloading software from the Web, the software manufacturer's Web site should provide this information.) Fortunately, additional RAM chips can often be added by plugging *memory modules,* which are circuit boards that contain memory chips, into a memory socket on the motherboard. Two types of memory modules are *SIMMs (single in-line memory modules)* and *DIMMs (dual in-line memory modules).* Whereas SIMMs can hold up to 9 RAM chips, DIMMs can hold up to 18. SIMMs are generally used to expand RAM on older computers, such as those with '386 and '486 microprocessors. DIMMs, which are faster, are used in Pentium II computers and most other Pentium computers.

ROM Chips

Unlike RAM, which is constantly being written on and erased, **ROM,** which stands for **read-only memory** and is also known as *firmware,* cannot be written on or erased by the computer user. (Firmware is a term used for software permanently stored on a chip.) In other words, RAM chips remember, temporarily, information supplied by you or a software program; ROM chips remember, permanently, information supplied by the manufacturer.

One of the ROM chips in a microcomputer contains instructions that tell the processor what to do when you first turn on, or boot, the computer. These instructions are called the *ROM bootstrap,* because they get the computer system going by helping it to "pull itself up by its bootstraps." To get the computer going, ROM performs a "power-on self-test" (POST). Another ROM chip helps the processor transfer information between the keyboard, screen, printer, and other peripheral devices to make sure all units are functioning properly. These instructions are called **ROM BIOS,** or **basic input/output system.** Fundamentally, ROM BIOS is an interface, a connector, and a translator between the computer hardware and the software programs that you run. (To be a true IBM clone, a computer must have the same ROM BIOS system as an IBM.) Still another ROM chip tells the computer how to construct each character displayed on the screen.

Three variations of ROM chips are used in special situations—*PROM, EPROM,* and *EEPROM:*

■ *PROM: PROM* chips, for *programmable read-only memory,* are blank chips on which the buyer, using special equipment, writes the program. Once the program is written, it cannot be erased. Some microcomputer software packages come on PROM units.

■ *EPROM: EPROM* chips, for *erasable programmable read-only memory,* are like PROM chips except that the contents can be erased, using special equipment, and new material can be written. Erasure is done with a special device that uses ultraviolet light.

■ *EEPROM: EEPROM* chips, for *electronically erasable programmable read-only memory,* can be reprogrammed using special electrical impulses. The advantage of EEPROM chips is that they need not be removed from the computer to be changed.

Other Forms of Memory

In addition to inserting SIMMs and DIMMs in expansion slots, as we mentioned earlier, a microcomputer's performance can be enhanced by adding other forms of memory, as follows:

■ *Cache memory:* In the most powerful computers and in high-end microcomputers, RAM is divided into two sections. One section is relatively large (several rows of chips) and is called *main RAM.* The other section is tiny—just a few chips. This is cache memory, which is much faster but also much more expensive than RAM. Pronounced "cash," **cache memory** is a special high-speed memory area that the processor can access quickly. Essentially, cache memory is a bridge between the processor and RAM. *(See Figure 2.8.)* A special "look-ahead program" transfers the data and instructions that were transferred from secondary storage to RAM from RAM to the processor. This allows the processor to run faster because it doesn't have to take time to swap instructions in and out of RAM. Large, complex programs and fast processors benefit the most from access to cache memory. There are several types of cache memory available. One type you see advertised frequently in computer magazine ads is *pipeline-burst cache,* which allows memory chips to be read from and written to at the same time.

Internal cache is built into the processor chip. External cache resides on fast chips located closer to the CPU than the RAM chips.

■ *Video memory:* Video memory or **video RAM** (**VRAM,** pronounced "vee-ram") chips are used to store display images for the monitor. The amount of

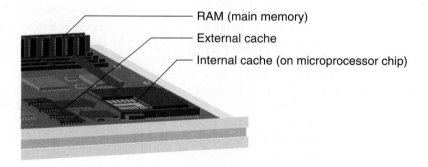

Figure 2.8 Memory cache speeds up the computer by storing data the computer has recently used.

RAM (main memory)

External cache

Internal cache (on microprocessor chip)

video memory determines how fast images appear and how many colors are available. Video memory chips are particularly desirable if you are running programs that display a lot of graphics. VRAM chips are usually located on a special video adapter card inserted in an expansion slot on the system board.

- *Flash memory:* Derived from EEPROMs and used primarily in portable computers, **flash memory,** or **flash RAM cards,** consist of circuitry on credit-card-size cards that can be inserted into slots connecting to the motherboard. Unlike standard RAM chips, flash memory is *nonvolatile.* That is, it retains data even when the power is turned off. Flash memory can be used not only to simulate main memory but also to supplement or replace hard disk drives for permanent storage. Some experts predict that flash RAM will eventually replace traditional CMOS RAM.

Ports: Connecting Peripherals

Microcomputers have different types of ports, depending on whether they use the PC or the Mac platform and how recent the model is. A **port** is a socket on the outside of the system unit that is connected by a bus to an expansion board on the inside of the system unit or connected directly to integrated circuitry on the motherboard. A port allows you to use a cable to plug in a peripheral device, such as a monitor, printer, or modem, so that it can communicate with the computer system.

Ports are of several types (*see Figure 2.9, next page*):

- *Parallel ports:* Lines connected to a **parallel port** allow 8 bits to be transmitted simultaneously, like cars on an eight-lane highway. Parallel lines move information faster than serial lines do, but they can transmit information efficiently only up to 15 feet (5.4 meters). Thus, parallel ports are used principally for connecting printers.

- *Serial ports:* Lines connected to a **serial port,** or *RS-232 port,* send bits one after the other in a single sequence, like cars on a one-lane highway. Serial lines are used to link equipment that is not close by. Serial ports are used principally for communications lines, modems, scanners, and mice—and, in the case of the Macintosh, the printer. (Serial ports are often called COM ports, for communications.) On the back of newer PCs is one 9-pin connector for serial port COM1, typically used for the mouse, and one 25-pin connector for serial port COM2, typically used for the modem.

- *Video adapter ports:* **Video adapter ports** are used to connect the video display monitor outside the computer to the video adapter card inside the system unit. Monitors may have either a 9-pin plug or a 15-pin plug. The plug must be compatible with the number of holes in the video adapter card.

- *SCSI ports:* Pronounced "scuzzy," a **SCSI** (short for **Small Computer System Interface) port** provides an interface for transferring data at high speeds for up to seven or fifteen SCSI-compatible devices, linked together in what is called a *daisy chain,* along an extended cable. *(See Figure 2.10.)* These devices include external hard disk drives, magnetic-tape backup units, scanners, and CD-ROM drives.

- *Game ports:* Game ports allow you to attach a joystick or similar game-playing device to the system unit.

- *Infrared ports:* These wireless, data-transfer ports are available on new computers and hardware peripherals such as printers. This type of connection uses a certain frequency of radio waves to transmit data, and so it requires an unobstructed line of sight between the transmitter and the receiver.

Figure 2.9 A port is a connector at the back of the computer where you plug in an external device. This allows instructions and data to flow between the computer and the device.

Serial Port

A serial port has either 9 or 25 pins. This type of port is known as a male connector. A serial port connects a modem or mouse.

A computer internally labels each serial port with the letters COM. The first serial port is named COM1, the second serial port is named COM2, and so on.

Keyboard Port

A keyboard port connects a keyboard. Keyboard ports are available in two sizes.

Game Port

A game port connects a joystick.

USB Port

Universal Serial Bus (USB) is a type of port that allows you to connect up to 127 devices using only one port. For example, you can use a USB port to connect a printer, modem, joystick, and scanner to your computer. Most new computers come with two USB ports.

Figure 2.10 Daisy chains

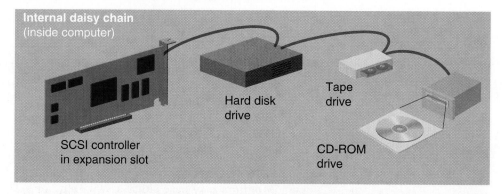

Internal daisy chain (inside computer)

Hard disk drive

Tape drive

CD-ROM drive

SCSI controller in expansion slot

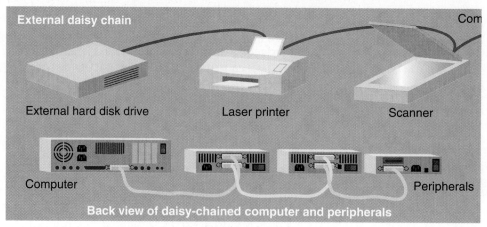

External daisy chain

Com

External hard disk drive

Laser printer

Scanner

Computer

Peripherals

Back view of daisy-chained computer and peripherals

Parallel Port

A parallel port has 25 holes. This type of port is known as a female connector. A parallel port connects a printer or tape drive.

A computer internally labels each parallel port with the letters LPT. The first parallel port is named LPT1, the second parallel port is named LPT2, and so on.

There are two enhanced types of parallel ports— Enhanced Parallel Port (EPP) and Extended Capabilities Port (ECP). These types of parallel ports increase the speed at which information flows between the computer and a device.

Monitor Port

A monitor port connects a monitor (display screen).

Expansion Slots and Cards

Most of today's microcomputers have *open architecture*—that is, they can easily be opened, so that users can add new devices and enhance existing capabilities. This spares users from having to buy a completely new computer every time they want to upgrade something. As with ports, microcomputers will have different numbers and kinds of expansion slots, based on the model.

Expansion slots, also called *bus slots*, are sockets on the motherboard into which you can plug expansion cards, after you open the system unit. *(Refer back to Figure 2.7.)* **Expansion cards**, or **adapter cards**, are circuit boards that provide more memory or control peripheral devices. Some slots are needed right away for ordinary peripherals; the remainder can be used for expansion later.

Among the types of expansion cards are the following:

■ *Memory cards:* As we mentioned in the section on RAM, memory expansion cards, called *memory modules*, allow you to add RAM chips, giving you more main memory.

■ *Video adapter cards:* These cards allow you to adapt different kinds of color video display monitors for your computer.

■ *Graphics accelerator cards:* These cards improve the performance of your computer when displaying graphics. For example, AGP (Accelerated Graphics Port) cards are designed to speed up your system's handling of 3-D graphics.

■ *Controller cards:* Controller cards are circuit boards that allow your microprocessor to work with the computer's various peripheral devices. For example, a disk controller card allows the computer to work with different kinds of hard disk and diskette drives.

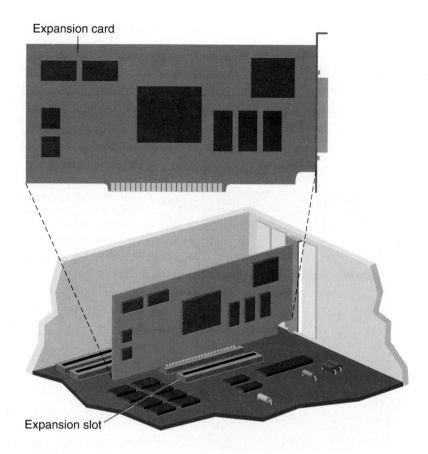

Expansion card

Expansion slot

■ *Other add-ons:* You can also add special circuit boards for modems, fax, sound, video capture, and networking, as well as coprocessor chips.

To install a new adapter card in your computer, you must plug the card into a bus slot, thus enabling the new device to communicate with the rest of the computer system. As we mentioned earlier (✔ p. 2.8), a bus line, or simply a bus, is a hardware pathway through which bits are transmitted within the processor and between the processor and other devices in the system unit. The computer's *internal bus* moves data around the microprocessor. *Expansion buses* and *local buses* move data between the processor and peripheral devices.

A computer bus provides parallel data transfer. For example, a 16-bit bus transfers 2 bytes (16 bits) at a time over 16 wires; a 32-bit bus transmits 4 bytes (32 bits) at a time over 32 wires, and so on.

Today, several bus designs are available:

■ *ISA:* The *Industry Standard Architecture* (ISA, pronounced "eye-suh") bus slot was developed by IBM in the late 1980s and has a 16-bit data bus. Although this standard is rather slow, several manufacturers still produce adapter cards for ISA bus slots. Therefore, most new computers still come with at least two ISA bus slots.

■ *PCI:* The *Peripheral Component Interconnect* bus slot has a 64-bit data bus and is the bus of choice for Pentium computers. Most Pentium computers contain at least two PCI bus slots, and the newer Pentium computers contain four or more.

■ *EISA:* The *Enhanced Industry Standard Architecture* (*EISA,* pronounced "ee-suh") bus is a 32-bit expansion bus for the IBM platform. EISA buses are more expensive than ISA buses, so they are used primarily on high-end micro-computers and network servers.

PCMCIA card

■ *PCMCIA:* The **PCMCIA** (short for **Personal Computer Memory Card International Association**) bus slot standard is used mostly in portable computers. It allows users to take advantage of credit-card-size peripherals, such as hard disk, memory, modem, and network cards. PCMCIA cards are referred to as *PC cards*.

A recently available type of connection is the Universal Serial Bus, which is actually both a port and a bus.

■ *USB:* The *Universal Serial Bus* is a new industry-wide standard that will eventually eliminate the need to install adapter cards. With this "plug and play" system, any new device, once plugged in, is configured automatically. Using a single USB port, you can plug in up to 127 devices, such as mice, modems, and keyboards, in a daisy chain. USB also supports *hot plugging*, which means you can plug in a device without turning off the computer. (With SCSI, you must turn off your equipment, connect the new device, then reboot the system.)

Because USB ports are faster than serial ports and more reliable than parallel ports, some industry hardware experts predict that USB ports and buses will replace other types of ports and buses. Indeed, the Apple iMac and G3 already come only with USB ports.

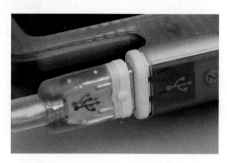

USB plug and port

2.5 Coming Attractions?

KEY QUESTION **What processing technologies might we use in the future?**

The old theological question of how many angels could fit on the head of a pin has become the technological question of how many *circuits* could fit there. Computer developers are obsessed with speed, constantly seeking ways to promote faster processing. Some of the most promising directions, already discussed, are RISC chips and parallel processing. Some other research paths being explored are the following:

■ *Gallium arsenide:* Silicon is the material of choice today for microprocessors, but there are other contenders. One is *gallium arsenide,* which allows electrical impulses to be transmitted several times faster than silicon can. Gallium arsenide also requires less power than silicon chips and thus can operate at higher temperatures. However, chip designers at present are unable to squeeze as many circuits onto a chip as they can with silicon.

A Texas police officer uses a laptop computer for field reports.

- *Superconductors:* Silicon, we have said, is a semiconductor: Electricity flows through the material with some resistance. This leads to heat buildup and the risk of circuits melting down. A *superconductor,* by contrast, is material that allows electricity to flow through it without resistance. The superconducting materials so far discovered are considered impractical because they are super-conductors only at subzero temperatures. Nevertheless, the search continues for a superconductor at room temperature—which would lead to circuitry 100 times faster than today's silicon chips.

- *Opto-electronic processing:* Today's computers are electronic, tomorrow's might be *opto-electronic*—using light, not electricity. With optical-electronic technology, a machine using lasers, lenses, and mirrors would represent the on/off codes of data with pulses of light.

  Light is much faster than electricity. Indeed, fiber-optic networks, which consist of hair-thin glass fibers instead of copper wire, can move information at speeds 3000 times faster than conventional networks. However, the signals get bogged down when they have to be processed by silicon chips. Opto-electronics chips would remove that bottleneck.

- *Nanotechnology:* Nanotechnology, nanoelectronics, nanostructures, nanofabrication—these terms are all associated with a measurement known as a nanometer. A *nanometer* is a billionth of a meter, which means we are operating at the level of atoms and molecules. A human hair is approximately 100,000 nanometers in diameter.

  In *nanotechnology,* molecules are used to create tiny machines for holding data or performing tasks. Experts attempt to do nanofabrication by building tiny nanostructures one atom or molecule at a time. When applied to chips and other electronic devices, the field is called nanoelectronics.

  Indeed, scientists have already forged layers of individual molecules into tiny computer switches. Researchers plan to assemble these switches and other diminutive components into devices called "chemically assembled electronic devices," or CAENs—machines that would be billions of times more powerful than today's personal computers. The new switches are the work of computer scientists and chemists at Hewlett-Packard Laboratories in Palo Alto, California, and at the University of California at Los Angeles. They hope to get the first CAEN components up and running within 10 years. The first prototype should be finished by 2002.

■ *Biotechnology:* Potentially, biotechnology could be used to grow cultures of bacteria that, when exposed to light, emit a small electrical charge, for example. The properties of this "biochip" could be used to represent the on/off digital signals used in computing.

Imagine millions of nanomachines grown from microorganisms processing information at the speed of light and sending it over far-reaching pathways. What kind of changes could we expect with computers like these?

Web Sites of Possible Interest

If you are already used to going online, you may want to check out these Web sites. Otherwise, wait until you have covered Chapters 7 and 8.

History (The Boston Computer Museum):
http://cityinsights.com/bocomput.htm
http://www.pbs.org/nerds/timeline/index.html

History of microprocessors:
http://web.islandnet.com/~kpolsson/comphist.htm

Tom's hardware site:
http://www.tomshardware.com

Kingston's "Ultimate Memory Guide":
http://www.kingston.com/king/mg0.htm

Remember that Internet and Web addresses may change. Also, you can find other sources of information by using a search tool and typing in the key search words Computer History, Microprocessors, and so on. (Search tools are covered in detail later on.)

Law

There are now about 1 million licensed attorneys in the United States, and their median yearly income is $60,000—good compared to some lines of work, of course. And $100,000 a year sounds even better, unless you divide it by the 60-hour weeks for 50 weeks a year that many lawyers work, which, points out legal consultant Hindi Greenberg, is "an hourly rate not much better than that paid to . . . paralegals."[a]

Nevertheless, a person with a law degree has lots of options, working not only as a practicing attorney but also in the growing industries that service law firms, such as computers and telecommunications. Or they may work in other fields to which their training in analytical thinking, communication, counseling, research, and so on are transferable.

Legal firms have long since learned the art of using computer technology to help them win cases. For years, lawyers have used the Lexis legal database to look up legal precedents. During the famous U.S. Justice Department antitrust suit against Microsoft, the lead prosecutor, David Boies, used a database package called Summation to pull together evidence from millions of pages of Microsoft's e-mail. He also used Trial Director to find and present damaging bits of video.[b]

As you might guess, a new species of legal eagle has come into being— the cyberlawyer. What makes cyberspace law so appealing, says one new practitioner, is that "It's a chance to think about first-level questions." Unlike so many other cases, in which the same issue has already been decided, law on the electronic frontier often deals with the unknown.[c] The court system is also being changed by technology. In recent years, state and federal courts have set up Web sites where lawyers and the public can access court schedules, download court documents, and obtain other legal information. Indeed, systems have been set up that allow users to electronically file motions with the court, which could cut down on the amount of paperwork.[d]

Finally, information technology has made the law more accessible to nonlawyers. The Internet is fast becoming a fertile breeding ground for litigation, as angry consumers form Web sites to post complaints and invite other people "interested in being class-action litigants" to send them e-mail that might entice an attorney to take the case on a contingency basis.[e] Families erroneously targeted by state computer "deadbeat dad" programs to cough up child support have launched counteroffensives using their own software to debunk government collection efforts.[f] The Quicken Family Lawyer program (which can be downloaded from *www.parsonstech.com*) helps people fill out legal documents, although it was apparently so good that a Texas judge ruled that it crossed the line into the illegal practice of law.[g]

Some Web sites of interest are the following: Free Advice (*www. freeadvice.com*) offers consumer-friendly advice on scores of legal issues. Lawyers.com (*www.lawyers.com*) has a database of 400,000 attorneys in the United States, so that you can search for an attorney by geographical area and by specialty. (Tips are given in a "Hiring a Lawyer" section. Law News Network (*www.lawnewsnetwork. com*), run by American Lawyer Media, offers legal news, as well as job listings.

Information Technology

Consider the following headlines:[a,b]

STUDENTS OPTING FOR LOW-TECH MAJORS

STEREOTYPE TURNS STUDENTS OFF OF HIGH-PAYING CAREER

Is there something wrong with this picture? Certainly students should major in whatever they want. But they could be passing up careers that pay upward of $50,000 a year.

Why is this? As one writer points out, students of all ages "perceive tech jobs to be for introverts, geeks, and geniuses. . . ."[c] This is an unfortunate misconception. Information-technology workers actually are pretty much like everyone else. It's not required that you be a genius or have quirky personality traits. Moreover, the field presents many exciting, challenging possibilities—positions that offer flexibility, travel, and other benefits.

Meanwhile, info-tech jobs go unfilled and—to cite another headline—"Techies Keep Laughing All the Way to the Bank."[d] The average starting pay for such jobs in 1999 was estimated to increase by 18.4% for programmers, 16.3% for database administrators, 14.8% for Web developers, 14.7% for Webmasters, 13.5% for software installers, and 12.4% for e-commerce specialists.[e]

Some digitally savvy students are paying their way through college by hiring themselves out as computer consultants, technical-support experts, and software developers. Stacy Peters-Walters, a senior majoring in special education at Dakota State University in South Dakota, taught herself how to use professional graphics software. She makes $20 an hour working 20 hours a week at her own one-woman company, offering Web design, technical support, and multimedia CD-ROM production. Dartmouth College sophomore Steve Magoun, a computer science major, also has a business in which he builds Web sites for various for-profit and nonprofit customers; it contributes about "four digits" to his tuition, he says.[f]

Of the three jobs most likely to be in increasing demand in the next 10 years, according to the Bureau of Labor Statistics, all are computer-technology based: systems analyst, computer scientist, and computer engineer. Median annual earnings for computer systems analysts and scientists who worked full time in 1996 were about $46,300. The top 10 percent earned more than $76,200. In 1997, according to Robert Half International Inc., starting salaries for info-tech workers employed by establishments with more than 50 employees were as follows: systems analysts, $46,000–$57,500; programmer-analysts, $39,000–$50,000; database administrators, $54,000–$67,500; network administrators, $36,000–$55,000; help-desk technicians, $25,000–$36,500; and software development specialists, $49,000–$67,500.

Of course, there are also superstars, just as there are in sports and entertainment. An executive with a California communications company reported he had lost a five-year programmer making $80,000 annually to a consultancy offering two years guaranteed at $300,000 per year.[g]

SUMMARY

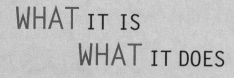

WHAT IT IS
WHAT IT DOES

WHY IT IS IMPORTANT

arithmetic/logic unit (ALU) (KQ 2.2, p. 2.8)   The part of the CPU that performs arithmetic operations and logical operations and that controls the speed of those operations.

Arithmetic operations are the fundamental math operations: addition, subtraction, multiplication, and division. Logical operations are comparisons, such as is "equal to" (=), "greater than" (>), or "less than" (<).

ASCII (American Standard Code for Information Interchange) (KQ 2.1, p. 2.4)   Binary code used in microcomputers; ASCII originally used 7 bits to form a character, but a zero was added in the left position to provide an 8-bit code, providing more possible combinations with which to form other characters and symbols (256 possible combinations).

ASCII is the binary code most widely used in microcomputers.

binary system (KQ 2.1, p. 2.4)   A two-state system (*bi-* means "two").

Computer systems use a binary system for data representation; two digits, 0 and 1, refer to the presence and absence of electrical current or a pulse of light. All data and programs that go into the computer are represented in terms of these numbers.

bus (KQ 2.2, p. 2.8)   Electrical pathway through which bits are transmitted within the CPU and between the CPU and other devices in the system unit. Common types include internal buses, local buses, and expansion buses.

The wider a computer's buses, the faster it operates.

byte (KQ 2.1, p. 2.7)   A group of 8 bits.

A byte holds the equivalent of a character—such as a letter or a number—in computer data-representation coding schemes. It is also the basic unit used to measure the storage capacity of main memory and secondary storage devices.

cache memory (KQ 2.4, p. 2.20)   Special high-speed memory area on a chip that the CPU can access quickly. A copy of the most frequently used instructions is kept in the cache memory so the CPU can look there first.

Cache memory, which supplements main memory, allows the CPU to run faster because it doesn't have to take time to swap instructions in and out of main memory. Large, complex programs benefit the most from having cache memory available.

central processing unit (CPU) (KQ 2.2, p. 2.8) The processor; it controls and manipulates data to produce information. In a microcomputer the CPU is usually contained on a single integrated circuit or chip called a *microprocessor.* This chip and other components that make it work are mounted on a circuit board called a *motherboard* (system board). More powerful computers have many processors.

chip (microchip) (KQ 2.2, p. 2.9) Small piece of silicon that contains thousands of microminiature electronic circuit components, mainly transistors.

control unit (KQ 2.2, p. 2.8) The part of the CPU that tells the rest of the computer system how to carry out a program's instructions.

coprocessors (KQ 2.2, p. 2.9) Additional processor chips that extend the capabilities and speed of the microprocessor.

EBCDIC (Extended Binary Coded Decimal Interchange Code) (KQ 2.1, p. 2.4) Coding scheme that uses 8 bits to form each byte.

execution cycle (E-cycle) (KQ 2.2, p. 2.13) Part of the machine cycle during which the ALU executes the instruction and stores the processed results in a register.

expansion card (adapter card) (KQ 2.4, p. 2.23) Add-on circuit board that provides more memory or a new peripheral-device capability. (The words *card* and *board* are used interchangeably.) Expansion cards are inserted into expansion slots inside the system unit.

expansion slots (KQ 2.4, p. 2.23) Socket on the motherboard into which users may plug an expansion card.

flash memory (flash RAM cards) (KQ 2.4, p. 2.21) Used primarily in notebook and subnotebook computers; consists of circuitry on credit-card-size cards that can be inserted into slots connecting to the motherboard.

gigabyte (G, GB) (KQ 2.1, p. 2.7) Approximately 1 billion bytes (1,073,741,824 bytes); a measure of storage capacity.

instruction cycle (I-cycle) (KQ 2.2, p. 2.12) Part of the machine cycle in which a single computer instruction is retrieved from memory and decoded.

The CPU is the "brain" of the computer.

Chips have made possible the development of small computers.

The control unit directs the movement of electronic signals between main memory and the arithmetic/logic unit. It also directs these electronic signals between the main memory and input and output devices.

Each coprocessor is dedicated to a special job, such as crunching numbers or handling graphics.

EBCDIC is commonly used in mainframes.

The completion time of the execution cycle determines how fast data is processed. The execution cycle is preceded by the instruction cycle.

Users can use expansion cards to upgrade their computers instead of having to buy entire new systems.

See *expansion card.*

Unlike standard RAM chips, flash memory is non-volatile—it retains data even when the power is turned off. Flash memory can be used not only to simulate main memory but also to supplement or replace hard disk drives for permanent storage.

Gigabytes are used to express the storage capacity of large computers, such as mainframes, although it is also applied to some microcomputer secondary storage devices.

Decoding means that the control unit alerts the circuits in the microprocessor to perform the specified operation. The instruction cycle is followed by the execution cycle.

kilobyte (K, KB) (KQ 2.1, p. 2.7)   Unit for measuring storage capacity; equals 1024 bytes (usually rounded off to 1000 bytes).

The sizes of stored electronic files are often measured in kilobytes.

machine cycle (KQ 2.2, p. 2.12)   Series of operations performed by the CPU to execute a single program instruction; it consists of two parts: an instruction cycle and an execution cycle.

The machine cycle is the essence of computer-based processing.

machine language (KQ 2.1, p. 2.6)   Binary code (language) that the computer uses directly. The 0s and 1s represent precise storage locations and operations.

For a program to run, it must be in the machine language of the computer that is executing it.

main memory (KQ 2.2, p. 2.11)   Also known as *memory, primary storage, internal memory,* or *RAM (random access memory)*; working storage that holds (1) data for processing, (2) the programs for processing the data, and (3) data after it has been processed and is waiting to be sent to an output, secondary storage, or communications device.

Main memory capacity determines the total size of the programs and data files a computer can work on at any given moment.

megabyte (M, MB) (KQ 2.1, p. 2.7)   About 1 million bytes (1,048,576 bytes).

Microcomputer main memory capacity is usually expressed in megabytes.

megahertz (MHz) (KQ 2.3, p. 2.15)   Measurement of microcomputer processing speed, controlled by the system clock; 1 MHz equals 1 million machine cycles per second.

Generally, the higher the megahertz rate, the faster a computer can process data. Currently microcomputers run at 133–400 MHz or more.

microprocessor (KQ 2.2, p. 2.8)   CPU (processor) consisting of miniaturized circuitry on a single chip; it controls all the processing in a computer.

Microprocessors enabled the development of microcomputers.

motherboard (KQ 2.4, p. 2.17)   Also called *system board;* the main circuit board in the system unit of a microcomputer.

This board contains the interconnecting assembly of important components, including CPU, main memory, other chips, and expansion slots.

parallel port (KQ 2.4, p. 2.21)   Part of the computer through which a parallel device, which transmits 8 bits simultaneously, can be connected.

Enables microcomputer users to connect to a parallel printer.

parity bit (KQ 2.1, p. 2.5)   Also called a *check bit;* an extra bit attached to the end of a byte.

Enables a computer system to check for errors during transmission. (The check bits are organized according to a particular coding scheme designed into the computer.)

PCMCIA (Personal Computer Memory Card International Association) (KQ 2.4, p. 2.25)   Bus standard for portable computers.

This standard enables users of notebooks and subnotebooks to insert credit-card-size peripheral devices called *PC cards,* such as modems and memory cards, into their computers.

port (KQ 2.4, p. 2.21)   Connecting socket on the outside of the computer system unit that is connected to an expansion board on the inside of the system unit. Ports are of six types: parallel, serial, video adapter, SCSI, game ports, and infrared ports.

Ports enable users to connect peripheral devices such as monitor, printer, and modem so that they can communicate with the computer system.

power supply (KQ 2.4, p. 2.16)   Device in the computer that converts AC current from the wall outlet to the DC current the computer uses.

The power supply enables the computer (and peripheral devices) to operate.

ROM (read-only memory) (KQ 2.4, p. 2.19)   Also known as *firmware;* a memory chip that permanently stores instructions and data that are programmed during the chip's manufacture and that cannot be changed or erased by the user. Three variations on the ROM chip are PROM, EPROM, and EEPROM. ROM is a nonvolatile form of storage.

ROM chips are used to store special basic instructions for computer operations such as those that start the computer and display characters on the screen.

ROM BIOS (basic input/output system) (KQ 2.4, p. 2.19)   ROM chip that helps the processor transfer information between the keyboard, screen, printer, and other peripheral devices to make sure all units are functioning properly.

ROM BIOS is an interface, a connector, and a translator between the computer hardware and the software programs that you run.

SCSI (Small Computer System Interface) port (KQ 2.4, p. 2.21)   Pronounced "scuzzy"; an interface for transferring data at high speeds for up to seven or fifteen SCSI-compatible devices, connected in a daisy chain.

SCSI ports are used to connect external hard disk drives, magnetic-tape backup units, and CD-ROM drives to the computer system.

serial port (KQ 2.4, p. 2.21)   Also known as RS-232 port; a port for connecting a cable that transmits 1 bit at a time, one after the other (instead of in parallel fashion).

Serial ports are used principally for connecting communications lines, modems, and mice to microcomputers.

system clock (KQ 2.3, p. 2.15)   Internal timing device that uses a quartz crystal to generate a uniform electrical frequency from which digital pulses are created.

The system clock controls the speed of all operations within a computer. The faster the clock, the faster the processing.

system unit (KQ 2.4, p. 2.15)   The box or cabinet containing the electrical components that do the computer's processing; usually includes processing components, RAM chips (main memory), ROM chips (read-only memory), power supply, expansion slots, and disk drives but not keyboard, printer, or often even the display screen.

The system unit integrates and protects many important processing and storage components.

terabyte (T, TB) (KQ 2.1, p. 2.7)   Approximately 1 trillion bytes (1,009,511,627,776 bytes).

The capacities of some forms of mass storage, or secondary storage for mainframes and supercomputers, are expressed in terabytes.

Unicode (KQ 2.1, p. 2.5)   Binary coding scheme developed by several big names in the computer industry. Unicode uses 2 bytes (16 bits) for each character, instead of 1 byte (8 bits). Thus, Unicode can handle 65,536 character combinations rather than ASCII's 256.

Ultimately, conversion to Unicode seems likely because it can handle more character combinations.

video adapter port (KQ 2.4, p. 2.21)   Part of the computer used to connect the video display monitor outside the computer to the video adapter card inside the system unit.

The video adapter port enables users to have different kinds of monitors, some having higher resolution and more colors than others.

video RAM (VRAM) (KQ 2.4, p. 2.20)   Chips that are used to display images for the monitor.

The amount of video memory determines how fast images appear and how many colors are available on the display screen.

1. Fill in the following blanks:

    a. A(n) _____ bit is an extra bit attached to a byte for purposes of checking for accuracy.

    b. A(n) _____ is about 1,000 bytes (1,024) bytes. A(n)

       _____ is about 1 million bytes (1,048,576 bytes).

       A(n) _____ is about 1 billion bytes (1,073,741,824 bytes).

    c. _____ is a binary programming language that the computer can run directly.

    d. The _____ is the part of the microprocessor that tells the rest of the computer system how to carry out a program's instructions.

    e. _____ refers to the number of bits the processor can hold in its registers, process at one time, and send through its local bus.

2. Label each of the following statements as either true or false.

    _____ Computer programmers write in programming languages that resemble machine language.

    _____ The bus connects a computer system's control unit and ALU.

    _____ The machine cycle is composed of the instruction cycle and the execution cycle.

    _____ Today's microprocessors have more transistors than those of the 1970s.

    _____ Main memory is nonvolatile.

3. List three binary data coding schemes:

    a. _____

    b. _____

    c. _____

4. Which of the following are components of the main processor?

    a. _____ ROM

    b. _____ RAM

    c. _____ control unit

    d. _____ ALU

    e. _____ coprocessor

5. Not all main processors are constructed in exactly the same way. List two common processor architectures for personal computers.

    a. _____

    b. _____

6. Define each of the following terms:
    a. machine cycle
    b. instruction cycle
    c. execution cycle

7. List three factors that you can use to differentiate one computer from another:

a. _____

b. _____

c. _____

8. The following might be contained on a computer's motherboard:

a. _____ RAM chips

b. _____ ROM chips

c. _____ microprocessor

d. _____ expansion boards

e. _____ keyboard

9. What are three variations of traditional ROM chips?

a. _____

b. _____

c. _____

10. To install a new adapter card in your computer, you must plug the card into a bus slot. List four common bus standards:

a. _____

b. _____

c. _____

d. _____

IN YOUR OWN WORDS

1. Answer each of the Key Questions listed at the beginning of the chapter.

2. What are parity bits used for?

3. What is the difference between ASCII and Unicode?

4. Why should units of capacity matter to computer users?

5. What are the main components of the processor?

6. Could a computer work without main memory? Why or why not?

7. How do MPP processors differ from CISC and RISC processors?

8. What's the difference between RAM and ROM?

9. What is the significance of the term *megahertz*?

10. What is a motherboard?

KNOWLEDGE IN ACTION

1. **Identifying Your Computer's Microprocessor and RAM Capacity.** If you're using the Windows 95 or Windows 98 operating system, you can easily determine what microprocessor and how much RAM is in your computer. To begin, click the Start button on the Windows desktop and then choose Settings, Control Panel from the menus. Then, locate the System icon in the Control Panel window and then double-click the icon.

   The System Properties dialog box will open, which contains four tabs: *General*, *Device Manager*, *Hardware Profiles*, and *Performance*. The name of your computer's microprocessor will display on the *General* tab. To see how much RAM is in your computer, click the *Performance* tab. Write down on a piece of paper what microprocessor and how much RAM is in your computer. When you're finished, close the System Properties dialog box by clicking its Close button (⊠) in the upper-right corner. Use the same procedure to close the Control Panel dialog box.

2. **Learning More About Blue Mountain.** SGI/Cray's Blue Mountain supercomputer is probably the most powerful computer in the world. Use an Internet search engine such as *www.yahoo.com* or *www.infoseek.com* to locate information on this computing giant. Through your investigation, determine why the computer was developed, how much RAM the computer has, and how large its hard disks are. Present your findings in a short report.

3. **PC Webopaedia.** The objective of this project is to introduce you to an online encyclopedia that's dedicated to computer technology. The *www.webopaedia.com* Web site is a superb resource for deciphering computer ads and clearing up difficult concepts. For practice, after visiting the site, type "main memory" into the Search text box and then press the Enter key. Print out the page that displays. Then, locate information on another processing topic that you find interesting and again print out your search result.

4. **A Processor in Every Pot?** Name at least five household appliances that use microprocessors (microcontrollers). Could any of these appliances function without the microprocessor? Select one of these products and describe what its microprocessor does.

5. **The Cutting Edge.** Using an Internet search engine, research one of the following technologies: biochips, tiny turbines, or single-electron transisters. What is the significance of this technology? Who is developing it? What impact do you think this will have on society? How is this technology being used today?

INPUT/OUTPUT HARDWARE

Interfaces Between You and the Computer

3

KEY QUESTIONS

You should be able to answer the following questions:

3.1 I/O, I/O, It's Off to Work We Go *How is input and output hardware used by a computer system?*

3.2 Input Hardware *What are three categories of input hardware, and what devices do they include?*

3.3 Output Hardware *What are the main characteristics of printers, plotters, multi-function devices, display screens, and audio output devices?*

3.4 In & Out: Devices That Do Both *How are terminals, smart cards, and touch screens used by a computer system?*

If, in a sudden fit of anti-technology disillusionment, you decided never to lay hands on a computer for the rest of your life, one system would still be hard to avoid. It's that universal gadget the ATM, the automated teller machine—the "magic money machine," as some people call it, built into the walls of banks, malls, and supermarkets everywhere.

Nearly half of American households already use an ATM at least once a month. Now, in a move that will probably affect your future, banks are recognizing that ATMs can be used to deliver all kinds of things besides $20 bills. ATMs in Las Vegas gambling casinos dispense $100 bills. In the future, look for machines that will cash checks down to the penny. In airports, variations on ATMs called *electronic ticketing machines* help travelers avoid lines and airlines save money. Some teller machines act like vending machines, selling plane and theater tickets, traveler's checks, bus passes, postage stamps, phone cards, and other documents. And, in a great leap beyond paper, a device called a Personal-ATM has been unveiled that you can install in your home. With this device, you can use your phone to download funds from your bank account onto a "smart card," a credit-card-like piece of plastic embedded with a computer chip and usable as a cash substitute.

Beyond one important fact—that they deal with money—why are ATMs of interest to us here? The reason is that this device exemplifies the two faces, or interfaces, by which people interact with the computer. These are *input,* as when we deposit a check into the machine, and *output,* as when it dispenses crisp green bills. In this chapter we explore input/output, or I/O, devices.

3.1 I/O, I/O, It's Off to Work We Go

KEY QUESTION **How is input and output hardware used by a computer system?**

Recall from Chapter 1 that *input* refers to data entered into a computer for processing—for example, from a keyboard or from a file stored on disk. *Output* refers to the results of processing, that is, data sent to the screen or the printer or to be stored on disk, or sent to another computer in a network (✔ p. 1.11).

In this chapter we focus on the common input and output devices that people deal with when they are working with a computer. *(See Figure 3.1.)*

Input hardware consists of devices that translate data into a form the computer can process. The people-readable form may be words like the ones in these sentences, but the computer-readable form consists of binary 0s and 1s, or off and on signals. **Output hardware** consists of devices that translate information processed by the computer into a form that humans can understand. The computer-processed information consists of 0s and 1s, which need to be translated into words, numbers, sounds, and pictures.

First we'll cover input hardware.

Figure 3.1

Common input and output devices

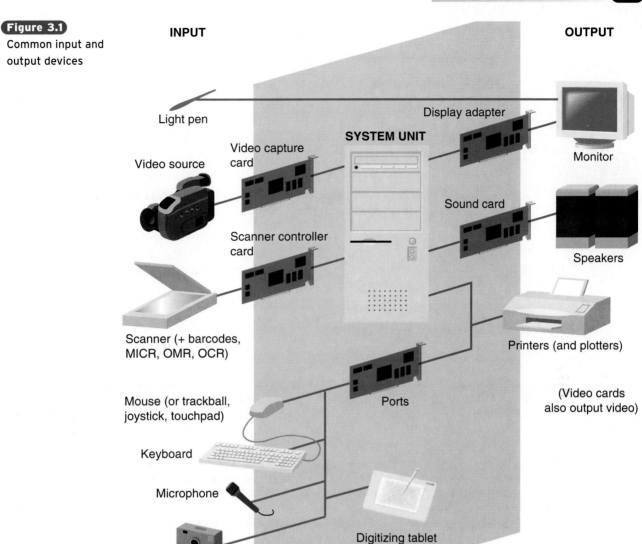

INPUT

OUTPUT

3.2 Input Hardware

KEY QUESTION **What are three categories of input hardware, and what devices do they include?**

One input device with which you are probably familiar is the keyboard. A **keyboard,** the first category of input hardware, converts letters, numbers, and other characters into electrical signals that are machine-readable by the computer's processor. The keyboard may look like a typewriter keyboard to which some special keys have been added. Or it may look like the keys on a bank's automatic teller machine or the keypad of a pocket computer used by a bread-truck driver.

You will also probably use some non-keyboard **pointing devices,** the second category of input hardware. These devices control the position of the cursor or pointer on the screen. Pointing devices include:

- Mice, trackballs, joysticks, and touchpads

- Light pens

- Digitizing tablets

- Pen-based systems

Because keyboard entry requires typing by people, the data input this way is less accurate than data input via non-keyboard **source-data entry devices,** the third category of input hardware. These include:

- Scanners, including bar code scanners, fax machines, and imaging systems

- Voice-recognition devices

- Audio input devices

- Video input devices

- Electronic cameras

- Sensors

- Human-biology input devices

Often keyboard, pointing, and source-data input devices are combined in a single computer system. A basic desktop-publishing system, for example, uses a keyboard, a mouse, and an image scanner. And some microcomputers have built-in scanners.

Keyboard Input

Even if you aren't a ten-finger typist, you can use a computer keyboard. *(See Figure 3.2.)* You should not feel intimidated by the number of keys, because you can easily undo mistakes.

Figure 3.2 Common keyboard layout

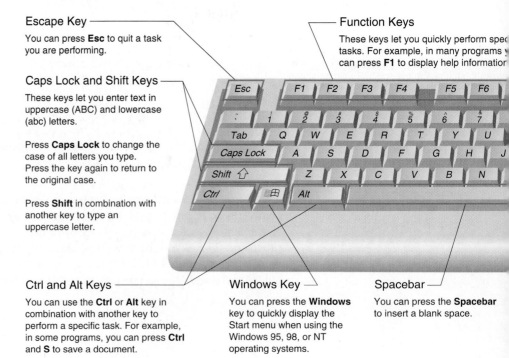

Escape Key
You can press **Esc** to quit a task you are performing.

Function Keys
These keys let you quickly perform spec tasks. For example, in many programs can press **F1** to display information

Caps Lock and Shift Keys
These keys let you enter text in uppercase (ABC) and lowercase (abc) letters.

Press **Caps Lock** to change the case of all letters you type. Press the key again to return to the original case.

Press **Shift** in combination with another key to type an uppercase letter.

Ctrl and Alt Keys
You can use the **Ctrl** or **Alt** key in combination with another key to perform a specific task. For example, in some programs, you can press **Ctrl** and **S** to save a document.

Windows Key
You can press the **Windows** key to quickly display the Start menu when using the Windows 95, 98, or NT operating systems.

Spacebar
You can press the **Spacebar** to insert a blank space.

QWERTY keyboard

■ *Standard typing keys: Typing keys* are the familiar QWERTY arrangement of letter, number, and punctuation keys found on any typewriter. QWERTY refers to the alphabet keys in the top left row on a standard typewriter keyboard.

The space bar and Shift, Tab, and Caps Lock keys do the same things on the computer that they do on a typewriter. (When you press the Caps Lock key, a light on your keyboard shows you are typing ALL CAPITAL LETTERS until you press the Caps Lock key again.)

An exception is the Enter (bent left arrow) key. The **Enter key,** sometimes called the Return key, is used to enter commands into the computer, in addition to beginning a new paragraph in a word processing system.

■ *Cursor-movement keys:* The **cursor,** also called the *insertion point,* is the symbol on the display screen that shows where data may be entered next. The **cursor-movement keys,** or arrow keys, are used to move the cursor around the text on the screen. These keys move the cursor left, right, up, or down.

The key labeled *PgUp* stands for *Page Up,* and the key labeled *PgDn* stands for *Page Down.* These keys move the cursor the equivalent of one page or one screen at a time up (toward the beginning of the document) or down (toward the end of the document).

■ *Numeric keys:* On a standard 101-key keyboard, previously known as an enhanced AT-style keyboard, a separate set of keys, 0 through 9, known as the **numeric keypad,** is laid out like the keys on a calculator. The numeric keypad has two purposes.

Whenever the Num Lock key is off, the numeric keys may be used as arrow keys for cursor movement and for other purposes such as PgUp, PgDn.

When the Num Lock key is on, the keys may be used for manipulating numbers, as on a calculator. A light is illuminated on the keyboard when the Num Lock key is pressed once and goes off when the Num Lock key is pressed again.

Backspace Key
You can press **Backspace** to remove the character to the left of the cursor.

Delete Key
You can press **Delete** to remove the character to the right of the cursor.

Status Lights
These lights indicate whether the **Num Lock** or **Caps Lock** features are on or off.

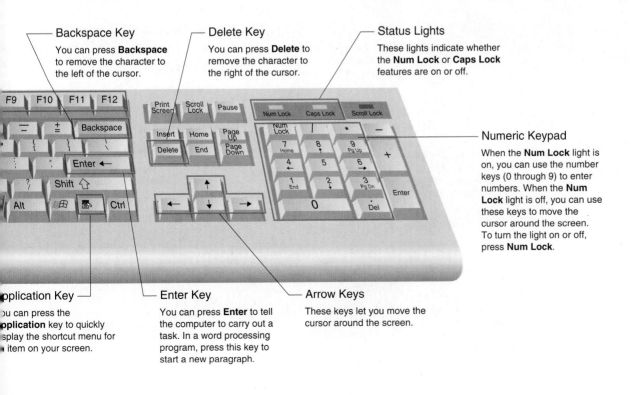

Numeric Keypad
When the **Num Lock** light is on, you can use the number keys (0 through 9) to enter numbers. When the **Num Lock** light is off, you can use these keys to move the cursor around the screen. To turn the light on or off, press **Num Lock**.

pplication Key
ou can press the **pplication** key to quickly splay the shortcut menu for item on your screen.

Enter Key
You can press **Enter** to tell the computer to carry out a task. In a word processing program, press this key to start a new paragraph.

Arrow Keys
These keys let you move the cursor around the screen.

Dr. Peter Torpey uses a Braille keyboard in his office at Xerox Corporation. Dr. Torpey, who is blind, also uses voice input.

For space reasons, portable computers often lack a separate numeric keypad—or the numeric keys may be superimposed on the typewriter letter keys and activated by the Num Lock key.

■   *Function keys:* **Function keys** are labeled with an F and a number, such as F1 and F2. They are used for issuing commands, not typing in characters. Desktop microcomputers usually have 12 function keys, portables often only 10.

The purpose of each function key is defined by the software you are using. For example, in one program, pressing F2 may print your document; in a different program, pressing F2 may save your work to disk. The documentation manual that comes with the software tells you how to use the function keys. Also, some companies make small templates that fit around or above the function keys and list the commands that the function keys correspond to.

Many keyboards also include built-in enhancements such as microphones, speakers, and volume control.

As computers have become more widespread, so has the incidence of various hand and wrist injuries. Accordingly, keyboard manufacturers have been giving a lot of attention to ergonomics. **Ergonomics** is the study of the physical relationships between people and their work environment; that is, it is the science of designing equipment for a safe and comfortable environment. Ergonomics deals with designing efficient and safe chairs, desks, and lights. It also recommends safe viewing distances from monitors. Keyboard manufacturers, as a result of ergonomic studies, have developed ergonomically sound keyboards to help prevent injuries and for use by physically challenged individuals. *(See Figure 3.3.)*

Figure 3.3   Ergonomic keyboards *(Top left)* A seven-year-old boy with cerebral palsy uses a toe-operated keyboard called a "liberator device." *(Top right)* ComKey ergonomic keyboard. *(Bottom right)* Keyboard for one hand, used at a rehabilitation center.

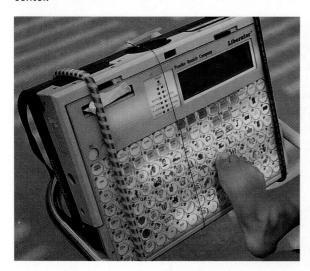

Warning!

Carpal Tunnel Syndrome (CTS)

Carpal Tunnel Syndrome is a Repetitive Stress Injury (RSI) whose symptoms include numbness, tingling, and pain in the fingers. The condition affects some workers who type without proper wrist support or type for long periods of time without breaks. You can avoid wrist strain when typing by keeping your elbows level with the keyboard and keeping your wrists straight and higher than your fingers.

Pointing Devices

One of the most natural of all human gestures, the act of pointing, is incorporated in several kinds of input devices.

Mice, Trackballs, Joysticks, and Touchpads

The principal pointing tools used with microcomputers are the mouse, the track-ball, the joystick, and the touchpad, all of which have variations. *(See Figure 3.4.)*

■ *Mouse:* A **mouse** is a device that is rolled about on a desktop to direct a pointer on the computer's display screen. When you move the mouse on your desk, the pointer on the screen moves in the same direction. The **mouse pointer** is the symbol that indicates the position of the mouse on the display screen. The pointer will change from an arrow to a pointing-finger icon, depending on the task you are performing. It also changes to the shape of an I-beam to indicate where text or other data may be entered. If you click on the left mouse button when the I-beam is positioned, a cursor—a blinking vertical line—appears in the text. What you type will be inserted here.

I-beam

Arrow

Figure 3.4 (a, b) Two types of mouse: two buttons and three buttons. (c) Trackball. (d) Joystick. (e) Touchpad.

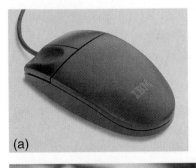

(a)

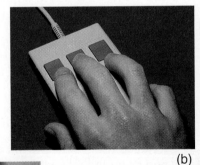

(b)

(c)

(d)

(e)

An iMac mouse, for the recent Apple Macintosh model

The mouse usually has a cable that is connected (by being plugged into a special port, or socket) to the microcomputer's system unit. This tail-like cable and the rounded "head" of the instrument are what suggested the name *mouse.* Some newer mouse types are wireless (cordless)—that is, they use battery-powered transmitters to send infrared signals to a battery-powered receiver hooked up to a serial port on the back of the computer. Some companies make mice in different sizes, to fit hands of different sizes.

On the bottom side of the mouse is a ball that translates the mouse movement into digital signals. On the top side are one to four buttons. Your software determines the use of the second, third, and fourth buttons; the first one is used for common functions, such as *clicking* and *dragging.* *(See Table 3.1.)*

Some brands of mouse, such as the Microsoft Intellimouse, have a wheel between the left and right mouse buttons with which one can scroll through the contents of a file.

Wheel

Depending on the software, many commands that can be executed with a mouse can also be performed through the keyboard. The mouse may make it easy to learn the commands for, say, a word processing program. However,

Table 3.1

LEARNING MOUSE LANGUAGE	
Term	**Definition**
	The directions you are most likely to encounter for using a mouse or a trackball are the following:
Point	Move the pointer to the desired spot on the screen, such as over a particular word or object.
Click	Tap—that is, press and quickly release—the left mouse button. A click often selects an item on the screen.
Double-click	Tap—press and release—the left mouse button twice, as quickly as possible. A double-click often opens a document or starts a program.
Drag	Press and hold the left mouse button while moving the pointer to another location.
Drop	Release the mouse button after dragging. Dragging and dropping makes it easy to move an item on the screen.
Right-click	Make a selection by using the button on the right side of the mouse. Doing so in the Windows 95/98 environment typically brings up a pop-up menu with options available to the object over which the cursor is positioned.
	Note: If you are left-handed, you can switch the functions of the left and right mouse buttons to make the mouse easier to use.

you may soon find that you can execute those commands more quickly through a combination of keystrokes on the keyboard.

Trackball mounted on a laptop's keyboard

■ *Trackball:* Another form of pointing device, the trackball, is a variant on the mouse. A **trackball** is a movable ball, on top of a stationary device, that is rotated with the fingers or palm of the hand. In fact, the trackball looks like a mouse turned upside down. Instead of moving the mouse around on the desktop, you move the trackball with the tips of your fingers.

Trackballs are especially suited to portable computers, which are often used in confined places such as on airline tray tables. Trackballs may appear on the keyboard, as shown to the left, or built into the right side of the screen. On some portables the trackball is a separate device that is clipped to the side of the keyboard.

■ *Joystick:* A **joystick** is a pointing device that consists of a vertical handle like a gearshift lever mounted on a base with one or two buttons. Named for the control mechanism that directs an airplane's fore-and-aft and side-to-side movement, joysticks are used principally in video games, in some computer-aided design systems, and in computerized robot systems. Special joysticks, such as SAM-JOYstick from RJ Cooper and Associates, are available for people with disabilities that don't let them use a mouse or a trackball.

■ *Touchpad:* **Touchpads** let you control the cursor/pointer with your finger. About the same size as a mouse, touchpads are flat, rectangular devices that use a very weak electrical field to sense your touch. As you move your finger-tip, the cursor follows the movement. You "click" by tapping your finger on the pad's surface or by pressing buttons on the top, back, or side of the pad. Many portable computers and desktop computers now include touchpads built into the keyboard.

Figure 3.5 Pros and cons of the mouse, trackball, and touchpad

Figure 3.5 gives some pros and cons of using mice, trackballs, and touchpads.

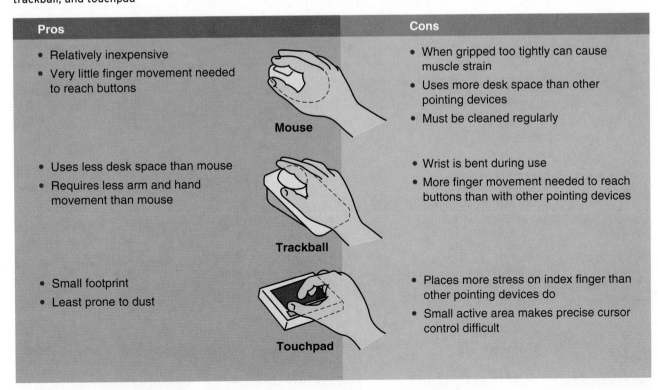

Pros		Cons
• Relatively inexpensive • Very little finger movement needed to reach buttons	**Mouse**	• When gripped too tightly can cause muscle strain • Uses more desk space than other pointing devices • Must be cleaned regularly
• Uses less desk space than mouse • Requires less arm and hand movement than mouse	**Trackball**	• Wrist is bent during use • More finger movement needed to reach buttons than with other pointing devices
• Small footprint • Least prone to dust	**Touchpad**	• Places more stress on index finger than other pointing devices do • Small active area makes precise cursor control difficult

Figure 3.6 Light pen. A microbiology lab technician uses a light pen to perform tests.

Light Pen

The **light pen** is a light-sensitive stylus, or pen-like device, connected by a wire to the computer terminal. The user brings the pen to a desired point on the display screen and presses the pen button, which identifies that screen location to the computer. *(See Figure 3.6.)* Light pens are used by engineers, graphic designers, and illustrators.

Digitizing Tablets

A **digitizing tablet** consists of a tablet connected by a wire to a stylus or puck. A stylus is a pen-like device with which the user "sketches" an image. A puck is a copying device with which the user copies, or traces, an image. *(See Figure 3.7.)*

When used with drawing and painting software, a digitizing tablet and stylus allow you to do shading and many other effects similar to those artists achieve with pencil, pen, or charcoal. Alternatively, when you use a puck, you can trace a drawing laid on the tablet, and a digitized copy is stored in the computer.

Digitizing tablets are used primarily in graphic design, computer animation, and engineering.

Figure 3.7 Digitizing tablets. *(Left)* A plastic surgeon generates images of a woman with different nose styles. *(Right)* An animator uses a digitizing tablet to create an image.

Pen-Based Systems

Pen-based computer systems use a pen-like stylus to enter handwriting and marks into a computer. *(See Figure 3.8.)* There is a good chance you will use one of these systems if you haven't already.

 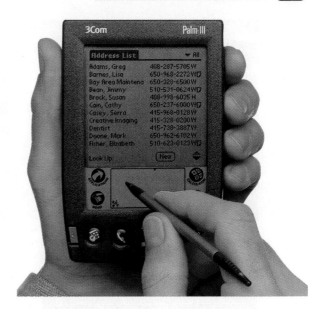

Figure 3.8 Pen-based computers. *(Left)* A shopper talks to a produce clerk, who is recording her comments about the produce. *(Right)* PalmPilot.

There are four types of pen-based systems:

- *Gesture recognition or electronic checklists: Gesture recognition* refers to a computer's ability to recognize various check marks, slashes, or carefully printed block letters and numbers placed in boxes. This type of pen-based system is incorporated in devices that resemble simple forms or checklists on handheld electronic clipboards, with an accompanying electronic pen or stylus. This type of small computer is used by meter readers, package deliverers, and insurance claims representatives.

- *Handwriting stored as scribbling:* A second type of pen-based system recognizes and stores handwriting. The handwriting is stored as a scribble and is not converted to typed text.

- *Handwriting converted, with training, to typed text:* Some pen-based devices can recognize your handwriting and transform it into typed text. These systems require that the machine be "trained" to recognize your particular (or even peculiar) handwriting. Moreover, the writing must be neat printing rather than script. The advantage of converting writing to typed text is that after conversion the text can be retrieved and later edited or further manipulated.

- *Handwriting converted, without training, to typed text:* The most sophisticated— and still mostly elusive—application of pen-based computers converts script handwriting to typed text without training.

Small handheld computers, called *PDAs (personal digital assistants)*, use pen-based input. Larger PDAs include small keyboards. However, the small models, called *palm computers*, do not include a keyboard and so rely on pen-based input. Popular palm computers include 3COM's PalmPilot *(see Figure 3.8)* and Palm III.

Source-Data Entry

As we mentioned earlier, source-data input devices do not require keystrokes to input data to the computer. In other words, data is entered from as close to the source as possible; people do not need to act as typing intermediaries. One of the most common source-data entry devices is the scanner.

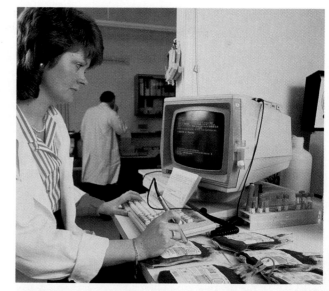

Figure 3.9 Bar-code readers. *(Top left)* Worker using a bar-code reader to check inventory. *(Top right)* Bar-code reader being used to enter details of units of blood into the hospital computer. *(Bottom left)* Worker using a bar-code reader to check a warehouse delivery. *(Bottom right)* United Parcel Service (UPS) worker scans package information into the UPS tracking system.

Scanning Devices

Scanners use laser beams and reflected light to translate hardcopy images of text, drawings, photos, and the like into digital form. The images can then be processed by a computer, displayed on a monitor, stored on a storage device, or communicated to another computer. Scanning devices include:

- Bar-code readers
- Mark- and character-recognition devices
- Fax machines
- Imaging systems

Bar-Code Readers **Bar codes** are the vertical zebra-striped marks you see on most manufactured retail products—everything from candy to cosmetics to comic books. In North America and, for example, in Australia, supermarkets, food manufacturers, and others have agreed to use a bar-code system called the *Universal Product Code.* Other bar-code systems are used on everything from Federal Express packages to railroad cars.

Bar-code readers are photoelectric scanners that translate the bar code symbols into digital code (ASCII or EBCDIC). *(See Figure 3.9.)* The price of a particular item is set within the store's computer and appears on the salesclerk's point-of-sale terminal and on your receipt. Records of sales are input to the store's computer and used for accounting, restocking store inventory, and weeding out products that don't sell well.

A recent innovation is the self-scanning bar-code reader, which grocers hope will extend the concept of self-service and help them lower costs. Here customers bring their groceries to an automated checkout counter, where they scan them and bag them. They then take the bill to a cashier's station to pay. To guard against theft, the bar-code scanner is able to detect attempts to pass off steak as peas.

Bar codes are also occasionally used on people. For example, when 1000 runners completed a 1996 relay race from Calistoga to Santa Cruz in northern California, they didn't have to wait four months to find out their times. Instead, they got the information at the finish line. Each runner wore a bar-code T-shirt, and handheld bar-code readers recorded runners' times at each of the race's thirty-six checkpoints.

Mark-Recognition and Character-Recognition Devices There are three types of scanning devices that translate certain types of marks and characters. They are usually referred to by their abbreviations MICR, OMR, and OCR.

■ *Magnetic-ink character recognition:* In **magnetic-ink character recognition (MICR),** a scanner translates the magnetically charged numbers printed at the bottom of bank checks and deposit slips. *(See Figure 3.10.)* MICR characters, which are printed with magnetized ink, are read by MICR equipment, producing a digitized signal. This signal is used by a bank's reader/sorter machine to sort checks.

■ *Optical mark recognition:* **Optical mark recognition (OMR)** uses a device that reads pencil marks and converts them into computer-usable form. Well-known examples are the OMR technology used to read the College Board Scholastic Aptitude Test (SAT), the Graduate Record Examination (GRE), and SCAN-TRON tests.

■ *Optical character recognition:* **Optical character recognition (OCR)** uses a device that reads special OCR character sets called OCR *fonts,* as well as typewriter and computer-printed characters, and converts them into machine-readable form. Examples that use OCR characters are utility bills and price tags on department-store merchandise. The *wand reader* is a common OCR scanning device. Some advanced OCR systems can recognize human handwriting, but generally the letters must be block printed. There is no standard

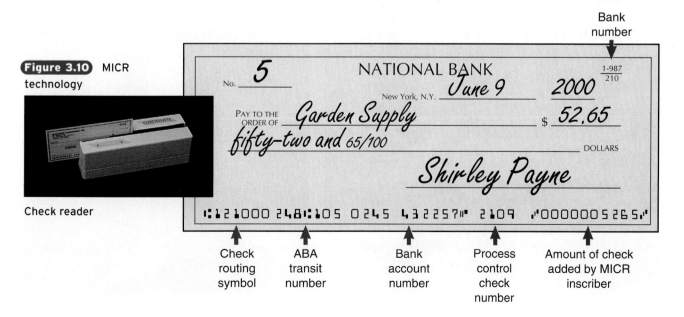

Figure 3.10 MICR technology

Check reader

Bank number

No. *5*   NATIONAL BANK   1-987 / 210

New York, N.Y. *June 9* *2000*

PAY TO THE ORDER OF *Garden Supply* $ *52.65*

fifty-two and 65/100 _____ DOLLARS

Shirley Payne

Check routing symbol | ABA transit number | Bank account number | Process control check number | Amount of check added by MICR inscriber

Figure 3.11 *(Left)* Stand-alone fax machine. *(Right)* Fax board.

that can be used to program computers to recognize script handwriting styles, because they vary so widely.

Using OCR can be five times faster than retyping a document into the computer. The important function of OCR is that, once the text appears on-screen, a user can copy it to a word processing program, spell check it, make corrections and additions, and save it.

Fax Machines A **fax machine**—or *facsimile transmission machine*—scans an image on paper and sends it as electronic signals over telephone lines to a receiving fax machine, which re-creates the image on paper. *(See Figure 3.11.)* (*Facsimile* means "an exact copy.") It can also scan and send an image to a fax *modem* (circuit board) inside a remote computer; this fax can be displayed on the screen, stored, or printed out by the computer's printer.

Imaging Systems An **imaging system**—or image scanner or graphics scanner—converts text, drawings, and photographs into digital form that can be stored in a computer system and then manipulated, stored, output, or sent via modem to another computer. *(See Figure 3.12.)* The system scans each image—

Figure 3.12 *(Left)* Checking the colors in a scanned magazine cover image. *(Right)* A graphics designer scans an image into his desktop publishing system.

Alice Springs, Australia nature conservancy workers check up on a wallaby by scanning the chip embedded under his skin.

color or black and white—with light and breaks it into light and dark dots or color dots, which are then converted to digital code. This is called *raster graphics,* which refers to the technique of representing a graphic image as a matrix of dots.

Imaging systems are used in document management, desktop publishing (DTP), and multimedia development. In DTP, the graphics scanner scans in artwork and photos that can then be positioned on a page of text, using desktop-publishing software. Other systems are available for turning paper documents—say, legal transcripts or financial records—into electronic files so that people can reduce their paperwork as well as the space required to store it. Internet and Web users scan photos into their computer systems to send to online friends or to post on Web pages.

Drum scanner—checking color values of scanned art in the printing industry

Scanners generally are flatbed, drum, or handheld. Flatbed and drum scanners are used for scanning high-quality color graphics. Flatbed scanners can scan single sheets and book-bound pages. Drum scanners are fed one sheet at a time; they cannot handle book-bound pages. Flatbed scanners scan at high resolutions—up to 2400 dots per inch (dpi), compared to 300–600 dpi for drum scanners. (The higher the resolution, the crisper the image but the longer the scanning time and the larger the image file.)

Handheld scanners are rolled by hand over the documents to be scanned. These scanners are generally used to scan in small images or parts of images. Their resolution is not very high.

Some manufacturers are building small scanners into portable computers—the user feeds a sheet of paper into a slot in the computer. Also, small scanners used just for snapshots and slides are available. Expensive 3-D scanners can convert small and medium-size objects into 3-D files.

Imaging-system technology has led to a whole new art or industry called *electronic imaging.* In electronic imaging, separate images are combined using scanners, digital cameras, video capture cards, and advanced graphic computers. This technology has become an important part of multimedia.

Slide scanner

Voice-Recognition

When you speak to a computer, can it tell whether you want to "recognize speech" or "wreck a nice beach"?

Voice-recognition systems, whereby you dictate input via a microphone, have faced considerable hurdles: different voices, pronunciations, and accents. In Atlanta, for instance, natives say "Tick a rat" (make a right turn, or "Take a right"). In New York City, they say "Gnome sane?" ("Do you know what I'm saying?") Such regionalisms pose real challenges to voice-recognition experts. With past voice-recognition systems, users had to use the software to train a particular computer to recognize their voices, and they had to pause between words rather than speak normally. Recently, however, the systems have measurably improved.

A **voice-recognition system,** using a microphone (or a telephone) as an input device, converts a person's speech into digital code by comparing the electrical patterns produced by the speaker's voice with a set of prerecorded patterns stored in the computer. *(See Figure 3.13.)*

Voice-recognition systems are finding many uses. Warehouse workers are able to speed inventory-taking by recording inventory counts verbally. Blind or paralyzed people can give verbal commands to their PCs rather than use the keyboard. Traders on stock exchanges can communicate their trades verbally. Astronauts who need to use two hands to make repairs in space can activate display screens in their helmet visors with spoken commands. Radiologists spend most of their time interpreting images such as X-rays and sending reports of their findings to other doctors. The reports traditionally have been dictated into a recording machine, transcribed by a secretary, and then corrected by the doctor—a process that often took days. Now, however, many radiologists use advanced voice-recognition systems to get their reports out much more rapidly.

Voice-recognition technology clearly has several advantages over traditional keyboard and mouse input. It protects users against repetitive stress injuries; it simplifies computing for beginning users; and it improves data-entry speed and can improve accuracy, if used properly.

Besides a microphone, a microcomputer voice-recognition system requires a sound board (discussed in the section on output), 180 MB or more of hard disk space, a fast processor, 32–64 MB of RAM (✔ p. 1.11), and a CD-ROM drive (discussed in the next chapter). Two popular programs are NaturallySpeaking from Dragon Systems and ViaVoice from IBM. Users talk in a natural manner and pace. The spoken words and punctuation immediately appear on the screen. Users can also do text editing and formatting via voice command, as well as manage files. These programs come with huge vocabularies that can be increased according to the user's needs. Special vocabularies—for example, for the medical and financial industries—are also available.

Both programs recommend short "conditioning" sessions to increase accuracy. In a conditioning session, the user reads a text supplied with the program into the microphone. The program then adjusts to the user's accent and intonation.

Audio Input Devices

Voice-recognition devices are only one kind of audio input device, which can translate music as well as other sounds. An **audio input device** records or plays analog sound and translates it for digital storage and processing. As we mentioned in Chapter 1, an *analog sound signal* represents a continuously variable wave within a certain frequency range. Such continuous fluctuations are usually represented with an analog device such as a cassette player. For the computer to process them, these variable waves must be converted to digital 0s and 1s, the language of the computer.

Figure 3.13 How a voice-recognition system works

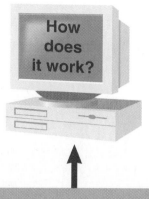

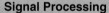

Speech

A person who's going to use speech recognition software must first go through an *enrollment.* This consists of the person dictating text that is already known to the software for 10 minutes to an hour. From this sampling, the software creates a table of *vocal references,* which are the ways in which the speaker's pronunciation of phonemes varies from models of speech based on a sampling of hundreds to thousands of people. *Phonemes* are the smallest sound units that combine into words, such as "duh," "aw" and "guh" in "dog." There are 48 phonemes in English. After enrollment, the speaker dictates the text he wants the software to transcribe into a microphone, preferably one that uses *noise-cancellation* to eliminate background sounds. The quality of the microphone and the computer's processing power are the most important hardware factors in speech recognition. The speaker can use continuous speech, which is normal speech without pauses between words.

Signal Processing

The sound wave is transformed into a sequence of codes that represent speech sounds.

Output

Computer recognizes word string and prints it on the screen.

Recognition Search

Using the data from 1, 2, and 3, the computer tries to find the best matching sequence of words as learned from a variety of examples.

1. Phonetic Models

Describe what codes may occur for a given speech sound.
  In the word *how,* what is the probability of the "ow" sound appearing between an H and a D?

2. Dictionary

Defines the phonetic pronunciation (sequence of sounds) of each word.
  How does it work
  haw daz it werk

3. Grammar

Defines what words may follow each other, using part of speech.
  How does <it> [work]
  adv vt pron v

There are two ways in which audio is digitized:

- *Audio board:* Analog sound, such as input through a microphone, goes through a special circuit board called an *audio board,* or a *sound card.* An *audio board* is an add-on (expansion) circuit board in a microcomputer that converts analog sound to digital sound and stores it for further processing and/or plays it back, providing output directly to speakers or an external amplifier. The three major sound standards are SoundBlaster, Ad Lib, and Windows. Some sound cards support all three standards. And some sound cards also have MIDI capability.

■ *MIDI board:* A *MIDI* (pronounced "middie") *board*—MIDI stands for Musical Instrument Digital Interface—provides a standard for the interchange of musical information between musical instruments, synthesizers, and computers. MIDI, which is based on a set of computer instructions rather than sample sounds, is widely used for multimedia applications. Most high-end sound cards have certain MIDI capabilities including ports for connecting external MIDI devices. For example, MIDI keyboards, also called *controllers,* and synthesizers can be plugged in to input music, which can then be stored, manipulated, and/or output.

Analog sound is converted to digital data via *sampling;* the sampling rate is the number of times per second analog sound is turned into a binary number by the computer. To digitize voice, the computer samples the sound waves 8000 times per second to attain AM-radio-quality output. Music is sampled 44,000 times per second to attain CD-quality output.

Video and Photographic Input

As with sound, most film and videotape is in analog form; the signal is a continuously variable wave. Thus, to be used by a computer, the signals that come from a VCR or a camcorder must be converted to digital form through a special video capture, or digitizing, card installed in the computer.

Two types of video cards are in common use:

■ *Frame-grabber video card:* Some video cards, called *frame grabbers,* can capture and digitize only a single frame at a time.

■ *Full-motion video card:* Other video cards, called *full-motion video cards* or *adapters,* can convert analog to digital signals at up to 30 frames per second (TV quality), giving the effect of a continuously flowing motion picture. *(See Figure 3.14.)*

Most video cameras are analog, but digital video cameras are also available. Unlike analog video cameras, which convert light intensities into infinitely variable signals, digital video cameras convert light intensities into discrete 0s and 1s. With the appropriate software, digital video can be transmitted (downloaded) directly to the computer. The main limitation in capturing full video is not input but storage. It takes a huge amount of storage space to store just 1 second of video.

Photographs can also be created digitally, avoiding the need for a scanner. The digital camera is a particularly interesting piece of hardware because it foreshadows major change for the entire industry of photography. Instead of using traditional (chemical) film, a digital camera captures images in electronic form for immediate viewing on a television, computer display screen, or attached LCD screen (such as that used to display charts on a classroom wall).

A **digital camera** uses a light-sensitive processor chip to capture photographic images in digital form on a memory card inserted in the camera. *(See Figure 3.15.)* The memory card can then be inserted into an adapter on the computer, and the contents can be copied onto the computer's hard disk for editing, storing, sending over the Internet, and printing out. Another type of digital camera stores 16 to 64 or 128 color shots in its flash memory chips, depending on the resolution. This type of camera is connected via a serial port so that (using special software) photos can be downloaded to the computer's hard drive. The memory-card process works faster than serial transmission. (Of course, photos can also be input to a computer via a scanner.)

Digital cameras have gone into wide use in journalism and industrial photography because the images are instantly available, can be deleted to make storage available for more photos, and can be transmitted over telephone lines and via satellite.

Figure 3.14 Changing analog video input to digital form

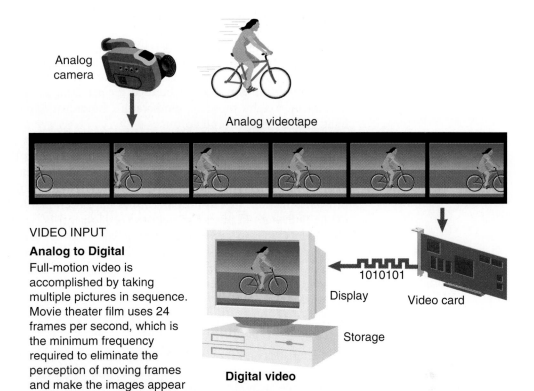

Analog camera

Analog videotape

VIDEO INPUT

Analog to Digital

Full-motion video is accomplished by taking multiple pictures in sequence. Movie theater film uses 24 frames per second, which is the minimum frequency required to eliminate the perception of moving frames and make the images appear visually fluid to the eye.

1010101

Display

Video card

Storage

Digital video

TV video generates 30 interlaced frames per second, which is actually transmitted as 60 half frames ("fields" in TV lingo) per second.

Video that has been digitized and stored in the computer can be displayed at varying frame rates, depending on the speed of the computer. The slower the computer, the jerkier the movement.

Figure 3.15 How a digital camera works

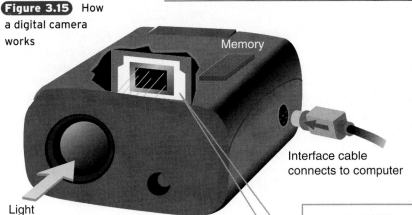

Memory

Interface cable connects to computer

Light

3. The digital information is stored in the camera's electronic memory, either built-in or removable.

4. Using an interface cable, the digital photo can be downloaded onto a computer, where it can be manipulated, printed, placed on a Web page, or e-mailed.

1. Light enters the camera through the lens.

2. The light is focused on the charge-coupled device (CCD), a solid-state chip made up of tiny, light-sensitive photosites. When light hits the CCD, it records the image electronically, just as film records images in a standard camera. The photosites convert light into electrons, which are then converted into digital information.

A look at CCDs

The smallest CCDs are 1/8 the size of a frame of 35 mm film. The largest are the same size as a 35 mm frame.

Smallest CCD

- Lower-end cameras start with 180,000 photosites.
- Professional cameras can have up to 6 million photosites.

CCD detail

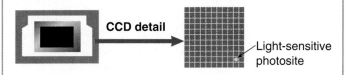

Light-sensitive photosite

Sensors

A **sensor** is a type of input device that collects specific kinds of data directly from the environment and transmits it to a computer. Although you are unlikely to see such input devices connected to a PC in an office, they exist all around us, often in invisible form. Sensors can be used for detecting all kinds of things: speed, movement, weight, pressure, temperature, humidity, wind, current, fog, gas, smoke, light, shapes, images, and so on.

Beneath the pavement, for example, are sensors that detect the speed and volume of traffic. These sensors send data to computers that can adjust traffic lights to keep cars and trucks away from gridlocked areas. In aviation, sensors are used to detect ice buildup on airplane wings or to alert pilots to sudden changes in wind direction. In California, sensors have been planted along major earthquake fault lines in an experiment to see if scientists can predict major earth movements. Sensors are also used by government regulators to monitor whether companies are complying with air-pollution standards. In New York City, a sensor called a *temperature pressure balancer* is mandated in new building construction; it maintains constant water temperature in the shower when a toilet is flushed somewhere else in the house.

Human-Biology Input Devices

Characteristics and movements of the human body, when interpreted by sensors, optical scanners, voice recognition, and other technologies, can become forms of input. Some examples are as follows:

- *Biometric systems: Biometric security devices* identify a person through a fingerprint, voice intonation, or other biological characteristic. For example, retinal-identification devices use a ray of light to identify the distinctive network of blood vessels at the back of a person's eyeball. Biometric systems are used in lieu of typed passwords to identify people authorized to use a computer system.

- *Line-of-sight systems:* Line-of-sight systems enable a person to use his or her eyes to point at the screen, a technology that allows users with physical disabilities to direct a computer. This is accomplished using a video camera mounted beneath the monitor in front of the viewer. When the user looks at a certain place on the screen, the video camera and computer translate that location into screen coordinates.

- *Cyber gloves and body suits:* Special gloves and body suits—often used in conjunction with "virtual reality," or the computer-generated simulation of reality—use sensors to detect body movements. The data for these movements is sent to a computer system. Similar technology is being used for human-controlled robot hands, which are used in nuclear power plants and hazardous-waste sites.

Multimedia Input Needs

In Chapters 1 and 2, we stated that multimedia systems have high system requirements. For example, you need a fast, powerful processor and some coprocessors. Throughout the section on input hardware, we mentioned some of the needs of a multimedia system. To recap—in addition to a keyboard and a mouse you need these for multimedia input:

- *Sound card:* All multimedia presentations now use sound.

- *Microphone:* The microphone provides sound input to the sound card.

- *Graphics scanner:* This allows you to include photos and art from outside sources.

- *Video capture card:* This card lets you digitize film and video segments for manipulation.

Input Controls: Preserving Data Integrity

No matter how sophisticated your input hardware is and how well designed your input methods are, you still run the risk of generating inaccurate or even useless information. The completeness and accuracy of information produced by a computer system will greatly depend on how much care was taken in capturing the raw data. An old computer-related saying summarizes this point: "Garbage In, Garbage Out" (GIGO). If you, the user, input incomplete and inaccurate data (Garbage In), then you can expect the information that is produced to be correspondingly incomplete and inaccurate (Garbage Out). How do you ensure that input data is accurate and complete?

Input controls include a combination of manual and computer-based control procedures designed to ensure that all input data has been accurately put into computer-usable form. A variety of control techniques can be used, depending on the design of the computer system and the nature of the processing activities taking place. System designers study these techniques and build them into systems. For example, computer software (a data-entry program) can include instructions to identify incorrect, invalid, or improper input data. Also, the computer can be programmed to run "reasonableness checks," by determining if input data exceeds specified limits or is out of sequence.

How important are input controls? Consider the modest-living couple who got a phone bill for $450,000 and spent months trying to convince the company it was a mistake. The customer service personnel and the data processing staff were probably trying to identify the glitch in the input control procedures. The computer doesn't make mistakes; the people who input data and monitor input procedures do. Even software writers are not infallible. Without input controls, mistakes might be impossible to detect or correct. Imagine the consequences this could have at the level of international trade, politics, and military activities.

Keiko, the "killer whale" known to moviegoers as the star of *Free Willy*, wears a transmitter that records heart and respiration rate to a computer chip that stores the data, which is later downloaded by researchers.

3.3 Output Hardware

KEY QUESTION **What are the main characteristics of printers, plotters, multifunction devices, display screens, and audio output devices?**

One of the most common output devices you will encounter is the monitor; another is the printer. Each of these devices is available in various forms, to match the needs of various types of users. First we'll discuss printers.

A **printer** is an output device that prints characters, symbols, and perhaps graphics on paper. (The printed output is generally referred to as *hardcopy* because it is in relatively permanent form. *Softcopy* refers to temporary images, such as those displayed on a monitor.) Printers are categorized according to whether or not the image produced is formed by physical contact of the print mechanism with the paper. *Impact printers* have contact; *nonimpact printers* do not.

Impact Printers

An impact printer has mechanisms resembling those of a typewriter: It forms characters or images by striking a mechanism such as a print hammer or wheel against an inked ribbon, leaving an image on paper. Impact printers are dying out; however, you may still come in contact with a dot-matrix printer. A *dot-matrix printer* contains a print head of small pins that strike an inked ribbon, forming characters or images. Print heads are available with 9, 18, or 24 pins; the 24-pin head offers the best print quality. Dot-matrix printers permit a choice between output of *draft quality,* a coarser-looking 72 dots per inch vertically, which may be acceptable for drafts of papers and reports, and *near-letter-quality,* a crisper-looking 144 dots per inch vertically, which is more suitable for a finished product to be shown to other people.

Dot-matrix printers print about 40–300 characters per second (cps) and can print some graphics, although the reproduction quality is poor. Color ribbons are available for limited use of color. Dot-matrix printers are noisy, inexpensive, and they can print through multipart forms, creating several copies of a page at the same time, which nonimpact printers cannot do.

Another type of impact printer is not used with microcomputers. Large computer installations use high-speed *line printers,* which print a whole line of characters at once rather than a single character at a time. Some, called *chain printers,* contain characters on a rotating chain; others, called *band printers,* contain characters on a rotating band. Speeds of up to 3000 lines a minute may be possible with these machines.

Nonimpact Printers

Nonimpact printers, used almost everywhere now, are faster and quieter than impact printers because they have fewer moving parts. Nonimpact printers form characters and images without direct physical contact between the printing mechanism and the paper.

Two types of nonimpact printers often used with microcomputers are *laser printers* and *ink-jet printers.*

■ *Laser printer:* Like a dot-matrix printer, a **laser printer** creates images with dots. However, as in a photocopying machine, these images are created on a drum, treated with a magnetically charged ink-like toner (powder), and then transferred from drum to paper. *(See Figure 3.16.)*

There are good reasons why laser printers are popular. They produce sharp, crisp images of both text and graphics, providing resolutions from 300 dpi up to 1200 dpi, which is near-typeset quality (NTQ). They are quiet and fast. They can print 4–32 text-only pages per minute for individual microcomputers, and more than 120 pages per minute for mainframes. (Pages with

Figure 3.16 Laser printer operation

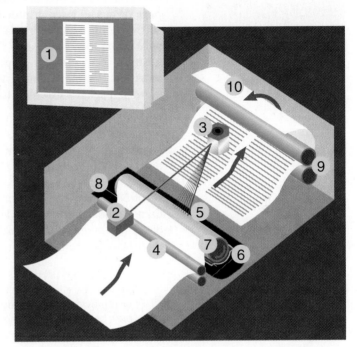

Laser Printer

1 The computer's software sends signals to the laser printer to determine where each dot of printing toner is to be placed on the paper.

2 The instructions from the printer's processor rapidly turn on and off a beam of light from a laser.

3 A spinning mirror deflects the laser beam so that the path of the beam is a horizontal line across the surface of a cylinder called the *drum*. As the laser beam is turned on and off, many tiny points of light are formed in a line across the surface of the drum. When the laser has finished flashing points of light across the entire width of the drum, the drum rotates— 1/300th of an inch in most laser printers—and the laser beam begins working on the next line of dots.

4 At the same time that the drum begins to rotate, a series of gears and rollers feeds a sheet of paper into the print engine along a path called the *paper train*. The paper train pulls the paper past an electrically charged wire that passes a static electrical charge to the paper. The charge may be either positive or negative, depending upon the design of the printer. For this example, we'll assume the charge is positive.

5 Where each point of light strikes the drum, it causes a negatively charged film—usually made of zinc oxide and other materials—on the surface of the drum to change its charge so that the dots have the same electrical charge as the sheet of paper. In this example, the light would change the charge from negative to positive. Each positive charge marks a dot that eventually will print black on paper. The areas of the drum that remain untouched by the laser beam retain their negative charge and result in white areas on the hard copy.

6 About halfway through the drum's rotation, the drum comes into contact with a bin that contains a black powder called *toner*. The toner in this example has a negative electrical charge—the opposite of the charges created on the drum by the laser beam. Because particles with opposite static charges attract each other, toner sticks to the drum in a pattern of small dots wherever the laser beam created a charge.

7 As the drum continues to turn, it presses against the sheet of paper being fed along the paper train. Although the electrical charge on the paper is the same as the charge of the drum created by the laser beam, the paper's charge is stronger and pulls the toner off the drum and onto the paper.

8 The rotation of the drum brings its surface next to a thin wire called the *corona wire*. Electricity passing through this wire creates a ring, or corona, around it that has a positive charge. The corona returns the entire surface of the drum to its original negative charge so that another page can be drawn on the drum's surface by the laser beam.

9 Another set of rollers pulls the paper through a part of the print engine called the *fusing system*. There, pressure and heat bind the toner permanently to the paper by melting and pressing a wax that is part of the toner. The heat from the fusing system is what causes paper fresh from a laser printer to be warm.

10 The paper train pushes the paper out of the printer, usually with the printed side down so that pages end up in the output tray in the correct order.

Laser printer

graphics print more slowly.) They can print in many fonts (type styles and sizes). (We discuss fonts in more detail in Chapter 6.) The more expensive models can print in different colors. Black-and-white laser printers cost about $400–$600; color costs about $1700–$2700.

Laser printers have built-in RAM chips to store documents output from the computer. If you are working in desktop publishing and printing complicated documents with color and many graphics, you will need a printer with a lot of RAM (check the printer RAM requirements on your software package). Laser printers also have their own ROM chips to store fonts and their own small dedicated processor. To be able to manage graphics and complex page design, a laser printer works with a page description language, a type of software that has become a standard for printing graphics on laser printers. A *page description language (PDL)* is software that describes the shape and position of letters and graphics to the printer. PostScript, from Adobe Systems, Inc., is one common type of page description language; HPGL, Hewlett-Packard Graphic Language, is another.

■ *Ink-jet printer:* Like laser and dot-matrix printers, ink-jet printers also form images with little dots. **Ink-jet printers** spray small, electrically charged droplets of ink from four nozzles through holes in a matrix at high speed onto paper. *(See Figure 3.17.)* A good ink-jet printer can be had for less than $400.

Ink-jet printers can print in color and are quieter and much less expensive than a color laser printer. However, they are slower (about 1–4 text-only pages per minute) and print in a somewhat lower resolution (300–720 dpi) than laser printers. Some new, expensive ink-jet printers print up to 1200 or

Figure 3.17 Ink-jet printer operation

Ink-jet printer

1 Four removable ink cartridges are attached to print heads with 64 firing chambers and nozzles apiece.

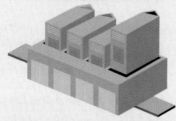

2 As the print heads move back and forth across the page, software instructs them where to apply dots of ink, what colors to use, and in what quantity.

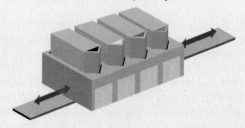

3 To follow those instructions, the printer sends electrical pulses to thin resistors at the base of the firing chambers behind each nozzle.

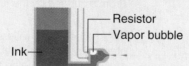

Resistor
Vapor bubble
Ink

5 A matrix of dots forms characters and pictures. Colors are created by layering multiple color dots in varying densities.

4 The resistor heats a thin layer of ink, which in turn forms a vapor bubble. That expansion forces ink through the nozzle and onto the paper at a rate of about 6,000 dots per second.

1400 dpi. High-resolution output requires the use of special coated paper, which costs more than regular paper. And, if you are printing color graphics at a high resolution on an ink-jet printer, it may take 10 minutes or more for a single page to finish printing.

A variation on ink-jet technology is the *bubble-jet printer,* which uses miniature heating elements to force specially formulated inks through print heads with 128 tiny nozzles. The multiple nozzles print fine images at high speeds. This technology is commonly used in portable printers.

Figure 3.18 provides some guidelines for choosing a printer. Information on this topic, as well as on acquiring any type of hardware, may be found on the Internet.

It's not uncommon these days to receive a crisply printed letter rendered on a word processor—in an envelope with a handwritten address. Why? Because the person writing the letter doesn't have, or doesn't know how to use, a printer envelope feeder for printing addresses. Envelope feeders and label printers are only one

Figure 3.18 Printer tips

Do I want a desktop or portable printer—or both? You'll probably find a desktop printer satisfactory (and less expensive than a portable). If you're on the road enough to warrant using a portable, see whether a *transportable* (small) or an *ultraportable* (smaller) would best suit you.

Do I need color, or will black-only do? Are you mainly printing text or will you need to produce color charts and illustrations (and if so, how often)? If you print lots of black text, consider getting a laser printer. If you might occasionally print color, get an ink-jet that will accept cartridges for both black and color.

Do I have other special output requirements? Do you need to print envelopes or labels? special fonts (type styles)? multiple copies? transparencies or on heavy stock? Find out if the printer comes with envelope feeders, sheet feeders holding at least 100 sheets, or whatever will meet your requirements.

Is the printer easy to set up? Can you easily put the unit together, plug in the hardware, and adjust the software (the driver programs) to make the printer work with your computer?

Is the printer easy to operate? Can you add paper, replace ink/toner cartridges, and otherwise operate the printer without much difficulty? (Make sure the printer is compatible with your computer.)

Does the printer provide the speed and quality I want? Will the machine print at least three pages a minute of black text and two pages a minute of color? Is the black dark enough and are the colors vivid enough?

Will I get a reasonable cost per page? Special paper, ink or toner cartridges (especially color), and ribbons are all ongoing costs. Ink-jet color cartridges, for example, may last 100–500 pages and cost $25–$30 new. Laser toner cartridges are cheaper and last longer. Ask the seller what the cost per page works out to. Are used cartridges recyclable?

Does the manufacturer offer a good warranty and good telephone technical support? Find out if the warranty lasts at least 2 years. See if the printer's manufacturer offers telephone support in case you have technical problems. The best support systems offer toll-free numbers and operate evenings and weekends as well as weekdays.

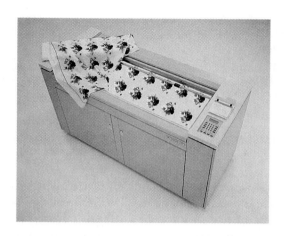

Figure 3.19 Plotters. *(Left)* Electrostatic. *(Right)* Ink-jet.

of several considerations to make when buying a printer. (Specialty printers that print nothing but envelopes and labels are also available for businesses that do large mailings.)

Plotters

A **plotter** is a specialized output device designed to produce high-quality graphics in a variety of colors. *(See Figure 3.19.)* Plotters are used for creating large hard-copy items, such as maps, architectural drawings, and 3-D illustrations. Such items are usually too large to be printed on regular printers.

The two principal kinds of plotters are *ink-jet* and *electrostatic*.

- *Ink-jet plotter:* Less expensive and slower than an electrostatic plotter, an *ink-jet plotter* uses ink-jets (like an ink-jet printer), and the paper is output over a drum, enabling continuous output.

- *Electrostatic plotter:* An *electrostatic plotter* is designed so that paper lies partially flat on a table-like surface. These plotters use toner in a manner similar to a photocopier. They are faster and more expensive than ink-jet plotters.

Installing a Printer or Plotter

Printers and plotters, like other peripheral devices such as mice, scanners, sound cards, and the like, must be installed. What does this mean? It means that the device's *driver* must be used to tell the computer what the device is and that it is attached to the system. A **driver** is a software program that links a peripheral device to the computer's operating system. It is written by programmers who understand the device's language and characteristics. The driver contains the machine language necessary to activate the device and perform the necessary operations. Drivers may come on disk with the peripheral device. In the case of fundamental peripherals such as the keyboard, diskette drive, and some hard disks, the drivers are included in the computer's BIOS chip (✔ p. 2.19). If you purchase a new peripheral—for example, a scanner—the documentation will tell you what steps to follow to install it.

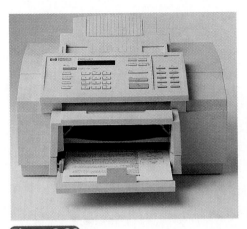

Figure 3.20

Multifunction device

Multifunction Printer Technology: One for All

Everything is becoming something else, and even printers are becoming devices that do more than print. For instance, fax machines are now available that can also function as an answering machine and a laser or ink-jet printer. Since 1990, Xerox Corp. has sold an expensive printer-copier-scanner that can be hooked into corporate computer networks.

Some recent hardware can do even more. **Multifunction devices** combine several capabilities, such as printing, scanning, copying, and faxing, all in one device. *(See Figure 3.20.)* Examples are the HP OfficeJet and the Canon MultiPass. By doing the work of four separate office machines at a price below the combined cost of buying these devices separately, the OfficeJet and the MultiPass offer budgetary and space advantages. Note, however, that these multifunction devices may not perform each of their functions as well as individual hardware devices dedicated to one function, and they operate more slowly than dedicated devices.

Monitors

As mentioned earlier, *softcopy* output generally refers to the display on a monitor, the output device that many people use the most. Monitors run under the control of a graphics display adapter card plugged into an expansion slot on the system board. The adapter allows information to leave the computer and appear on the monitor. (If you are working with graphics and video, such as in multimedia applications, this card will also have a graphics coprocessor, accelerator circuitry, and video support.) The display adapter comes with its own RAM, called *VRAM,* or *video RAM.* VRAM controls the resolution of images displayed on the monitor, as well as the number of colors and the speed at which the images are displayed. In addition, the more video memory you have, the higher the resolution and the more colors you can display. A video display adapter with 1 megabyte of memory will support 16.7 million colors.

The size of a screen is measured diagonally from corner to corner in inches, just like television screens. For microcomputers, 14- to 21-inch screens are common. Larger screens are often used by people in desktop publishing and multimedia production in order to view two facing pages of a book or magazine at the same time. Of course, pocket-size computers have even smaller screens. To give themselves a larger screen size, some portable-computer users buy a larger desktop monitor (or a separate docking station) to which the portable can be connected. Near the display screen are control knobs that, as on a television set, allow you to adjust brightness and contrast.

Cathode-Ray Tubes (CRTs)

The **cathode-ray tube (CRT)** is a vacuum tube used as a display screen in a computer or video display terminal. CRTs are the most common softcopy output devices used with desktop computer systems; this technology is also used in standard TV sets. The CRT's screen display is made up of small picture elements (dots), called *pixels* for short. A **pixel** is the smallest unit on the screen that can be turned on or off or made different shades. A stream of bits defining the image is sent from the computer to the CRT's electron gun, where electrons are activated according to the bit patterns. *(See Figure 3.21, next page.)* The front of the CRT screen is coated inside with phosphor. When a beam of electrons from the electron gun (deflected through a yoke) hits the phosphor, it lights up selected pixels to generate an image on the screen.

Pixels

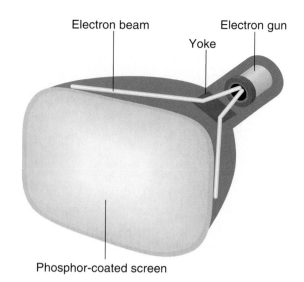

Electron beam

Yoke

Electron gun

Phosphor-coated screen

Figure 3.21 How a CRT works. *(Top)* A stream of bits from the computer's CPU is sent to the electron gun, which converts the bits into electrons. The gun then shoots a beam of electrons through the yoke, which deflects the beam. When the beam hits the phosphor coating on the inside of the CRT screen, a number of pixels light up, making the image on the screen. *(Botttom)* Each character on the screen is made up of small dots called pixels, short for *picture elements.*

Flat-Panel Displays

If CRTs were the only existing technology for computer screens, we would still be carrying around 25-pound (12-kilogram) "luggables" instead of lightweight notebooks and pocket PCs. CRTs provide bright, clear images, but they consume power and space and are relatively heavy. The larger the CRT screen, the deeper the unit.

Compared to CRTs, **flat-panel displays** are much thinner, weigh less, and consume less power. They have been used for years in portable computers, and now they are available for desktop computers. A current limitation is cost: an LCD for a desktop microcomputer costs 2–3 times as much as an equivalent monitor based on CRT technology. Also, flat-panel displayed images are not always as good as CRT images, and flat-panel images cannot be clearly viewed from an angle.

Flat-panel displays consist of two plates of glass separated by a substance that may be activated in particular ways.

Flat-panel displays may be characterized in terms of: (1) the substance between the plates of glass and (2) the arrangement of the transistors in the screens.

■ *Substances between plates—LCD or EL:* Two common types of technology are used in flat-panel display screens: *liquid-crystal display* and *electroluminescent display.* (*See Figure 3.22.*)

A **liquid-crystal display (LCD)** consists of a substance called *liquid crystal,* the molecules of which line up in a particular way. Under an applied voltage, the molecular alignment is disturbed, which changes the optical properties of the liquid crystal in the affected area. As a result, light—usually backlighting behind the screen—is blocked or allowed through to create an image.

An **electroluminescent (EL) display** contains a substance that glows when it is charged by an electric current. A pixel is formed on the screen when current is sent to the intersection of the appropriate row and column. The combined voltages from the row and column cause the screen to glow at that point.

■ *Arrangement of transistors—active-matrix or dual-scan (passive-matrix):* Flat-panel screens are either active-matrix or dual-scan displays, according to where their transistors are located.

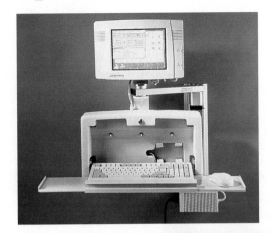

Figure 3.22 Flat-panel displays. *(Top left)* LCD display for a specialized display screen used in a hospital. *(Top right)* EL display for laptops. *(Bottom)* Full-size ViewSonic desktop flat-panel LCD screen.

In an *active-matrix display*, each pixel on the screen is controlled by its *own* transistor. Active-matrix screens are much brighter and sharper than dual-scan screens, but they are more complicated and thus more expensive.

In a *dual-scan display,* which used to be called *passive-matrix display,* two transistors control a whole row or column of pixels each, at the same time. Dual-scan provides a sharp image for monochrome (one-color) screens but is more subdued for color. The advantage is that dual-scan displays are less expensive and use less power than active-matrix displays.

Screen Clarity

Whether for CRT or flat-panel, screen clarity depends on three qualities: *resolution, dot pitch,* and *refresh rate.*

■ *Resolution:* The clarity or sharpness of a display screen is called its **resolution;** the more pixels there are per square inch, the better the resolution. Resolution is expressed in terms of the formula *columns of pixels* × *rows of pixels.* Thus, a screen with 640 × 480 pixels has a total of 307,200 pixels. This screen will be less clear and sharp than screens with higher resolutions. Standard screen resolutions are 640 × 480, 800 × 600, 1024 × 768, 1280 × 1024, and 1600 × 1200. Some display adapters can handle all these resolutions, while others may go only as high as 1024 × 768.

■ *Dot pitch:* **Dot pitch** is the amount of space between pixels; the closer the dots, the crisper the image. A .28 dot pitch means dots are 28/100ths of a millimeter apart. Generally, a dot pitch of less than .31 will provide clear images. Multimedia and desktop publishing users typically use .25 mm dot pitch monitors.

■ *Refresh rate:* **Refresh rate** is the number of times per second that the pixels are recharged so that their glow remains bright. Refresh is necessary because the phosphors hold their glow for just a fraction of a second. The higher the refresh rate, the more solid the image looks on the screen—that is, it doesn't flicker. The refresh rate should be at least 72 Hz (Hertz).

Color

Display screens can be either *monochrome* or *color.*

■ *Monochrome:* **Monochrome display screens** display only one color on a background—usually black on white, amber on black, or green on black. The number of shades of the one color that the monitor can display is referred to as *gray-scale.* Monochrome screens are dying out. However, you may still encounter them in some offices.

■ *Color:* **Color display screens,** also called *RGB monitors* (for red, green, blue), can display between 16 colors and 16.7 million colors, depending on their type. The number of colors is referred to as the *color depth,* or *bit depth.* Most software today is developed for color, and—except for some pocket PCs—most microcomputers today are sold with color display screens.

There are different standards for monitors, and they support different color depths.

■ *VGA:* **VGA,** for *video graphics array,* will support 16 to 256 colors, depending on resolution. At 320 × 200 pixels it will support 256 colors; at the sharper resolution of 640 × 480 pixels it will support 16 colors, which is called *4-bit color.*

■ *SVGA:* **SVGA,** for *super video graphics array,* will support 256 colors at higher resolution than VGA. SVGA has two graphics modes: 800 × 600 pixels and 1024 × 768. SVGA is called *8-bit color.* Most new computer systems offer SVGA.

■ *XGA:* Also referred to as *high-resolution display,* **XGA,** for *extended graphics array,* supports up to 16.7 million colors at a resolution of 1024 × 768 pixels. Depending on the video display adapter memory chip, XGA will support 256, 65,536, or 16,777,216 colors. At its highest quality, XGA is called *24-bit color,* or *true color.*

Note: The more colors and the higher the refresh rate and the resolution, the harder the display adapter has to work, and the more expensive it is. And the higher the settings, the slower the adapter may operate. Also, for a display to work, video display adapters and monitors must be compatible. Your computer's software and the video display adapter must also be compatible. Thus, if you are changing your monitor or your video display adapter, be sure the new one will still work with the old. Most monitors today can accommodate resolutions greater than SVGA, depending on the video card connected to them.

Bit-Mapped Displays

The computer uses bits (0s and 1s) to describe each pixel's attributes—its color and position. On monochrome screens, one bit represents one pixel on the screen. For color monitors, several bits represent one pixel. Bit-mapped display screens permit the computer to manipulate pixels on the screen individually, enabling the software to create a greater variety of images. Today most screens can display text and graphics—icons, charts, graphs, and drawings.

Future Display Technology

Home TV designs favor image brightness and compact size, whereas computer screens need to be engineered for higher resolution and sharp images. For technical reasons, it's difficult to make the image on a computer screen as bright as one on a TV screen. However, the development of HDTV (high-definition television) may change that and create a convergence between the TV and the computer monitor markets. The reason for this is that HDTV specifications call for resolution of up to 1920 × 1080 pixels, which is more than adequate for desktop computer screen displays.

Another promising new approach for computer screen technology is FED (field emission display). In FED, dozens or hundreds of tiny electron emitters are placed behind each pixel, in a panel where each pixel is controlled directly—as with an active-matrix LCD—but the light is emitted by the phosphors at that individual pixel, as in a CRT.

Audio Output Hardware

In the following sections we describe the hardware devices that enable voice output and sound output, also considered to be softcopy output.

Voice Output

Voice output devices convert digital data into speech-like sounds. These devices are no longer very unusual. You hear such forms of voice output on telephones ("Please hang up and dial your call again"), in soft-drink machines, in cars, in toys and games, and recently in vehicle-navigation devices. Two types of voice output technology exist: *speech coding* and *speech synthesis*.

Speech coding uses actual human voices speaking words to provide a digital database of words that can be output as voice sounds. That is, words are codified and stored in digital form. Later they may be retrieved and translated into voices as needed. The drawback of this method is that the output is limited to whatever words were previously entered into the computer system. However, the voice output message does sound more convincingly like real human speech.

Speech synthesis uses a set of 40 basic speech sounds (called *phonemes*) to electronically create any words. No human voices are used to make up a database of words; instead, the computer converts stored text into voices. For example, with one Apple Macintosh program, you can type in *Wiyl biy ray5t bae5k*—the numbers elongate the sounds. The computer will then speak the synthesized words, "We'll be right back." Such voice messages are usually understandable, though they don't sound exactly human.

Some uses of speech output are simply frivolous or amusing. You can replace your computer start-up beep with the sound of James Brown screaming "I feel goooooood!" Or you can attach a voice annotation to a financial analysis document to say "I know this figure looks high, Bob, but trust me."

But some uses are quite serious. For people with disabilities, for example, computers help to level the playing field. A 39-year-old woman with cerebral palsy had little physical dexterity and was unable to talk. By pressing keys on the laptop computer bolted to her wheelchair, she was able to construct the following voice-synthesized message: "I can do checkbooks for the first time in my life. I cannot live without my computer."

Sound Output

Sound output devices produce digitized sounds, ranging from beeps and chirps to music. All these sounds are nonverbal. PC owners can customize their machines to greet each new program with the sound of breaking glass or to moo like a cow every hour. Or they can make their computers express the distinctive sounds available (from the book/disk combination *Cool Mac Sounds*) under the titles "Arrgh!!!" or "B-Movie Scream." To exercise these possibilities, you need both the necessary software and the sound card, or digital audio circuit board (such as SoundBlaster). The sound card plugs into an expansion slot in your computer, but it is commonly integrated with the motherboard on newer computers.

A sound card is also required in making computerized music. There are two types of sound output technology for music: *FM synthesis* and *virtual acoustics.*

In *FM synthesis,* a synthesizer mimics different musical instruments by drawing on a library of stored sounds. Sounds are generated by combining wave forms of different shapes and frequencies. This is the kind of music-synthesis technology embodied in the pioneering Moog synthesizer, invented in 1964, and the Yamaha DX-7 synthesizer. It is also used in 95% of the circuit boards that offer advanced sound in IBM-compatible computers. The drawback, however, is that even the best synthesized music doesn't sound truly life-like; electronic instruments can't capture all the nuances of real instruments.

In *virtual acoustics,* instead of storing a library of canned sounds, the device stores a software model of an actual instrument, such as a clarinet. Thus, a set of formulas in the software represent how tightly a musician's lips press against the clarinet's mouthpiece reed. On a virtual-acoustics synthesizer, the musician can simulate "blowing" on the instrument either by breathing into a sensor or by pushing a pedal. This triggers a special microprocessor that simulates the airflow and resonances of an actual clarinet.

In either case, the digital sound outputs go to a mixer, a device that balances and controls music and sounds. They can then flow through stereo speakers or be recorded. Microcomputers often come with a sound speaker, although these speakers often have a rather tinny quality. For good sound, you will need to connect external speakers.

Multimedia Output Needs

Clearly, the various kinds of audio outputs and their devices are important components of multimedia systems. Some software developers are working on applications not only for entertainment but also for the business world.

With the advances and refinements in output, more and more materials are available in *polymedia* form. That is, someone's intellectual or creative work—whether words, pictures, sound, or animation—may appear in more than one form. For instance, you could be reading this chapter printed in a traditional bound book. Or you might be reading it in a "course pack," printed on paper through some sort of electronic delivery system. Or it might appear on a computer display screen. Or it could be in multimedia form, adding sounds, animated graphics, and video to the text.

Thus, information technology changes how ideas are communicated.

If you are working in multimedia or want to run multimedia applications on your computer, you will need the following output hardware items:

■ Sound card

■ Headphones

■ Speakers

3.4 In & Out: Devices That Do Both

KEY QUESTION How are terminals, smart cards, and touch screens used by a computer system?

Terminals

People working on a large computer system are usually connected to the main, or host, computer via terminals. A **terminal** is an input/output device that uses a keyboard for input and a monitor for output. *(See Figure 3.23.)*

Terminals are either dumb or intelligent.

- *Dumb:* A *dumb terminal* can be used only to input data to and receive information from a computer system; it cannot do any processing on its own.

    For example, airline clerks use dumb terminals at airport ticket and check-in counters. Another example is a *portable terminal,* a mobile terminal that can be connected to a main computer system through wired or wireless communications. A parking control officer might use a handheld wireless dumb terminal to send data to a central computer to identify cars with unpaid parking tickets.

- *Intelligent:* An *intelligent terminal* has built-in processing capability and RAM but does not have its own storage capacity. Intelligent terminals are not as powerful as microcomputers and are not designed to operate as stand-alone machines. They are often found in local area networks in an office. Users share applications software and data stored on a server.

    Some companies are marketing a type of intelligent terminal as a "network computer." This machine, less expensive than a microcomputer, would be hooked up to the Internet, which would provide the necessary software and data via servers also connected to the Internet.

Microcomputers are also sometimes used in business as terminals. This trend is occurring not only because their prices have come down but also because they reduce the processing and storage load on the main computer system.

Some terminals are built specifically to accomplish certain tasks—for example, the point-of-sale terminal and the automated teller machine.

- A **point-of-sale (POS) terminal** combines the input capabilities of a cash-register-type keypad, an optical scanner for reading price tags, and/or a

Figure 3.23 Terminals. *(Left)* The Hong Kong Stock Exchange networks hundreds of terminals to a central computer. *(Right)* During surgery, a medical technician monitors the patient's heart rate and blood pressue on terminals hooked up to equipment in the operating room.

Figure 3.24 POS terminal. Clerk at a jeans store scans in a price on a price tag.

magnetic stripe reader for reading credit cards with the output capabilities of a monitor and a receipt printer. Some POS terminals are hooked up to a central computer for credit checking and inventory updating; others are stand-alone machines that store daily transactions until they can be downloaded to the main computer for processing. POS terminals are found in most department stores. *(See Figure 3.24.)*

■ The *automated teller machine (ATM)* reads the encoded magnetic stripe on the ATM card and provides output in the form of display on a monitor and printed records of transactions.

Smart Cards and Optical Cards

It has already come to this: Just as many people collect stamps or baseball cards, there is now a major worldwide collecting mania for used wallet-size telephone debit cards. These are the cards by which telephone time is sold and consumed in many countries. Generally the cards are collected for their designs, which bear likenesses of anything from Elvis Presley to Felix the Cat to Martin Luther King. The cards have been in use in Europe for more than 15 years, and about 500 U.S. phone companies are now selling them.

Most of these telephone cards are examples of "smart cards." They are prepaid cards that tally remaining cash balances as calls are made. An even more sophisticated technology is the optical card.

■ *Smart card:* A **smart card** looks like a credit card but contains a microprocessor and memory chip that are used for identification and financial transactions, as well as storing small databases, such as an individual's medical records. When inserted into a reader, the card transfers data to and from a central computer; it can store basic financial or other records. More secure than a magnetic stripe card, it can be programmed to self-destruct if the wrong password is entered too many times.

In France, where the smart card was invented, you can buy telephone debit cards at most cafés and newsstands. You insert the card into a slot in the phone, wait for a tone, and dial the number. The time your call lasts is automatically calculated on the chip inside the card and deducted from the balance of time paid for. The French also use smart cards as bank cards, and some people carry their medical histories on them.

Students at Florida State University use smart cards to pay tuition, eat in the cafeteria, borrow library books, rent videos, and gain access to dormitories and online study groups. In Asia, where the cards are popular, they often store not only cash transactions but also personal and corporate data such as medical histories and security clearances. In Finland, smart cards are used to link older individuals and people with disabilities to ambulance services, emergency units, and pharmacies. The U.S. Department of Defense is looking at replacing traditional military dog tags with smart cards that include service and family data. Some observers think that business travelers will soon have a personal smart card that can be used for many purposes, such as buying airline tickets, reserving rental cars, checking into hotels—even opening the door to their hotel rooms. Once back at the office, they will be able to transfer all their travel expenses electronically onto an expense report. There will be no need to keep paper receipts.

Indeed, smart cards may eventually eliminate the need for cash—or, at least, that's the hope of many banks, credit card issuers, universities, and the U.S. government. Why? Smart cards can save the cost of collecting, counting, securing, and transferring cash. Some smart cash cards come with small handheld readers that tally the card's cash balance.

Yifat Mabary uses a smart card to make a purchase at the Royale Kosher Bakery in New York City.

■ *Optical card:* The conventional magnetic-stripe credit card holds the equivalent of a half page of data. The smart card with a microprocessor and memory chip holds the equivalent of 30 pages. The optical card presently holds about 2000 pages of data. Optical cards use the same type of technology as music compact disks but look like silvery credit cards. Optical cards are plastic, laser-recordable, wallet-type cards used with an optical card reader. Because they can cram so much data (6.6 megabytes) into so little space, they may become popular in the future. For instance, a person's health card would have enough room not only for his or her medical history and health-insurance information but also for digital images, such as electrocardiograms, low-resolution chest X-rays, and ultrasound pictures of a fetus. A book containing 1000 pages of text plus 150 detailed drawings could be mailed on an optical card in a 1-ounce first-class letter. One manufacturer of optical library-card systems suggested that people might wish to store personal information on their cards, such as birth certificates and insurance policies.

Touch Screens

A **touch screen** is a video display screen that has been sensitized to receive input from the touch of a finger. *(See Figure 3.25, next page.)* Behind the screen, which is covered with a plastic layer, there are invisible beams of infrared light. The user can, for example, input requests for information by pressing on displayed buttons and then see the requested information displayed as output on the screen.

Because touch screens are easy to use, they can convey information quickly. They are often used in automatic teller machines, in directories conveying tourist information in airports and hotels, in fast-food restaurants (to select menu items), and in preschool multimedia education. Touch screens' inability to display large amounts of information limits their use with microcomputers, although some applications do exist.

Now You See It, Now You Don't

Of course, as with input technology, improvements are continually being made in output hardware systems. Retinal display systems are one example—images projected pixel by pixel, or point of light by point of light, from an outside source directly onto the retina of a viewer's eye.

Figure 3.25 Touch screens. *(Left)* Elizabeth Young uses a touch screen at Duke University Medical Center to provide information about her medical history. The software allows her to answer questions by touching options. *(Right)* A hotel touch screen provides information about hotel services.

Imagine you are a soldier facing a minefield. You scan the lethal ground in front of you, and suddenly the buried mines appear before your eyes, enabling you to pick a path to safety. Unfortunately, that kind of X-ray road map is not yet available, but within a few years, experts predict, the technology will be ready—not just for the military but also for surgeons, mechanics, and anyone else who needs to visualize complex information.

Retinal displays allow viewers to see information on what appears to be a translucent computer screen hanging a few feet in front of them. In fact, there is no screen; the image exists only inside the eye. Soldiers will be able to use virtual displays to see mines as they are projected from helmet-mounted, ground-penetrating radar. Surgeons will be able to call up high-resolution X-rays of patients as they lie on the operating table. Mechanics will see color-coded diagrams of the miles of wiring under a jet airplane's skin as they work on it.

Web Sites of Possible Interest

There are many links to the Web sites of hardware companies around the world. The following resource is a time saver. (Remember, if you're not familiar with surfing the Internet, we'll be covering that topic soon.)
http://www-atp.llnl.gov/atp/companies.html

Hundreds of links to hardware vendors and computer magazine Web sites can be found at:
http://guide.sbanetweb.com

For more information about how to choose a monitor:
http://hawks.ha.md.us/hardware/monitors.html
http://www.hardwarecentral.com/hardware/monitors/

For printer information:
http://www.connectworld.net/c9.html

For scanners:
http://www.scanshop.com
http://www.infomedia.net/scan

Law Enforcement

If the police officer who pulls you over for speeding knows your name before you've even stepped out of your car, it's not because he or she is psychic. It's probably because the patrol car has an M.D.T.—a mobile data terminal, or small computer—which revealed you as the car owner when the officer queried it about your license-plate number. A particular advantage of the system is that a patrol officer can run license checks directly with the department of motor vehicles, without having to ask a harried radio dispatcher to drop everything and do it. Patrol cars can also communicate directly with each other in an environment "that resembles an online chat room," as one writer puts it.[a]

Computers have been used in law enforcement almost from the beginning of the computer age. Among the most valuable tools are databases. New York City reduced serious crime by 27% between 1993 and 1995 in part by using databases coupled with computerized crime-mapping software that enables beat cops to identify different kinds of crime clusters and trends and to fight them block by block. For example, maps revealed that police had been making drug arrests where they were easiest rather than where most citizens complained of drug sales, in hard-to-infiltrate public-housing complexes; vice cops were thereupon reassigned in more effective ways. Computerized crime mapping, says criminologist John Eck, "is probably the greatest technological innovation to hit policing in decades."[b] The U.S. Immigration and Naturalization Service uses databases to store information about certain frequent business travelers to the U.S. These individuals, who have been previously checked out; can avoid long waits at the border by simply inserting an identity card into a machine and placing a hand into an identity analyzer.[c]

Police investigating crime scenes now also benefit by wearing lightweight computers that are housed in weatherproof vests. The setup includes a digital camera, a laser range finder for exact measurements, and databases full of scientific and legal data. A version called Team Finder uses satellite technology—a GPS, or Global Positioning System receiver—to record the location of each piece of evidence as it's tagged with a bar-code label.[d,e] Police with a court warrant may also slip a GPS receiver into a suspect's car, then track his or her movements on a laptop computer.[f]

As might be expected, the Internet has also become a law-enforcement tool. For instance, the Web is being used as a virtual post office wall to display wanted pictures of fugitives. The FBI has been posting its 10 "most wanted" on the Internet since 1995. Now other agencies and businesses, ranging from the Commodity Futures Trading Commission to Wells Fargo Bank, are using the Web to do the same thing.[g,h] On their days off, three San Jose, California, police officers have used a Web page, as well as a cable-TV show and a newspaper, to publicize more than 2000 fugitives and have helped police nab more than 200 suspects.[i] Also in San Jose, a 3-year-old who had been abducted was spotted in hours, rather than days, thanks to a system of computers, scanners, color printers, and modems that provided quick dissemination to the public of thousands of high-quality color photos of the missing boy.[j]

Readers interested in news about the criminal justice system may wish to check APB Online (*www.apbonline.com*).

Genealogy

When Marilyn Arnold of Falls Church, Virginia, went online for the first time, she decided to type the key world "genealogy" just to see what showed up. Within an hour, however, she had located several other people who were researching her family surnames and had sent them queries.[a] Thus has the personal computer helped a growing number of people find out about their ancestral roots.

Genealogy—the tracing of family history through past generations—"can be enormously fascinating," points out one writer, "but serious research has traditionally required a lot of legwork, time, and money."[b] No wonder, then, that it used to be only the well off who could afford to have professional genealogists document their family trees. Today, however, information technology has had two important consequences: (1) It makes it easier for ordinary people to do their own amateur ancestor hunting. (2) Or, if they are too time-starved to do it themselves, they are now better able to afford computer-assisted researchers at reasonable prices. Writer Lettice Stuart of Houston earns a good living selling her services as a "personal historian" producing family histories for ordinary people.[c]

Still, family-history research is not yet at the push-button stage. When *USA Today* reporter Jefferson Graham began his search, he says, "my fantasy was that all the important records—marriage, birth, census, etc.—would be fully searchable from home via Internet databases. Not yet. You still have to go to libraries and use microfilm, but the Web often can point you in the right direction."[d] Brian Leverich, an Internet genealogy pioneer, estimates that only 1 percent of public records are now online, although this will no doubt change. The Church of Jesus Christ of Latter-day Saints (more commonly known as the Mormons) has extensive genealogical research facilities around the country, but it has only begun to put this information online.[e] New York's Ellis Island—the immigration station through which flowed the forebears of nearly half the U.S. population—has plans for a complex database project to reconstruct immigrant histories, which are now not even listed in alphabetical order by name, but the program is still in its early stages.[f]

Some people begin their pursuit of family lore by typing the names of kinfolk (or their own last name) into an online phone directory like Switchboard, which holds the addresses of 100 million-plus U.S. residents. On a whim, Margie Newton, of Concord, California, typed in "Schouten," her maiden name, and the screen filled with 84 Schoutens, which led her to launch a genealogical journey in cyberspace.[g] A better approach, however, is to go to one of the major genealogy sites, such as RootsWeb, the USGenWeb Project, or Cyndi's List. There are also sites for particular ethnic groups, such as those of black and Jewish ancestry.

Some popular genealogy Web sites are the following: Cyndi's List of Genealogy Sites on the Internet (*www.cyndislist.com*); the National Genealogical Society (*www.ngsgenealogy.org*); RootsWeb (*www.rootsweb.com*); and the USGenWeb Project (*www.usgenweb.org*). For African-Americans there are Afrigeneas (*www.msstate.edu/Archives/History/afrigen*) and Christine's Genealogy Website (*ccharity.com*). For Jews, there are JewishGen (*www.jewishgen.org*) and the International Association of Jewish Genealogical Societies (*www.jewishgen.org/ajgs*).

WHAT IT IS
WHAT IT DOES

WHY IT IS IMPORTANT

audio input device (KQ 3.2, p. 3.16) Device that records or plays analog sound and translates it for digital storage and processing.

Audio input devices, such as audio boards and MIDI boards, are important for multimedia computing.

bar-code reader (KQ 3.2, p. 3.12) Photoelectric scanner, found in many retail stores, that translates bar code symbols on products into digital code.

With bar-code readers and the appropriate computer system, retail clerks can total purchases and produce invoices with increased speed and accuracy; and stores and other businesses can monitor inventory and services with greater efficiency.

bar codes (KQ 3.2, p. 3.12) Vertical striped marks of varying widths that are imprinted on retail products and other items; when scanned by a bar-code reader, the code is converted into computer-usable digital input.

Bar codes may be used to input data about many items, from food products to overnight packages to railroad cars, for tracking and data manipulation.

cathode-ray tube (CRT) (KQ 3.3 p. 3.27) Vacuum tube used as a display screen in a computer or video display terminal. Images are represented on the screen by individual dots or "picture elements" called *pixels.*

This technology is found not only in the screens of desktop computers but also in television sets and flight-information monitors in airports.

cursor (KQ 3.2, p. 3.5) Movable symbol on the display screen that shows the user where data may be entered next.

All applications software packages use cursors to show users where their current work location is on the screen.

cursor-movement keys (KQ 3.2, p. 3.5) Also called *arrow keys;* used to move the cursor around the text on the screen.

These keys move the cursor left, right, up, or down.

digital camera (KQ 3.2, p. 3.18) Electronic camera that uses a light-sensitive silicon chip to capture photographic images in digital form.

Unlike traditional cameras, digital cameras produce images in digital form that can be transmitted directly to a computer's hard disk for manipulation, storage, and/or printing out.

digitizing tablet (KQ 3.2, p. 3.10) Tablet connected by a wire to a pen-like stylus, with which the user sketches an image, or to a puck, with which the user copies an image.

A digitizing tablet can be used to achieve shading and other artistic effects or to "trace" a drawing, which can be stored in digitized form.

dot pitch (KQ 3.3, p. 3.29)   Amount of space between pixels (dots); the closer the dots, the crisper the image.

Dot pitch is one of the measures of display-screen crispness.

driver (KQ 3.3, p. 3.26)   Software program that links a peripheral device to the computer's operating system.

The driver contains the machine language necessary to activate the device.

electroluminescent (EL) display (KQ 3.3, p. 3.28) Flat-panel display that uses a substance that glows when it is charged by an electric current. A pixel is formed on the screen when current is sent to the intersection of the appropriate row and column. The combined voltages from the row and column cause the screen to glow at that point.

EL display is used in portable computers.

Enter key (KQ 3.2, p. 3.5)   Also called the *Return key;* used to enter commands into the computer.

Executing commands is a key function of using a computer.

ergonomics (KQ 3.2, p. 3.6)   Study, or science, of the physical and psychological relationships between people and their work environment.

Ergonomic principles are used in designing ways to use computers to further productivity while avoiding stress, illness, and injuries.

fax machine (KQ 3.2, p. 3.14)   Short for *facsimile transmission machine;* input device for scanning an image and sending it as electronic signals over telephone lines to a receiving fax machine, which re-creates the image on paper, or to a fax modem.

Fax machines permit the transmission of text and graphic data over telephone lines quickly and inexpensively.

flat-panel displays (KQ 3.3, p. 3.28)   Display screens that are much thinner, weigh less, and consume less power than CRTs. Flat-panel displays consist of two plates of glass separated by a substance that may be activated in particular ways. Liquid-crystal displays (LCDs) and electroluminescent (EL) displays differ in terms of the properties of the substance between the plates. Active-matrix and dual-scan (passive-matrix) displays differ in terms of their transistor configuration.

Flat-panel displays are used in portable computers, for which CRTs are not practical (because of their large size).

function keys (KQ 3.2, p. 3.6)   Computer keyboard keys that are labeled F1, F2, and so on; usually positioned along the top or left side of the keyboard.

Function keys are used to issue commands. Precisely how they are used depends on the software.

imaging system (KQ 3.2, p. 3.14)   Also known as *image scanner,* or *graphics scanner;* input device that converts text, drawings, and photographs into digital form that can be stored in a computer system.

Image scanners have enabled users with desktop publishing software to readily input images into computer systems for manipulation, storage, and output. Imaging systems are also used in document management and multimedia development.

ink-jet printer (KQ 3.3, p. 3.24)   Nonimpact printer that forms images with little dots. Ink-jet printers spray small, electrically charged droplets of ink from four nozzles through holes in a matrix at high speed onto paper.

Because they produce high-quality images on special paper, they are often used in graphic design and desktop publishing. However, ink-jet printers are slower than laser printers and print at a lower resolution on regular paper.

input controls (KQ 3.2, p. 3.21) Combination of manual and computer-based control procedures designed to ensure that all input data has been accurately put into computer-usable form.

Without input controls, mistakes might be impossible to detect or correct.

input hardware (KQ 3.1, p. 3.2) Devices that take data and programs that people can read or comprehend and convert them to a form the computer can process. Devices are of two types: keyboard entry and source-data entry.

Input hardware enables data to be put into computer-processable form.

joystick (KQ 3.2, p. 3.9) Pointing device that consists of a vertical handle like a gearshift lever mounted on a base with one or two buttons; it directs a cursor or pointer on the display screen.

Joysticks are used principally in video games, computer-aided design systems, and in computerized robots.

keyboard (KQ 3.2, p. 3.3) Typewriter-like input device that converts letters, numbers, and other characters into electrical signals that the computer's processor can read.

Keyboards are the most popular kind of input device.

laser printer (KQ 3.3, p. 3.22) Nonimpact printer similar to a photocopying machine; images are created on a drum, treated with a magnetically charged ink-like toner (powder), and then transferred from drum to paper.

Laser printers produce much better image quality than do dot-matrix printers and can print in many more colors; they are also quieter. Laser printers, along with page description languages, enabled the development of desktop publishing.

light pen (KQ 3.2, p. 3.10) Light-sensitive pen-like input device connected by a wire to a computer terminal; the user brings the pen to a desired point on the display screen and presses the pen button, which identifies that screen location to the computer.

Light pens are used by engineers, graphic designers, and illustrators for making drawings.

liquid-crystal display (LCD) (KQ 3.3, p. 3.28) Flat-panel display that consists of a substance called *liquid crystal,* the molecules of which line up in a particular way. Under an applied voltage, the molecular alignment is disturbed, which changes the optical properties of the liquid crystal in the affected area. As a result, light—usually backlighting behind the screen—is blocked or allowed through to create an image.

LCD is useful not only for portable computers but also as a display for various electronic devices, such as watches and radios.

magnetic-ink character recognition (MICR) (KQ 3.2, p. 3.13) Type of scanning technology that reads magnetized-ink characters printed at the bottom of checks and converts them to computer-acceptable digital form.

MICR technology is used by banks to sort checks.

mouse (KQ 3.2, p. 3.7) Pointing device that is rolled about on a desktop to position a cursor or pointer on the computer's display screen.

For many purposes, it is easier to communicate commands to a computer with a mouse than with a keyboard. For microcomputers, a mouse is needed to use most graphical user interface programs and to draw illustrations.

mouse pointer (KQ 3.2, p. 3.7)   Symbol on the display screen whose position is directed by movement of a mouse.

The position of the mouse pointer indicates where information may be entered or a command (such as clicking, dragging, or dropping) may be executed. Change in the shape of the pointer indicates that a particular function may be performed at that point.

multifunction device (KQ 3.3, p. 3.27)   Single hardware device that combines several capabilities, such as printing, scanning, copying, and faxing.

A multifunction device can do the work of several office machines at a price below the combined cost of buying these devices separately.

numeric keypad (KQ 3.2, p. 3.5)   Laid out like the keys on a calculator; used for manipulating numbers and for directional purposes.

The numeric keypad has two purposes: Whenever the Num Lock key is off, the numeric keys may be used as arrow keys for cursor movement. When the Num Lock key is on, the keys may be used for manipulating numbers, as on a calculator.

optical character recognition (OCR) (KQ 3.2, p. 3.13)   Type of scanning technology that reads special preprinted characters and converts them to computer-usable form. A common OCR scanning device is the wand reader.

OCR technology is frequently used with utility bills and price tags on department-store merchandise.

optical mark recognition (OMR) (KQ 3.2, p. 3.13) Type of scanning technology that reads pencil marks and converts them into computer-usable form.

OMR technology is frequently used for grading multiple-choice and true/false tests, such as parts of the College Board Scholastic Aptitude Test and SCANTRON tests.

output hardware (KQ 3.1, p. 3.2)   Hardware that translates information processed by the computer into a form that humans can understand.

Without output devices, computer users would not be able to view or use their work.

pen-based computer system (KQ 3.2, p. 3.10)   Input system that uses a pen-like stylus to enter handwriting and marks into a computer. The four types of systems are gesture recognition, handwriting stored as scribbling, personal handwriting stored as typed text, and standard handwriting "typeface" stored as typed text.

Pen-based computer systems benefit people who don't know how to type or don't want to type or who need to make routinized kinds of inputs such as check marks.

pixel (KQ 3.3, p. 3.27)   Short for *picture element;* smallest unit on the screen that can be turned on and off or made different shades.

Pixels are the building blocks that allow text and graphical images to be presented on a display screen.

plotter (KQ 3.3, p. 3.26)   Specialized output device designed to produce high-quality graphics in a variety of colors. Two common types of plotters are flatbed and drum.

Plotters are especially useful for creating maps and architectural drawings, although they may also produce less complicated charts and graphs.

pointing devices (KQ 3.2, p. 3.4)   Input devices that control the position of the cursor or pointer on the screen.

Pointing devices include mice, trackballs, joysticks, light pens, digitizing tablets, and pen-based systems.

point-of-sale (POS) terminal (KQ 3.4, p. 3.33)   Terminal that combines the input capabilities of a cash-register-type keypad, optical scanner, and magnetic-stripe reader with the output capabilities of a monitor and a printer.

POS terminals record customer transactions at the point of sale and also store data for billing and inventory purposes.

printer (KQ 3.3, p. 3.22)   Output device that prints characters, symbols and perhaps graphics on paper. Printers are categorized according to whether the image produced is formed by physical contact of the print mechanism with the paper. Impact printers have contact; nonimpact printers do not.

Printers provide one of the principal forms of computer output.

refresh rate (KQ 3.3, p. 3.30)   Number of times per second that screen pixels are recharged so that their glow remains bright.

The higher the refresh rate, the more solid the image looks on the screen.

resolution (KQ 3.3, p. 3.29)   Clarity or sharpness of a display screen; the more pixels there are per square inch, the better the resolution. Resolution is expressed in terms of the formula *horizontal pixels × vertical pixels.* A screen with 640 × 480 pixels has a total of 307,200 pixels. This screen will be less clear and sharp than a screen with 800 × 600 (equals 480,000) or 1024 × 768 (equals 786,432) pixels.

Users need to know what screen resolution is appropriate for their purposes.

scanner (KQ 3.2, p. 3.12)   Source-data input device that translates hardcopy images of text, drawings, and photos into digital form.

Scanners simplify the input of complex data. The images can be processed by the computer, manipulated, displayed on a monitor, stored on a storage device, and/or communicated to another computer.

sensor (KQ 3.2, p. 3.20)   Type of input device that collects specific kinds of data directly from the environment and transmits it to a computer.

Sensors can be used for detecting speed, movement, weight, pressure, temperature, humidity, wind, current, fog, gas, smoke, light, shapes, images, and so on.

smart card (KQ 3.4, p. 3.34)   Card similar to a credit card but containing a microprocessor and memory chip that can be used to input data.

Telephone users may buy a smart card that lets them make telephone calls until the total cost limit programmed into the card has been reached. Smart cards may eventually take the place of cash.

sound output devices (KQ 3.3, p. 3.31)   Audio output device that produces digitized, nonverbal sounds, ranging from beeps and chirps to music. It includes software and a sound card or digital audio circuit board.

PC owners can customize their machines to announce new programs and certain functions with particular sounds. Sound output is also used in multimedia presentations.

source-data entry device (KQ 3.2, p. 3.4)   Also called *source-data automation;* non-keyboard data-entry device. The categories include scanning devices; magnetic-stripe cards; smart and optical cards; voice-recognition devices; audio input devices; video input devices; electronic cameras; sensors; and human-biology input devices.

Source-data entry devices lessen reliance on keyboards for data entry and can make data entry more accurate.

SVGA (super video graphics array) (KQ 3.3, p. 3.30)   Graphics board standard that supports 256 colors at higher resolution than VGA. SVGA has two graphics modes: 800 × 600 pixels and 1024 × 768. Called *8-bit color.*

Super VGA is a higher-resolution version of video graphics array (VGA). It is the standard most commonly used today.

terminal (KQ 3.4, p. 3.33)   Input/output device that uses a keyboard for input and a monitor for output.

Terminals are generally used to input data to and output data from large computer systems, such as a mainframe.

touchpad (KQ 3.2, p. 3.9)   Flat, rectangular input device that uses a very weak electrical field to sense your touch.

Touchpads let you control the cursor/pointer with your finger.

touch screen (KQ 3.4, p. 3.35)   Video display screen that has been sensitized to receive input from the touch of a finger. It is often used in automatic teller machines and in directories conveying tourist information.

Because touch screens are easy to use, they can convey information quickly and can be used by people with no computer training; however, the amount of information offered is usually limited.

trackball (KQ 3.2, p. 3.9)   Movable ball, on top of a stationary device, that is rotated with the fingers or palm of the hand; it directs a cursor or pointer on the computer's display screen.

Unlike a mouse, a trackball is especially suited to portable computers, which are often used in confined places.

VGA (video graphics array) (KQ 3.3, p. 3.30) Graphics board standard that supports 16 to 256 colors, depending on resolution. At 320 × 200 pixels it will support 256 colors; at sharper resolution of 640 × 480 pixels it will support 16 colors. Called *4-bit color*.

VGA is still used, although SVGA is taking over.

voice output device (KQ 3.3, p. 3.31)   Audio output device that converts digital data into speech-like sound. Two types of voice output technology exist: speech coding and speech synthesis.

Voice output devices are a common technology, found in telephone systems, soft-drink machines, and toys and games.

voice-recognition system (KQ 3.2, p. 3.16)   Input system that converts a person's speech into digital code; the system compares the electrical patterns produced by the speaker's voice with a set of pre-recorded patterns stored in the computer.

Voice-recognition technology is useful for inputting data in situations in which people are unable to use their hands or need their hands free for other purposes.

XGA (extended graphics array) (KQ 3.3, p. 3.30) Graphics board display standard, also referred to as *high resolution;* supports up to 16.7 million colors at a resolution of 1024 × 768 pixels. Depending on the video display adapter memory chip, XGA will support 256, 65,536, or 16,777,216 colors. At its highest quality, XGA is called *24-bit color,* or *true color.*

XGA offers the most sophisticated standard for color and resolution.

1. Fill in the following blanks:
   a. One of the easiest ways to categorize input hardware is whether or not it uses a(n) _____.
   b. _____ determines what the function keys on a keyboard do.
   c. Keyboard manufacturers have been giving a lot of attention to the study of the physical relationships between people and their work environment, a field called _____.
   d. _____ _____ are designed to ensure the accuracy of input data.
   e. A(n) _____ terminal is entirely dependent for all of its processing activities on the computer system to which it is hooked up.

2. List four hardware devices you might need to create a multimedia presentation.
   a. _____
   b. _____
   c. _____
   d. _____

3. What three characteristics determine the clarity of a computer screen?
   a. _____
   b. _____
   c. _____

4. Label each of the following statements as either true or false.

   _____ QWERTY describes a common keyboard layout.

   _____ Scanners use laser beams and reflected light to translate photos into digital form.

   _____ Photos taken with a digital camera can be downloaded to a computer's hard drive.

   _____ On a computer screen, the more pixels that appear per square inch, the higher the resolution.

   _____ Display screens can be either monochrome or color.

5. Describe the purpose for each of the following:
   a. cursor-movement keys
   b. Enter key
   c. function keys
   d. numeric keypad keys

6. List four examples of non-keyboard pointing devices:
   a. _____
   b. _____
   c. _____
   d. _____

7. From the following list, select those devices that are considered non-keyboard source-data entry devices.
   a. voice-recognition devices
   b. video input devices
   c. light pen
   d. electronic camera
   e. digitizing tablet

8. List three types of scanning devices.

   a. _____

   b. _____

   c. _____

9. Printers are categorized according to whether or not the image is produced by physical contact of the print mechanism with the paper. The two main categories of printers are:

   a. _____

   b. _____

IN YOUR OWN WORDS

1. Answer each of the Key Questions that appear at the beginning of this chapter.

2. What are function keys used for? How do you know which key does what?

3. Why would you use a trackball, a joystick, or a touchpad instead of a mouse?

4. Why does source-data entry pose less of a problem for accuracy of input data than does keyboard entry?

5. What does the term *ergonomics* mean?

6. What are input controls?

7. What are plotters typically used for?

8. What are device drivers used for?

9. What is a pixel?

10. What is a terminal?

KNOWLEDGE IN ACTION

1. **Taking Stock.** List the input and output devices that are part of the computer system you use at school, work, or home. Identify each device as either an input or output device, and describe what each device is used for.

2. **Output Requirements.** Visit a local computer or electronics store and locate five separate software packages. Write down the name of each software program and what its output requirements are, if any. What type of printer is required? What type of screen display is required?

3. **Input, Input, Everywhere.** During the next week, make a list of all the input devices you notice—in stores, on campus, at the bank, in the library, on the job, at the doctor's, and so on. At the end of the week, report on the devices you have listed and in what environment they were used.

4. **Working Smart.** Using your Web browser, visit the *http://www.smartcrd.com/info/whatis/faq.htm* site. At this address, you'll find answers to commonly asked questions about smart cards. Print this document out and then answer the following questions in your own words: (a) How can smart cards benefit consumers? (b) What is the Smart Card Forum? (c) What types of businesses are implementing smart card technology?

5. **Shopping for a Printer.** Visit a local electronics store or an online shopping site (such as *www.buydirect.com* or *www.insight.com*) and write down the names of five printers that are for sale. For each printer, identify the following information: (a) type of printer, such as laser or ink-jet, (b) the printer's resolution, and (c) the cost of the printer. Is it PC-compatible or Mac-compatible?

Now that you've come up with an idea for your Web business, it's time to consider the design of your site, where to store your site, and what hardware you'll need to get started. Keep in mind that initially you will run your business from a single computer. Perhaps after your business grows, you'll invest in additional processing power.

For anyone who has visited the Amazon.com site, it is obvious that careful planning went into the design of its hardware, software, and content. The site is very easy to navigate and makes you want to browse its "aisles." Let's look at some tips that will help you create a winning Web site for your online business.

PLANNING THE CONTENT DESIGN OF YOUR SITE

No matter if you only have one employee (you) and your company headquarters is an arm's length from your refrigerator and sink full of dishes, customers will take you seriously if your site is professional in design and contains complete and accurate information. You can either create the site yourself or hire a Web consultant with graphics experience to assist you.

When planning the design of your site, your attention should first focus on developing a clearly defined message. The text and graphics you choose to populate your site should all support your message. Without saying it directly, Amazon's message is "Welcome to our site and stay a while. We're here to serve you." After an introductory visit to the site, the Amazon.com Home page even customizes itself and addresses you by name!

Your color scheme, or the collection of colors you use throughout your site, should also support your message. (Don't use psychedelic colors, for example, if your theme is traditional in nature.) Amazon.com uses predominantly black text on a white background, in keeping with how text often appears on a printed page. To make things interesting, the site uses a few additional colors as well.

Consider asking a few people to review your color scheme before you actually implement it. You don't want customers to shop somewhere else simply because they were turned off by your choice of colors!

PLANNING YOUR HOME PAGE

The first page customers will see when they go to Yourname.com is your Home page. Think of your Home page as the online equivalent of a brochure or reception area where first impressions are all-important. As exemplified by the Amazon.com Home page, your Home page should make customers feel welcome and provide an entry point to the other pages of your site. And it should load fast. Web users are an impatient lot. If it takes more than 30 seconds before all the fancy graphics you've built into your Home page appear on the screen, your customers will probably decide to shop somewhere else. This doesn't mean that your Home page has to be boring—it's relatively simple to create fast-loading graphics (but these steps are beyond the scope of the current discussion). In general, you want your Home page to:

1. *Make a good (and fast) first impression.* You can accomplish this with a well-thought-out theme and color scheme, and by including fast-loading graphics.

2. *Provide a means for navigating your site.* You can accomplish this the most easily using a Menu bar that provides links to the other areas (pages) of your site. Like Amazon.com, you will want to include the same navigation scheme on every page of your site.

3. *Highlight the latest news.* Users like to read "news" about your business. Consider including a navigation button that links to a list of press releases about you, and your company, products, and services.

4. *Provide a means for customers to contact you.* This can be accomplished with a navigation button or by including a link to your e-mail address at the bottom of the Home page.

PLANNING WHERE TO HOST YOUR SITE

An important decision to make when planning your Web site involves deciding where you will host your site, or store it. You can purchase your own computer to act as the server or rent space on another computer, either from your Internet access provider or from another company that specializes in renting out space for Web sites. If you're running your business from a single computer and are new to the Internet, we don't recommend that you take on the technical challenges of running your own server computer. It will be much simpler for you to rent space for your site from an access provider for $20 to $300 per month, depending on your needs. Customers will still be able to access your business 24 hours per day, 7 days per week, and you'll have full use of your desktop machine. Also, your provider will most likely use high-speed Internet connections so that your Web pages will flow to the Internet at swifter speeds than if they were originating from your computer. A note of caution: Beware of access providers that charge you per transaction (such as a nine-cent fee for credit card purchases), by the number of "hits" your Web site generates, or by the number of megabytes served to browsers each month.

CHOOSING THE RIGHT TOOLS

Before you embark on constructing a Web site, ensure that you have the right tools. First, you'll need a computer system on which you'll develop your Web site and support future business operations. Note that Web development doesn't require a high-end machine—you really only need a text editor for writing HTML. Following is a list of some general system requirements for your computer.

PC Configuration

Hard disk	4 GB or more
RAM	48 MB or more
Processor	200 MHz or more
Modem	56 kbps or more
Backup drive	Yes
Multimedia support	Yes

When you consider your computer system in terms of the everyday operation of your business, ensure that you have plenty of hard disk space for future software purchases and data inputs, including invoice data, personnel information, and general record keeping. You might also consider purchasing a laptop if you'll need to access your site from the road.

WHAT DO YOU THINK?

1. Map out on paper what you want to appear on your Home page. What navigation links will you include? Describe the theme and color scheme that you will incorporate into your site. Feel free to search the Web for ideas and information to help when designing your site.

2. Visit the Projectcool Web site (www.projectcool.com) and then explore the Sightings link to obtain examples of well-designed Web sites. What sites do you find particularly appealing? Why?

3. Research the costs of hosting your site with an Internet access provider in your area. Perform your research using an Internet search engine or by looking up "Internet Services" in your phone book's yellow pages and then calling for more information.

4. Describe the hardware that you think you'll need to run your business. Think in terms of the computer(s) you will use to develop a Web site and manage the business from an accounting and database standpoint.
   a. Visit a computer store to help you determine prices for the various parts of your system(s). If you want to do your shopping on the Web, visit the Buy.com Web site (www.buy.com).
   b. What kind of backup device(s) will serve the backup needs of your business? Why?
   c. What is the overall cost of the hardware you want to purchase?

CHAPTER 4

STORAGE HARDWARE

Preserving Data and Information

No longer supporting actors to high-powered computers, storage devices are moving toward center stage. Equipment for storing programs and data for later retrieval and use—that is, storage hardware, or more formally, secondary storage hardware—has traditionally been used to support a computer's needs. Now, with the explosive growth in World Wide Web sites and business stockpiling of customer and market-research data, the world of computing is becoming storage-centered.

M ost new computers today come with a high-capacity hard disk drive for storing applications software and data files, a diskette drive for sharing data files with others via lower-capacity diskettes, a CD-ROM drive for installing or using software and games, and a hard disk cartridge drive for backup. Before we describe how these and similar devices work, let us cover some storage fundamentals, including those elements that are common to all secondary storage devices and types of files.

This first chapter starts you on your way by presenting a brief overview of computers—hardware, software, and other concepts. Later chapters will cover these topics in detail.

4.1 Storage Fundamentals

KEY QUESTION   What is the difference between primary and secondary storage, and what are the basic types of files?

As you learned in the previous chapter, the data you are working on is stored in RAM (primary storage) in an electrical state during processing (✔ p. 1.11). Because RAM is an electrical state, data in RAM disappears when you turn off the power to your computer. Therefore, before you turn your microcomputer off, you must save your work onto a storage device that stores data permanently (until it is erased)—such as a diskette or a hard disk—rather than electrically. When saved to a **secondary storage** device, your data will remain intact even when the computer is turned off.

In addition to data, computer software programs must be stored in a computer-usable form. A copy of software instructions must be retrieved from a permanent storage device and placed into RAM before processing can begin. The computer's operating system determines where and how data and programs are stored on the secondary storage devices.

In very general terms, a secondary storage device can be thought of as a file cabinet. You store data there until you need it. Then you open the drawer, take out the appropriate folder (file), and place it on the top of your desk (in primary storage, or RAM), where you work on it—perhaps writing a few things in it or

Saved by firefighters from a burning house, this laptop was melted shut and written off as dead until the disk doctors came to the rescue. Chris Bioss, a "recovery engineer," specializes in retrieving data from damaged hard drives.

throwing away a few pages. Note that in the case of electronic documents on a computer, you are actually taking out a *copy* of the desired file and putting it on the desktop. An old version of the file remains in the file cabinet (secondary storage) while the copy of the file is being edited/updated on the desktop (in RAM). When you are finished with the file, you take it off the desktop (out of primary storage) and return it to the cabinet (secondary storage). Thus the updated file replaces the old file.

Common Elements of Storage Technology

Magnetic tape, diskettes, hard disks, and other storage devices have several features in common. In Chapter 2, we explained the meanings of kilobytes, megabytes, gigabytes, and terabytes in conjunction with RAM capacity (✔ p. 2.14). The same terms are also used to measure the data capacity of secondary storage devices. To repeat:

■ *Kilobyte:* (abbreviated K or KB) is equivalent to 1024 bytes.

■ *Megabyte:* (abbreviated M or MB) is 1 million bytes (rounded off).

■ *Gigabyte:* (G or GB) is 1 billion bytes (rounded off).

■ *Terabyte:* (T or TB) is about 1 trillion bytes.

The amount of data in a file in your personal computer might be expressed in kilobytes or megabytes. The amount of data being stored in a remote database accessible to you over a communications line could well be expressed in gigabytes or terabytes.

The process of retrieving information from a storage device is referred to as **reading**. When information is read from secondary storage, it is copied from the storage device to primary storage (RAM). You will also hear the phrases *loading an application* or *opening a file* to describe retrieving information from a storage device. The process of copying information to a storage device is referred to as **writing**. The action of *saving a file,* for example, involves writing to a storage device. In the context of computer storage, the mechanism that makes reading and writing possible is generally referred to as a *drive*. Storage drives are designed to work with a specific type of storage device. For example, magnetic tape drives work with magnetic tape, diskette drives work with diskettes, hard disk drives work with hard disks, and so on.

Information is read from and written to a storage device according to a specific method, called a *data access method.* The method used affects its speed and its usefulness for certain applications.

■ **Sequential storage** means that data is stored in sequence, such as alphabetically. *(See Figure 4.1, next page.)* Tape storage falls in the category of sequential storage. Thus, you would have to search a tape past all the information from A to J, say, before you got to K. Sequential storage is ideal when information must be accessed in sequential order; however, it bogs down when information must be accessed randomly.

■ Hard disks and other types of disks, by contrast, generally fall in the category of **direct access storage** (although data can be stored sequentially). In direct access storage, also called *random access storage,* the computer can go directly to the information you want. Such storage is ideal when information must be accessed in random order; however it slows down when information must be accessed sequentially.

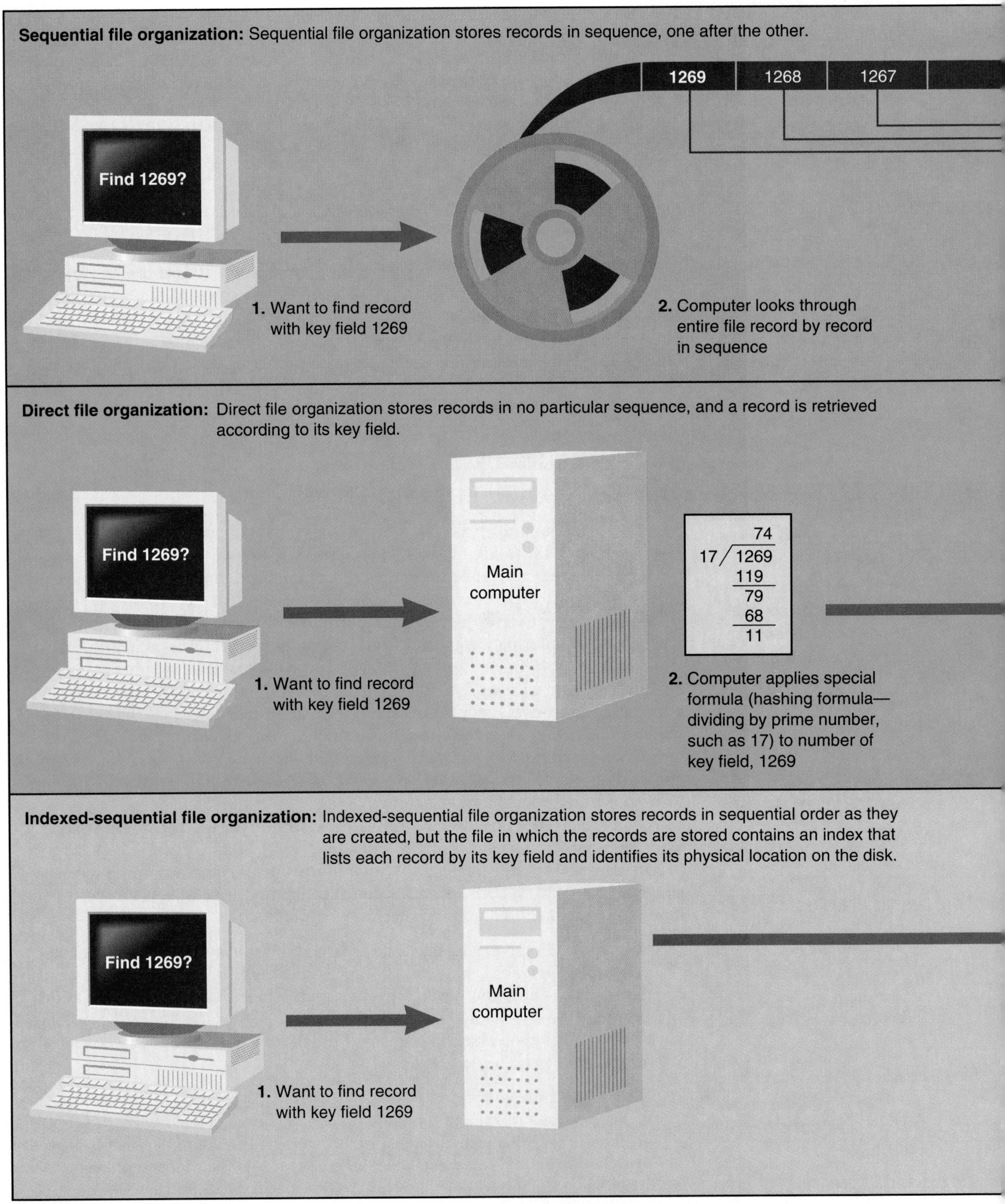

Sequential file organization: Sequential file organization stores records in sequence, one after the other.

1269	1268	1267

Find 1269?

1. Want to find record with key field 1269

2. Computer looks through entire file record by record in sequence

Direct file organization: Direct file organization stores records in no particular sequence, and a record is retrieved according to its key field.

Find 1269?

Main computer

$$17 \overline{\smash{\big)}\, 1269} \begin{array}{r} 74 \\ \underline{119} \\ 79 \\ \underline{68} \\ 11 \end{array}$$

1. Want to find record with key field 1269

2. Computer applies special formula (hashing formula—dividing by prime number, such as 17) to number of key field, 1269

Indexed-sequential file organization: Indexed-sequential file organization stores records in sequential order as they are created, but the file in which the records are stored contains an index that lists each record by its key field and identifies its physical location on the disk.

Find 1269?

Main computer

1. Want to find record with key field 1269

Figure 4.1 Three methods of data storage: sequential, direct, and indexed-sequential

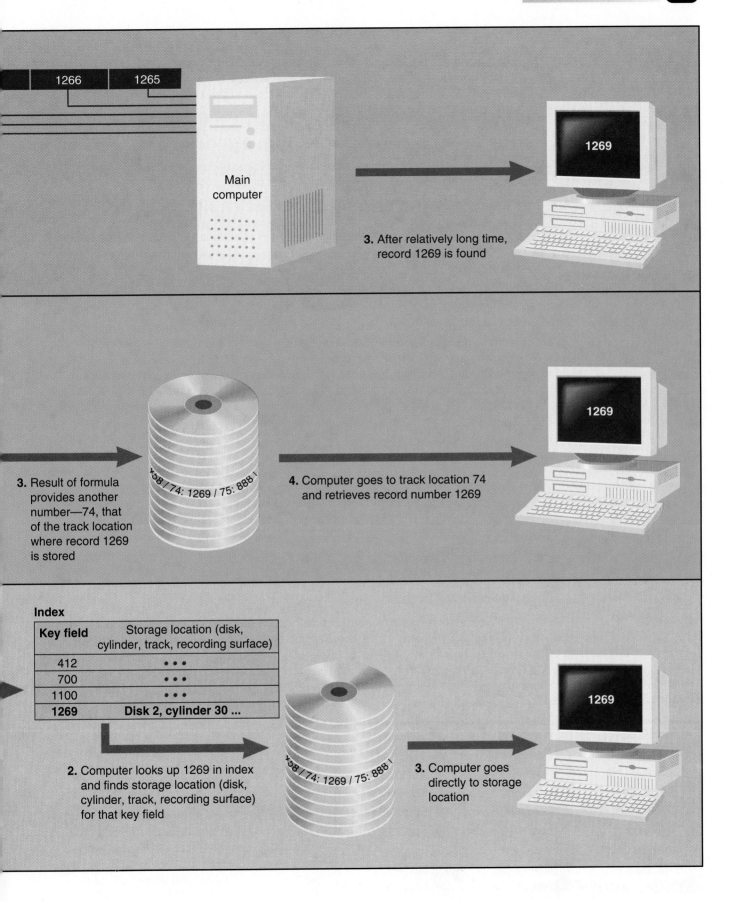

1266   1265

Main computer

3. After relatively long time, record 1269 is found

1269

3. Result of formula provides another number—74, that of the track location where record 1269 is stored

x58 / 74: 1269 / 75: 888

4. Computer goes to track location 74 and retrieves record number 1269

1269

Index

Key field	Storage location (disk, cylinder, track, recording surface)
412	• • •
700	• • •
1100	• • •
1269	**Disk 2, cylinder 30 ...**

2. Computer looks up 1269 in index and finds storage location (disk, cylinder, track, recording surface) for that key field

x58 / 74: 1269 / 75: 888

3. Computer goes directly to storage location

1269

- The *Indexed-Sequential Access Method (ISAM)* has some of the advantages of both the sequential and direct forms of storage. Indexed-sequential file organization stores data in sorted order. However, the file in which the data is stored contains an index that lists the data by key fields and identifies the physical locations on the disk. This type of file organization results in quick data access, either sequentially or randomly. ISAM requires the use of a magnetic or optical disk. (*Note:* Another type of storage is VSAM, for Virtual Sequential Access Method, which is common in IBM mainframes.)

No matter what drive or data access method is used, data is always stored in the form of a file. We take a closer look at files in the next section.

Types of Files

A file is a collection of data or information treated as a unit by the computer. However, not all files can be used by all software programs; cross-platform compatibility and applications software compatibility are issues here.

Some common types of files are these:

- *Program files:* **Program files** contain software instructions. **Source program files** contain high-level computer instructions in their original form, as written by the programmers. These instructions must be translated into machine-language instructions (✔ p. 2.6) in order for the processor to use them. The files that contain the machine-language instructions are called **executable files** (or *binary files*).

- *Data files:* **Data files**, often called *document files*, contain data, not programs—that is, they contain material that you or someone else has created and stored using applications software.

- *ASCII files:* **ASCII files** are text-only (no formatting, such as boldface or italic, and no graphics). The characters are in ASCII code (✔ p. 2.4). This file format is used to transfer documents between incompatible platforms, such as IBM and Macintosh.

- *Image files:* **Image files** contain digitized graphics.

- *Audio and video files:* **Audio files** contain digitized sound. **Video files** contain digitized video images.

A file name consists of a unique *name*, which describes its contents, and a three-character *extension*, which describes its type. (*Note:* Macintosh-based computers don't use extensions.) An example of a file name is "Report.doc" where "Report" is the name and ".doc" is the extension. Extensions are often added automatically by the applications software. There are literally hundreds of known file extensions; Table 4.1 identifies a few common ones. As we see, image files may have many different extensions, depending on the software that creates them.

How does the operating system software—called the OS—know where to store and locate all the different types of files on a secondary storage device? Some OSs use **FATs,** or **file allocation tables.** This part of the OS keeps track of where everything is stored on disk by maintaining a sort of indexed table with entries of locations for all file names. Files are not usu-

Examples of file extensions

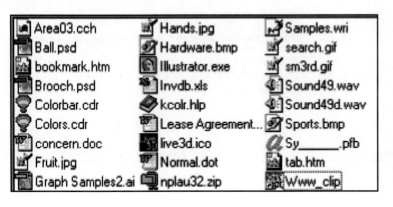

Table 4.1

EXAMPLES OF PC FILE EXTENSIONS	
File Type	**Extension**
Source program file	.COM
Source executable file	.EXE
System support file	.DLL
Microsoft Word data file	.DOC
Microsoft Excel data file	.XLS
Microsoft Access data file	.MDB
ASCII file	.TXT
Encapsulated PostScript image file	.EPS
Tagged image file	.TIF
Still image file (compressed according to the standards of the Joint Photographic Experts Group)	.JPG
Graphics interchange format image file	.GIF
Windows bitmap image file	.BMP
Audio files	.WAV .MID
Video files	.MPG .AVI

ally stored with all their data intact in one place. Instead, they are stored in *clusters*—that is, in groups of data spread out in different locations on the same disk. The FAT tracks the cluster locations. In Macintosh computers, the tracking of file locations is handled by the part of the OS called the *Finder*. (On the newest disks, each file may indeed be stored in one place.)

How does the user keep track of the files on the computer—that is, how do you find them? The OS uses a filing system that displays the names of the files in each folder. Some folders are created by the OS and applications software programs for their own use; others are created by the user as they are needed. For example, you might open the folder called PSYCHOLOGY REPORT and see the files CHAPT1, CHAPT2, CHAPT3, and so on, listed in order. The type of OS that you have determines the filing system.

What Can You Do with Files Besides Filing Them?

When you work with common software applications such as word processing programs, spreadsheets, and graphics programs, you will become familiar with the basic functions of file management. In addition to naming, saving, and opening files, file management also involves *copying*, *renaming*, and *deleting* files, and *printing* files. If your files are huge, taking up a lot of space on your hard disk, you may want to use special software to *compress* them (a topic we cover in Chapter 5). Additional file-management procedures involve *importing* a file so that you can use it in the current software application and *exporting* a file to a software format different from the current one.

Now that we have covered storage and file fundamentals, we turn to the secondary storage devices you are likely to encounter:

■ Tape

■ Diskette

■ Hard disk

■ Optical disk

4.2 Tape Storage

KEY QUESTION **How is data represented on magnetic tape?**

Magnetic tape used to be a common secondary storage medium for large computer systems. These days, however, it is used primarily for backup and archiving of data. **Magnetic tape** is thin plastic tape that has been magnetically coated for storing data as magnetic spots. On large computers, tapes are used on magnetic-tape units (reels) and in cartridges. On microcomputers, tapes are used only in cartridges. **Cartridge tape units,** also called *tape streamers,* are used to back up data from a hard disk onto a tape cartridge. *(See Figure 4.2.)*

A cartridge tape unit using ¼-inch cassettes (*QIC,* or *Quarter-Inch Cartridge standard*) fits into a standard bay in the microcomputer system cabinet and uses low-cost minicartridges that can store up to 20 GB of data on a single tape. A more advanced form of cassette, adapted from technology used in the music industry, is the digital audio tape (DAT), which uses 2- or 3-inch cassettes and stores 2–24 GB. DATs are used for very high-quality audio recording and data backup. More expensive digital linear tape (DLT) provides capacities from 10 GB to 70 GB.

Since tapes are sequential-access media, using them for backup is generally a slow process. As a result, many users opt to use removable hard disk cartridges as backup media, as we will discuss shortly. (Prices of drives and tape/disk cartridges are always factors in deciding on a backup method.)

Figure 4.2 Cartridge tape units

4.3 Diskette Storage

KEY QUESTION **What are the characteristics of diskettes?**

A **diskette,** or *floppy disk,* is a removable, round, flat piece of mylar plastic that, like tape, stores data and programs as magnetized spots. More specifically, data is stored as electromagnetic charges on a metal oxide film that coats the mylar plastic. Data is represented by the presence or absence of these charges, following standard patterns of data representation (such as ASCII). A square plastic case protects the mylar disk from being touched. Diskettes are often called "floppy" because the mylar disk is flexible, not rigid.

The most common size of diskette is 3½ inches in diameter. *(See Figure 4.3.)* Larger and smaller sizes of diskettes also exist, although they are not standard on most microcomputers. Usually, one diskette drive (floppy drive) is built into the microcomputer's system cabinet. *(See Figure 4.4.)*

Figure 4.3 Diskettes

Diskette drive

Figure 4.4 Diskette drive on a system unit

How a Disk Drive Works

A **disk drive** is a computer hardware device that holds, spins, reads from, and writes to magnetic (or optical) disks. How exactly does it work?

In the case of a floppy drive, a diskette is inserted into a slot, called the *drive gate,* or *drive door,* in the front of the drive housing. *(See Figure 4.5.)* This clamps the diskette in place over the spindle of the drive mechanism so that the drive can operate. An access light goes on when the disk is in use. After using the disk, you retrieve it by pressing an eject button. (*Note:* Do not remove the disk when the access light is on!)

Figure 4.5 Cutaway view of a diskette drive

When a diskette is inserted into the drive, it presses against a system of levers. One lever opens the metal plate, or shutter, to expose the data access area.

Other levers and gears move two read/write heads until they almost touch the diskette on both sides.

The drive's circuit board receives signals, including data and instructions for reading/ writing that data from/to disk, from the drive's controller board. The circuit board translates the instructions into signals that control the movement of the disk and the read/write heads.

A motor located beneath the disk spins a shaft that engages a notch on the hub of the disk, causing the disk to spin.

When the heads are in the correct position, electrical impulses create a magnetic field in one of the heads to write data to either the top or bottom surface of the disk. When the heads are reading data, they react to magnetic fields generated by the metallic particles on the disk.

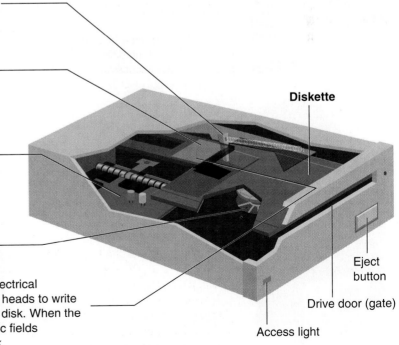

Diskette

Eject button

Drive door (gate)

Access light

The device by which data is transferred from a disk to the computer, and from the computer to the disk, is the disk drive's read/write head. The diskette spins inside its case, and the read/write head moves back and forth over the data access area. Outside the drive, the diskette's data access area is covered by a metal protective plate (or shutter). This plate slides aside when you insert the diskette into the drive. *(Refer back to Figure 4.5.)*

Characteristics of Diskettes

Diskettes have the following characteristics:

■ *Tracks and sectors:* On a diskette, data is recorded in rings called **tracks,** which are neither visible grooves nor a single spiral. Rather, they are closed concentric rings. *(See Figure 4.6.)* The number of tracks on a diskette is measured in *TPI,* or *tracks per inch.* The higher the TPI, the more data the diskette can hold.

Each track is divided into **sectors.** Sectors are invisible wedge-shaped sections used by the computer for storage reference purposes. The number of sectors on the diskette varies according to the recording density—the number of bits per inch (see "Data capacity" in this list). Each sector typically holds 512 bytes of data. When you save data from your computer to a diskette, it is

Figure 4.6 Parts of a diskette

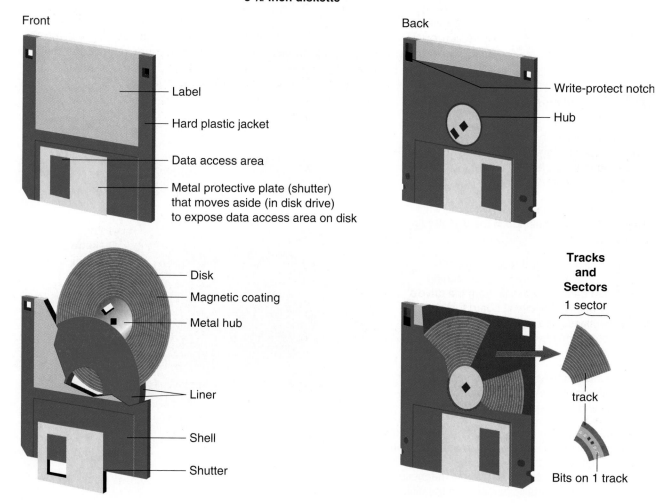

3 1/2-inch diskette

Front

- Label
- Hard plastic jacket
- Data access area
- Metal protective plate (shutter) that moves aside (in disk drive) to expose data access area on disk

Back

- Write-protect notch
- Hub

- Disk
- Magnetic coating
- Metal hub
- Liner
- Shell
- Shutter

Tracks and Sectors

1 sector

track

Bits on 1 track

distributed by tracks and sectors on the disk. That is, the system software uses the point at which a sector intersects a track to reference the data location; the software spins the disk and positions the read/write head at that location.

■ *Unformatted versus formatted diskettes:* When you buy a new box of diskettes, the box may state that they are "formatted." However, if they are not formatted, you have a task to perform before you can use the disks with your computer and disk drive. Unformatted disks are manufactured without tracks and sectors in place. **Formatting**—or **initializing,** as it is called on the Macintosh—means preparing the disk so that the computer's operating system software can write information on it. This includes defining the tracks and sectors on it, as well as setting up the FAT (✔ p. 4.6). The software documentation (user's manual) that comes with your microcomputer tells you what commands to enter to format your diskettes. (*Note:* If you ever put a formatted disk with data already written to it into the drive and reformat it, *all* data will be lost during the reformatting process.)

■ *Data capacity:* Not all diskettes hold the same amount of data. A diskette's capacity depends on its *recording density*—that is, the number of bits per inch that can be written onto the surface of the disk. Today most diskettes are **high-density (HD)** and can store 1.44 MB (PCs) or 1.2 MB (Macs). This data capacity translates into approximately 250–300 text pages. Diskettes with higher capacities are also available. For example, Sony has developed a High Capacity Floppy Disk Drive System (HiFD) that stores 200 MB on a diskette. HiFD drives are faster than current diskette drives and can also read and write on standard 1.44 MB diskettes.

■ *Write-protect features:* Diskettes have features to prevent someone from accidentally writing over—and thereby obliterating—data on the diskette or making changes to program files. To write-protect your diskette, you press a lever toward the edge of the diskette, uncovering a hole (which appears on the lower right side, viewed from the back). (*See Figure 4.7.*)

Figure 4.7 Write-protect features. For data to be written to this disk, a small piece of plastic must be closed over the tiny window on one side of the disk. To protect the disk from being written to, you must open the window. (Using the tip of a pen helps.)

Writable

Write-protect
window closed

Write-protected

Write-protect
window open

> ### Taking Care of Diskettes
>
> There are a number of rules for taking care of diskettes. In general, they boil down to the following:
>
> ■ *Don't touch diskette surfaces:* Don't touch anything visible through the protective case, such as the data access area on the disk surface.
>
> ■ *Be careful with the protective plate:* Don't throw diskettes into your pocket or backpack because eventually the rough handling makes the protective plate lift away from the plastic case. After that happens, the plate gets caught in the drive. If you forcibly withdraw the diskette, the plate will sometimes come off, rendering the diskette useless and the drive unusable until someone fishes out the piece of metal.
>
> ■ *Handle diskettes gently:* Don't try to bend them or put weights on them. (Don't use them for coffee or soft-drink coasters. Moisture can seep underneath the sliding metal plate and damage the disk surface.)
>
> ■ *Avoid risky physical environments:* Disks don't do well in sun or heat (such as in glove compartments or on top of steam radiators). They should not be placed near magnetic fields (including those created by nearby telephones or electric motors). They also should not be exposed to chemicals (such as cleaning solvents) or spilled coffee or alcohol.
>   Most experts say that airport security systems will not damage disks. However, if you are unconvinced of this, hand your diskettes (and portable computer, if you wish) to a security guard before walking through the checkpoint.
>
> ■ *Don't leave a diskette in the drive:* Take the diskette out of the drive when you're done. If you leave the diskette in the drive, the read/write head remains resting on the diskette surface.

4.4 Hard Disks

KEY QUESTION **What are the characteristics of hard disks, and what types of hard disks are available?**

Magnetic bits on a disk surface, caught by a magnetic force microscope. The dark stripes are 0 bits; the bright stripes are 1 bits.

Comparing the use of diskettes to hard disks is like discovering the difference between moving your household in several trips in a small sports car and doing it all at once with a moving van. Whereas a high-density 3½-inch diskette can hold as much as 1.44 megabytes of data, most personal computers today come configured with hard disks that hold between 4 and 10 gigabytes, or more. You can store approximately 1.2 million pages on a 4-GB hard drive. Indeed, at first with a hard disk you may feel you have more storage capacity than you'll ever need. However, after a few months you may worry that you don't have enough—especially if you're using multimedia or graphics-oriented programs, because digital video and graphic-intensive data require immense amounts of storage.

Diskettes are made out of flexible material, which makes them floppy. By contrast, **hard disks** are thin but rigid metal or glass platters covered with a substance that allows data to be held in the form of magnetized spots. Hard disks are also tightly sealed within an enclosed unit to prevent any foreign matter—dust or smoke, for example—from getting inside. Data may be recorded on both sides of the disk platters.

We'll now describe the following aspects of hard disk technology, as well as virtual memory and the MR head:

■ Nonremovable internal hard disk drives of microcomputers

■ Variations of microcomputer hard disks

■ Hard disk technology for large computer systems

Nonremovable Internal Hard Disk Drives of Microcomputers

In microcomputers, hard disks are platters sealed inside a hard disk drive that is built into the system unit and cannot be removed. This internal drive is installed in a *drive bay,* a slot or opening in the computer cabinet. From the outside of a microcomputer, a hard disk drive is not visible; it looks simply like part of the front panel on the system cabinet. Inside, however, are a disk or disks on a drive spindle, read/write heads mounted on an actuator (access) arm that moves back and forth, and power connections and circuitry. *(See Figure 4.8.)* The most common disk sizes today are 1 and 3½ inches. The operation is much the same as for

Figure 4.8

Nonremovable internal microcomputer hard disk drive, photo and cutaway view. The hard disk drive is sealed inside the system cabinet and is not accessible.

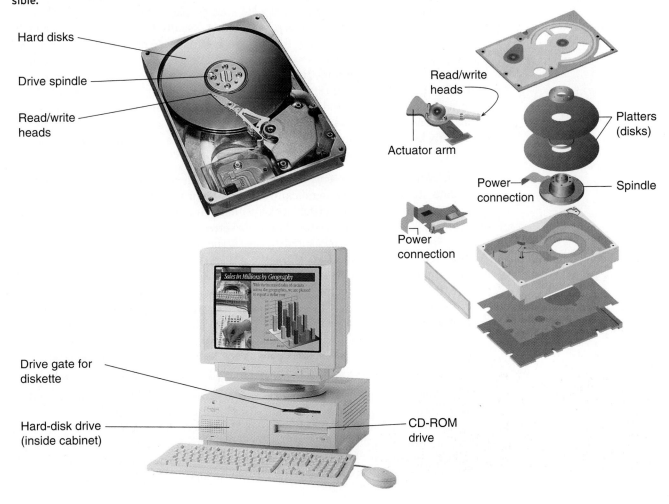

Hard disks

Drive spindle

Read/write heads

Read/write heads

Actuator arm

Platters (disks)

Power connection

Spindle

Power connection

Drive gate for diskette

Hard-disk drive (inside cabinet)

CD-ROM drive

Figure 4.9 Cylinders

In a stack of disks, access arms slide in and out to specific tracks. They use the cylinder method to locate data—the same track numbers lined up vertically one above the other form a "cylinder."

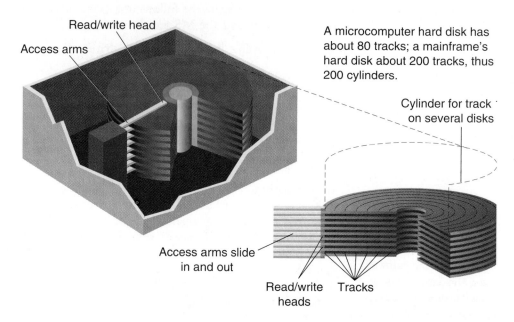

Read/write head

Access arms

A microcomputer hard disk has about 80 tracks; a mainframe's hard disk about 200 tracks, thus 200 cylinders.

Cylinder for track on several disks

Access arms slide in and out

Read/write heads   Tracks

a diskette drive; the read/write heads locate specific pieces of data according to track and disk surface number. Whereas diskettes usually have 135 tracks per inch (TPI), hard disks have thousands; whereas an HD diskette may have 18 sectors, a hard disk may have up to 64.

Secondary storage systems that use several hard disks don't use the sector method to locate data. Rather they use what is known as the *cylinder method.* Because the access arms holding the read/write heads all move together, the read/write heads are always over the same track on each disk at the same time. All the tracks with the same track number, lined up one above the other, thus form a cylinder. *(See Figure 4.9.)*

- *Hard disk advantages—capacity and speed:* We mentioned that hard disks have a data storage capacity significantly greater than that of diskettes. As for speed, hard disks allow faster access to data than do diskettes, because a hard disk spins several times faster than a diskette.

    Speed is generally measured by *seek time, latency,* and *access time.* **Seek time** refers to the time it takes for the read/write head to move to the correct track, measured in *milliseconds,* or *ms* (1000th of a second). A fast hard disk drive may have a seek time of 6 ms. After the head reaches the correct track, it must wait for the disk to rotate until the head is positioned over the correct sector; this rotation time is called **latency,** which may be about 5 ms for a hard drive. If you add seek time to latency, you get the total **access time** (in our example, 11 ms). In advertisements for hard drives, these numbers are figured as averages.

- *Disadvantage—possible "head crash":* In principle a hard disk is quite a sensitive device. As opposed to the read/write head in a diskette drive, the read/write head in a hard disk drive does not actually touch the disk but rather rides on a cushion of air about 0.000001 inch thick. (It has been said that the read/write head flying over the hard disk surface is comparable to a jet plane flying 6 inches above the earth's surface.[1]) The disk is sealed from impurities within a container, and the whole apparatus is manufactured under sterile conditions. Otherwise, a smoke particle, a human hair, or a fingerprint is all it would take to cause what is called a *head crash.*

In a head crash, the surface of the read/write head or particles on its surface come into contact with the disk surface, causing the loss of some or all of the data on the disk. An incident of this sort could, of course, be a disaster if the data has not been backed up. There are firms that specialize in trying to retrieve (for a hefty fee) data from crashed hard disks, though this cannot always be done.

A head crash can also be caused by jarring the hard disk when it is in use, so caution should be exercised. In recent years, computer magazines have evaluated the durability of portable computers containing hard disks by submitting them to drop tests. Most of the newer machines are surprisingly hardy. However, the possibility of hard disk failure always exists—whether in portable or in desktop computers.

Two common types of hard disk architectures are used in microcomputers: EIDE and SCSI.

Don't need for exam →

- *EIDE:* **EIDE,** or **Enhanced Integrated Drive Electronics,** refers to a type of hardware interface widely used to connect hard disks and CD-ROM drives to a PC via a bus (✔ p. 2.14). EIDE connects via a flat ribbon cable to an expansion board called a *host adapter,* which plugs into an expansion slot on the motherboard (✔ p. 2.17). With EIDE drives, the controller electronics are contained on a printed circuit board within the drive itself, so that the adapter is a fairly simple circuit board. An inexpensive EIDE host adapter can control four hard drives (one of which may be a CD-ROM or optical disk drive), two diskette drives, two serial ports, a parallel port, and a game port (✔ p. 2.21). EIDE can attain data transfer rates up to 16.6 MB per second. Because of its low cost, EIDE is increasingly being used instead of SCSI, the drive interface we describe next.

- *SCSI:* **SCSI (small computer system interface,** ✔ p. 2.21) is the drive interface used on Mac computers and high-end PCs, including multimedia workstations and network servers. SCSI allows the connection of 7–15 peripheral devices in a daisy chain hookup to a single expansion board. SCSI-2 can attain transfer rates of 20–40 MB per second; ultra 3 SCSI, 160 MB per second.

Sue Smith of the Marin, California, Humane Society scans a pet cat to identify its owner. The Society has implanted more than 15,000 pets with microchips (*right*) containing the owner's name, address, and phone number—data that is then logged into a nationwide database.

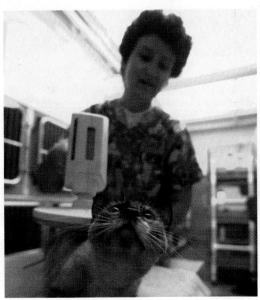
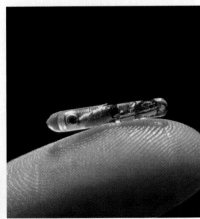

Microcomputer Hard Disk Variations: Power & Portability

If you have a microcomputer with limited hard disk capacity, the following options can provide additional power or portability:

■ *External hard disk drives:* If you don't have room in the system unit for another internal hard disk but need additional storage, consider adding an external hard disk drive. Some detached external hard disk drives can store gigabytes of data. You can also attach several external hard drives via a SCSI interface.

■ *Removable disks:* **Hard disk cartridges,** or *removable hard disks,* consist of one or more platters enclosed along with read/write heads in a hard plastic case. The case is inserted into an internal cartridge drive connected to a microcomputer (or in an external drive, in older computers). A cartridge, which is not much larger than a floppy disk, may hold as much as 2 gigabytes of data. These cartridges are often used to transport huge files, such as desktop-publishing files with color and graphics and multimedia video segments. They are also frequently used for backing up data because, although they are more expensive, they are much faster than tape cartridges and hold much more data than diskettes. Removable magnetic disks and drives come in either EIDE, SCSI, or parallel configurations. Some popular hard disk cartridge systems are SyQuest's SyJet drive and Iomega's Zip and Jaz drives. *(See Figure 4.10.)* A SyJet cartridge holds 1.5 GB. Zip cartridges each hold 100 MB, and Jaz cartridges hold 1 or 2 GB. Note that cartridges made for one type of drive cannot be used in another type of drive.

Figure 4.10 Removable hard disk cartridges and drives

View of several forms of computer storage disk drives. From top to bottom: Zip drive, external hard disk drive, CD-ROM drive, SyQuest hard disk cartridge drive, and a floppy disk drive in a system unit.

Virtual Memory: Using Disk Space to Increase RAM

Virtual memory uses disk space to extend primary memory (RAM), enabling users to run larger software programs than would otherwise be possible. Your operating system, such as Microsoft Windows, divides virtual memory into *pages* of uniform size. When the instructions in a virtual-memory page are needed, they are copied from the disk into RAM. For example, when making up this book, we used the Mac PowerPC 9500's virtual memory function to run QuarkX-Press desktop-publishing software at the same time as Adobe PhotoShop, which was used to manipulate photos inserted on the book's pages. Note that virtual memory can make it seem as if your computer is running more slowly, because of the extra work the computer has to do to retrieve software instructions.

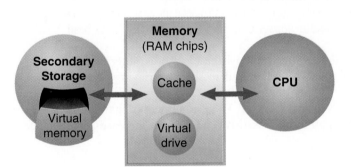

Hard Disk Technology for Large Computer Systems

The large databases offered by such organizations as CompuServe, America Online, and Dialog, as well as the predicted movies-on-demand through cable and wireless networks and most Internet and World Wide Web locations, depend on secondary storage devices for large computers.

Three types of secondary storage devices are available for large computers:

■ *Removable packs:* A removable-pack hard disk system contains 6–20 hard disks, of $10\frac{1}{2}$- or 14-inch diameter, aligned one above the other in a sealed unit. Capacity varies; some packs range into the terabytes.

These removable hard disk packs resemble a stack of phonograph records, except that there is space between disks to allow access arms to move in and out. Each access arm has two read/write heads—one reading the disk surface below, the other the disk surface above. However, only one of the read/write heads is activated at any given moment.

■ *Fixed disk drives:* Fixed disk drives are high-speed, high-capacity disk drives that are housed (sealed) in their own cabinets. Although not removable or portable, they are now more common than removable packs, because of their greater storage capacity and reliability. A single mainframe computer might have 20–100 such fixed disk drives attached to it.

RAID unit

■ *RAID storage system:* A fixed disk drive sends data to the computer along a single path. A **RAID (redundant array of inexpensive disks)** storage system, which consists of two or more disk drives within a single cabinet or connected along a SCSI chain, sends data to the computer along several parallel paths simultaneously. Response time is thereby significantly improved.

The RAID system not only holds more data than a fixed disk drive within the same amount of space but is also more reliable because if one drive fails, others can take over.

Future Hard Disk Technology: The MR Head

Since its introduction in 1955, the magnetic storage industry has constantly increased the performance and capacity of hard disk drives. Today, applications like multimedia, video, audio, and graphical user interfaces, along with increasing program sizes, demand ever greater storage capacity.

The read/write head technology that has sustained the hard disk drive industry to date is based on the voltage produced when a permanent magnet (that is, the disk) moves past a wire-wrapped magnetic core (that is, the read/write head). Over the years, various improvements have been made to this arrangement to increase recording density; however, the ability to manufacture these heads cost-effectively is nearing its natural limit. Thus, if disk storage technology is to continue to provide increased capacity and performance, a new recording head technology is needed. This new technology is the magnetoresistive (MR) read head (MRH).

In traditional read/write head technology, the head must alternately perform conflicting tasks: writing data on the disk and reading (retrieving) previously written data. MRH technology avoids this problem by separating the write and read functions into two physically distinct heads. This fundamental change in read/write technology will enable the disk drive industry to increase performance well into the 21st century.

4.5 Optical Disks

KEY QUESTION **What are optical disks, and how are they used?**

By now optical disk technology is well known to most people. An **optical disk** is a removable disk on which data is written and read through the use of laser beams; there is no mechanical arm, as with diskettes and hard disks. The most familiar form of optical disk is the one used in the music industry. Like a miniature phonograph record, a compact disk, or CD, is an audio disk using digital code that can hold up to 74 minutes (2 billion bits' worth) of high-fidelity stereo sound.

Recording data

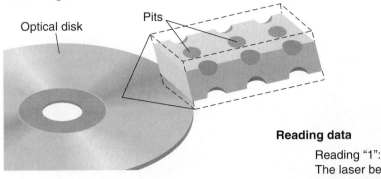

Optical disk

Pits

Reading data

Reading "1":
The laser beam reflects off the smooth surface; this is interpreted as a 1 bit.

Reading "0":
The laser beam enters a pit and is not reflected; this is interpreted as a 0 bit.

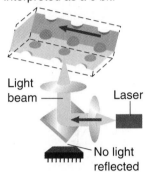

Lens

Semi-transparent mirror

Laser

Reflected beam

Light beam

Laser

No light reflected

Figure 4.11 Optical disks. *(Top)* Writing data: A high-powered laser beam records data by burning tiny bits onto the surface of the disk. *(Right)* Reading data: A low-powered laser beam is reflected from smooth areas, which are interpreted as 1 bits, and is not reflected from pitted areas, which are interpreted as 0 bits.

The optical disk technology that revolutionized the music business with music CDs is doing the same for secondary storage with computers. A single optical CD-ROM disk may hold 650 megabytes of data, although 1-GB CD-ROMs are also available. A 650-MB CD-ROM can hold 250,000 pages of text, or more than 7000 photos or graphics, or 19 hours of speech, or 74 minutes of video. Although some disks are used strictly for digital data storage, many are used to distribute multimedia programs that combine text, visuals, and sound.

In the principal types of optical disk technology, a high-power laser beam is used to represent data by burning tiny pits into the surface of a hard-plastic disk. To read the data, a low-powered laser light scans the disk surface: Pitted areas are not reflected and are interpreted as 0 bits; smooth areas are reflected and are interpreted as 1 bits. *(See Figure 4.11.)* Because the pits are so tiny, a great deal more data can be represented than is possible in the same amount of space on a diskette or on many hard disks.

The optical disk technology used with computers consists of these main types:

- CD-ROM disks
- CD-R disks
- CD-RW disks
- DVD/DVD-ROM

CD-ROM Disks

For microcomputer users, the best-known type of optical disk is the CD-ROM. **CD-ROM,** which stands for **compact disk–read-only memory,** is an optical disk format used to hold software programs and data such as prerecorded text, graph-

Figure 4.12 Notebook computers with CD-ROM drives

ics, and sound. Like music CDs, a CD-ROM is a read-only disk. *Read-only* means that the disk's content is recorded at the time of manufacture and cannot be written on or erased by the user, a feature that makes CD-ROMs excellent media for software distribution and copyrighted image catalogs.

Most microcomputers have built-in CD-ROM drives. *(See Figure 4.12.)* Users can also purchase external CD-ROM drives. The drives come either in a SCSI configuration for Macs or PCs, or in an EIDE configuration (✔ p. 4.15) available only for PCs. In the former case, you will also need a SCSI adapter card; in the latter case, an EIDE-controller adapter card. Since all CD-ROMs conform to the same format, it's possible for your CD-ROM drive to play music CDs.

Whereas at one time a CD-ROM drive was only a single-speed drive, now there are many different speeds, ranging from four-speed (4×) to forty-speed (40×). The faster the drive spins, the more quickly it can deliver data to the processor. Table 4.2 lists the most common CD-ROM speeds and their associated data transfer rates.

Table 4.2

CD-ROM SPEEDS	
Speed	**Data Transfer Rate Per Second**
4×	600 K
6×	900 K
8×	1.2 MB
10×	1.6 MB
12×	1.8 MB
16×	2.4 MB (maximum)
24×	3.6 MB (maximum)
32×	4.8 MB (maximum)
40×	6 MB (maximum)

CD-ROM drives used to handle only one disk at a time. Now, however, there are multidisk drives that can handle up to 100 disks. (Such drives are sometimes called *jukeboxes,* or *CD changers.*)

Clearly, CD-ROM has become an important data-storage medium. CD-ROM disks are commonly used for storing applications programs, encyclopedias, catalogs, games, edutainment software (education software that feels and looks like a game), magazines and books, and movies.

CD-R Disks

CD-R, which stands for **compact disk–recordable,** is a CD format that allows users with CD-R drives to write data, only once, onto a specially manufactured disk that can then be read by a standard CD-ROM drive. Once the data is recorded, it can't be written over (changed). One of the most interesting examples of CD-R technology is the Photo CD system. *(See Figure 4.13.)* Developed by Eastman Kodak, Photo CD is a technology that allows photographs taken with an ordinary 35-millimeter camera to be stored digitally on an optical disk. You can shoot up to 100 color photographs and take them to a local photo shop for processing. A week later you will receive back not only conventional negatives and snapshots but also the images on a CD-ROM disk. Depending on your equipment, you can then view the disk using any compatible CD-ROM drive. The drive could be for an IBM PC or a Macintosh or one of Kodak's own Photo CD players, which attaches directly to a television set.

 **Figure 4.13** Photo CD system

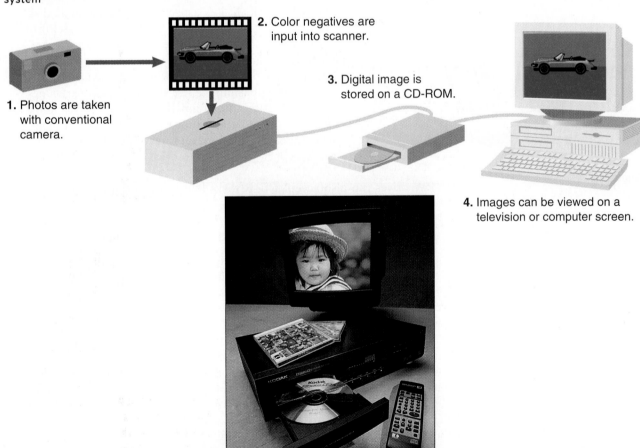

2. Color negatives are input into scanner.

3. Digital image is stored on a CD-ROM.

1. Photos are taken with conventional camera.

4. Images can be viewed on a television or computer screen.

Photo CD is particularly significant for the impact it will have on the manipulation of photographs. With the right software, you can flip, crop, and rotate photos, incorporate them into desktop-publishing materials, and print them out on laser printers. Commercial photographers and graphics professionals can manipulate images at the level of pixels, or picture elements (the dots of color that make up a picture). One possibility is to merge images from different sources—for example, to superimpose the heads of show-business figures in place of the U.S. presidents on Mount Rushmore. Because the image is digital, it can be taken apart pixel by pixel and put back together in many ways. This helps photo professionals further their range; however, it also presents a danger that the credibility of photographs will be compromised.

CD-RW Disks

The **CD-RW (compact disk–rewritable)** format allows users to erase data so that the disk can be used over and over again. The most common type of erasable and rewritable optical disk is probably the *magneto-optical disk (MO),* which uses aspects of both magnetic disk and optical disk technologies. Such disks are useful to people who need to save successive versions of large documents, handle databases, back up large amounts of data and information, or work in multimedia production or desktop publishing. These disks come in cartridges that are inserted into compatible external drives hooked up to the computer. Imation's *SuperDisk* uses a magnetic/optical technology, and the SuperDisk drive can also accept floppy diskettes. Most MO disks hold about 250 MB.

Superdisk

CD-RW drives can also accept CD-R disks and CD-ROMs.

DVD-ROM: The "Digital Convergence" Disk

According to the various industries sponsoring it, DVD isn't an abbreviation for anything. (The letters used to stand for "digital video disk" and later, when its diverse possibilities became obvious, for "digital versatile disk.") But this is the designation that Sony/Philips (with its Multi Media CD) and Toshiba/Time Warner (with its Super Density disk) agreed to in late 1995, when they avoided a "format war" by joining forces to meld their two advanced disk designs into one. Suffice it to say that **DVD-ROM** is a silvery, 5-inch optically readable digital disk that looks like an audio compact disk but can store 4.7–17 gigabytes, allowing great data storage, studio-quality video images, and theater-like surround sound. *(See Figure 4.14.)* Actually, the home-entertainment version is called simply the DVD. The computer version of the DVD is called the DVD-ROM disk. It represents a new generation of high-density CD-ROM disks, with write-once and rewritable capabilities.

(a)

(b) Inside a DVD disk

Four feature-length films can fit on a single DVD disk, which is CD-size but can hold about 25 times more information.

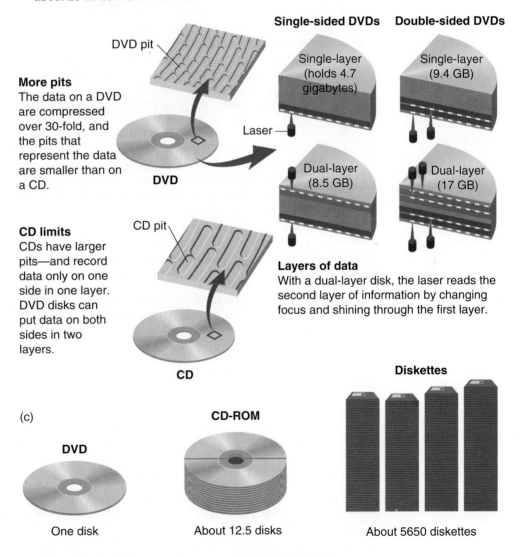

Single-sided DVDs   **Double-sided DVDs**

DVD pit

More pits
The data on a DVD are compressed over 30-fold, and the pits that represent the data are smaller than on a CD.

DVD

Laser

Single-layer (holds 4.7 gigabytes)

Single-layer (9.4 GB)

Dual-layer (8.5 GB)

Dual-layer (17 GB)

CD limits
CDs have larger pits—and record data only on one side in one layer. DVD disks can put data on both sides in two layers.

CD pit

Layers of data
With a dual-layer disk, the laser reads the second layer of information by changing focus and shining through the first layer.

CD

Diskettes

(c)

CD-ROM

DVD

One disk

About 12.5 disks

About 5650 diskettes

Figure 4.14 DVD: A new era of data storage. *(a)* This DVD disk can hold 4.7–17 GB of information. *(b)* Recording on a DVD disk. *(c)* Comparative capacities of DVD, CD-ROM, and diskettes.

Manufacturers are aggressively developing DVD erasing/writing machines and DVD-compatible computers. All these devices should be able to play any CD-ROM or audio CD, finally producing a single player for any CD/DVD disk. DVD technology is expected to replace the VHS videotape now used in VCRs (video cassette recorders).

How does a DVD work? Like a CD or CD-ROM, the surface of a DVD contains microscopic pits, which represent the 0s and 1s of digital code that can be read by a laser. The pits on the DVD, however, are much smaller and closer together than those on a CD, allowing far more information to be represented there. The new generation of lasers used in DVD technology produce a beam that can focus on pits roughly half the size of those on current audio CDs. Another important development is that the DVD format allows for *two layers* of data-defining pits on each side of the disk. Finally, engineers have succeeded in squeezing more data into fewer pits, principally through data compression.

Besides being designed from the outset to work with the full range of electronic, television, and computer hardware, the major characteristics of the DVD are as follows:

■ *More storage capacity, faster data transfer:* A single-layer, single-sided disk will hold 4.7 gigabytes of information, or a library of 300-page novels, or 7 hours of music. (This compares with 650 megabytes or 74 minutes of playing time on today's single-sided music CD.) Indeed, all ratings versions of a film (PG, PG-13, R, and so on) could be included. Parents could use a special password to protect children from selecting versions that are adult-only. A double-layer, double-sided DVD can hold 17 gigabytes of data.

■ *Better audio:* "A Toshiba demonstration clip of the train wreck scene from *The Fugitive* put me right in the midst of squealing brakes and crunching metal," wrote an observer of a DVD prototype, "thanks to a 5.1-channel digital surround-sound specification."[2] The specification allows for six separate audio tracks. It also permits up to eight language translations, which means movie makers could put a number of languages on one disk. In time, there might be some new ultra-high-fidelity audio applications.

One important matter: DVD players will be backward compatible—that is, able to play today's audio compact disks.

■ *Better video:* Picture quality can visibly surpass that currently delivered on videocassettes. In fact, the DVD is designed to offer the superb images found on the new digital satellite system (DSS). In its DVD-ROM form, it will deliver full-screen video that looks like television, rather than expanses of fuzzy blocks (called *pixelation*).

■ *DVD-ROM and recordable and rewritable capabilities:* Software publishers now employ so much space-eating video and animation in their programs that they are rapidly running out of room on standard 680-megabyte CD-ROM disks. Thus, they and computer makers decided they had to enter the DVD standards fray to push for a single DVD design that could be used for data storage as well as for movies and music. They also wanted the new drives to be able to read today's CD-ROM disks. The result is the DVD-ROM disk.

We are now entering one of those periods familiar to computer users in which exciting new technology simultaneously delights and frustrates consumers. The delight, of course, will be that DVD-ROMs will store a lot more information and enable you to see movies and listen to music on your personal computer. (Movies such as *Blade Runner, Mars Attacks!, Casablanca, Doctor Zhivago,* and *Gone with the Wind* are already available for DVD players.) The frustration will be that many kinds of hardware will soon become obsolete or irrelevant, and there will be lots of changes until everything shakes down.

4.6 The Importance of Backup

KEY QUESTION **Why do computer users need backup?**

Even with the best of care, any disk can suddenly fail for reasons you can't understand. Many computer users have found themselves unable to retrieve data from a diskette that worked perfectly the day before, because some defect has damaged a track or sector. Hard disks can crash. Any computer system—large or small—can be hit by fire or flood.

Thus, users and companies should always be thinking about backup. As we've mentioned, backup is the name given to tapes, diskettes, or disks that store copies of programs and data stored elsewhere. The best protection if you're writing, say, a make-or-break research paper is to make two copies of your data. One copy may be on your hard disk, certainly, but duplicates should be on tape, diskettes, or removable hard disk cartridges—or even recordable CD-ROMs, if available.

If you're backing up less than 10 MB, diskettes may work fine. If you're backing up more than that, tape or disk cartridges would be more efficient. If you work with files daily, you would be most secure if you backed up all your files every day. If you work with files only occasionally, you need to determine how often backup is needed. And remember to keep the backup media in a different place. If your computer system and your backup tapes are in the same structure and the place burns down, your backup is obviously worthless.

Some microcomputer software programs provide automatic backup. For example, with Colorado Scheduler, you insert your tape cartridge into the tape drive and click the mouse button on the Colorado Scheduler icon; the computer takes care of the rest. Almost all large computer systems have scheduled automatic backup—either of all files (*full backup*) or only those files that have changed since the last backup session (*incremental backup*).

Note that some storage media last longer than others. Tape will deteriorate within 5–15 years, depending on how it's stored. Hard disk cartridges such as Zip and Jaz have a shelf life of about 10 years, according to the manufacturers. MO drives are more expensive but also more durable. The life span of a CD-ROM disk is almost unlimited. Thus you need to determine how long you will need to archive your backup material before deciding on a storage medium. Also, be sure to have a timed backup strategy. For example, if you add and change data every day, set your backup software to back up those files every night. And you could keep two storage cartridges: a working one and one stored in a safe place. Then exchange the cartridges weekly.

4.7 Other Forms of Secondary Storage

KEY QUESTION **What is flash memory?**

The revolution in secondary-storage technology will probably continue throughout our lifetime and will have a profound effect on the way information is handled and business is conducted. In the next section we describe flash memory, a robust variation on conventional computer-memory chips that we mentioned in Chapter 2. Finally, we will look at some noteworthy developments involving advanced storage technology.

Flash-Memory Cards

Disk drives, whether for diskettes, hard disks, or CD-ROMs, all involve moving parts—and moving parts can break. Flash-memory cards have no moving parts. **Flash-memory,** or **flash RAM, cards** consist of circuitry on credit-card-size cards that can be inserted into slots connecting to the motherboard. They can hold up to 100 megabytes of data.

A videotape produced for Intel, which makes flash-memory cards, demonstrates their advantage: In one scene, engineers strap a memory card onto one electric paint shaker and a disk drive onto another. Each storage device is linked to a personal computer running identical graphics programs. Then the engineers switch on the paint shakers. Immediately, the disk drive fails, its delicate recording heads smashed against its spinning metal platters. The flash-memory card takes the licking and keeps on computing.

As we described in Chapter 2, flash memory is only one of the options available with PCMCIA slots, which were designed primarily for small portable computers. PCMCIA slots in a computer's system cabinet allow users to insert credit-card-size peripherals (PC cards) measuring about 2.1 by 3.4 inches. Besides flash-memory cards, you can plug in modems, hard drives, and adapters for communicating over local area networks (LANs).

Note that flash-memory cards are not infallible. Their circuits wear out after repeated use, limiting their life span.

Advanced Storage Technology

Scientists keep finding new ways to put more and more data on storage media. IBM is actively developing an optical recording system capable of storing 350 million bits per square inch. The company has said it expects to soon reach densities of 10 billion bits a square inch. Such densities would mean that a $3\frac{1}{2}$-inch disk drive could contain all the text of ten thousand 300-page novels.

In what has been called "the world's smallest Etch-a-Sketch," physicists at NEC Corp. in Tokyo used a sophisticated probe—a tool called a scanning tunneling microscope (STM)—to paint and erase tiny lines roughly 20 atoms thick. This development could someday lead to ultra-high-capacity storage devices for computer data.

Web Sites of Possible Interest

Computer companies:
http://www-atp.llnl.gov/atp/companies.html

Computer product reviews:
http://www.anandtech.com
http://www.computers.com
http://www.reviewfinder.com

Agriculture

In 1996, Alan Greenspan, chairman of the Federal Reserve Board, spoke of a historic transition—"one of those rare, perhaps once-in-a-century events"—by which technology was re-ordering the economy. "The advent of the transistor and the integrated circuit," he said, "and, as a consequence, the emergence of modern computer, telecommunication, and satellite technologies have fundamentally changed the structure of the American economy."[a]

Nowhere is the shift more pronounced than in agriculture. A century ago, America changed from an agrarian to an industrial economy. Now it is moving from the Industrial Age to the Information Age—and farmers are decreasing even further, with their numbers expected to drop 273,000 between 1994 and 2005, according to the U.S. Bureau of Labor Statistics.[b] Part of the reason for this decline is computer technology. But part of the reason also is the weakening of farm markets brought about by recessions that began in East Asia in 1997—and those U.S. farmers who invested in new technology actually weathered that storm better.[c] For those who remain, agriculture will be high-tech indeed.

Lloyd and Disa McPherson, dairy farmers near Stuarts Draft, a small Virginia town in the Blue Ridge Mountains, own not only milking machines, tractors, and barns. They also have a desktop microcomputer, with which they visit World Wide Web sites to check prices for the grains they feed their Holsteins and Jerseys. "To get this information before," Lloyd says, "we had to make telephone calls—lots of them. On the Internet, it's easy to find and we can check it whenever we want."[d]

Others use Web sites for marketing purposes. Greg Nolan, co-owner of the Bar 5 Simmental Stock Farms cattle ranch in Douglas, Manitoba, Canada, created a series of Web pages to advertise the ranch's breeding stock. On the Net, Nolan figures, he can not only reach potential customers at low cost but also compete better with larger businesses. "On the Internet, it's all the same," he says. "Whether you're IBM or the Bar 5, you're on a level playing field."[e]

Arlen Ruestman's business card lists not only his telephone number but also the exact latitude and longitude of his corn and soybean farm in Toluca, Illinois. It's his way of promoting what is known as *precision farming,* the use of global-positioning–satellite (GPS) technology to control costs and boost crop yields. "With GPS," says one account, "farmers map and analyze their fields for characteristics such as acidity and soil type, feed the data into computers, and pick up signals from space [satellites] that calibrate their actions as they drive over their fields. So instead of covering a large tract with a uniform amount of seeds, fertilizers, or herbicides, for example, they can spread just the right amount needed on each square yard."[f]

Frances Swain, 27, is the technology manager on Tom Door's 3800-acre farm in Marcus, Iowa, near Sioux City. The son of a used-car dealer, Swain's reddish hair is greased back like a 1950's rocker. He has a passion for computers but describes himself as "not in love with crops or pigs or cows." Nevertheless, he represents a new breed of worker that, according to agricultural economists, American farmers will need because they will have "to rely heavily on technology and information systems to compete with nations that have cheaper land and labor."[g]

WHAT IT IS
WHAT IT DOES
WHY IT IS IMPORTANT

access time (KQ 4.4, p. 4.14)   The sum of the seek time and latency.

The faster a disk's access time, the faster data is retrieved.

ASCII files (KQ 4.1, p. 4.6)   Text-only files (no formatting, such as boldface or italic, and no graphics).

This format is used to transfer documents between incompatible platforms, such as IBM and Macintosh. ASCII files may use the .TXT file name extension.

audio files (KQ 4.1, p. 4.6)   Files that contain digitized sound.

.WAV and .MID (MIDI) files are audio files.

cartridge tape units (KQ 4.2, p. 4.8) Also called *tape streamers;* secondary storage used to back up data from a hard disk onto a tape cartridge.

Cartridge tape units are often used with microcomputers as a backup method and with larger systems for archival purposes.

CD-R (compact disk—recordable) (KQ 4.5, p. 4.21)   CD format that allows users to write data once only onto a specially manufactured disk that can be read by a standard CD-ROM drive.

Home users can do their own recordings in CD format. CD-R can be used, for example, for recording photos and as a backup medium.

CD-ROM (compact disk—read-only memory) (KQ 4.5, p. 4.19)   Optical-disk form of secondary storage that holds more data—including photographs, art, sound, and video—than diskettes and some hard disks. Like music CDs, a CD-ROM is a read-only disk. CD-ROM disks will not play in a music CD player.

CD-ROM disks are used in multimedia, education, and entertainment.

CD-RW (compact disk–rewritable) (KQ 4.5, p. 4.22)   Optical disk that allows users to erase data so that the disk can be used over and over again (as opposed to CD-ROMs, which can only be read and CD-Rs, which can be written to only once). The most common type of erasable optical disk is probably the magneto-optical disk, which uses aspects of both magnetic disk and optical disk technologies.

Such disks are useful to people who need to save successive versions of large documents, handle enormous databases, back up large amounts of data and information, or work in multimedia production or desktop publishing.

data files (KQ 4.1, p. 4.6)   Files that contain data, not programs; also called *document files.*

Data files contain material that a user has created and stored using applications software programs. The program may add an extension, such as .DAT.

direct access storage (KQ 4.1, p. 4.3) Storage media that allow the computer direct access to a storage location without having to go through what's in front of it.

Direct access storage (disk) is much faster than sequential storage (tape).

disk drive (KQ 4.3, p. 4.9) Computer hardware device that holds, spins, reads from, and writes to magnetic or optical disks.

Without disk drives, disks cannot be used. Disk drives can be internal (built into the computer system cabinet) or external (connected to the computer by a cable).

diskette (KQ 4.3, p. 4.8) Also called *floppy disk;* a removable secondary storage medium; consisting of a round, flexible mylar disk coated with a metal oxide film, which stores data as electromagnetic charges. Data is represented by the presence or absence of these electromagnetic charges, following standard patterns of data representation (such as ASCII). The plastic casing of the diskette protects the mylar disk from being touched by human hands. Diskettes are called "floppy" because the mylar disk is flexible, not rigid. The common diskette size is now 3½ inches.

Diskettes are used on all microcomputers.

DVD-ROM (KQ 4.5, p. 4.22) Five-inch optical disk that looks like a regular audio CD but can store 4.7 gigabytes of data on a side, in the single-layer version, or 8.5 GB in the dual-layer version.

DVD-ROMs provide great storage capacity, studio-quality images, and theater-like surround sound.

EIDE (Enhanced Integrated Drive Electronics) (KQ 4.4, p. 4.15) Type of hardware interface widely used to connect hard disks to an IBM-type PC.

EIDE is popular because of its low cost and is increasingly being used to connect tape drives and CD-ROM drives to PCs.

executable files (KQ 4.1, p. 4.6) Files that contain machine-language instructions.

Executable files, which may use the extension .EXE, contain the machine-language instructions the computer needs to run programs.

file allocation table (FAT) (KQ 4.1, p. 4.6) Function of the operating system that keeps track of where everything is stored on disk, by maintaining a sort of indexed table with entries of locations for all file names.

FATs are needed for the computer system to find files.

flash-memory (flash RAM) cards (KQ 4.7, p. 4.26) Circuitry on credit-card-size cards (PC cards) that can be inserted into slots connecting to the computer's motherboard.

Flash-memory cards are variations on conventional computer-memory chips; however, unlike standard RAM chips, flash memory is nonvolatile: It retains data even when the power is turned off. Flash memory can be used not only to simulate main memory but also to supplement or replace hard disk drives for permanent storage.

formatting (initializing) (KQ 4.3, p. 4.11) Preparing diskettes so that the operating system can write information on them. This process includes defining the tracks and sectors (the storage layout). Formatting is carried out by one or two simple computer commands.

Diskettes cannot be used until they have been formatted. Nowadays most diskettes are sold preformatted.

hard disk (KQ 4.4, p. 4.12)   Secondary storage medium; a rigid disk made out of metal and covered with a magnetic recording surface. Like diskettes and tape, it holds data in the form of magnetized spots. Hard disks are tightly sealed within an enclosed unit to prevent contamination by any foreign matter. Data may be recorded on both sides of the disk platters.

Hard disks hold much more data than diskettes do. Nearly all microcomputers now use hard disks as their principal storage medium. Hard disk drives can be internal or external; removable disks may also be used.

hard disk cartridge (KQ 4.4, p. 4.16)   One or more removable hard disk platters enclosed along with read/write heads in a hard plastic case. The case is inserted into an external cartridge system connected to the computer.

A hard disk cartridge, which is removable and easily transported in a briefcase, may hold gigabytes of data. Hard disk cartridges, such as SyQuest, Zip, and Jaz, are often used for transporting large graphics files and for backing up data.

high-density (HD) diskette (KQ 4.3, p. 4.11)   Diskette that can store 1.2–1.44 megabytes.

Most microcomputers use HD diskettes.

image files (KQ 4.1, p. 4.6)   Files that contain digitized graphics.

Users working with graphics must learn how to use various types of graphics files, such as .EPS, .JPG, .TIF, .GIF, and .BMP.

latency (KQ 4.4, p. 4.14)   The time it takes for the hard disk to rotate so that the head is positioned over the correct sector.

Latency for a fast hard disk drive may be about 5 milliseconds.

magnetic tape (KQ 4.2, p. 4.8)   Thin plastic tape coated with a substance that can be magnetized; data is represented by magnetized or nonmagnetized spots. Tape can store files only sequentially.

Tapes are used in reels, cartridges, and cassettes. Today "mag tape" is used mainly to provide backup, or duplicate storage, and for archiving .

optical disk (KQ 4.5, p. 4.18)   Removable disk on which data is written and read by means of laser beams.

Optical disks hold much more data than many magnetic disks and have been instrumental in the development of the multimedia industry.

program files (KQ 4.1, p. 4.6)   Files containing software instructions.

Contrast with *data files*.

RAID (redundant array of inexpensive disks) (KQ 4.4, p. 4.18)   Storage system consisting of two or more disk drives within a single cabinet or connected along a SCSI chain that sends data to the computer along several parallel paths simultaneously. Response time is thereby significantly improved.

A RAID system not only holds more data than a fixed disk drive within the same amount of space but also is more reliable because if one drive fails, others can take over. RAID systems are commonly used for servers and multimedia systems.

read (KQ 4.1, p. 4.3)   Computer activity whereby data represented in the magnetized spots on a disk (or tape) are converted to electronic signals and transmitted to primary storage (RAM) in the computer.

Reading allows stored data and information to be transferred to a place where it can be manipulated.

SCSI (small computer system interface) (KQ 4.4, p. 4.15)   Peripheral-device interface used on Mac computers and some high-end PCs.

Using SCSI, 8–16 peripheral devices may be connected in a daisy chain hookup to a single expansion board.

secondary storage (KQ 4.1, p. 4.2) Equipment that stores data and programs permanently on disk or tape.

Secondary storage is nonvolatile—that is, saved data and programs are permanent, or remain intact, when the power is turned off. Secondary storage meets computer users' need for far greater storage capacity than is available through primary storage (RAM).

sectors (KQ 4.3, p. 4.10) On a diskette, up to 18 invisible wedge-shaped sections used by the computer for storage reference purposes.

When users save data from computer to diskette, it is distributed by tracks and sectors on the disk. That is, the system software uses the point at which a sector intersects a track to reference the data location; the software spins the disk and positions the read/write head at that location.

seek time (KQ 4.4, p. 4.14) The time it takes for the read/write head to move to the correct track, measured in *milliseconds*, or *ms* (1000th of a second).

Seek time varies in different hard disks. A fast hard disk may have a seek time of 6 milliseconds.

sequential storage (KQ 4.1, p. 4.3) Data stored in sequence, such as alphabetically.

Sequential storage is the only type of storage provided by tape, which is used mostly for archiving and backup.

source program files (KQ 4.1, p. 4.6) Files containing high-level computer instructions.

These instructions must be translated into machine language in order for the processor to use them.

tracks (KQ 4.3, p. 4.10) The rings on a diskette along which data is recorded. Each track is divided into eight or nine sectors.

See *sectors*.

video files (KQ 4.1, p. 4.6) Files that contain digitized video images.

.MPG and .AVI are common video file extensions.

virtual memory (KQ 4.4, p. 4.17) Type of hard drive space that mimics primary memory (RAM).

When RAM space is limited, virtual memory allows users to run more software at once, provided the computer's CPU and operating system are equipped to use it. The system allocates some free disk space as an extension of RAM—that is, the computer swaps parts of the software program between the hard disk and RAM as needed.

write (KQ 4.1, p. 4.3) Computer activity whereby data processed by the computer is recorded onto a disk (or tape).

Writing allows users to save data and information to secondary storage media.

EXERCISES

1. Fill in the following blanks:

   a.   A(n) _____ is about 1 trillion bytes.

   b.   The process of retrieving information from a storage device is referred to as _____ and the process of copying information to a storage device is referred to as _____.

   c.   _____ is always a sequential access storage device.

   d.   A(n) _____ is a removable disk on which data is written and read through the use of laser beams.

   e.   _____ is the name given to a diskette, disk cartridge, or tape that is a duplicate or copy of data that is stored elsewhere.

2. List two advantages that hard disks have over diskettes.

   a.   _____

   b.   _____

3. What kinds of secondary storage do large computer systems use?

   a.   _____

   b.   _____

   c.   _____

4. How do the following terms relate to disk storage?
   a.   tracks
   b.   sectors
   c.   formatting
   d.   write-protect features

5. Describe each of the following file types:
   a.   program files
   b.   data files
   c.   ASCII files
   d.   image files

6. Label each of the following statements as either true (T) or false (F).

   _____ Magnetic tape can handle only sequential data storage and retrieval.

   _____ Hard disks may be affected by a head crash when particles on the read/write heads come into contact with the disk's surface.

   _____ To use a diskette, you usually need a disk drive, but not always.

   _____ One advantage of using diskettes is that they aren't susceptible to extreme temperatures.

   _____ EIDE and SCSI are two common types of hard disk architecture.

7. Briefly compare the following data access methods:
   a.   sequential storage
   b.   direct access storage
   c.   indexed-sequential access method (ISAM)

8. List three advantages of DVD-ROMs:

a. _____

b. _____

c. _____

9. What are five things you can do with a file?

a. _____

b. _____

c. _____

d. _____

e. _____

10. List four rules for taking care of diskettes.

a. _____

b. _____

c. _____

d. _____

IN YOUR OWN WORDS

1. Answer each of the Key Questions that appear at the beginning of this chapter.

2. What is a file?

3. What is a file allocation table?

4. Why is a diskette sometimes called a floppy disk?

5. What is a hard disk?

6. What does disk formatting do?

7. Does a microcomputer user need both a hard drive and a diskette drive? Why or why not?

8. What is a CD-RW disk?

9. What is a cartridge tape unit and what is it typically used for?

10. What is a flash-memory card?

KNOWLEDGE IN ACTION

1. **Determining Your Computer's Hard Disk Capacity.** If you're using the Windows 95 or Windows 98 operating system, you can easily determine the storage capacity of your computer. To begin, double-click the "My Computer" icon on the Windows desktop. Then, right-click the hard disk icon, which is in the shape of a rectangle. The icon may have a name like "Hard disk (C:)" or "Hard disk (D:)." From the right-click menu, choose Properties. By referring to the information displayed in the Properties dialog box, write down the hard disk's capacity, amount of used space, and amount of free space.

When you're finished, close the Properties dialog box by clicking its Close button (⊠) in the upper-right corner. Use the same procedure to close the "My Computer" window.

2. **Navigating a Hard Disk.** If you're using the Windows 95 or Windows 98 operating system, you can easily navigate the contents of your computer's hard disk. To begin, double-click the "My Computer" icon on the Windows desktop. Then, double-click the hard disk icon, which is in the shape of a rectangle. The icon may have a name like "Hard disk (C:)" or "Hard disk (D:)." If necessary, maximize the current window by clicking its Maximize button (▢) in the upper-right corner.

In Windows, folders are used to organize groups of files. The Windows folder icon looks like a manila folder. How many folders are displaying in the current window? How many files are displaying? (*Note:* Files are represented by something other than a folder icon.)

To open a folder, you double-click it. Double-click a folder icon to display the contents of that folder. What is the name of the folder you double-clicked? How many folders and files are stored in it? To move to the previous folder view, click the Back button on the toolbar. Close the current window by clicking its Close button (⊠) in the upper-right corner. Use the same procedure to close any other windows that are open on the Windows desktop.

3. **Going Shopping.** Visit the *www.buycomp.com* Web site and then identify the brand name and price of the following storage devices: (a) 4-GB hard drive, (b) 40× CD-ROM drive, and (c) Jaz drive. Because different models are available for each of these components, also provide a description.

4. **Scanning a Computer Ad.** Cut out an advertisement from a newspaper or magazine that features a new microcomputer system. Circle all the terms that are familiar to you now that you've read the first four chapters of this text. Define these terms on a separate sheet of paper. Is this computer expandable? How much does the computer cost? Is the monitor included in the price?

5. **Getting a Free Personal Computer**. Visit the *www.free-pc.com* Web site to learn more about obtaining a Free-PC. What is required from you to obtain a Free-PC? What processing, input/output, and storage components are standard in a Free-PC? Under what circumstances must you return your Free-PC?

Answers to Self-Test Exercises: 1a. terabyte 1b. reading, writing 1c. magnetic tape 1d. optical disk 1e. backup 2. capacity, speed 3. removable packs, fixed disk drives, RAID storage systems 4a. Tracks are the rings on a diskette along which data is recorded. Each track is divided into eight or nine sectors. 4b. On a diskette, up to 18 invisible wedge-shaped sectors are used by the computer for storage reference purposes. 4c. Formatting means preparing diskettes so that the operating system can write information on them. This process includes defining the tracks and sectors (the storage layout). 4d. Diskettes have features to prevent someone from accidentally writing over—and thereby obliterating—data on the diskette or making changes to program files. To write-protect your diskette, you press a lever toward the edge of the diskette, uncovering a hole (which appears on the lower right side, viewed from the back). 5a. Files containing software instructions. 5b. Files that contain data, not programs; also called *document files.* 5c. Text-only files (no formatting, such as bold-face or italic, and no graphics). 5d. Files that contain digitized graphics. 6. T, T, F, F, T 7. In sequential storage, data is stored in sequence, such as alphabetically. In direct access storage, storage media allows the computer direct access to a storage location without having to go through what's in front of it. ISAM has some of the advantages of both the sequential and direct forms of storage. Indexed-sequential file organization stores data in sorted order. However, the file in which the data is stored contains an index that lists the data by key fields and identifies the physical locations on the disk. This type of file organization results in quick data access, either sequentially or randomly. 8. more storage capacity, better transfer rate, better audio, better video 9. name, save, open, rename, delete, print, compress, import, export 10. Don't touch the diskette surface, be careful with the protective plate, handle diskettes gently, avoid risky physical environments, don't leave a diskette in the drive.

SYSTEM SOFTWARE

The Director

CHAPTER 5

KEY QUESTIONS

You should be able to answer the following questions:

5.1 Two Basic Software Types: For the Computer & for the User *What is system software and applications software?*

5.2 System Software Components *What functions does system software perform?*

5.3 Common Operating Systems: Platforms *How does Windows 98 compare to other microcomputer operating systems?*

5.4 The Future: Is the Web Changing Everything? *What is a network computer, and how does it involve the Internet and Java?*

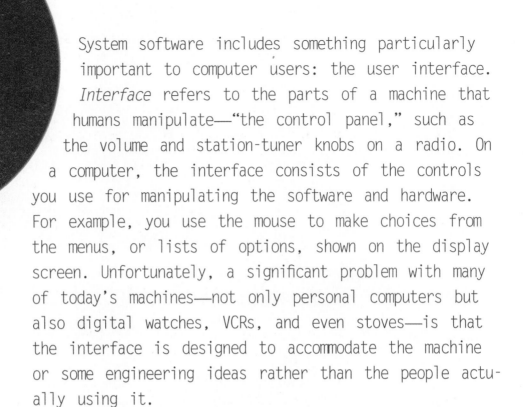

System software includes something particularly important to computer users: the user interface. *Interface* refers to the parts of a machine that humans manipulate—"the control panel," such as the volume and station-tuner knobs on a radio. On a computer, the interface consists of the controls you use for manipulating the software and hardware. For example, you use the mouse to make choices from the menus, or lists of options, shown on the display screen. Unfortunately, a significant problem with many of today's machines—not only personal computers but also digital watches, VCRs, and even stoves—is that the interface is designed to accommodate the machine or some engineering ideas rather than the people actually using it.

Good interfaces are intuitive, like the twin knobs on an old radio; anyone, whether novice or sophisticate, can use them at once. Bad interfaces force us to relearn the required behaviors every time. A poorly designed software interface may include a bewildering array of menus and icons. Of course, you can prevail over a bad interface if you repeat the procedures often enough. That's why you can become familiar with a befuddling word processor you use all the time but not with the cumbersome e-mail system you use intermittently.

In this chapter we embark on a discussion of software programs and the interfaces you can use to control them. When you get hands-on experience with software, you will find that some programs are relatively easy to use but some are not. Don't be too hard on yourself if you have difficulty with particular software. Remember that it should be the software designer's job to take your needs into account, not the other way around.

5.1 Two Basic Software Types: For the Computer & for the User

KEY QUESTION What is system software and applications software?

No such thing as software existed in the earliest computers. Instead, to change computer instructions, technicians actually had to rewire the equipment. Then, in the 1950s, computer scientists began to use punched cards to store program instructions. In the mid-1950s, high-speed storage devices that were developed for ready retrieval eliminated the need for hand-wired control panels. Since that time, the sophistication of computer hardware and software has increased exponentially. Software is created by software programmers, who code instructions using special programming languages, such as C++. (This topic is covered in more detail in Chapter 10.)

With the appearance of the microcomputer in the late 1970s, computer hardware and software became accessible to more people because they became more affordable, easier to use, and flexible enough to handle very specific job-related tasks. Because of this accessibility, a large pool of applications software has been created to satisfy almost any user's requirements. In other words, you do not have to be a technical specialist to use computer software to solve complicated and tedious problems. However, you will be entering the job race without your running shoes if you do not understand the uses of—and the differences among—types of system software and applications software.

To help you understand the differences among types of software, let us repeat the definitions for applications and system software.

- ■ **System software** works "behind the scenes"; it "underlies" applications software. These programs start up the computer and function as the principal coordinator of all hardware components and applications software programs. Without system software loaded into the RAM (✔ p. 2.11) of your computer, your hardware and applications software are useless.

- ■ **Applications software** consists of computer programs designed to satisfy a user's needs. The task or problem may require, for example, word processing, computations for payroll processing, creation of animation, maintenance of different types of data in different types of files, the design of a full-color magazine or a new artificial heart valve, or the preparation of forms and documents. Applications software communicates to system software all file management and resource requests (use of peripheral devices). (Applications software is covered in detail in the next chapter.)

Every application works through "layers" in the computer to get to the hardware and perform the desired result. Think of the applications software layer as what the computer is doing and the system software as how the computer does it. Both system software and applications software must be purchased by the user. (System software and some applications software are usually shipped with and included in the price of a microcomputer.)

For large computer systems, the choice of system software tends to be made by computer specialists and the hardware vendor, and the applications software is often custom-written for the

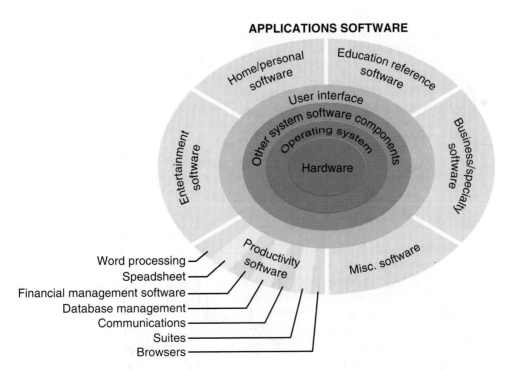

system; this type of software is called *custom software.* For microcomputer systems, most applications software is usually purchased at a store, direct from the manufacturer, or via mail order or online from a catalog. (There is much more applications software to choose from than system software.) Applications software purchased off the shelf is often referred to as *off-the-shelf,* or *packaged, software.* Microcomputer users generally receive system software along with the computer they purchase or use at work.

If you are a microcomputer user starting from scratch, you should first identify your processing needs. Then choose your applications software. Next choose compatible hardware models and system software that will allow you to use your applications software efficiently and to expand your system if necessary. By choosing your applications software first, you will ensure that all your processing requirements will be satisfied. You won't be forced to buy a software package that is your second choice simply because your first choice wasn't compatible with the hardware or system software already purchased.

When you go to work in an office, chances are that the computer hardware and system software will already be in operation; so if you have to choose anything, it will most likely be applications software to help you do your job. If you do find yourself in a position to choose applications software, make sure not only that it will satisfy the processing requirements of your job, but also that it is compatible with your company's existing hardware, system software, and applications software.

5.2 System Software Components

KEY QUESTION What functions does system software perform?

Without system software you won't be able to use any applications software. System software tells the computer how to interpret data and instructions; how to communicate with peripheral equipment like printers, keyboards, and disk drives; how to manage files; and how to use the hardware in general. Also, it allows you, the user, to interact with the computer. System software comprises a large number of instructions that can be grouped into three basic parts:

1. Operating system
2. Utilities
3. Language translators

As a computer user, you will have to use system software, so it is important to understand the role it plays in the computer system.

Operating System: In Control

The **operating system (OS),** the most important system software component, consists of the master programs, called the **supervisor,** that manage the basic operations of the computer. These programs reside in RAM (main memory) while the computer is on and provide resource management services of many kinds; for example, they run and store other programs and store and process data. The operating system allows you to concentrate on your own tasks or applications rather than on the complexities of managing the computer. Interpreting the commands you give, the OS runs programs and allows you to interact with the programs while they are running.

Figure 5.1 Booting process. When you turn on the computer, the processor (CPU) automatically begins executing the part of the operating system's start-up system located in ROM (1). These instructions help load the operating system from the hard disk into RAM (2), and then they pass control to the OS.

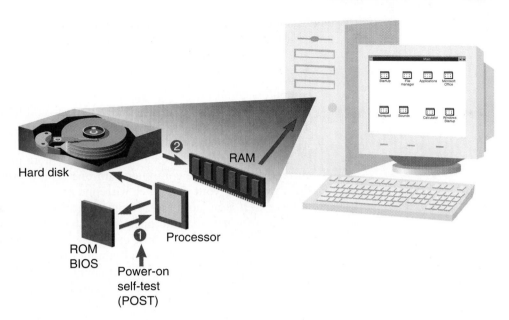

The operating system is automatically loaded into main memory soon after you turn on, or "boot," the computer. The term *booting* refers to the process of loading parts of the operating system into a computer's main memory, usually from hard disk. *(See Figure 5.1.)* This loading is accomplished by a program (called the *bootstrap loader* or *boot routine*) stored permanently in the computer's electronic circuitry. When you turn on ("power up") the machine, the program performs an automatic *power-on self-test (POST),* which usually tests RAM, the keyboard, and the disk drives. If the tests are successful, the computer boots itself. (If the tests are unsuccessful, the computer reports the error by emitting a series of beeps and displaying an error message on the display screen.) During booting, as already mentioned, parts of the operating system are loaded from disk into memory. The parts of the OS that always remain in memory while the computer is on are called *resident.* Less frequently used parts of the OS are copied from disk when needed and are called *nonresident,* or *transient.*

The operating system includes **BIOS** (the **basic input/output system**), which manages the essential peripherals such as the keyboard, screen, disk drives, and parallel and serial ports (✔ p. 2.21). BIOS also manages some internal services such as time and date. This is the part of the operating system that tests the computer when you power up. After running the autostart program, it loads the rest of the operating system and turns control over to it. BIOS is usually stored on one or more ROM chips (✔ p. 2.19) or flash memory chips (✔ p. 2.21).

The operating system controls additional functions, such as *managing programs and data, managing memory, handling input and output,* and *coordinating some network communications functions.*

Managing Programs and Data

A computer is required to perform many different jobs at once. It locates and accesses files and programs requested by users and by other programs. In word processing, for example, it accepts input data, stores the data on a disk, and prints out a document—seemingly simultaneously. Some computers can also handle more than one program at the same time—word processing, spreadsheets, database management—displaying them in separate windows on the screen. Other computers can accommodate the needs of several different users at the same time. How does the computer keep everything straight? Among the ways operating systems manage operations more efficiently are multitasking, multiprogramming, time-sharing, and multiprocessing. Not all operating systems can do all these things.

■ *Multitasking—executing more than one program concurrently:* Earlier microcomputers could do only *single-tasking*, whereby an OS could run only one application program at a time. Thus, users would have to shut down the application program they were working in before they opened another application, which was inconvenient. Today, multitasking operating systems are used.

Multitasking is the execution of two or more programs by one user concurrently on the same computer with one central processor. You may be writing a report on your computer with one program while another program plays a music CD. How does the computer handle both programs at once?

The answer is that the operating system directs the processor to spend a predetermined amount of time executing the instructions for each program, one at a time. In essence, a small amount of each program is processed, and then the processor moves to the remaining programs, one at a time, processing small parts of each. This cycle is repeated until processing is complete. The processor speed is usually so fast that it may seem as if all the programs are being executed at the same time. However, the processor is still executing only one instruction at a time, no matter how it may appear to the user. Because processors work so much faster than peripheral devices, it can accomplish several processing tasks while waiting for, say, a printer to finish outputting a document.

Microcomputer users working on a system with multitasking capabilities will become familiar with the terms *foreground* and *background*. If, for example, your computer is printing out your psychology report while you are creating some graphs for your marine biology report, the printing will occur in the *background;* that is, the processor will allocate less time to it than to what is in the *foreground*—the current application you are working in. Background processing is noninteractive, low-priority processing; foreground processing is interactive, high-priority processing. With some operating systems you can specify the percentage of processor time spent on foreground and background applications.

■ *Multiprogramming—concurrent execution of different users' programs:* **Multiprogramming** is the execution of two or more programs on a *multiuser* operating system. As with multitasking, the processor spends a certain time executing each user's program but, because it works so quickly, all the programs seem to be running at the same time. (Multiprogramming is essentially a multiple-user version of multitasking.)

■ *Time-sharing—round-robin processing of programs for several users:* In **time-sharing,** a single computer processes the tasks of several users at different stations in round-robin fashion. Time-sharing is the operative principle when several users are linked by a communications network to a single computer. The computer will first work on one user's task for a fraction of a second, then go on to the next user's task, and so on.

How is this done? The answer is through *time slicing.* Because computers operate so quickly, they can alternately apportion slices of time (fractions of a second) to various tasks. Thus, the computer may rapidly switch back and forth among different tasks, just as a hairdresser or dentist works with several clients or patients concurrently. The users are generally unaware of the switching process.

Multitasking and time-sharing differ slightly. With multitasking, the processor directs the programs to take turns accomplishing small tasks or events within the programs. These events may be making a calculation,

The "steps of God" are what the Balinese call their elaborate network of rice terraces. For centuries, the complex water systems that nourished this land were maintained by "water priests," who combined religious ritual with water management in a system that worked with the environment. With the help of American-developed software, the Balinese rice farmers now use computers to combine the benefits of the old and the new to manage the terraces.

searching for a record, printing out part of a document, and so on. Each event may take a different amount of time to accomplish. With time-sharing, the computer spends a fixed amount of time with each program before going on to the next one.

Time-sharing is used by some companies' travel agents scattered around the country. The central computer allows the agents to make reservations at the same time. Time-sharing can also allow a research center's scientists and engineers to work on different projects at the same time.

■ *Multiprocessing—simultaneous processing of two or more programs by multiple processors:* **Multiprocessing** is processing done by two or more computers or processors linked together to perform work simultaneously—that is, at precisely the same time. This can entail processing instructions from different programs or different instructions within the same program at the same time.

Multiprocessing goes beyond multitasking, which works with only one processor. In both cases, the processing should be so fast that, by spending a little bit of time working on each program in turn, several programs can be run at the same time. With both multitasking and multiprocessing, the operating system keeps track of the status of each program so that it knows where it left off and where to continue processing. But an operating system capable of multiprocessing is much more sophisticated than that required for multitasking.

Multiprocessing can be done in several ways. One is by coprocessing, whereby the controlling processor works together with coprocessors (✔ p. 2.9), each of which handles a particular task, such as creating display-screen graphics or performing high-speed mathematical calculations. Many microcomputer systems have coprocessing capabilities.

Another way to perform multiprocessing is by parallel processing (✔ p. 2.11), whereby several full-fledged processors work together on the same tasks, sharing memory. Parallel processing is often used in large computer systems designed to keep running if one of the processors fails. These systems are called *fault-tolerant systems;* they have many processors and redundant components such as memory and input, output, and storage devices. Fault-tolerant systems are used, for example, in airline reservation systems.

Managing Memory

The operating system apportions available memory among jobs as necessary. One common technique of dealing with memory shortages is via *virtual memory* (✔ p. 4.17), which implements the hardware and operating system to mimic actual memory (RAM) when this memory space is limited. This allows users to work with larger documents and run more software at once. When the processor needs information held in virtual memory addresses, it moves the information to RAM addresses and moves other information out of RAM and into virtual memory addresses in secondary storage, most commonly the hard disk. This process is called *swapping,* or *paging.* The use of virtual memory will slow performance, but it provides the user with more flexibility.

Handling Input and Output

The OS, as we mentioned, manages essential peripheral devices and allows the computer to communicate with them. It does this via device drivers. **Drivers** comprise software programs that support specific peripheral devices. Each driver contains the detailed machine language (✔ p. 2.6) necessary to control a specific device. The OS commands the driver, which in turn commands the peripheral device.

Note that no OS includes all the device drivers that exist today. Some drivers may have to be purchased separately, usually along with the device.

Coordinating Some Network Communications Functions

It used to be that network communications functions were handled by a separate net work operating system (NOS). Now, however, some communications functions are included in the regular OS, to meet personal network connection needs. Business network administration needs usually still require a separate NOS, such as Netware or Windows NT, which we cover shortly.

Utility Programs: Helping Hands

Utility programs, the second part of system software, are generally used to support, enhance, or expand existing programs in a computer system. Many operating systems have utility programs built in for common purposes. Additional utility programs are available separately. Examples of utility programs are:

Need to know Utility Programs

- *Backup:* Suddenly your hard disk drive fails, and you have no more programs or files. Fortunately, we hope, you have used a **backup utility** to make a backup, or duplicate copy, of the information on your hard disk. Examples of separate backup utilities are Norton Backup (from Symante) and Colorado Scheduler.

- *Data recovery:* A **data recovery utility** is used to restore data that has been physically damaged or corrupted. Data can be damaged by viruses (see following), bad software, hardware failure, and power fluctuations that occur while data is being written/recorded.

- *Virus protection:* If there's anything that can make your heart sink faster than the sudden failure of your hard disk, it may be the realization that your computer system has been invaded by a virus. A virus consists of hidden programming instructions that are buried within a program or code in a data file (✔ p. 4.6). Sometimes they copy themselves to other programs, causing havoc. Sometimes the virus is merely a simple prank that pops up a message. Other times, however, it can destroy programs and data and wipe your hard disk

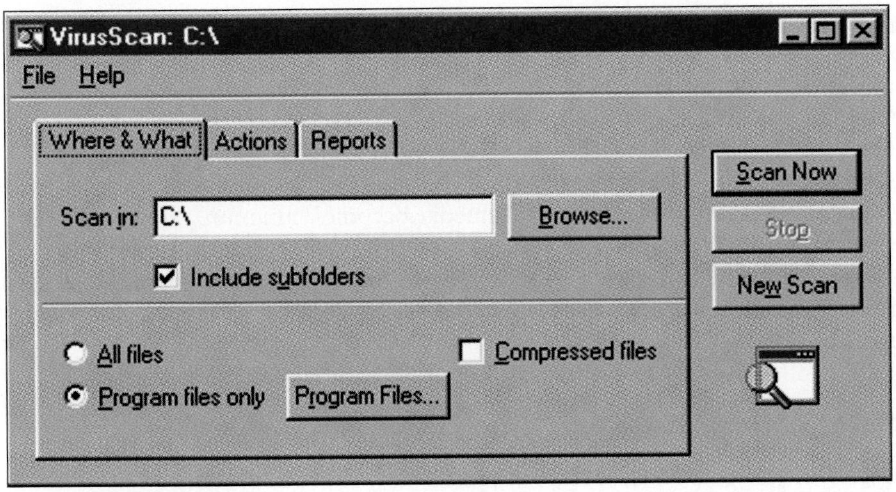

```
┌─────────────────────────────────────────────────────────┐
│ 🔲 VirusScan: C:\                              _ □ ✕     │
├─────────────────────────────────────────────────────────┤
│  File   Help                                             │
│                                                          │
│  ┌─────────────┐                                         │
│  │Where & What │ Actions │ Reports                       │
│  ┌──────────────────────────────────────┐    ┌────────┐ │
│  │                                       │    │Scan Now│ │
│  │  Scan in:  [C:\            ]  Browse… │    └────────┘ │
│  │                                       │    ┌────────┐ │
│  │       ☑ Include subfolders            │    │  Stop  │ │
│  │                                       │    └────────┘ │
│  │  ○ All files        ☐ Compressed files│    ┌────────┐ │
│  │  ◉ Program files only  [Program Files…]│   │New Scan│ │
│  │                                       │    └────────┘ │
│  └──────────────────────────────────────┘              │
└─────────────────────────────────────────────────────────┘
```

Scanning software dialog box, asking whether you want to scan your hard drive (C:\) for viruses

clean. Viruses are spread when people exchange diskettes or download (make copies of) files from computer networks.

Fortunately, antivirus software is available. **Antivirus software** is a utility program that scans hard disks, diskettes, and memory to detect viruses. Some utilities destroy the virus on the spot. Others notify you of possible viral behavior. Note that new viruses are constantly being developed. Thus, you need the type of antivirus software that can detect unknown viruses and that also offers frequent, free updates; such updates are usually available online, to be downloaded. Popular antivirus software utilities are Norton Antivirus, Dr. Solomon's Anti-Virus Toolkits, McAfee's VirusScan, and Webscan.

Note: Though it's a good idea to install an antivirus utility on your computer, virus risks are sometimes exaggerated. With few exceptions, if you don't boot your computer with a foreign diskette, directly run programs downloaded from a network, open files attached to e-mail, or use illegally copied program diskettes, your risk of virus infection is low. *(See Table 5.1.)*

■ *Data compression:* As you continue to store files on your hard disk, it will eventually fill up. You then have several choices. You can delete old files to make room for the new. You can buy a hard-disk cartridge drive and some cartridges and transfer files and programs to those. Or you can use a **data compression utility.** Data compression utilities remove redundant elements, gaps, and unnecessary data from a computer's storage space so that fewer bits

[handwritten margin notes:]
Data compression on exam.
Data compression:
① Normal data
② Compressed data
Pressed file is needed to compress and decompress the data.
If normal data is damaged → file is lost. If compressed data is lost, everything compressed will be damaged.

Table 5.1

┌──┐
│   **PREVENTION FIRST**   │
├──┤
│ McAfee offers these tips to help you avoid viruses.   │
│   │
│ ■ Never start your computer from an unknown diskette. Always │
│   make sure your diskette drive is empty before turning on or│
│   restarting your computer.   │
│   │
│ ■ Run virus-scanning software on a new diskette before   │
│   executing, installing, or copying its files into your   │
│   system.   │
│   │
│ ■ If you download or install software from a network server │
│   (including the Internet), bulletin board, or online   │
│   service, always run scanning software on the directory you │
│   placed the new files in before executing them.   │
│   │
│ ■ Create a start-up diskette containing the scan program.   │
│   Make sure this disk is write-protected so that it cannot   │
│   become infected.   │
│   │
│ ■ Scan files attached to e-mail before you open them.   │
└──┘

are required to store or transmit data. Given today's huge-capacity hard disks, you may never fill yours up. Still, data compression remains an issue.

With the increasing use of large graphic, sound, and video files, data compression is necessary both to reduce the storage space required and to reduce the time needed to transmit such large files over a network. You may also want to compress a file to fit on a diskette, for portability.

As the use of sophisticated multimedia becomes common, compression/decompression will be increasingly taken over by built-in hardware boards that specialize in this process. That will leave the main processor free to work on other things, and compression/decompression software utilities will become obsolete.

The following box lists the most common data compression formats.

Data Compression: Getting More from Less

Data-compression techniques can be divided into two major families: lossy and lossless. These two techniques differ in the trade-off between data quality and storage space. Lossy data compression involves a certain loss of accuracy in exchange for a high degree of compression. This type of compression is often used for graphics files and digital voice files. Lossless compression involves techniques that generate an exact duplicate with a lower degree of compression. This is achieved by removing redundant data elements. Lossless compression is often used with database records, spreadsheets, and word processing files.

Several standards exist for compression, particularly of visual data. If you record and compress in one standard, you cannot play the data back in another. The main reason for the lack of agreement is that different industries have different priorities. What will satisfy the users of still photographs, for example, will not work for users of moving images. Also keep in mind that some compression/decompression techniques—sometimes called *codecs*—require special hardware, along with the software utility.

■ *Lossy compression utilities:* These compression schemes use ratios of 1:10 up to 1:50, meaning that the compressed files are about 1/10 to 1/50 of the original size.
  (1) JPEG ("jay-peg," Joint Photographers Experts Group): This is a compression program for still images. Motion-JPEG can be used for digital video storage and editing but not transmission. There are more than 30 types of JPEG programs, which can cause compatibility problems. (File extension [✔ p. 4.6] is .JPG.)
  (2) MPEG ("em-peg," Motion Pictures Experts Group): This is a compression program for storage, editing, and transmission of video images. MPEG keeps a complete, detailed image for the first frame (or key frame) of a video segment. For subsequent frames, only the information that changes is stored. Key frames with complete information (called *intra-coded frames*, or *I-frames*) are placed at regular intervals to maintain picture quality. The MPEG standard is supported by IBM, Apple, AT&T, and many other manufacturers and carriers. (File extension is .MPG.)

■ *Lossless compression utilities:* These compression schemes use a ratio of about 1:4 and are used for text files and graphics files. Most of these programs, along with decompression programs, can be downloaded free via the Internet.

NAME	FILE EXTENSION	MICROCOMPUTER TYPE (PLATFORM)
WINZIP	.ZIP	PC
ARC	.ARC	PC
PAK	.PAK	PC
Windows Install	.xx$	PC
StuffIt	.SIT	Mac
PackIt	.PIT	Mac
DiskDoubler	.DD	Mac
Apple Link	.PKG	Mac
Self-Extracting	.SEA	Mac

Of course, other compression software programs exist, but the foregoing are some of the common ones.

To use one of these programs—say, WINZIP—on a file downloaded from a server on the Internet, you would do the following:

1. While online, designate the location (folder) on your hard disk where you want the downloaded file to be placed.

2. Download the file.

3. Go offline.

4. Load WINZIP, which has previously been installed on your hard disk, by double-clicking on its folder or icon.

5. After WINZIP is open, use its menu option to open the downloaded file into WINZIP and designate the disk location (folder) where you want to save the decompressed file. (It can be the same place you put it when you downloaded it, or not.)

You can also "zip" (compress) the file again later.

Note that if you download a compressed multimedia file, you will need the appropriate software that supports the decompression and playback of sound and video to hear and view the presentation. *Multimedia utilities*, or *extensions*, may or may not include their own compression/decompression programs. Some multimedia utilities come packaged with the system software—QuickTime for the Mac and AVI (audio/video interleave) for Windows-equipped PCs.

Defragmentation: When a file is stored on a disk, the computer tries to put the elements of data next to one another. However, this is not always possible because previously stored data may be taking up locations that prevent this. Then, after the user has saved and deleted many files, there remain many scattered areas of stored data that are too small to be used efficiently. This is called *fragmentation*. It causes the computer to run slower than if all the data in a file were stored together in one location. Utility programs called **defraggers** are available to *defragment* the disk, thus rearranging the data so that the data units of each file are repositioned together (contiguously) in one location on the disk. (*Note:* You can also defragment a file by simply saving it under a different name onto a disk that has ample space available.)

Many other utilities exist, such as those for transferring files back and forth between a desktop microcomputer and a laptop. They are often offered by companies other than those making the operating system. Later the operating system developers may incorporate these features as part of a product. (*Note:* Independent, or external, utilities must be compatible with your system software; check the software packaging and user documentation.)

Language Translators

A **language translator**—system software's third component—is software that translates a program written by a programmer in a language such as C++ into machine language (✔ p. 2.6), which the computer can understand. All system software and applications software must be turned into machine language for execution by the computer. (Language translators, including compilers and interpreters, are covered in Chapter 10.)

System Software Interfaces

As we mentioned at the beginning of the chapter, the **user interface** provides the means for you to communicate with the computer; it controls the manner of interaction between the user and the operating system. The old type of interface is *command-driven.* *(See Figure 5.2.)* In this type of interface, the user must type in strings of characters to issue commands; the mouse cannot be used. The command-driven interface was followed by the *menu-driven interface.* *(See Figure 5.2.)* In this case, the user issues commands by means of menus—on-screen lists of options to choose from. Choices can be made by clicking the mouse or by using the keyboard. The menu-driven interface was greatly improved by the development of the **graphical user interface (GUI**, pronounced "gooey"). *(See Figure 5.2.)* First developed by Xerox, the GUI was adapted by Apple for its Macintosh machines and was later introduced by Microsoft in its PC system software called *Windows.* In addition to menus, GUIs employ pictorial figures called *icons* to represent tasks, functions, and programs; for example, a trash can may represent a delete-file function.

Another feature of the GUI is the use of windows (lowercase "w"). **Windows** divide up the display screen into sections. Each window may show different output—for instance, a word processing document in one and a spreadsheet in another.

Finally, the GUI permits liberal use of both the keyboard and the mouse. The mouse serves as a pointing device; it allows you to move the cursor to a particular icon or place on the display screen. The function represented by the icon can be activated by pressing (clicking) buttons on the mouse. Or, using the mouse, you can move ("drag") an image from one side of the screen to the other or change its size.

GUI has become the standard microcomputer system software interface. *(See Figure 5.3.)*

Figure 5.2 Examples of command-driven *(top)*, menu-driven *(middle)*, and graphical user *(bottom)* interfaces

Figure 5.3 The GUI is now the common interface between the user, applications software, and the operating system.

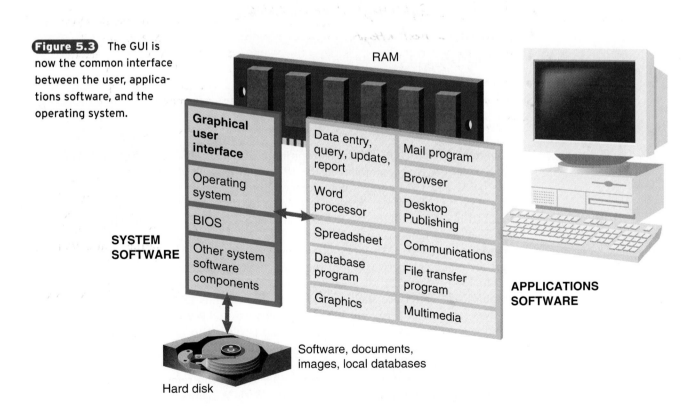

5.3 Common Operating Systems: Platforms

KEY QUESTION **How does Windows 98 compare to other microcomputer operating systems?**

The type of processor used in a computer determines the type of machine language it uses. And the computer's operating system is created to work with that particular type of machine language. Thus, the processor model and the operating system determine the **platform**—that is, the type of computer architecture, or family; the PC and the Apple Macintosh are two common platforms. For the most part, software created for one type of platform will not run, without special arrangements, on other platforms. Once you understand the platform, you can begin to understand what the particular computer system is capable of. As a microcomputer user, you'll have to learn not only the applications software you want to use but also, to some degree, the relevant operating system.

Common operating systems used on mainframes and midsize computers are MVS, VM, OS/390, and VAX/VMS. In this section, we describe the following microcomputer operating systems:

- DOS and Windows 3.x
- Windows 9x
- Windows NT / Windows 2000
- OS/2 Warp
- UNIX _ first attempt at universal interface.
- Linux _ next attempt.
- Mac OS
- NetWare

DOS and Windows 3.x

Command-driven **DOS** (in English, pronounced "dahss")—short for **Disk Operating System**—was very popular in the 1980s and early 1990s and runs primarily on PCs (IBM and IBM-compatible microcomputers). IBM's version of DOS is called *PC-DOS* and Microsoft's version is called *MS-DOS* (for IBM-compatibles). Except for subtle differences, PC-DOS and MS-DOS are identical. Microsoft launched its original version, MS-DOS 1.0, in 1981, and there have been several upgrades since then. MS-DOS 7.0 was issued in 1996 and includes enhanced support for managing networks and the latest microprocessors.

In 1985, Microsoft released Windows 1.0, an *operating environment* that lays a graphical user interface shell around DOS and extends DOS's capabilities. Version 2.0 was released in 1988, but it wasn't until version 3.0 was released in 1990 that Windows really took off and created an industry tied to its GUI, multitasking capabilities, and ability to manage large amounts of memory. There have been several releases of Windows 3—3.0, 3.1, and 3.11. (*Note:* The number before the period refers to a version. The number after the period refers to a release, which has fewer refinements than a new version.) With **Windows 3.x,** you display your work in one or more *windows* on the desktop. You can easily switch and move data among windows. Although Windows 3.x improves DOS's capabilities, DOS still has many shortcomings and has been succeeded by other, more versatile operating systems. Windows 3.x is becoming obsolete, replaced by Windows 9x and later versions.

Windows 9x

Windows 95, released in 1995, was the major upgrade designed to replace DOS and Windows 3.x. A true multitasking operating system, Windows 95 does not require the separate MS-DOS program. The GUI is not the shell; instead it is integrated into the operating system. Like Windows 3.x, Windows 95 uses windows and a desktop. *(See Figure 5.4.)* Among the many features included in Windows 95 are support for longer filenames, e-mail, fax transmission, multimedia, and Plug and Play, which simplifies the process of installing new hardware.

Most important, though, is the fact that Windows 95 is a *32-bit operating system*, meaning that it can work with 32 bits of data at one time. This is twice as much as can be processed by any version of DOS, which can only work with data in 16-bit chunks. What this means to you is that applications written for Windows 95 run faster and you can work with multiple applications at the same time without a noticeable delay. Also, with Windows 95, you are able to realize the potential and power of today's more sophisticated microprocessors.

Windows 98, which models its interface after Windows 95, includes several enhanced capabilities over Windows 95—primarily, its support of the Internet. *(See Figure 5.5, next page.)* With Windows 98, you can open documents stored locally on your computer, documents stored on your company's network, and documents stored on the Web without having to open a separate Web-browser window. In addition, Windows 98 provides support for huge hard disks, state-of-the-art hardware such as DVD disks (✔ p. 4.22) and the Universal Serial Bus standards (✔ p. 2.25), and additional commands for customizing the user interface.

A simplified version of Windows 9x, Windows CE, is used for palmtop computers.

Figure 5.4 Windows 95 screen, showing the Desktop with program and directory icons

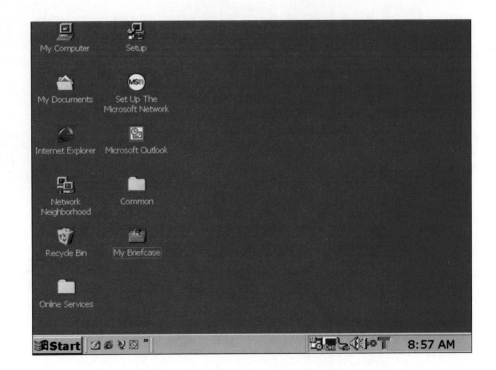

Figure 5.5 Windows 98 screen

Outlook Express: Part of Microsoft's browser, Internet Explorer, that enables you to use e-mail.

Microsoft Network: Click here to connect to Microsoft Network (MSN), the company's online service.

Norton Protected: Click here to activate anti-virus software.

Network Neighborhood: If your PC is linked to a network, click here to get a glimpse of everything on the network.

My Documents: Where your documents are stored unless you specify otherwise.

My Computer: Gives you a quick overview of all the files and programs on your PC.

Documents: Multitasking capabilities allow users to smoothly run more than one program at once.

Start menu: After clicking on the start button, a menu appears, giving you a quick way to handle common tasks. You can launch programs, call up documents, change system settings, get help, and shut down your PC.

Start button: Click for an easy way to start using the computer.

Taskbar: Gives you a log of all programs you have opened. To switch programs, click on the icon buttons on the taskbar.

Multimedia: Windows 98 features sharper graphics and improved video capabilites.

Japanese and American members of the Mormon church journey via wagon train from Nebraska to Utah, re-enacting a trip taken by Mormons to escape religious persecution more than 150 years ago. Using a solar-powered laptop with wireless modem, Osamu Sekiguchi of Tokyo posts his impressions of the journey to a Japanese Web site.

Windows NT / Windows 2000

Whereas Windows 9x is basically consumer-oriented, **Windows NT,** for New Technology, is business-oriented. Providing a similar interface to Windows 9x, it is a multitasking, multiprocessing operating system with built-in support for large networks of computers—that is, Windows NT is a *multiuser* system. Multiuser platforms support workgroup computing, situations in which LANs (✔ p. 1.14) are set up to allow users to share files, databases, and applications. Windows NT 4.0 is designed to run on workstations (✔ p. 1.14) or other powerful computer systems. Windows NT 5.0 will work on new notebooks.

There are two basic versions of Windows NT. Windows NT Server, for heavy-duty networking, can support up to 32 processors, whereas Windows NT Workstation supports 1–2 processors.

Microsoft is working on Windows 2000 (Win2000), which will combine the Windows NT line with Windows 9x. Indeed, Microsoft's goal is to produce the first operating system that runs everything from laptops to dumb terminals in networks to huge office computers.

1993	Windows NT 3.1	6.1 million lines of code
1994	Windows NT 3.5	8.3 million lines of code
1995	Windows NT 3.51	10.1 million lines of code
1996	Windows NT 4.0	18.9 million lines of code
2000	Windows 2000	30 million lines of code

OS/2 Warp

OS/2 (there is no OS/1) was initially released in April 1987 as IBM's contender for the next mainstream operating system. **OS/2**—for **Operating System 2**—was designed to run on IBM and IBM-compatible microcomputers. Unfortunately, because of an array of management and marketing disasters, IBM slipped far behind Microsoft in developing an installed base for OS/2. (In fact, IBM and Microsoft were once partners in developing OS/2. Then Microsoft decided to put all its efforts into backing Windows and later Windows NT.)

In late 1994 IBM unveiled a souped-up version of OS/2, called OS/2 Warp. OS/2 Warp is similar to Windows NT. But despite spending $2 billion on OS/2 in its struggle against Windows, the company failed to increase its market share. IBM has even started shipping Windows NT on some of its lower-end systems. Although the future of OS/2 Warp is uncertain, IBM continues to support its approximately 10 million Warp users. The latest versions of Warp are available online and can be downloaded from IBM's Web site.

UNIX

UNIX was invented more than two decades ago by American Telephone & Telegraph (AT&T), making it the oldest operating system still used today. *(See Figure 5.6.)* **UNIX** is a multiuser, multitasking operating system with built-in networking capability. Because it can run with relatively simple modifications on most types of computers—from micros to minis to mainframes—UNIX is called a *portable* operating system. The primary users of UNIX are government agencies, universities, large corporations, and banks, which use the software for everything from airplane-parts design to currency trading to Web site management. Indeed, the developers of the Internet built it around UNIX because of its ability to keep large systems with hundreds of processors churning out transactions for months or even years without fail. For that reason, companies such as PepsiCo's Taco Bell chain use UNIX to link in-store cash registers to back-office servers for inventory control and labor scheduling. Red Roof Inn trusts UNIX servers to run the daily operations of its 280 locations. Even one of the world's fastest systems—a supercomputer at the U.S. Department of Energy's Sandia National Laboratory—is controlled by a variant of UNIX. The supercomputer, which is used to simulate nuclear explosions and other situations, is powered by more than 9000 Pentium Pro microprocessors (🖛 p. 2.11, parallel processing).

Will UNIX endure? Rapid advances by Windows NT Server have convinced some industry analysts that it will overtake UNIX. However, UNIX vendors maintain that the UNIX market is still healthy. They hang their hopes on the network computing movement and the emergence of the Internet as a computing environment. No other operating system, they believe, is better suited for manag-

Figure 5.6 UNIX screen

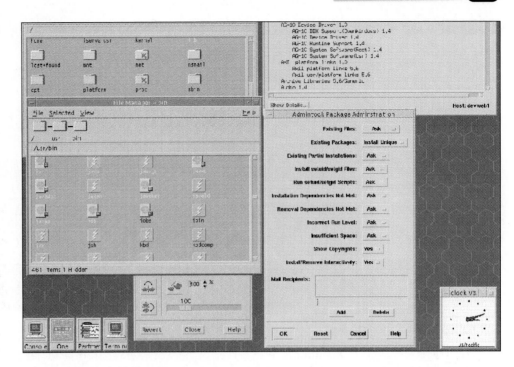

ing transactions conducted on large servers connected to the Internet than the operating system on which the "network of networks" was built.

In addition, hardware manufacturers such as Compaq, Hewlett-Packard, and IBM are promoting convergence strategies that would lead to tools for uniting and managing UNIX *and* NT devices on corporate networks.

Linux

Another PC-compatible operating system option is **Linux,** a version of UNIX. *(See Figure 5.7, next page.)* Linus Torvalds developed Linux in 1990 while he was a computer science student at Helsinki University in Finland. He developed it as freeware, offering UNIX's power without the hefty price. Free Linux versions can be downloaded from hundreds of Internet sites.

While Linux has ample power to run many Windows-based applications, few software developers currently design their software to be used specifically with Linux. However, some software manufacturers are supporting Linux. Corel has released a Linux version of WordPerfect 8, Netscape offers a Linux-compatible version of its browser Navigator 4.04, and Caldera offers a Linux office suite, Star Office. Indeed, Red Hat Software (Red Hat Linux 5.2) and other commercial Linux distributors have simplified installation. Linux currently lacks a GUI, but Red Hat Gnome and K Desktop Environment will soon take care of that.

Some hardware manufacturers are also supporting Linux. Compaq, Dell, and Hewlett-Packard are shipping some server computers with Linux instead of Windows NT.

And Alexandre Julliard, a young Swiss programmer, has been coordinating an international project that is intended to let PC users run their normally Windows-dependent programs in Linux. The project is known as Wine, short for Windows Emulator. (*Emulation* refers to the ability of one type of software to imitate software of a different technical standard so completely that the difference is virtually invisible to the user.)

Figure 5.7 Linux screen

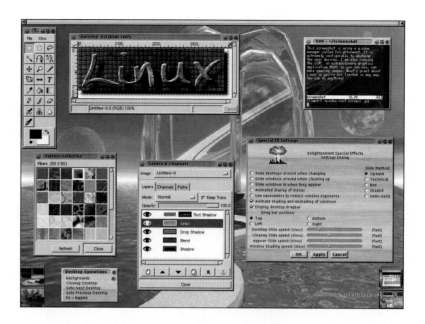

Linux is ideal for users needing the performance and stability of UNIX to maintain a Web server or network server from a PC at low cost. It also fits adventurous users who want the freedom to use their strong technical skills to develop their own applications. New users without some UNIX experience may have to wait a while before using this OS.

Mac OS

Mac OS, formerly called *Macintosh Operating System*, is designed to run on Apple's Macintosh line of computers and compares closely to Windows 9x. *(See Figure 5.8.)* The Macintosh has always had one outstanding feature: It is easy to use, and the easy-to-use interface has generated a strong legion of fans. After almost a decade of Macintoshes costing more than comparable PCs, Apple cut its prices. The result was to bring Macs more into line with equipment from IBM, Compaq, Dell, and others. The latest version of Mac OS is 8.5, released in 1998.

With all the favorable publicity about ease of use for the Macintosh, is there a downside? Indeed there is: Because Mac computers make up only about 4% of the personal computer market, only about 7000 commercial applications packages have been written for Macs. By contrast, some 30,000 or more applications packages are available for DOS and Windows computers. However, its graphics capabilities still make the Macintosh a popular choice for people working in commercial art, desktop publishing, prepress operations, multimedia, and engineering design. Within large organizations it has also been an efficient machine for people for whom extensive training does not pay—whether temporary secretaries or senior executives. Those wanting to sample a truly wide range of program offerings, however, may need to look elsewhere.

(*Note*: The Mac GE line is commonly used for desktop publishing and other complex applications. The ¡Mac, introduced in 1998, is used for basic applications such as word processing and easy Internet connections.)

Figure 5.8 Mac OS screen. "HD" stands for "hard disk." The window shows what's on the hard disk. The System folder holds system software and related files; the Aplications folder holds applications software and related files. Suitcases hold different fonts. The Laser Jet folder holds the printer driver.

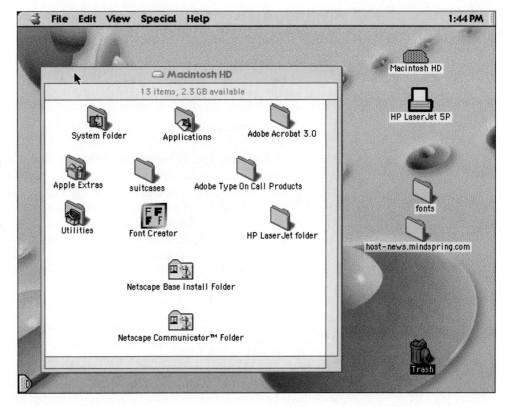

NetWare

As we mentioned (✔ p. 5.8), a network needs network operating system (NOS) software to provide it with multiuser, multitasking capabilities. The operating system facilitates communications, resource sharing, and security, thereby providing the basic framework of the LAN. The NOS consists of modules that are distributed throughout the LAN environment. Some NOS modules reside in servers, while others reside in the clients. The client is generally a hardware device or a microcomputer hooked up to the network. The server (✔ p. 1.15) is a computer that contains large amounts of memory, so that multiple clients can share the server's resources while still performing certain functions independently. Servers also manage the data.

Developed by Novell during the 1980s, *NetWare* has been the most popular operating system for orchestrating microcomputer-based LANs throughout a company or campus. NetWare 5.0 was released in 1998.

Can you continue to use, say, MS-DOS on your office personal computer while it is hooked up to a LAN running NetWare? Indeed you can. NetWare provides a shell around your own operating system. If you want to work "off network" ("stand-alone"), you run the microcomputer's regular operating system—DOS, OS/2, Mac OS, UNIX, or Windows. If you want to work "on network," you respond to another prompt and type in whatever password will admit you to the network.

5.4 The Future: Is the Web Changing Everything?

KEY QUESTION **What is a network computer, and how does it involve the Internet and Java?**

Nothing stands still. The major system software developers toil on the versions to come, works in progress to which they have given fanciful code names such as Memphis and Cyberdog. However, almost without warning, the Internet and the World Wide Web have dramatically changed the picture.

Today personal computing is still complicated because of the existence of conflicting standards. Could it be different tomorrow, as more and more people join the trend toward networked computers and access to the World Wide Web?

As we've seen, there are different hardware and software standards, or platforms. Developers of applications software, such as word processors or database managers, need to make different versions to run on different platforms. Networking complicates things even further. Text, photos, sound files, video, and other kinds of data come in so many different formats that it's difficult to maintain the software needed to use them.

Today microcomputer users who wish to access online data sources must provide not only their own computer, modem, and communications software but also their own operating system software and applications software. *(See Figure 5.9, top.)*

Could this change in the future?

Today you are responsible for making sure that your computer system will be compatible with others you have to deal with. For instance, if a Macintosh user sends you a file, it's up to you to find out how to translate the file so that it will work on your PC. What if the responsibility for ensuring compatibility between different systems were left to online service providers?

In this future model, you would use your Web software to access the World Wide Web and take advantage of applications software anywhere on the network. *(See Figure 5.9, bottom.)* Whatever operating system ran on your computer would not matter. Applications software would become nearly disposable: You would download applications software and pay a few cents or a few dollars for each use. If you decided to use particular software frequently, you could store it on your own computer. However, you wouldn't have to worry about buying the right software, since it would be available online whenever you needed it.

Bloatware or the Network Computer?

Bloatware is a colloquial name for software that is so crowded (bloated) with features that it requires a powerful microprocessor and enormous amounts of main memory and hard-disk storage capacity in order to run efficiently. In other words, the software application suffers from "featuritis." Bloatware, of course, fuels the movement toward upgrading, in which users must buy more and more powerful hardware to support the software.

Against this, among other things, engineers have proposed the idea of the "network computer" or "hollow PC." In this approach—which not everyone accepts—the expensive PCs with muscular microprocessors and operating systems would be replaced by network computers costing perhaps $500 or less. Also

Figure 5.9 Online personal computing—today and tomorrow. *(Top)* Today users provide their own operating system software and their own applications software and are usually responsible for installing it on their micro-computers. They are also responsible for any upgrades of hardware and software. Data can be input or downloaded from online sources. *(Bottom)* Tomorrow, according to this model, users would not have to worry about operating systems or even about having to acquire and install (and upgrade) their own applications software. Using a universal browser, they could download not only data but also different kinds of applications software from online sources.

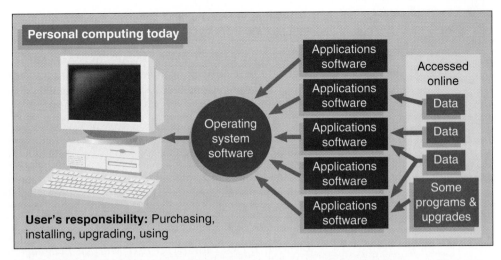

Personal computing today

Applications software

Applications software

Operating system software

Applications software

Applications software

Applications software

Accessed online

Data

Data

Data

Some programs & upgrades

User's responsibility: Purchasing, installing, upgrading, using

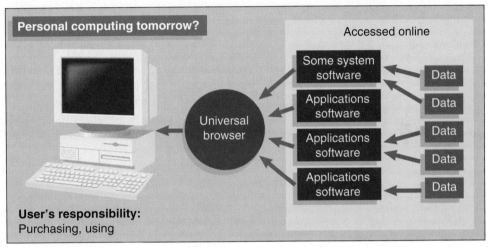

Personal computing tomorrow?

Some system software

Applications software

Universal browser

Applications software

Applications software

Accessed online

Data

Data

Data

Data

Data

User's responsibility: Purchasing, using

known as the *Internet PC,* the *network computer (NC)* would theoretically be a "hollowed-out" computer, perhaps without even a hard disk, serving as a mere terminal or entry point to the online universe. The computer thus becomes a peripheral to the Internet, and remote servers would supply most software, processing, and information needs.

This concept of the stripped-down computer is also referred to as a *thin client.* The thin-client strategy is to replace existing desktop personal computers with a new generation of ultracheap computers. Thin clients are being developed by a consortium of, among others, IBM, Sun Microsystems, Netscape Communications, and Apple Computer according to a standard called the *NC Reference Profile.* Microsoft and Intel are sticking with their own versions of network PCs. Indeed, Microsoft has bought WebTV Networks with the plan of turning the WebTV (✔ p. 1.24) into more than a home entertainment gadget by developing NT servers for this device.

Some people in business and industry applaud the trend toward thin clients; critics, however, have raised such questions as the following:

- *Aren't high-speed connections required?* Even users equipped with the fastest modems would find downloading even small programs (applets) very time-consuming. Doesn't the network computer ultimately depend on faster connections than are possible with the standard telephone lines and modems now in place?

■ *Would an NC be reliable?* What if the communications channels go down? What if they're busy?

■ *Would users go for it?* Would computer users really prefer scaled-down generic software that must be retrieved from the Internet each time it is used? Would a pay-per-use system tied to the Internet really be cheaper in the long run?

The Jolt from Java

Thin clients will use new programming languages such as Java to download software code as needed and then execute it. What is Java? The arrival of Java in 1995 is a tale told in three acts:

■ *Act I—the creation of HTML:* Perfected by researcher Tim Berners-Lee in Geneva, *HTML,* for *HyperText Markup Language,* lets people create graphical onscreen documents for the Internet that can easily be linked by words and pictures to other documents. Hypertext, which will be covered in more detail in Chapter 8, has been used to link documents on stand-alone personal computers. What is noteworthy about HTML is that it links documents wherever they are stored, including anywhere on the sprawling universe of the Internet.

Berners-Lee distributed HTML standards around the world via the Internet for free, and soon other researchers were creating and linking HTML documents. Quickly it became apparent that HTML documents were an ideal medium for publishing and annotating scientific papers, research materials, reference works, and the like. These rich HTML documents collectively became a distinct domain within the Internet, a realm we now call the World Wide Web.

■ *Act II—the appearance of Web browsers:* Very soon millions of HTML documents had appeared on the Web, but there was no easy way to locate them and view them. In 1993, Marc Andreeson and colleagues at the University of Illinois's National Center for Supercomputer Applications created the first Web browser software called *Mosaic.* The first version was for Sun workstations; later versions were developed for Macintoshes and Windows PCs. Andreeson went on to join James Clark in founding *Netscape,* which makes a popular Web browser called *Netscape Navigator.* (Netscape has since been purchased by AOL, America Online.)

As both the number of Web sites and the number of viewers using browsers increased, people began to wish that Web pages would do more than just sit there. Java was one solution to this problem.

■ *Act III—enter Java:* Ace programmer James Gosling wrote Java for Sun Microsystems as part of an unsuccessful effort to develop equipment for interactive television. Java is a programming language that enables a Web page to deliver, along with the visual content, tiny application programs called *applets* (mini-applications) that, when downloaded, can make Web pages interactive.

"Applets," says one report, "can create dancing advertising, self-updating scoreboards, moving stock ticker marquees, even animated cartoons. . . . Think of Java applets as just-in-time software that you can simply throw away after each use. If you want to look at the same Web page again, the Internet will furnish a fresh copy of both the information and the applet."[1]

The significance of Java is that Sun wrote versions of it to run on all the major computers and then gave them away, so that anyone wanting to use applets to create "active content" (such as animated weather maps) on Web sites could use them. The result was a whole new style of computing built around the Internet.

Web Sites of Possible Interest

http://www.microsoft.com/win95/
http://www.microsoft.com/win98/
http://www.microsoft.com/ntworkstation/
http://www.microsoft.com/ntserver/
http://www.linux.org
http://www.redhat.com
http://www.apple.com
http://www.ibm.com
http://www.novell.com

Most people buy computers for what they can do—usually that means the applications they can run. Applications like Adobe PhotoShop and QuarkXpress (mainstays of the publishing industry) will probably continue to run better on the Mac. And people who were trained to use these applications on the Mac will continue to prefer the Mac to run them. Artists who have added multiple SCSI disks to their systems to deal with their [many] 80-MB PhotoShop files really don't want to try the same trick with Windows 9x. It's still not as easy on Windows 9x.

UNIX on the desktop these days means mostly high-end workstations or systems running either Linux or some other free UNIX-alike (like FreeBSD). High-end workstation users fit into the same category as Mac users: They have their applications . . . and have little incentive to switch right now.

At the low end, many users are trying Linux. They're finding what you'd expect: It's extremely flexible, it doesn't crash easily, it isn't a resource hog.

. . . If you believe that the Wintel [Windows/Intel] monopoly is a bad idea, then Java is a godsend—it'll run on anything, anywhere.

Switching horses entirely off Windows isn't something a lot of people are contemplating. Analyst groups like IDC say that the Mac is losing desktop market share and will continue to lose it. Linux is growing in share, but corporations are still nervous about running what they perceive as unsupported software (though many Linux vendors, as well as the Linux community, offer support).

And Windows NT is gaining in mindshare . . .

Finally, Linux won't run Microsoft Office . . . Remember: It comes back to applications, and Linux desktop applications—even the good ones like Star Office and ApplixWare—still don't have the familiarity and, more important, the near universality of applications like Microsoft Office. Even though Applix-Ware can read most Office file formats, users who have trained on Office will need to be retrained . . . Plus, these free UNIX-alikes still look like UNIX . . .

In short, the future of UNIX and the Macintosh on the desktop is a niche role, performing one or two critical functions. It's not about the quality of the OSs; in many ways, these OSs are better than Windows. It's about perception; it's about availability of applications; and it's about universality—sometimes it's just easier to run the same software as everybody else.

Reasons to Switch to Another OS

✔ Potentially more stable
✔ Potentially easier to use
✔ Potentially less expensive to run
✔ Potentially more secure

Photography

HOLD IT! *Click!*

Or will the *click* come from a mouse button rather than from a camera shutter? Photography is undergoing radical changes, moving from a film, or chemical-based, medium to a digital one.

Filmless digital cameras, which record images on memory chips, are fast gaining in popularity among news organizations, such as Associated Press photographers covering the Super Bowl. "The cameras really . . . perform quite spectacularly," says the AP's executive photo editor.[a]

The Associated Press, however, can afford top-of-the-line cameras. Many professional photographers have continued to stick with film, since, as one report suggests, "the only digital cameras that come close to film's quality cost as much as a new car."[b] Affordable filmless cameras can sometimes produce somewhat grainy images, and so their initial uses have been for jobs requiring the quick recording or relaying of information. Thus, they have been well received by insurance investigators, real-estate brokers, advertising agencies, aircraft-maintenance shops, and designers of World Wide Web home pages on the Internet. Still, as more and more imaging chips are produced by standard chip-making methods, quality should improve and camera prices fall.

Digital photography has been described by technology writer Stephen Manes as being "like Polaroid photography with a Xerox copier and fax machine attached."[c] With a digital camera, you don't need to visit a photofinisher. Instead, right after you take the picture, as Manes says, "you can transmit your photos of earthquake damage to your insurance agent, incorporate your friends' leering mugs into your home page for all the world to laugh at, or use retouching software and your ink-jet printer to print hundreds of copies of a faked picture proving you are a personal friend of Oprah's."

The ability to use a scanner to input conventional photos into computers has existed for some time. Photo developers can then take the scanned photos and put them on a flexible disk or CD-ROM. With a digital camera, however, photographers can simply transfer the images, via a cable, directly into a Macintosh or Windows-based microcomputer. They can then use imaging software to touch up, reconstruct, stretch, squeeze, distort, or completely alter the pictures.

The software also allows photographers to insert photos into greeting cards or into digital "picture postcards" that can be sent to someone via e-mail. In addition, they can plug the digital camera directly into a television set to provide impromptu slide shows. If you have your portrait taken at a professional photographers, with the right digital equipment the proofs can be made available immediately on a computer screen so additional poses can be shot if necessary. Though still in their infancy, desktop photography and digital imaging are clearly giving photographers many new tools. Kodak and Intel have teamed up in a $150 million marketing campaign to make it easier for consumers to put photos online.[d,e]

"Everything—the popularity of digital cameras, cheaper prices for scanners, the popularity of color printers and the Internet, and low-cost photo-editing software—point to a boom in [the photography] market," says the vice president of Life Picture Inc., developer of photo-editing products.[f]

WHAT IT IS
WHAT IT DOES   WHY IT IS IMPORTANT

antivirus software (KQ 5.2, p. 5.9) Software utility that scans hard disks, diskettes, and memory to detect viruses; some antivirus utilities also destroy viruses.

Computer users must find out what kind of antivirus software to install on their systems for protection against damage and shutdown.

applications software (KQ 5.1, p. 5.3) Software that performs useful tasks for the user.

Applications software such as word processing, spreadsheet, database manager, graphics, and communications packages provide convenient tools for increasing people's productivity.

backup utility (KQ 5.2, p. 5.8)   Operating system utility that makes a duplicate copy of contents of a disk.

Backing up is an essential function; users should back up all their work so that they don't lose it if the original disks are destroyed.

BIOS (basic input/output system) (KQ 5.2, p. 5.5)   Part of the operating system that manages the essential peripherals such as the keyboard, screen, disk drives, and parallel and serial ports. It also manages some internal services such as time and date.

This is the part of the operating system that tests the computer upon booting via an autostart program and loads the OS into memory.

data compression utility (KQ 5.2, p. 5.9)   Software utility that removes redundant elements, gaps, and unnecessary data from computer files so that less space is required to store and transmit data.

Many of today's files, with graphics, sound, and video, require huge amounts of storage space; data compression utilities allow users to reduce the space required.

data recovery utility (KQ 5.2, p. 5.8) System software utility used to restore data that has been physically damaged or corrupted on disk or tape.

Disks and tapes can be damaged by viruses, bad software, hardware failure, and power fluctuations that occur while data is being written/recorded.

defraggers (KQ 5.2, p. 5.12)   Utility programs that rearrange the data on a disk so that the data units of each file are repositioned together in one location on the disk.

Fragmentation causes the computer to run more slowly than if all the data in a file were stored together in one location. Defraggers help fix this problem.

DOS (disk operating system) (KQ 5.3, p. 5.15)   Older command-driven microcomputer operating system that runs primarily on IBM and IBM-compatible microcomputers.

DOS used to be the most common microcomputer operating system. It is still used on many microcomputers, although it is being replaced by OSs with graphical user interfaces.

drivers (KQ 5.2, p. 5.8)   Components of system software; programs that control specific peripheral devices.

Drivers are needed so that the computer's operating system can recognize and run peripheral hardware.

graphical user interface (GUI) (KQ 5.2, p. 5.13) User interface that uses images to represent options. Some of these images take the form of icons, small pictorial figures that represent tasks, functions, and programs.

GUIs are easier to use than command-driven interfaces and menu-driven interfaces; they permit liberal use of the mouse as a pointing device to move the cursor to a particular icon or place on the display screen. The function represented by the icon can be activated by pressing (clicking) buttons on the mouse.

language translator (KQ 5.2, p. 5.13) System software that translates a program written in a computer language (such as C++) into the language (machine language) that the computer can understand.

Without language translators, software programmers would have to write all programs in machine language (0s and 1s), which is difficult to work with.

Linux (KQ 5.3, p. 5.20) Freeware version of UNIX.

Linux can be useful to PC users who have to maintain a Web server or a network server.

Mac OS (KQ 5.3, p. 5.20) Formerly called Macintosh Operating System, system software for the Macintosh.

Although Macs are not as common as PCs, many people believe they are easier to use. Macs are often used for graphics and desktop publishing.

multiprocessing (KQ 5.2, p. 5.7) Operating system software feature that allows two or more computers or processors linked together to perform work simultaneously. (Whereas *concurrently* means "at almost the same time," *simultaneously* means "at precisely the same time.")

Multiprocessing is faster than multitasking and time-sharing. In microcomputers, specialized microprocessors called *coprocessors* employ multiprocessing for specialized tasks such as creating display-screen graphics and performing high-speed mathematical calculations.

multiprogramming (KQ 5.2, p. 5.6) Operating system software feature that allows the execution of two or more programs on a *multiuser* system. Program execution occurs concurrently, not simultaneously.

See *multitasking.*

multitasking (KQ 5.2, p. 5.6) Operating system software feature that allows the execution of two or more programs concurrently on a single-user system.

Allows the computer to rapidly switch back and forth among different tasks. The user is generally unaware of the switching process and is able to use more than one application program at the same time.

operating system (OS) (KQ 5.2, p. 5.4) Principal piece of system software in any computer system; consists of the master set of programs that manage the basic operations of the computer. The operating system remains in main memory until the computer is turned off.

These programs act as an interface between the user and the computer; for instance, they run and store other programs and store and process data. The operating system allows users to concentrate on their own tasks or applications rather than on the complexities of managing the computer.

Operating System 2 (OS/2) (KQ 5.3, p. 5.18) PC operating system designed by IBM, less popular than Windows 9x.

Like Windows 95, OS/2 does not require DOS to run underneath it, and it has an integrated GUI. OS/2 can also run most DOS, Windows, and OS/2 applications programs simultaneously, which means users don't have to throw out their old applications to take advantage of new features. OS/2 is not used on as many microcomputers as Windows, for which many more applications programs have been written.

platform (KQ 5.3, p. 5.14) The particular hardware or software standard on which a computer system is based—for example, an IBM platform or a Macintosh platform.

Users need to be aware that, without special arrangements or software, different platforms are not compatible.

supervisor (KQ 5.2, p. 5.4) Central component of the operating system. It resides in main memory while the computer is on and directs other programs to perform tasks to support applications programs.

Were it not for the supervisor program, users would have to stop one task—for example, writing—and wait for another task to be completed—for example, printing a document.

system software (KQ 5.1, p. 5.3) Programs that start up the computer and function as the principal coordinator of all hardware components and applications software programs.

Applications software cannot run without system software. System software has three components: the operating system, utilities, and language translators.

time-sharing (KQ 5.2, p. 5.6) Operations system software feature whereby a single large computer processes the tasks of several users at different stations in round-robin fashion.

Time-sharing and multitasking differ slightly. With time-sharing, the computer spends a fixed amount of time with each program before going on to the next one. With multitasking the computer works on each program until it reaches a logical stopping point—for example, until it has to wait for more data to be input.

UNIX (KQ 5.3, p. 5.19) Operating system originally developed by AT&T for multiple users, with built-in networking capability, the ability to run multiple tasks at one time, and versions that can run on all kinds of computers.

Because it can run with relatively simple modifications on many different kinds of computers, from micros to minis to mainframes, UNIX is said to be a "portable" operating system. UNIX is used mainly by large corporations and banks, for everything from designing airplane parts to currency trading. The Internet is based on the UNIX OS.

user interface (KQ 5.2, p. 5.13) Part of the operating system (or operating environment) that allows users to communicate, or interact, with it. There are three types of user interfaces: command-driven, menu-driven, and graphical. The last type is easiest to use.

Without user interfaces, no one could use a computer system.

utility programs (KQ 5.2, p. 5.8) System software component generally used to support, enhance, or expand existing programs in a computer system.

System software has many utility programs built in. Other external utility programs are available separately. Examples of utilities are data recovery, backup, virus protection, data compression/decompression, and defragmentation.

windows (KQ 5.2, p. 5.13) Feature of graphical user interfaces such that the display screen is divided into sections. Each window is dedicated to a specific purpose.

Using this feature, an operating system (or operating environment) can display several windows on a computer screen, each showing a different output, such as a word processing document, a spreadsheet, and graphics.

Windows 3.x (KQ 5.3, p. 5.15) Operating environment from Microsoft that places a GUI shell around the MS-DOS/PC-DOS operating system.

The Windows operating environment made DOS easier to use; far more applications have been written for Windows than for DOS alone.

Windows 95/98 (KQ 5.3, p. 5.16) Successor to Windows 3.x; true PC-compatible operating system, with an integrated GUI.

Windows has become the most common system software used on microcomputers.

Windows NT (New Technology) (KQ 5.3, p. 5.18) Operating system intended to support large networks of computers and high-end workstations.

Microsoft may eventually merge Windows 95/98 and Windows NT into one powerful operating system for microcomputers.

1. Fill in the following blanks:

   a. _____ _____ is a collection of related programs designed to perform a specific task for the user.

   b. A(n) _____ _____ is software that translates a program written by a programmer into machine language.

   c. _____ is the concurrent execution of different users' programs.

   d. _____ _____ utilities remove redundant elements, gaps, and unnecessary data from a computer's storage space.

   e. _____ is the round-robin processing of programs for several users.

2. Label each of the following statements as either true (T) or false (F).

   _____ A program that can defragment a disk is referred to as a defragger.

   _____ The operating system resides in RAM at all times when your computer is on.

   _____ System software starts up the computer and functions as the principal co-ordinator of all hardware components.

   _____ UNIX is the oldest operating system in use today.

   _____ Whereas Windows NT is basically consumer-oriented, Windows 9x is business-oriented.

3. Define each of the following:
   a. booting
   b. GUI
   c. platform
   d. BIOS
   e. command-driven

4. List five microcomputer operating systems.

   a. _____

   b. _____

   c. _____

   d. _____

   e. _____

5. Define each of the following operating system functions:
   a. multitasking
   b. multiprogramming
   c. time-sharing
   d. multiprocessing

6. Systems software comprises a large number of instructions that can be grouped into the following basic parts:

   a. _____

   b. _____

   c. _____

7. Describe each of the following types of utility programs:
   a. backup
   b. data recovery
   c. virus protection
   d. data compression
   e. defragmentation

8. List four peripherals managed by the BIOS portion of an operating system.

   a. _____

   b. _____

   c. _____

   d. _____

9. The operating system controls several functions including:

   a. _____

   b. _____

   c. _____

10. Describe each of the following in a few sentences:
    a. Windows 9x
    b. Windows 2000
    c. UNIX

IN YOUR OWN WORDS

1. Answer each of the Key Questions that appear at the beginning of this chapter.

2. What happens when you boot your computer?

3. Why can't you run your computer without system software?

4. Why is multitasking useful?

5. What is a network computer?

6. What is an operating system and how is it loaded into memory?

7. What is a device driver?

8. What is a utility program?

9. What is antivirus software used for?

10. What is the significance of Java?

KNOWLEDGE IN ACTION

1. **Evaluating Your System Software.** Determine what system software is used on the computers in the computer lab at school. If necessary, ask your instructor or lab assistant. Once you've identified the name and version of the operating system, use the system software's reference manual or other library resources to answer the following questions: (a) What is the name and version of the system software? (b) Is it a command-driven interface or a GUI interface? (c) Does the system software support multitasking? (d) Do you need a password before you can use the computers in your lab?

2. **Exploring Java.** Reportedly, Sun Microsystem's Scott McNealy is dedicating huge sums of money to get Java technology into as many appliances and products as possible. Already, Java technology is used in cars, smart cards, and key chains. To find out more about Java, visit the Java Home page at *http://java.sun.com*. Answer the following questions: (a) Click the "Java in the Real World" hyperlink and then select five examples of Java technology in action that interest you. Describe each of your chosen examples in a few sentences. (b) Click the "Applets" link and then locate the "Other Applets" section. Execute a few of the applets in this category. Write down the name of the applets you executed and what each did. (c) Click the "Employment" link and then locate the list of employment categories. Click an employment category link that interests you. Write down a list of three jobs that sound interesting.

Self-Test Exercises: Answers: 1a. applications software 1b. language translator 1c. multiprogramming 1d. data compression 1e. time-sharing 2. T, T, T, T, F 3a. The term *booting* refers to the process of loading parts of the operating system into a computer's main memory, usually from hard disk. This loading is accomplished by a program (called the *bootstrap loader* or *boot routine*) stored permanently in the computer's electronic circuitry. When you turn on ("power up") the machine, the program performs an automatic *power-on self-test (POST)*, which usually tests RAM, the keyboard, and the disk drives. If the tests are successful, the computer boots itself. 3b. User interface that uses images to represent options. Some of these images take the form of icons, small pictorial figures that represent tasks, functions, and programs. 3c. *Platform refers* to the type of computer architecture, or family; the PC and the Apple Macintosh are two common platforms. For the most part, software created for one type of platform will not run, without special arrangements, on other platforms. 3d. *BIOS* refers to the *basic input/output system,* which is part of the operating system. It manages the essential peripherals and some internal activities, such as time and date. It also is the part of the operating system that tests the computer when you power up. 3e. With a command-driven interface, the user must type in strings of characters to issue commands; the mouse cannot be used. 4. DOS/Windows 3.x, Windows 9x, Windows NT, OS/2 Warp, UNIX, Linux, Mac OS 5a. Operating system software feature that allows the execution of two or more programs concurrently on a single-user system. 5b. Operating system software feature that allows the execution of two or more programs on a *multiuser system.* Program execution occurs concurrently, not simultaneously. 5c. Operations system software feature whereby a single large computer processes the tasks of several users at different stations in round-robin fashion. 5d. Operating system software feature that allows two or more computers or processors linked together to perform work simultaneously. (Whereas *concurrently* means "at almost the same time," *simultaneously* means "at precisely the same time.") 6. operating system, utilities, language translators 7a. Backup is a duplicate (a copy) of data and programs. 7b. Data recovery involves restoring data that has been physically damaged or corrupted. 7c. Virus protection involves using antivirus software to scan hard disks, diskettes, and memory to detect viruses. 7d. Data compression utilities remove redundant elements, gaps, and unnecessary data from a computer's storage space so that fewer bits are required to store or transmit data. 7e. When a file is stored on a disk, the computer tries to put the elements of data next to one another. However, this is not always possible because previously stored data may be occupying locations that prevent this. Then, after the user has saved and deleted many files, there remain many scattered areas of stored data that are too small

to be used efficiently. This is called *fragmentation.* It causes the computer to run slower than if all the data in a file were stored together in one location. Utility programs called *defraggers* are available to *defragment* the disk, thus rearranging the data so that the data units of each file are repositioned together (contiguously) in one location on the disk. 8. keyboard, screen, disk drives, parallel and serial port devices 9. managing programs and data, handling input and output, coordinating some network communications functions, managing memory. 10. *Answers will vary.*

APPLICATIONS SOFTWARE:

The User's Tools

Getting the computer and the peripherals—the hardware—is only the beginning. You may have agonized over your hardware purchase for months, but it's your choice of software that will really determine the utility—or uselessness—of your new PC.

There are thousands of programs to choose from—games alone number more than 2500—and some of them can make your life far easier and more productive than you might imagine. But others, unfortunately, don't even begin to live up to the magic promotional phrase "ease of use." Even software programs advertised as "user friendly" are too complex for many people. However, that will no doubt change. Hardware and software manufacturers know that they will achieve growth and profits only by making their products as easy to use as possible.

For you, however, there's no point in waiting. By setting your mind to learning software, you can begin to extend the range of your productivity. And when the software itself becomes better, so will you.

6.1 Applications Software Tools

KEY QUESTION What are the five basic categories of applications software?

Computer software has become a multibillion-dollar industry. More than a thousand companies have entered the applications software industry, and they have developed a wide variety of products. Applications software can be acquired directly from a software manufacturer or from the growing number of businesses that specialize in the sale and support of microcomputer hardware and software. Most independent and computer chain stores devote a substantial amount of shelf space to applications software programs; some businesses specialize in selling only software.

If you can't find off-the-shelf software to meet your needs, you can develop your own. If you don't know how to do it yourself, you can have the computer professionals within your own organization develop the software, or you can hire outside consultants to do it. Unfortunately, hiring a professional to write software for you can easily cost ten times more than off-the-shelf software.

Basically, there are four categories of applications software. *(See Figure 6.1.)* *Basic productivity software* consists of programs found in most offices and probably on all campuses, on personal computers and on larger computer systems. Most of the common applications software packages used today are productivity tools. *Business and specialty software,* often called *vertical market software,* consists of programs developed for a specific business or industry. Whatever your occupation, you will probably find it also has specialty software tools available to it. This is true whether your career is dairy farmer, building contractor, police officer, dance choreographer, or chef.

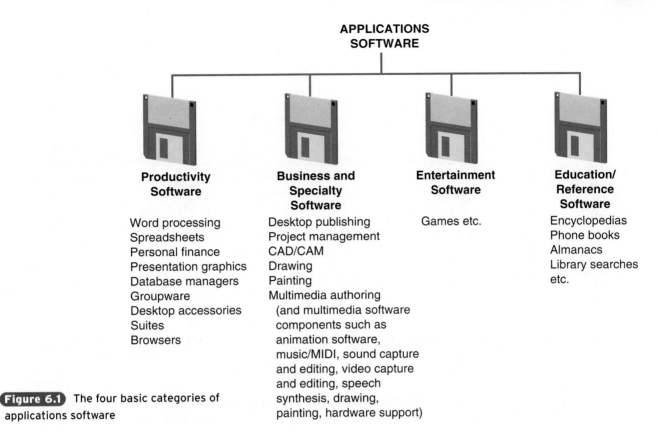

Figure 6.1 The four basic categories of applications software

Entertainment software consists of action and adventure games that can be played at home through a television set or personal computer or in an entertainment arcade of the sort found in shopping malls. *Education and reference software* is used to educate and entertain. Because of the popularity of videogames, many educational software companies have been blending educational content with some of the features popular in games. Computers alone won't boost academic performance, but they can have a positive effect on student achievement in all major subject areas, preschool through college. In addition to educational software, library search and reference software has become popular. For instance, there are CD-ROMs with encyclopedias, phone books, voter lists, mailing lists, maps, home-remodeling how-to information, and reproductions of famous art.

Many people will buy an applications software program just because it was recommended by a friend. They do not bother to evaluate whether the program offers all the features and processing capabilities necessary to meet their needs. While it's much easier in the short run to simply take the friend's recommendation, in the long run a lot of extra time and money may be spent. Knowing what software is available—and how to evaluate it—is vital to satisfy processing requirements.

■ *Productivity tools:* These are the programs found in most offices and probably all campuses. Their purpose is simply to make users more productive when performing general tasks. Examples are word processing, spreadsheet, personal finance, presentation graphics, database management, group collaboration, desktop and personal information management, integrated, and web browsing applications.

It may still be possible to work in an office in some countries without knowing any of these programs. However, that won't be the case in the 21st century.

■ *Specialty tools:* Knowledge of specialized programs is a necessity in some occupations and businesses (as desktop publishing is for people in publications work). You should have at least a nodding acquaintance with them because they are general enough to be used in many vocations and professions. Many specialty software tools exist today. Examples include desktop-publishing, project management, computer-aided design and manufacturing (CAD/CAM), drawing and painting, and multimedia authoring software.

Don't worry if you don't know all these terms; you will by the end of the chapter. However, before we discuss the different types of productivity and specialty software tools, we need to go over some of the features common to most kinds of applications software packages.

6.2 Common Features of Applications Software

KEY QUESTION **What features are common to most applications software?**

Although applications software packages differ in their use of specific commands and functions, most of them have some features in common:

abcl

↑

Insertion point
(blinking bar)

■ *Insertion point:* The **insertion point** *(left)* is the movable symbol on the display screen that shows you where you may enter data next. You can move the insertion point around using either the keyboard's directional arrow keys (✔ p. 3.5) or by clicking with the mouse.

■ *Scrolling:* **Scrolling** *(right)* is the activity of moving quickly upward or downward through the text or other screen display. A standard computer screen displays only 20–22 lines of standard-size text. Of course, most documents are longer than that. Using the directional arrow keys or a mouse, you can move (scroll) through the display screen and into the text above and below it.

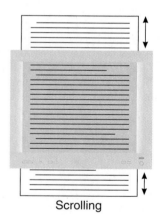

Scrolling

Windows

■ *Windows:* As we mentioned in the last chapter in the section on GUIs (✔ p. 5.13), a **window** is a rectangular section of the display screen with a title bar on top. Each window may show a different display, such as a word processing document in one and a spreadsheet in another.

■ *Menu bar:* A **menu bar** is a row of menu options displayed across the top or the bottom of the screen. (Recall that a menu is a list of command options, or choices [✔ p. 5.13].)

Menu bar

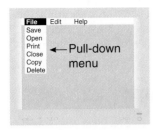

← Pull-down menu

Rocky, the assistant

Icons

Pull-down menu: A **pull-down menu** *(left)* is a list of command options, or choices, that is "pulled down" out of the menu bar. Pull-down menus can be opened by keystroke commands or by "clicking" (pressing) the mouse button while pointing to the title in the menu bar and then dragging the mouse pointer down. Some menus "pop up" from the menu bar and so are called **pop-up menus.**

Help menu and screens: A **Help menu** *(right)* offers a choice of Help screens, specific displayed explanations of how to perform various tasks, such as printing out a document. Having a set of Help screens is like having a built-in electronic instruction manual. Help features also include searchable topic indexes and online glossaries.

Help may also be available in the form of an *assistant.* In this case, the applications program leads you through a series of questions to determine exactly what you need help with. Then it leads you through the steps to accomplish your objective. The assistant appears as an icon or cartoon character you click on *(left).*

Buttons: In a graphical interface, **buttons** *(right)* are used to represent file names and the popular features and functions.

Button on Toolbar

Buttons are usually identified by a small graphic, called an **icon** *(left).* Most applications use *toolbars* to group related buttons.

Toolbars: A **toolbar** is a row of on-screen buttons, usually appearing immediately below the menu bar, used to activate a variety of functions of the applications program. Toolbars can often be customized and moved around on the screen.

Dialog box: A **dialog box** *(right)* is a box that appears on the screen. It is used to collect information from the user and to display helpful messages.

Default values: **Default values** are the standard settings employed by the computer when the user does not specify an alternative. For example, unless you specify particular margin widths in your page setup, the word processing program will use the manufacturer's default values.

Macros: A **macro** is a feature that allows you to use a single keystroke, command, or toolbar button to automatically issue a predetermined series of commands. Thus, you can consolidate several keystrokes or menu selections into only one or two keystrokes. Although many people have no need for macros, you will find them quite useful if you need to continually repeat complicated patterns of keystrokes.

macro → miniprograms + set of instructions that are repeated over and over. (used for repetitive tasks)

OLE: Many software applications have the ability to integrate applications using **OLE (object linking and embedding).** This feature enables you to embed an object created using one application (such as graphics) into another application (such as word processing). Changes made to the embedded object affect only the document that contains it. Objects can also be linked. In this case, changes made to the object are automatically made in all the linked documents that contain it. Thus OLE facilitates the sharing and manipulating of information. An object may be a document, worksheet, chart, picture, or even a sound recording.

OLE

Clipboard — hidden area where programs are placed.

■ *Clipboard:* Many applications software programs allow you to copy an item from one document and then paste it into another document or application—or copy an item and place the copy in another part of the same document. The **Clipboard** is the area where the copy is held before it is pasted. (The Clipboard can hold only one item at a time.)

■ *Tutorials and documentation:* How are you going to learn a given software program? Most commercial packages come with tutorials. A **tutorial** is an instruction book or program that takes you through a prescribed series of steps to help you learn the product.

Tutorials must be contrasted with documentation. **Documentation** is a user manual or reference manual that is a narrative and graphical description of a program. Documentation may be instructional, but features and functions are usually grouped by category for reference purposes. For example, in word processing documentation, all cut-and-paste features are grouped together so that you can easily look them up if you have forgotten how to perform them. Documentation may come in booklet form or on diskette or CD-ROM; it may also be available online from the manufacturer.

Compatibility Issues: What Goes with What?

Compatibility: pick software then hardware. + software that can be run on hardware system.

As we mentioned in the last chapter (✔ p. 5.13), all system software and applications software must be turned into machine language for execution by the computer. Different computer families use different machine language coding. Thus each applications software program must be written to "talk" to the system software and its language translator. Applications software written, for example, for an IBM PC will not—without conversion—run on a Macintosh. This is why it's important to determine your applications software needs first—to determine what you want the computer to do for you—and then to select compatible hardware and system software. In a situation where you will need to transfer files among different platforms, you will have to consider conversion options.

Some experts predict that, sometime soon, compatibility will no longer be an issue, as the computer industry works toward universal standards and compatibility. However, that time has not yet come.

Now that we have taken a look at some of the features shared by different types of applications software packages, let's briefly examine the most common types of productivity software tools. After that, we'll consider some common specialty tools.

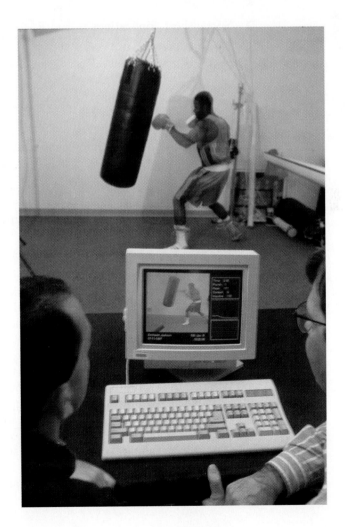

Pummeling the smartest punching bag on earth, Olympic boxer Kerry Deshawn Jackson works out at the U.S. Olympic Training Center. The bag is outfitted with a censor designed to gauge the force of the punches. The data is graphed on a computer.

6.3 Productivity Software Tools

KEY QUESTION **What are several productivity software tools?**

Let's get right to the point: What do most people use software for? The answer hasn't changed in a decade. If you don't count games, by far the most popular applications are (1) word processing and (2) spreadsheets, according to the Software Publishers Association. Moreover, studies show that most people use only a few basic features of these programs, and they use them for rather simple tasks. For example, most documents produced with word processing software are one-page letters, memos, or simple reports. And most of the time people use spreadsheets simply to add up numbers.

This is important information. If you are this type of user, you may have no more need for fancy software and hardware than an ordinary commuter has for an expensive Italian race car. However, you may need to become a "power user," learning all the software features available, in order to keep ahead in your career. Moreover, in this age of multimedia, you may wish to do far more than current software and hardware allow, in which case you need to be continually learning what computing and communications can do for you.

Let us now look at the various types and uses of productivity software for:

- Word processing

- Spreadsheet applications

- Personal finance

- Presentation graphics

- Database management

- Group collaboration

- Desktop and personal information management

- Integrated applications

- Web browsing

(Note: We discuss communications software in Chapters 7 and 8.)

Word Processing Software

One of the first typewriter users was Mark Twain. However, the typewriter, that long-lived machine, has gone to its reward. Indeed, if you have a manual typewriter, getting it repaired is almost as difficult as finding a blacksmith. What, then, is the alternative? Word processing.

Word processing software allows you to use computers to create, edit, store, and print documents. You can easily insert, delete, and move words, sentences, and paragraphs—without ever using an eraser. Word processing programs also offer a number of features for "dressing up" documents with variable margins, type sizes, and styles. The user can do all these manipulations on screen, in "wysiwyg" fashion, before printing out hardcopy. (*Wysiwyg* stands for "what you see is what you get," meaning that the screen displays documents exactly as they will look when printed.)

Word processing software also offers additional features, such as spelling checkers, as we shall describe.

Creating Documents

Creating a document means entering text, using the keyboard. As you type, word wrap automatically continues text on the next line when you reach the right margin. That is, the text "wraps around" to the next line.

Editing Documents

Editing is the act of making alterations in the content of your document. Some features of editing are *insert and delete; undelete; search and replace; cut, copy, and paste; spelling checker; grammar checker;* and *thesaurus.*

- *Insert and delete: Inserting* is the act of adding to the document. You simply place the cursor wherever you want to add text and start typing; the existing characters will move aside.

   Deleting is the act of removing text, usually using the Delete or Backspace keys.

- The *Undelete,* or *Undo,* command allows you to change your mind and restore text that you have deleted. Some word processing programs offer as many as 100 layers of "undo," allowing users who delete several blocks of text, but then change their minds, to reinstate one or more of the blocks.

- *Search and replace:* The *Search* command, or *Find* command, allows you to find any word, phrase, or number that exists in your document. The *Replace* command allows you to automatically replace it with something else.

- *Cut, copy, paste:* Typewriter users were accustomed to using scissors and glue to "cut and paste" if they wanted to move a paragraph or block of text from one place to another in a manuscript. With word processing, you can easily select the portion of text you want to move and then use the *Cut* or *Copy* command to remove it or copy it. Then use the *Paste* command to insert it somewhere else.

- *Spelling checker, grammar checker, thesaurus:* Many writers automatically run their completed documents through a *spelling checker,* which tests for incorrectly spelled words. (Some programs have an Auto Correct function that automatically fixes such common mistakes as transposed letters—"teh" instead of "the.") Another feature is a *grammar checker,* which flags poor grammar, wordiness, incomplete sentences, awkward phrases, and excessive use of the passive voice.

   If you find yourself stuck for the right word while you're writing, you can call up an on-screen thesaurus, which will present you with the appropriate word or alternative words.

Formatting Documents

Formatting means determining the appearance of a document. *(See Figure 6.2, next page.)* There are many choices here.

- *Type:* You can decide what typeface and type size you wish to use. A particular typeface and size is called a **font.** All variations of a particular typeface are called a *font family. (See Figure 6.3, page 6.11.)* You can specify whether the font should be underlined, *italic,* or **boldface.**

- *Spacing and columns:* You can choose whether you want the lines to be *single-spaced* or *double-spaced* (or something else). You can specify whether you want text to be *one column* (like this page), *two columns* (like many magazines and books), or *several columns* (like newspapers).

Figure 6.2 Word 2000 screen showing the Format pull-down menu. This menu offers many options for changing the formatting of a document or part of it. A menu item with an arrowhead (▶) offers even more options.

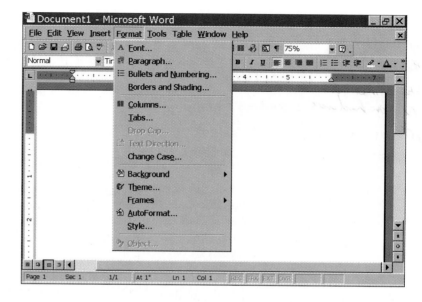

■ *Margins and justification:* You can indicate the dimensions of the page borders, or *margins*—left, right, top, and bottom—around the text.

You can specify whether the text should be *justified* or not. *Justify* means to align text evenly between left and right margins, as is done, for example, with most newspaper columns. *Ragged right* means to not align the text evenly on the right, as is done with many business letters (text is left-justified). *Ragged left* means the left side of the text is not evenly aligned (text is right-justified), and centered means that each line of text is centered on the page.

This text is right- and left-justified. This style is often used in newspaper columns.	This text is left-justified and ragged right. This style is often used in business letters.	This text is right-justified and ragged left. This style is often used in ads and brochures.	This text is centered. This style is often used in headings.

■ *Pages, headers, footers:* You can indicate *page numbers* and *headers* or *footers.* A *header* is common text (such as a date or document name) that is printed at the top of every page. A *footer* is the same thing printed at the bottom of every page.

■ *Other formatting:* You can specify *borders* or other decorative lines, *shading, tables,* and *footnotes.* You can even pull in ("import") *graphics* or drawings from files in other software programs.

It's worth noting that word processing programs (and indeed most forms of applications software) come from the manufacturer with default settings. Thus, for example, most word processing programs will automatically prepare a document single-spaced, justified, and with 1-inch right and left margins unless you alter these default settings, which is easy to do.

Printing Documents

Most word processing software gives you several options for printing. For example, you can print several copies of a document. You can print *individual pages* or a *range of pages.* You can even *preview* a document before printing it out. *Previewing* (print previewing) means viewing a document on screen to see what it will look like in printed form. Whole pages are displayed in reduced size.

Examples of fonts:

ABCDEFGHIJK   10-point Times Roman regular

ABCDEFGHIJK 14-point Ariel Bold

ABCDEFGHIJK 24-point Trump Medieval Italic

Type glossary:

Font   A character set in a particular size and type design (typeface)
Point   Unit of measurement of type size; 12 points equal 1 pica.
Pica   Unit of measurement of page elements, such as margin width; 6 picas equal 1 inch.
Leading   Unit of measurement between lines of type; for example, space (10 + 2 = 12) between lines.
            10/12 lines would be closer together than 10/14 lines.

Type basics:

Many characteristics give fonts different looks—from the ornate to the plain, text-book style. Some fonts are more readable and better for reports and documents. Some are unique or formal and may be better for a logo or invitation.

But how do font designers give their fonts different looks? One of the most common ways to change a font is to add a *serif* or leave the font *sans serif* (without a serif). This serif is a little "foot" or "hat" added to the letters. Designers also can adjust some of the type characteristics, maybe making a loop a little wider, raising an ascender, or giving a jaunty lift to the ear on a *g*. They can change the *pitch* of letters, which is how much horizontal room they get. The pitch may be *fixed* or *monospaced*, meaning each letter gets the same amount of room, or it may be *proportional*, so that the spacing depends on the width of the particular character. Finally, they can give letters or numerals a different weight, which is the thickness, or a different style, such as straight up or italics.

To give you an idea of what designers have to play around with, here we've assembled a chart illustrating the names of all the parts of a typeface design.

f i t ness
Monospaced type

fitness
Proportional type

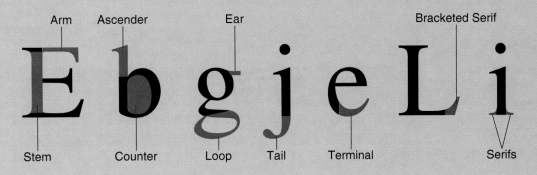

Arm   Ascender   Ear   Bracketed Serif

Stem   Counter   Loop   Tail   Terminal   Serifs

Figure 6.3 Font fundamentals

Some word processors even come close to desktop-publishing programs in enabling you to prepare professional-looking documents with different type faces and sizes. However, as we shall see later, desktop-publishing programs do far more.

Today, popular word processing programs are Microsoft Word for the PC, Word for the Mac, Corel WordPerfect for the PC, and WordPerfect for the Mac.

Spreadsheet Software

What is a spreadsheet? Traditionally, it was simply a grid of rows and columns, printed on special green paper, that was used by accountants and others to produce financial projections and reports. A person making up a spreadsheet often spent long days and weekends at the office penciling tiny numbers into countless tiny rectangles. When one figure changed, the totals and other formulas based on that number had to be recomputed—and ultimately there might be wastebaskets full of discarded spreadsheets.

In the late 1970s, Daniel Bricklin was a student at the Harvard Business School. One day he was staring at columns of numbers on a blackboard when he got the idea for computerizing the worksheet. The result, VisiCalc, was the first of the electronic spreadsheets. An electronic **spreadsheet** allows users to create tables and financial schedules by entering data into rows and columns arranged as a grid on a display screen. *(See Figure 6.4.)* A spreadsheet document is called a *worksheet.*

The electronic spreadsheet quickly became the most popular small-business program and convinced the business world that the microcomputer is an invaluable business tool. Unfortunately for Bricklin, VisiCalc was shortly surpassed by Lotus 1-2-3, a sophisticated program that combines the spreadsheet with database and graphics programs. Today the principal spreadsheet programs are Microsoft Excel and Lotus 1-2-3.

Figure 6.4 The Excel 2000 for Windows electronic spreadsheet is a computer-based version of the traditional paper spreadsheet. When one number is changed, all related numbers in the spreadsheet are automatically recalculated.

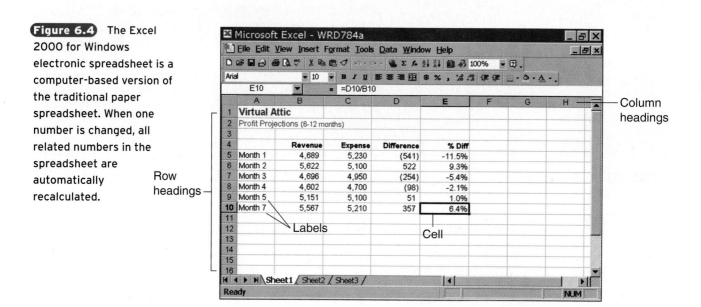

Principal Features

Spreadsheet software worksheets include the following features:

■ *Columns and rows: Column headings* appear across the top ("A" is the name of the first column, "B" the second, and so on). *Row headings* appear down the left side ("1" is the name of the first row, "2" the second, and so forth).

■ *Cells, cell addresses, and cell pointer:* The place where a row and a column intersect is called a **cell,** and its position is called a **cell address.** For example, "A1" is the cell address for the top left cell, where column A and row 1 intersect. A *cell pointer* indicates where data is to be entered. The cell pointer can be moved around like the insertion point in a word processing program.

■ *Values:* A number, date, or formula entered in a cell is called a *value.* The values are the actual numbers used in the worksheet—dollars, percentages, grade points, temperatures, or whatever.

■ *Formulas, functions, recalculation:* Now we come to the reason the electronic spreadsheet has taken offices by storm. **Formulas** are instructions for calculations. For example, a formula might be +A1+A2+A3, meaning to add the contents of cells A1, A2, and A3.

    Functions are built-in formulas that perform common calculations. For instance, a function might sum or average a range of numbers or round off a number to two decimal places. An example of a function is SUM(A1:A3), meaning "Sum (add) all the numbers in the cells with cell addresses A1 through A3."

    After the values have been plugged into the spreadsheet, the formulas and functions can be used to calculate outcomes. What is revolutionary, however, is the ease with which the spreadsheet does recalculation. *Recalculation* is the process of recomputing values automatically, either as an ongoing process as data is being entered or afterward, with the press of a key. With this simple feature, the hours of mind-numbing work required to manually rework paper spreadsheets has become a thing of the past.

    The recalculation feature has opened up whole new possibilities for decision making. As a user, you can create a plan, put in formulas and numbers, and then ask yourself, "What would happen if we change that detail?"—and immediately see the effect on the bottom line. This is called the *what if* function. For example, if you're buying a new car, the "what if" function lets you consider various options: Any number of things can be varied: total price ($10,000? $15,000?), down payment ($2000? $3000?), interest rate on the car loan (7%? 8%?), or number of months to pay (36? 48?). You can keep changing the "what if" possibilities until you arrive at a monthly payment figure that you're comfortable with.

    Spreadsheets can be linked with other spreadsheets. The feature of *dynamic linking* allows data in one spreadsheet to be linked to and automatically update data in another spreadsheet. Thus, the amount of data being manipulated can be enormous.

Analytical Graphics: Creating Charts

Another useful feature of spreadsheet packages is the ability to create analytical graphics. Presented in spreadsheet forms, as rows and columns of numbers, financial data is not always easy to comprehend. Whether viewed on a monitor or printed out, **analytical graphics,** or **business graphics,** help make sales figures, economic trends, and the like easier to comprehend and analyze.

Figure 6.5 Analytical graphics. Bar charts, line charts, and pie charts are used to display numerical data in graphical form.

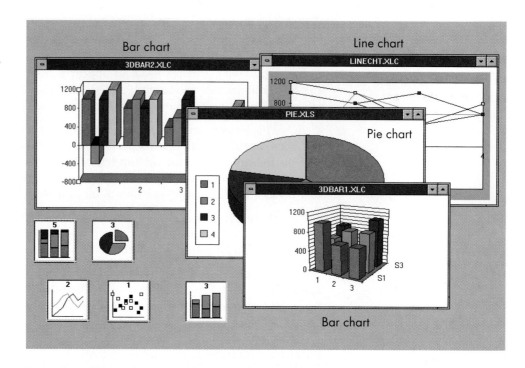

The principal examples of analytical graphics are bar charts, line graphs, and pie charts. *(See Figure 6.5.)* Quite often these charts can be displayed or printed out so that they look three-dimensional. Spreadsheets can even be linked to more exciting graphics, such as digitized maps.

Personal Finance Software

Personal finance software lets you keep track of income and expenses, write checks, and plan financial goals. *(See Figure 6.6.)* Such programs don't promise to make you rich, but they can help you manage cash and investments, or maybe even get you out of trouble.

Many personal finance programs include a calendar and a calculator, but the principal features are the following.

- *Tracking of income and expenses:* The programs allow you to set up various account categories for recording income and expenses, including credit card expenses. (Some personal finance program developers even offer a Visa credit card that sends you monthly statements via your modem or a diskette for direct entry into your computer.)

- *Checkbook management:* All programs feature checkbook management, with an on-screen check writing form and check register that look like the ones in your checkbook. Checks can be purchased to use with your computer printer. Some programs even offer a nationwide electronic payment service (through BillPay USA or CheckFree) that lets you pay your regular bills automatically, even depositing funds electronically into the accounts of the people owed.

- *Reporting:* All programs compare your actual expenses with your budgeted expenses. Some will compare this year to last year.

- *Income tax:* All programs offer tax categories, for indicating types of income and expenses that are important when you're filing your tax return. Most personal finance programs are also able to interface with a tax-preparation program.

Figure 6.6 M.Y.O.B. accounting screen. Personal finance software allows users to write and print out checks, among many other things.

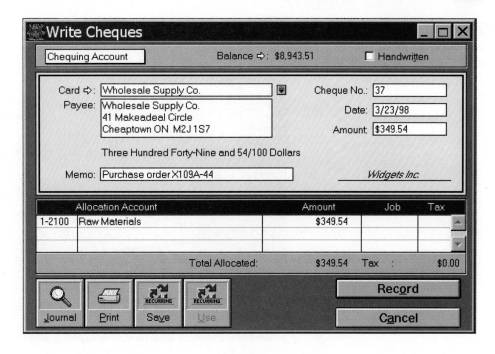

■ *Other:* Some of the more versatile personal finance programs offer financial-planning, retirement-planning, and portfolio-management features. Quicken Deluxe also provides interactive tutorials and counseling sessions with leading financial consultants via a multimedia help system.

Quicken (there are versions for DOS, Windows, and Macintosh) seems to have generated a large following, but other personal finance programs exist as well. They include Kiplinger's CA-Simply Money, Managing Your Money, Microsoft Money, Simply Accounting, M.Y.O.B., and WinCheck. Some offer enough features that you could use them to manage a small business.

In addition, tax software programs provide virtually all the forms you need for filing income taxes. Tax programs make complex calculations, check for mistakes, and even unearth deductions you didn't know existed. (The principal tax programs are Andrew Tobias' TaxCut, Kiplinger TaxCut, TurboTax/MacInTax, Personal Tax Edge, and CA-Simply Tax.) Finally, there are investment software packages, such as StreetSmart from Charles Schwab and Online Xpress from Fidelity, as well as various retirement-planning programs.

Presentation Graphics

Computer graphics can be highly complicated, such as those used in special effects for movies (for instance, *Titanic* and *Antz*). Here we are concerned with just one kind of graphics, called *presentation graphics.*

Presentation graphics are part of presentation software, which uses graphics and data/information from other software tools to communicate or make a presentation to others, such as clients or supervisors. Presentations may make use of some analytical graphics—bar, line, and pie charts—but they most often include bulleted lists. *(See Figure 6.7, next page.)* Examples of well-known presentation software packages are Microsoft PowerPoint, Aldus Persuasion, Lotus Freelance Graphics, and SPC Harvard Graphics.

Some presentation software packages provide artwork called clip art that can be electronically cut and pasted into the graphics. These programs also allow you to use electronic painting and drawing tools for creating lines, rectangles, and just

Figure 6.7 Presentation graphics—an advertisement

about any other shape. Depending on the system's capabilities, you can add text, animated sequences, and sound. Presentation graphics are frequently output to the screen or printed on transparency acetates.

Presentation software packages are also used in kiosks, multimedia training, and lectures. (A *kiosk* is a small, self-contained, booth-like structure. Multimedia kiosks dispense information via computer display.)

Database Management System Software

In its most general sense, a database is any electronically stored collection of data in a computer system. In its more specific sense, a *database* is a collection of interrelated files in a computer system. These computer-based files are organized according to their common elements, so that they can be retrieved easily. Sometimes called a *database manager* or *database management system (DBMS)*, **database software** is a program that controls the structure of a database and access to the data. *(See Figure 6.8.)*

Benefits of Database Software

Because it can access several files at one time, database software is much better than the old file managers (also known as flat-file management systems) that used to dominate computing. A *file manager* is a software package that can access only one file at a time. With a file manager, you could call up a list of, say, all students at your college majoring in English. You could also call up a separate list of all students from Wisconsin. But you could not call up a list of English majors from Wisconsin, because the relevant data is kept in separate files. Database software allows you to do that.

Figure 6.8 Microsoft 2000 Access screen. Database management software can manage huge amounts of data.

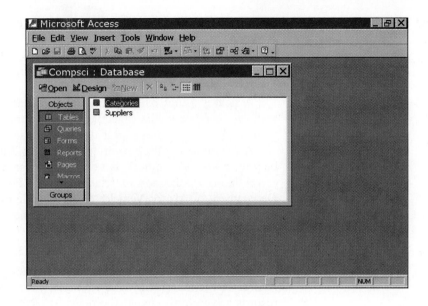

Databases are a lot more interesting than they used to be. Once they included only text. Digital technology has added new kinds of information—not only documents but also pictures, sound, and animation. *(See Figure 6.9.)* It's likely, for instance, that your personnel record in a future company database will include a picture of you and perhaps even a clip of your voice. If you go looking for a house to buy, you will be able to view a real estate agent's database of video clips of homes and properties without leaving the realtor's office. Today the principal database programs are Microsoft Access, Microsoft Visual FoxPro, Oracle, and Claris Filemaker Pro. A multimedia program called Instant Database allows users to attach sound, motion, and graphics to forms. You can also attach these elements using OLE (✔ p. 6.6).

Databases have gotten easier to use, but they still can be difficult to design. Even so, the trend is toward making such programs easier for both database creators and database users.

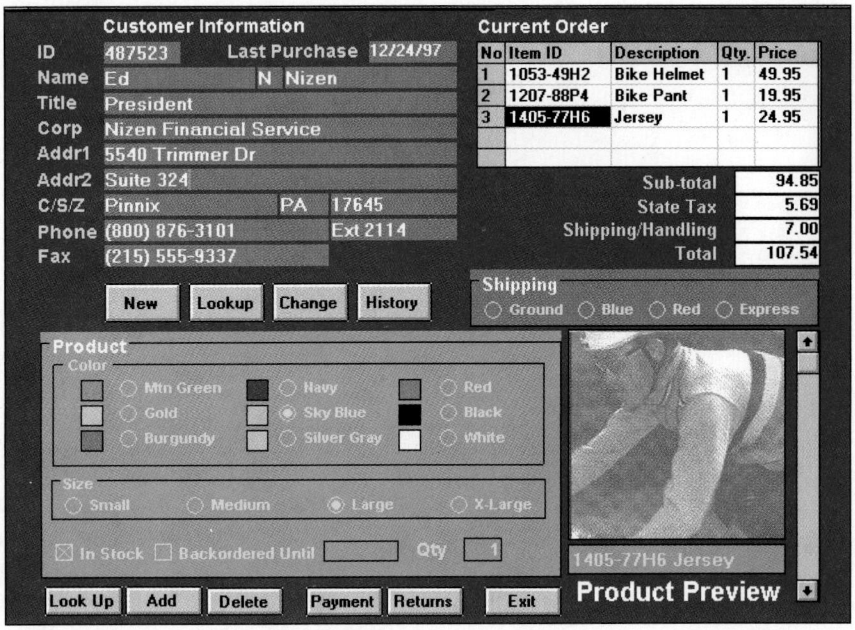

Figure 6.9 Graphical data. Increasingly, database software is used to store not only text but also graphics, sound, and animation.

Principal Features of Database Software

Some features of databases are as follows:

■ *Organization of a database:* A database is organized—from smallest to largest items—into *fields, records,* and *files.*

A **field** is a unit of data consisting of one piece of information, whether text, numbers, or media object (graphic, sound bite). Examples of a field are your name, your address, your driver's license number, *or* your photograph.

A **record** is a collection of related fields. An example of a record would be your name *and* address *and* driver's license number *and* photograph.

A **file** is a collection of related records. For example, a file in your state's Department of Motor Vehicles could include everyone who received a driver's license on the same day, including their names, addresses, and driver's license numbers.

Database software allows records to be easily added, deleted, and revised.

■ *Select and display:* The beauty of database software is that you can locate records in the file quickly. For example, your college may maintain several records about you—one at the registrar's, one in financial aid, one in the housing department, and so on. Any of these records can be called up on a computer display screen for viewing and updating. Thus, if you move, your address field will need to be changed in all databases. Each database is quickly corrected by finding your record. Once displayed, the address field can be changed. This field need be changed only once; it will automatically be updated in all other files.

■ *Sort:* With database software you can easily change the order of records in a file. Normally, records are entered into a database in the order they occur—for example, by the date a person registered to attend college. However, all these records can be sorted in different ways—by state, by age, or by Social Security number.

■ *Calculate and format:* Many database software programs contain built-in mathematical formulas. This feature can be used, for example, to find the grade-point averages for students in different majors or in different classes. Such information can then be organized into different formats and printed out.

■ *Queries:* Database software allows you to query files and get answers—for example, "What are the grade-point averages of the students in Spanish 101?"

■ *Reports:* Database software will also generate reports that sort and group data. You can publish these reports on paper or the Web, or simply view them on the screen.

Groupware

Most microcomputer software is written for people working alone. **Groupware** is software that is used on a network and serves a group of users working together on the same project. Groupware improves productivity by keeping you continually notified about what your colleagues are thinking and doing, and vice versa.

Groupware is essentially of four types:

■ *Basic groupware:* Exemplified by Lotus Notes, this kind of groupware uses an enormous database containing work records, memos, and notations and combines it with a messaging (e-mail) system. It is information-centered and allows people to do workgroup computing, focusing on the information being processed. Thus, a company like accounting giant Coopers & Lybrand uses

Just outside Tokyo, Japan, an indoor computer-driven "winter" sports facility—the largest in the world—enables ski buffs to ski all year. The system uses microprocessors to keep the snow falling, the lifts running, and the temperatures at 26° F.

Lotus Notes software to let co-workers organize and share financial and tax information. It can also be used to relay advice from outside specialists, speeding up audits and answers to complex questions from clients.

Groupware is more than just multiuser software, which allows users on a network to access the same data; groupware does this but also allows users to coordinate and keep track of an ongoing project.

■ *Workflow software:* Workflow software, exemplified by ActionWorkflow System and ProcessIt, helps workers understand and redesign the steps that make up a particular process—thus, it is process-centered. It governs the tasks performed and coordinates the transfer of the information required to carry out the tasks. It also routes work automatically among employees and helps organizations reduce paper-jammed bureaucracies.

■ *Meeting software:* Examples of meeting software are Microsoft NetMeeting, Netscape's Collaborator, and Ventana's GroupSystems V, which allow people to have computer-linked meetings. With this software, people "talk," or communicate, with one another at the same time by typing on microcomputer keyboards.

■ *Scheduling software:* Scheduling software such as Microsoft Outlook, Microsoft SchedulePlus, and Powercore's Network Scheduler 3 use a microcomputer network to coordinate co-workers' electronic datebooks or appointment calendars so they can figure out a time when they can all get together. (*Note:* Scheduling software is useful only if everyone uses it regularly and consistently—otherwise appointment information and the like will be missing.)

Groupware has changed the kind of behavior required for success in an organization. For one thing, it requires workers to take more responsibility. Ethically, of course, when you are contributing to a group project of any kind, you should try to do your best. However, when your contribution to the project is clearly visible to all, as happens with groupware, you have to do your best. In addition, using e-mail or groupware means you need to use good manners and be sensitive to others while you're online.

Figure 6.10 Outlook 2000 screen. This desktop accessory is showing a daily schedule.

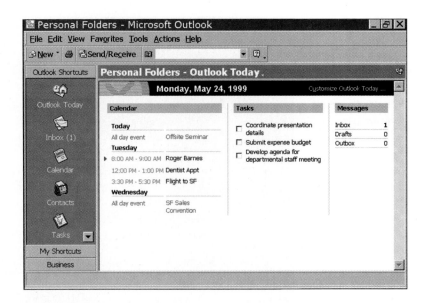

Desktop Accessories and PIMs

Pretend you are sitting at a desk in an old-fashioned office. You have a calendar, clock, calculator, Rolodex-type address file, and notepad. Most of these items could also be found on a student's desk. How would a computer and software improve on this arrangement? Many people find ready uses for types of software known as *desktop accessories* and *personal information managers (PIMs)*.

■ *Desktop accessories:* A **desktop accessory,** or *desktop organizer,* is a software package that provides an electronic version of tools or objects commonly found on a desktop: calendar, clock, card file, calculator, and notepad. *(See Figure 6.10.)*

Some desktop accessory programs come as standard equipment with system software (such as Microsoft Windows). Others, such as Borland's Side-Kick or Lotus Agenda, are available as separate programs to run in your computer's main memory while you are running other software. Some are principally scheduling and calendaring programs; their main purpose is to enable you to do time and event scheduling.

Suppose, for example, you are working on a word processing document and someone calls to schedule lunch next week. You can simply enter a command that "pops up" your appointment calendar, type in the appointment, save the information, and then return to your interrupted work. Other features, such as a calculator keypad, a scratch pad for typing in notes to yourself, and a Rolodex-type address and phone directory (some with an automatic telephone dialer), can be displayed on the screen when needed.

■ *Personal information managers:* A more sophisticated program is the **personal information manager (PIM),** a combination word processor, database, and desktop accessory program that organizes a variety of information. Examples of PIMs are Commence, Ecco, and Lotus Organizer. (PIMs are often integrated into e-mail and groupware products.)

Lotus Organizer, for example, looks much like a paper datebook on the screen—down to simulated metal rings holding simulated paper pages. The program has screen images of section tabs labeled Calendar, To Do, Address, Notepad, Planner, and Anniversary. The Notepad section lets users enter long documents, including text and graphics, that can be called up at any time.

Integrated Software and Software Suites

What if you want to take data from one program and use it in another—say, call up data from a database and use it in a spreadsheet? You can try using separate software packages, but one may not be designed to accept data from the other. Two alternatives are the collections of software known as *integrated software* and *software suites*.

Integrated Software: "Works" Programs

Integrated software packages combine the features of several applications programs—such as word processing, spreadsheet, database, graphics, and communications—into one software package. These so-called "works" collections give good value because the entire bundle often sells for $100 or less. The principal representatives are AppleWorks, ClarisWorks, Lotus Works, Microsoft Works, and PerfectWorks.

Some of these programs have assistants that help you accomplish various tasks. Thus, Microsoft's Works for Windows 95 helps you create new documents using any of 39 "task wizards." The wizards lead you through the process of creating a letter, for example, which permits you to customize as many features as you want.

Integrated software packages are less powerful than the corresponding single-purpose programs, such as a word processing program or a spreadsheet. But that may be fine, because single-purpose programs may be more complicated than you need. For instance, you may have no use for a word processor that will create an index. Moreover, single-purpose programs demand more computer resources. Microsoft Word takes up about 20 megabytes on your hard disk, whereas Microsoft Works takes only 7 megabytes.

However, system software such as Windows makes the advantage of sharing information in integrated programs redundant, since the user can easily shift between applications programs that are *completely different*. In addition, integrated programs are largely being replaced in the Windows environment by software suites, as we discuss next.

Software Suites: "Office" Programs

Software suites, or simply suites, are applications—like spreadsheet, word processing, graphics, communications, and groupware—that are bundled together and sold for a fraction of what the programs would cost if bought individually.

"Bundled" and "unbundled" are jargon words frequently encountered in software and hardware merchandising. *Bundled* means that components of a system are sold together for a single price. *Unbundled* means that a system has separate prices for each component.

The principal suites, sometimes called "office" programs, are Office from Microsoft, SmartSuite from Lotus, and Perfect Office from Corel. Microsoft's Office 2000 consists of programs that separately would cost perhaps $1500 but as a suite cost roughly $700. A trade-off, however, is that such packages require a lot of hard-disk storage capacity.

Web Browsers

The Internet, that network of millions of interconnected networks, "is just a morass of data, dribbling out of [computers] around the world," says one writer. "It is unfathomably chaotic, mixing items of great value with cyber-trash." This is why browser software has caught people's imaginations, he states. "A browser cuts a path through the tangled growth and even creates a form of memory, so each path can be retraced."[1]

We cover the Internet in detail in Chapter 8. Here let us consider briefly just a part of it, one that you may find particularly useful.

The World Wide Web

The most exciting part of the Internet is probably that fast-growing region or subset of it known as the World Wide Web. The *World Wide Web,* or simply the *Web,* consists of hundreds of thousands of intricately interlinked sites—called *home pages*—set up for on-screen viewing in the form of colorful magazine-style "pages" with text, images, and sound.

To be connected to the World Wide Web, you need a modem and an automatic setup with an online service or Internet access provider (described in Chapter 8), which often provides the browser software for exploring the Web. (The reverse is also true: If you buy some Web browsers, they will help you find an access provider.) A **Web browser,** or simply browser, is software that enables you to "browse through" and view Web sites. You can move from page to page by clicking on or selecting a hyperlink—either underlined text or a graphic—or by typing in the address of the destination page.

There are a great many browsers, including some unsophisticated ones offered by Internet access providers and some by the large commercial online services such as America Online, CompuServe, and Prodigy. However, the recent battle royal for Web browser prominence has been between Netscape, which produces Navigator and Communicator, and Microsoft, which offers Microsoft Explorer.

6.4 Specialty Applications Software Tools

KEY QUESTION **What are some types of specialty applications software?**

After learning some of the productivity software just described, you may wish to extend your range by becoming familiar with more specialized programs. For example, you might first learn word processing and then move on to desktop publishing, the technology used to prepare much of today's printed information. Or you may want to move beyond presentation graphics and learn how to prepare animation and special effects. Let us consider the following examples of these specialized tools, although these are but a handful of the thousands of programs available:

- Desktop-publishing software

- Project management software

- Computer-aided design (CAD) and manufacturing (CAM) software

- Drawing and painting software

- Multimedia authoring software

Desktop-Publishing Software

Not everyone can set up a successful desktop-publishing business, because many complex layouts require experience, skill, and knowledge of graphic design and of typography. Indeed, use of these programs by nonprofessional users can lead to rather unprofessional-looking results. Nevertheless, the availability of microcomputers and reasonably inexpensive software has opened up a career area formerly reserved for professional typographers, compositors, and printers. **Desktop publishing,** abbreviated **DTP,** involves using a microcomputer and mouse, scanner, laser or ink-jet printer, and DTP software for mixing text and graphics to produce high-quality printed output for commercial printing. *(See Figure 6.11.)* Often the printer is used primarily to get an advance look before the completed job is sent to an imagesetter for even higher-quality output. (Imagesetters generate images directly onto film, which is then given to the printer for platemaking and printing.) Professional desktop-publishing programs are QuarkXPress and PageMaker. Microsoft Publisher is a "low-end," consumer-oriented DTP package. Some word processing programs, such as Word and WordPerfect, have many DTP features but at nowhere near the level of sophistication of the aforementioned packages.

Desktop-publishing software has the following characteristics:

■ *Mix of text with graphics:* Unlike traditional word processing programs, desktop-publishing software allows you to manage and merge precisely typographically aligned text with graphics. Indeed, while laying out a page on screen, you can make the text flow, liquid-like, around graphics such as photographs. Among many other things, you can make art drop behind text or text drop out from (print white in) art. You can make text columns uneven and art bleed out into the margin. You can resize art, silhouette it, change the colors, change the texture, flip it upside down, and make it look like a photo negative.

Figure 6.11 How DTP uses other files. Text is composed with a word processor, graphics are drawn with drawing and painting programs, and photographs and other artwork are scanned in and manipulated with appropriate software. Data from these files is integrated using desktop-publishing software, then printed out on a laser printer or sent to an imagesetter. *(Continues on next two pages.)*

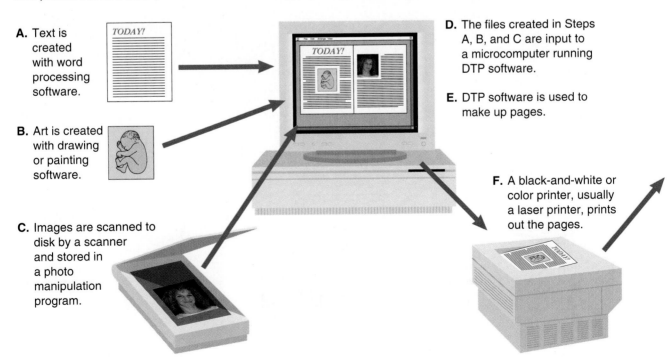

A. Text is created with word processing software.

B. Art is created with drawing or painting software.

C. Images are scanned to disk by a scanner and stored in a photo manipulation program.

D. The files created in Steps A, B, and C are input to a microcomputer running DTP software.

E. DTP software is used to make up pages.

F. A black-and-white or color printer, usually a laser printer, prints out the pages.

■ *Varied type and layout styles:* As do word processing programs, DTP programs provide a variety of fonts. Additional fonts can be purchased on disk or downloaded online. You can also create all kinds of rules, borders, columns, and page numbering styles. A style sheet in the DTP program enables you to choose and record the settings that determine the appearance of the pages and to save document templates, or master documents, that can be used repeatedly. This may include defining the size and typestyle of text and headings, the numbers of columns of type on a page, and the width of lines and boxes.

■ *Use of files from other programs:* It's not usually efficient to do word processing, drawing, and painting within the DTP software. Thus, text is usually composed on a word processor, such as Word or WordPerfect, artwork is created with drawing and painting software, such as Adobe Illustrator or CorelDRAW, and photographs are scanned in and then manipulated and stored using Adobe PhotoShop or other photo-manipulation or imaging software. Prefabricated art may also be obtained from disks containing clip art, or "canned" images that can be used to illustrate DTP documents. The DTP program is used to integrate all these files. On the display screen you can look at your work one page or two facing pages at a time (in reduced size). Then you can see it again after it is printed out.

This book is an example of the use of QuarkXPress to combine Word, Adobe Illustrator, and Photoshop files: It was laid out electronically by one of the authors. The Quark files and the art files were then sent to a prepress house for certain refinements, color separation, and film imposition. Then the book went to the printer. (It could just as easily have been output electronically or placed on the Web.)

Project Management Software

A desktop accessory/PIM can help you schedule your appointments and do some planning. That is, it can help you to manage your own life. But what if you need

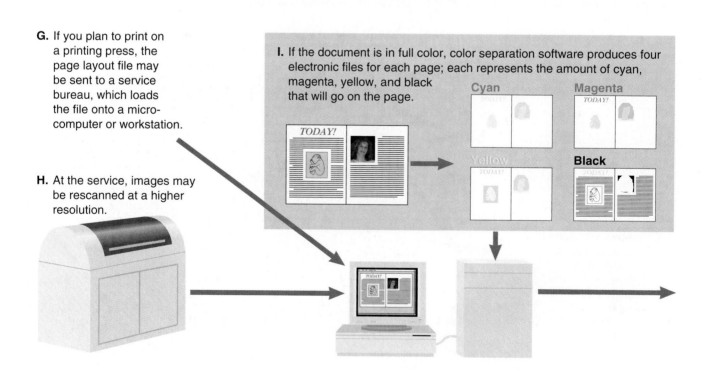

G. If you plan to print on a printing press, the page layout file may be sent to a service bureau, which loads the file onto a microcomputer or workstation.

H. At the service, images may be rescanned at a higher resolution.

I. If the document is in full color, color separation software produces four electronic files for each page; each represents the amount of cyan, magenta, yellow, and black that will go on the page.

Cyan   Magenta

Yellow   **Black**

to manage the lives of others to accomplish a full-blown project, such as steering a political campaign or handling a nationwide road tour for a band? Strictly defined, a project is a one-time operation consisting of several tasks that must be completed during a stated period of time. The project can be small, such as an advertising campaign for an in-house advertising department, or large, such as construction of an office tower or a jetliner.

Project management software is a program used to plan, schedule, and control resources—people, costs, and equipment—required to complete a project on time. For instance, the associate producer on a feature film might use such software to keep track of the locations, cast and crew, materials, dollars, and schedules needed to complete the picture on time and within budget. The software would show the scheduled beginning and ending dates for a particular task, called a *milestone*— such as shooting all scenes on a certain set—and then the date that task was actually completed. Examples of project management software are Harvard Project Manager, Microsoft Project for Windows, Project Scheduler 4, SuperProject, and Time Line.

Two important tools available in project management software are Gantt charts and PERT charts. *(See Figure 6.12, next page.)* A *Gantt chart* uses lines and bars to indicate the duration of a series of tasks. The time scale may range from minutes to years. The Gantt chart allows you to see whether tasks are being completed on schedule. A *PERT chart* (Program Evaluation Review Technique) shows not only timing but also relationships among the tasks of a project. The relationships are represented by lines that connect boxes describing the tasks.

Even project management software has evolved into new forms. For example, a program called ManagePro for Windows is designed to manage not only goals and tasks but also the people charged with achieving them. "I use it to track projects, due dates, and the people who are responsible," says the director of management information systems at a Lake Tahoe, Nevada, timeshare condominium resort. "And then you can get your reports out either on project information, showing progress on all the steps, or a completely different view, showing all the steps that have to be taken by a given individual."[2]

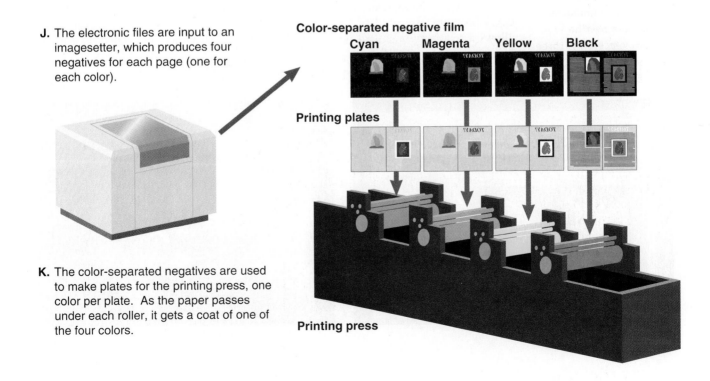

J. The electronic files are input to an imagesetter, which produces four negatives for each page (one for each color).

Color-separated negative film

Cyan   Magenta   Yellow   Black

Printing plates

K. The color-separated negatives are used to make plates for the printing press, one color per plate. As the paper passes under each roller, it gets a coat of one of the four colors.

Printing press

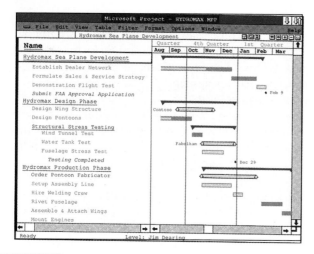

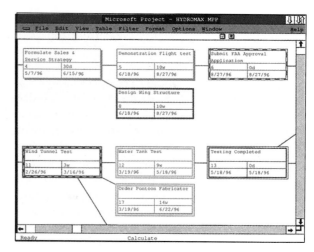

Figure 6.12 Project management software. *(Left)* Gantt chart from Microsoft Project. *(Right)* PERT chart from Microsoft Project.

Computer-Aided Design (CAD) and Manufacturing (CAM) Software

Computers have long been used in engineering design. **Computer-aided design (CAD)** programs are software programs for the design of products and structures. CAD programs, which are now available for microcomputers, help architects design buildings and work spaces and engineers design cars, planes, electronic devices, roadways, bridges, and subdivisions. One advantage of CAD software is that the product can be drawn in three dimensions and then rotated on the screen so the designer can see all sides. *(See Figure 6.13.)*

Examples of CAD programs for beginners are Autosketch, CorelCAD, Easy-CAD2 (Learn CAD Now), and TurboCAD. One CAD program, Parametric, allows engineers to do "what if" overhauls of designs, much as users of electronic spreadsheets can easily change financial data. This feature can dramatically cut design time. For instance, using Parametric, Motorola was able to design its Micro Tac personal cellular telephone in 9 months instead of the usual 18. Yet not all CAD programs are used by technical types; a version available now, for example, allows a relatively unskilled person to design an office. Other programs are avail-

Figure 6.13 CAD. *(Left)* Screens from Autodesk CAD system. *(Right)* CAD screen of an automobile brake assembly. The designer can draw in three dimensions and rotate the figures on the screen.

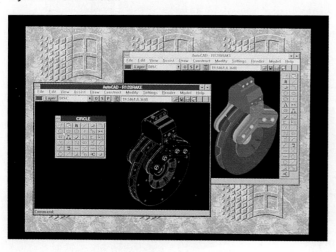

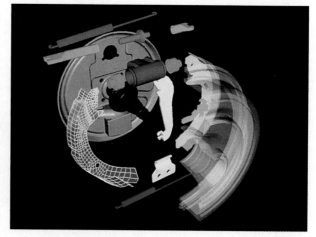

able for designing homes. These programs include "libraries" of options such as cabinetry, furniture, fixtures, and, in the landscaping programs, trees, shrubs, and vegetables.

A variant on CAD is *CADD,* for *computer-aided design and drafting,* software that helps people do drafting. CADD programs include symbols (points, circles, straight lines, and arcs) that can be used to put together graphic elements, such as the floor plan of a house. An example is Autodesk's AutoCAD.

CAD/CAM—for computer-aided design/computer-aided manufacturing—software allows CAD product designs to be input into an automated manufacturing system that makes the products. For example, CAD and its companion CAM brought a whirlwind of enhanced creativity and efficiency to the fashion industry. Some CAD systems allow designers to electronically drape digitally generated mannequins in flowing gowns or tailored suits that don't exist, or twist imaginary threads into yarns, yarns into weaves, weaves into sweaters without once touching needle to garment. The designs and specifications are then input into CAM systems that enable robot pattern-cutters to automatically cut thousands of patterns from fabric, with only minimal waste. Whereas previously the fashion industry worked about a year in advance of delivery, CAD/CAM has cut that time to 8 months—a competitive edge for a field that feeds on fads.

Drawing and Painting Software

It may be no surprise to learn that commercial artists and fine artists are abandoning the paintbox and pen-and-ink for software versions of palettes, brushes, and pens. The surprise, however, is that an artist can use mouse and pen-like stylus to create computer-generated art as good as that achievable with conventional artist's tools. More surprising, even nonartists can be made to look good with these programs.

There are two types of computer art programs: drawing and painting.

■ *Drawing programs:* A **drawing program** is graphics software that allows users to design and illustrate objects and products. CAD and drawing programs are similar. However, CAD programs provide precise dimensioning and positioning of the elements being drawn, so that they can be transferred later to CAM programs. Also, CAD programs lack the special effects for illustrations that come with drawing programs.

A program named Sketcher, for example, is described as having 12 different "paper" textures from which to choose, mimicking a range of surfaces from plain paper to canvas. There are even more choices in pencils, chalks, air brushes, pens, felt pens, markers, charcoals, and a variety of brush types. Drawing with a charcoal-like tool is just like drawing with real paper and charcoal, except neater. Other drawing programs are CorelDRAW, Adobe Illustrator, and Macromedia Freehand.

■ *Painting programs:* Whereas drawing programs are generally vector-based programs *(see box, next page),* painting programs are raster-based color. **Painting programs** are graphics programs that allow users to simulate painting on screen. A mouse or a tablet stylus is used to simulate a paintbrush. The program allows you to select "brush" sizes and shapes, as well as colors from a color palette.

The difficulty with using painting programs is that a powerful computer system is needed because color images take up so much main memory and disk storage space. In addition, these programs require sophisticated color printers of the sort found in specialized print shops called service bureaus.

Vector Graphics Versus Bit-Mapped Graphics

In vector graphics, geometric formulas are used to represent pictures. In bit-mapped graphics, the picture image is created using a complex series of dots, or pixels (✔ p. 3.27). Bit-mapped graphics are often called *raster graphics.*

You will need to understand these two methods and how they function in today's graphics systems if you are to master computer graphics. If you create an image on the computer, but you don't know which method is used, you will become aware of it as soon as you try to manipulate the image. Drawing programs create vector graphics; painting programs and scanning produce bit-mapped graphics.

In vector graphics, you can manipulate parts of the whole in ways not possible with bit-mapped graphics. For example, the size of vector-graphic images can be changed without adversely affecting the graphic quality. And individual parts of a graphic can be rotated or easily made to disappear behind or overprint other parts of the graphic. However, vector-graphics programs have trouble with, for instance, lots of tiny squiggles, since they try to view each squiggle as made up of many tiny arcs. In addition, these programs do not store the color of each pixel as you are working. Instead, they store a memo about a geometric shape and the color of the entire shape. Vector graphics are best for high-contrast art such as logos, weather maps, architectural drawings, and bright-colored charts. Also, many word processing programs include basic drawing programs for creating simple illustrations to insert in text documents.

In bit-mapped graphics programs, the colors of all the individual pixels are stored in RAM while you're painting. Thus, you need lots of RAM if your screen is large and if you are using lots of colors. Bit-mapped graphics are good for representing continuous ranges of colors with soft edges, such as impressionist paintings and photographs. However, enlarging and reducing a bit-mapped graphic image too much can make the dots ungainly or too fine to reproduce well. Also, bit-mapped graphics take up more storage space than vector graphics.

Software programs exist that convert vector graphics to bit-mapped graphics, and vice versa, and that allow both types of graphics to be used in the same document. Common vector-graphic file extensions (✔ p. 4.6) are .EPS (encapsulated PostScript), .DCS (desktop color separator), and .WMF (Windows meta file). Common bit-mapped graphic file extensions are .TIF (tagged image file format), .BMP (bitmap), and .GIF (graphics interchange format).

How can nonartists be made to look good with these programs? Consider the "Auto van Gogh" feature offered by a painting program called Painter. After you feed your scanned photograph or other digital image into the program, just a few clicks of the mouse will render it in Vincent van Gogh's style of multicolored brush strokes. Other programs such as Kai's PowerGoo can be used to "morph" (alter) scanned-in or created illustrations. *(See Figure 6.14.)*

Multimedia Authoring Software

Multimedia authoring software enables creators to combine not only text and graphics but animation, video, voice, and sound effects as well. A multimedia system is a combination of hardware and software that incorporates multiple media within a desktop computer system. In previous chapters you learned what hardware is necessary to play multimedia presentations. When you buy a multimedia item on CD-ROM, it basically needs to be compatible with your system to run. However, who puts those complicated multimedia presentations together? Project

Figure 6.14 Morphed illustration in PowerGoo

managers; creative directors; content and subject matter experts; writers, editors, and researchers; graphic designers; photographers; image processing specialists; sound designers; musicians; voice talent; audio engineers; animators; and video professionals, to name a few. These people work with various types of software programs, depending on their specialties. Then multimedia authoring software is used to synchronize the parts of the whole and ready the product for distribution.

Because people tend to remember much more of what they hear and see—as opposed to what they only hear or only see—multimedia has become a useful tool in many areas, such as information management, training, interactive learning, electronic publishing, entertainment, and communications. For example, Atlanta won the bid for the 1996 Olympics on the strength of a multimedia presentation that put the Olympic committee "inside" the stadium, which had yet to be built.

Professionals who develop multimedia projects have special hardware needs—equipment to record and copy their own CD-ROMS and/or DVDs, particular types of sound boards and audio controllers, video boards, compression/decompression-compatible hardware, graphics cards and accelerators, microphones, music synthesizers, projection options, and so forth. And, as mentioned, they need authoring software. Some of the common authoring tools, which differ in levels of sophistication and authoring method, are Microsoft Powerpoint and Hypercard for the Mac (presentation-graphics level), Macromedia Authorware and Macromedia Director, AimTech IconAuthor, Asymetrix Toolbook, and Action! for Macintosh and Windows. Basically, authoring tools allow the creator to sequence and time the occurrence of events, determining which previously created graphics, sound, text, and video files come into action when. The software also allows the creator to determine the type and level of user interaction. For example, does each event require the user to answer a question with a keyboarded "yes" or "no" before the program can proceed?

Multimedia creation on a simple level—such as generating presentation graphics with Microsoft PowerPoint for a business or educational presentation—is accessible to many users. However, multimedia on the most sophisticated level, using Director or Toolbook, for instance, requires quite a bit of knowledge and training.

6.5 Installing & Updating Applications Software

KEY QUESTION What does installing software involve?

Installing Applications Software

You can buy a videotape, CD-ROM, or audiotape, insert it into its player, and view or listen to it by simply pressing a button. This is not the case with software, no matter whether it is systems software or applications software. To use it in your microcomputer, you must first install it. Installation means copying and usually decompressing (✔ p. 5.9) program files from a CD-ROM or other medium to your hard disk. Directions for installing come with the instructions (documentation) accompanying the software. Additional advice is available, sometimes through a toll-free 800 number, from the software manufacturer.

The installation program may also ask you to specify what kind of microcomputer and monitor you are using, whether you are using a hard disk, and so on. Once installed, the software program will store most of your responses in a special file (.INI) on the disk. Each time you load the software, it will refer to this file.

Software Versions and Releases

Every year or so, software developers find ways to enhance their products and put forth a new *version* or new *release*.

■ *Version:* A version is a major upgrade in a software product. Versions are usually indicated by numbers such as 1.0, 2.0, 3.0, and so forth. The higher the number preceding the decimal point, the more recent the version.

■ *Release:* A release is a minor upgrade. Releases are usually indicated by a change in the number after the decimal point—3.0, then 3.1, then perhaps 3.11, then 3.2, and so on.

Mindful that many users may avoid a new "X.0" version on the theory that not all the bugs have been worked out yet, some software developers have departed from this system. In 1995, for example, Microsoft decided to call its new operating system "Windows 95" (✔ p. 5.16) instead of "Windows 4.0."

Most software products are upward compatible (or "forward compatible"). *Upward compatible* means that documents created with earlier versions of the software can be processed successfully on later versions. Thus, you can use the new version of a word processing program, for instance, to get into and revise the file of a term paper you wrote on an earlier version of that program. However, downward-compatible ("backward-compatible") software is less common. *Downward compatible* means that software developed for a new version of a software product can be run on older versions. For example, if you can run your new word processing program on your old operating system then the new package is downward compatible.

Although we cover most of the ethical and societal issues related to computerization in Chapter 14, before we close this chapter on applications software we do need to raise the ethical issues of copying intellectual property, including software.

6.6 Ethics & Intellectual Property Rights: When Can you Copy?

KEY QUESTION   How serious is it to violate a software copyright?

Information technology has presented legislators and lawyers—and you—with some new ethical questions regarding rights to intellectual property. **Intellectual property** consists of the products, tangible or intangible, of the human mind. There are three methods of protecting intellectual property: *patents* (as for an invention), *trade secrets* (as for a formula or method of doing business), and *copyrights* (as for a song or a book).

What Is a Copyright?

Of principal interest to us is copyright protection. A **copyright** is the exclusive legal right that prohibits copying of intellectual property without the permission of the copyright holder. Copyright law protects books, articles, pamphlets, music, art, drawings, movies—and, yes, computer software. Copyright protects the *expression* of an idea but not the idea itself. Thus, others may copy your idea for, say, a new shoot-'em-up videogame but not your particular variant of it. Copyright protection is automatic and lasts a minimum of 50 years; you do not have to register your idea with the government (as you do with a patent) in order to receive protection.

These matters are important because digital technology has made the act of copying far easier and more convenient than in the past. Copying a book on a photocopier might take hours, so people felt they might as well buy the book. Copying a software program onto another floppy disk, however, might take just seconds.

With the help of microchips, cattle farmer Greg Hermes-meyer employs ultrasound to gauge the meat and fat content of a cow.

Digitization threatens to compound the problem. For example, current copyright law doesn't specifically protect copyright material online. Says one article:

> Copyright experts say laws haven't kept pace with technology, especially digitization, the process of converting any data—sound, video, text—into a series of ones and zeros that are then transmitted over computer networks. Using this technology, it's possible to create an infinite number of copies of a book, a record, or a movie and distribute them to millions of people around the world at very little cost. Unlike photocopies of books or pirated audiotapes, the digital copies are virtually identical to the original.[3]

Piracy, Plagiarism, and Ownership of Images and Sounds

Three copyright-related matters deserve our attention: software and network piracy, plagiarism, and ownership of images and sounds.

- *Software and network piracy:* It may be hard to think of yourself as a pirate (no sword or eyepatch) when all you've done is make a copy of some commercial software for a friend. However, from an ethical standpoint, an act of piracy is like shoplifting the product off a store shelf—even if it's for a friend.

  Piracy is theft or unauthorized distribution or use. A type of piracy is to appropriate a computer design or program. This is the kind that Apple Computer claimed in a suit (since rejected) against Microsoft and Hewlett-Packard alleging that items in Apple's interface, such as icons and windows, had been copied.

  Software piracy is the unauthorized copying of copyrighted software. One way is to copy a program from one floppy disk to another. Another is to download a program from a network and make a copy of it.

  Network piracy is using electronic networks to distribute unauthorized copyrighted materials in digitized form. Record companies, for example, have protested the practice of computer users' sending unauthorized copies of digital recordings over the Internet.

  The easy rationalization is to say, "I'm just a poor student, and making this one copy or downloading only one digital recording isn't going to cause any harm." But that single act of software piracy, multiplied millions of times, is causing the software publishers a billion-dollar problem. They point out that the loss of revenue cuts into their budget for offering customer support, upgrading products, and compensating their creative people. Piracy also means that software prices are less likely to come down; if anything, they are more likely to go up.

  If publishers, broadcasters, movie studios, and authors are to take a chance on developing online and multimedia versions of their intellectual products, they need to be assured that they can cover their costs and make a reasonable return. Piracy threatens their ability to do so. Unless piracy can be curtailed—perhaps by the development of anticopying technology and by laws that make it a crime to disable that technology—the Information Superhighway may remain empty of traffic because no one wants to put anything on the road.

- *Plagiarism:* **Plagiarism** is the expropriation of another writer's text, findings, or interpretations and presenting it as one's own. Information technology puts a new face on plagiarism in two ways. On the one hand, it offers plagiarists new opportunities to go far afield for unauthorized copying. On the other hand, the technology offers new ways to catch people who steal other people's material.

Fingerprint databases enable law enforcement officers to compare a set of fingerprints against 8,000,000 stored prints in 75 minutes—a search that would take more than 40 years to conduct manually.

Because their overheads are low, electronic online journals are willing to publish papers that attract a small number of readers. With the explosion in the number of such journals, it is very hard to keep track of all the academic and scientific papers published there. Correspondingly, it may be difficult to know when a work has been plagiarized.

■ *Ownership of images and sounds:* Using computers, scanners, digital cameras, and the like, your power to alter images and sounds is almost unlimited. What does this mean for the original copyright holders? An unauthorized sound snippet of a soul musician's famous howl can be electronically transformed by digital sampling into the background music for dozens of rap recordings. Images can be appropriated by scanning them into a computer system, then altered or placed in a new context.

The line between artistic license and infringement of copyright is not always clear-cut. In 1993, a federal appeals court in New York upheld a ruling against artist Jeff Koons for producing ceramic art of some puppies. It turned out that the puppies were identical to those that had appeared in a postcard copyrighted by a California photographer. But what would have been the judgment if Koons had scanned in the postcard, changed the colors, and rearranged the order of the puppies to produce a new postcard?

In any event, to avoid lawsuits for violating copyright, a growing number of artists who have recycled material have taken steps to protect themselves. This usually involves paying flat fees or a percentage of their royalties to the original copyright holders.

These are the general issues you need to consider when you're thinking about how to use someone else's intellectual property in the Digital Age. Now let's see how software fits in.

Public Domain Software, Freeware, and Shareware

No doubt most of the applications programs you will study in conjunction with this book will be commercial software packages, with brand names such as Microsoft Word or Lotus 1-2-3. However, there are a number of software products that are available to you—often over the Internet—as *public domain software, freeware,* and *shareware.*

■ *Public domain software:* **Public domain software** is not protected by copyright and thus may be duplicated by anyone at will. Public domain programs have been donated to the public by their creators. They are often available through sites on the Internet or through computer users groups. A users group consists of individuals who share interests and trade information about computer systems.

You can duplicate public domain software without fear of legal prosecution. (Beware: Downloading software through the Internet may introduce viruses [✔ p. 5.8] when you run the programs.)

■ *Freeware:* **Freeware** is software that is available free of charge. Freeware is usually distributed through the Internet or computer users groups.

Why would any software creator let the product go for free? Sometimes developers want to see how users respond so that they can make improvements in a later version.

Freeware developers often retain all rights to their programs, so that technically you are not supposed to duplicate and distribute it further. Still, there is no problem about your making several copies for your own use.

■ *Shareware:* **Shareware** is copyrighted software that is distributed free of charge but requires users to pay a fee in order to receive technical help, documentation, or upgrades. Shareware, too, is distributed primarily by communications connections such as the Internet. An example of shareware is WinZip, a program for decompressing/compressing computer files (✔ p. 5.11), which you can obtain from the Internet.

Is there any problem about making copies of shareware for your friends? Actually, the developer is hoping you will do just that. That's the way the program gets distributed to a lot of people—some of whom, the software creator hopes, will make a contribution or pay a registration fee for advice or upgrades.

Because shareware is copyrighted, you cannot use it as the basis for developing your own program in order to compete with the developer.

Proprietary Software and Types of Licenses

Proprietary software is software whose rights are owned by an individual or business, usually a software developer. The ownership is protected by the copyright, and the owner expects you to buy a copy in order to use it. The software cannot legally be used or copied without permission.

Software manufacturers don't sell you the software so much as sell you a license to become an authorized user of it. What's the difference? In paying for a **software license,** you sign a contract in which you agree not to make copies of the software to give away or for resale. That is, you have bought only the company's permission to use the software and not the software itself. This legal nicety allows the company to retain its rights to the program and limits the way its customers can use it. The small print in the licensing agreement allows you to make one copy (backup copy or archival copy) for your own use.

There are several type of licenses:

■ *Shrink-wrap licenses:* **Shrink-wrap licenses** are printed licenses inserted into software packages and visible through the clear plastic wrap or printed directly on the plastic wrap. The use of shrink-wrap licenses eliminates the need for a written signature, since buyers know they are entering into a binding contract by merely opening the package. Each shrink-wrap license is for a single system.

- *Single-user licenses:* A **single-user license** limits the use of the software in a network to one user at a time.

- *Multiple-user licenses:* A **multiple-user license** allows more than one person in a network to use the software. Each user is assigned a license, and only these people may use the software.

- *Concurrent-use license:* A **concurrent-use license** allows a specified number of software copies to be used at the same time. If, for example, the concurrent-use license is for 10 users, any 10 users in the company may use the software at the same time.

- *Site licenses:* A **site license** permits a customer to make as many copies of a software product as necessary for use just within a given facility, such as a college computer lab or a particular business.

The Software Police

Industry organizations such as the Software Publishers Association (hotline for reporting illegal copying: 800-388-7478) are going after software pirates large and small. Commercial software piracy is now a felony, punishable by up to five years in prison and fines of up to $250,000 for anyone convicted of stealing at least ten copies of a program or more than $2500 worth of software. Campus administrators are getting tougher with offenders and are turning them over to police.

Web Sites of Possible Interest

Freeware:
http://www.freewarenow.com
http://mirror.apple.com

Jewish and Hebrew software:
http://www.virtualjerusalem.com/gate

Non-English software:
http://www.threeweb.ad.jp/logos

Software archives:
http://www.filez.com
http://www.jumbo.com
http://www.pcworld.com/fileworld
http://www.shareware.com

Automobile Manufacturing

It's already come to this:

Concerned about the distracting effects on drivers not only of cellular phones but also of gadgets like satellite navigation systems and car-mounted personal computers, auto makers and federal regulators are setting up industry safety guidelines. This is a legitimate concern, since car manufacturers have unveiled high-tech options that will enable car drivers and passengers to download e-mail, surf the Internet, and receive faxes.

"The bottom line is we're very cognizant of driver overload and driver distraction," says one engineering manager.[a]

Coming down the road in the automobile industry is a cornucopia of gadgetry, some of it already available. Before you leave on a trip, there are a variety of Web sites you can consult that offer maps to your destination, weather forecasts en route, and suggested points of interest. Or you can install a car-based global-positioning device, like Street Pilot GPS, which will use signals from satellites to tell you where you are and plot your course.[b] Some luxury cars (Lexus, BMW) come with car-navigation systems as an option.[c] Or if you're a commuter who wants to avoid tie-ups, you can subscribe to a paging service such as RoadCast (from AirTouch Paging) which displays continuously updated traffic messages on a calculator-size pager.[d]

Under the hood in your car, microprocessors control acceleration, transmission, braking, traction, air bags, climate control, and antitheft systems. On cars with stability-control systems (Cadillac, Mercedes-Benz), it's no longer necessary for a driver to turn into the direction of a skid. Sensors tell the position of the steering wheel and the car's intended direction, as well as wheel speed and sideways acceleration, and automatically feed data to onboard computers that correct the skid.[e,f] Newer vehicles also have night-vision displays that sense infrared energy coming from animals and people along the roadway who are invisible to the human eye, sonar devices to help you back into tight parking places, and "smart" cruise-control systems that will keep you a minimum distance from the car in front of you.[g] Some cars also feature voice-recognition systems that lets you control climate, audio, and cell-phone systems with your voice. ("Phone dial 555-1212" or "Temperature 70 degrees.")[h,i]

Finally, there are the somewhat scary developments of "steering-wheel offices" and "road theater." In the new "network vehicle," workaholic road warriors can mount a laptop computer on the steering wheel, plug an extra cell phone into the cigarette lighter, and check their e-mail on the PC screen mounted in place of the car radio in their dashboards.[j,k,l] Meanwhile, in the back seat, other passengers can watch movies and TV, play video games, and browse the Web on flat-screen monitors.[m,n]

The following are some Web sites of interest: *www.MapsOnUs.com* offers free directions and maps, *www.FreeTrip.com* suggests points of interest on your travel route, *www.Weather.com* provides forecasts en route. Vehicle price guides are provided by Kelleys Blue Book (*www.kbb.com*) and Edmund's (*www.edmund.com*). Car-buying tips are offered by Consumer Reports Online (*www.consumerreports.com*). "Vehicle satisfaction scores" are provided on *www.autopacific.com*.

Sports

"There's no reason for an umpire to call balls and strikes," says Peter Teitelbaum, a professor of health and sports science at the University of Dayton. "Let's have a real, computer-generated strike zone."[a]

Is this what baseball will become? Computers have entered sports as they have everything else.

The high-technology heart of professional sports may be secondary storage hardware, wherein reside the databases with their vast compilations of statistics. However, computers are present in many other ways as well. "Armed with notebook computers, fax modems, and specialized software," says one report on professional basketball, "the teams compile scouting reports, analyze statistics, and create models to predict what players and teams might do in specific game situations. In a matter of minutes and a few keystrokes, the machines permit coaches to do work that used to take hours of laborious sorting through statistics sheets and play diagrams."[b]

The National Football League has borrowed the same technology that physicians use for sonograms in order to produce still-image photos from video films. Whereas at one time coaches on the sidelines used runners (or even nylon cord and shower-curtain hooks) to convey Polaroid photos of game movements taken from the booth high above the field, today they rely on sophisticated video printers to spit out almost instantaneous images to enable them to evaluate formations and plays. "It's a good coaching tool," says Tom Donahoe, director of football operations for the Pittsburgh Steelers. "The game happens so fast. Sometimes, the picture verifies what you saw. Sometimes, it shows you something else."[c]

In competitive sailing races, such as America's Cup, onboard computers provide data on weather and wave conditions from sensors, and the information is transmitted to sealed displays. A sophisticated navigation system takes readings from satellites twice a second. Hull designs are created by computer-controlled modeling machines. Models are hooked to digital sensors and put through tests in water-filled tanks. During actual competition, laser beams are bounced off competitors to provide information on rival boats' speed and distance.[d]

Computers are present in amateur sports as well. Runners in the London Marathon attach microchips to their shoelaces which, when they run over strategically placed mats, send information to a computer system that computes how fast they are going.[e] At bowling alleys, players checking in are assigned lanes by clerks using a Windows NT local area network; the bowlers then punch in their names at a terminal that keeps score automatically, and pin spotters are activated by infrared cameras taking digital images of the pins.[f] Microprocessors are now used in snowboards, skis, water skis, and mountain bicycles in devices called "piezoelectric modules" to control vibrations.[g]

And for sports fans in need of hourly fixes of scores, statistics, and news updates, the Internet is tailor-made for them, since sports material can be updated constantly from anywhere around the world.[h,i,j]

Some Web sites for sports information or news are: *www.audionet.com, www.cbs.sports. com, www/cnnsi.com, www/finalfour. net, www/sportsticker.com, espn.sportzone.com, www.totalsports. com, www.nba.com, www. majorleaguebaseball.com, www.nhl.com,* and *www.olympic.com.*

WHAT IT IS
WHAT IT DOES

WHY IT IS IMPORTANT

analytical graphics (KQ 6.3, p. 6.13) Also called *business graphics;* graphical forms representing numerical data. The principal examples are bar charts, line graphs, and pie charts.

Numerical data is easier to analyze in graphical form than in the form of rows and columns of numbers, as in electronic spreadsheets.

button (KQ 6.2, p. 6.5) Simulated on-screen button (a kind of icon) that is activated ("pushed") by a mouse click (or other pointing device) to issue a command.

Buttons make it easier for users to enter commands.

(CAD/CAM) computer-aided design/computer-aided manufacturing (KQ 6.4, p. 6.26) Applications software that allows products designed with CAD to be input into a computer-based manufacturing (CAM) system that makes the products.

CAD/CAM systems have greatly enhanced creativity and efficiency in many industries.

cell (KQ 6.3, p. 6.13) In an electronic spreadsheet, the rectangle where a row and a column intersect.

The cell is the smallest working unit in a spreadsheet. Data and formulas are entered into the cells.

cell address (KQ 6.3, p. 6.13) In an electronic spreadsheet, the position of a cell—for example, "A1," where column A and row 1 intersect.

Cell addresses provide location references for spreadsheet users.

Clipboard (KQ 6.2, p. 6.6) Area where cut or copied material is held before it is pasted.

The Clipboard allows you to copy or cut an item from one document and then paste it into another part of the same document, another document, or another application.

concurrent-use license (KQ 6.6, p. 6.35) License that allows a specified number of software copies to be used at the same time.

If, for example, the concurrent-use license is for 10 users, any 10 users in the company may use the software at the same time.

copyright (KQ 6.6, p. 6.31) Body of law that prohibits copying of intellectual property without the permission of the copyright holder.

Copyright law aims to prevent people from taking credit for and profiting unfairly from other people's work.

database software (KQ 6.3, p. 6.16) Applications software for maintaining a database. It controls the structure of a database and access to the data.

Database manager software allows users to organize and manage huge amounts of data.

+ Big 3 software packages
+ Common features of Windows Software

+ font, typeface
+ proportionate vs. fixed spacing.
+ integrated software
(works vs. suites)

+ field, record, file.

default values (KQ 6.2, p. 6.5) Settings automatically used by a program unless the user specifies otherwise, thereby overriding them.

Users need to know how to change default settings in order to customize their documents.

desktop accessory (KQ 6.3, p. 6.20) Also called *desktop organizer*, software package that provides electronic counterparts of tools or objects commonly found on a desktop: calendar, clock, card file, calculator, and notepad.

Desktop accessories help users to streamline their daily activities.

desktop publishing (DTP) (KQ 6.4, p. 6.23) Applications software that, along with a microcomputer, mouse, scanner, and printer, is used to mix text and graphics, including photos, to produce high-quality printer output. Some word processing programs also have many DTP features. Text is usually composed first on a word processor, artwork is created with drawing and painting software, and photographs are scanned in. Prefabricated clip art and photos may also be obtained from disks (CD-ROM and/or floppy) containing clip art.

Desktop publishing has reduced the number of steps, the time, and the money required to produce professional-looking printed projects.

dialog box (KQ 6.2, p. 6.5) In a graphical user interface, a box that appears on the screen and is used to collect information from the user and to display helpful messages.

Dialog boxes make software easier to use.

documentation (KQ 6.2, p. 6.6) User's manual or reference manual that is a narrative and graphical description of a program. Documentation may be instructional, but usually features and functions are grouped by category.

Documentation helps users learn software commands and use of function keys, solve problems, and find information about system specifications.

drawing program (KQ 6.4, p. 6.27) Applications software that allows users to design and illustrate objects and products.

Drawing programs are vector-based and are best used for straightforward illustrations based on geometric shapes.

field (KQ 6.3, p. 6.18) Unit of data consisting of one piece of information, whether text, numbers, or media object (sound bite, graphic).

Examples of a field are your name, your address, your driver's license number, *or* your photo.

file (KQ 6.3, p. 6.18) Collection of related records.

A file in your state's Department of Motor Vehicles might include, for example, everyone who received a driver's license on the same day, including their names, addresses, and driver's license numbers.

font (KQ 6.3, p. 6.9) A particular typeface and size.

Once the font is set, you can make headings or emphasized words stand out by adding bold, italic, or underlined styles.

formatting (KQ 6.3, p. 6.9) Determining the appearance of a document.

There are many ways to format a document, including using different typefaces, boldface, italics, variable spacing, columns, and margins. The document's format should match the needs of its users.

formula (KQ 6.3, p. 6.13) In an electronic spreadsheet, instruction for calculations that are entered into designated cells. For example, a formula might be SUM(A5:A15), meaning "Sum (add) all the numbers in the cells with cell addresses A5 through A15."

When spreadsheet users change data in one cell, all the cells linked to it by formulas will automatically recalculate their values.

freeware (KQ 6.6, p. 6.34) Software that is available free of charge.

Freeware is usually distributed through the Internet. Users can make copies for their own use but are not free to make unlimited copies.

groupware (KQ 6.3, p. 6.18) Applications software that is used on a network and serves a group of users working together on the same project.

Groupware improves productivity by keeping users continually notified about what their colleagues are thinking and doing.

Help menu (KQ 6.2, p. 6.5) Applications software feature that offers instructions for using other software features; includes Help screens, searchable indexes, and online glossaries.

Help menus provide a built-in electronic instruction manual.

icon (KQ 6.2, p. 6.5) Small pictorial figure that represents a task, function, program, file, or disk. The function or object represented by the icon can be activated by clicking on it.

The introduction of icons has simplified the use of software.

insertion point (KQ 6.2, p. 6.4) Also called the *cursor*; movable symbol on the display screen that shows the user where data may be entered next. The insertion point is moved around with the keyboard's directional arrow keys or by means of the mouse.

All applications software packages use insertion points to show users their current work location on the screen.

integrated software package (KQ 6.3, p. 6.21) Applications software that combines several applications programs into one package—usually electronic spreadsheet, word processing, database management, graphics, and communications programs.

Integrated software packages offer greater flexibility than separate single-purpose programs.

intellectual property (KQ 6.6, p. 6.31) Consists of the products, tangible or intangible, of the human mind.

Such property can be protected by copyright, the exclusive legal right that prohibits copying without the permission of the copyright holder.

macro (KQ 6.2, p. 6.5) Software feature by means of which a single keystroke, command, or toolbar button may be used to automatically issue a predetermined series of commands.

Macros increase productivity by consolidating several command keystrokes into one or two.

menu bar (KQ 6.2, p. 6.4) A row of menu options displayed across the top or bottom of the screen.

Menu bars make software easier to use.

multimedia authoring software (KQ 6.4, p. 6.28) Special applications software that enables creators to combine not only text and graphics but also animation, video, music, voice, and sound effects, as well as a measure of user interaction, into multimedia productions.

Because people tend to remember much more of what they both hear and see, multimedia has become a useful tool in many areas, including education, professional training and simulation, and entertainment.

multiple-user license (KQ 6.6, p. 6.35) License that allows more than one person in a network to use the software.

Each user is assigned a license, and only these people may use the software.

network piracy (KQ 6.6, p. 6.32) The use of electronic networks for unauthorized distribution of copyrighted materials in digitized form.

If piracy is not controlled, creative people may not want to make their intellectual property and copyrighted material available in digital form.

OLE (object linking and embedding) (KQ 6.2, p. 6.5) Means by which the user can embed an object created using one application (such as graphics) into another application (such as word processing).

OLE facilitates the sharing and manipulating of information.

painting program (KQ 6.4, p. 6.27) Raster-graphics program that allows the user to simulate painting, in color, on the screen.

Painting programs are good for art with soft edges and many colors.

personal finance software (KQ 6.3, p. 6.14) Applications software that helps users track income and expenses, write checks, and plan financial goals.

Personal finance software can help people manage their money more effectively.

personal information manager (PIM) (KQ 6.3, p. 6.20) Combined word processor, database, and desktop accessory software to organize information.

PIMs offer an electronic version of an appointment calendar, to-do list, address book, notepad, and similar daily office tools, all in one place.

plagiarism (KQ 6.6, p. 6.32) Expropriation of another writer's text, findings, or interpretations and presenting them as one's own.

Information technology offers plagiarists new opportunities to go far afield for unauthorized copying, yet it also offers new ways to catch these people.

pop-up menu (KQ 6.2, p. 6.5) A menu that "pops up" from the menu bar.

Pop-up menus make programs easier to use.

presentation graphics (KQ 6.3, p. 6.15) Graphical forms used to communicate or make a presentation of data to others, such as clients or supervisors.

Presentation graphics programs, part of presentation software packages, may employ analytical graphics but look much more sophisticated, thanks to the use of texturing patterns, complex color, and three-dimensional images.

project management software (KQ 6.4, p. 6.25) Applications software used to plan, schedule, and control the resources—people, costs, and equipment—required to complete a project on time.

Project management software increases the ease and speed of planning and managing complex projects.

proprietary software (KQ 6.6, p. 6.34) Software whose rights are owned by an individual or business.

Ownership of proprietary software is protected by copyright. This type of software must be purchased to be used. Copying is restricted.

public domain software (KQ 6.6, p. 6.34) Software that is not protected by copyright and thus may be duplicated by anyone at will.

Public domain software offers lots of software options to users who may not be able to afford much commercial software. Users may download such software from the Internet for free and make as many copies as they wish.

pull-down menu (KQ 6.2, p. 6.5) A list of command options, or choices, that is "pulled down" out of the menu bar.

Like other menu-based and GUI features, pull-down menus make software easier to use.

record (KQ 6.3, p. 6.18) Collection of related fields.

An example of a record would be your name and address and driver's license number *and* photograph.

scrolling (KQ 6.2, p. 6.4) Moving quickly upward or downward through text or other screen display, using directional arrow keys or the mouse.

Normally a computer screen displays only 20–22 lines of text. Scrolling enables users to view an entire document, no matter how long.

shareware (KQ 6.6, p. 6.34) Copyrighted software that is distributed free of charge, usually over the Internet; users must make a payment to the copyright holder in order to receive technical help, documentation, or upgrades.

Along with public domain software and freeware, shareware offers yet another inexpensive way to obtain new software.

shrink-wrap license (KQ 6.6, p. 6.34) Printed license inserted into the software packaging and visible through the clear plastic wrap.

The use of shrink-wrap licenses eliminates the need for a written signature, since buyers know they are entering a binding contract by opening the wrapping.

single-user license (KQ 6.6, p. 6.35) License that limits the use of the software in a network to one user at a time.

Only one person is licensed to use the software.

site license (KQ 6.6, p. 6.35) License that permits a customer to make multiple copies of a software product for use only within a given facility.

Site licenses eliminate the need to buy many copies of one software package for use in, for example, an office or a computer lab.

software license (KQ 6.6, p. 6.34) Contract by which users agree not to make copies of proprietary software to give away or to sell.

Software manufacturers don't sell people software so much as licenses to become authorized users of the software.

software piracy (KQ 6.6, p. 6.32) Unauthorized copying of copyrighted software—for example, copying a program onto a diskette for a friend.

Software piracy represents a serious loss of income to software manufacturers and tends to increase the prices of programs.

software suite (KQ 6.3, p. 6.21) Several applications software packages—like spreadsheet, word processing, graphics, communications, and groupware programs—bundled together and sold for a fraction of what they would cost if bought individually.

Software suites can save users a lot of money.

spreadsheet (KQ 6.3, p. 6.12) Also called *electronic spreadsheet*; applications software that simulates a paper worksheet and allows users to create tables and financial schedules by entering data and/or formulas into rows and columns displayed as a grid on a screen. If data is changed in one cell, values in other cells specified in the spreadsheet will be automatically recalculated.

The popularity of spreadsheet programs is largely responsible for the widespread adoption of the microcomputer as a business tool.

toolbar (KQ 6.2, p. 6.5) A row of on-screen buttons used to activate a variety of functions of the applications program.

Toolbars can often be customized and moved around on the screen.

tutorial (KQ 6.2, p. 6.6) Instruction book or program that takes users through a prescribed series of steps to help them learn the product.

Tutorials, which accompany applications software packages as booklets or on disk, enable users to practice new software in a graduated fashion and, accordingly, to learn in an effective manner. Tutorials may also be available online via the Internet.

Web browser (KQ 6.3, p. 6.22) Software that enables people to view Web sites on their computers.

Without browser software, users' access to the part of the Internet called the World Wide Web is impossible.

window (KQ 6.2, p. 6.4) Feature of graphical user interfaces; a rectangle that appears on the screen and displays information from a particular part of a program.

Using the windows feature, you can display several windows on the screen, each showing a different application program such as word processing, spreadsheets, and graphics, or showing different files within the same application.

word processing software (KQ 6.3, p. 6.8) Applications software that enables users to create, edit, revise, store, and print documents.

Word processing software allows you to easily create, change, and produce attractive documents such as letters, memos, reports, and manuscripts.

EXERCISES

1. Fill in the following blanks:

a. _____ _____ software allows you to create and edit documents.

b. A(n) _____ is a collection of interrelated files in a computer system.

c. New applications software must be _____ by the user before it can be used.

d. _____ is the activity of moving quickly upward or downward through the text or other screen display.

e. Workflow software, meeting software, and scheduling software are all considered _____ .

2. Label each of the following statements as either true or false.

_____ Word processing and database management are the two most popular applications.

_____ Electronic spreadsheet software enables you to perform "what-if" calculations.

_____ A worksheet is composed of fields, records, and files.

_____ You can access the World Wide Web using multimedia authoring software.

_____ OLE is used to collect information from the user and display helpful messages.

3. Describe each of the following terms:
   a. icon
   b. toolbar
   c. macro
   d. Clipboard

4. What is word processing software used for?

a. _____

b. _____

c. _____

d. _____

5. Describe each of the following spreadsheet terms:
   a. cell
   b. cell address
   c. formula

6. List four features of personal finance software.

a. _____

b. _____

c. _____

d. _____

7. Define each of the following terms:
   a. intellectual property
   b. copyright
   c. software piracy
   d. network piracy

8. Define the following database terms:
   a. field
   b. record
   c. file

9. What are the following types of software used for?
   a. project management software
   b. desktop-publishing software
   c. personal information manager (PIM)

IN YOUR OWN WORDS

1. Answer each of the Key Questions that appear at the beginning of this chapter.

2. What is the difference between software productivity tools and specialty tools?

3. What's the difference between drawing and painting software?

4. What's the difference between a software version and a release?

5. How does a shrink-wrap license differ from a site license?

6. What would you say to a person who asks for a copy of a new applications program you just bought?

7. What is the difference between freeware and shareware?

8. What are CAD programs used for?

9. What is the difference between integrated software and a software suite?

KNOWLEDGE IN ACTION

1. **Choosing Software.** If you were in the market for a new microcomputer today, what software would you want to use on it? What system software would you choose? Make a list of each type of applications software that you think you would use and describe why.

2. **Purchasing Software.** Visit the following company Web sites to obtain more information about their respective integrated programs and software

suites: (a) Microsoft Office 2000—*www.microsoft.com/office*, (b) Corel WordPerfect Suite 8—*www.corel.com/products/wordperfect*, and (c) Ability Office 98—*www.ability.com*. For each product, list its name, capabilities, and price, if available.

3. **Exploring Shareware.** Shareware is copyrighted software that is distributed free of charge, but requires you to pay a fee later to receive technical help, documentation, or upgrades. Several Web sites include libraries of shareware programs and it's worth browsing them to see if any programs might be of interest. Visit the *www.winfiles.com* site and identify three shareware programs that you find interesting. For each program, state its name, the operating system it runs on, and its capabilities. Also, describe the contribution you must make to receive technical support.

4. **Creating a Document.** If you are using Windows 9x, do the following to create a short document. Click the Start button on the Windows taskbar and then choose Programs, Accessories, Word-Pad from the menus. Windows' word processing application will open. The insertion point is blinking in the upper-left corner of the document area. Type the following: "Word processing software allows you to easily insert, delete, and move words, sentences, and paragraphs. Word processing programs also offer a number of features for dressing up documents with variable margins, type sizes, and styles." If your computer is hooked up to a printer, print the document by clicking the Print button on the toolbar. (Hint: The Print button is represented by a printer icon.) To exit WordPad, click the Close button (☒) in the upper-right corner of the application window. When WordPad prompts you to save your work, use the mouse to click the No command button.

Answers to Self-Test Exercises   1a. word processing
1b. database   1c. installed   1d. scrolling   1e. groupware
2. F, T, F, F, F   3a. Small pictorial figure that represents a
task, function, program, file, or disk. The function or
object represented by the icon can be activated by clicking
on it.   3b. A row of on-screen buttons used to activate a
variety of functions of the applications program.
3c. Software feature by means of which a single keystroke,
command, or toolbar button may be used to automatically
issue a predetermined series of commands.   3d. Area
where cut or copied material is held before it is pasted.
4. creating documents, editing documents, formatting documents, printing documents   5a. In an electronic spreadsheet, the rectangle where a row and a column intersect.
5b. In an electronic spreadsheet, the position of a cell—for
example, "A1," where column A and row 1 intersect.
5c. In an electronic spreadsheet, instruction for calculations
that are entered into designated cells. For example, a formula might be SUM(A5:A15), meaning "Sum (add) all the
numbers in the cells with cell addresses A5 through A15."
6. tracking of income and expenses, checkbook management, reporting, income tax   7a. Intellectual property consists of the products, tangible or intangible, of the human
mind. There are three methods of protecting intellectual
property: patents (as for an invention), trade secrets (as for
a formula or method of doing business), and copyrights (as
for a song or a book).   7b. A copyright is the exclusive
legal right that prohibits copying of intellectual property
without the permission of the copyright holder. Copyright
law protects books, articles, pamphlets, music, art, drawings, movies—and, yes, computer software. Copyright protects the expression of an idea but not the idea itself.
7c. Software piracy is the unauthorized copying of copyrighted software. One way is to copy a program from one
floppy disk to another. Another is to download a program
from a network and make a copy of it.   7d. Network piracy is using electronic networks to distribute unauthorized
copyrighted materials in digitized form. Record companies,
for example, have protested the practice of computer users'
sending unauthorized copies of digital recordings over the
Internet.   8a. Unit of data consisting of one piece of
information, whether text, numbers, or media object
(sound bite, graphic).   8b. Collection of related fields.
8c. Collection of related records.   9a. Project management
software is a program used to plan, schedule, and control
resources—people, costs, and equipment—required to
complete a project on time.   9b. Desktop publishing,
abbreviated DTP, involves using a microcomputer and
mouse, scanner, laser or ink-jet printer, and DTP software
for mixing text and graphics to produce high-quality printed output for commercial printing.   9c. A personal information manager (PIM) combines word processing, database, and desktop accessory program to organize a variety
of information.

EPISODE 3

PLANNING FOR COMMERCE AT YOUR SITE

Imagine if someone pointed you in the direction of a pile of four-by-fours and construction tools and said "build something." There's no saying what you would come up with. The possibilities are almost as varied when you consider options for constructing a Web site for presenting your products and supporting financial transactions.

The degree to which you make it easy for customers to find out about your products, make selections, and provide payment information, will directly affect the success of your online business. Amazon.com has been very successful in these areas. As one Amazon.com customer commented, "Your site is dangerous. I could easily spend half my salary here. I love bookstores and libraries, but frankly, I find more of the titles I want on your site, and they're so easy to order, and the interface is so friendly that I think this new vice is going to corrupt me permanently."

CREATING AN ONLINE CATALOG

How you present your product(s) can be determined to a large extent by how many products you sell. If you carry just a few products, a simple listing, perhaps in a table format, that includes the name, description, and price for each product might work just fine. A more interesting approach would be to use graphical representations of your products that are linked to pages containing more detailed information. With this approach, users selectively reveal more information about the products they're interested in. Let's look at how you might obtain more information about the book entitled *Encore Provence*, by Peter Mayle, as featured on Amazon.com's Home page on May 21, 1999.

Step 1:
One method you can use to find out more about *Encore Provence* is to click the book's cover graphic. (Note: Another method would be to click the Encore Provence link.)

Going South

After a four-year break from his cherished turf, Peter Mayle returned to France to write *Encore Provence*. His prose is as evocative as ever, whether he's describing the terrain, the people, or the cuisine. Don't miss his fine essay on that crucial Provençal implement--the corkscrew!

Excerpt

40% off

Step 2:
After clicking the graphic, the following screen appears. At this point, click the read an excerpt link, located on the left side of the screen.

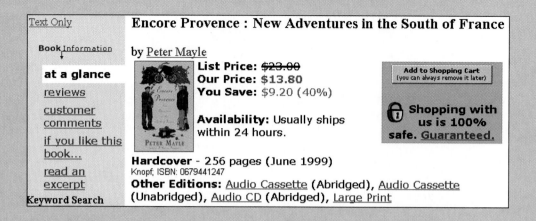

Step 3:

An excerpt of the book appears. After reading the excerpt, you may decide to purchase the book by clicking the Add to Shopping Cart link that appears in the blue box near the top of the screen.

From Chapter One

I think it was the sight of a man power-washing his underpants that really brought home the differences, cultural and otherwise, between the old world and the new.

It was a cold, still morning in early winter, and the pulsing thumpthump, thumpthump of a high-pressure hose echoed through the village. Getting closer to the sound, it was possible to see, over a garden wall, a laundry line totally devoted to gentlemen's underwear in a stimulating assortment of colors. The garments were under attack, jerking and flapping under the force of the water jet like hanging targets in a shooting gallery. Standing some distance away, out of ricochet range, was the aggressor, in cap and muffler and ankle-high zippered carpet slippers. He had adopted the classic stance of a soldier in combat, feet spread apart, shooting from the hip, a merciless hail of droplets raking back and forth. The underpants didn't stand a chance.

Step 4:

Details such as price, page length, and availability will now appear on the screen.

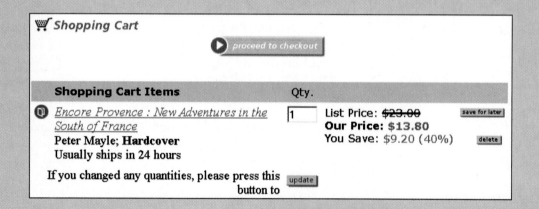

If you sell many products, consider building a search capability into your site or organizing your products into categories. Amazon.com has done both. With Amazon.com's search tools, for example, you can locate a book (or other product) based on its title, subject, author, keyword, publication date, or ISBN. To find out what books are available in a broader topic area, such as the topic of starting a Web-based business, you might be better off browsing through Amazon.com's categories and subcategories until you target a book of interest.

TAKING ORDERS AND COLLECTING PAYMENT

A common method for taking orders is to simply include contact information, such as your business address, phone number, fax number, and e-mail address, at the bottom of every page in your site. Customers can then use one of these contact points to obtain additional information about your products or to place an order. This method works well if your online catalog contains a few products. If your online catalog contains many products, consider automating your transaction processing system using Web shopping carts and interactive forms. A customer can easily add products to or take products out of a virtual shopping cart prior to making the actual decision to purchase. Amazon.com employs this latter approach.

SECURITY CONCERNS

Some of your customers may not feel comfortable about providing financial details, such as credit card numbers, over the Internet. To make customers feel more at ease, consider giving them options such as talking to someone to complete the order.

Additional methods for collecting payment involve personal checks, purchase orders, membership systems, and electronic money. But as Web authors David Cook and Deborah Sellers put it ". . . [E]ither trust the human or the machine. And many users who would balk at entering their number via the Internet would easily use their cordless or cellular phone, both of which are extremely open to eavesdropping."[1] Software-based commerce servers are available which attempt to make the Internet secure for credit card transactions.

TRACKING INVENTORY

Now that your customer has done his job by providing order and payment information, you must do your part by shipping the product quickly, and ideally, providing the customer with an e-mail notice describing the status of the order. Amazon.com customers are notified within 15 minutes of placing an order that the order was received. Keeping good track of inventory through the use of a database application that is constantly updated with order information will help you chart current inventory levels, so that you can replenish inventory when necessary. Amazon.com's order database, for example, is directly linked to its inventory database. Good inventory management will ensure that you have product in stock, your orders are shipped promptly, and that customer relations remain strong.

CHOOSING SOFTWARE

Much of the software you'll need to create your Web site is available for free on the Internet. For starters, you'll need a software tool called an *HTML (hypertext markup language) editor*, such as Microsoft FrontPage, that you will use to build your Web site and a graphics program that will let you work with a broad range of graphics files. If this topic is starting to sound a bit technical, remember that your expert Web consultant can take care of creating your site for you. In this Episode, continue to focus on "what" you want to do, not "how" you're going to do it.

Below we provide some general software recommendations for gaining access to the Internet and using some of its features. Much of this software may be included in your computer's system software. Otherwise, your access provider can provide you with most of this software.

- *Internet connection software*—This type of software is necessary for you to establish a connection between your computer and the Internet. This software may already be built into your computer's system software.

- *Web browser software*—Browser software enables you to view your Web site.

- *E-mail software*—With e-mail software, you can receive and send electronic messages to anyone on the Internet.

- *Usenet software*—With Usenet software, you can read, post, and reply to messages in the many thousands of newsgroups on the Internet. Usenet provides an excellent means for you to advertise your business to people with a specific interest in your product.

- *FTP (File Transfer Protocol)*—This software provides your primary means of sending and receiving files when you're not using the Web. You would use FTP, for example, to update your Web site if it is located remotely on your provider's computer.

Keep in mind that as you continue to develop your business, you'll come up with additional software requirements.

WHAT DO YOU THINK?

1. Describe the specific features of the Yourname.com online catalog. What method have you chosen to present your products? Why?

2. How do you plan to take customer orders at Yourname.com? Why? If you plan to use an interactive order form, provide an example of how you want your form to look (using pen and paper or design software), and then describe the rationale behind the specific features of your form.

3. How have you decided to collect payment from your customers? Why?

4. How do you plan to keep track of inventory? If you will be using a database management system, what fields will you include in your inventory database?

CHAPTER 7

COMMUNICATIONS TECHNOLOGY

Starting Along the Information Superhighway

"Computers and communications: These are the parents of the Information Age," says one writer. "When they meet, the fireworks begin."[1] What are those fireworks? One dramatic consequence of information and communications technologies is that conventional meanings of time and space are changing. Says one expert, "The physical locations we traditionally associate with work, leisure, and similar pursuits are rapidly becoming meaningless."[2]

Through communications and connectivity, computers, telephones, and wireless devices are being linked by invisible networks everywhere. In this chapter we describe the basics of communications technology. In the next chapter we describe some of the things you can do with this technology.

7.1 Using Computers to Communicate: Technological Basics

KEY QUESTION **What do you need to communicate online through a microcomputer?**

Figure 7.1 Analog and digital signals. An analog signal represents a continuous electrical signal in the form of a wave. A digital signal is discontinuous, expressed as discrete bursts in on/off electrical pulses.

Communications, or *telecommunications,* refers to the transfer of data (*communications*) from a transmitter—also called a sender or a source—to a receiver—also called a sink—across a distance (*tele,* from ancient Greek, meaning "far off"). Some form of electromagnetic energy—electricity, radio waves, or light—is used to represent the data or code, which is transmitted through a physical medium—for example, wire, cable, or the atmosphere. Additionally, some intermediate devices may be required to set up a path for the data transfer and to maintain adequate signal strength. The data transmitted can be voice, text, video, images, sound, or a combination of these (multimedia).

Recall from Chapter 1 (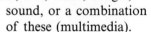 p. 1.6) that data can be transmitted by two types of signals, *analog* and *digital.* (*See Figure 7.1 for a review.*) In a way they resemble analog and digital watches. An analog watch shows time as a continuum. A digital watch shows time as discrete numeric values.

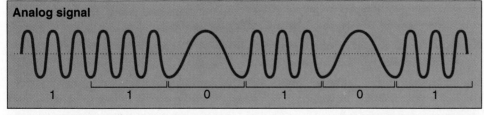

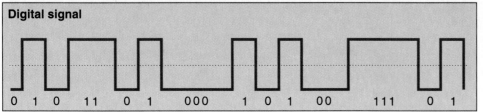

An entomologist enters data on a laptop computer, deep in the rain forest in Belize, Central America.

Analog Signals: Continuous Waves

Telephones, radios, and televisions—the older forms of communications technology—were designed to work with an analog signal. An *analog signal* is a continuous electrical signal in the form of a wave called a *carrier wave*.

Two characteristics of analog carrier waves that can be altered are frequency and amplitude.

- *Frequency:* **Frequency** is the number of times a wave repeats during a specific time interval—that is, how many times it completes a *cycle* in a second.

- *Amplitude:* **Amplitude** is the height of a wave within a given period of time. Amplitude is actually the strength or volume—the loudness—of a signal.

Both frequency and amplitude can be modified by making adjustments to the wave. Indeed, it is by such adjustments that an analog signal can be made to express a digital signal, as we shall explain.

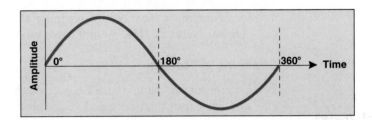

Digital Signals: Discrete Bursts

You have learned that a *digital signal* uses on/off or present/absent electrical pulses in discontinuous, or discrete, bursts, rather than a continuous wave. This two-state signal represents the two-state binary language of 0s and 1s that computers use. That is, the presence of an electrical pulse can represent a 1 bit, its absence a 0 bit.

Actually, the transmission of data as discrete (digital) signals is not as new as you might think. In the mid-1880s, Samuel Morse developed the Morse code, which on paper consisted of a series of dots and dashes. Thus the letter V, for example, consisted of three dots and a dash (... –). However, the actual transmission of this character via telegraph wires and telegraphing equipment consisted of three short signals ("taps") and one long signal, each signal being separated by a pause.

The Modem: The Great Translator

Computers use digital signals. However, many of our present communications lines, such as telephone and microwave, are still analog. To get around this problem, we need a **modem**—short for *mo*dulator/*dem*odulator—to convert digital signals into analog form (a process known as *modulation*) for transition over phone lines. A receiving modem at the other end of the phone line then converts the analog signal back to a digital signal (a process known as *demodulation*). (*See Figure 7.2, next page.*)

Modulation/demodulation does not actually change the wave form of an analog signal into the on/off form of the digital signal. Rather, it changes the form of the wave. For instance, the frequency might be changed. A normal wave cycle within a given period of time might represent a 1, but more frequent wave cycles within a given period might represent a 0. Or, the amplitude might be changed. A

Figure 7.2 How modems work. A sending modem translates digital signals into analog waves for transmission over phone lines. A receiving modem translates the analog signals back into digital signals.

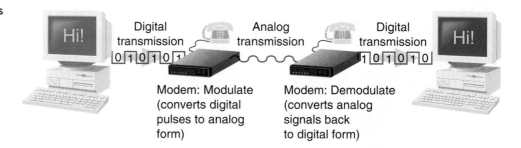

loud sound might represent a 1 bit, a soft sound might represent a 0 bit. That is, a wave with normal height (amplitude) might signify a 1, a wave with smaller height a 0. *(See Figure 7.3.)* The wave itself does not assume the boxy on/off shape represented by the true digital signal.

From this we can see that modems are a compromise. They cannot transmit digital signals in a way that delivers their full benefits. As a consequence, communications companies have been developing alternatives, such as the Integrated Services Digital Network (ISDN) and cable modems, discussed shortly.

Choosing a Modem

Two criteria for choosing a modem are whether you want an internal or external one, and what transmission speed you wish:

■ *External versus internal:* Modems are either internal or external. *(See Figure 7.4.)* An external modem is a box that is separate from the computer. The box may be large or it may be portable, pocket size. A cable connects the modem to a port in the back of the computer. A second line connects the modem to a standard telephone jack. There is also a power cord that plugs into a standard AC wall socket. The advantage of the external modem is that it can be used with different computers. Thus, if you buy a new microcomputer, you will probably be able to use your old external modem.

An internal modem is a circuit board that plugs into a slot inside the system cabinet or that is integrated into the motherboard (✔ p. 2.17). Nowadays most new microcomputers come with an internal modem already installed. Advantages of the internal modem are that it doesn't take up extra space on your desk and doesn't have a separate power cord.

For laptop computers, modems are on PC (PCMCIA) cards (✔ p. 25).

Figure 7.3 Modifying an analog signal. A modem may modify an analog signal to carry the on/off digital signals of a computer in two ways. (*Top*) The frequency of wave cycles is altered so that a normal wave represents a 1 and a more frequent wave within a given period represents a 0. (*Bottom*) The amplitude (height) of a wave is altered so that a wave of normal height represents a 1 and a wave of lesser height represents a 0.

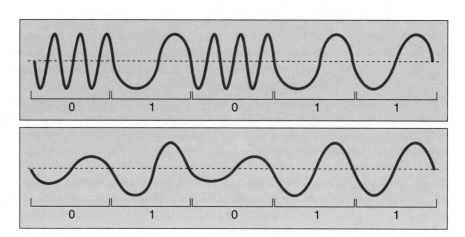

[Handwritten margin note:] Internal modem → modem plugs into computer. External modem → modem is located on external box.

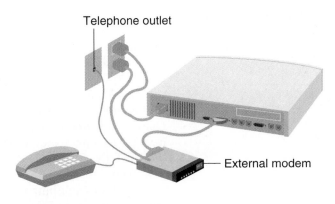

Telephone outlet

External modem

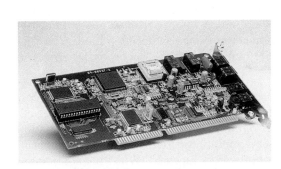

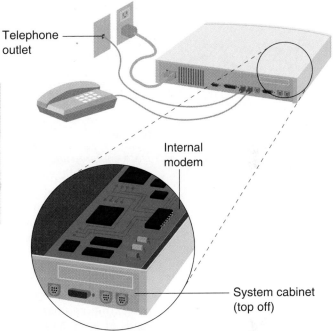

Telephone outlet

Internal modem

System cabinet
(top off)

Figure 7.4 External versus internal modems. An external modem is a box that is outside the computer (*top*). An internal modem is a circuit installed in an expansion slot inside the system cabinet (*bottom*).

■ *Transmission speed:* Because most modems use standard telephone lines, users are charged the usual rates by phone companies, whether local or long-distance. Users are also often charged by online services for time spent online. Accordingly, *transmission speed*—the speed at which modems transmit data—becomes an important consideration. The faster the modem, the less time you need to spend on the telephone line.

Transmission speeds are typically expressed in terms of **bits per second (bps)** or, more likely, **kilobits per second (Kbps).** Today's modems typically operate at speeds of 28,800 bps (or 28.8 Kbps), 33.6 Kbps, or 56 Kbps. To give you an idea of how the speed of your modem might affect you, a ten-page single-spaced letter can be transmitted by a 28.8-Kbps modem in about 10 seconds, and by a 56-Kbps modem in about 5 seconds.

Note: The type and condition of phone lines affect modem speed—for example, many phone lines max out at 28.8 Kbps or 33.6 Kbps. Also, when two modems are connected, they will run at the speed of the slower one.

Modems used to be manufactured using different standards. That meant that not every 56 Kpbs modem would work with every Internet service provider. However, a standard called *V.90* was developed for new 56 Kbps modems. (Software updates are available for older 56 Kbps modems.) Thus, all new 56 Kbps modems are compatible.

Communications Software

To communicate via modem, your microcomputer requires communications software. *Communications software* manages the transmission of data between computers. Today, many communications software functions are taken care of by the system software (for example, Windows 98). In addition, communications software is also supplied by many online services, such as CompuServe and America Online, and Internet service providers, such as Mindspring. Macintosh users also have Smartcom; Windows users have Smartcom, Crosstalk, Wincom, Comm Works, Telix, Crosstalk, Procomm Plus, and HyperTerminal; OS/2 Warp users have HyperAccess.

Besides establishing connections among computers, communications software may perform other functions:

- *Error correction:* Static on telephone lines can introduce errors into data transmission, or "noise." Noise is an extraneous signal that causes distortion in the data signal. Noise can be caused by power line spikes, poorly fitting electrical contacts, or strong electrical/magnetic signals coming from nearby power lines or equipment such as air conditioners and X-ray machines. Although such "noise" may not affect voice transmission very much, it can garble high-speed data transmission. When acquiring a modem and its accompanying software, you should inquire whether it incorporates error-correction features.

- *Data compression:* As we mentioned in Chapter 5 (✔ p. 5.9), data compression reduces the volume of data in a message, thereby reducing the amount of time required to send data from one modem to another. The communications software does this by replacing repeating patterns with symbols that indicate what the pattern is and how often it is repeated. When the compressed message reaches the receiver, the symbols are then replaced and the full message is restored. With text and graphics, a message may be compressed to as much as one-tenth of its original size.

- *Remote control:* Remote-control software allows you to control a microcomputer from another microcomputer in a different location, perhaps even thousands of miles away. One part of the program is in the machine in front of you, the other in the remote machine. Such software is useful for travelers who want to use their home machines from afar. It's also helpful for technicians trying to assist users with support problems. Examples of remote-control software for microcomputers are Carbon Copy, Commute, Norton PCAnywhere, and Timbuktu/Remote.

- *Terminal emulation:* Mainframes and minicomputers are designed to be accessed by terminals, not by microcomputers, which have a different operating system. Terminal emulation software allows you to use your microcomputer to simulate a mainframe or minicomputer terminal. That is, the software tricks the large computer into acting as if it is communicating with a terminal. (Some system software, such as Windows 95, includes terminal emulation software.)

Don't need → ## ISDN, Cable Modems, ADSL, and Dishes: Faster, Faster, Faster!

Users who find themselves banging the table in frustration as their 28.8-Kbps modem takes 25 minutes to transmit a 1-minute low-quality video from a Web site are about to get some relief. The most immediate contenders to replace standard phone modems are *ISDN, cable modems, ADSL,* and *satellite dish.*

■ *ISDN lines:* **ISDN** stands for **Integrated Services Digital Network,** which consists of hardware and software that allow voice, video, and data to be communicated as digital signals over traditional copper-wire telephone lines, called *POTS* (*plain old telephone system*). Capable of transmitting up to 128 Kbps, ISDN lines are up to five times faster than conventional phone modems. ISDN also supports two phone lines so that you can talk on the phone on one line while connecting to the Internet on the other.

Provided by many telephone companies, ISDN is not cheap, costing perhaps two or three times as much as regular monthly phone service. Installation could also cost $350 or more if you need a phone technician to wire your house and install the software in your PC; and you need to purchase a special ISDN connector box or adapter card, to which you connect your microcomputer, fax machine, modem, and telephone. Nevertheless, with the number of people now working at home and/or surfing the Internet, demand has pushed ISDN orders off the charts.

■ *ADSL:* A recent hardware and software technology called *Asymmetric Digital Subscriber Line (ADSL)* is considered by many to be the successor to ISDN. It was developed by Bellcore Labs, the biggest research consortium in the United States, jointly owned by the seven regional Bell operating companies. Microsoft, Compaq, and Intel are promoting ADSL through various phone companies. Experts predict that by 2002, about 2.7 million people will be using ADSL on regular telephone lines (POTS).

■ *Cable modems:* Cable companies say that a cable modem can carry digital data more than 1000 times faster (up to 30 Mbps) than POTS lines, and they've found that usage shoots up when the service is connected. **A cable modem** connects a personal computer to a cable-TV system that offers online services. Unlike regular cable set-top boxes, which allow only one-way data transmission, cable modems handle two-way transmission. Most experts choose cable modem in areas where it's available, because it's faster than ADSL. Presently about 30% of cable homes are wired for two-way connectivity. By 2002, about 13.6 million people are expected to be using cable modems.

■ *Dishes:* Satellite dishes offer yet another improvement in data transmission speed. Hughes Network Systems offers a 36-inch satellite dish called the Convergence Antenna that transmits 15 times faster than a standard high-speed modem. Instead of, for example, connecting to the Internet through telephone lines, users subscribe to Hughes's satellite Internet service, called DirecPC. Thus a 90-second animation clip that normally takes an hour to download arrives in less than two minutes. (We discuss satellites in more detail later in the chapter.)

Hardware	Speed	Installation Cost	Local Use Cost	Availability
ISDN	128 Kbps	$350–$700	About $30–$125 per month	Most major cities
ADSL	90–680 Kbps (upload)– 640 Kbps–8 Mbps (download)	$400–$800	About $30–$200 per month	Trial areas in major cities
Cable	96 Kbps (upload)– 30 Mbps (download)	$300–$500	About $30–$40 per month	Some major cities
Satellite dish	400 Kbps–33.6 Mbps	$650	About $50–$150 per month	Widespread

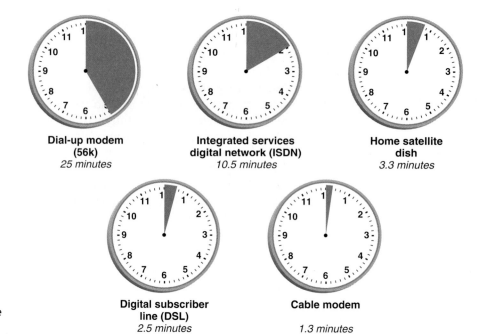

Dial-up modem (56k)
25 minutes

Integrated services digital network (ISDN)
10.5 minutes

Home satellite dish
3.3 minutes

Digital subscriber line (DSL)
2.5 minutes

Cable modem
1.3 minutes

Downloading *The Times.* Time typically needed to download a 10 MB file (about the file size of all the words, except advertising, in ten copies of the newspaper).

7.2 Communications Channels: The Conduits of Communications

KEY QUESTION **What is a communications channel?**

If you are of a certain age, you may recall when two-way individual communications were accomplished mainly in two ways. They were carried by (1) a telephone wire or (2) a wireless method such as shortwave radio. Today there are many kinds of communications channels, although they are still wired or wireless. A **communications channel** is the path—the physical medium—over which data travels in a telecommunications system from its source to its destination. Channels are also called *links, lines,* or *media.*

Let us now look at some common channel types.

- Twisted-pair wire
- Coaxial cable
- Fiber-optic cable
- Microwave systems
- Satellite systems
- Other wireless systems

Twisted-Pair Wire

The telephone line that runs from your house to the pole outside, or underground, is probably twisted-pair wire. **Twisted-pair wire** consists of two strands of insulated copper wire, twisted around each other. They are then covered in another layer of plastic insulation. *(See Figure 7.5.)* There are two types of twisted-pair wire: *UTP (unshielded twisted pair)* and *STP (shielded twisted pair).*

Because so much of the world is already served by twisted-pair wire, or POTS, it will no doubt continue to be used for years, both for voice messages and for modem-transmitted computer data. However, twisted pair can be slow, and it also does not protect well against electrical interference, called *noise*. It is still used to connect parts of a LAN over short distances, but it will certainly be superseded by better communications channels, wired or wireless.

Coaxial Cable

Coaxial cable, commonly called "co-ax," consists of insulated copper wire wrapped in a solid or braided metal shield, then in an external cover. Co-ax is widely used for cable television and to connect parts of a LAN over longer distances. The extra insulation makes coaxial cable much better at resisting noise than twisted-pair wiring. Moreover, it can carry voice and data at a faster rate (up to about 200 Mbps, compared to 16–100 Mbps for twisted-pair wire). Often many coaxial cables will be bundled together.

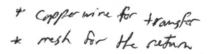

Handwritten note: + Copper wire for transfer / + mesh for the return

Figure 7.5 Three types of wired communications channels. (*Top left*) Twisted-pair wire. This type does not protect well against electrical interference. (*Top right*) Coaxial cable. This type is shielded against electrical interference. It can also carry more data than twisted-pair wire. (*Bottom right*) When coaxial cable is bundled together, as here, it can carry more than 40,000 conversations at once. (*Bottom left*) Fiber-optic cable. Thin glass strands transmit pulsating light instead of electricity. These strands can carry computer and voice data over long distances.

Fiber-Optic Cable

A **fiber-optic cable** consists of hundreds or thousands of thin strands of glass that transmit not electricity but rather pulsating beams of light. These strands, each as thin as a human hair, can transmit billions of pulses per second, each "on" pulse representing one bit. When bundled together, fiber-optic strands in a cable 0.12 inch thick can support a quarter- to a half-million voice conversations at the same time. Moreover, unlike electrical signals, light pulses are not affected by random electromagnetic interference in the environment. Thus, they have much lower error rates than normal telephone wire and cable. In addition, fiber-optic cable is lighter and more durable than twisted-wire and coaxial cable.

The main drawbacks until recently have been cost and the material's inability to bend around tight corners. Now we have *graded-index plastic optical fiber*, which is cheaper, lighter, and more flexible than glass fibers. The plastic flexible fiber is said to handle loops and curves with ease and thus will be better than glass for curb-to-home wiring. The new fibers can transmit 1 trillion bits (1 terabit) per second per fiber.

Denver-based Qwest Communications International began laying fiber-optic cables along railway lines in 1996. AT&T has already laid 41,000 miles, and NorthEast Optic Network is installing 600 miles of fiber-optic cable along the U.S. east coast. Japan's Fujitsu and Australia's Alcatel are constructing an 18,000-mile undersea fiber-optic cable looping from Australia and New Zealand to the United States and then back through Hawaii and Fiji to Australia.

Microwave Systems

Wired forms of communications, which require physical connection between sender and receiver, will not disappear any time soon, if ever. For one thing, fiber-optic cables can transmit data communications 10,000 times faster than microwave and satellite systems can. Moreover, they are resistant to illegal data theft.

Still, some of the most exciting developments are in wireless communications. After all, there are many situations in which it is difficult to run physical wires.

Microwave systems transmit voice and data through the atmosphere as high-frequency radio waves. These frequencies are used not only to operate microwave ovens but also to transmit messages between ground-based earth stations and satellite communications systems.

Nowadays you see dish- or horn-shaped microwave antennas nearly every-where—on towers, buildings, and hilltops. *(See Figure 7.6.)* Why, you might wonder, do people have to interfere with nature by putting a microwave dish on top of a mountain? The reason is that microwaves cannot bend around corners or around the earth's curvature; they are line-of-sight. *Line-of-sight* means that there must be an unobstructed view between transmitter and receiver. Thus, microwave stations need to be placed within 25–30 miles of each other, with no obstructions in between. The size of the dish varies with the distance (perhaps 2–4 feet in diameter for short distances, 10 feet or more for long distances). A string of microwave relay stations will each receive incoming messages, boost the signal strength, and relay the signals to the next station.

More than half of today's telephone system uses dish microwave transmission. However, the airwaves are becoming so saturated with microwave signals that future needs will have to be satisfied by other channels, such as satellite systems.

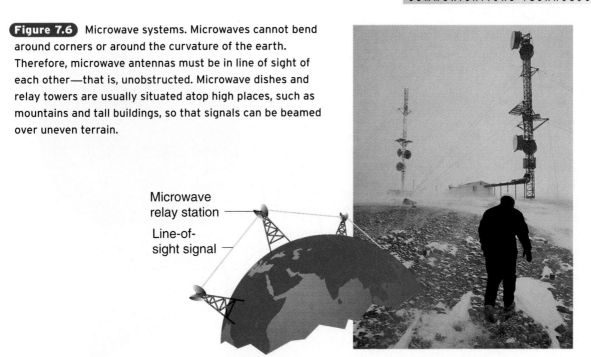

Figure 7.6 Microwave systems. Microwaves cannot bend around corners or around the curvature of the earth. Therefore, microwave antennas must be in line of sight of each other—that is, unobstructed. Microwave dishes and relay towers are usually situated atop high places, such as mountains and tall buildings, so that signals can be beamed over uneven terrain.

Microwave relay station

Line-of-sight signal

Satellite Systems

To avoid some of the limitations of microwave earth stations, communications companies have added microwave "sky stations"—communications satellites. **Communications satellites** are microwave relay stations in orbit around the earth. Traditionally, the orbit has been 22,300 miles above the earth, although some systems are much lower. Because their speed matches the earth's rate of rotation, they appear to an observer on the ground to be stationary in space—that is, they travel in a *geostationary orbit (GEO)*. Consequently, microwave earth stations are always able to beam signals to a fixed location above. The orbiting satellite has solar-powered receivers and transmitters (transponders) that receive the signals, amplify them, and retransmit them to another earth station. *(See Figure 7.7, next page.)* The satellite contains many communications channels and receives both analog and digital signals from earth stations.

Other satellite networks use *medium-earth orbits (MEOs)*, about 5000–10,000 miles from earth, or *low-earth orbits (LEOs)*, only 400–800 miles up. Among other things, these satellites would offer wireless phone, messaging, paging, and related services, as well as satellite-to-home TV signals.

To transmit a signal from a ground station to a satellite is called *uplinking.* The signal is then *downlinked* to, for example, a TV station.

Other Wireless Systems

Of course, mobile wireless communications have been around for some time. The Detroit Police Department started using two-way car radios in 1921. Mobile telephones were introduced in 1946. Today, however, we are witnessing an explosion in mobile wireless use that is making worldwide changes.

Figure 7.7
Communications satellite

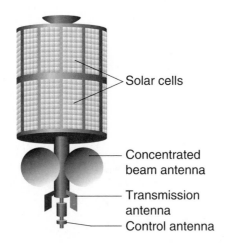

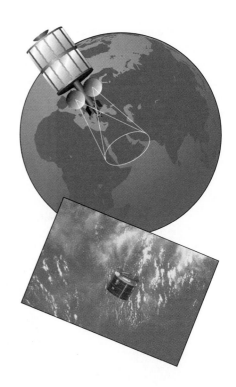

■ *Global Positioning System (GPS):* A $10 billion infrastructure developed by the U.S. military in the mid-1980s, **GPS,** for **Global Positioning System**, consists of a series of earth-orbiting satellites that continuously transmit timed radio signals for use in identifying earth locations. A GPS receiver with a display screen—handheld or mounted in a vehicle, plane, or boat—can pick up transmissions from any four satellites, interpret the information from each, and calculate to within a few hundred feet or less the receiver's longitude, latitude, and altitude. The accuracy of GPSs is expected to improve to plus or minus a few feet.

Military units use this system to determine exactly where they are. It is also used for civilian purposes such as tracking trucks and taxis, locating stolen cars, orienting hikers and campers, and aiding in surveying, and it has become standard safety equipment on boats. Filmmakers use GPS to track the sun and time their sunrise and sunset shots so they don't get shadows. Some GPS receivers include map software for finding your way around, such as the Guidestar system available with some rental cars.

The NavTalk cell phone includes a GPS receiver that uses NavTalk software. The display shows your position. If the person you're calling is also using NavTalk, your display will show that person's position as well.

A spin-off of GPS, called *LPS (Local Position System)*, uses radio frequency identification (RFID) technology to track both people and objects throughout the interior of a bulding. LPS units are often used in security systems.

A blind man with a guide dog uses a special GPS computer device to help navigate his way.

Various types of satellites

Geostationary Earth orbit (GEO)

SPACEWAY
Subscribers access service with $1,000 terminal, 26-inch dish antenna.

Satellites: 8
Orbits: Geostationary, 22,300 miles above equator
Operational in: First global region in 1999, rest in 2000
Cost: $3 billion
Speed: 16 kilobits per second to 6 megabits per second
Applications: Ordinary fixed telephone service in developing areas, fax, videoconferencing, data, broadband multimedia, such as from Internet
Investor: Hughes Electronics

Medium-Earth orbit (MEO)

ICO GLOBAL COMMUNICATIONS
A London-based private offshoot of INMARSAT, ICO has 47 telecommunications investors and COMSAT, Hughes.

Satellites: 10
Orbits: Inclined 45 degrees to equator, 6,434 miles up
Operational in: 2000
Cost: $3.7 billion
Applications: Hand-held dual-mode mobile phones that talk to satellites and cellular systems; phones for cars, ships, aircraft; fixed phones in developing areas

ODYSSEY
Founded by TRW Inc. and Teleglobe Inc. to offer worldwide mobile phone service

Satellites: 12
Orbits: Inclined 50 degrees to equator, 6,434 miles up
Operational in: 2001
Cost: $3.2 billion
Applications: Hand-held dual mode phones, other personal communications services, largely in developing nations

Low-Earth orbit (LEO)

GLOBALSTAR
A simple, beefy system for worldwide mobile and fixed-phone service

Satellites: 48
Orbits: Inclined 52 degrees to equator, 763 miles up
Operational in: Fall 1998 (partial), full in 1999
Cost: $2.5 billion
Applications: Hand-held dual-mode phones, fixed ordinary phones, paging, low-speed data
Partners: Loral Space & Communications, Qualcomm Inc.

IRIDIUM
Designed so business travelers can call anywhere from anywhere

Satellites: 66
Orbits: Near polar orbit at 421.5 miles up
Operational in: Sept. 1998
Cost: $5 billion
Applications: Hand-held dual-mode phones, paging, low-speed data, fax
Investors: Motorola, Raytheon, Lockheed Martin, Sprint, Khrunichev State Research, 12 others

ORBCOMM
95-pound minisatellites to provide message services for industry, outdoors enthusiasts

Satellites: 28
Orbits: Inclined 45 and 70 degrees to equator, 480 miles up
Operational in: 1997
Cost: $330 million
Applications: Data messages from individuals; tracking of barges, truck trailers; remote monitoring of industrial installations, oil wells
Partners: Orbital Sciences Corp., Teleglobe Inc.

TELEDESIC
"Internet in the Sky" aims to make broadband multimedia connections anywhere just like fiber-optic cables.

Satellites: 840
Orbits: Near polar orbits, 420 miles up
Operational in: 2002
Cost: $9 billion
Applications: Broadband multimedia for corporate intranets, Internet, videoconferencing, up to 28 megabits per second
Investors: Bill Gates, Craig McCaw

■ *Pagers:* Once stereotyped as devices for doctors and drug dealers, pagers are now consumer items. Commonly known as *beepers*, for the sound they make when activated, pagers are simple radio receivers to which data is sent from a special radio transmitter. Often the pager has its own telephone number. When the number is dialed from a phone, the call goes by way of the transmitter straight to the designated pager.

Today's pagers are available in pocket sizes and designer colors. Pagers also do more than beep, transmitting full-blown alphanumeric text and other data. Newer ones are mini-answering machines, capable of relaying digitized voice messages.

Pagers are efficient for transmitting one-way information—emergency messages, news, prices, stock quotations, mortgage rates, delivery-route assignments, even sports news and scores—at low cost to single or multiple receivers. Recently some companies have introduced two-way paging. This technology allows customers to send a preprogrammed acknowledgment ("Will be late—stuck in traffic") after they have received a message. Eventually, paging companies hope these two-way devices will evolve into full-fledged handheld communicators.

■ *Analog cellular phone:* Analog cellular phones are designed primarily for communicating at 824–894 MHz by voice through a system of ground-area cells. Each cell is hexagonal in shape, usually 8 miles or less in diameter, and is served by a transmitting-receiving tower. Calls are directed between cells by a mobile telephone switching office (MTSO). Movement between cells requires that calls be handed off by the MTSO. *(See Figure 7.8.)*

Figure 7.8 Cellular connections

Calling from a cellular phone:
When you dial a call on a cellular phone, whether on the street or in a car, the call moves as radio waves to the transmitting-receiving tower that serves that particular cell. The call then moves by wire or microwaves to the mobile telephone switching office (MTSO), which directs the call from there on—generally to a regular local phone exchange, after which it becomes a conventional phone call.

Receiving a call on a cellular phone:
The MTSO transmits the number dialed to all the cells it services. Once it finds the phone, it directs the call to it through the nearest transmitting-receiving tower.

On the move:
When you make calls to or from phones while on the move, as in a moving car, the MTSO's computers sense when a phone's signal is becoming weaker. The computers then figure out which adjacent cell to "hand-off" the call to and find an open frequency in that new cell to switch to.

1. A call originates from a mobile cellular phone.
2. The call wirelessly finds the nearest cellular tower using its FM tuner to make a connection.
3. The tower sends the signal to a Mobile Telephone Switching Office (MTSO) using traditional telephone network land lines.
4. The MTSO routes the call over the telephone network to a land-based phone or initiates a search for the recipient on the cellular network.
5. The MTSO sends the recipient's phone number to all its towers, which broadcast the number via radio frequency.
6. The recipient's phone "hears" the broadcast and establishes a connection with the nearest tower. A voice line is established via the tower by the MTSO.

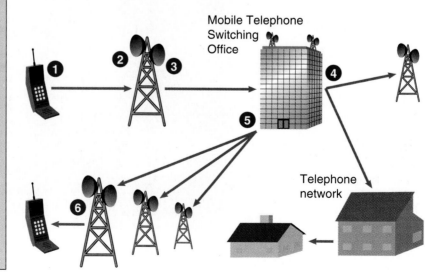

Mobile Telephone Switching Office

Telephone network

Handing off voice calls between cells poses only minimal problems. However, handing off data transmission (where every bit counts), with the inevitable gaps and pauses as one moves from one cell to another, is much more difficult. In the long run, data transmissions will probably have to be handled by the technology we discuss shortly, packet radio.

■ *Digital cellular phone:* Cellular telephone companies are trying to rectify the problem of faulty data transmission by switching from analog to digital. Digital cellular phone networks turn your voice message into digital bits, which are sent through the airwaves, then decoded back into your voice by the cellular handset. Unlike analog cellular phones, digital phones can handle e-mail messages, paging, and some headline news items in addition to voice transmission. But these features won't work if the user is traveling outside the digital network service area. And you'll be able to make and receive nondigital phone calls only if your unit is equipped to function both in digital and analog modes.

Despite advances in wireless technology, North American cell phones remain useless outside North America. Travelers wishing to use cell phones abroad have to rent temporary units. But the World Trade Organization (WTO) is hoping to change to change that by standardizing worldwide telecommunications systems. The agreement, set to be implemented by 69 nations over the next six to seven years, provides a framework for an eventual global system that will be low in cost, high in quality, and extremely efficient.

A digital cell phone costs two or three times more than an analog one, but the monthly bill may be less, especially for heavy users. Digital phone networks promise clearer sound, although some consumers don't agree.

Nokia cell phone connected to a PC-card modem, which will be inserted into a slot on the side of the laptop computer.

■ *Packet radio:* Packet-radio-based communications use a nationwide system of radio towers that send data to handheld computers.

Packet radio is the basis for services such as RAM Mobile Data and Ardis. The advantage of packet-radio transmission is that the wireless computer identifies itself to the local base station, which can transmit over as many as 16 separate radio channels. Packet switching encapsulates the data in "envelopes," which ensures that the information arrives intact.

Packet-radio data networks are useful for mobile workers who need to communicate frequently with a corporate database. For example, National Car Rental sends workers with handheld terminals to prowl parking lots, recording the location of rental cars and noting the scratches and dents. They can thereby easily check a customer's claim that a car was already damaged or find out quickly when one is stolen.

(*Left*) Nokia cell phone and electronic organizer. (*Right*) Motorola StarTac cell phone and electronic organizer, which can display faxes and e-mail.

7.3 Factors Affecting Communications Among Devices

KEY QUESTION **What factors affect how fast data is transmitted over a communications channel?**

Having gotten a good look at the kinds of communication channels available, we can take a brief look at other factors that affect data transmission. The whole topic of communications technology is quite complicated and very technical. However, in this age of communicating via computers, you need to be familiar with some of the other basic factors that affect data transmission, including the following:

- Transmission rate—frequency and bandwidth
- Line configurations—point-to-point versus multipoint
- Serial versus parallel transmission
- Direction of transmission—simplex, half-duplex, and full-duplex
- Transmission mode—asynchronous versus synchronous
- Packet switching
- Multiplexing
- Protocols

Transmission Rate: Higher Frequency, Wider Bandwidth, More Data

Transmission rate is a function of two variables: frequency and bandwidth.

- *Frequency:* The amount of data that can be transmitted on a channel depends on the wave frequency—the cycles of waves per second. Frequency is expressed in hertz: 1 cycle per second equals 1 hertz. The more cycles per second, the more data that can be sent through that channel.

  A twisted-pair telephone wire operating at a frequency of 4000 hertz might send only 1 kilobyte of data in a second. A coaxial cable of 100 megahertz might send 10 megabytes. And a fiber-optic cable of 200 trillion hertz might send 1 gigabyte.

- *Bandwidth:* **Bandwidth** is the difference between the highest and lowest frequencies—that is, the range of frequencies. Data may be sent not just on one frequency but on several frequencies within a particular bandwidth, all at the same time. Thus, the greater the bandwidth of a channel, the more frequencies it has available and hence the more data that can be sent through that channel. The rate of speed of data through the channel is expressed in bits per second (bps), kilobits per second (Kbps), or megabits per second (Mbps).

Line Configurations: Point-to-Point and Multipoint

There are two principal line configurations, or ways of connecting communications lines: point-to-point and multipoint.

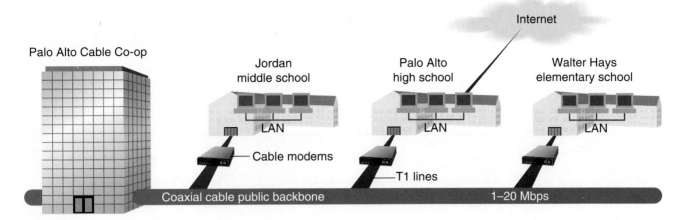

Figure 7.9 Three schools in Palo Alto, California, share T1 access to the Internet over a wide area network that uses the local cable TV system as its high-speed backbone.

■ *Point-to-point:* A *point-to-point line* directly connects the sending and receiving devices, such as a terminal with a central computer. This arrangement is appropriate for a private line whose sole purpose is to keep data secure by transmitting it from one device to another. A point-to-point line may be public or private (leased). In 1958, as an improvement to its telephone service, Bell Labs developed the T1 line, which uses special signaling techniques and multiplexers to increase the capacity of existing copper long-distance lines. The T1 line can carry 24 signals on a single set of twisted copper wires. Since long-distance calls are now handled mostly by microwave, satellite, and fiber-optic systems, T1 lines—although expensive—are often used as leased (private, or dedicated) point-to-point lines for high-speed data transmission between offices or schools and, for example, companies that provide access to the Internet. *(See Figure 7.9.)*

■ *Multipoint:* A *multipoint line* is a single line that connects several communications devices to one computer. Often on a multipoint line only one communications device, such as a terminal, can transmit at any given time.

Serial and Parallel Transmission

Data is transmitted in two ways: serially and in parallel.

■ *Serial data transmission:* In **serial data transmission,** bits are transmitted sequentially, one after the other. *(See Figure 7.10, next page.)* This arrangement resembles cars proceeding down a one-lane road.

  Serial transmission is the way most data flows over a twisted-pair telephone line. It is found in communications lines, modems, and most mice. The plug-in board for a microcomputer modem usually has a serial port.

■ *Parallel data transmission:* In **parallel data transmission,** bits are transmitted through separate lines simultaneously. The arrangement resembles cars moving in separate lanes at the same speed on a multilane freeway.

  Parallel lines move information faster than serial lines do, but they are efficient for up to only 15 feet. Thus, parallel lines are used, for example, to transmit data from a PC's processor to a printer.

  Parallel transmission may also be used within a company's facility, for terminal-to-main-computer data transmission.

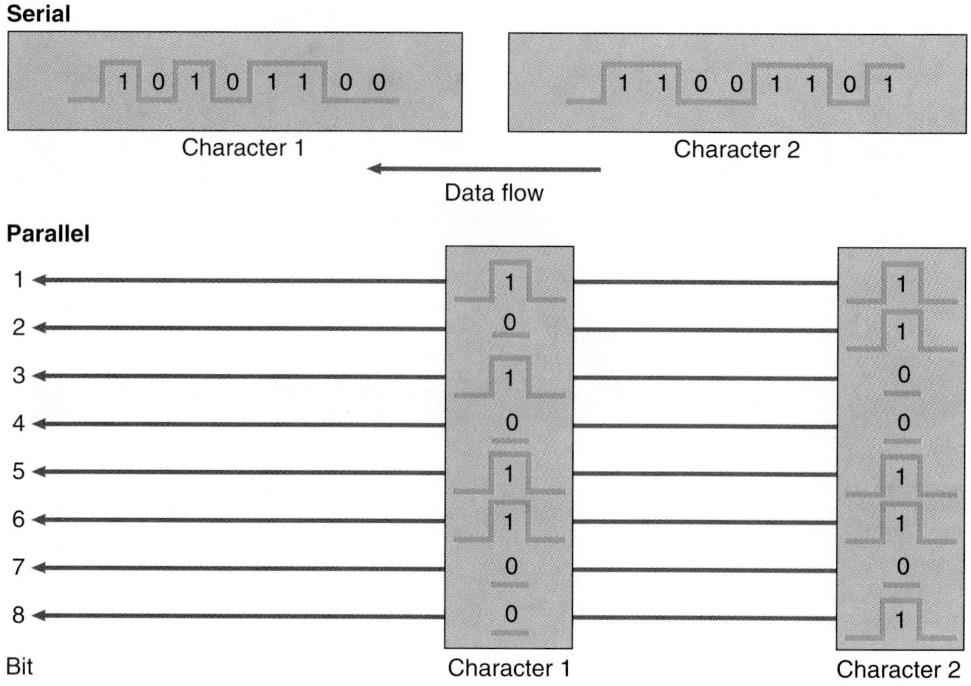

Figure 7.10 Serial and parallel data transmission

Serial

Parallel

Direction of Transmission: Simplex, Half-Duplex, and Full-Duplex

When two computers are in communication, data can flow in three ways: simplex, half-duplex, or full-duplex. These are fancy terms for easily understood processes. *(See Figure 7.11.)*

- *Simplex transmission:* In **simplex transmission,** data can travel in only one direction. An example is a traditional television broadcast, in which the signal is sent from the transmitter to your TV antenna. There is no return signal. Some computerized data collection devices also work this way (such as seismograph sensors that measure earthquakes).

- *Half-duplex transmission:* In **half-duplex transmission,** data travels in both directions but only in one direction at a time. This arrangement resembles traffic on a one-lane bridge; the separate streams of cars must take turns. Half-duplex transmission is seen with CB or marine radios, in which both parties must take turns talking. This is the most common mode of data transmission used today.

- *Full-duplex transmission:* In **full-duplex transmission,** data is transmitted back and forth at the same time. This arrangement resembles automobile traffic on a two-way street. An example is two people on the telephone talking and listening simultaneously. Full-duplex transmission is sometimes used in large computer systems. It is also available for some new microcomputer modems and software to support truly interactive collaboration using products like Microsoft NetMeeting.

Transmission Mode: Asynchronous Versus Synchronous

Suppose your computer sends the word CONGRATULATIONS! to someone as bits and bytes over a communications line. How does the receiving equipment

Figure 7.11 Transmission directions: Simplex, half-duplex, and full-duplex

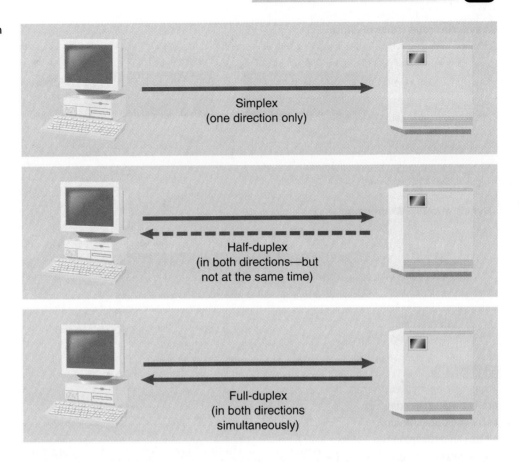

Simplex
(one direction only)

Half-duplex
(in both directions—but
not at the same time)

Full-duplex
(in both directions
simultaneously)

Personal computers use asynchronous transmission

know where one byte (or character) ends and another begins? This matter is resolved through either *asynchronous transmission* or *synchronous transmission.* (*See Figure 7.12, next page.*)

■ *Asynchronous transmission:* This method, used with most microcomputers, is also called *start-stop transmission.* (*Asynchronous* comes from the ancient Greek word meaning "not timed.") In **asynchronous transmission** data is sent one byte (or character) at a time. Each string of bits making up the byte is bracketed, or marked off, with special control bits. That is, a "start" bit represents the beginning of a character, and a "stop" bit represents its end.

Most microcomputers use asynchronous transmission—at only one byte at a time, with start and stop pulses, this is a relatively slow method. As a result, asynchronous transmission is not used when great amounts of data must be sent rapidly. Its advantage is that the data can be transmitted whenever it is convenient for the sender.

■ *Synchronous transmission:* Instead of using start and stop bits, **synchronous transmission** sends data in blocks (*synchronous* means "timed"). Start and stop bit patterns, called *sync bytes,* are transmitted at the beginning and end of the blocks. These start and end bit patterns synchronize internal clocks in the sending and receiving devices so that they are in time with each other.

This method is rarely used with microcomputers because it is more complicated and more expensive than asynchronous transmission. (However, some microcomputer modems will convert the asynchronous signals from the computer's serial port into synchronous signals on the transmission line.) It also requires careful timing between sending and receiving equipment. It is appropriate for large computer systems that need to transmit great quantities of data quickly.

Asynchronous transmission

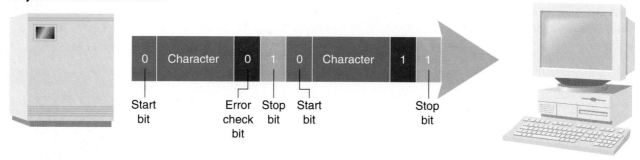

Synchronous transmission

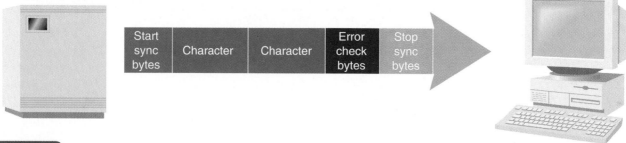

Figure 7.12

Transmission modes. There are two ways that devices receiving data transmissions can determine the beginning and ends of strings of bits (bytes, or characters). (*Top*) Asynchronous transmission. Each character is preceded by a "start" bit and followed by a "stop" bit. (*Bottom*) Synchronous transmission. Messages are sent in blocks, with start and stop patterns of bits, called *sync bytes*, before and after the blocks. The sync bytes synchronize the timing of the internal clocks between sending and receiving devices.

Packet Switching: Getting More Data on a Network

A **packet** is a maximum-fixed-length block of data for transmission. The packet also contains instructions about its destination. In **packet switching,** electronic messages are divided into packets for transmission over a wide area network to their destination, through the most expedient routes. (A wide area network, discussed shortly, is a communications network that covers a wide geographical area, such as a state or a country.) The benefit of this technique is that it can handle high-volume traffic in a network. It also allows more users to share a network, thereby offering cost savings. Packet switching is particularly appropriate for sending messages over long distances—for instance, across the country. Accordingly, it is used in large networks such as Telenet, Tymnet, and AT&T's Accunet.

Here's how packet switching works: A sending computer breaks an electronic message apart into packets. The various packets are sent through a communications network—often by different routes, at different speeds, and sandwiched in between packets from other messages. Once the packets arrive at their destination, the receiving computer reassembles the packets into proper sequence to complete the message. Packet switching is suitable for data, but not real-time voice and video, transmission.

Packet switching is contrasted with *circuit switching,* by which the transmitter has full use of the circuit until all the data has been transmitted and the circuit is terminated. Circuit switching is used by the telephone company for its voice networks to guarantee steady, consistent service for telephone conversations. A newer technology, called *asynchronous transfer mode,* or *ATM,* combines the efficiency of packet switching with some aspects of circuit switching and can thus handle both data and real-time voice and video. ATM is designed to run on high-bandwidth fiber-optic cables.

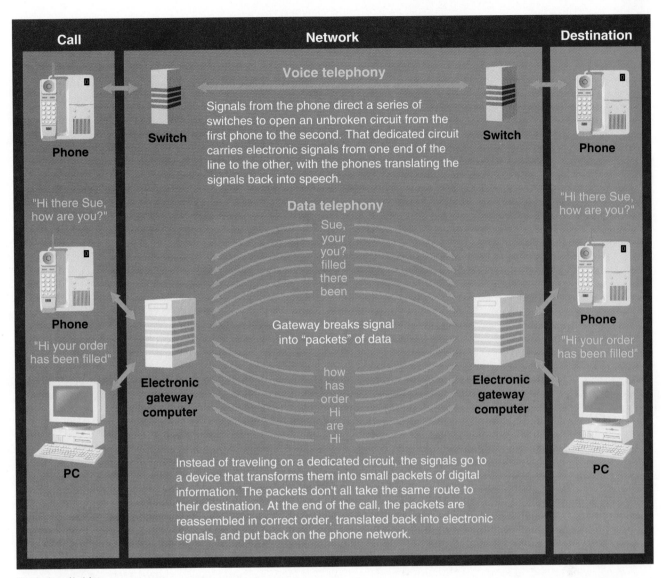

Call	Network	Destination

Phone — **Switch**

Voice telephony

Signals from the phone direct a series of switches to open an unbroken circuit from the first phone to the second. That dedicated circuit carries electronic signals from one end of the line to the other, with the phones translating the signals back into speech.

Switch — **Phone**

"Hi there Sue, how are you?"

"Hi there Sue, how are you?"

Data telephony

Sue,
your
you?
filled
there
been

Phone

"Hi your order has been filled"

Gateway breaks signal into "packets" of data

Phone

"Hi your order has been filled"

Electronic gateway computer

how
has
order
Hi
are
Hi

Electronic gateway computer

PC

Instead of traveling on a dedicated circuit, the signals go to a device that transforms them into small packets of digital information. The packets don't all take the same route to their destination. At the end of the call, the packets are reassembled in correct order, translated back into electronic signals, and put back on the phone network.

PC

Packet switching

A turtle goes home to the waters of San Diego, California, almost a year after being found, inexplicably, in the frigid waters of Prince William Sound. Glued to his back is a two-pound satellite transmitter that will provide information about this endangered species—the East Pacific Green turtle—that has never before been available.

Multiplexing: Enhancing Communications Efficiencies

Communications lines nearly always have far greater capacity than a single micro-computer or terminal can use. Because operating such lines is expensive, it's more efficient if several communications devices can share a line. This is the rationale for multiplexing. **Multiplexing** is the transmission of multiple signals over a single communications channel.

Three types of devices are used to achieve multiplexing—*multiplexers, concentrators,* and *front-end processors:*

■ *Multiplexers:* A *multiplexer* is a device that merges several low-speed transmissions into one high-speed transmission. *(See Figure 7.13.)* Depending on the model, 32 or more devices may share a single communications line. Messages sent by a multiplexer must be received by a multiplexer of the same type. The receiving multiplexer sorts out the individual messages and directs them to the proper recipient.

■ *Concentrators:* Like a multiplexer, a concentrator is a piece of hardware that enables several devices to share a single communications line. However, unlike a multiplexer, a *concentrator* collects data in a temporary storage area. In other words, unlike a multiplexer, which spreads the signals back out again on the receiving end, the concentrator has a receiving computer to perform that function.

■ *Front-end processors:* The most sophisticated of these communications-management devices is the front-end processor, a computer that handles communications for mainframes. A *front-end processor* is a smaller computer that is connected to a larger computer and assists with communications functions. It transmits and receives messages over the communications channels, corrects errors, and relieves the larger computer of routine computational tasks.

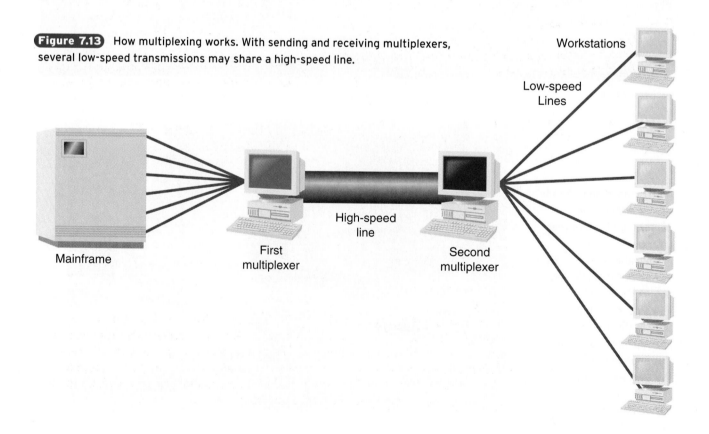

Figure 7.13 How multiplexing works. With sending and receiving multiplexers, several low-speed transmissions may share a high-speed line.

Workstations

Low-speed Lines

Mainframe

First multiplexer

High-speed line

Second multiplexer

Sometimes the term *front-end processor* is used synonymously with the term *communications controller,* although this latter device is usually less sophisticated. (A communications controller handles communications between a computer and peripheral devices such as terminals and printers.) In a local area network, the functions of a front-end processor are performed by a *network adapter.* This is simply a printed circuit board inserted into a workstation or server (✔ pp. 1.14–1.15).

Protocols: The Rules of Data Transmission

All this information on data transmission may seem unduly technical for an ordinary computer user. Fortunately, when you sit down to send a message through a telecommunications system, you won't usually have to think about these details. Experts will already have taken care of them for you in sets of rules called *protocols.*

The word *protocol* is used in the military and in diplomacy to express rules of precedence, rank, manners, and other matters of correctness. (An example would be the protocol that specifies who will precede whom into a formal reception.) Here, however, a **protocol,** or *communications protocol,* is a set of conventions governing the exchange of data between hardware and/or software components in a communications network.

Protocols are built into the hardware or software you are using. The protocol in your communications software, for example, will specify how receiver devices will acknowledge sending devices, a matter called *handshaking.* Handshaking establishes the fact that the circuit is available and operational. It also establishes the level of device compatibility and the speed of transmission. Protocols will also specify the type of electrical connections used, the timing of message exchanges, error-detection techniques, and so on.

In the past, not all hardware and software developers subscribed to the same protocols. As a result, many kinds of equipment and programs have not been able to work with one another. In recent years, more developers have agreed to subscribe to a standard of protocols called OSI. Backed by the International Standards Organization, **OSI** (short for **Open Systems Interconnection**) is an international standard that defines seven layers of protocols, or software responsibilities, for worldwide computer communications. *(See Figure 7.14, next page.)* We provide information about some specific protocols in the next chapter.

Now that we have covered the basic principles of communications technology, we turn to one of the main uses of that technology: networks.

7.4 Communications Networks

KEY QUESTION **What are communications networks and what advantages do they provide?**

Whether wired, wireless, or both, all the channels we've described can be used singly or in mix-and-match fashion to form networks. A **network,** or *communications network,* is a system of interconnected computers, telephones, or other communications devices that can communicate with one another and share applications and data. It is the tying together of so many communications devices in so many ways that is changing the world we live in.

Figure 7.14 The seven layers of the ISO standard for worldwide communications, which defines a framework for implementing protocols

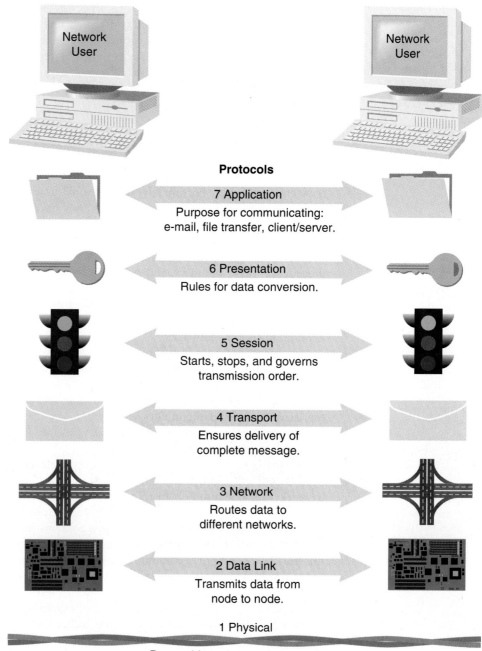

Protocols

7 Application
Purpose for communicating:
e-mail, file transfer, client/server.

6 Presentation
Rules for data conversion.

5 Session
Starts, stops, and governs
transmission order.

4 Transport
Ensures delivery of
complete message.

3 Network
Routes data to
different networks.

2 Data Link
Transmits data from
node to node.

1 Physical

Passes bits onto connecting medium.

A network requires a network operating system—NOS—to manage network resources. It may be a completely self-contained operating system, such as Net-Ware (✔ p. 5.21), or it may require an existing operating system such as Windows 98 or OS/2 in order to function.

Here we will consider the following aspects of networks:

■ Types of networks—wide area, metropolitan area, and local

■ Some network features

■ Advantages of networks

Types of Networks: Wide Area, Metropolitan Area, and Local

Networks are categorized principally in the following three sizes:

■ *Wide area network:* A **wide area network (WAN)** is a communications network that covers a wide geographical area, such as a state or a country. Some examples of computer WANs are Tymnet, Telenet, Uninet, and Accunet. The Internet links together hundreds of computer WANs. Of course, most telephone systems—long-distance, regional, and local—are WANs.

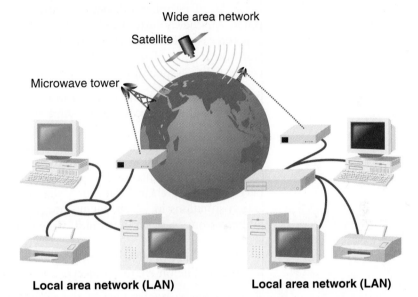

Wide area network

Satellite

Microwave tower

Local area network (LAN)   **Local area network (LAN)**

Don't need →
~~MAN~~ MAN

■ *Metropolitan area network:* A **metropolitan area network (MAN)** is a communications network covering a geographic area the size of a city or suburb. The purpose of a MAN is often to avoid long-distance telephone charges. Cellular phone systems are often MANs.

■ *Local network:* A **local network** is a privately owned communications network that serves users within a confined geographical area. The range is usually within a mile—perhaps one office, one building, or a group of buildings close together, such as a college campus. Local networks are of two types: private branch exchanges (PBXs) and local area networks (LANs), as we discuss shortly.

All these networks may consist of various combinations of computers, storage devices, and communications devices.

Some Network Features: Hosts and Nodes; Downloading and Uploading

Many computer networks, particularly large ones, are served by a host computer. A **host computer,** or simply a *host,* is the main computer in a system of computers and/or terminals connected by communications links. The host is responsible for overall control of the system. On a local area network, some of the functions of the host may be performed by a server. A **server** is a computer shared by several users in a network.

node –
User computer

A **node** is simply a device that is attached to a network. A node may be a microcomputer, terminal, storage device, or some peripheral device.

As a network user you can download and upload files. **Download** means that you retrieve files from another computer and store them in your computer. **Upload** means that you send files from your computer to another computer.

Advantages of Networks

The following advantages are particularly true for LANs, although they apply to MANs and WANs as well.

- *Sharing of peripheral devices:* Laser printers, disk drives, and scanners are examples of peripheral devices—that is, hardware that is connected to a computer. Any newly introduced piece of hardware is often quite expensive, as was the case with color laser printers. To justify their purchase, companies want them to be shared by many users. Usually the best way to do this is to connect the peripheral device to a network serving several computer users.

- *Sharing of programs and data:* In most organizations, people use the same software and need access to the same information. It could be expensive for a company to buy one copy of, say, a word processing program for each employee. Rather, the company will usually buy a network version of that program that will serve many employees.

  Organizations also save a great deal of money by letting all employees have access to the same data on a shared storage device. This way the organization situations in which, for instance, some employees update customer addresses on their own machines while other employees remain ignorant of such changes.

  Finally, network-linked employees can, using groupware (✔ p. 6.18), work together online on shared projects.

- *Better communications:* One of the greatest features of networks is electronic mail, as we have seen. With e-mail everyone on a network can easily keep others posted about important information. Thus, the company eliminates the delays encountered with standard interoffice mail delivery or telephone tag.

- *Security of information:* Before networks became commonplace, an individual employee might be the only one with a particular piece of information, stored in his or her desktop computer. If the employee was dismissed—or if a fire or flood demolished the office—no one else in the company might have any knowledge of that information. Today such data would be backed up or duplicated on a networked storage device shared by others.

- *Access to databases:* Networks also enable users to tap into numerous databases, whether the private databases of a company or the public databases of online services.

7.5 Local Networks

KEY QUESTION What is a local area network?

Although large networks are useful, many organizations need to have a local network—an in-house network—to tie together their own equipment. Here let's consider the following aspects of local networks:

- Types of local networks—PBXs and LANs

- Types of LANs—client-server and peer-to-peer

- Components of a LAN

- Topology of LANs—star, ring, bus, hybrid, and FDDI

Types of Local Networks: PBXs and LANs

The most common types of local networks are PBXs and LANs.

- *Private branch exchange (PBX):* A **private branch exchange (PBX)** is a private or leased telephone switching system that connects telephone extensions in-house. It also connects them to the outside telephone system.

   A public telephone system consists of "public branch exchanges"—thousands of switching stations that direct calls to different branches of the network. A private branch exchange is essentially the old-fashioned company switchboard. You call in from the outside, the switchboard operator says "How may I direct your call?" and you are connected to the extension of the person you wish to talk to.

   Newer PBXs can handle not only analog telephones but also digital equipment, including computers. However, because older PBXs use existing telephone lines, they may not be able to handle the volumes of electronic messages found in some of today's organizations. These companies may be better served by LANs.

- *Local area network (LAN):* PBXs may share existing phone lines with the telephone system. Local area networks usually require installation of their own communication channels, whether wired or wireless. A **local area network (LAN)** (pronounced "lan") is a local network consisting of a communications link, network operating system, microcomputers or workstations, servers, and other shared hardware. Such shared hardware might include printers, scanners, and storage devices.

Types of LANs: Client-Server and Peer-to-Peer

Local area networks are of two principal types: client-server and peer-to-peer. *(See Figure 7.15, next page.)*

- *Client-server LANs:* A **client-server LAN** consists of requesting microcomputers, called *clients,* and supplying devices that provide a service, called *servers.* The server is a computer that manages shared information or devices, such as laser printers. One piece of the NOS resides in each client machine and another resides in each server. The NOS allows the remote drives on the servers to be accessed as if they were local drives on the client machine. The server is usually a powerful microcomputer with a lot of RAM and secondary storage capacity. Client-server networks, such as those run under Novell's NetWare operating system, are the most common type of LAN.

   Another example of a client-server hookup is a user's microcomputer at home connected to America Online (AOL). The user uses the GUI (✔ p. 5.13) and browser software (✔ p. 6.22) on his or her *client* machine. When initiating an Internet session, that software runs with software installed on AOL's communications *server.* That way the two devices communicate effectively without requiring that the Internet communications software be downloaded from the server to the client as part of every Internet session.

[handwritten note in left margin:] Server networks better than peer-to-peer networks

Figure 7.15 Two types of LANs: client-server and peer-to-peer. (*Top*) Client-server LAN. Individual microcomputer users, or *clients,* share the services of a centralized computer called a *server.* In the case shown here, the server is a file server, via which users share files and programs. (*Bottom*) Peer-to-peer LAN. Computers share equally with one another without having to rely on a central server.

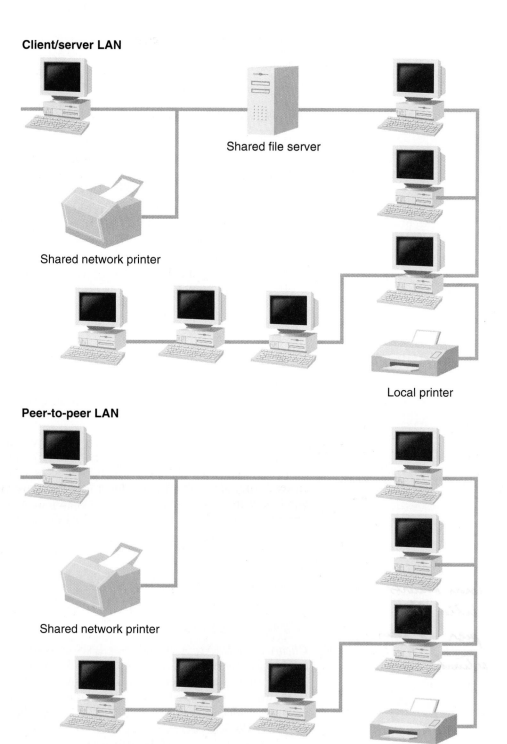

Client/server LAN

Shared file server

Shared network printer

Local printer

Peer-to-peer LAN

Shared network printer

Local printer

There may be different servers for managing different resources—files and programs, databases, printers. The one you may hear about most often is the file server. A **file server** is a computer that stores the programs and data files shared by users on a LAN. It acts like a disk drive but is in a remote location. (In a NetWare client-server system, any files stored on client machines cannot be accessed by other clients. Windows NT does allow such access.)

A *database server* is a computer in a LAN that stores data. Unlike a file server, it does not store programs. A *print server* is a computer in a LAN that controls one or more printers. It stores the print-image output from all the microcomputers on the system. It then feeds the output to one or more printers one document at a time. *Fax servers* are dedicated to managing fax transmissions, and *mail servers* manage e-mail. *Communications servers* translate packets on a network and allow all nodes access to its modems.

- *Peer-to-peer:* The word *peer* denotes an individual who is equal in standing with another (as in the phrases "peer pressure" or "jury of one's peers"). A **peer-to-peer LAN** is one in which all microcomputers on the network communicate directly with one another without relying on a server—that is, the NOS allows each station to be both client and server. Thus, files stored on one peer machine can be accessed by other peer machines. Peer-to-peer networks are less expensive than client-server networks and work effectively for up to 25 computers. Beyond that they slow down under heavy use. Thus, they are appropriate for networking in small groups, as for workgroup computing. Software used includes LANtastic by Artisoft, Localtalk by Apple, and Microsoft's Windows NT Server, Windows NT Workstation, and Windows 95/98.

Many LANs mix elements from both client-server and peer-to-peer models.

Components of a LAN

Local area networks are made up of several standard components. *(See Figure 7.16, next page.)*

- *Connection or cabling system:* LANs do not use the telephone network. Instead, they use some other cabling or connection system, either wired or wireless. Wired connections may be twisted-pair wiring, coaxial cable, or fiber-optic cable. Wireless connections may be infrared or radio-wave transmission. Wireless networks are especially useful if computers are portable and are moved often. However, wireless LANs transmit at relatively slow speeds compared to wired LANs.

- *Microcomputers/workstations with interface cards:* Two or more microcomputers or workstations are required, along with network interface cards. A **network interface card,** inserted into an expansion slot (✔ p. 2.23) in a microcomputer, enables the computer to send and receive messages on the LAN.

- *Network operating system:* As we mentioned earlier, the network operating system software manages the activity of the network—it provides it with multiuser, multitasking (✔ p. 5.6) capabilities. Depending on the type of network, the main operating system software may be stored on a server, on each microcomputer on the network, or a combination of both.

    In addition to supporting multitasking and multiuser access, LAN operating systems provide for recognition of users based on passwords, user IDs, and terminal IDs.

    Examples of network operating systems are Novell's NetWare, Microsoft's Windows NT Server, and IBM's PC LAN. As mentioned in Chapter 5, you can also establish peer-to-peer networking using Microsoft Windows for Workgroups, Windows 95/98, and Windows NT Workstation.

- *Other shared devices:* Printers, fax machines, scanners, storage devices, and other peripherals may be added to the network as necessary and shared by all users.

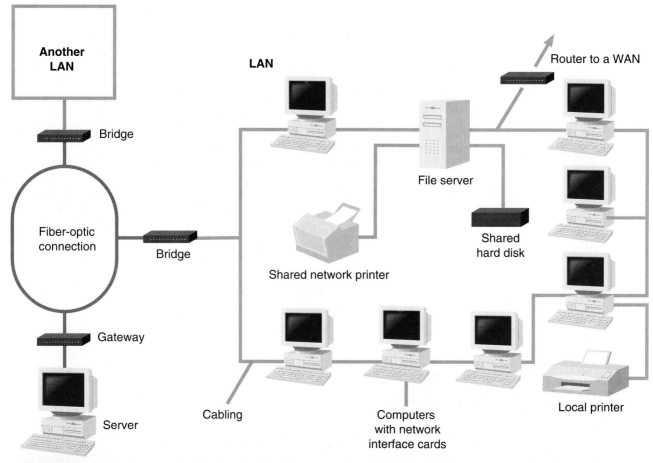

Figure 7.16 Components of a typical LAN.

■ *Bridges, routers, and gateways:* A LAN may stand alone, but it may also connect to other networks, either similar or different in technology. Hardware and software combinations are used as interfaces to make these connections.

A **bridge** is an interface used to connect the same types of networks. Bridges operate at the bottom two levels of the OSI protocol model, providing physical layer and data link layer connectivity. Bridges extend the physical reach of a LAN, passing traffic from one LAN segment to another on the basis of the packet's address. They also have buffers that can store messages to forward later in case of traffic congestion.

A **router** is a highly intelligent device that supports connectivity between both like and unlike LANs and between LANs and WANs/MANs. Routers operate at the bottom three of the OSI model's seven layers of protocol. The router is able to view the network as a whole; bridges, in contrast, view the network only on a link-by-link basis.

A **gateway** performs all functions of bridges and routers, including protocol conversion at all seven layers of the OSI model. For example, an online information service such as CompuServe acts as a gateway, via servers, for your microcomputer's connection to the Internet (a WAN). A gateway supplies entrances to dissimilar networks by tearing down a packet of information from one network and restructuring it for a different network's protocol.

Bridges are protocol-independent; routers are protocol-dependent. Bridges are faster than routers because they do not have to deal with protocol reading. Gateways are the slowest of the three. Network designers determine which types of bridges, gateways, and routers to use depending on what types of networks and e-mail systems they are connecting, how fast things need to work, and how much everything is going to cost.

Topology of LANs

Networks can be laid out in different ways. The physical layout, or shape, of a network is called a *topology.* The five basic topologies are *star, ring, bus, hybrid,* and *FDDI.*

- *Star network:* In a **star network,** all microcomputers and other communications devices are connected to a central *hub,* such as a file server or host computer, usually via UTP (unshielded twisted pair). Electronic messages are sent through the central hub to their destinations at rates of 1–100 Mbps. The central hub monitors the flow of traffic. A PBX system is an example of a star network.

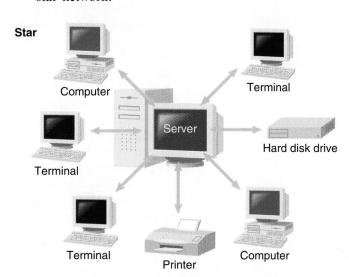

Star

Computer
Terminal
Server
Hard disk drive
Terminal
Terminal
Printer
Computer

The advantage of a star network is that, if a connection is broken between any communications device and the hub, the rest of the devices on the network will continue operating. The primary disadvantage is that a hub failure is catastrophic.

- *Ring network:* In a **ring network,** all microcomputers and other communications devices are connected in a continuous loop. Electronic messages are passed around the ring in one direction, with each node serving as a repeater, until they reach the right destination. There is no central host computer or server. Rings generally are UTP, STP, or fiber-optic cable with transmission speeds of 16 Mbps. An example of a ring network is IBM's Token Ring Network, in which a bit pattern (called a "token") determines which user on the network can send information.

The advantage of a ring network is that messages flow in only one direction. Thus, there is no danger of collisions. The disadvantages are the current speed limit and the relatively high cost.

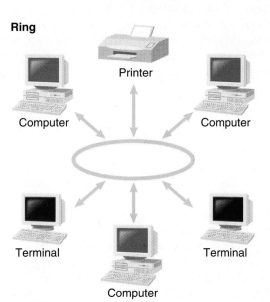

Ring

Printer
Computer
Computer
Terminal
Terminal
Computer

Bus

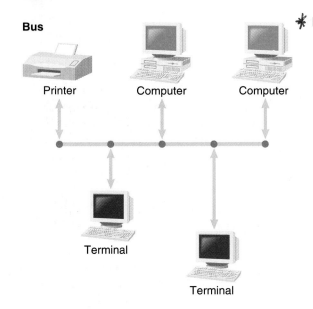

Printer   Computer   Computer

Terminal

Terminal

✳ ■ *Bus network:* The bus network works like a bus system at rush hour, with various buses pausing in different bus zones to pick up passengers. In a **bus network,** all communications devices are connected to a common cable, called a *bus,* using co-ax, STP, or UTP. There is no central computer or server, and data transmission is bidirectional at a rate of about 1–10 Mbps. Each communications device transmits electronic messages to other devices. If some of those messages collide, the device waits and tries to retransmit.

An example of a bus network is Xerox's Ethernet. LAN technology was first developed at the Xerox Research Center in Palo Alto, California. That concept, originally known as the Altos Aloha Network, became known as *ethernet,* from *luminiferous ether,* the mythological omnipresent passive medium once thought to support the transmission of electromagnetic energy through a vacuum.

When Xerox standardized the technology in 1979, they officially named it Ethernet, which quickly became the LAN standard. It is now a common LAN configuration.

The advantage of a bus network is that it is relatively inexpensive to install. The disadvantage is that, if the bus fails, the entire network fails.

Almost all networks are hybrid (mixture of star, ring, bus)

■ *Hybrid network:* **Hybrid networks** are combinations of star, ring, and bus networks. For example, a small college campus might use a bus network to connect buildings but star and ring networks within certain buildings.

■ *FDDI network:* A newer and higher-speed—and more costly—network is FDDI (pronounced "fiddy"), short for Fiber Distributed Data Interface. Capable of transmitting 100–200 Mbps, a **FDDI network** uses fiber-optic cable with a duplex token ring topology. The FDDI network is used for such high-tech purposes as electronic imaging, high-resolution graphics, and digital video.

The main disadvantages of this type of network are its high cost and the fragility of the fiber-optic cable. Should the primary ring fail, the network can continue operating via the secondary cable ring, which is typically located in the same cable sheath as the primary ring. However, if there are problems on both rings, the network will fail.

F D D I

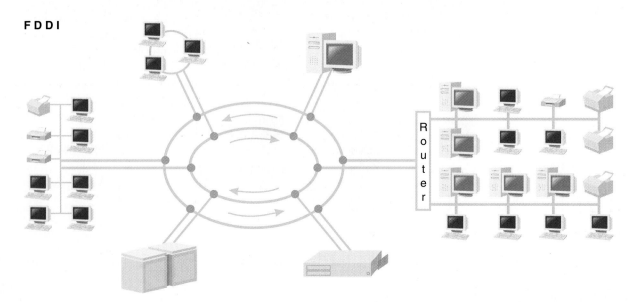

In Alsmeer, Netherlands, an early-morning flower auction takes place. Buyers bid electronically, via a LAN, for the flowers. Within three hours, buyers will have snapped up 17,000,000 flowers. By noon, the flowers will be on jets, bound for shops around the world.

7.6 Networking at Work

KEY QUESTION **What options does networking give you?**

Networked environments provide users with several options. We will take them in order, more or less, from simpler to more complex activities. Specifically, we will discuss:

- Fax Messages _ *picture (may or may not be words) that goes from computer to computer (or fax)*
- Voice Mail
- Electronic Mail _ *words sent*
- Videoconferencing and V-Mail
- Workgroup Computing and Groupware
- Electronic Data Interchange
- Intranets and Extranets
- Telecommuting
- The Virtual Office

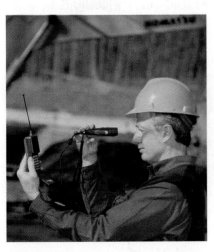

Fax Messages

Recall from Chapter 3, in the section on scanners (✔ p. 3.12), that fax stands for "facsimile transmission," or reproduction. A **fax** may be sent by a dedicated fax machine, which scans paper documents, or by fax modem, a circuit board inside the computer. The message then travels over a communications link, usually a phone line, to a receiving computer or fax machine.

A field worker views a fax message received via a wireless computer display and a cell phone.

Voice Mail

Like a sophisticated telephone answering machine, **voice mail** digitizes incoming voice messages and stores them in the recipient's "voice mailbox" in digitized form. It then converts the digitized versions back to voice messages, which may be retrieved by dialing in from any phone or via newer micro- and notebook computers and entering one's user ID.

Voice mail systems also allow callers to deliver the same message to many people within an organization by pressing a single key. They can forward calls to the recipient's voice mail box, which can be accessed from home, hotel, or on the road. They allow the person checking messages to speed through them or to slow them down. He or she can save some messages and erase others and can dictate replies that the system will send out.

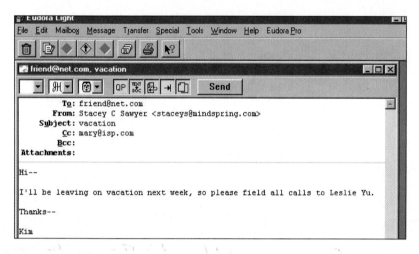

Electronic Mail

As previously discussed (✔ p. 1.21), **e-mail,** or **electronic mail,** links computers by wired or wireless connections and allows users, through their keyboards and the use of a user ID, to post messages and to read responses on their display screens. If you're part of a company, university, or other large organization, you may get e-mail services as part of an established network. Otherwise you can sign up with a commercial online service (America Online, CompuServe, Microsoft Network), e-mail service (such as MCI Mail), or Internet access provider (such as Pipeline USA, Mindspring). E-mail software is also included in browser software.

E-mail has both advantages and disadvantages:

- *Advantages of e-mail:* Like voice mail, it helps people avoid playing phone tag or coping with paper and stamps. A message can be as simple as a birthday greeting or as complex and lengthy as a report with supporting documents and links to additional online services (including attached video and sound files). It can be quicker than a fax message and more organized than a voice mail message. By reading the list of senders and topics displayed on the screen you can quickly decide which messages are important. Also, e-mail software automatically creates an archive of all sent and received messages. Sending an e-mail message usually costs as little as a local phone call (or less) but it can go across several time zones and be read at any time. Indeed, some e-mail messages are now received as voice mail by the software and can be played back as such.

- *Disadvantages of e-mail:* You might have to sort through scores or even hundreds of messages a day, a form of junk mail brought about by the ease with which anyone can send duplicate copies of a message to many people. Your messages are far from private and may be read by e-mail system operators and others (such as your employer); thus, experts recommend you think of e-mail as a postcard rather than a private letter. Mail that travels via the Internet often takes a circuitous route, bouncing around various computers in the country, until one of them recognizes the address and delivers the message. Thus, although a lot of messages may go through in a minute's time, others may be hung up because of system overload, taking hours and even days. Last, users should not let their e-mail pile up; all those messages may be taking up space on some system's server. (Some systems will automatically delete messages left on the server longer than the time limit allows.)

The U.S. Postal Service has begun to offer e-mail with features of first-class mail, including "postmarks" and return receipts. Telephone companies are offering phones with small screens for displaying e-mail sent through their e-mail centers. And in some cases, you can already hear your e-mail via telephone. Octel Communications and Microsoft have introduced technology that combines voice mail and e-mail functions. This hardware-and-software product will, for example, allow you to listen to a computerized voice read your e-mail via a car phone on your way to work. You could also phone in messages to the e-mail center, which will then transfer the messages as e-mail to their recipients.

Videoconferencing and V-Mail

Videoconferencing, also called *teleconferencing,* is the use of television video and sound technology as well as computers to enable people in different locations to see, hear, and talk with one another. At one time, videoconferencing consisted of people meeting in separate conference rooms that were specially equipped with television cameras. Now videoconferencing software and equipment can be installed on microcomputers, with a camera and microphone to capture the person speaking and a monitor and speakers for the person being spoken to.

Videoconferencing is still somewhat problematic. The audio- and video-capturing abilities of today's computers are very sophisticated; however, traditional phone lines handle only voice transmission well. If you can't afford to spend thousands of dollars on a special dedicated line, you will have to live with the less-than-optimal quality of videoconferencing over regular phone lines. And even in this case, the more you spend, the better the quality will be. For instance, relatively inexpensive ($150) CineVideo from CINECOM comes with a black-and-white camera and microphone. More expensive systems, such as Sony Electronics' TriniCom 500, run on ISDN lines and cost around $2000. The high-end systems that run on dedicated lines such as a T1 can cost in the tens of thousands of dollars.

The requirements for a videoconference over phone lines are a camera, a way to get video on your computer (usually via a video capture card), a modem, a sound card, videoconferencing software, a microphone, and speakers.

A relatively new development is an initiative to deliver *v-mail,* or *video mail*— video messages that are sent, stored, and retrieved like e-mail. One version would use the Proshare Windows-based videoconferencing product, Oracle's Media Server—a computer storage system developed for movies-on-demand technologies—and ISDN telephone lines.

Sarajevo, Bosnia, and Fort Bragg, North Carolina: Army Lieutenant Frank Holmes, stationed in Bosnia, talks to his wife, Amanda, and daughter, Morgan, 5,000 miles away in North Carolina, using ProShare videoconferencing technology.

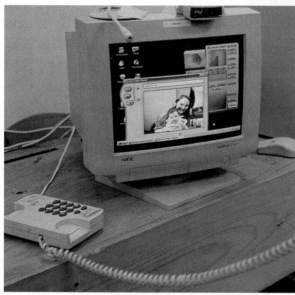

Workgroup Computing and Groupware

Workgroup computing, also called *collaborative computing,* enables teams of coworkers to use networks of microcomputers to share information and cooperate on projects. Workgroup computing is made possible not only by networks and microcomputers but also by *groupware* (✔ p. 6.18). You'll recall that groupware is software that allows two or more people on a network to work on the same information at the same time.

In general, groupware permits office workers to collaborate with colleagues and tap into company information through computer networks. It also enables them to link up with crucial contacts outside their organization—a customer in Nashville, or a supplier in Hong Kong, for example.

The best-known groupware is Lotus Notes. Notes has been compared to jazz music. "Like jazz, Notes carries a free-wheeling, improvisational quality," says one writer. "For example, it lets individuals tailor their main menu of options, giving them more control over what information they can retrieve and what programs they can run. It also lets companies easily customize programs."[3] Among its advantages, Notes can run on a variety of operating systems and allows users to send e-mail via several online services. It also lets users create and store all kinds of data—text, audio, video, pictures—on common databases. Notes 4.0 lets users create documents that can be displayed on the Web and use a built-in browser to surf the Web. In addition, Notes has the advantages of offering better security and the ability to synchronize multiple kinds of databases.

Electronic Data Interchange

Paper handling is the bane of organizations. Paper must be transmitted, filed, and stored. It takes up much of people's time and requires the felling of innumerable trees. Is there a way to accomplish the same business tasks without using paper?

One answer lies in business-to-business transactions conducted via a computer network. **Electronic data interchange (EDI)** is the direct electronic exchange of standard business documents—such as purchase orders, invoices, and shipping documents—between organizations' computer systems. For example, Wal-Mart has electronic ties to major suppliers like Procter & Gamble, allowing both companies to track the progress of an order or other document through the supplier company's computer system.

To use EDI, organizations wishing to exchange transaction documents must have compatible computer systems, or else go through an intermediary. For example, many colleges are now testing or using EDI to send transcripts and other educational records, as a cost-effective alternative to standard paper handling. Software organizations are urging that such schools adopt a standardized format (called SPEEDE/EXPRESS) as a common language to facilitate the task.

Intranets and Extranets

It had to happen: First, businesses found that they could use the World Wide Web to get information to customers, suppliers, or investors. FedEx, for example, saved millions by putting up a server in 1994 that enabled customers to click through Web pages to trace their parcels, instead of having FedEx customer-service agents do it. It was a short step from that to companies starting to use the same technology *inside*—in internal Internet-like networks called *intranets*. **Intranets** are internal corporate networks that use the infrastructure and standards of the Internet and the World Wide Web.

One of the greatest considerations of an intranet is security—making sure that sensitive company data accessible on intranets is protected from the outside world. The means for doing this is security software called *firewalls*. A **firewall** is a security program that connects the intranet to external networks, such as the Internet. It blocks unauthorized traffic from entering the intranet and can also prevent unauthorized employees from accessing the intranet.

Taking intranet technology a few steps further, extranets may change forever the way business is conducted. Whereas intranets are internal systems, designed to connect the members of a specific group or single company, **extranets** are extended intranets connecting not only internal personnel but also select customers, suppliers, and other strategic offices. As intranets do, extranets offer security and controlled access. By using extranets, large companies can, for example, save millions in telephone charges for fax documents.

Ford Motor Co. has already introduced an extranet that connects more than 15,000 Ford dealers worldwide. Called FocalPt, the network supports sales and servicing of cars, with the aim of providing support to Ford customers during the entire life of their cars.

A traveling salesman contacts his office via cell phone and laptop computer.

Telecommuting

Working at home with telecommunications between office and home is called **telecommuting.** Many companies, particularly high-technology ones, are encouraging telecommuting because they have found it boosts morale and improves productivity. The reasons for telecommuting are quite varied. One may be to eliminate the daily drive, reducing traffic congestion, energy consumption, and air pollution. Another may be to take advantage of the skills of homebound workers with physical disabilities (especially since the passage of the Americans with Disabilities Act). Parents with young children, as well as "lone eagles" who prefer to live in resort areas or other desirable locations, are other typical telecommuter profiles.

Another term for telecommuting is *telework.* However, telework includes not only those who work at least part time from home but also those who work at remote or satellite offices, removed from organizations' main offices. Such satellite offices are sometimes called *telework centers.* An example of a telework center is the Riverside Telecommuting Center, in Riverside, California, supported by several companies and local governments. The center provides office space that helps employees who live in the area avoid lengthy commutes to downtown Los Angeles. However, these days an office can be virtually anywhere.

The Virtual Office

The term *virtual office* borrows from "virtual reality" (artificial reality that projects the user into a computer-generated three-dimensional space). The **virtual office** is a nonpermanent and mobile office run with computer and communications technology. Employees work not in a central office but from their homes, cars, and other new work sites. They use pocket pagers, portable computers, fax machines, and various phone and network services to conduct business.

In Bangkok, Thailand, commuters work as they wait in gridlocked traffic, riding in an office on wheels—a specially equipped rental van with laptops, fax machines, cell phones, and modems.

Could you stand not having a permanent office at all? Here's how one variant, called *hoteling,* would work: You call ahead to book a room and speak to the concierge. However, your "hotel" isn't a Hilton, and the "concierge" isn't a hotel employee who handles reservations, luggage, and local tours. Rather, the organization is Ernst & Young, an accounting and management consulting firm. The concierge is an administrator who handles scheduling of available office cubicles—of which there is only one for every three workers.

Hoteling works for Ernst & Young because its auditors and management consultants spend 50 to 90% of their time in the field, in the offices of clients. When they need to return to their local E&Y office, they call a few hours in advance. The concierge consults a computerized scheduling program and determines which cubicles are available on the days requested. He or she chooses one and puts the proper nameplate on the office wall. The concierge then punches a few codes into the phone to program its number and voice mail. When employees come in, they pick up personal effects and files from lockers and take them to the assigned cubicles.

What makes hoteling possible, of course, is computer and communications technology. Computers handle the cubicle scheduling and reprogramming of phones. Employees can carry their work around with them, because it is stored on the hard drives of their laptops. Cellular phones, fax machines, and e-mail permit employees to stay in touch with supervisors and co-workers.

So-called blue-collar workers are also now working out of virtual offices. For example, truckers may now be required to carry laptops with which they keep in touch via satellite with headquarters. They may also have to take on tasks previously never dreamed of. These include faxing sales invoices, hounding late-paying customers, and training people to whom they deliver high-tech office equipment.

Other workers—field service representatives, salespeople, and roving executives—also find that to stay competitive they must bring office technology with them. Many people, however, find that technology creates an electronic leash—pagers, cell phones, and e-mail take over their life.

As we noted at the beginning of this chapter, information technology is blurring time and space, eroding the barriers between work and private life. Some people thrive on it, but others hate it.

Web Sites of Possible Interest

National Telecommunications and Information Administration:
http://www.ntia.doc.gov/

Modems
http:///www.modemhelp.com/

Cable modem
http://www.cablemodems.com/

ISDN
http://www.heise.de/doc/FAQ/comp/dcom/isdn

ADSL
http://www.adsl.com/adsl_forum.html

Map of underwater telecommunications cables
http://w3.lab.kdd.co.jp/kdd/cable/

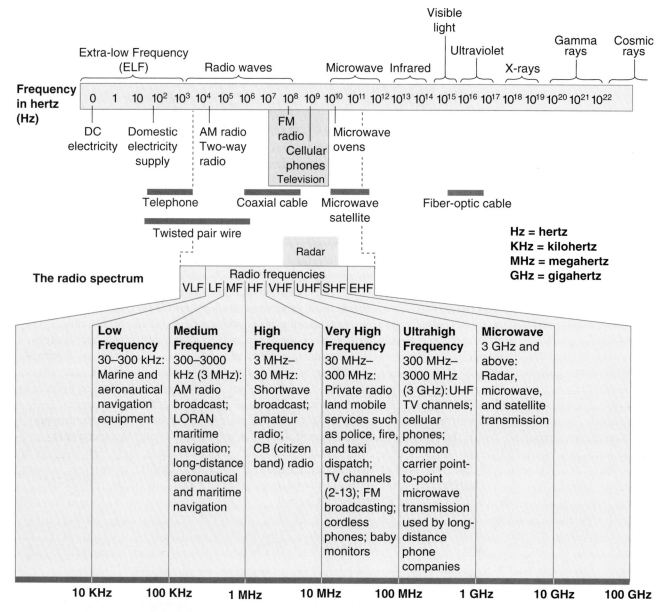

The electromagnetic spectrum

The radio spectrum

Radar

Radio frequencies

VLF | LF | MF | HF | VHF | UHF | SHF | EHF

Hz = hertz
KHz = kilohertz
MHz = megahertz
GHz = gigahertz

Low Frequency	**Medium Frequency**	**High Frequency**	**Very High Frequency**	**Ultrahigh Frequency**	**Microwave**
30–300 kHz: Marine and aeronautical navigation equipment	300–3000 kHz (3 MHz): AM radio broadcast; LORAN maritime navigation; long-distance aeronautical and maritime navigation	3 MHz–30 MHz: Shortwave broadcast; amateur radio; CB (citizen band) radio	30 MHz–300 MHz: Private radio land mobile services such as police, fire, and taxi dispatch; TV channels (2-13); FM broadcasting; cordless phones; baby monitors	300 MHz–3000 MHz (3 GHz): UHF TV channels; cellular phones; common carrier point-to-point microwave transmission used by long-distance phone companies	3 GHz and above: Radar, microwave, and satellite transmission

10 KHz   100 KHz   1 MHz   10 MHz   100 MHz   1 GHz   10 GHz   100 GHz

Frequencies for wireless data communications

Cellular	Private land mobile	Narrowband PCS	Industrial	Common carrier paging	Point-to-multipoint Point-to-point	PCS	Industrial
824–849 MHz 869–894 MHz	896–901 MHz 930–931 MHz Includes RF packet radio services	901–902 MHz 930–931 MHz	902–928 MHz Unlicensed commercial use such as cordless phones and LANs	931–932 MHz Includes national paging services	932–935 MHz 941–944 MHz	1850–1970 MHz 2130–2150 MHz 2180–2200 MHz	2400–2483.5 MHz Unlicensed commercial use such as LANs

Home Networks

Until recently, the giant housing developer Kaufman & Broad Home Corp. could safely predict which options would be most popular with new home buyers: wall-to-wall carpeting in the den, a pool in the back yard, or no-wax flooring in the kitchen. But in January [1998], something unexpected happened: In the solidly middle-class San Francisco suburb of Union City, more than 80% of home buyers at its Rosecrest housing development opted for the installation of a built-in computer network. In fact, it became the best-selling option. Kaufman & Broad adjusted its strategy, and home networking is now a standard feature for all its California developments, even those in farming communities.

From California's Bay Area to North Carolina's Research Triangle, home builders are equipping new housing developments with state-of-the-art computer networks. At the new Harbor Side and Presidential Estates developments in Florida's Coral Gables, for instance, buyers of $220,000 to $470,000 homes can ask builders to install systems that allow families to share high-speed Internet access as well as data with every PC in the house. The system turns off the curling iron that was accidentally left burning on the bathroom counter during the morning's mad dash to get out the door. It welcomes its owners home after work by switching on the house lights 20 minutes before they pull in the driveway. Homes can also be networked to one another and to nearby schools and stores, creating what could be termed a NAN, or neighborhood area network. . . . [The] new Canyon Gate and Stone Gate communities in suburban Houston—where new homes go for between $200,000 and $500,000—sit next to a new public school, which will be connected to every home. The link lets students who are home sick retrieve and hand in homework electronically or videoconference into classroom discussions and exams. And . . . report cards and progress reports can be e-mailed to parents directly. . . .

Home networking, once an expensive plaything for high-tech hobbyists, is becoming attractive to ordinary folks who rely on the services they use at work and want the same at home. And they can have it with the proliferation of high-speed services such as cable, ISDN, and ADSL modems. . . .

There are good reasons why it makes sense to install the complex web of cabling and hardware at the same time a house's walls are erected. First, there is the financial issue. Retrofitting a home is expensive—about $5000 to wire a 3000-square-foot house. For a new home, the typical cost is between $2500 and $3500. . . .

The most reliable networks are laid out with a type of twisted-pair cabling called "category five," what techies call "Cat 5." This conduit ushers data and video to the home's computer equipment and televisions, through a device called a hub, a boxy piece of hardware with ports for each connection. Some forward-thinking folks are preparing their homes for fiber optics, when it becomes [readily] available. That calls for "Smurf tubing," named for its electric blue color that matches the hue of the cartoon elves of the 1980s. Smurf tubing is designed to protect hair-thin . . . fiber optics [fibers].

Whatever the cable, installing it into an existing house is an arduous and untidy process no matter how it's handled. Technicians must drill holes in walls, tunneling from one room to the next. In older homes, where that's impossible, cabling is tacked along floors and doorway runners, leaving a college dorm-room aesthetic.

But sharing data and devices is certainly available to the majority of people, who live in analog homes. There are several basic, relatively inexpensive . . .

home networking kits that can hook up two PCs. SOHOware Network Plus, Linksys Network Starter Kit, and NetGear Network Starter Kit . . . all come with several Cat 5 cables, a hub, and two Ethernet cards, which connect a PC to the cabling. Warning: Going this route compels you not only to open up your PCs and fit the cards into empty slots but also to disguise cables. . . . You can tote a laptop or two around the house and stay online wirelessly with Proxim's Symphony cordless modem; it connects your laptop at 56 Kbps, when you fit the receiver card into your laptop's PCMCIA slot. . . .

One of the most exciting possibilities, Jini, was recently announced by Sun Microsystems, designers of the Java programming language. Like Java, Jini is a type of software designed to run on any kind of device on a network—be it wired or wireless. . . . Jini enables devices to actually "talk" to each other automatically, circumventing the need to install special software drivers. Because of this, devices designed to work with Jini—which will likely range from Epson printers and Canon digital cameras to Nokia and Ericsson digital cellular phones—are instantly part of the network and available to use as soon as, and wherever, they are turned on. Gadgets using Jini can communicate no matter what kind of network they're on—a digital camera tethered to the network via cabling could, for example, send a photo to a cellular phone with an LCD [liquid crystal display] panel. . . .

Source: Susan Gregory Thomas, "Home Network," *U.S. News & World Report.*

Retailing (E-Tailing)

Could what happened to farming also happen to retailing?

In 1900, 40% of employed Americans worked on farms. Now fewer than 3% do, because technology enables farmers to produce more food with fewer workers. During the next 100 years, could the same thing happen to the retail industry?

Technology writer Kevin Maney thinks it might. The Internet, he points out, "allows one 'store' like Amazon.com to act like a chain of thousands of stores. A handful of smart managers, a bunch of computers, and a central warehouse can do the job of a sea of retail store clerks and stock boys."[a] In addition, Web shopping sites have a built-in price advantage over brick-and-mortar stores because they don't have to pay for the physical facilities or as much staffing.

Indeed, although fewer than one in five of the largest U.S. retailers sell their wares on the Internet, Web retailing is already big business, with consumers spending more than $10 billion online in 1997. Over 10% of that was spent at a single Web site—netMarket, an online discount service offering more than 1 million items for sale to its dues-paying members. The secret for retail success, according to netMarket's founder, is to guarantee low prices, all-in-one convenience, and an incentive to pay for membership-based shopping.[b]

Are there any limitations to what can be sold on the Internet? Computers, books, and airline tickets seem obvious. But what about groceries?

"You can't exactly sniff cantaloupes over your modem," points out one writer.[c] Even so, online grocery shopping is predicted to be a $60 billion to $85 billion business by 2007—some 15% of U.S. households.[d] Two pioneer online supermarkets, Peapod and NetGrocer, have been joined by new endeavors, HomeGrocer.com (partly owned by Amazon.com), Webvan, and WholeFoods.com.

The challenges for all these Internet food ventures are daunting: Even designing a Web site shopping menu can be difficult because the profusion of groceries makes them hard to categorize. Figuring out how to deliver items, particularly perishable ones (drop off at customer's workplace? put in refrigerated box in the garage?), is one of the biggest headaches. And many people don't want to pay the surcharges to support grocery delivery. Even filling orders can be an expensive task, since most online grocers have clerks wheeling carts through a warehouse filling individual customer orders. Webvan has tried to solve this problem by building a mechanized warehouse in which machines zip groceries around so that a single worker can fill several orders.[e,f,g,h]

A growing number of Web sites, particularly of the nongrocery variety, offer software "agents" or "shopbots" to help you compare online products and prices.

Some online groceries (not all of them are national yet) are Hannaford's HomeRuns (www.homeruns.com), HomeGrocer (www.homegrocer.com), NetGrocer (www.netgrocer.com), Peapod (www.peapod.com), ShopLink (www.shoplink.com), Streamline (www.streamline.com), Webvan Group (www.webvan.com), and WholeFoods. com (www.wholefoods.com). Two Web malls are NetMarket (www. netmarket.com) and Spiegel (www.spiegel. com). Two shopping bots are MySimon (www. mysimon.com) and BotSpot (www.BotSpot.com).

WHAT IT IS / WHAT IT DOES

WHY IT IS IMPORTANT

amplitude (KQ 7.1, p. 7.3)   In analog transmission, the height of a wave within a given period of time.

Amplitude refers to strength or volume—the loudness of a signal.

All pc's are **asynchronous transmission** (KQ 7.3, p. 7.19)   Also called *start-stop transmission;* data is sent one byte (character) at a time. Each string of bits making up the byte is bracketed with special control bits; a "start" bit represents the beginning of a character, and a "stop" bit represents its end.

This method of communications is used with most microcomputers. Its advantage is that data can be transmitted whenever convenient for the sender. Its drawback is that transmitting only one byte at a time makes it relatively slow. Asynchronous transmission is not suitable when great amounts of data must be sent rapidly.

bandwidth (KQ 7.3, p. 7.16)   Difference between the lowest and highest frequencies transmitted in a particular channel or system

Different telecommunications systems use different bandwidths for different purposes. The wider the bandwidth, the faster data can be transmitted.

bits per second (bps) (KQ 7.1, p. 7.5) Measurement of data transmission speeds. Most modems today transmit at 28,800, 33,600, and 56,000 bps (28.8 Kbps, 33.6 Kbps, and 56 Kbps, respectively).

The faster the modem, the less time online and therefore the less expense.

bridge (KQ 7.5, p. 7.30)   Interface that enables similar networks to communicate.

Smaller networks (local area networks) can be joined together to create larger area networks.

bus network (KQ 7.5, p. 7.32)   Type of network in which all communications devices are connected to a common channel, with no central server. Each communications device transmits electronic messages to other devices. If some of those messages collide, the device waits and tries to retransmit.

The advantage of a bus network is that it is relatively inexpensive to install. The disadvantage is that, if the bus itself fails, the entire network fails.

cable modem (KQ 7.1, p. 7.7)   Modem connecting a PC to a cable-TV system that offers online services, as well as TV.

Cable modems transmit data faster than standard modems.

client-server LAN (KQ 7.5, p. 7.27) Type of local area network (LAN); it consists of requesting microcomputers, called *clients,* and supplying devices that provide a service, called *servers.* The server is a computer that manages shared information or devices, such as laser printers.

Client-server networks are the most common type of LAN. Compare with *peer-to-peer LAN.*

coaxial cable (KQ 7.2, p. 7.9)   Type of communications channel; commonly called *co-ax*, it consists of insulated copper wire wrapped in a solid or braided metal shield, then in an external cover.

Coaxial cable is much better at resisting noise than twisted-pair wiring. Moreover, it can carry voice and data at a faster rate.

communications (KQ 7.1, p. 7.2)   Also called *telecommunications;* the electronic transfer of information from one location to another. Also refers to electromagnetic devices and systems for communicating data.

Communications systems have helped to expand human communication beyond face-to-face meetings to far-reaching electronic connections, sometimes called the *global village.*

communications channel (KQ 7.2, p. 7.8)   The path—the physical medium—over which data travels in a telecommunications system from its source to its destination.

Today there are many kinds of communications channels, wired and wireless.

communications satellites (KQ 7.2, p. 7.11)   Microwave relay stations that orbit the earth, most at an altitude of 22,300 miles above the equator. Because their speed matches the earth's rate of rotation, they appear stationary in space, and thus microwave earth stations can beam signals to a fixed location above. The satellite has solar-powered receivers and transmitters (transponders) that receive the signals, amplify them, and retransmit them to another earth station.

An orbiting satellite contains many communications channels and receives both analog and digital signals from ground microwave stations anywhere on earth.

download (KQ 7.4, p. 7.26)   To retrieve files online from another computer and store them in the user's own microcomputer. Compare with *upload.*

Downloading enables users of online systems to quickly scan file names and then save the files for later reading; this reduces the time spent online and the corresponding charges.

electronic data interchange (EDI) (KQ 7.6, p. 7.37)   Direct electronic exchange of standard business documents—such as purchase orders, invoices, and shipping documents between organizations' computer systems.

EDI allows companies to eliminate standard paper handling and its costs.

e-mail (electronic mail) (KQ 7.6, p. 7.34)   System in which computer users, linked by wired or wireless communications lines, use their keyboards to post messages and to read responses on their display screens.

E-mail allows users to send messages to recipients' "mailboxes"—files stored on the computer system. It is a much faster way of transmitting written messages than traditional mail services.

extranet (KQ 7.6, p. 7.37)   Extended intranet that uses Internet and Web technology to connect not only internal personnel in a company but also select customers, suppliers, and other strategic offices.

Extranets allow companies network security and controlled access and save millions in telephone charges for fax documents.

fax (KQ 7.6, p. 7.33)   Stands for *facsimile transmission* or reproduction; a message sent by dedicated fax machine or by fax modem.

A fax message may transmit a copy of text and/or graphics for the price of a telephone call.

FDDI network (KQ 7.5, p. 7.32)   Short for *Fiber Distributed Data Interface*; a type of local area network that uses fiber-optic cable with a duplex token ring topology.

The FDDI network is used for such high-tech purposes as electronic imaging, high-resolution graphics, and digital video.

fiber-optic cable (KQ 7.2, p. 7.10)   Type of communications channel consisting of hundreds or thousands of thin strands of glass that transmit pulsating beams of light. These strands, each as thin as a human hair, can transmit billions of pulses per second, each "on" pulse representing 1 bit.

When bundled together, fiber-optic strands in a cable 0.12 inches thick can support a quarter- to a half-million simultaneous voice conversations. Moreover, unlike electrical signals, light pulses are not affected by random electromagnetic interference in the environment, and thus fiber-optic channels have much lower error rates than telephone wire and cable.

file server (KQ 7.5, p. 7.28)   Type of computer used on a local area network (LAN) that acts like a disk drive and stores the programs and data files shared by users of the LAN.

A file server enables users of a LAN to all have access to the same programs and data.

firewall (KQ 7.6, p. 7.37)   Software used in corporate networks (intranets and extranets) to prevent unauthorized people from accessing the network.

Firewalls are necessary to protect an organization's network against theft and corruption.

frequency (KQ 7.1, p. 7.3)   Number of times a radio wave repeats during a specific time interval—that is, how many times it completes a cycle in a second; 1 Hertz = 1 cycle per second.

The higher the frequency—that is, the more cycles per second—the more data can be sent through a channel.

full-duplex transmission (KQ 7.3, p. 7.18)   Type of data transmission in which data is transmitted back and forth at the same time, unlike simplex and half-duplex transmission.

Full-duplex is frequently used between computers in large computer systems.

gateway (KQ 7.5, p. 7.30)   Interface that enables dissimilar networks to communicate with one another.

With a gateway, a local area network may be connected to a larger network, such as a wide area network.

GPS (Global Positioning System) (KQ 7.2, p. 7.12)   System of a series of earth-orbiting satellites that continuously transmit timed radio signals used to identify locations on earth.

A GPS receiver—handheld or mounted in a vehicle, plane, or boat—can pick up transmissions from any four GPS satellites, interpret the information from each, and calculate the receiver's longitude, latitude, and altitude to within a few hundred feet or less.

half-duplex transmission (KQ 7.3, p. 7.18)   Type of data transmission in which data travels in both directions but only in one direction at a time, as with CB or marine radios; both parties must take turns talking.

Half-duplex is a common transmission method with microcomputers, as when logging onto an electronic bulletin board system.

host computer (KQ 7.4, p. 7.25)   The central computer that controls a network. On a local area network, the host's functions may be performed by a computer called a *server*.

The host is responsible for managing the entire network.

hybrid network (KQ 7.5, p. 7.32)   Type of local area network (LAN) that combines star, ring, and bus networks.

A hybrid network can link different types of LANs. For example, a small college campus might use a bus network to connect buildings but star and ring networks within certain buildings.

intranet (KQ 7.6, p. 7.37)   Internal corporate network that uses the infrastructure and standards of the Internet and the World Wide Web.

Intranets can connect all types of computers and provide information in multimedia form.

ISDN (Integrated Services Digital Network) (KQ. 7.1, p. 7.7) Hardware and software system standard for transmitting voice, video, and data simultaneously as digital signals over traditional telephone lines.

The main benefit of ISDN is speed. It allows people to send digital data much faster than most modems can now deliver on the analog voice network.

kilobits per second (Kbps) (KQ 7.1, p. 7.5) Thousand bits per second, a measure of data transmission speed.

See *bits per second (bps)*.

local area network (LAN) (KQ 7.5, p. 7.27) Network that serves users within a confined geographical area; consists of a communications link, network operating system, microcomputers or workstations, servers, and other shared hardware such as printers or storage devices. LANs are of two principal types: client-server and peer-to-peer.

LANs have replaced large computers for many functions and are considerably less expensive. However, LANs have neither the great storage capacity nor the security of mainframes.

local network (KQ 7.4, p. 7.25) Privately owned communications network that serves users within a confined geographical area. The maximum range is usually a mile.

Local networks are of two types: private branch exchanges (PBXs) and local area networks (LANs).

metropolitan area network (MAN) (KQ 7.4, p. 7.25) Communications network that covers a geographic area the size of a city or a suburb.

The purpose of a MAN is often to avoid long-distance telephone charges. Many cellular phone systems are often MANs.

microwave systems (KQ 7.2, p. 7.10) Communications systems that transmit voice and data through the atmosphere as super-high-frequency radio waves. Microwaves are electromagnetic waves that vibrate at 1 billion hertz per second or higher.

Microwave frequencies are used to transmit messages between ground-based stations and satellite communications systems. More than half of today's telephone system uses microwave transmission.

modem (KQ 7.1, p. 7.3) Short for *mo*dulator/*de*modulator; device that converts digital signals into a representation of analog form (modulation) to send over phone lines; a receiving modem then converts the analog signal back to a digital signal (demodulation).

A modem enables users to transmit data from one computer to another by using standard telephone lines instead of special communication lines such as fiber-optic or cable.

multiplexing (KQ 7.3, p. 7.22) The transmission of multiple signals over a single communications channel.

Multiplexing allows several communications devices to share one line at the same time. Three types of devices are used to achieve multiplexing—*multiplexers, concentrators,* and *front-end processors.*

network (KQ 7.4, p. 7.23) Also called *communications network;* a system of interconnected computers, telephones, or other communications devices that can communicate with one another and share applications and data.

Networks allow users to share peripheral devices, programs, and data and to have access to databases.

network interface card (KQ 7.5, p. 7.29) Circuit board inserted into an expansion slot in a microcomputer that enables it to send and receive messages on a local area network.

Without a network interface card, a microcomputer cannot be used to communicate on a LAN.

node (KQ 7.4, p. 7.25)   Any device that is attached to a network.

OSI (Open Systems Interconnection) (KQ 7.3, p. 7.23)   International standard that defines seven layers of protocols, or software responsibilities, for worldwide computer communications.

packet (KQ 7.3, p. 7.20)   Fixed-maximum-length block of data for transmission. The packet also contains instructions about its destination.

packet switching (KQ 7.3, p. 7.20)   Technique for dividing electronic messages into packets—fixed-length blocks of data—for transmission to their destination over a network, through the most expedient route. A sending computer breaks an electronic message apart into packets, which are sent through a communications network via different routes and speeds At their destination, a receiving computer reassembles them into proper sequence to complete the message.

parallel data transmission (KQ 7.3, p. 7.17)   Method of transmitting data in which bits are sent through separate lines simultaneously.

peer-to-peer LAN (KQ 7.5, p. 7.29)   Type of local area network (LAN); all microcomputers on the network communicate directly with one another without relying on a server.

private branch exchange (PBX) (KQ 7.5, p. 7.27)   Private or leased telephone switching system that connects telephone extensions in-house and link them to the outside telephone system.

protocol (KQ 7.3, p. 7.23)   Set of conventions governing the exchange of data between hardware and/or software components in a communications network.

ring network (KQ 7.5, p. 7.31)   Type of local area network (LAN) in which all communications devices are connected in a continuous loop and messages are passed around the ring until they reach the right destination. There is no central server.

router (KQ 7.5, p. 7.30)   Highly intelligent device that supports connectivity between both like and unlike LANs and between LANs and WANs/MANs. Routers operate at the bottom three layers of the OSI model.

serial data transmission (KQ 7.3, p. 7.17)   Method of data transmission in which bits are sent sequentially, one after the other, through a single line.

A node may be a microcomputer, terminal, storage device, or some peripheral device, any of which enhance the usefulness of the network.

In the past, not all hardware and software developers subscribed to the same protocols. As a result, many kinds of equipment and programs have not been able to work with one another.

By creating data in the form of packets, a transmission system can deliver the data more efficiently and economically, as in packet switching.

The benefit of packet switching is that it can handle high-volume traffic in a network. It also allows more users to share a network, thereby offering cost savings.

Unlike serial lines, parallel lines move information rapidly, but they are efficient for only up to 15 feet. Thus, parallel lines are used, for example, to transmit data from a computer's CPU to a printer.

Peer-to-peer networks are less expensive than client-server networks and work effectively for up to 25 computers. Thus, they are appropriate for networking in small groups.

Newer PBXs can handle not only analog telephones but also digital equipment, including computers.

Protocols specify how receiver devices acknowledge sending devices, along with the type of connections used, the timing of message exchanges, error-detection techniques, etc.

The advantage of a ring network is that messages flow in only one direction, so there is no danger of collisions. The disadvantages are the current speed limit and the relatively high cost.

Routers are able to view the network as a whole; bridges, in contrast, view the network only on a link-by-link basis.

Serial transmission is found in communications lines, modems, and some mice.

server (KQ 7.4, p. 7.25) Computer shared by several users in a network.

simplex transmission (KQ 7.3, p. 7.18) Type of transmission in which data travels in only one direction; there is no return signal.

star network (KQ 7.5, p. 7.31) Type of local area network in which all microcomputers and other communications devices are connected to a central hub, such as a file server. Electronic messages are routed through the central hub to their destinations. The central hub monitors the flow of traffic.

synchronous transmission (KQ 7.3, p. 7.19) Type of transmission in which data is sent in blocks. Start and stop bit patterns, called *sync bytes,* are transmitted at the beginning and end of the blocks. These start and end bit patterns synchronize internal clocks in the sending and receiving devices.

telecommuting (KQ 7.6. p. 7.38) Way of working at home and communicating with ("commuting" to) the office by phone, fax, and computer.

twisted-pair wire (KQ 7.2, p. 7.9) Type of communications channel consisting of two strands of insulated copper wire, twisted around each other.

upload (KQ 7.4, p. 7.26) To send files from a user's microcomputer to another computer. Compare with *download.*

videoconferencing (KQ 7.6, p. 7.35) Also called *teleconferencing;* form of conferencing using video cameras and monitors that allow people at different locations to see, hear, and talk with one another.

virtual office (KQ 7.6, p. 7.38) A nonpermanent and mobile office run with computer and communications technology.

voice mail (KQ 7.6, p. 7.34) System in which incoming voice messages are stored in a recipient's "voice mailbox" in digitized form. The system converts the digitized versions back to voice messages when they are retrieved. With voice mail, callers can direct calls within an office using buttons on their Touch-Tone phone.

wide area network (WAN) (KQ 7.4, p. 7.25) Communications network that covers a wide geographical area, such as a state or a country.

With servers, users on a LAN can share several devices, as well as data.

Some computerized data collection devices, such as seismograph sensors that measure earthquakes, use simplex transmission.

The advantage of a star network is that, if a connection is broken between any communications device and the hub, the rest of the devices on the network will continue operating. The primary disadvantage is that a hub failure is catastrophic.

Synchronous transmission is rarely used with microcomputers because it is more complicated and more expensive than asynchronous transmission. It is appropriate for computer systems that need to transmit great quantities of data quickly.

Telecommuting can help ease traffic and the stress of commuting by car and extend employment opportunities to those who need or want to stay at home.

Twisted-pair wire has been the most common channel or medium used for telephone systems. It is relatively slow and does not protect well against electrical interference.

Uploading allows microcomputer users to easily exchange files with each other over networks.

Videoconferencing allows people in different locations around the world to meet and share presentations.

Employees work not in a central office but from their homes, cars, and customers' offices. They use pocket pagers, portable computers, fax machines, and various phone and network services to conduct business.

Voice mail enables callers to deliver the same message to many people, to forward calls, to save or erase messages, and to dictate replies.

The Internet links together hundreds of computer WANs. Most telephone systems are WANs.

1. Fill in the following blanks:

   a. A(n) _____ converts digital signals into analog signals for transmission over phone lines.

   b. _____ transmission sends data in both directions simultaneously, similarly to two trains passing in opposite directions on side-by-side tracks.

   c. A(n) _____ _____ network is a communications network that covers a wide geographical area, such as a state or a country.

   d. _____ cable transmits data as pulses of light rather than as electricity.

   e. In _____ transmission data is sent one byte (or character) at a time.

2. Label each of the following statements as either true or false.

   _____ Frequency and amplitude are two characteristics of analog carrier waves.

   _____ The current limitation of cable modems is that they don't provide much on-line interactivity.

   _____ You must purchase special hardware and software before you can use ISDN technology.

   _____ All communications channels are either wired or wireless.

   _____ Parallel transmission is faster than serial transmission.

3. Define each of the following:
   a. intranet
   b. extranet
   c. workgroup computing
   d. electronic data interchange

4. List five components of a local area network.

   a. _____

   b. _____

   c. _____

   d. _____

   e. _____

5. Define each of the following:
   a. wide area network
   b. metropolitan area network
   c. local network

6. What are four functions of communications software?

   a. _____

   b. _____

   c. _____

   d. _____

7. Define the following terms:
   a. simplex transmission
   b. half-duplex transmission
   c. full-duplex transmission

8. What are four advantages of using networks?

   a. _____

   b. _____

   c. _____

   d. _____

9. Provide a brief description of each of the following LAN topologies:
   a. star network
   b. ring network
   c. bus network
   d. hybrid network
   e. FDDI network

IN YOUR OWN WORDS

1. Answer each of the Key Questions that appear at the beginning of this chapter.

2. What is a communications protocol?

3. How can a modem's data-transmission speed affect you?

4. What does "POTS" stand for? What are some limitations of POTS? Why do coaxial cable and fiber-optic cable offer improvements?

5. Why is bandwidth a factor in data transmission?

6. What are multiplexers used for?

7. What's the difference between a LAN and a WAN?

8. What is an intranet?

9. How are cable modems an improvement over traditional phone modems?

10. What is a firewall?

KNOWLEDGE IN ACTION

1. **Researching Your School's Network**. Are the computers at your school or work connected to a network? If so, what are the characteristics of the network? What advantages does the network provide in terms of hardware and software support? What types of computers are connected to the network (microcomputers, minicomputers, and/or mainframes)? Specifically, what software/hardware is allowing the network to function?

2. **Researching Cable Modems**. A lot of information about cable modems is available on the Internet at the Cable Datacom News site at *www.cabledatacomnews.com/cmic*. Visit this site and then locate the following information, summarizing your results in a two-page report: (a) Provide statistics about current and future usage of cable modems, (b) list the names of three companies who manufacture cable modems and provide information about their products, (c) list three Internet Service Providers (ISPs) who provide service over cable lines, (d) list three Web addresses where your classmates can find out more about cable modems.

3. **GPS Applications.** In this chapter, we discussed several applications for the Global Positioning System. Using an Internet search engine, obtain three additional examples of GPS technology in action. (Note: An excellent online resource is Trimble Navigation's GPS site at *www.trimble.com/gps*.) Summarize your findings in a two-page report.

4. **Distance Education.** Distance learning, or distance education, uses electronic links to extend college campuses to people who otherwise would not be able to take college courses. Is your school or someone you know involved in distance learning? If so, research the system's components and uses. What hardware and software do students need in order to communicate with the instructor and classmates? Prepare a short report on this topic.

Answers to Self-Test Exercises: 1.a modem 1b. full-duplex 1c. wide area 1d. fiber-optic 1e. asynchronous 2. T, T, T, T, T 3a. Internal corporate network that uses the infra-structure and standards of the Internet and the World Wide Web. 3b. Extended intranet that uses Internet and Web technology to connect not only internal personnel but also select customers, suppliers, and other strategic offices. 3c. Also called *collaborative computing;* technology that enables teams of co-workers to use networks of microcomputers to share information and coop-erate on projects. Workgroup computing is made possible not only by networks and microcomputers but also by groupware. 3d. Direct electronic exchange of standard business documents—such as purchase orders, invoices, and shipping documents between organizations' computer systems. 4. connection or cabling system, microcomputers with interface cards, network operating system, bridges, routers, gateways, other shared devices 5a. Communica-tions network that covers a wide geographical area, such as a state or a country. 5b. Communications network that covers a geographic area the size of a city or a suburb. 5c. Network that serves users within a confined geographical area; consists of a communications link, network operating system, microcomputers or workstations, servers, and other shared hardware such as printers or storage devices. LANs are of two principal types: client-server and peer-to-peer. 6. error correction, data compression, remote control, ter-minal emulation 7a. Type of transmission in which data travels in only one direction; there is no return signal. 7b. Type of data transmission in which data travels in both directions but only in one direction at a time, as with CB or marine radios; both parties must take turns talking. 7c. Type of data transmission in which data is transmitted back and forth at the same time, unlike simplex and half-duplex transmission. 8. sharing of peripheral devices, sharing of programs and data, better communications, security of information, access to databases 9a. Type of local area network in which all microcomputers and other communications devices are connected to a central hub, such as a file server. Electronic messages are routed through the central hub to their destinations. The central hub monitors the flow of traffic. 9b. Type of local area network (LAN) in which all communications devices are connected in a continuous loop and messages are passed around the ring until they reach the right destination. There is no central server. 9c. Type of network in which all communications devices are connected to a common channel, or bus, with no central server. Each communica-tions device transmits electronic messages to other devices. If some of those messages collide, the device waits and tries to retransmit. 9d. Type of local area network (LAN) that combines star, ring, and bus networks. 9e. Short for *Fiber Distributed Data Interface;* a type of local area net-work that uses fiber-optic cable with a duplex token ring topology.

THE INTERNET AND THE WORLD WIDE WEB

Working Online

8

The Internet is changing the nature of human existence. It affects personal communication, education, commerce, entertainment, and virtually every other aspect of our lives. But what *is* the Internet?

8.1 The Internet

KEY QUESTION **What are the Internet, its connections, its features, and its addresses?**

Called "the mother of all networks," the **Internet** is an international network connecting up to 400,000 smaller networks in more than 200 countries. These networks are formed by educational, commercial, nonprofit, government, and military entities. Each of these small autonomous networks on the Internet makes its own decision about what resources to make available on the Internet. There is no single authority that controls the Internet overall.

According to the *Computer Industry Almanac,* as of February 10, 1999, there are approximately 147 million Net users worldwide, with some countries represented as follows:

	millions		millions
United States	76	Italy	2.14
Japan	9.75	Spain	1.98
United Kingdom	8.1	Netherlands	1.96
Germany	7.14	Taiwan	1.65
Australia	4.36	China	1.58
France	2.79	Finland	1.57
Sweden	2.58	Norway	1.34

One recent projection claimed that, by the middle of the year 2000, 2 billion people will have access to the Internet.

Although English is the dominant language of the Internet, according to Euro-Marketing Associates, 44% of users employ a language other than English on the Net. The most popular non-English languages:

Spanish	24%	Swedish	4%
Japanese	22%	Italian	4%
German	13%	Dutch	4%
French	10%	Others	13%
Chinese	6%		

Where Did the Internet Come From?

Created by the U.S. Department of Defense in 1969 (under the name ARPAnet—ARPA was the department's Advanced Research Project Agency), the Internet was built to serve two purposes. The first was to share research among military, industry, and university sources. The second was to provide a system for sustaining communication among military units in the event of nuclear attack. Thus, the system was designed to allow many routes among many computers, so that a message could arrive at its destination by many possible ways, not just a single path. This original network system was largely based on the Unix operating system (✔ p. 5.19).

With the many different kinds of computers being connected, engineers had to find a way for the computers to speak the same language. The solution developed was *TCP/IP,* the Unix communications protocol standard since 1983 and the heart of the Internet. **TCP/IP, for Transmission Control Protocol/Internet Protocol,** is the standardized set of computer protocols (✔ p. 7.23) that allow different computers on different networks, using different operating systems, to communicate with each other—thus making the Internet appear to the user to operate as a single network. TCP/IP breaks data and messages into packets of information of about 1500 characters each, gives them a destination, and formats them with error-protection bits. Each packet travels via the fastest route possible. On the Internet, this route may change in seconds. Thus, the last packet sent may arrive first at the destination. For this reason, TCP/IP is needed to reassemble the packets into their original order.

Connecting to the Internet

The networks that make up the Internet are connected by high-speed phone lines and special hardware, making it nearly impossible for you to connect directly to the Internet with a microcomputer. Universities, colleges, and most large businesses have dedicated, high-speed phone lines that provide a *direct connection* to the Internet. If you're a student, this may be the best deal, because the connection is free or low cost. Otherwise, you will need to establish a *dial-up connection* to the Internet.

In general, establishing a dial-up connection to the Internet involves the following steps:

1. *Locate a communications line for your computer.* In addition to a standard computer system, you need access to a standard telephone line or a cable line (✔ p. 7.7).

2. *Ensure that your computer is configured with a phone and modem.* As you know, before you can communicate over standard phone lines, your computer system must have an installed modem. If you plan to use a cable line, be sure your computer is configured with a special cable modem for communicating over cable lines. If you are using ISDN, your phone company will have to install special ISDN hardware.

3. *Choose an access provider and then connect to the Internet.* You have two basic choices here. You can subscribe to an Internet Service Provider or to a commercial online service.

    Internet Service Providers (ISPs) are local or national companies that provide access to the Internet for a monthly fee. Essentially, an ISP is a small network that connects to the high-speed communications links that make up the Internet's backbone—the major supercomputer sites and educational and research foundations within the United States and throughout the world. As you decide on which ISP to use, consider seeking the advice of friends or reading published reviews of ISPs. Two examples of national ISPs are Mindspring and Sprynet.

Opening an account with an ISP requires that you select from a list of payment plans that resemble those used by cable-TV and telephone companies. As with cable TV, you may be charged a fee for basic service, with additional fees for specialized or enhanced services. You will also be charged by your telephone company for your time on the line, just as when making a regular phone call. However, most ISPs offer local access numbers. Thus, unless you live in a rural area, you will not be paying long-distance phone charges. All told, the typical user may pay $10–$30 a month to use an ISP.

Once you have contacted an ISP and paid the required fee, the ISP will provide you with information about phone numbers for connections and about how to set up your computer and modem to dial into their network of servers. Most of today's operating systems, such as Microsoft Windows 98, include wizards that lead you step by step through setting up a dial-up account with an ISP and then connecting to the Internet. Or your provider may supply all the software for establishing a connection.

Online services (✔ p. 1.22) provide a friendly alternative to using ISPs. An **online service**, such as America Online (AOL), Compuserve, or Microsoft Network (MSN), acts as a sort of tour guide to the vast offerings of the Internet. Although the Internet offers the same information as online services, many users prefer online services because the information is packaged. Online services charge for organizing and filtering the information and for providing user-friendly access to it. When you subscribe to a commercial online service, you're given communications software for connecting to the Internet. Although subscribing to an online service may not be the cheapest way to connect to the Internet, it may be the easiest. Subscription charges are $20–$40 a month, or more.

Tips for Choosing an ISP

■ *Is the ISP connection a local call?* Some ISPs are local, some are national. Be sure to select an ISP in your local calling area, or the telephone company will charge you by the minute for your ISP connection.

■ *How much will it cost?* Ask about setup charges, and ask if the ISP will waive those charges if you use the setup features of your operating system, such as Windows 95/98. (A microcomputer's OS uses a protocol called *PPP*, which stands for *point-to-point protocol*, to access an ISP or other online resource via serial lines.) Ask what the fee is per month, for how many hours. Ask what software is included when you join. Also ask what Web page services the ISP provides: Can it design a page for you? Store the page you design? How much do these Web services cost? If you install a Web page on the ISP's server, can you send files to it— for example, to update it—via standard file transfer protocol?

■ *How good is the service?* Ask how long the ISP has been in business, how fast it has been growing, what the peak periods are, and how frequently busy signals occur. (Before you sign up with an ISP, dial its local access number from your home phone at various times to see how often you get a busy signal.) Ask if customer service (a help line or online help site) is available evenings and weekends as well as during business hours. Is it toll-free? Also, review the technical capabilities of your provider (for example, do they offer support for cable lines?).

■ *What e-mail software does it offer?* Can you access your e-mail through another ISP?

What Can You Use the Internet For?

Following are some of the popular Internet tools at your disposal:

■ *World Wide Web*—the multimedia portion of the Internet: The Web is surely one of the most exciting phenomena of our time. The fastest-growing part of the Internet (growing at perhaps 4% per month in number of users), the World Wide Web is the most graphically inviting and easily navigable section of it. The **World Wide Web**, or simply "the Web," consists of an interconnected system of sites, or servers, all over the world that can store information in multimedia form—sounds, photos, and video, as well as text. We describe the World Wide Web in more detail shortly.

■ *E-mail*: The World Wide Web is getting a lot of attention, but for many people the main attraction of the Internet is electronic mail (✔ p. 1.21). There are millions of users of e-mail in the world, and although half of them are on private corporate networks, a great many of the rest are on the Internet.

Bleeding Sailor Performs Self-Surgery via E-Mail

A sailor with a badly infected arm, alone on a boat in the middle of the stormy South Atlantic. A scalpel and some gauze down below, near the laptop computer. A doctor in Boston, reaching the sailor with an e-mail connection that worked only when the sun was shining.

Put together with a satellite link, perseverance, and quite a bit of luck, those elements came together last week to save a Russian sailor's life in the middle of the open sea.

Viktor Yazykov, a competitor in the perilous Around Alone sailing contest, which pits solo sailors against each other in a race around the world, operated on his own arm . . . with instructions e-mailed from Dr. Daniel Carlin in Boston.

The surgery was makeshift at best. Bungee cords, a bottle of red wine, and some chocolate became instant medical supplies for a sailor who had to become an instant surgeon almost entirely on his own.

Bleeding heavily after slicing into his own elbow with the scalpel, Yazykov wondered whether he would die. His solar-powered computer connection shut down on him just after Carlin's step-by-step e-mail on how to perform the operation arrived at nightfall, leaving Yazykov to handle the emergency with no outside advice for hours. . . .

[H]e lashed down his tiller and went to his cabin. He thought the operation would take only a few minutes. He did not get back on deck for almost 22 hours. . . .

When he woke up, Carlin directed him by e-mail to apply direct pressure to the wound, which Yazykov did. He finished the first leg of the race, making it to Cape Town, and is expected to make a full recovery.

April Lynch, *San Francisco Chronicle*

Mayaguez, Puerto Rico. The movement of this rare show horse, a Paso Fino, has traditionally been evaluated visually. A new computer device created by the researchers at the University of Puerto Rico allows breeders and judges at horse competitions to now evaluate the horses electronically.

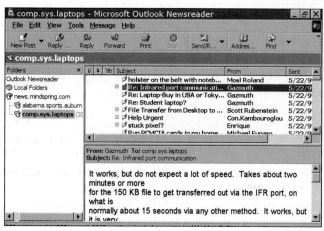

■ *Usenet newsgroups*—electronic discussion groups: One of the Internet's most interesting features goes under the name *Usenet*, short for "user network," which is essentially a giant dispersed bulletin board. **Usenet newsgroups** are electronic discussion groups that focus on a specific topic, the equivalents of AOL's or Compuserve's "forums." They are one of the most lively and heavily trafficked areas of the Net. Newsgroups are divided into abbreviated hierarchies of topics, such as alt (alternative subjects), biz (business topics), and comp (computer-related topics). These major hierarchies are divided into subcategories, and further subcategories. The action of joining a newsgroup is called "subscribing."

■ *Mailing lists*—e-mail-based discussion groups: Combining e-mail and newsgroups, mailing lists—called **listservs**—allow anyone to subscribe (generally at no charge) to an e-mail mailing list on a particular subject or subjects and to post messages. The mailing-list sponsor then sends those messages to everyone else on that list. Thus, newsgroup listserv messages appear automatically in your mailbox; you do not have to make the effort of accessing the newsgroup. (As a result, it's necessary to download and delete mail almost every day, or your mailbox will quickly become full.) There are more than 3000 electronic mailing-list discussion groups.

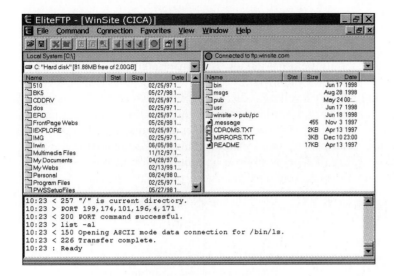

■ *FTP*—for transferring files around the world: Many Net users enjoy "FTPing"—cruising the system and checking into some of the tens of thousands of so-called FTP sites; these sites, which predate the Web, offer interesting free files to copy (download). Using **FTP,** for **File Transfer Protocol,** you can connect to a remote computer called an FTP site and transfer publicly available files to your own microcomputer's hard disk. The free files offered cover nearly anything that can be stored on a computer, including software, games, photos, maps, art, music, books, and statistics. (Remember: Scan all downloaded files and programs for viruses before opening them! (✔ p. 5.8)

Some 2000-plus FTP sites (so-called *anonymous FTP sites*) are open to anyone; others can be accessed only by means of a password. You can also use FTP to upload (transfer) your files to an FTP site.

■ *Telnet*—to connect to remote computers: An older Internet technology, **Telnet** is a terminal emulation protocol that allows you to connect (log on) to remote computers. This feature, which allows microcomputers to communicate successfully with mainframes, enables you to tap into Internet computers and public-access files as though you were connected directly instead of, for example, through your ISP site. Many public and university libraries employ Telnet to make their library catalogs available on the Internet, so that users can access the catalogs at home as if they were seated at one of the terminals in the library.

■ *Gopher*—an older browsing tool: A software program called *Gopher* has been used to browse the resources of the Internet for some time. A **Gopher** organizes information using hierarchical menus, or lists of items, from which you can choose. Each menu leads to files, Internet resources, data, or anything else you might search for on the Internet. Since the introduction of the World Wide Web, gophers are not as prevalent. Today they are used mainly for scholastic research, since many libraries, universities, colleges, and government facilities maintain information on Gopher servers. *Gopherspace* is the term used to describe the collection of all interconnected Gopher servers.

Many online sites have a set of FAQs—Frequently Asked Questions—that newcomers, or "newbies," are expected to become familiar with. Most FAQs offer *netiquette*—or "net etiquette"—guides to appropriate behavior while online. Examples of netiquette blunders are typing with the CAPS LOCK key on—the Net equivalent of yelling—discussing subjects not appropriate to the situation, using inappropriate language, repeating points made earlier, and improper use of the software. *Spamming*, or sending unsolicited e-mail, is especially irksome; examples of *spam* include chain letters, advertising, and junk mail. Something that helps smooth communication in the online culture is the use of *emoticons*, keyboard-produced pictorial representations of expressions:

:-)	happy face	:-@	scream
:-(	sorrow or frown	<g>	grin
:-O	shock, surprise	<BTW>	by the way
:-/	sarcasm	<IMHO>	in my humble opinion
;-)	wink	<FYI>	for your information
:-|	anger	<nc>	no comment
:/	hmmmmm	<jk>	just kidding
;-D	laugh		

Internet Addresses

Similar to residential and business addresses, *Internet addresses* are used to identify an individual or resource on the Internet. Before you can send an e-mail message, you must know the recipient's e-mail address. Likewise, before you can display a Web page, you must know the address for the Web page. Each Internet address, whether for e-mail, the Web, or another resource, must be unique. The Internet's addressing scheme was developed in 1984 and is called the **Domain Name System (DNS)**.

E-Mail Addresses

Break into individual pieces → Internet Addresses

E-mail addresses are composed of a user ID, followed by an @ ("at") symbol, followed by a domain name. *(See Figure 8.1.)* A *domain* is simply a location on the Internet. Consider the following address:

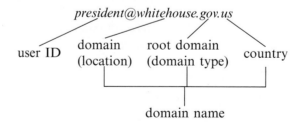

The user ID tells who is at the address—in this case, *president* is the recipient. The domain, which is located after the @ symbol, tells the location and type of address. Domain name components are separated by periods (called "dots"). The *location* portion of the address provides specific information about where the message should be delivered, and the root domain describes the type of location. Currently there are six root domain types.

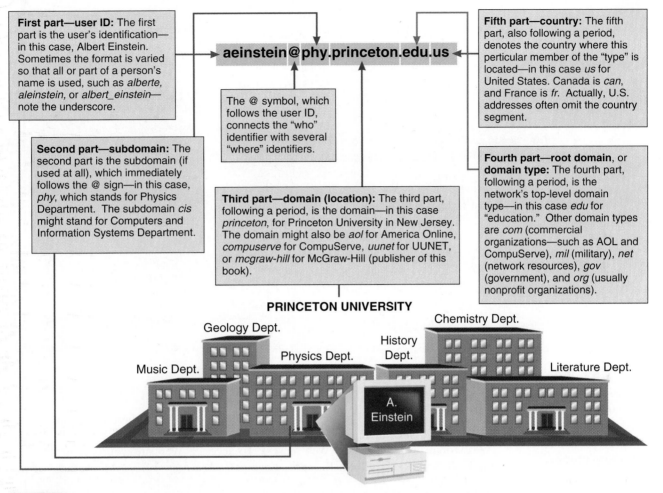

First part—user ID: The first part is the user's identification—in this case, Albert Einstein. Sometimes the format is varied so that all or part of a person's name is used, such as *alberte*, *aleinstein*, or *albert_einstein*—note the underscore.

Second part—subdomain: The second part is the subdomain (if used at all), which immediately follows the @ sign—in this case, *phy*, which stands for Physics Department. The subdomain *cis* might stand for Computers and Information Systems Department.

aeinstein@phy.princeton.edu.us

The @ symbol, which follows the user ID, connects the "who" identifier with several "where" identifiers.

Third part—domain (location): The third part, following a period, is the domain—in this case *princeton*, for Princeton University in New Jersey. The domain might also be *aol* for America Online, *compuserve* for CompuServe, *uunet* for UUNET, or *mcgraw-hill* for McGraw-Hill (publisher of this book).

Fifth part—country: The fifth part, also following a period, denotes the country where this particular member of the "type" is located—in this case *us* for United States. Canada is *can*, and France is *fr*. Actually, U.S. addresses often omit the country segment.

Fourth part—root domain, or **domain type:** The fourth part, following a period, is the network's top-level domain type—in this case *edu* for "education." Other domain types are *com* (commercial organizations—such as AOL and CompuServe), *mil* (military), *net* (network resources), *gov* (government), and *org* (usually nonprofit organizations).

PRINCETON UNIVERSITY

Geology Dept.   Physics Dept.   History Dept.   Chemistry Dept.

Music Dept.   A. Einstein   Literature Dept.

Figure 8.1 What an Internet address means. This example shows how an e-mail message might find its way to a hypothetical address, Albert Einstein in the Physics Department of Princeton University.

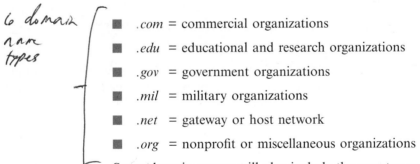

6 domain name types

- *.com* = commercial organizations
- *.edu* = educational and research organizations
- *.gov* = government organizations
- *.mil* = military organizations
- *.net* = gateway or host network
- *.org* = nonprofit or miscellaneous organizations

Some domain names will also include the country name, as in our example ("us," for United States). Another example of an e-mail address is that of the Free Software Foundation,

> *gnu@prep.ai.mit.edu*

where *gnu* is the recipient, *prep.ai.mit* are the components of the location, and *edu* indicates the root domain, or type of organization. An individual who subscribes to an online information address, such as America Online, might have an address that looks like *jimbob@aol.com*.

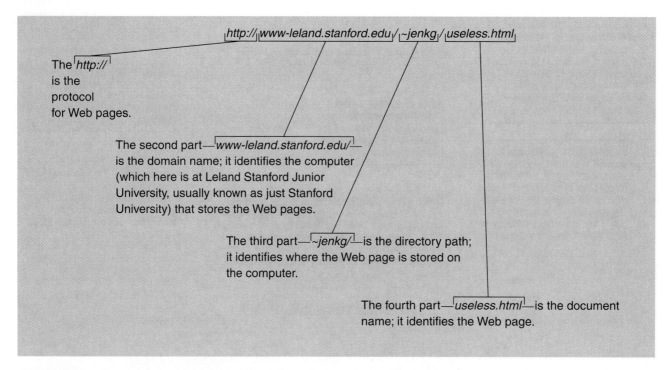

Figure 8.2 Meaning of a URL address. This example is the URL for Deb & Jen's Land O'Useless Facts, which consists of bizarre trivia submitted by readers.

* Breakup web address into parts.

Web Addresses

The places you might visit on the Web are called *Web sites*; there are easily a few million such sites throughout the world. More specifically, a **Web site** is a file or files stored on a computer (Web server). To access a Web site, you type in its address, or **URL** (**Uniform Resource Locator**). *(See Figure 8.2.)* An example of a URL is

   http://www.mcgraw-hill.com

where *http* stands for **Hypertext Transfer Protocol (HTTP)**, which is the protocol for transferring Web files. The *www* portion of the address stands for "World Wide Web" and the last part of the name, *mcgraw-hill.com*, domain name, *com* being the root domain. Another example of a Web address is

   http://www.mcgraw-hill.com/cit/concepts/info.html

where the *cit* and *concepts* portion of the URL refer to a specific location on the McGraw Hill site and the last part of the name, *info.html*, refers to a specific document named "info." The format, or language, used for files on the Web is called **Hypertext Markup Language (HTML)**, thus the *html* extension. *(See Figure 8.3.)*

Who Controls the Domain Name System?

How do you register a domain name? You can hire a company to do it for you, for setup fees ranging from $100 to $250, or you can do it yourself, by visiting the Internet Assigned Numbers Authority (iana), a subsidiary of the Internet Corporation for Assigned Names and Numbers (ICANN), which currently administers domain-name registration in the United States, at *www.iana.org.* Click on Domain Name Services, then on How to Get a Domain Name and fill out the form. Your name cannot be used by anyone else. (Of course, you cannot choose a name that has already been registered.)

Figure 8.3 Examples of HTML code

Every Web page has the same basic structure:

```
<html>
<head>
<title>The Home Page Title</title>
</head>
<body>

The text to appear on the Web page.

</body>
</html>
```

Each tag is enclosed in "<" and ">" as "<command>," with no spaces between the command and its enclosing less-than and greater-than signs. Most of the commands come in pairs. For instance, the body section is started with "<body>" and finished with the command and a leading slash in "</body>." To make words appear in italics, you'll use the commands "<i>" and "</i>." Thus, a line of HTML written with

```
The speed of the new processor is <i> really
</i> amazing!
```

will appear on the browser as

The speed of the new processor is *really* amazing!

As is apparent, the HTML source of the page looks very flat compared to what the user will see.

Other types of text formatting you can use include:

- `<b>... </b>`
  Make the text be in bold.
- `<u>... </u>`
  Underline the text.
- `<tt>... </tt>`
  Present the text in a typewriter font.
- `<em>... </em>`
  Show the text for emphasis.
- `<strong>... </strong>`
  Provide more emphasis than `<em>`.

You can show section headings with different character sizes. This makes it possible to clearly display sections and subsections. The tags vary in size from `<H1>`, the largest, through `<H6>` for the smallest. Each is closed out with `</H1>` through `</H6>`. The most common use of these tags is to identify sections of the Web page devoted to different topics:

```
<h1>Hardware</h1>
<h3>Processors</h3>
<h3>Disk Cartridges</h3>
```

```
<h1>Software</h1>
<h3>Word Processing</h3>
<h3>Spreadsheets</h3>
```

The result would be as follows:

Hardware
Processors
Disk Cartridges

Software
Word Processing
Spreadsheets

8.2 The World Wide Web

KEY QUESTION **How do you browse and search the Web, experience multimedia, and design Web pages?**

The World Wide Web is the most graphically inviting and easily navigable section of the Internet. Note two distinctive features:

1. *Multimedia form:* Whereas Gopher and Telnet deal with text, the Web provides information in multimedia form—graphics, video, and audio as well as text. You can still access Gopher, FTP, and the like through the Web, but the Web offers capabilities not provided by these earlier Internet tools.

2. *Use of hypertext:* Whereas Gopher is a menu-based approach to accessing Net resources, the Web uses a hypertext format. **Hypertext** is a system that directly links documents scattered across many Internet sites, so that an underlined or highlighted word or phrase in one document becomes a connection to a document in a different place.

Popular Uses of the Web

Here's a guide to what most people use the Web for:

■ *Performing research:* The Web provides access to a vast amount of research material, including resources from libraries, museums, and research institutions. A small sampling includes the Microsoft Encarta site (*www.encarta.com*), which lets you search through an online encyclopedia; the Internet Public Library (*www.ipl.com*), an online collection of reference material including magazines, newspapers, almanacs, and encyclopedias; and the Library of Congress Web site (*www.loc.gov*), which includes online exhibits, photographs, catalogs, and publications.

■ *Chatting:* Some Web sites provide chat rooms, which are a way to socialize with a group of other individuals interactively and in a casual manner. Participants can type in messages for the group to view; other group members can respond immediately. Many types of chat rooms also allow private messages to be sent to specific individuals. A wide range of chat rooms exists. Some are designed for discussions on specific topics, while others are simply for socializing. Some chat rooms are monitored for proper etiquette and content, out of a concern, for example, that children may participate; others are totally uncensored.

■ *Obtaining news:* You can expect to get the latest news on the Web, because most major news sites are updated throughout the day. A small sampling of news sites includes MSNBC (*www.msnbc.com*), ESPN Sportszone (*espn.sportszone.com*), and the New York Times (*www.nytimes.com*).

■ *Downloading software:* Many users download freeware, shareware (✔ p. 6.34), and commercial software from the Web. The Shareware.com site, for example, provides access to over 250,000 files. (*Note:* Don't forget about the possibility of viruses when downloading.)

■ *Taking classes:* Most colleges now offer courses via the Web, enabling you to earn college credit, diplomas, and degrees from home using your computer.

- *Arranging travel plans:* Using Easy Sabre (*www.easysabre.com*) or Travelshopper (*www.travelshopper.com*), you can search for flights and book reservations through the computer and have tickets sent to you by FedEx. You can also refer to weather maps, which show regions of interest (for example, *www.weather.com*). In addition, you can review restaurant guides, such as the Zagat Restaurant Directory (*www.zagat.com*).

- *Shopping:* If you can't stand parking hassles, limited store hours, and check-out lines, the Web may provide a shopping alternative. At the Internet Mall (*www.internetmall.com*), you'll find over 25,000 links to online merchants selling anything from flowers and clothing to computers and electronics. Online bookstores include Amazon.com (*www.amazon.com*) and Barnes and Noble (*BarnesandNoble.com*). CDNow (*www.cdnow.com*) is a great online store if you're into music. Basically, if you want to buy it, you'll find it on the Web.

- *Managing investments:* Several investment brokerages have Web sites where you can invest money and keep tabs on your portfolio and on the stock market as a whole.

Browsing the Web

Information on a Web site is stored on "pages." The **home page** is the main page or first screen you see when you access a Web site, but there are usually other pages or screens. The terms *Web site* and *home page* tend to be used interchangeably, although a site may have many pages.

A **Web browser** is software that translates HTML documents and allows you to view Web pages on your computer screen (✔ p. 6.22). You can also use browser software to navigate other parts of the Internet. Examples of Web browsers are Internet Explorer and Netscape Navigator. Several methods exist for browsing the Web, but by far the easiest (and most fun) involves using the mouse to click on underlined or highlighted words and images, known as **hyperlinks**. (*See Figure 8.4.*) To see if something is a link, move the mouse pointer over it. If the mouse pointer changes to a hand, you're pointing to a link. When you click a link, you are telling your Web browser to retrieve and then display a page from a

Figure 8.4 Hyperlinks and hand icon

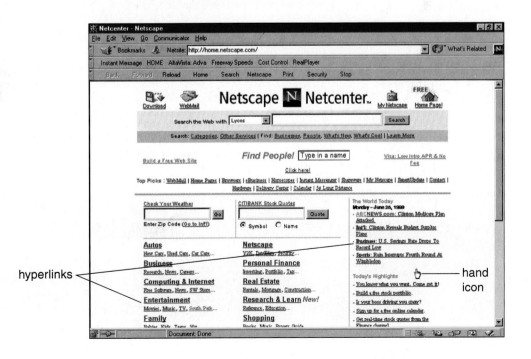

The first (text-only) browser was released in January 1992. Mosaic, the first general public browser, was released in September, 1993; Netscape Navigator in December 1994; and Microsoft Internet Explorer in November 1995.

Web site. In just a few seconds, you can easily click your way to Web sites located around the world. Another way to browse involves typing the address, or URL, of a Web page directly into the address area of the browser window.

Suppose you want to go back to some Web pages you have viewed. You can use either a history list or a bookmark. With a **history list**, the browser records the Web pages you have viewed during a particular connection session. During that session, if you want to return to a site you visited earlier, you can click on that item in the history list. When you exit the browser, the history list is usually canceled. (Check to see if your browser saves your history of sites visited *after* you disconnect. If so, anyone with access to your computer can view this list.) **Bookmarks**, also called *favorite places,* consist of titles and URLs of Web pages listed for easy reference. You compile your own bookmark list by adding Web pages that you think you will visit frequently in the future. With these bookmarks stored in your browser, you can easily return to those pages in a future session by clicking on the listings.

Some common examples of Web page components are shown in the accompanying figure. *(See Figure 8.5.)*

When you find something on the Web that is too long to read online or that you want to review later, you have the option of printing it or saving it to your computer's hard disk. Most browsers also support FTP, so that you can download files stored on the Internet.

Figure 8.5 Some common Web page components

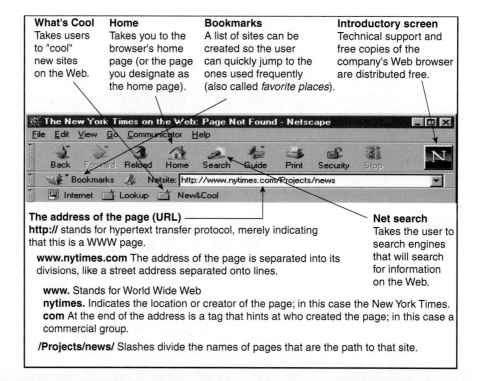

What's Cool Takes users to "cool" new sites on the Web.

Home Takes you to the browser's home page (or the page you designate as the home page).

Bookmarks A list of sites can be created so the user can quickly jump to the ones used frequently (also called *favorite places*).

Introductory screen Technical support and free copies of the company's Web browser are distributed free.

The address of the page (URL)
http:// stands for hypertext transfer protocol, merely indicating that this is a WWW page.

www.nytimes.com The address of the page is separated into its divisions, like a street address separated onto lines.

www. Stands for World Wide Web
nytimes. Indicates the location or creator of the page; in this case the New York Times.
com At the end of the address is a tag that hints at who created the page; in this case a commercial group.

/Projects/news/ Slashes divide the names of pages that are the path to that site.

Net search Takes the user to search engines that will search for information on the Web.

Like "Bookmarks."

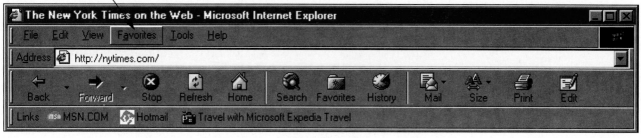

Internet *cookies* are data files created and sent to a user's computer by Web servers. They record what pages you've visited at a Web site and keep track of your online purchases, electronic transactions, and other information. When you revisit the Web site, the browser will automatically look for the cookie on your hard disk. When it finds the cookie, the browser sends the information stored in the cookie to the Web server. While cookies can help Web server administrators build profiles of visitors and can save a user's password to a particular site, critics say that they can also invade privacy—for example, revealing users' behavior to direct marketers without the users' knowledge.

Users have the option of simply deleting cookies from their hard disks or purchasing a utility such as Pretty Good Privacy's PGPcookie.cutter, which blocks cookies.

Searching the Web

There's a Web site for every interest: America's Job Bank, CIA World Factbook, Four11 (phone numbers), Internet Movie Database, Library of Congress, NASA Spacelink, New York Times, Recipe Archives, Rock and Roll Hall of Fame, TV Guide Online, U.S. Census Information, Woody Allen Quotes, and on and on.

Unfortunately, there's no central registry of cyberspace keeping track of the comings and goings of Web sites. However, there are several ways to find information. First, several books, updated every year, list the URLs of hundreds of popular Web sites—for example, *1001 Really Cool Web Sites* from Jamsa Press. In addition, magazines and newspapers are a good source for information about Web sites. You can also use online search tools—*search engines* and *directories*—to locate the URLs of sites on topics that interest you. *(See Figure 8.6, pp. 16–19.)* **Directories** are lists of Web sites classified by topic. The process by which directories are created is that people submit Web pages to a group of other people, who classify and index them. Yahoo! is an example of a directory. **Search engines** allow you to find specific documents through keyword searches and menu choices. Without relying on directories, search engines use software indexers (called *spiders*) to "crawl" around the Web and build indexes based on what they find. Excite, Go, and Lycos are search engines. Another is Deja News (*www.dejanews.com*), which is used for searching Usenet newsgroups.

To access a directory or search engine by means of a browser, you can type the search site's URL in directly or use procedures specific to the browser.

Experiencing Multimedia on the Web

As we've said, what really distinguishes the World Wide Web from the rest of the Internet—and what largely accounts for its popularity—is that it provides information in *multimedia* form—graphics, animation, video, and audio as well as text.

At its current stage of evolution, the technology may require users to do some extra work in order to activate Web multimedia on their own computers. Thus, you may have to use so-called plug-in programs to run certain multimedia components of a Web page within the browser window. **Plug-ins** (sometimes called *add-ons*) are programs downloaded from a vendor's Web site that enhance your Web browser's capabilities. Many plug-ins are free, at least free for a trial period. They are often used to improve animation, video, and audio.

Popular plug-ins are Real Audio (for audio: *www.realaudio.com*), Shockwave (for animation: *www.macromedia.com*), Live 3D (for virtual reality: *www.netscape.com*), VivoActive (for video: *www.vivo.com*), and CU-SeeMe (for videoconferencing: *www.wpine.com*).

Figure 8.6 A field guide to Web search sites

Try some of the search engines.

Guide to Web Search Sites

Excite
www.excite.com
Good searches on broad general topics, Excite adds interesting extras like a simultaneous search of the Web, news headlines, sports scores and company information — and groups the relevant results on a single page. Some reviewers have complained that the search results aren't always relevant.

Dogpile
www.dogpile.com
This metasearch site can go through 13 Web search engines, as well as more than two dozen on-line news services or other types of sources, and sorts the results by the search engine that found them. While this is not the most useful presentation if you just want the facts, it's a good way to check which search engine works best for you.

Yahoo
www.yahoo.com
A human-compiled directory of Web sites, Yahoo doesn't help you search for the contents of individual Web pages. It's excellent for researching broad general topics, but tends to return too many results, many of them irrelevant.

Go
www.go.com
When searching for Web pages, news stories, and Usenet postings, Go produces very accurate and relevant results. But according to Search Engine Watch (*www.searchenginewatch.com*), it has a much smaller index of Web pages than many others.

Ask Jeeves
www.askjeeves.com
An excellent beginner's site that's also good for anyone's general queries, Ask Jeeves leads you through questions to help narrow your search, and also simultaneously searches six other sites for relevant Web pages. Its ability to interpret natural language queries makes it easy to learn but also makes constructing precise queries difficult.

Hotbot
www.hotbot.com
This is the search engine of *Wired* magazine, whose search engine Inktomi also powers Snap.com's and Yahoo's Web searches. It is an excellent tool for finding specific information. In addition to a thorough and up-to-date index, it provides an easy interface for constructing precise search queries — but this requires extra effort up front.

Lycos

www.lycos.com

Lycos provides a good selection of advanced search capabilities, like the ability to search for specific media types (JPEG files, Java scripts, and so on). Its advanced search, Lycos Pro, provides even more options. But general Web searches can produce checkered results. Also, Lycos's index of Web pages is small.

Northern Light

www.nlsearch.com

In addition to its index of Web pages, Northern Light searches through pay-per-view articles from periodicals not generally available on the Web. It sorts its results into topic headings, which can prove very useful.

Alta Vista

www.altavista.net

Another excellent tool for exhaustive and precise searches, Alta Vista makes it harder than Hotbot does for beginners to construct precise queries but, once you've mastered its search syntax, it's quick and easy to use. Its results, however, can include many duplicates. Alta Vista also includes a powerful photo finder (you can search more than 11 million images): *http://image.altavista.com/cgi-bin/avncgi*

Metacrawler

www.metacrawler.com

This is a metasearch site, simultaneously searching Yahoo, Excite, and five other search engines, then aggregating the results. It's excellent for getting a quick hit of what's out there. But if you don't see what you want in the results, its limited search options make it tough to issue really precise queries.

Internet Sleuth

www.isleuth.com

Internet Sleuth is a 3000-strong collection of specialized online databases, which can also simultaneously search up to six other search sites for Web pages, news, and other types of information. It's excellent for highly specialized searches in any subjects in its detailed directory — but the metasearch results aren't sorted intuitively.

Direct Hit

www.directhit.com

Search engine spitting back too many results? Try Direct Hit at *www.directhit.com*, which takes your search term, polls major search engines, and show the 10 most popular sites.

Steps to Smart Searching

PICK YOUR SITE

No one site is good for every search. Search directories like Yahoo and Lycos's Top 5% are good for researching general topics. Search engines like Hotbot and Alta Vista are better for very specific information. Metasearch sites like Dogpile and Metacrawler cast the net a little wider on searches for specific information by using more than one search engine.

PICK YOUR WORDS

Most search engines do a poor job when seeking out a single word. Increase the number of words to increase the scope of your search. And pick the words well — many search engines ignore common words like 'the,' 'and,' and 'Web.'

USE THE PHRASE THAT PAYS

Enter the two words Strawberry Fields in a search box, and you could get results as diverse as W. C. Fields and strawberry shortcake. Yahoo, Alta Vista, Hotbot and others recognize words in quotes — "Strawberry Fields" — as a phrase. Metacrawler and others provide phrase searching as an option.

TAKE ADVANTAGE OF THE OPERATORS

Most search sites use code words or symbols called operators to make searches more precise. The operators vary from site to site, but the common ones are AND, OR, NOT, quotation marks, and the plus and minus signs (see the accompanying table, top right, for details on how to use them).

USE BROWSER CLICK TRICKS

When checking out results, view them in a new browser window so you can quickly return to the results page without clicking the browser's Back button. In most browsers, you can open a link in a new browser window by holding down the Shift key while clicking on the link. And if a page fails to load the first time you click on a link, try clicking again.

CHECK YOUR SPELLING

Many Web sites are riddled with spelling errors but, for the sites that are worth finding, correct spelling helps. Ask Jeeves and Go Network provide spelling help for the orthographically challenged. Also, vary the styling of terms, so that a search for CD-ROM, for example, will also turn up CDROM or CD ROM.

COVER ALL THE BASES

If you're looking for gardening tips, for example, you may need to account for several different words — garden, gardens, gardening, gardener, and so on. Go Network and Lycos handle plurals and word stems automatically. Alta Vista uses a different approach, the wildcard character. Enter garden* and you'll get results on all the different options. Search sites that don't recognize word stems or wildcards need you to think up variants by yourself and search for them all (for instance, garden OR gardening OR gardens).

ASK FOR DIRECTIONS

Not every search site works the same way, but all of them provide a help section and tips. A couple of minutes spent checking the help pages can pay dividends later.

DON'T STICK AROUND

If you don't find what you're looking for in the first couple of results screens, either go back and enter a different set of search terms or move on to another search site.

Netscape's Navigator/Communicator and Microsoft's Internet Explorer come equipped with one particularly interesting add-on: *telephony,* a way to make use of the Internet for inexpensive long-distance calls. If two users have the same software, they can communicate by voice with microcomputer microphones and speakers, while paying only their local dial-up connection charge. That means users can call anyone in the world and talk as long as they like for the ISP monthly charge.

How Operators Work

" " (quotation marks) enclose words to search for a phrase: "Strawberry Fields Forever"

AND connects two or more words, all of which must appear in the results: Strawberry AND Fields AND Forever

OR connects two or more search words, any of which may appear in the results: Strawberry Fields OR Strawberryfields

NOT excludes the word after it from the results: Strawberry Fields NOT W.C.

- (minus sign), like NOT, excludes the word that follows it: Strawberry Fields -W.C.

+(plus sign) precedes a word that must appear: +Strawberry +Fields

Note that it's possible to string together several operators to construct a very precise query. To exclude certain cover versions of a certain song, for example, you could try: "Strawberry Fields" AND "The Beatles" NOT "Sandy Farina" NOT "Nashville Superpickers"

Designing Web Pages

Charlotte Buchanan and her two colleagues own GlamOrama, a Seattle-based apparel store. When they took their boutique online, by designing their own Web site, they broke even within six months. Using a credit card, customers can buy items from GlamOrama's catalog.

Before you can put a business online, you must design a Web page and perhaps online order forms. Professional Web page designers can do that for you, or you can do it yourself, using a menu-driven program included with your Web browser or a Web-page design software package such as Microsoft FrontPage or Adobe PageMill.

Once your home page is designed, complete with links, you will want to rent space on your ISP's server. The ISP, which will charge you according to how many megabytes of space your Web site files take up on the server, will give you directions on how to copy the files to the server via modem. (When you sign up with an ISP for Internet access, it will typically provide a small amount of server space that you can use for uploading your Web page.)

Web Design Sensitivity

Imagine how you would react if you logged onto a Web site and were greeted by a hand flashing an obscene gesture. You would probably be upset and fire off an outraged e-mail to the Webmaster. At the very least, you probably wouldn't visit the Web site aain.

This is exactly how some Internet users feel when they visit two popular [San Francisco] Bay Area-based Web sites—one a technical magazine, the other an online brokerage. The sites each display a "thumbs up" icon to indicate, respectively, a computer product or stock that is a "good buy." Although the symbol is popular on U.S. Web sites, it is a rude gesture to Iranians.

What these companies fail to realize is their Web sites actually broadcast globally, and though the content may work well with a U.S. audience, it could have an unintended meaning in other cultures. . . .

[M]ost U.S.-based Web sites are built for a U.S.-centric audience. Although most companies realize the World Wide Web is a medium that can be accessed around the globe, few consider diverse audiences when developing their Internet sites.

Another American symbol that does not translate well across cultures is the dog. You may have heard the phrase, "Nothing sells a product better than babies or puppies." That might be true for a U.S. audience that views dogs as man's best friend, but it does not hold true for a Chinese audience, because dogs are not so revered in Asia. . . .

But symbols and icons are not the only issues to consider when developing a Web site for a multicultural audience. It is also important to consider the language and the culture of the customer. Many companies simply translate English Web pages into foreign languages, sometimes with disastrous results that can confuse and frustrate the reader.

For example, when a major U.S. warehouse store launched its Latin American site in Spanish, all the accents were missing. In Spanish, missing accents are like missing letters. Without the accents, the Web site was laughable and made little sense.

Another common side effect of simply translating a site often occurs in Web-based order forms. Many companies use order forms that cannot be processed unless every address field is filled in completely. Although these forms work well for U.S. customers, they do not work with international addresses where states and ZIP codes do not exist. . . .

Clearly, in this global economy, companies limited by U.S.-focused Web sites will miss out on sales to a diverse Internet audience. American companies that take advantage of the Web best will be the ones that recognize that their Web markets and communications are indeed worldwide.

Wei-Tai Kwok, "Online Sensitivity," *San Jose Mercury News*

Push Technology: Web Sites Come Looking for You

Whereas it used to be that people went out searching the World Wide Web, now the Web is looking for us. The driving force behind this is **push technology** or *webcasting*, defined as software that enables information to find consumers rather than consumers.

"Pull" is basic surfing: You go to a Web site using a browser and pull down the information to your desktop. "Push," however, consists of information delivery from various sites to your PC by means of special software. Here's how it works. Several services offer personalized news and information, based on a profile that you define when you register with them and download their software. You select the categories, or channels, of interest—sports news from the *Miami Herald,* stock updates on Pfizer or Merck pharmaceuticals, weather reports from Iceland—and the provider sends what you want as soon as it is available or at times scheduled by you. The push software PointCast, for example, displays headlines as a screensaver; when you click on the headlines, you're transported to news summaries. Click again and you're zapped to the point of origin. (Note that information can be pushed to you as soon as it is available only if your computer is constantly connected.)

Among the push-media programs available are BackWeb, Ifusion, InCommon, Intermind, Marimba, PointCast, and Wayfarer. Netscape has a push-media product called Netcaster, part of its Communicator software. Microsoft has Active Channels as part of its Internet Explorer browser suite. Each company has lined up many media sources, such as Disney and CNN, to supply "channels" of pushed information.

Push technologies have come in for their share of criticism. Push is valuable if you know what you want, if you don't have a lot of time, and if you want to receive something regularly. Average home users, however, may find push services slow and distracting. Downloading is slow on an average PC, and many of the channels mainly offer teasers, which means that, to find out what you want, you have to go online and pull up the publisher's normal Web site, with its profit-generating advertisements. Worse, many channels don't really allow you to customize the news you want. Corporate technology managers have also become concerned that a constant stream of pushed information will gum up their internal networks. As a result, push software developers are trying to find ways to reshape the content delivered so that it is more useful.

8.3 Online Services: Who Should Use Them?

KEY QUESTION **How might you choose between subscribing to an online service and an Internet Service Provider?**

Before the use of the Internet became common and before the World Wide Web was developed, online services allowed computer users to access many sources of information. Today, there are several online services, but four are considered mainstream. They are:

■ America Online (AOL)—with more than 10 million subscribers

■ CompuServe—about 7.5 million

■ Microsoft Network (MSN)—about 3 million

■ Prodigy—about 1 million

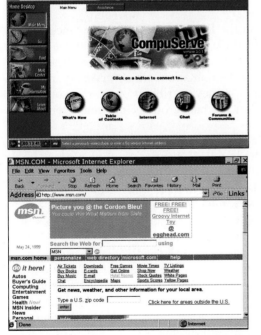

About a million subscribers are enrolled in small online services, which measure their membership in the hundreds rather than the millions. Examples are The WELL and Women's Wire in the San Francisco Bay Area and ECHO (East Coast Hang Out) in New York. Still others—Dialog, Dow Jones News/Retrieval, Nexis, Lexis—may principally be considered collections of databases rather than department-store-like online services.

Why would someone want to subscribe to an online service when most of its content can be accessed directly on the Web? As we mentioned earlier, online services package information so that you can more quickly and easily find what you're looking for. If you're unsure of whether to choose an online service or ISP for Internet access, remember that you can always change your mind later on by canceling your subscription.

Online Services Versus Portals: Is There a Difference?

The dividing line between "online service" and "portal" seems to be disappearing. Originally, a portal was a search engine that had expanded to provide many of the functions previously offered only by online services. Now, a Web *portal* is a doorway to the Web—in other words, a Web site that provides a good starting

point for exploring the Internet. Web portals allow you to quickly search for information on the Web, chat, and access e-mail simply by typing a word or a phrase. They also let you browse through categories such as travel, sports, and business to find information that interests you. Browsers (such as Netscape Netcenter, associated with the browser Netscape Navigator), search engines (such as Excite and Yahoo!), and online services (such as America Online) can also be portals. Portals aim to be the first place Web surfers go online and the home base for all their Internet activities. Portal sites make money by selling advertising space.

Niche portals are portals that target a certain interest. Women, for instance, can head to iVillageInc. or Chickclick. ESPN has created a sports portal.

8.4 New Internet Technologies

KEY QUESTION What are the characteristics of telephone, radio, TV, and 3-D Internet technologies?

Where are we headed as the Internet expands in scope and capabilities? Let's take a look.

Before 1989, people communicated on the Internet by sending text messages and some graphics. Then came the World Wide Web, and now all kinds of other media—multimedia—are possible. First came colorful graphics and images, which now enliven so many home pages. Then came animation, which makes graphics even more interesting; thanks to animation, a moving ribbon of sports scores or stock prices may scroll across the screen, or the backgrounds and characters in a video game may change

Audio on the Web is also now available, in two forms—as sound files that can be downloaded, and as ongoing "streaming audio." Want to hear what's on a band's new CD? Music companies often promote their new releases by allowing interested consumers to download samples as sound files, which can be played on a multimedia computer's sound system. *Streaming audio* allows you to listen to sound while downloading it from the Web to your computer. This has opened up interesting telephone and radio applications, as we shall describe.

Similarly, video on the Web comes in two forms—as video files that can be downloaded, and as "streaming video." Movie companies and film archives allow you to download short segments from movies available (though it may take some time) and then play them back for viewing on your computer. *Streaming video* allows you to view video as it is downloaded to your computer. Web video has also led to some interesting new uses, which we'll discuss.

As these technologies evolve, we may use the Internet and the Web as phone line, radio network, television network, and 3-D theater.

■ *Telephones on the Net:* "Hey, Pops, you there?" The voice coming through the PC speakers, from a college dorm 150 miles away, was remarkably clear. The man switched on his computer microphone. "Pops here," he replied.[1]

With Internet **telephony**—using the Net to make phone calls, either one-to-one or for audioconferencing—it's possible to make long-distance phone calls that are surprisingly inexpensive. Sending overseas telephone calls via the Net, in fact, costs only a small fraction of international phone charges. (Calls to London from San Francisco, for instance, cost only 16 cents a minute versus $1.09 under a basic AT&T plan. Qwest Communications and a few other carriers already provide calls over the Net for 5–7.5 cents a minute.)

Telephony can be performed using a PC with a sound card and a microphone, a modem linked to a standard Internet service provider, and the right software: Netscape Conference (part of Netscape Communicator) or Microsoft NetMeeting (part of Microsoft Internet Explorer). With NetMeeting, you can also view applications over the Net, so your telephone partner and you can work on a report at the same time, while talking about it on the Internet phone.

In addition, you can make Net phone calls from your PC to ordinary phones. Or you can make your call on an ordinary phone, by placing a call to a phone company, which in turn connects to a gateway to the Internet and converts your voice to digital information for transmission over the Net. Another gateway company converts that digital information back to a voice signal and sends it to a telephone company, which routes it to the receiving party. *(See Figure 8.7.)*

Figure 8.7 How Internet telephony works

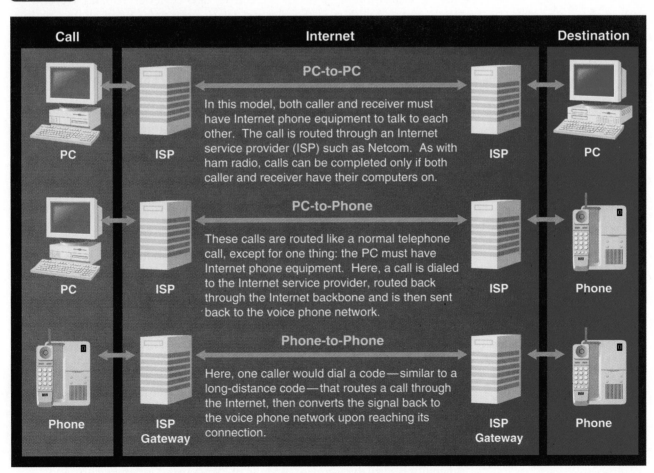

PC-to-PC
In this model, both caller and receiver must have Internet phone equipment to talk to each other. The call is routed through an Internet service provider (ISP) such as Netcom. As with ham radio, calls can be completed only if both caller and receiver have their computers on.

PC-to-Phone
These calls are routed like a normal telephone call, except for one thing: the PC must have Internet phone equipment. Here, a call is dialed to the Internet service provider, routed back through the Internet backbone and is then sent back to the voice phone network.

Phone-to-Phone
Here, one caller would dial a code—similar to a long-distance code—that routes a call through the Internet, then converts the signal back to the voice phone network upon reaching its connection.

■ *Radio on the Net:* Science journalist David Einstein received an inquiry in the mail. "I read an article recently that talked about special software for picking up Internet radio. What I am looking for is something that would be able to receive uninterrupted Grateful Dead music."[2]

The answer, Einstein replied in his column, was software known as RealPlayer (downloadable for free at *www.real.com*). With this, Einstein added, "you can listen to continuous Grateful Dead music by going to *www.deadradio.com*."

Desktop radio broadcasting—both music and spoken programming—has been a reality since 1995, when RealAudio software was unveiled. RealAudio compresses sound so that it can be played in real time, even though sent over telephone lines. You can, for instance, listen to 24-hour-a-day net.radio, which features "vintage rock," or English-language services of 19 shortwave outlets from World Radio Network in London. "The implications of the new technology are enormous," says one computer writer. "It could provide a global soapbox for political parties, religious movements, and other groups that lack access to broadcast services."[3]

■ *Television on the Net:* You can already visit the Web on television, as with Web TV. But can you get television programs over the Internet? RealPlayer (*www.real.com*) offers live, television-style broadcasts over the Internet, for viewing on your PC screen. You download RealPlayer, install it, and then point your browser to a site featuring RealVideo. That will produce a streaming-video television image in a window a few inches wide.

"Considering that you're seeing and hearing the broadcast on your computer, it seems nothing short of incredible," says reviewer Thomas Weber. "But compared with even the cheapest television set, the picture looks pretty bad."[4]

Weber tuned into a politician delivering a speech on the Web site of the C-SPAN cable television network and found the image "ghostly and jerky." When he switched over to MSNBC, "a car commercial went haywire, creating a mishmash of colors."

The problem is the speed of most people's Internet modems. RealPlayer, Weber found, actually does a pretty good job of adapting to the available speed, skipping parts of the picture when necessary to keep from interrupting the flow. But until high-speed Net connections are commonplace, watching Internet television on a PC will be a headache.

For the past couple of years, several television broadcasters (such as NBC, CNN, and MTV) have used a technology called *Intercast,* which simultaneously delivers TV broadcasts and selected Web pages to your PC. (You'll need a TV tuner/decoder card or a new microcomputer with such circuitry built in.) The main appeal is that you can access Web home pages related to the television program. For example, as MSNBC anchor Brian Williams talks about Iraq, you could get background information about the region from the Web.

■ *3-D on the Net:* Three-dimensionality may be one of the tougher challenges. So far, the computer can't update images as fast as the human eye, so that walking through 3-D cyberstores usually feels like staggering, which can make some people feel sick.

Still, several companies are trying to bring 3-D to the Web, using software technology called VRML (for Virtual Reality Modeling Language). Silicon Graphics offers a 3-D viewer called VRML2 to supplement browsers, so that, for instance, users can zoom in on a realistic image of a car they want to buy. Microsoft and Netscape have agreed to popularize the standard, and the capability is available on new versions of Netscape's Communicator and Microsoft's Explorer.

What about bringing the sense of touch to the Internet? That, too, seems to be (literally) within reach. A device called the Phantom from SensAble Technologies, based on what's known as force-feedback technology, gives you the feeling you are actually touching and manipulating objects on your PC screen. Thus, you could seem to grasp the handle of a screwdriver on screen and tell whether it was hard plastic or rubber.

8.5 Net Loss?

KEY QUESTION **What are some of the downside issues relating to use of the Internet and Web?**

Although we focus on issues of ethics, privacy, and security in Chapter 14, we will briefly discuss here some other downside issues related to use of the Internet and the Web. Although you may not agree with some of the concerns, they are still worth considering.

A basic problem with information available on the Internet and the Web is that it is often impossible to know where the information has come from, who has paid for it, and whether it is reliable. And how does one know if the creators of the information source or the Web page are who they say they are? For example, you might be preparing a research paper on the Holocaust and access a seemingly relevant Web site that is actually run by people who are Holocaust "revisionists" —that is, they don't believe the Holocaust occurred. If these people don't identify themselves as such, how can you evaluate the information they offer?

And, in spite of the many conveniences offered by the Internet and the Web, many people are concerned about the adverse effect current modes of information presentation may have on young people's education and capacity for critical thinking. Whereas the pre-TV and pre-computer generations learned to think linearly— that is, in an inductive/deductive fashion, building new learning on the foundation of related material that was already understood—many younger people are more used to an entertainment-related, information-bite style of presentation, which seems to engender shorter attention spans and a lessened ability to think things through. Clearly, this style is very prevalent on the Web. The following are some specific areas of concern.[5]

■ *The Internet isn't a library. It's a television.* It has been argued that using the Internet in the classroom is like using a super television that can be turned on at any time and tuned in to any of 100,000 unrestricted channels, only a tiny fraction of which are dedicated to educational programming—and many of those include commercials.

■ *The Internet isn't about information. It's about marketing.* Many people feel that the Internet erases the already blurry line between information and corporate marketing. That is, many presentations ignore the traditional division of editorial content and advertising in quality print publications.

■ *Kids want to use the Internet for entertainment.* Are the behavior patterns that dictate how kids use the Web already established? It may be too late to establish the Web as primarily an educational medium. Kids already know how to use the Web—for games and entertainment. Does this mindset hinder the ability and/or willingness to stick to one train of thought and research a topic thoroughly?

■ *Other reliable high-tech resources are better for educational uses than the Internet.* For example, thousands of educational CD-ROM software packages are available—most in multimedia format.

What about the consequences of substituting online time for real-life time? Comments Clifford Stoll, physicist, astronomer, and author of *Silicon Snake Oil: Second Thoughts on the Information Highway:*[6]

> I cannot imagine my life 50 years from now being spent online. Indeed, I hope my life 10 or 20 years from now will be spent with relatives, friends, and neighbors. I hope I'll spend more time in coffee shops and less time on the Net. . . . I've been on the Internet since 1975. I'm not afraid of computers. I don't feel our problem is fear of computers. Quite the opposite. I feel our problem is a blind love affair with the Internet. Some day soon, we'll wake up and say, "Oh my god. Look at all the time I've wasted online." Is this not obvious? To me, talk about a virtual community, and artificial neighborhood, and artificial life—come on. For me, real warmth, love, and compassion come from real people, real neighborhoods, real life and real friends and real family.

Web Sites of Possible Interest

Portals:
http://www.aol.com	*http://snap.com*
http://excite.com	*http://yahoo.com*
http://hotbot.com	*http://zap.com*
http://infoseek.com	*http://ivillage.com*
http://lycos.com	*http://chickclick.com*
http://netcenter.com	*http://ESPN.SportsZone.com*

Web directories:
Harley Hahn's Internet Web Yellow Pages: *http://www.harley.com*

Job Searches

The digital revolution is changing everything it touches, and the job market is no exception. Until recently several large, all-purpose Web sites have assisted people in finding internships and jobs and helped companies fill job vacancies. Now, however, job-related sites have mushroomed, and there are many additional sites relating to specific jobs and professions, such as accounting, medicine, engineering, and law. Some of these sites charge fees; others don't. Here are a few. You can also go to the Web sites of individual companies to see if they are hiring.

Don't forget: The rules of creating a good resume still apply, even if it's in electronic form, ready to be e-mailed or faxed. Applications software, such as Professional Web Resume, can help you create a professional résumé. Keep your résumé to three pages or less. Also, you may have to produce your résumé in four different forms: a word processor document, an ASCII (text-only, ✔ p. 2.4) file, an HTML-coded file (✔ p. 8.10), and a hard copy. The word processor document can be printed and faxed or copied and pasted *into* an e-mail message. (Don't send your résumé as an e-mail attachment; many companies won't open the attachment out of fear of viruses or because of incompatibility issues.) The ASCII file is what you submit to job-related sites. An HTML-coded résumé can be posted as a Web page or submitted to job boards. And you may still need hard copy to send to companies that still use "snail mail" (regular mail). If you are planning to reply to online job ads, make sure to find out what form of résumé the company requires.

www.jobtrak.com/jobguide	The Riley Guide to Internet Job Searching
www.jobweb.org/occhandb.htm	The Occupational Outlook Handbook
www.collegegrad.com	College Grad Job Hunter
www.occ.com	Online Career Center
www.ajb.dni.us	America's Job Bank
www.careermosaic.com	Career Mosaic
www.monster.com	The Monster Board
www.careermag.com/news/ indes.html	Career Magazine Jobline Database
http://classifieds.yahoo.com	Yahoo!Classifieds
www.bizwomen.com/	Bizwomen
www.4work.com	4Work
www.cweb.com/	CareerWEB
www.espan.com	E-Span Interactive Employment Network
www.financialjobs.com	Accounting-related jobs
www.healthsearchusa.com	Jobs in the health industry
www.engineeringjobs.com	Engineering jobs
www.attorneysatwork.com	Jobs in the field of law
www.careercentral.com	Career Central
www.careerpath.com	Career Path
www.ilm-jobs.com	Industrial Light + Magic

For a report on predicted needs for people to work in information technology fields, go to *www.itaa.org* for an electronic copy of "Help Wanted: The IT (Information Technology) Workforce Gap at the Dawn of a New Century," issued by the Information Technology Association of America.

Currently there are not enough people to support, run, and develop U.S. computer networks. According to some estimates, there's a shortage of about 345,000 people to fill information technology jobs.

Auctions

Stratis Morfogen, 31, a third-genera-tion "fish guy," grew up watching auc-tioneers and buyers at New York City's Fulton Fish Market haggle over the price of seafood. But his father thought Morfogen was crazy to build his own fish-auction Web site (*www.Fultonstreet.com*)—that is, until 300 orders started coming in each day averaging $90 each.[a]

Today millions of buyers and sell-ers are linking up at online auctions, where everything is available from comic books to wines, from used cars to Caribbean cruises, from Frank Zappa memorabilia to Lincoln arti-facts. With the electronic auction boom, points out one writer, "Sud-denly, the 'junk' in someone's attic in Duluth has become the treasure in someone else's house in Downey."[b] More than 500 Web sites now wield an electronic gavel and within four years are expected to lure about 6.5 million buyers, or 10% of all online pur-chasers.[c] The Internet is also changing the tradition-bound art and antiques auction business (dominated by such venerable names as Sotheby's, Christie's, and Butterfield & Butter-field), giving bidders more choices and cheaper fees.[d]

There are generally two types of auction sites: (1) person-to-person auc-tions (such as eBay) that connect buy-ers and sellers for a listing fee and a commission on sold items, and (2) ven-dor-based auctions (such as Bid.com, Surplus Action, and OnSale) that buy merchandise and sell them at dis-count.[e] To become a bidder, you regis-ter with a site, providing your name, address, and sometimes a credit-card number. Sellers provide a description or scanned photo of what they want to sell and name a starting bid. Buyers submit bids over periods of time rang-ing from hours to weeks, and the high-est bidder wins. Buyer and seller then arrange for payment and delivery. The auction site, which cataloged the mer-chandise and perhaps provided a search engine to help find items, then collects a percentage.

What's to prevent ripoffs? After all, you probably don't know anything about the other person in the transac-tion. Many auction sites, such as eBay, solicit comments from buyers about each seller, then post the results; sell-ers who receive too many complaints are barred from doing future business on the site. For items worth more than $100, after you've made a deal, you're advised to use an online escrow ser-vice to act as an impartial third party that holds funds until the transaction is complete; escrow services generally charge about 5% of the transaction (and the fee is not refundable). Thus, if you're a buyer, you would send your money to the escrow service (or let them charge your credit card), the seller would ship you merchandise by a reputable method such as UPS or FedEx, and if you're satisfied with the goods you then authorize the escrow service to release the funds.[f,g]

In addition, experts and consumer organizations offer these tips:[h,i,j] (1) Buy from sites—and individuals—with a proven track record. You can check out a company by contacting the Bet-ter Business Bureau. (2) Be wary of claims about antiques and collectibles. (3) Don't get caught up in "auction fever"; research the value of an item in advance so you won't overpay.

Popular auction sites that sell everything are eBay (*www.ebay.com*), First Auction (*www.firstauction.com*), and Auction Universe (*www. auctionuniverse.com*). Onsale (*www.onsale.com*), Ubid (*www.uBid.com*), and EZBid.com (*www.Ezbid.com*) offer computers, electronics, and other merchandise. Priceline (*www.priceline.com*) is an auction site for airline tickets.

WHAT IT IS
WHAT IT DOES

WHY IT IS IMPORTANT

bookmarks (KQ 8.2, p. 8.14)   Also called *favorite places;* titles and URLs of Web pages, listed for easy reference. Users compile personal bookmark lists of sites they expect to visit frequently in the future.

The user can connect to a site of interest simply by clicking on the bookmark listing, without the need to find the address again from other sources.

directory (KQ 8.2, p. 8.15)   On the Web, a list of Web sites classified by topic; it is created by people who index submitted Web sites.

Directories are useful for browsing—looking at Web pages in a general category and finding items of interest. *Search engines* may be more useful for hunting specific information.

Domain Name System (DNS) (KQ 8.1, p. 8.8)   Addressing system for the Internet that uses six root domain designations: *.com, .edu, .gov, .mil, .net, .org.* An address—for example, *president@ whitehouse.gov.us*—proceeds from the specific to the general.

A domain name is necessary for sending and receiving e-mail and for many other activities on the Internet.

FTP (File Transfer Protocol) (KQ 8.1, p. 8.7)   Feature of the Internet whereby users can connect their PCs to remote computers and transfer (download) publicly available files.

FTP enables users to copy free files of software, games, photos, music, and so on.

Gopher (KQ 8.1, p. 8.7)   Internet program that allows users to use a system of menus to browse through and retrieve files stored on different computers.

Gophers can simplify Internet searches.

history list (KQ 8.2, p. 8.14)   A record made by Web browser software of the Web pages a user has viewed during a particular connection session.

The history list makes it easy to revisit a particular site after surfing various sites. The list is not usually saved after the user ends that Web session; however, a *bookmark* can be used to revisit the site in the future.

home page (KQ 8.2, p. 8.13)   The first page (main page)—that is, the first screen—seen upon accessing a Web site.

The home page provides a menu or explanation of the topics available on that Web site.

hyperlinks (KQ 8.2, p. 8.13)   Underlined words or highlighted items in a Web site's page that indicate links to other sites (via hypertext). The mouse pointer changes to a hand icon when it passes over a hyperlink. To go to one of the linked sites, just click on the hyperlink.

Hyperlinks are easy-to-recognize visual cues that allow you to find other Web sites related in theme to the one you are currently viewing.

hypertext (KQ 8.2, p. 8.12)　A system that directly links documents scattered across many Internet sites, so that an underlined or highlighted word or phrase in one document becomes a connection to a document in a different place.

Hypertext links many documents by topics.

Hypertext Markup Language (HTML) (KQ 8.1, p. 8.10)　The format language used for formatting files on the Web.

HTML code is an essential means of formatting Web programs and documents.

Hypertext Transfer Protocol (HTTP) (KQ 8.1, p. 8.10)　The protocol for transferring HTML files on the Web.

See *Hypertext Markup Language.*

Internet (KQ 8.1, p. 8.2)　International network composed of up to 400,000 smaller networks. Created as ARPAnet in 1969 by the U.S. Department of Defense, the Internet was designed to share research among military, industry, and university sources and to sustain communication in the event of nuclear attack.

Today the Internet is essentially a self-governing noncommercial community offering both scholars and the public such features as information gathering, electronic mail, and discussion and newsgroups.

Internet service provider (ISP) (KQ 8.1, p. 8.3) Local or national company that provides unlimited public access to the Internet and the Web for a flat fee.

Unless they subscribe to an online information service or have a direct network connection, microcomputer users need an ISP to connect to the Internet.

listserv (KQ 8.1, p. 8.6)　Electronic mailing lists that combine functions of e-mail and newsgroups.

Anyone connected to the Internet can subscribe to listserv services. Subscribers receive information on particular subjects and can post e-mail to other subscribers.

online service (KQ 8.1, p. 8.4)　Company that provides access to databases, electronic meeting places, and the Internet to subscribers equipped with telephone-linked microcomputers; examples include CompuServe and America Online.

Online services offer user-friendly access to a wealth of services, from electronic mail to home shopping to video games to enormous research facilities to discussion groups.

plug-ins (KQ 8.2, p. 8.15)　Also called *add-ons;* in Web software, programs that enhance the capabilities of a Web browser—for example, by improving animation, video, or audio or providing telephony.

Plug-in programs can activate multimedia components of Web pages if the receiving computer doesn't already have that capability.

push technology (KQ 8.2, p. 8.20)　Also called *webcasting;* software that enables information on the Web to find consumers. The consumer selects a "channel" or category of interest, and the provider sends information as it becomes available or at scheduled times.

Users can see the latest news on a topic; usually they receive a short notification like a sports score or headline and can then go to a Web site to see more complete information.

search engine (KQ 8.2, p. 8.15)　Search tool that allows the user to find specific documents through key-word searches or menu choices. It uses software indexers (spiders) to "crawl" around the Web and build indexes based on what they find in available Web pages.

Search engines, along with directories, allow users to find Web sites of interest to them.

TCP/IP (Transmission Control Protocol/Internet Protocol) (KQ 8.1, p. 8.3)   Standardized set of guidelines (protocols) that allow computers on different networks to communicate efficiently with one another.

Unix-based TCP/IP is the standard protocol of the Internet.

telephony (KQ 8.4, p. 8.23)   Making phone calls to other users over the Internet; all callers need the same telephonic software, a microcomputer with a microphone, a sound card, a modem, and a link to an Internet service provider.

Telephony on the Internet is less expensive than standard phone calls, especially international calls. It can also support audioconferences in which participants view and work on documents together.

Telnet (KQ 8.1, p. 8.7)   Internet feature that allows microcomputer users to connect (log on) to remote computers as if they were directly connected to those computers.

With Telnet, users can peruse large databases and library card catalogs.

URL (Uniform Resource Locator) (KQ 8.1, p. 8.10)   Address that points to a specific site on the Web.

Addresses are necessary to distinguish among Web sites.

Usenet newsgroups (KQ 8.1, p. 8.6)   Electronic discussion groups that focus on a specific topic.

Usenet newsgroups are among the most lively and heavily trafficked areas of the Net.

✳ **Web browser** (KQ 8.2, p. 8.13)   Graphical user interface software used to browse through Web sites.

Users can't surf the Web without a browser.

Web site (KQ 8.1, p. 8.10)   File(s) stored on a computer (Web server) as part of the World Wide Web.

Each Web site focuses on a particular topic. The information on a site is stored on "pages." The starting page is called the *home page.*

World Wide Web (KQ 8.1, p. 8.5)   Interconnected (hyperlinked) system of sites on the Internet that store information in multimedia form.

Web software allows users to view information that includes not just text but graphics, animation, video, and sound. The types of information available on the Web are limitless.

SELF-TEST EXERCISES

1. Fill in the following blanks:

   a. The _____ is the most extensive network in the world.

   b. _____ is an Internet protocol that lets you connect to a remote computer and download files to your computer's hard disk.

   c. _____ _____ _____ are local or national companies that provide unlimited public access to the Internet for a monthly fee.

   d. The format of files stored on the Web is _____ .

   e. One method to access a Web site using browser software involves typing in the site's address, called a(n) _____ .

2. Label each of the following statements as either true or false.

   _____ When you click a hyperlink, you're telling your Web browser to retrieve and then display a page from a Web site.

   _____ TCP/IP allows different computers using different operating systems to communicate with each other efficiently.

   _____ Two methods for connecting to the Internet include signing up with an ISP or subscribing to an online information service.

   _____ Web addresses always use the @ ("at") sign.

   _____ The Internet's addressing scheme is called the Domain Name System (DNS).

3. Define the following Web-related terms:
   a. Web browser
   b. hyperlinks
   c. history list
   d. bookmarks
   e. hypertext

4. List five activities people commonly perform on the Web.

   a. _____

   b. _____

   c. _____

   d. _____

   e. _____

5. What steps must you follow to establish an Internet connection from your microcomputer?

   a. _____

   b. _____

   c. _____

6. What questions should you ask before choosing an ISP?

   a. _____

   b. _____

   c. _____

   d. _____

7. Provide an example of a Web address and an e-mail address:

   Web address: _____

   e-mail address: _____

8. Describe the significance of the following new Internet technologies:
   a.   telephones on the Internet
   b.   radio on the Internet
   c.   television on the Internet

9. What are two costs associated with using an ISP or online service?

   a. _____

   b. _____

10. Provide five examples of Internet tools:

   a. _____

   b. _____

   c. _____

   d. _____

   e. _____

IN YOUR OWN WORDS

1. Answer each of the Key Questions that appear at the beginning of this chapter.

2. For searching the Web, what is the difference between a directory and a search engine?

3. What is an Internet Service Provider?

4. What is an online service?

5. What is FTP used for?

6. What is a Usenet newsgroup?

7. What are plug-in programs used for?

8. What is meant by the phrase *push technology*?

9. What is the significance of the TCP/IP protocols?

10. What is a portal?

KNOWLEDGE IN ACTION

1. **Purchasing a Computer.** Pretend that you need to purchase a computer for home use in business-related (school-related) tasks. Review a current computer magazine or visit an online shopping site such as Intuit.com to choose a system that will satisfy your needs. Make sure that your system is configured with a modem. Include the following in a report:

■ Who manufactures your chosen system?

■ How much does the system cost?

■ Provide a description of the system (input, processing, storage, output, communications components).

■ What software is included?

2. **Finding an Effective Use of Multimedia.** Some Web sites go overboard with multimedia effects, while others don't include enough. Locate a Web site that you think makes effective use of multimedia. What is the purpose of the site? What types of media are used at the site? Why is the site's use of multimedia effective?

3. **Learning More About Online Services.** Using your Web browser, visit the CompuServe site (*www.compuserve.com*). There are several activities you can perform here without being a member. First, determine what you must do to become a new CompuServe member. Second, locate the "Overview" link on the Home page and then click it to obtain more information about CompuServe. Third, participate in a forum on a topic that interests you and then describe the experience. Present your findings in a 1–2 page report.

4. **Using the Web to Find a Job.** Visit the links presented in this chapter's Career box. What three sites do you think will be particularly helpful in finding a future job? Why? Provide a description of the three sites in a report.

Answers to self-test exercises: 1a. Internet   1b. File Transfer Protocol, or FTP   1c. Internet service providers
1d. HTML, or Hypertext Markup Language   1e. URL, or Uniform Resource Locator   2. T, T, T, F, T
3a. Graphical user interface software used to browse through Web sites.   3b. Underlined words or highlighted items in a Web site's page that indicate links to other sites (via hypertext). The mouse pointer changes to a hand icon when it passes over a hyperlink. To go to one of the linked sites, just click on the hyperlink.   3c. A record made by Web browser software of the Web pages a user has viewed during a particular connection session.   3d. Also called *favorite places;* titles and URLs of Web pages, listed for easy reference. Users compile personal bookmark lists of sites they expect to visit frequently in the future.   3e. A system that directly links documents scattered across many Internet sites, so that an underlined or highlighted word or phrase in one document becomes a connection to a document in a different place.   4. perform research, obtain the latest news, download free software, arrange travel plans, shop, manage investments
5. locate a communications line for your computer, ensure that you computer is configured with a modem, choose an ISP or online service and then connect to the Internet 6. Is the ISP connection a local call? How much will it cost? How good is the service? What e-mail software does it offer? 7. *Answers will vary.* 8. *Answers will vary.* 9. telephone charges, subscription charges 10. any five of the following: World Wide Web, e-mail, Usenet newsgroups, mailing lists, FTP, Telnet, Gopher

EPISODE 4

When you think of traffic, the first thought that comes to mind most probably isn't a happy one. But when it comes to your Web site, traffic, and lots of it, is a good thing. It means that you've been successful in advertising your site and that customers find value in your products. If you receive a lot of repeat traffic, it means that customers enjoyed the experience and convenience of shopping at your site. With your site construction efforts well underway, let's focus on ways to advertise your site and encourage repeat visits.

In Amazon.com's first year of business, December 1995, the number of average daily visits to the Amazon.com site was 2200. By March 1997, the number of daily visits had grown to approximately 80,000, with repeat customers accounting for 40% of Amazon.com's orders. Since 1997, Amazon.com has continued to grow at an impressive rate. In addition to discounted pricing, Amazon.com offers customers engaging content and personalized services. In this Episode, we look at some general strategies for promoting traffic to your site and review the Amazon.com formula for success in more detail.

ESTABLISHING A WEB PRESENCE

Once your site is up and running, make sure to list it on all the major search engines and directories. Most customers will use a search engine or directory to begin a search for a specific product or service on the Internet. You can do this yourself by loading your browser and then going to the search engine or list that you want your address added to. Look on the top or bottom of the Home page for directions on submitting your address (www.yourname.com) to the list. For example, to add your site to the Yahoo search engine, go to the site (http://www.yahoo.com) and then click the How to Suggest a Site link, located on the bottom of the first page. The over 200 search engines and directories on the Internet have also given rise to companies such as WebPromote (http://www.webpromote.com), which generate revenue from assisting businesses with the important step of establishing a Web presence. At some point, you may become curious about what sites have links to your Web site. One way to obtain this information is to use the AltaVista search engine (http://www.altavista.com) and then type in `link: yourname.com` into the search field. A list of every site that references your site will appear.

GETTING YOUR SITE BOOKMARKED

The ability to bookmark a Web address using your browser lets you visit the site later without having to type in its corresponding URL. The process of using a bookmark is similar in concept to using the speed-dial function on your telephone or executing a macro. It stands to reason that customers will only bookmark your site if you provide compelling content. Amazon.com's engaging content and personalized services have factored greatly into its high percentage of repeat customers. At the Amazon.com site, you have access to author interviews, entertaining editorial content, and synopses. As well, you have the opportunity to post reviews, discuss your favorite books with other customers, and provide feedback to authors. In short, Amazon.com's dynamic content is worth checking out every once in a while.

ADVERTISING YOUR SITE

Some sites, such as Yahoo!, are visited by thousands of visitors a day. These sites often generate additional revenue through *banner advertising*, whereby you pay a fee to include your own banner ad on the top and bottom of the highly-trafficked page. A banner ad typically contains a graphic that is linked to your site. By clicking the graphic, the user becomes a potential customer.

GATHERING CUSTOMER INFORMATION

The more information you have about your customers, such as their specific areas of interest, the better off you will be when trying to target their needs in the future. The question now is how do you get Sam and Suzie Surfer to take a moment to provide information to you about themselves without annoying them? One method is to give the customer the option of filling out a customer survey. Perhaps include a humorous graphic on a Web page that links to a customer survey form. Make sure to ask customers for their e-mail address and if they would be open to receiving periodic information about your latest products and promotions.

LISTENING TO YOUR CUSTOMERS

By including e-mail addresses so that customers can contact you with questions, comments, or complaints, you improve the chances that customers will want to do business with you in the future. Standard e-mail addresses include info@yourname.com for general inquiries, webmaster@yourname.com for Web site inquiries, and sales@yourname.com for inquiries about products and services. Consider including contact links on the bottom of your Home page or on a separate Contacts page that your customer can easily navigate to. Remember also that by replying promptly to messages, your customers will know that their concerns are important to you.

SITE SECURITY CONSIDERATIONS

Many security options are available to ensure that your Web site is secure from hackers, sometimes called *Internet graffiti artists*, who have enough knowledge about the Internet to access or change the files at your Web site. Make sure to talk with your access provider or system administrator to ensure that not just anybody has access privileges to your Web files. Also, consider changing the password you use to access your Web site on a weekly basis.

WHAT DO YOU THINK?

1. In a 1–2 page report, analyze the steps you've taken in Episodes 1–4 to plan your Web-based business. Think of your Web business as a system and structure your report, as much as possible, according to the systems development life cycle (SDLC).

2. What specific features are you going to include at your site in order to inspire customers to visit again?

3. How do think you will establish a Web presence? Describe the process you will follow. How will you advertise your site? Will you advertise on highly-trafficked sites using a banner? Why/why not?

4. What method(s) will you use to gather demographic information about your customers? How will you use this information to your advantage in the future? Will your use of this information also be beneficial to your customers?

5. What contact information do you plan to include at your site? Why?

6. What procedures do you plan to follow in order to protect your site from unwanted visitors. Feel free to research your response using current computer publications and by performing a search for this topic on the Internet.

INFORMATION SYSTEMS ANALYSIS AND DESIGN

The Systems Development Life Cycle

9

No matter what your position in an organization, you will undoubtedly come in contact with a systems development life cycle (SDLC)—the process of setting up a business system, or an information system. Before we discuss this systems approach to solving problems, let's ask a basic question: What *is* a system?

A *system* is defined as a collection of related components that interact to perform a task in order to accomplish a goal. Any organization that uses information technology will have a computer-based information system consisting of hardware, software, data/information, procedures, people, and communications setups (✔ p. 1.5). *(See Figure 9.1 for a review.)* These work together to provide management with information for running the organization.

Systems do not work very well. The point of *systems analysis and design* is to ascertain how a system works and then take steps to make it better. Often, a systems approach is used to define, describe, and solve a problem or to meet an objective—for example, to produce multimedia CD-ROMs.

From time to time, organizations need to change their information systems, in response to new marketing opportunities, modified government regulations, the introduction of new technology, merger with another company, or other developments. For instance, a major cable-TV company may need to set up a billing sys-

Figure 9.1 Review of components of a computer-based information system

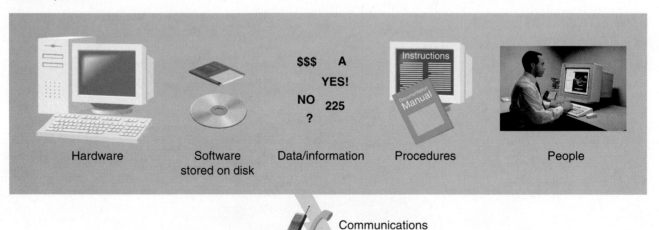

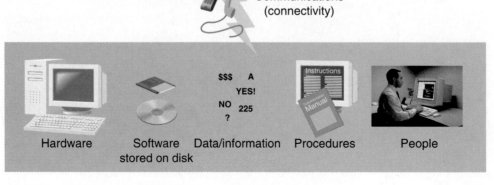

tem for movies-on-demand, or, on a smaller scale, a two-person graphic design business may want to change its invoice and payment system. When change is needed, the time is ripe for applying the principles of systems analysis and design.

The formal process by which organizations build systems is known as the **systems development life cycle (SDLC).** The extent to which your job brings you in contact with your company's SDLC will vary depending on a number of factors, such as the size of the organization, your job description, your relevant experience, and your educational background. In large companies the SDLC usually involves clearly defined standards and procedures. Although the technical aspects of each phase of the cycle will undoubtedly be handled by information specialists, users will always interface with these specialists. As we'll see, users play a vital role in systems development.

User Participation in Systems Development: Helping to Avoid System Failure

Many general users of computers assume they will have little to do with the analysis and development of information systems. However, in your professional life, you may participate in an SDLC in many ways. For example:

■ You may need to explain to systems analysts how the current system works in your department: the manual procedures you use, what you do to support an existing computer-based system, and the current business terminology and purpose of the system.

■ You may attend a meeting where problems with the current system and ways of improving it are discussed. Indeed, in progressive companies, management may *require* employee input in developing new systems through a process called *JAD (joint applications development),* which uses highly organized, intensive workshops to bring together system owners, users, analysts, and designers to jointly define and design systems.

■ You may be required to provide systems analysts and designers with the departmental objectives and requirements that the system must meet. For instance, if you want the new system to produce useful reports, you should plan to give the information specialists recommendations on how these reports should look and what information or data they should contain.

■ You may be involved in the approval of projects and budgets as a member of a special steering committee (a managing committee that determines the order in which business will be taken up).

■ As the development of a new system nears completion, you will probably help evaluate it and test whether it works as expected.

■ You may have to help prepare some of the documentation generated during system development.

■ You will attend briefings and training sessions to learn how the new system will affect your job and what its new operating procedures will be.

■ And, you will end up using the new system. This may involve preparing data for input, processing data, and/or using information produced by the system.

The importance of user input should not be underrated. Indeed, sometimes systems fail because their components and functions are not clearly defined in terms of user objectives and are not adequately controlled, with the consequence that user requirements are not met. In some cases user input is simply disregarded. Other reasons why systems fail include:

- *Lack of communication:* Sometimes failures can be traced to a breakdown in communications among users, management, and information specialists. Vague definitions of the project and of project goals can be included here.

- *Continuation of a project that should have been canceled:* Often it's tempting to continue an unviable project simply because of the investment already made (called *sunk costs*). Analysts should reevaluate the project—including costs and schedules—at each phase of its development to determine if it remains feasible. Superficial project reviews and status reports can lead to disaster.

- *The failure of two or more portions of the new system to fit together properly:* Such a failure of *systems integration* often results when different portions of the systems are worked on by technical specialists who do not communicate well or who have different priorities and objectives.

- *Politics:* A successful outcome is unlikely in a project environment characterized by political maneuvering, interpersonal manipulation, and hidden motives.

- *Lack of management support:* Lack of support from management is usually infectious: Lower-level employees, as well as outside consultants, may lose confidence in and enthusiasm for the project, and their work may suffer.

- *Technological incompetence:* Perhaps the skills of the people working on the project are not up to the challenge. It may be, for example, that a technical systems engineer has been promoted to manage a project component and, although competent at the previous job level, proves incompetent as a manager. The tendency to promote employees to their level of incompetence is often referred to as the Peter Principle (formulated by Laurence Peter in a 1969 book of the same name).

- *Major changes in available technology in the middle of a project:* If new generations of software and hardware appear, the project may be abandoned and the SDLC started all over again.

- *Lack of user training:* As we'll discuss later in the chapter, user training is essential for the success and acceptance of a new system.

Responses to systems failure vary. Project leaders may be fired. Usually the systems requirements are reassessed, a smaller system that can be more easily controlled is developed to meet the highest-priority requirements.

In most large companies, a great deal of money is allocated for information processing functions (hardware, software, and staff support); a systems development project that costs more than $1 million is not uncommon. The development process may involve hundreds, even thousands, of individual tasks, performed by many people within the organization—often within several different subdivisions of the organization. This multiplicity of effort can lead to conflicting objectives and poor coordination. If system development bogs down, the final product may be delayed; the final cost may be more than double the original estimate. To avoid such difficulties, the SDLC—along with project management software (✔ p. 6.25) and other software tools to be discussed—is used as a guideline to direct and administer the development process and to control the financial expenditures. In other words, following a structured procedure—the SDLC—brings order to the development process.

In a small company, the financial outlay on project development may be much less. However, following the steps of the SDLC is no less important. A few of the risks of ignoring these steps are the following:

■ *The new system does not meet the users' needs:* If the information gathered by the systems analysts and designers is inaccurate or incomplete, the software will not do what the users need or will be too complex.

■ *Unnecessary hardware is acquired:* If personal computers and printers are sitting idle most of the time, then probably far too much money has been invested without a clear definition of how much processing power is needed.

■ *Insufficient hardware may be acquired:* For example, users may be frustrated by poor system response time.

■ *Software may be inadequately tested and thus may not perform as expected:* Users tend to rely heavily on the accuracy and the completeness of the information provided by the computer. However, if software is not adequately tested before use, undetected programming errors may produce inaccurate or incomplete information, or the system may lock up or perform unexpectedly.

9.1 Systems Development Life Cycle (SDLC)

KEY QUESTION **What are the six phases of the SDLC?**

Different organizations may refer to the systems development life cycle by different names—such as *applications development cycle, systems development cycle,* or *structured development life cycle*—or, indeed, sometimes by no name at all. However, the general objectives remain the same. The number of steps necessary to complete the cycle may also vary from one company to another, depending on the level of detail necessary to effectively administer and control systems development. One way to look at systems development is to divide it into six phases (*see Figure 9.2, next page*).

■ *Phase 1: Preliminary investigation*

■ *Phase 2: Systems analysis*

■ *Phase 3: Systems design*

■ *Phase 4: Systems development/acquisition*

■ *Phase 5: Systems implementation*

■ *Phase 6: Systems maintenance*

■ *When the system becomes obsolete, the SDLC begins again with another preliminary investigation, and a new system is developed.*

Are the Phases Distinct? Not Always

Keep in mind that, although we speak of six separate SDLC phases, one phase does not necessarily have to be completed before the next one begins. In other words, the phases often overlap; some activities in all phases are interrelated and interdependent and thus are called *cross-life-cycle activities.* These activities include fact-finding, documentation and presentation, estimation and measurement, feasibility analysis, project management, and process management.[1]

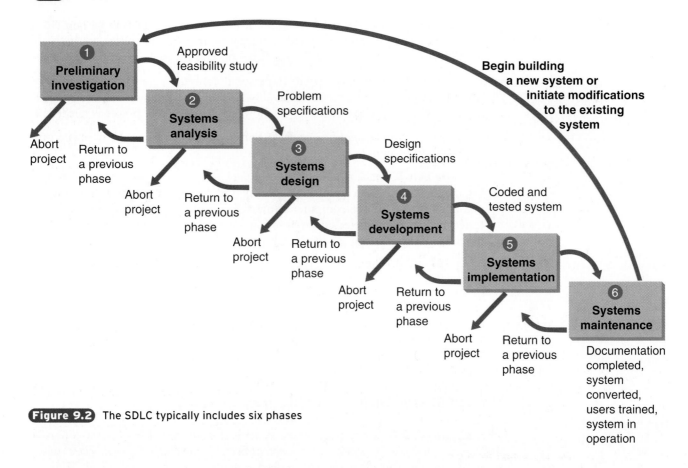

Figure 9.2 The SDLC typically includes six phases

- *Fact-finding:* Information gathering/data collection—using observation of the existing system, research, meetings, interviews, questionnaires, sampling, and so forth—about systems, requirements, and preferences

- *Documentation:* Recording facts and specifications for a system

- *Presentation:* Formally packaging documentation for review by users and managers

- *Estimation:* Approximate evaluation of the time, effort, cost, and benefits of developing systems

- *Measurement:* Measuring and analyzing developer productivity and quality (perhaps including costs)

- *Feasibility analysis:* Determining how beneficial the development of the system would be to the organization

- *Project management:* Ongoing activity by which the systems analyst plans, delegates, directs, and controls the project, so as to develop an acceptable system within the allotted time and budget

- *Process management:* Ongoing activity that establishes standards for activities, methods, tools, and products of the SDLC

The SDLC of a building versus the SDLC of an information system

SDLC Phases	Building a New Factory	Creating a New Information System
1	**Preliminary investigation** Management determines the existing building is too small; analyst (architect) does initial study to determine preliminary costs and constraints of new building.	Management determines there is a problem with the existing information system; systems analyst does initial study to determine preliminary costs and constraints.
2	**Systems analysis** Architect investigates the problems with the existing building and the requirements for the new building.	Analyst investigates the problems in the existing system and the requirements for the new system.
3	**Systems design** Architect creates detailed drawings of the proposed new building.	Analyst creates detailed diagrams, charts, models, and prototypes of components of the proposed new system.
4	**Systems development** The contractor, monitored by the architect, builds the factory. Building inspectors examine the factory for quality and safety.	The programmers, monitored by the analysts, build the system. Testers test the systems for quality.
5	**Systems implementation** Machinery and people are moved into the new factory, and production begins.	Data, people, and procedures are converted from the old system to the new; final documentation is compiled; users are trained; the new system is put into operation.
6	**Systems maintenance** The factory must be maintained and repaired by the maintenance crew until the day when it's determined to be obsolete, at which point the SDLC begins again for a new building.	The information system must be maintained, repaired, and enhanced by analysts and maintenance programmers until it is suspected to be obsolete. Then the SDLC begins again for a new system.

Who Participates? Basically, Everyone

To get a systems analysis/development project going, sometimes all it takes is a single individual who believes that something badly needs changing. An employee may influence a supervisor. A customer or supplier may get the attention of someone in higher management. Top management on its own may decide to take a look at a system that seems inefficient. A steering committee may be formed to decide which of many possible projects should be worked on.

Participants in the project are of three types:

■ *Users:* As mentioned, the system under discussion should always be developed in consultation with users, whether floor sweepers, research scientists, or customers, internal users, telecommuting users, or external users (such as those using electronic data interchange (✔ p. 7.37). Indeed, inadequate user involvement in analysis and design can be a major cause of system failure or lack of acceptance. In many cases, a system that works is never fully adopted, because users don't feel involved in its development.

■ *Management:* Managers within the organization should be consulted about the system. Managers also make the major decisions about changing or not changing the system and about purchases.

■ *Technical staff:* Members of the company's information systems department—systems analysts, software programmers, and networking staff—need to be involved. For one thing, they may well have to carry out and execute the project, or, if not, to work with outside IS people contracted to do the job.

The computer professional generally in charge of the SDLC is the head **systems analyst,** also called a *systems engineer* or a *project leader. (See Figure 9.3.)* This person, who is a member of the information systems department—or perhaps from an outside consulting firm—studies the information and communication needs of an organization and determines what changes are required to deliver better information to people who need it, when they need it. "Better" information means information that is **c**omplete, **a**ccurate, **r**elevant, and **t**imely ("CART"). The systems analyst achieves this goal through the problem-solving method of systems analysis and design—the "systems approach." Large and complex projects usually require the services of several systems analysts specializing in different areas of information systems—such as databases, software programming, client-server programming, personal computing (also called *end-user computing*), and networks/telecommunications.

Occasionally steering committees are formed to help decide how to get started—that is, which systems development projects to work on first. The steering committee, which includes individuals from each department in the organization, hears reports from experts about the advantages, disadvantages, and costs of a particular project. On that basis, the committee decides whether it is in the organization's interest to implement the project. If so, the systems development life cycle proceeds.

Figure 9.3 The SDLC typically includes six phases

JOB DESCRIPTION:

The systems analyst gathers and analyzes information about current systems and any new requirements for any new systems. He or she uses that information to plan modifications to existing systems or to design new systems. The analyst introduces the specifications through formal presentations and documentation. The analyst supervises the coding and testing of new programs, site preparation, documentation and training, conversion, and maintenance.

DUTIES:
- Apply fact-gathering techniques to study current systems and develop requirements for proposed information systems.
- Develop solutions to business system problems.
- Design procedures for data collection and processing.
- Use structured diagramming and documentation methods to illustrate and define both existing and proposed information systems.
- Estimate requirements for time and resources, and estimate benefits.
- Perform cost-benefit analysis on any proposed system solution.
- Supervise site preparation.
- Choose hardware and software.
- Use prototyping techniques to develop abbreviated systems quickly during analysis and design.
- Evaluate system designs for quality and ease of maintenance.
- Design input forms, output reports, and display formats.
- Incorporate security measures into a system design.
- Supervise coding, testing, and quality control.
- Supervise user documentation and training.
- Oversee conversion to new system.
- Supervise maintenance and change control after the system is in operation.
- Establish system development standards.
- Keep current with developments in the field of computer technology.

EXPERIENCE AND SKILLS:
- Bachelor's degree in computer science, information science, accounting, statistics, or business. Graduate degree is desirable.
- Experience as a programmer.
- Training in systems analysis and design.
- Experience or training in business systems.
- Effective verbal and written communications skills.
- Experience or training in management skills.

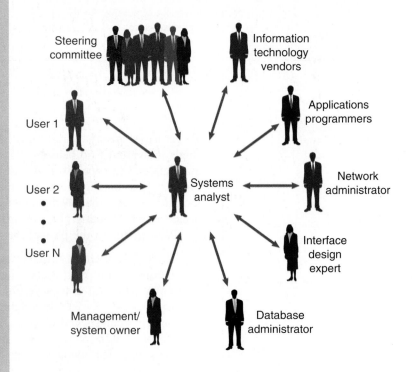

All the processes and tools used in the SDLC cannot be covered in one chapter of an introductory text. However, in the following sections, we outline the basic principles.

9.2 The First Phase: Conduct a Preliminary Investigation

KEY QUESTION **What is the objective of the first phase of the SDLC?**

The objectives of **Phase 1, preliminary investigation,** are to conduct a preliminary analysis, propose alternative solutions, describe the costs and benefits of each solution, and submit a preliminary plan with recommendations. *(See Figure 9.4.)* This phase is often called a *feasibility study.*

1. Conduct the Preliminary Analysis

In this step, you need to find out what the organization's objectives are and to explore the nature and scope of the problems under study.

■ *Determine the organization's objectives:* Even if a problem pertains to only a small segment of the organization, you cannot study it in isolation. You need to find out what the overall objectives of the organization are and how groups and departments within the organization interact. Then you need to examine the problem in that context.

To define the objectives of the organization, you can do the following:

(1) Read internal documents about the organization, such as original corporate charters, prospectuses, annual reports, procedures manuals, and e-mail.

(2) Read external documents about the organization, such as news articles, accounts in the business press, reports by securities analysts, and audits by independent accounting firms. You should also read material on the competition (as in trade magazines, investors services' newsletters, and annual reports).

Figure 9.4 Phase 1

1. Conduct preliminary analysis. This includes stating the objectives, defining nature and scope of the problem.
2. Propose alternative solutions: leave system alone, make it more efficient, or build a new system.
3. Describe costs and benefits of each solution.
4. Submit a preliminary plan with recommendations.

(3) Interview important executives within the company, as well as key users within the particular area you are concerned with. Some face-to-face interviews may be possible, but, if you're dealing with people over a wide geographical area, expect to spend a lot of time on the phone or using e-mail and/or videoconferencing.

From these sources, you can find out what the organization is supposed to be doing and, to some extent, how well it is meeting those goals. Also, you must try to understand the "corporate culture," the set of shared attitudes, values, goals, and practices that characterize the company.

Note that systems analysis does not focus only on information technology. In *business process redesign (BPR)*, principles of systems analysis are applied to the goal of dramatically changing and improving the fundamental business processes of an organization, *independent of information technology.* Interest in BPR was driven by the discovery that most current information systems and applications have merely automated existing inefficient business processes. BPR analysis focuses almost entirely on noncomputer processes. Each process is studied and analyzed for bottlenecks, value returned, and opportunities for elimination or streamlining. The last stop is to examine how information technology might best be applied to the improved business processes. In this chapter, however, we *are* focusing on computer-based information systems.

■ *Determine the nature and scope of the problems:* You may already have a sense of the nature and scope of a problem. However, with a fuller understanding of the goals of the organization, you can now take a closer look at the specifics. Is too much time being wasted on paperwork? on waiting for materials? on nonessential tasks? How pervasive is the problem within the organization? outside of it? What people are most affected? And so on. Your reading and your interviews should give you a sense of the character of the problem.

2. Propose Alternative Solutions

In delving into the organization's objectives and the specific problems, you may have already discovered some solutions. Other possible solutions may be generated by interviewing people inside the organization, clients or customers, suppliers, and consultants and by studying what competitors are doing. With this data, you then have three choices. You can leave the system as is, improve it, or develop a new system.

■ *Leave the system as is:* Often, especially with paper-based or nontechnological systems, the problem really isn't bad enough to justify the measures and expenditures required to get rid of it.

■ *Improve the system:* Sometimes changing a few key elements in the system—upgrading to a new computer or new software, or doing a bit of employee retraining, for example—will do the trick. Modifications might be introduced over several months, if the problem is not serious.

■ *Develop a new system:* If the existing system is truly harmful to the organization, radical changes may be warranted. A new system would not mean just tinkering around the edges or introducing some new piece of hardware or software. It could mean changes in every part and at every level.

3. Describe Costs and Benefits

Whichever of the three alternatives is chosen, it will have costs and benefits. In this step, you need to indicate what these are.

The changes or absence of changes will have a price tag, of course, and you need to indicate what it is. Greater costs may result in greater benefits, which, in turn, may offer savings. The benefits may be both tangible—such as cost savings—and intangible—such as worker satisfaction. A process may be speeded up, streamlined through the elimination of unnecessary steps, or combined with other processes. Input errors or redundant output may be reduced. Systems and subsystems may be better integrated. Users may be happier with the system. Customers or suppliers may interact more efficiently with the system. Security may be improved. Costs may be cut.

4. Submit a Preliminary Plan

Now you need to wrap up all your findings in a written report, submitted to the executives (probably top managers) who are in a position to decide in which direction to proceed—make no changes, change a little, or change a lot—and how much money to allow the project. You should describe the potential solutions, costs, and benefits and indicate your recommendations. If management approves the feasibility study, then the systems analysis phase can begin.

9.3 The Second Phase: Do a Detailed Analysis of the System

KEY QUESTION **What tools are used in the second phase of the SDLC to analyze data?**

The objectives of **Phase 2, systems analysis,** are to gather data, analyze the data, and write a report. *(See Figure 9.5.)* Systems analysis describes *what* a system is already doing and *what* it should do to meet the needs of users. Systems design—the next phase—specifies *how* the system will accommodate the objective.

Figure 9.5 Phase 2

1. Gather data, using written documents, interviews, questionnaires, observations, and sampling.
2. Analyze the data, using CASE tools, data flow diagrams, systems flowcharts, connectivity diagrams, grid charts, and decision tables.
3. Write a report.

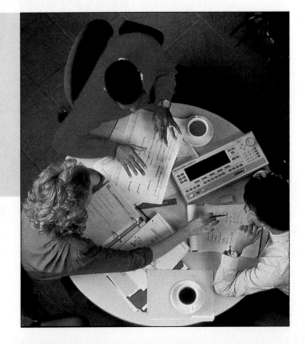

In this second phase of the SDLC, you will follow the course prescribed by management on the basis of your Phase 1 feasibility report. We are assuming that you have been directed to perform Phase 2—to do a careful analysis of the existing system, in order to understand how the new system you propose would differ. This analysis will also consider how people's positions and tasks will have to change if the new system is put into effect. In general, it involves a detailed study of: [2]

■ The information needs of the organization and all users

■ The activities, resources, and products of any present information systems

■ The information systems capabilities required to meet the established information needs and user needs

1. Gather Data

In gathering data, systems analysts use a handful of tools, most of them not terribly technical. They include written documents, interviews, questionnaires, observation, and sampling.

■ *Written documents:* A great deal of what you need is probably available in the form of written documents: reports, forms, manuals, memos, business plans, policy statements, and so on. Documents are a good place to start because they tell you how things are or are supposed to be. These tools will also provide leads on people and areas to pursue further.

   One document of particular value is the organization chart. *(See Figure 9.6.)* An organization chart shows levels of management and formal lines of authority.

■ *Interviews:* Interviews with managers, workers, clients, suppliers, and competitors will also give you insights. Interviews may be structured or unstructured.

Figure 9.6 Example of an organization chart

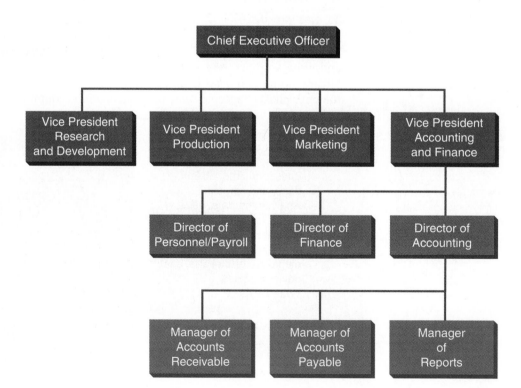

—*Structured interviews* include only questions you have planned and written out in advance. By sticking with this script, you can ask a number of people identical questions and compare their answers.

—*Unstructured interviews* also include questions prepared in advance, but you can vary from the line of questions and pursue other subjects if it seems productive.

Again, JAD sessions may be used.

■ *Questionnaires:* Questionnaires are useful for getting information from large groups of people when you can't get around to interviewing everyone. Questionnaires may also yield more information if respondents can be anonymous. In addition, this tool is convenient, is inexpensive, and yields a lot of data. However, people may not return their forms, results can be ambiguous, and with anonymous questionnaires you'll have no opportunity to follow up.

■ *Observation:* No doubt you've sat in a coffee shop or on a park bench and just done "people watching." This can be a tool for analysis, too. Through observation you can see how people interact with one another and how paper moves through an organization. Observation can be nonparticipant or participant. If you are a *nonparticipant* observer, and people know they are being watched, they may falsify their behavior in some way. If you are a *participant* observer, you may gain more insights by experiencing the conflicts and responsibilities of the people you are working with.

■ *Sampling:* If your data-gathering phase involves a large number of people or a large number of events, it may simplify things to study just a sample. That is, you can do a sampling of the work of 5 people instead of 100, or 20 instances of a particular transaction instead of 500.

2. Analyze the Data

Once the data is gathered, you need to come to grips with it and analyze it. Many analytical tools, or modeling tools, are available. Modeling tools enable a systems analyst to present graphic (pictorial) representations of a system. Examples are CASE tools, data flow diagrams, systems flowcharts, connectivity diagrams, grid charts, decision tables, and object-oriented analysis.

■ *CASE tools:* CASE (computer-aided software engineering) tools—software programs that automate many activities in the SDLC—are also used to analyze various aspects of a system. We cover these tools in more detail in the next section.

■ *Data flow diagrams:* A **data flow diagram (DFD),** also called a *process model,* graphically shows the flow of data through a system—that is, the essential processes of a system along with inputs, outputs, and files. *(See Figure 9.7, next page.)* CASE tools may be used to assist in diagramming activities.

In analyzing the current system and preparing data flow diagrams, the systems analyst must also prepare a data dictionary, which is then used and expanded during all remaining phases of the SDLC. A **data dictionary** defines all the elements that make up the data flow. Among other things, it records what each data element is by name, how long it is (how many characters), and where it is used (files in which it will be found), as well as any numerical values assigned to it. This information is usually entered into a data dictionary software program.

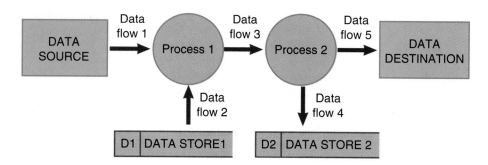

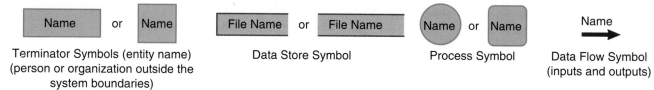

Explanation of standard data flow diagram symbols

Terminator Symbols (entity name)
(person or organization outside the
system boundaries)

Data Store Symbol

Process Symbol

Data Flow Symbol
(inputs and outputs)

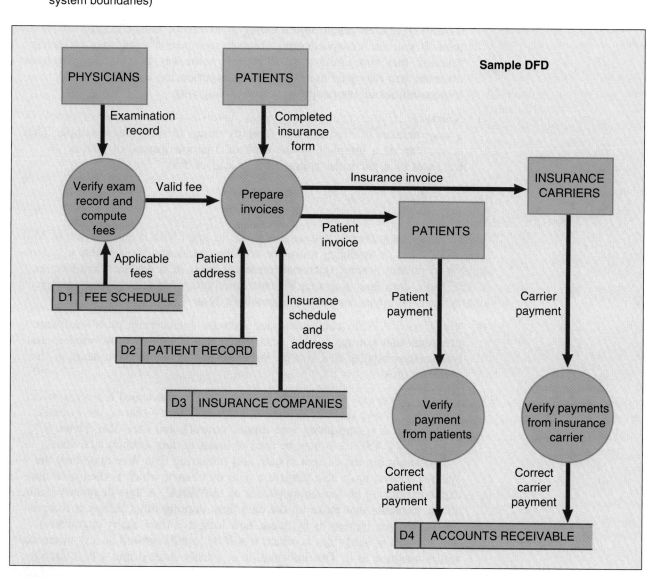

Figure 9.7 Data flow diagram

■ *Systems flowcharts:* Another tool is the **systems flowchart,** also called the *system flow diagram. (See Figure 9.8.)* A systems flowchart diagrams the major inputs, outputs, and processes of a system. In some cases a systems flowchart can be used in place of a DFD; in other cases, it is a useful supplement.[3]

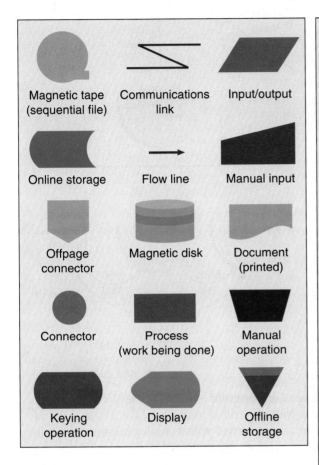

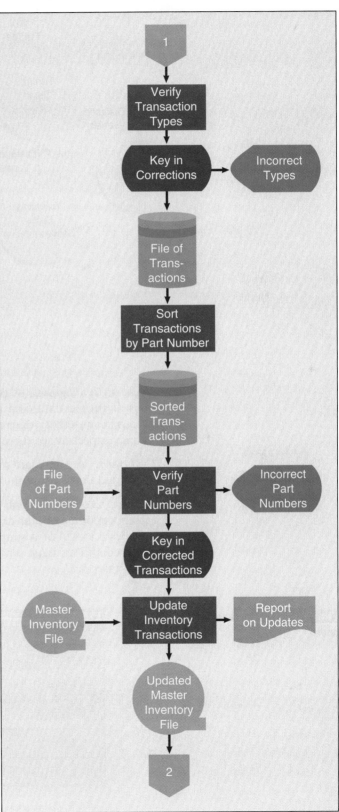

Figure 9.8 System flow diagram: symbols used and sample

Figure 9.9 Example of a connectivity diagram (speed of communications lines must also be considered)

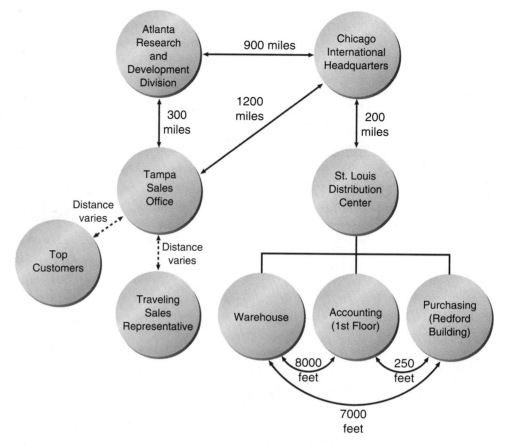

■ *Connectivity diagrams:* A **connectivity diagram** is used to map network connections of people, data, and activities at various locations. *(See Figure 9.9.)* Because connectivity diagrams are concerned with communications networks, we may expect to see these in increasing use.

■ *Grid charts:* A **grid chart** shows the relationship between data on input documents and data on output documents. *(See Figure 9.10.)*

■ *Decision tables:* A **decision table** shows the decision rules that apply when certain conditions occur and what actions to take. That is, a decision table provides a model of a simple, structured decision-making process. It shows which conditions must take place in order for particular actions to occur. *(See Figure 9.11.)*

Figure 9.10 Sample grid chart

Forms (input)	Reports (output)		
	Report A	**Report B**	**Report C**
Form 1	✓	✓	
Form 2			✓
Form 3	✓	✓	

	1	2	3	4	5	6	7	8	9	10	11	12
Invoice Amount	<100	<100	<100	<100	100-1000	100-1000	100-1000	100-1000	>1000	>1000	>1000	>1000
Invoice Age	10 or less	10 or less	>10	>10	10 or less	10 or less	>10	>10	10 or less	10 or less	>10	>10
Payment Discount	Y	N	Y	N	Y	N	Y	N	Y	N	Y	N
Authorize Payment	X	X	X	X	X		X	X				
Set Invoice Aside						X						
Put Invoice on CRR									X	X	X	X

Key

<100 = less than $100	10 or less = less than or equal to 10 days
100 – 1000 = $100 to $1000 inclusive	>10 = greater than 10 days
>1000 = greater than $1000	Y = yes
CRR = cash requirements report	N = no

Figure 9.11 Sample decision table

■ *Object-oriented analysis (OOA):* For the past 30 years, most systems development strategies have deliberately given separate consideration to data and to processes. Although most systems analysis and design methods have attempted to combine data and process models, the results have been less than fully successful. Object technologies and techniques attempt to eliminate the separation of concerns about data and process. Instead data and processes that act on the data are combined, or *encapsulated,* into things called *objects*—"building blocks" made of software routines. The only way to create, delete, change, or use the data in an object (called *properties*) is through one of its encapsulated processes (called *methods*). The systems and software development strategy is changed to focus on the "assembly" of the system from a library of reusable objects. Of course, the objects must be defined, designed, and constructed. An analyst using OOA techniques studies existing objects to see if they can be reused or adapted for new uses and defines new and modified objects that will be combined with existing objects into a useful business computing application.[4]

3. Write a Report

Once you have completed the analysis, you need to document this phase. This report to management should have three parts. First, it should explain how the existing system works. Second, it should explain the problems with the existing system. Finally, it should describe the requirements for the new system and make recommendations on what to do next.

At this point, not a lot of money will have been spent on the project. If the costs of proceeding seem prohibitive, the managers reading the report may well call a halt. Otherwise, you will be called on to move to Phase 3.

9.4 The Third Phase: Design the System

KEY QUESTION **At the conclusion of the third phase of the SDLC, what should have been created?**

The objectives of **Phase 3, systems design,** are to do a preliminary design and then a detail design and to write a report. *(See Figure 9.12.)* In this third phase of the SDLC, you will essentially create a rough draft and then a detail draft of the proposed information system.

1. Do a Preliminary Design

A preliminary design describes the general functional capabilities of a proposed information system. It reviews the system requirements and then considers major components of the system. Usually several alternative systems (called *candidates*) are considered, and the costs and the benefits of each are evaluated.

Some tools that may be used in the preliminary design and the detail design are the following:

Figure 9.12 Phase 3

1. Do a preliminary design, using CASE tools, prototyping tools, and project management software, among others.
2. Do a detail design, defining requirements for output, input, storage, and processing and system controls and backup.
3. Write a report.

Figure 9.13 Iconix offers many CASER tools. This screen is from one of their banking system tools. It shows a model for an ATM transaction. The purchaser of the CASE tool would enter details relative to the particular situation.

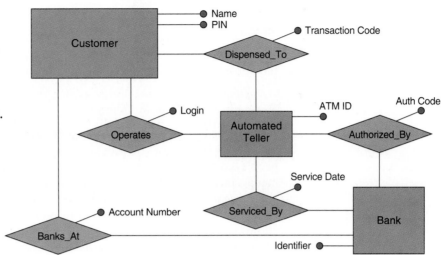

■ *CASE tools:* As we mentioned earlier, **CASE** (for **computer-aided software engineering**) **tools** are software programs that automate various activities of the SDLC in several phases. *(See Figure 9.13.)* This technology is intended to speed up the process of developing systems and to improve the quality of the resulting systems. Examples of such programs are Excelerator, Iconix, System Architect, Rational Rose, and Powerbuilder.

CASE tools may be used at almost any stage of the systems development life cycle, not just design. So-called *front-end CASE tools,* or *upper-CASE tools,* are used during the first three phases—preliminary investigation, systems analysis, systems design—to help with early analysis and design. So-called *back-end CASE tools,* or *lower-CASE tools,* are used during the later stages—systems development and implementation—to help in coding and testing, for instance. (There is some overlap between front-end and back-end CASE tools because analysts have never reached agreement on exactly when systems design ends and system development begins.)

CASE tools can be used for many functions. Among them are these:

—*Diagramming:* Drawing diagrams of system components and models, which can be linked to other components.

—*Prototyping:* **Prototyping** refers to using workstations, CASE tools, and other software applications to build working models (experimental versions) of system components—such as inputs, outputs, and various programs—so that they can be quickly tested and evaluated. Thus a **prototype** is a limited working system developed to test out design concepts. A prototype allows users to find out immediately how a change in the system might benefit them. Then the prototype can be refined and included in the final working system. For example, a systems analyst might develop a menu as a possible screen display, which users could try out. The menu can then be redesigned or fine-tuned, if necessary. Prototyping is also often used to build user interfaces (✔ p. 5.13).

—*Reporting:* Reports can be extracted from the CASE tool's database.

—*Managing quality:* CASE tools can analyze models, descriptions, and prototypes for consistency, completeness, and conformance to rules.

—*Supporting decisions:* Some CASE tools help systems analysts estimate and analyze feasibility.

—Organizing documentation: CASE tools can assemble, organize, and report information for review by system owners, users, and designers.

—Generating code: Some applications software code, or significant portions of the application, can be automatically generated.

—Testing: CASE tools help the system designers and developers test databases and application programs.

■ *Project management software:* As we described in Chapter 6, project management software consists of programs used to plan, schedule, and control the people, costs, and resources required to complete a project on time. Project management software often uses Gantt charts and PERT charts.

A *Gantt chart* uses lines and bars to indicate the duration of a series of tasks. The time scale may range from minutes to years. The Gantt chart allows you to see whether tasks are being completed on schedule. A *PERT (Program Evaluation Review Technique) chart* shows not only timing but also relationships (dependencies) among the tasks of a project, some of which must be completed before others can begin. The relationships are indicated by arrows joining numbered circles that represent events. Elapsed time is indicated alongside the arrows.

2. Do a Detail Design

A detail design describes how a proposed information system will deliver the general capabilities described in the preliminary design. The detail design usually considers the following parts of the system, in this order: output requirements, input requirements, storage requirements, processing and networking requirements, and system controls and backup.

■ *Output requirements:* The first thing to determine is what you want the system to produce. In this first step, the systems analyst determines what media the output will be—whether hardcopy and/or softcopy—and designs the appearance or format of the output, such as headings, columns, and menus.

Boeing's new 777 airplanes feature a digital phone service, allowing laptop users to send and receive faxes and log onto the Internet. Seat-back power outlets eliminate the need to change batteries after a few hours in the air.

■ *Input requirements:* Once you know the output, you can determine the inputs. Here, too, you must define the type of input, such as keyboard or source data entry (✔ p. 3.4). You must determine in what form data will be input and how it will be checked for accuracy. You also need to figure out what volume of data the system can be allowed to take in.

■ *Storage requirements:* Using the data dictionary as a guide, you need to define the files and databases in the information system. How will the files be organized? What kind of storage devices will be used? How will they interface with other storage devices inside and outside of the organization? What will be the volume of database activity?

■ *Processing and networking requirements:* What kind of computer or computers will be used to handle the processing? What kind of operating system and applications software will be used? Will the computer or computers be tied to others in a network? Exactly what operations will be performed on the input data to achieve the desired output information? What kinds of user interface are desired?

■ *System controls and backup:* Finally, you need to think about matters of security, privacy, and data accuracy. You need to prevent unauthorized users from breaking into the system, for example, and snooping in private files. You need to devise auditing procedures and to set up specifications for testing the new system (Phase 4). Finally, you need to institute automatic ways of backing up information and storing it elsewhere in case the system fails or is destroyed.

3. Write a Report

All the work of the preliminary and detail designs will end up in a large, detailed report. When you hand over this report to senior management, you will probably also make some sort of presentation or speech.

9.5 The Fourth Phase: Develop/Acquire the System

KEY QUESTION What general tasks do systems analysts perform in the fourth phase of the SDLC?

In **Phase 4, systems development/acquisition,** the systems analysts or others in the organization acquire the software, acquire the hardware, and then test the system. *(See Figure 9.14, next page.)* This phase begins once management has accepted the report containing the design and has "greenlighted" the way to development. Depending on the size of the project, this phase will probably involve substantial expenditures of money and time. However, at the end you should have a workable system.

1. Acquire Software

During the design stage, the systems analyst may have had to address what is called the "make-or-buy" decision; if not, that decision certainly cannot be

Figure 9.14 Phase 4

1. Acquire software.
2. Acquire hardware.
3. Test the system.

avoided now. In the make-or-buy decision, you decide whether you have to create a program—have it custom-written—or buy it. Sometimes programmers decide they can buy an existing software package and modify it rather than write it from scratch.

If you decide to create a new program, then the question is whether to use the organization's own staff programmers or to hire outside contract programmers (*outsource* it). Whichever way you go, the task could take months. (Programming is an entire subject unto itself, and we address it in Chapter 10.)

2. Acquire Hardware

Once the software has been chosen, the hardware to run it must be acquired or upgraded. It's possible you will not need to obtain any new hardware. It's also possible that the new hardware will cost millions of dollars and involve many items: microcomputers, minicomputers, mainframes, monitors, modems, and many other devices. The organization may prefer to lease rather than buy some equipment, especially since chip capability has traditionally doubled about every 18 months.

3. Test the System

With the software and hardware acquired, you can now start testing the system in two stages: first *unit testing* and then *system testing*. (If CASE tools have been used throughout the SDLC, testing is minimized because any automatically generated program code is more likely to be error free.)

■ *Unit testing:* In **unit testing,** test (made-up, or sample) is run through the individual parts of the program. If the program is written as a collaborative effort by multiple programmers, each part of the program is tested separately.

■ *System testing:* In **system testing,** the parts are linked together, and test data is used to see if the parts work together. At this point, actual organization data may also be used to test the system. The system is also tested with erroneous data and with massive amounts of data to see if it can be made to fail ("crash").

At the end of this long process, the organization will have a workable information system, one ready for the implementation phase. (Figure 9.15 summarizes the tools used in phases 2–4.)

Figure 9.15 Summary of Phases 2–4

Phase 2	Phase 3	Phase 4
CASE tools	CASE tools and	CASE tools
Data flow diagrams	prototyping	Programming
Systems flowcharts	Project management	languages
Connectivity diagrams	software	
Grid charts		
Decision tables		
Object-oriented analysis		

9.6 The Fifth Phase: Implement the System

KEY QUESTION **What tasks are typically performed in the fifth phase of the SDLC?**

Whether the new information system involves a few handheld computers, an elaborate telecommunications network, or expensive mainframes, **Phase 5, systems implementation,** will involve some close coordination to make the system not just workable but successful. (*See Figure 9.16.*)

1. Convert to the New System

Conversion from the old information system to the new one involves converting hardware, software, and files.

■ *Hardware conversion* may be as simple as taking away an old PC and plunking a new one down in its place. Or it may involve acquiring new buildings and putting in elaborate wiring, climate-control, and security systems.

Figure 9.16 Phase 5

1. Convert hardware, software, and files through one of four types of conversions: direct, parallel, phased, or pilot.
2. Compile final documentation.
3. Train the users.

■ *Software conversion* means making sure the applications that worked on the old equipment also work on the new.

■ *File,* or *data, conversion* means converting the old files to new ones without loss of accuracy. For example, can the paper contents from the manila folders in the personnel department be input to the system with a scanner? Or do they have to be keyed in manually, with the consequent risk of errors being introduced?

There are four strategies for handling conversion: direct, parallel, phased, and pilot. *(See Figure 9.17.)*

■ *Direct approach:* **Direct implementation** (also called *plunge implementation*) means the user simply stops using the old system and starts using the new one. The risk of this method should be evident: What if the new system doesn't work? If the old system has truly been discontinued, there is nothing to fall back on.

Figure 9.17 Four implementation strategies

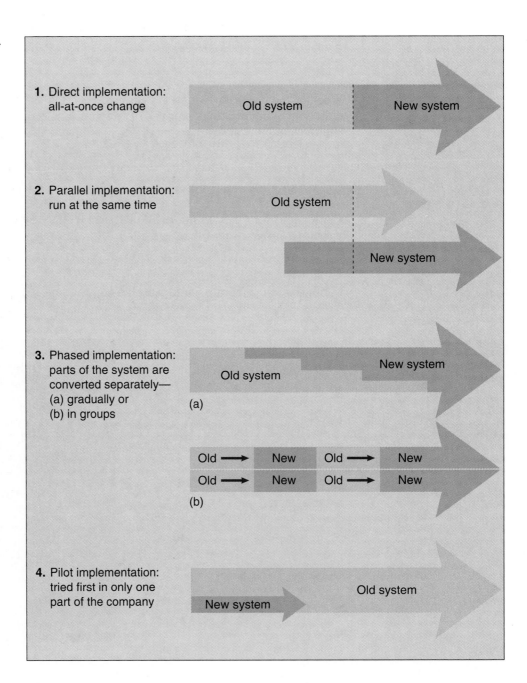

- *Parallel approach:* In **parallel implementation,** the old and new systems are operated side by side until the new system has shown it is reliable, at which time the old system is discontinued. Obviously there are benefits in taking this cautious approach. If the new system fails, the organization can switch back to the old one. The downside of this method is the expense of keeping two systems going at the same time.

- *Phased approach:* **Phased implementation** means that parts of the new system are phased in separately—either at different times (parallel) or all at once in groups (direct).

- *Pilot approach:* **Pilot implementation** means that the entire system is tried out but only by some users. Once the reliability has been proved, the system is implemented with the rest of the intended users. The pilot approach still has its risks, since all of the users in a particular group are taken off the old system. However, the risks are confined to only a small part of the organization.

    In general, the phased and pilot approaches are the most favored. Phased is best for large organizations in which people are performing different jobs. Pilot is best for organizations in which everyone performs the same task (such as order taking at a direct-mail house).

2. Compile Final Documentation

Developing good documentation is an important aspect of all phases of the SDLC. Examples include manuals of operating procedures and sample data-entry display screens, forms, and reports. Of course, if CASE tools have been used, much of the documentation will have been automatically generated and updated during the SDLC. *(See Figure 9.18.)*

3. Train the Users

Back in Chapter 1, we pointed out that people are important elements in a computer-based information system. Nevertheless, some organizations have neglected the role of users when implementing a new computer system. An information system, however, is no better than its users. Hence, training is *essential.*

Figure 9.18 What documentation includes

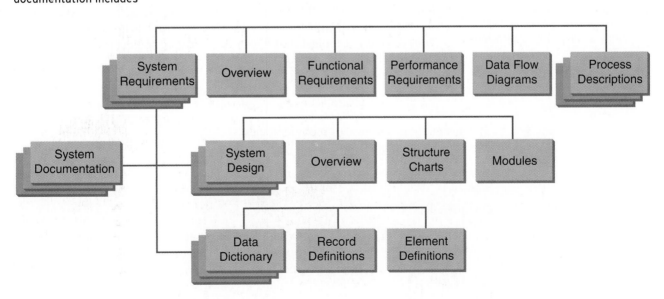

Training tools range from documentation (instruction manuals) to videotapes to live classes to one-on-one, side-by-side teacher-student training. Sometimes training is conducted by the organization's own staff; at other times it is contracted out. Some companies build interactive multimedia presentations and electronic performance support systems (EPSS) to train and support users.

9.7 The Sixth Phase: Maintain the System

KEY QUESTION **What two tools are often used in the maintenance phase of the SDLC?**

Phase 6, systems maintenance, adjusts and improves the system by having system audits and periodic evaluations and by making changes based on new conditions.

Even with the conversion accomplished and the users trained, the system won't just run itself. There is a sixth—and never-ending—phase in which the information system must be monitored to ensure that it is effective. Maintenance includes not only keeping the machinery running but also updating and upgrading the system to keep pace with new products, services, customers, government regulations, and other requirements.

Two maintenance tools are auditing and evaluation.

The sixth phase is to keep the system running through system audits and periodic evaluations.

- *Auditing:* Auditing means an independent review of an organization's information system to see if all records and systems are as they should be. Often a systems analyst will design an *audit trail*, which helps independent auditors trace the record of a transaction from its output back through all processing and storage to its source.

- *Evaluation:* Auditing, which is usually done by an accountant, is one form of evaluation. Other evaluations may be done by the head systems analyst, by outside systems analysts, or by a user or client who is able to measure the workings of the system against some preset criteria.

Once the system is old enough to present new problems, the SDLC is started all over again to design and develop a replacement. In large corporations, a typical SDLC can be measured in years, not months or weeks.

Web Sites of Possible Interest

Systems analysis and design methodologies:
http://www.ac.com/index.html

Working in an IS department:
http://www.computerworld.com

CASE tools:
http://www.casewise.com

The Movies

"In computers, we know there are going to continue to be bazillions of jobs," says Jan Millsapps, chair of the cinema department at San Francisco State University, where cinema arts programs lead to degrees in multimedia and animation. "But artists are expanding the possibilities. . . . More and more the art of these students will be the movie stars of the future."[a]

Star Wars: Episode I—The Phantom Menace, Titanic, Con Air, Apollo 13, Twister, Independence Day, and similar movies melding live action and animation have made computer artists stars themselves. The $115 million *Star Wars: Episode I*, for instance, has 1965 digital shots out of about 2200, and even when film was used it was scanned into computers to be tweaked with animated effects, lighting, and the like. Entire beings were created on computers by artists working on designs developed by producer George Lucas and his chief artist, Doug Chiang.[b]

Why are computer artists in demand? Because the price of hiring star actors costs so much—some make $20 million a film—animation, though not cheap, looks more and more like a bargain. Moreover, the special effects are readily understood by audiences in foreign countries, which major studios increasingly count on to make a film profitable. The soaring demand for computer-generated imagery—not only for movies but also for TV ads and video games—has produced an expansion in digital-animation training programs by colleges and trade schools ranging from the University of Washington, to San Francisco State University, to Ex'pression Center for New Media in Emeryville, California.[c,d]

But animation is not the only area in which computers are revolutionizing movies. Digital editing has radically transformed the way films are assembled. Says one report, "Traditional film editing was always a funky, hands-on proposition: reeling and unreeling spools of film, cutting and gluing pieces of celluloid together, working amid a sea of film that sometimes got trampled underfoot." Today, by contrast, "150 miles of film can be stored on hard drives and an editor with the press of a key or the click of a mouse can instantly access any visual or audio moment in the film."[e] Thus, hundreds of variations of a scene can be stored and called up for review and comparison. A crowd of extras can be multiplied into an army of thousands. In *Star Wars: Episode I*, for example, a shot of 100,000 characters (many of them aliens) cheering in a stadium did not entail a crowd that big but was mostly digitally created. Moreover, editors can create their own dissolves and fades, instead of having to ship the film out to an optical shop to accomplish these tasks.

Computer techniques have been used to extend the lives of damaged classic films, as in the digital remastering of the 1969 Peter Fonda movie *Easy Rider*.[f] They have even been used to develop digitally created actors—called "synthespians"—such as the late John Wayne in a Coors beer ad.[g] However, real present-day actors are also realizing some benefits from the computer, as when they receive last-minute casting calls through such electronic "cybercasting" services as Castnet and The Link.[h] Screenwriters looking to sell their scripts can also post their work without charge on Web sites that may catch the eye of a producer.[i]

Even nonprofessionals can get into movie-making as new computer-related products come to market. Digital video capture and editing systems are now available for under $1000, enabling amateurs to turn home videotapes into digital data and edit them. Digital camcorders, which offer outstanding picture and sound quality, are dropping in price.[j,k]

WHAT IT IS
WHAT IT DOES WHY IT IS IMPORTANT

✱ (CASE) computer-aided software engineering tools (KQ 9.4, p. 9.19)   Software for computer-automated system design and modification.

CASE tools may be used in almost any phase of the SDLC, not just design. So-called *front-end CASE tools* are used during the first three phases—preliminary analysis, systems analysis, systems design—to help with the early analysis and design. So-called *back-end CASE tools* are used during two later phases—systems development and implementation—to help in coding and testing, for instance.

connectivity diagram (KQ 9.3, p. 9.16) Modeling tool used to map network connections of people, data, and activities of various locations.

Because connectivity diagrams are concerned with communications networks, their use is increasing.

data dictionary (KQ 9.3, p. 9.13) Record of all the elements of data that make up the data flow in a system.

In analyzing a current system and preparing data flow diagrams, systems analysts must prepare a data dictionary, which is used and expanded during subsequent phases of the SDLC.

✱ data flow diagram (DFD) (KQ 9.3, p. 9.13)   Also called a *process model;* modeling tool that graphically shows the flow of data through a system.

A DFD diagrams the processes that change data into information.

decision table (KQ 9.3, p. 9.16)   Modeling tool showing the decision rules that apply when certain conditions occur and what actions to take.

A decision table provides a model of a simple, structured decision-making process. It shows which conditions must take place in order for particular actions to occur.

direct implementation (KQ 9.6, p. 9.24)   Also called *plunge implementation;* method of system conversion in which the users simply stop using the old system and start using the new one.

The risk of this method is that there is nothing to fall back on if the new system proves unsatisfactory.

grid chart (KQ 9.3, p. 9.16)   Modeling tool that shows the relationship between data on input documents and data on output documents.

Grid charts are used in the systems design phase of the SDLC.

parallel implementation (KQ 9.6, p. 9.25)   Method of system conversion whereby the old and new systems are operated side by side until the new system has shown it is reliable.

If the new system fails, the organization can switch back to the old one. The downside is the expense of operating two systems simultaneously.

phased implementation (KQ 9.6, p. 9.25) Method of system conversion whereby parts of the new system are phased in gradually, perhaps over several months, or all at once, in groups.

This conversion strategy is prudent, though it can be expensive.

pilot implementation (KQ 9.6, p. 9.25) Method of system conversion whereby the entire system is tried out by only some users. Once the reliability has been proved, the system is implemented with the rest of the intended users.

The pilot approach has risks, since all the users of a particular group are taken off the old system. However, the risks are confined to a small part of the organization.

preliminary investigation (KQ 9.2, p. 9.9) Phase 1 of the SDLC; the purpose is to conduct a preliminary analysis (determine the organization's objectives, determine the nature and scope of the problem), propose alternative solutions (leave the system as is, improve the efficiency of the system, or develop a new system), describe costs and benefits, and submit a preliminary plan with recommendations.

The preliminary investigation lays the groundwork for the other phases of the SDLC.

prototype (KQ 9.4, p. 9.19) Limited working system developed to test out design concepts.

A prototype allows users to find out immediately how a change in the system might benefit them. Then the prototype can be refined and included in the final working system.

prototyping (KQ 9.4, p. 9.19) Building a model or experimental version of all or part of a system so that it can be quickly tested and evaluated.

Prototyping is part of the preliminary design stage of Phase 3 of the SDLC.

systems analysis (KQ 9.3, p. 9.11) Phase 2 of the SDLC; the purpose is to gather data (using written documents, interviews, questionnaires, observation, and sampling), analyze the data, and write a report.

The results of systems analysis will determine whether the system should be redesigned.

systems analyst (KQ 9.1, p. 9.8) Information specialist who performs systems analysis, design, and implementation.

Using the problem-solving method of systems analysis and design, the systems analyst studies the information and communications needs of an organization to determine how to deliver information that is more accurate, timely, and useful.

systems design (KQ 9.4, p. 9.18) Phase 3 of the SDLC; the purpose is to do a preliminary design and then a detail design and to write a report.

Systems design is one of the most crucial phases of the SDLC.

systems development/acquisition (KQ 9.5, p. 9.21) Phase 4 of the SDLC; hardware and software for the new system are acquired and tested. The fourth phase begins once management has approved development.

In this phase, the organization may be required to invest substantial time and money.

systems development life cycle (SDLC) (KQ 9.1, p. 9.3)   Six-phase process that many organizations follow during systems analysis and design: (1) *preliminary investigation;* (2) *systems analysis;* (3) *systems design;* (4) *systems development;* (5) *systems implementation;* (6) *systems maintenance.* Phases often overlap, and a new one may start before the old one is finished. After the first four phases, management must decide whether to proceed to the next phase. User input and review is a critical part of each phase.

The SDLC is a comprehensive tool for solving organizational problems, particularly those relating to the flow of computer-based information.

systems flowchart (KQ 9.3, p. 9.15)   Also called *system flow diagram;* modeling tool that uses many symbols to diagram the input, processing, and output of data in a system as well the interaction of all the parts in a system.

A systems flowchart graphically depicts the major inputs, outputs, and processes of a system.

systems implementation (KQ 9.6, p. 9.23)   Phase 5 of the SDLC; the purpose is to convert the hardware, software, and files to the new system and to train the users; compilation of final documentation is also done.

This phase involves putting design ideas into operation.

systems maintenance (KQ 9.7, p. 9.26)   Phase 6 of the SDLC; the purpose is to adjust and improve the system through system audits and periodic evaluations.

Systems won't run themselves; they must be maintained.

system testing (KQ 9.5, p. 9.22)   Part of Phase 4 of the SDLC; the parts of a new program are linked together, and test (sample) data is used to see if the parts work together.

In addition to sample test data, actual data used within the organization may be used in system testing. Also, erroneous data and massive amounts of data may be used to see if the system can be made to fail.

unit testing (KQ 9.5, p. 9.22)   Part of Phase 4 of the SDLC; individual parts of a new program are tested, using test (sample) data.

If the program is written as a collaborative effort by multiple programmers, each part of the program is tested separately. See *system testing.*

1. Fill in the following blanks:

   a. A _____ is a collection of related components that interact to perform a task in order to accomplish a goal.

   b. In the case of _____ _____ the old system is halted on a given date and the new system is activated.

   c. The modeling tool used by the systems analyst to focus on the flow of data through a system is called a(n) _____ _____ _____ .

   d. The situation in which the old system and the new system are running at the same time for a specified period is called _____ implementation.

   e. The process of building a small, simple model of a new information system is called _____ .

2. Label each of the following statements as either true or false.

   a. _____ Users are rarely involved in systems development.

   b. _____ During the system testing phase of the SDLC, the system is often fed erroneous data.

   c. _____ Software and hardware are acquired in the systems development phase of the SDLC.

   d. _____ Gantt charts are used to automate various activities in the SDLC.

   e. _____ Data dictionaries are used to define the elements of data that make up a data flow diagram.

3. What are each of the following tools used for?
   a. grid chart
   b. system flowchart
   c. decision table
   d. connectivity diagram

4. Differentiate each of the following:
   a. direct implementation
   b. parallel implementation
   c. phased implementation
   d. pilot implementation

5. Define each of the following terms:
   a. system
   b. systems development life cycle
   c. systems analyst

6. List four reasons why a system might fail:

   a. _____

   b. _____

   c. _____

   d. _____

7. Provide four examples of cross-life-cycle activities:

a. _____

b. _____

c. _____

d. _____

8. Describe the roles that each of the following play in the SDLC:
a. users
b. management
c. technical staff

9. What four steps constitute the first phase of the SDLC?

a. _____

b. _____

c. _____

d. _____

10. List four methods for gathering data in the second phase of the SDLC.

a. _____

b. _____

c. _____

d. _____

IN YOUR OWN WORDS

1. Answer each of the Key Questions that appear at the beginning of this chapter.

2. List the six phases of the SDLC.

3. What is the purpose of the systems development phase of the SDLC?

4. What is the difference between a structured and unstructured interview?

5. What are CASE tools used for?

6. What is a steering committee?

7. What is a prototype?

8. What is the purpose of the sixth phase of the SDLC?

9. In what phase of the SDLC are connectivity diagrams, grid charts, and decision tables used?

KNOWLEDGE IN ACTION

 1. **Exploring Object-Oriented Development Tools.** Rational Software is a company that specializes in selling object-oriented development tools. Visit this company's Web site (*www.rational.com*) to learn more about the company's product offerings. Specifically, describe each of the following products in a two-page report: Rational Suite, Rational Rose, and Rational TestMate. For each product, include a product overview and a list of features and benefits.

2. **Exploring CASE Tools.** Using an Internet search engine, identify a company that develops CASE tools. In a few paragraphs, describe what this company's CASE tools are used for.

3. **Exploring Project Failure.** Have you participated in a project that failed? Why did it fail? Based on what you know now, what might you have done to help the project succeed?

4. **Creating a Data Flow Diagram.** Design a system that would handle the input, processing, and output of a simple form of your choice. Use a data flow diagram to illustrate the system.

Answers to Self-Test Exercises: 1a. system 1b. direct implementation 1c. data flow diagram 1d. parallel 1e. prototyping 2. F, T, T, F, T 3a. A grid chart is a mod-eling tool that shows the relationship between data on input documents and data on output documents. 3b. Also called *system flow diagram,* a system flowchart is a modeling tool that uses many symbols to diagram the input, processing, and output of data in a system as well the interaction of all the parts in a system. 3c. A deci-sion table is a modeling tool showing the decision rules that apply when certain conditions occur and what actions to take. 3d. A connectivity diagram is a model-ing tool used to map network connections of people, data, and activities of various locations. 4a. Also called *plunge implementation,* direct implementation is a method of system conversion in which the users simply stop using the old system and start using the new one. 4b. Method of system conversion whereby the old and new systems are operated side by side until the new system has shown it is reliable. 4c. Method of system conversion whereby parts of the new system are phased in gradually, perhaps over several months, or all at once, in groups. 4d. Method of system conversion whereby the entire system is tried out by only some users. Once the reliability has been proved, the system is implemented with the rest of the intended users. 5a. A *system* is defined as a collec-tion of related components that interact to perform a task in order to accomplish a goal. 5b. Six-phase process that many organizations follow during systems analysis and design: (1) *preliminary investigation;* (2) *systems analysis;* (3) *systems design;* (4) *systems development;* (5) *systems implementation;* (6) *systems maintenance.* Phases often overlap, and a new one may start before the old one is finished. After the first four phases, management must decide whether to proceed to the next phase. User input and review is a critical part of each phase. 5c. Information specialist who performs systems analysis, design, and implementation. 6. Responses may include any four of the following: lack of communication, contin-uation of a project that should have been canceled, fail-ure of two or more portions of the system to work together properly, politics, lack of management support, technological incompetence, major changes in available technology, and lack of user training. 7. Responses may include any four of the following: fact-finding, documen-tation, presentation, estimation, measurement, feasibility, and project management. 8. *Answers may vary.* 9. Conduct the preliminary study, propose alternative solu-tions, describe costs and benefits, submit a preliminary plan. 10. Responses may include any four of the follow-ing: written data, interviews, questionnaires, observation, and sampling.

SOFTWARE PROGRAMMING AND LANGUAGES

Where Your Software Comes From

10

KEY QUESTIONS

You should be able to answer the following questions:

10.1 Programming: A Five-Step Procedure *What are the five steps of the program-development cycle?*

10.2 Five Generations of Programming Languages *How do low-level programming languages compare to high-level programming languages?*

10.3 High-Level Programming *What are the characteristics of the common high-level programming languages?*

10.4 Object-Oriented and Visual Programming *How do object-oriented and visual programming compare?*

10.5 Internet Programming: HTML, XML, VRML, Java, & ActiveX *What are the main characteristics of HTML, XML, VRML, Java, and ActiveX?*

By the time we are adults, our minds have become set in various patterns of thinking that affect how we respond to new situations and new ideas. These mind-sets, which are the result of our personal experiences and the social environments in which we have grown up, determine what ideas we think are important and, conversely, what ideas we ignore.

If we are to function effectively in a complex society, we must learn to liberate ourselves from confining mind-sets and to think critically. Critical thinking involves sorting out conflicting claims, weighing the evidence for them, letting go of personal biases, and arriving at reasonable views. It means actively seeking to understand, analyze, and evaluate information in order to solve specific problems. "Before making important choices," says one writer, clear thinkers "try to clear emotion, bias, trivia and preconceived notions out of the way so they can concentrate on the information essential to making the right decision."[1] All it takes is practice. Critical thinking is essential to the problem-solving process of the systems development life cycle (SDLC) (✔ p. 9.3) in general and of programming in particular.

10.1 Programming: A Five-Step Procedure

KEY QUESTION What are the five steps of the program-development cycle?

People often think of programming as simply typing words and numbers into a computer. This is part of it, but only a small part. Basically, programming is a method of problem solving that employs algorithms. An **algorithm** is a set of ordered steps used to solve a problem. (*Algorithm* essentially means the same thing as *logic*.)

What a Program Is

To see how programming works, consider what a program is. A **program** (also called *software*) is a list of instructions that the computer must follow to process data into information. The instructions consist of statements written in a programming language, such as Visual BASIC. **Programming,** also called *software engineering,* is a multistep process for creating that list of instructions. Only one of those steps (the step called *coding*) consists of sitting at the keyboard and typing in code.

Traditionally, the steps of the program development cycle are as follows. *(See Figure 10.1.)* Newer approaches to creating programs—discussed later in the chapter—may adapt these steps to their particular needs.

1. Clarify the programming needs
2. Design the program

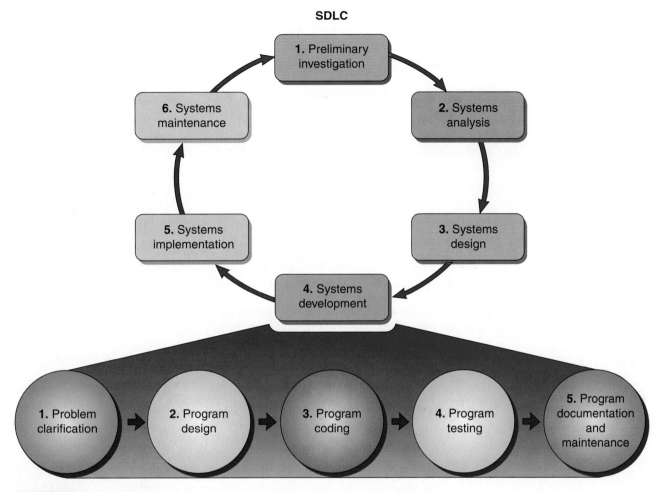

SDLC

Figure 10.1 Programming is traditionally a five-step problem-solving process. It constitutes phase 4.1 of the systems development life cycle (SDLC).

> 3. Code the program
>
> 4. Test the program
>
> 5. Document and maintain the program

Please note that these steps often overlap or are performed concurrently. For example, documentation needs to be collected throughout the entire development cycle. Also, recall that program development constitutes Phase 4.1 of the systems development life cycle (✔ p. 9.21).

The First Step: Clarify the Programming Needs

This step requires performing six mini-steps. They include clarifying objectives, output, input, and processing tasks, and then studying their feasibility and finally documenting them. Let us consider these six mini-steps.

1. Clarify Objectives and Users

You solve problems all the time. A problem might be deciding whether to take a required science course this term or next. Or you might try to solve the problem of grouping your classes so that you can also fit a job into your schedule. In such cases you are specifying your objectives. Programming works the same way. You need to write a statement of the objectives you are trying to accomplish—the problem you are trying to solve. If the problem is that your company's systems analysts have designed a new computer-based payroll processing system and brought it to you as the programmer, you need to clarify the programming needs.

You also need to identify who the users of the program will be. Will they be people inside the company, outside, or both? What kind of skills will they bring?

2. Clarify Desired Outputs

Make sure you understand the outputs—what the system designers want to get out of the system—before you study the inputs. For example, what kind of hard-copy is wanted? What information should the outputs include? This step may require several meetings with systems designers and users to make sure you're creating what they want.

3. Clarify Desired Inputs

Once you know the kind of outputs required, you can think about input. What kind of input data is needed? What form should it appear in? What is its source?

4. Clarify the Desired Processing

Here you make sure you understand the processing tasks that must occur in order for input data to be processed into output data.

5. Double-Check the Feasibility of Implementing the Program

Is the program you're supposed to create consistent with the present budget? Will it require hiring a lot more staff? Will it take too long to accomplish?

Sometimes programmers decide they can buy an existing program and modify it rather than write it from scratch.

6. Document the Analysis

Throughout program clarification, programmers must document everything they do. This includes writing objective specifications of the entire process being described.

The Second Step: Design the Program

Assuming the decision is to make, or custom-write, the program, you can then move on to the design phase. It used to be that programmers took a seat-of-the-pants approach; programming was considered an art, not a science. Today, however, most programmers use a design approach called *structured programming*. **Structured programming** takes a top-down approach that breaks programs into modular forms. It also uses standard logic tools called *control structures*. The point of structured programming is to make programs more efficient and better organized (more readable), and to have better notations so that they have clear and correct descriptions.

In structured programming, the software is designed in three mini-steps. First, the program logic is determined through a top-down approach, on the basis of program modules and a hierarchy chart. Then it is designed in detailed form, either in narrative form, using pseudocode, or graphically, using flowcharts. Finally, the design is tested with a structured walkthrough. Let's consider the three mini-steps of program design in more detail.

1. Determine the Program Logic, Using a Top-Down Approach

Laying out the program logically is like outlining a lengthy term paper before you write it. **Top-down program design** proceeds by identifying the function of the program and then breaking it down, in hierarchical fashion, to specify the processing steps, or *modules*, required to perform that function, down to the lowest level of detail. After the program is designed, the actual coding of the modules proceeds.

Modularization simplifies program design by allowing the individual program modules to be developed and tested separately.

A module (sometimes called a *subprogram* or *subroutine*) is a self-contained processing step, consisting of logically related program statements. An example of a module might be a programming instruction that simply says, "Open a file, find a record, and show it on the display screen." It is best if each module has only a single function, just as an English paragraph should have a single, complete thought. This rule limits the module's size and complexity.

Top-down program design can be represented graphically in a *hierarchy chart*. A hierarchy chart, or structure chart, illustrates the overall purpose of the program and identifies all the modules needed to achieve that purpose and the relationships among them. *(See Figure 10.2.)* The program must move upward through the chart in sequence, from one module to the next, until all have been processed. There must be three principal modules corresponding to the three

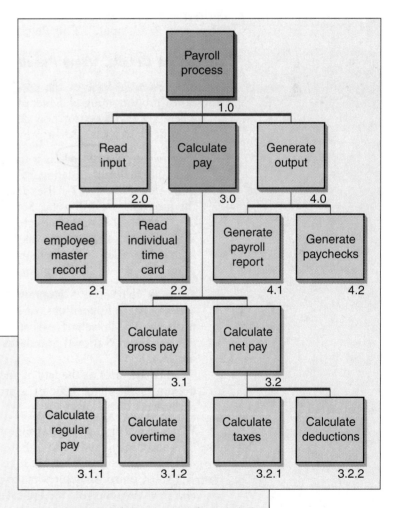

Figure 10.2 A hierarchy chart. This represents a top-down design for a payroll program. Here the modules, or processing steps, are represented from the highest level of the program down to details. The three principal computing operations—input, processing, and output—are represented by the modules in the second layer: "Read input," "Calculate pay," and "Generate output." Before tasks at the top of the chart can be performed, all the ones below must be performed. Each module represents a logical processing step.

Rules of Module Design

1. Each module must be of manageable size—fewer than 50 program instructions.

2. Each module should be independent and have a single function.

3. The functions of input and output are clearly defined in separate modules.

4. Each module has a single entry point (execution of the program module always starts at the same place) and a single exit point (control always leaves the module at the same place).

5. If one module refers to or transfers control to another module, the latter module returns control to the point from which it was "called" by the first module.

Figure 10.3 Pseudocode

If a list of payroll tasks looks like this:

Read name, hourly rate, hours worked
Calculate gross pay and net pay
Write name, gross pay and net pay
Write name, gross pay, net pay

The pseudocode would look like this:

READ name, hourly rate, hours worked
Gross pay = hourly rate times hours worked
Net pay = Gross pay minus 15
WRITE name, Gross pay, Net pay

principal computing operations—input, processing, and output. (In Figure 10.2 they are "Read input," "Calculate pay," and "Generate output.")

2. Design Details, Using Pseudocode, Flowcharts, and Control Structures

Once the essential logic of the program has been determined, through the use of top-down programming and hierarchy charts, you can go to work on the details.

There are two ways to show details—write them (using pseudocode) and draw them (using flowcharts). Most projects employ both methods.

■ *Pseudocode:* **Pseudocode** is a tool for designing a program in narrative form using normal human-language statements to describe the logic and processing flow. *(See Figure 10.3.)* Pseudocode is like an outline or summary form of the program you will write. Sometimes pseudocode is used simply to express the purpose of a particular programming module in somewhat general terms. With the use of such terms as IF, THEN, or ELSE, however, the pseudocode follows the rules of control structures, an important aspect of structured programming, as we shall explain.

■ *Program flowcharts:* A **program flowchart** graphically presents the detailed series of steps (algorithms, or logical flow) needed to solve a programming problem. The flowchart uses standard symbols—called ANSI symbols, after the American National Standards Institute, which developed them. *(See Figure 10.4.)*

The symbols at the left of the drawing might seem clear enough. But how do you establish the logic of a program? How can you reason it out so it will really work? The answer is to use control structures as explained next.

When you're trying to determine the logic behind something, you use words like "if" and "then" and "else." (For example, you might reason something like this: "If she comes over, then we'll go out to a movie, or else I'll just stay in and watch TV.") Control structures make use of the same words. A **control structure,** or *logic structure,* controls the logical sequence in which computer program instructions are executed. In structured program design, four basic control structures are used to form the logic of a program: sequence, selection, case, and iteration (or loop). *(See Figure 10.5, p. 8.)* (Additional variations of these four basic structures are also used.) These tools allow you to write structured programs and take a lot of the guesswork out of programming.

	Symbol	Name	Use

ANSI standard symbols for program flowcharts

Terminal — Indicates the beginning and end of a program.

Process — A calculation or assigning of a value to a variable.

Input/Output (I/O) — Any statement that causes data to be input to a program (INPUT, READ) or output from the program, such as printing on the display screen or printer.

Figure 10.4 Examples of a program flowchart and explanation of flowchart symbols

Decision — Program decisions. Allows alternate courses of action based on a condition. A decision indicates a question that can be answered *yes* or *no* (or *true* or *false*).

Predefined Process — A group of statements that together accomplish one task. Used extensively when programs are broken into modules.

Connector — Can be used to eliminate lengthy flowlines. Its use indicates that one symbol is connected to another. Also used as the termination of IF-THEN-ELSE logic. *(See Figure 10.5.)*

Three sample flowcharts. Can you determine what each will do?

Flowlines and Arrowheads — Used to connect symbols and indicate the sequence of operations. The flow is assumed to go from top to bottom and from left to right. Arrowheads are only required when the flow violates the standard direction.

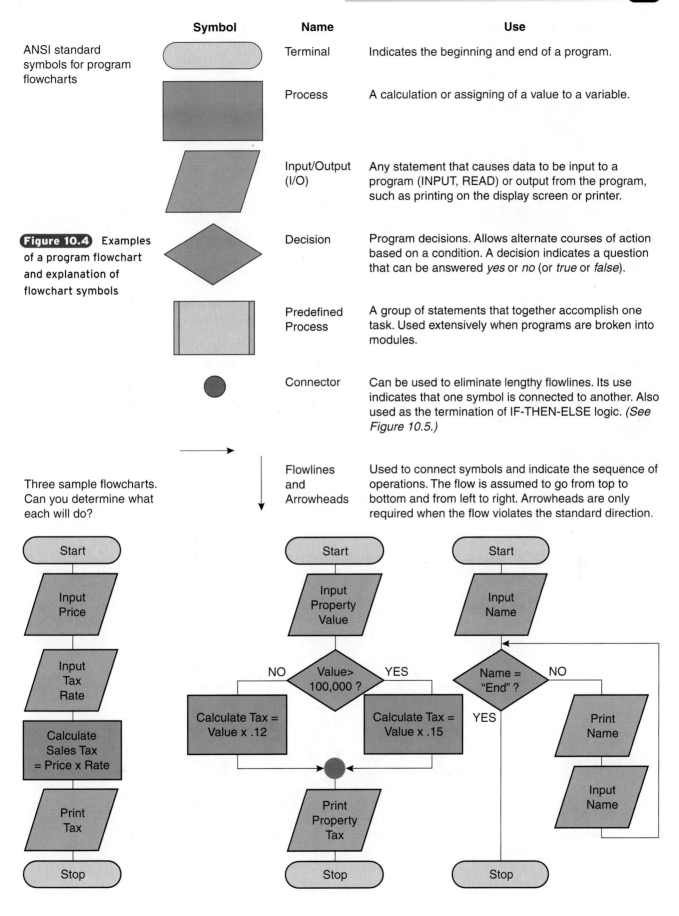

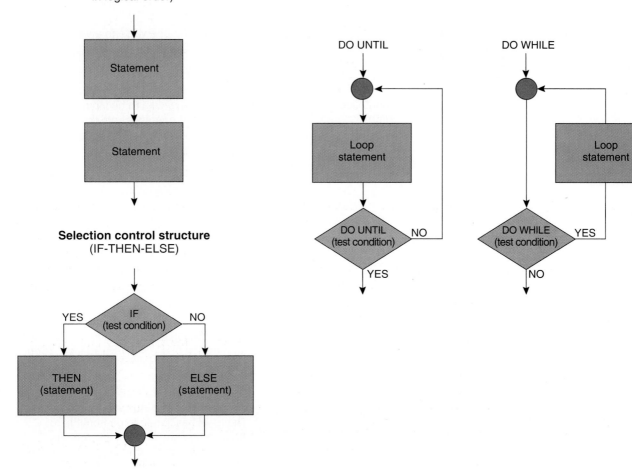

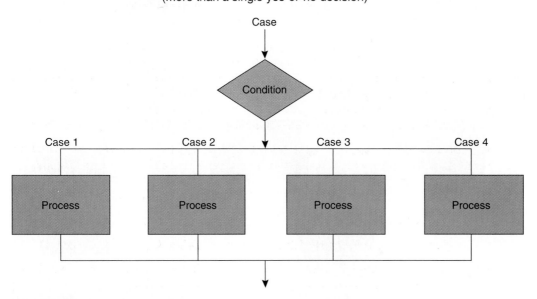

Figure 10.5 The four control structures used in structured program design to form the logic of a program: sequence, selection, case, and iteration (loop)

Children come from around the world to seek medical treatment at St. Jude's Children's Hospital. The hospital's learning center helps the children keep up with their classmates back home, and teachers work on-site using computers featuring the latest in educational software.

Any control structure must have only one entry and one exit; that is, the control structure is entered at a single point and exited at another single point. (Modules, as noted in Figure 10.2, rule 4, also have only one entry and one exit.) This helps simplify the logic so that others following in a programmer's footsteps are better able to make sense of the program. (In the days before this requirement was instituted, programmers could have all kinds of variations, leading to the kind of incomprehensible program known as *spaghetti code.*)

Let us consider the four control structures:

■ In the **sequence control structure,** one program statement follows another in logical order. In the example shown in Figure 10.5, there are two green boxes ("statement" and "statement"). One box could say "Open file," the other "Read a record." There are no decisions to make, no choices between "yes" or "no." The boxes logically follow one another in sequential order.

■ The **selection control structure**—also known as an *IF-THEN-ELSE structure*—represents a choice. It offers two or more paths to follow at points in the program where a decision must be made. An example of a selection structure is as follows:

IF a worker's hours in a week exceed 40
THEN overtime hours equal the number of hours exceeding 40
ELSE the worker has no overtime hours.

■ The **case control structure** is a variation on the usual selection control structure that involves more than a single yes-or-no decision. The case structure allows several alternatives, or "cases," to be presented. ("IF Case 1 occurs, THEN do thus-and-so. IF Case 2 occurs, THEN follow an alternative course." And so on.) The case control structure saves the programmer the trouble of having to indicate a lot of separate IF-THEN-ELSE conditions.

■ The **iteration control structure** (also known as the *loop* structure) is a structure in which a process may be repeated as long as a certain condition remains true. There are two types of iteration structures—DO UNTIL and DO WHILE. An example of a DO UNTIL structure is as follows:

DO read in employee records UNTIL there are no more employee records.

An example of a DO WHILE structure is as follows:

DO read in employee records WHILE—that is, as long as—there continue to be employee records.

What seems to be the difference between the two iteration structures? It is simply this: If there are several statements that need to be repeated, you need to decide when to stop repeating them. You can decide to stop them at the beginning of the loop, using the DO WHILE structure. Or you can decide to stop them at the end of the loop, using the DO UNTIL structure. The DO UNTIL iteration means that the loop statements will be executed at least once, because the iteration statements are executed before the program checks whether to stop.

3. Do a Structured Walkthrough

No doubt you've had the experience, after having read over your research paper or project several times, of being surprised when a friend (or instructor) pointed out some things you missed. The same thing happens to programmers.

In the **structured walkthrough,** a programmer leads other people in the development team through a design segment. The structured walkthrough, the final part of the design phase, consists of a formal review process in which others—fellow programmers, systems analysts, and perhaps users—scrutinize ("walk through") the programmer's design work. They review the parts of the program for errors, omissions, and duplications in processing tasks. Because the whole program is still on paper at this point, these matters are easier to correct than they will be later. Some programmers get very nervous before a structured walkthrough, as if it were a test of their competence. Others see it as merely a cooperative endeavor.

The Third Step: Code the Program

Once the design has been developed and reviewed in a walkthrough, the next step is the actual writing of the program, called **coding.** Coding consists of translating the logic requirements from pseudocode or flowcharts into a programming language—the letters, numbers, and symbols arranged according to syntax rules (language rules) that make up the program. Coding is what many people think of when they think of programming, although it is only one of the five steps.

1. Select the Appropriate Programming Language

A **programming language** is a language used to write instructions for the computer. Examples are Visual BASIC and C++. Not all languages are appropriate for all uses. Some have strengths in mathematical and statistical processing, whereas others are more appropriate for database management. Thus, in selecting the language, you will need to consider factors such as what purpose the program is designed to serve and what languages are already being used in the organization or field you are in.

2. Follow the Syntax

For a program to work, you have to follow the **syntax,** the rules of the programming language that specify how words and symbols are put together. Programming languages have their own grammar just as human languages do. But computers are probably a lot less forgiving if you use these rules incorrectly.

The Fourth Step: Test the Program

Program testing involves running various tests—such as desk-checking and debugging (also called *alpha testing*)—and then running actual (real) data to make sure the program works.

Figure 10.6 The first actual case of a "bug" being found in a computer dates from 1945, when a moth was discovered lodged in the wiring of the Mark I computer. The moth disrupted the execution of the program.

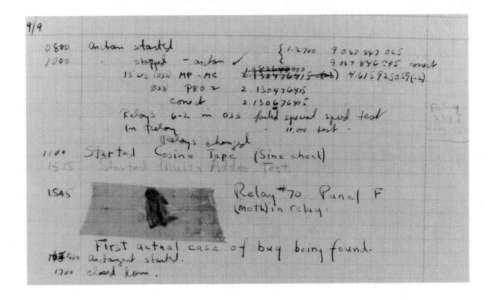

1. Perform Desk-Checking

Desk-checking is simply reading through, or checking, the program to make sure that it's free of errors and that the logic works. In other words, desk-checking is like proofreading. This step should be taken before the program is actually run on a computer.

2. Debug the Program

Once the program has been desk-checked, further errors, or "bugs," will doubtless surface. *(See Figure 10.6.)* **Debugging** means detecting, locating, and removing all errors in a computer program. Mistakes may be syntax errors or logic errors. **Syntax errors** are caused by typographical errors and incorrect use of the programming language. These are usually the easiest bugs to fix. Debugging utility programs (sometimes called *diagnostics*) check program syntax and display syntax-error messages. **Logic errors** are caused by incorrect use of control structures.

3. Run Real-World Data

After desk-checking and debugging, the program may run fine—in the laboratory. However, it then needs to be tested with real data, called *beta testing*. Indeed, it is even mandatory to test it with bad data—data that is faulty, incomplete, or in overwhelming quantities—to see if you can make the system crash. Users, after all, may be far more heavy-handed, ignorant, and careless than programmers have anticipated.

The testing process may involve several trials using different test data before the programming team is satisfied the program can be released. Even then, some bugs may remain, but there comes a point at which the pursuit of errors becomes uneconomical. This is one reason many users are nervous about using the first version (version 1.0) of a commercial software package.

The Fifth Step: Document and Maintain the Program

Preparing the program documentation is the fifth step in programming. The resulting **documentation** consists of written, graphic, and electronic descriptions of what a program is and how to use it. Preparing documentation is not just an end-stage process of programming. It has been (or should have been) going on throughout all previous programming steps. Documentation is needed for everyone who will be involved with the program—users, operators, and programmers.

1. Prepare User Documentation

When you buy a commercial software package, such as a spreadsheet, it is usually accompanied by user documentation. Such documentation should explain both how to use the software and how to exploit it. It should also include information on what a user should do on encountering an error. User documentation can take many forms, including "Getting Started" tutorials, User Guides, Reference Manuals, and online help. It is usually written by hired technical writers.

2. Prepare Operator Documentation

The people who run large computers are called *computer operators.* Because they are not always programmers, they need to be told what to do when the program malfunctions. The operator documentation gives them this information.

3. Write Programmer Documentation

Long after the original programming team has disbanded, the program may still be in use. If, as often happens, one-fifth of the programming staff leaves every year, after five years there may be no one left who knows anything about the software. Programmer documentation offers the keys to understanding the program's underlying logic and operation.

4. Maintain the Program

A word about maintenance: Maintenance is any activity designed to keep programs in working condition, error-free, and up to date. It includes adjustments, replacements, repairs, measurements, tests, and so on. The rapid changes typical of modern organizations in their products, marketing strategies, accounting systems, and so on call for corresponding changes in their computer systems. Thus, documentation must be available to help programmers make those adjustments.

The five steps of the programming process and their substeps are summarized in Figure 10.7.

10.2 Five Generations of Programming Languages

KEY QUESTION How do low-level programming languages compare to high-level programming languages?

As we've said, a programming language is a set of rules that tells the computer what operations to perform. Programmers, in fact, use these languages to create other kinds of software. Many programming languages have been written, some with colorful names (SNOBOL, HEARSAY, DOCTOR, ACTORS, JOVIAL). Each is suited to solving particular kinds of problems. What do all these languages have in common? Simply this: Ultimately, programs written in a particular language must be reduced to digital form—1s or 0s—because that is all the computer can understand.

Figure 10.7 The five steps of traditional programming

Step	Activities
Step 1: Problem definition	1. Specify program objectives and program users. 2. Specify output requirements. 3. Specify input requirements. 4. Specify processing requirements. 5. Study feasibility of implementing program. 6. Document the analysis.
Step 2: Program design	1. Determine program logic through top-down approach and modularization, using hierarchy chart. 2. Design details using pseudocode and/or flowcharts (preferably with control structures). 3. Test design with structured walkthrough.
Step 3: Program coding	1. Select the appropriate high-level programming language. 2. Code the program in that language, following the syntax carefully.
Step 4: Program testing	1. Desk-check the program to discover errors. 2. Run the program and debug it (alpha testing). 3. Run real-world data (beta testing).
Step 5: Program documentation and maintenance	1. Write user documentation. 2. Write operator documentation. 3. Write programmer documentation. 4. Maintain the program.

There are five levels or generations of programming languages. They start at the lowest level with (1) machine language. They range up through (2) assembly language, (3) high-level languages, and (4) very-high-level languages. At the highest level are (5) natural languages. Programming languages are said to be *lower level* when they are closer to the language that the computer itself uses—the 1s and 0s. They are called *higher level* when they are closer to the language people use—more like English, for example.

First introduced in 1945, programming languages have evolved over the years. The births of the generations are as follows. *(See Figure 10.8, next page.)*

■ First generation, 1945—machine language

■ Second generation, mid-1950s—assembly language

■ Third generation, early 1960s—high-level languages: FORTRAN, COBOL, C, BASIC, and Pascal

■ Fourth generation, early 1970s—very-high-level languages: NOMAD and FOCUS

■ Fifth generation, early 1980s—natural languages

Let us consider these five generations.

Figure 10.8 The five generations of programming languages

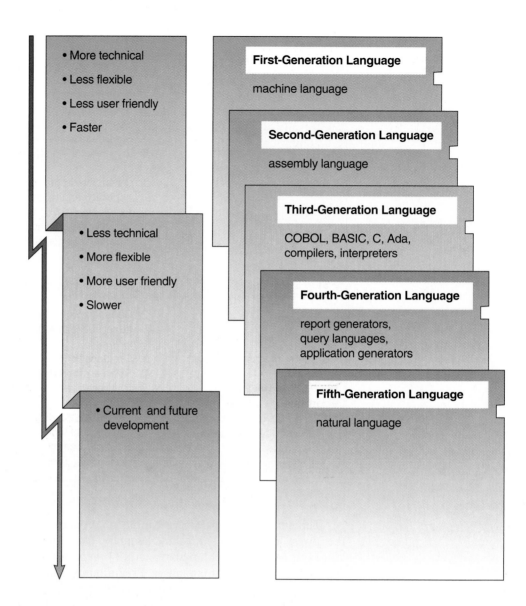

- More technical
- Less flexible
- Less user friendly
- Faster

- Less technical
- More flexible
- More user friendly
- Slower

- Current and future development

First-Generation Language

machine language

Second-Generation Language

assembly language

Third-Generation Language

COBOL, BASIC, C, Ada, compilers, interpreters

Fourth-Generation Language

report generators, query languages, application generators

Fifth-Generation Language

natural language

First Generation: Machine Language

The lowest level of language, **machine language** is the basic language of the computer, representing data as 1s and 0s (✔ p. 2.6). *(See Figure 10.9.)* Machine language programs vary from computer to computer; that is, they are machine dependent.

These binary digits, which correspond to the on and off electrical states of the computer, clearly are not convenient for people to read and use. Believe it or not, though, programmers did work with these mind-numbing digits. When the next generation of programming languages—assembly language—came along there must have been great sighs of relief.

Second Generation: Assembly Language

Assembly language is a low-level language that allows a programmer to use abbreviations or easily remembered words instead of numbers. *(Refer to Figure 10.9 again.)* For example, the letters MP could be used to represent the instruction MULTIPLY, and STO to represent STORE.

Figure 10.9 *(Top)*
Machine language is all
binary Os and 1s—very
difficult for people to work
with. *(Middle)* Assembly
language uses abbrevia-
tions for major instructions
(such as MP for MULTIPLY).
This is easier for people to
use, but still quite difficult.
(Bottom) Third-generation
languages use English
words.

```
First generation
Machine language

11110010 01110011 1101 001000010000 0111 000000101011
11110010 01110011 1101 001000011000 0111 000000101111
11111100 01010010 1101 001000010010 1101 001000011101
11110000 01000101 1101 001000010011 0000 000000111110
11110011 01000011 0111 000001010000 1101 001000010100
10010110 11110000 0111 000001010100

Second generation
Assembly language

                    PACK  210(8,13),02B(4,7)
                    PACK  218(8,13),02F(4,7)
                    MP    212(6,13),21D(3,13)
                    SRP   213(5,13),03E(0),5
                    UNPK  050(5,7),214(4,13)
                    OI    054(7),X'F0'

Third generation
COBOL

     MULTIPLY HOURS-WORKED BY PAY-RATE GIVING GROSS-PAY ROUNDED
```

As you might expect, a programmer can write instructions in assembly language more quickly than in machine language. Nevertheless, it is still not an easy
language to learn, and it is so tedious to use that mistakes are frequent. Another
drawback is that, like machine language, assembly language varies from computer
to computer—it is machine dependent.

We now need to introduce the concept of a language translator. Because a
computer can execute programs only in machine language, a translator or con-
verter is needed if the program is written in any other language. A **language translator** is a type of system software (✔ p. 5.13) that translates a program written in
a second- or higher-generation language into machine language.

Language translators are of three types:

■ Assemblers

■ Compilers

■ Interpreters

An assembler, or assembler program, is a program that translates the assembly-
language program into machine language. We describe compilers and interpreters
in the next section.

Third Generation: High-Level Languages

A high-level language is an English-like language, such as COBOL and BASIC.
(Refer back to Figure 10.9.) Such languages allow users to write in a familiar
notation, rather than numbers or abbreviations. Most high-level languages are not
machine dependent—they can be used on more than one kind of computer.

As we mentioned, assembly language requires an assembler as a language
translator. The translator for high-level languages is, depending on the language,
either a compiler or an interpreter.

■ *Compiler—execute later:* A **compiler** is software that looks at an entire high-
level program before translating it into machine language. The programming
instructions of a high-level language are called the *source code.* The compiler
translates source code into machine language, which in this case is called the
object code. With compilers, the object code can be saved and run later. That

Figure 10.10 Compiler. This language translator converts the high-level language (source code) into machine language (object code) before the computer can execute the program.

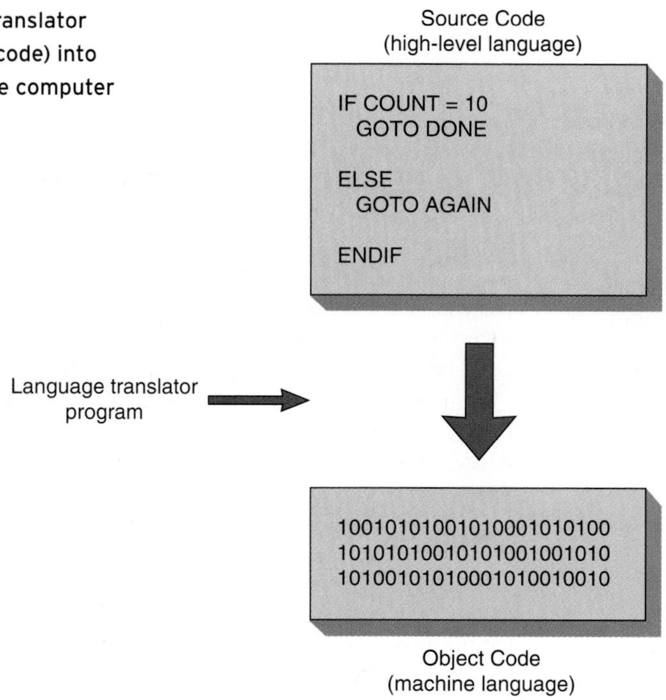

Source Code
(high-level language)

```
IF COUNT = 10
    GOTO DONE

ELSE
    GOTO AGAIN

ENDIF
```

Language translator
program →

```
10010101001010001010100
10101010010101001001010
10100101010001010010010
```

Object Code
(machine language)

is, the object code doesn't have to be recompiled. As a result, compiled programs run faster than interpreted programs, as we describe next. *(See Figure 10.10.)*

Examples of high-level languages using compilers are C and COBOL.

■ *Interpreter—execute immediately:* An **interpreter** is software that converts high-level language statements into machine language one at a time, in succession. Unlike compilers, which must look at an entire program before converting it into machine language, interpreters provide programmers with immediate feedback regarding the accuracy of their coded instructions. However, as mentioned previously, a program that must be interpreted runs more slowly than a compiled program. Interpreters are sometimes used by programmers when developing a program and in education to allow students to program interactively.

+ Interpreter slower than compiler.

Examples of high-level languages that use an interpreter are BASIC and LISP.

Third-generation, high-level languages are also known as *procedural languages.* The corresponding programs set forth precise procedures, or series of instructions, and the programmer has to follow a proper order of actions to solve a problem. To do that, the programmer has to have a detailed knowledge of programming and of the computer that the program will run on. Suppose you want to take a taxi to a theater showing a particular movie. If you tell the taxi driver precisely how to get to the theater, that's procedural. You have to know how to get there yourself, and you will probably get there efficiently. However, if you simply tell the taxi driver to "take me to see movie X," then you're saying only what you want, which is nonprocedural. In this case, you may not get to the theater in an efficient manner.

Fourth-generation languages are nonprocedural, as we shall explain.

Fourth Generation: Very-High-Level Languages

Very-high-level languages are often called *4GLs,* for *4th-generation languages.* Compared with third-generation languages, 4GLs are much more user-oriented and allow programmers to develop programs with fewer commands, although they also require more computing power. 4GLs are called *nonprocedural* because programmers and even users can write programs that only tell the computer what they want done, without specifying all the procedures for doing it. That is, they do not have to specify all the programming logic or otherwise tell the computer how the task should be carried out. This saves programmers a lot of time because they do not need to write as many lines of code as they do with procedural languages. 4GLs are also called *RAD (rapid application development) tools.*

Fourth-generation languages consist of report generators, query languages, application generators, and interactive database management system programs. Some 4GLs are tools for end-users, some are tools for programmers.

[handwritten: 7 part of 4th Generation Languages. →]

- ■ *Report generators:* A *report generator,* also called a *report writer,* is a program for end-users that is used to produce a report. The report may be a printout or a screen display. It may show all or part of a database file. You can specify the format in advance—columns, headings, and so on—and the report generator will then produce data in that format.

  Report generators were the precursor to today's query languages.

- ■ *Query languages:* A *query language* is an easy-to-use language for retrieving data from a database management system. The query may be expressed in the form of a sentence or near-English command. Or the query may be obtained from choices on a menu.

  Examples of query languages are SQL (for structured query language) and Intellect.

- ■ *Application generators:* An *application generator* is a programmer's tool that generates applications programs from descriptions of the problem rather than by traditional programming. The benefit is that the programmer does not need to specify how the data should be processed. The application generator is able to do this because it consists of modules preprogrammed to accomplish various tasks.

  Programmers use application generators to help them create parts of other programs. For example, the software is used to construct on-screen menus or types of input and output screen formats. NOMAD and FOCUS, two database management systems, include application generators. *[handwritten: different syntax, logic]*

4GLs may not entirely replace third-generation languages because they are usually focused on specific tasks and hence offer fewer options. Still, they improve productivity because programs are easy to write.

Fifth Generation: Natural Languages

Natural languages are of two types. The first are ordinary human languages: English, Spanish, and so on. The second are programming languages that use human language to give people a more natural connection with computers. Some of the query languages mentioned above under 4GLs might seem pretty close to human communication, but natural languages try to be even closer.

With 4GLs, you can type in some rather routine inquiries. An example of a request in FOCUS might be:

SUM SHIPMENTS BY STATE BY DATE.

Natural languages allow questions or commands to be framed in a more conversational way or in alternative forms. For example, with a natural language, you might be able to state:

I WANT THE SHIPMENTS OF PERSONAL DIGITAL ASSISTANTS FOR ALABAMA AND MISSISSIPPI BROKEN DOWN BY CITY FOR JANUARY AND FEBRUARY. ALSO, I NEED JANUARY AND FEBRUARY SHIPMENTS LISTED BY CITIES FOR PERSONAL COMMUNICATORS SHIPPED TO WISCONSIN AND MINNESOTA.

Natural languages are part of the field of study known as *artificial intelligence* (discussed in detail in Chapter 13). Artificial intelligence (AI) is a group of related technologies that attempt to develop machines to emulate human-like qualities, such as learning, reasoning, communicating, seeing, and hearing.

The dates of the principal programming languages are shown in the accompanying two-page timeline. *(See Figure 10.11.)*

10.3 High-Level Programming

KEY QUESTION **What are the characteristics of the common high-level programming languages?**

Many of the older, traditional high-level (third-generation) programming languages are being replaced in the mainstream by more modern programming tools, as we will discuss shortly. However, a sizable number of older computer-based information systems whose code was created using traditional languages are still maintained. Thus, programmers need to be familiar with these languages as well as with newer languages. Following are short descriptions of some common high-level programming languages.

Figure 10.11 Timeline for development of programming languages and formatting tools

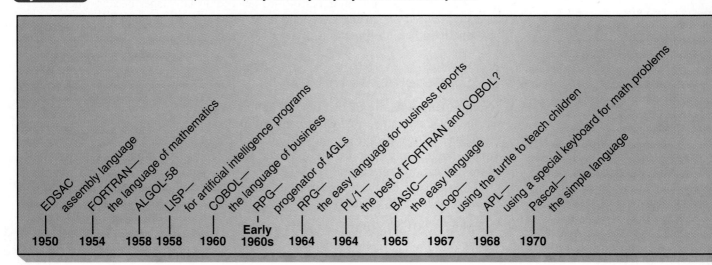

FORTRAN: The Language of Mathematics

*+ Math ; Sunching ;
not a lot of
user input*

Developed in 1954 by IBM, **FORTRAN** (for **FOR**mula **TRAN**slator) was the first high-level language. *(See Figure 10.12, next page.)* Originally designed to express mathematical formulas, it is still the most widely used language for mathematical, scientific, and engineering problems. It is also useful for complex business applications, such as forecasting and modeling. However, because it cannot handle a large volume of input/output operations or file processing, it is not used for more typical business problems.

As do all programming languages, FORTRAN has both advantages and disadvantages.

■ *Advantages:* (1) FORTRAN can handle complex mathematical and logical expressions. (2) Its statements are relatively short and simple. (3) FORTRAN programs developed on one type of computer can often be modified to work on other types.

■ *Disadvantages:* (1) FORTRAN does not handle input and output operations to storage devices as efficiently as some other high-level languages. (2) It has only a limited ability to express and process nonnumeric data. (3) It is not as easy to read and understand as some other high-level languages.

COBOL: The Language of Business

*+ a lot of control
input /output*

Formally adopted in 1960, **COBOL** (for **COmmon Business Oriented Language**) has been the most frequently used business language for large computers. *(Refer again to Figure 10.12.)* Its most significant attribute is that it is extremely readable. For example, a COBOL line might read:

MULTIPLY HOURLY-RATE BY HOURS-WORKED GIVING GROSS-PAY

First standardized in 1968 by the American National Standards Institute (ANSI), the language has been revised several times.

Writing a COBOL program resembles writing an outline for a research paper. The program contains four divisions—Identification, Environment, Data, and Procedure. The divisions in turn are broken into sections, which are divided into paragraphs, which are further divided into sentences. The Identification Division identifies the name of the program and the author (programmer) and perhaps some other helpful comments. The Environment Division describes the computer

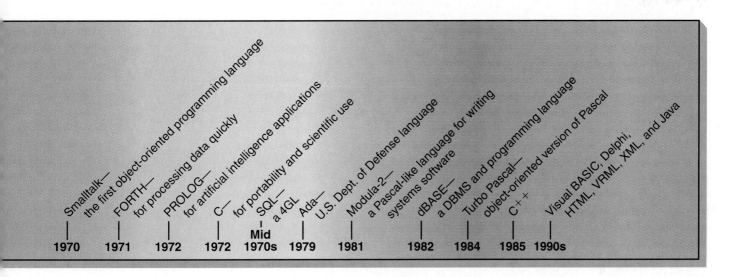

FORTRAN

```
IF (XINVO .GT. 500.00) THEN

    DISCNT = 0.07 * XINVO

ELSE

    DISCNT = 0.0

ENDIF

XINVO = XINVO – DISCNT
```

COBOL

```
OPEN-INVOICE-FILE.
    OPEN I-O INVOICE FILE.

READ-INVOICE-PROCESS.
    PERFORM READ-NEXT-REC THROUGH READ-NEXT-REC-EXIT UNTIL END-OF-FILE.
    STOP RUN.

READ-NEXT-REC.
    READ INVOICE-REC
        INVALID KEY
            DISPLAY 'ERROR READING INVOICE FILE'
            MOVE 'Y' TO EOF-FLAG
            GOTO READ-NEXT-REC-EXIT.
    IF INVOICE-AMT > 500
        COMPUTE INVOICE-AMT = INVOICE-AMT – (INVOICE-AMT * .07)
        REWRITE INVOICE-REC.

READ-NEXT-REC-EXIT.
    EXIT.
```

C

```
if (invoice_amount > 500.00)

    DISCOUNT = 0.07 * invoice_amount;

else

    discount = 0.00;

invoice_amount = invoice_amount – discount;
```

BASIC

```
10  REM       This Program Calculates a Discount Based on the Invoice Amount
20  REM           If Invoice Amount is Greater Than 500, Discount is 7%
30  REM           Otherwise Discount is 0
40  REM
50  INPUT "What is the Invoice Amount"; INV.AMT
60  IF INV.AMT A> 500 THEN LET DISCOUNT = .07 ELSE LET DISCOUNT = 0
70  REM           Display results
80  PRINT "Original Amt", "Discount", "Amt after Discount"
90  PRINT INV.AMT, INV.AMT * DISCOUNT, INV.AMT – INV.AMT * DISCOUNT
100 END
```

Pascal

```
if INVOICEAMOUNT > 500.00 then

    DISCOUNT := 0.07 * INVOICEAMOUNT

else

    DISCOUNT := 0.0;

INVOICEAMOUNT := INVOICEAMOUNT – DISCOUNT
```

Figure 10.12 How five third-generation languages handle the same statement

on which the program will be compiled and executed. The Data Division describes what data will be processed. The Procedure Division describes the actual processing procedures.

These are the advantages and disadvantages of COBOL.

■ *Advantages:* (1) It is machine independent, meaning that it can be run on different platforms. (2) Its English-like statements are easy to understand, even for a nonprogrammer. (3) It can handle many files, records, and fields. (4) It easily handles input/output operations.

■ *Disadvantages:* (1) Because it is so readable, it is wordy. Thus, even simple programs are lengthy, and programmer productivity is reduced. (2) It cannot handle mathematical processing as well as some other languages.

C: For Portability and Scientific Use

C is the language's entire name, and it does not stand for anything. Developed at Bell Laboratories, **C** is a general-purpose, compiled language that works well for microcomputers and is portable among many computers. *(Refer back to Figure 10.12.)* It is widely used for writing operating systems and utilities. C is also the programming language used most commonly in commercial software development, including games, robotics, and graphics. It is now considered a necessary language for programmers to know.

Here are the advantages and disadvantages of C:

■ *Advantages:* (1) C works well with microcomputers. (2) It has a high degree of portability—it can be run without change on a variety of computers. (3) It is fast and efficient. (4) It enables the programmer to manipulate individual bits in main memory.

■ *Disadvantages:* (1) C is considered difficult to learn. (2) Because of its conciseness, the code can be difficult to follow. (3) It is not suited to applications that require a lot of report formatting.

BASIC: The Easy Language

BASIC was developed by John Kemeny and Thomas Kurtz in 1965 for use in training their students at Dartmouth College. By the late 1960s, it was widely used in academic settings on all kinds of computers, from mainframes to PCs. Now its use has extended to business.

BASIC (for **Beginner's All-purpose Symbolic Instruction Code**) has been the most popular microcomputer language and is considered the easiest programming language to learn. *(Refer again to Figure 10.12.)* Although it is available in compiler form, the interpreter form is more popular with first-time and casual users. This is because it is interactive, meaning that user and computer can communicate with each other during the writing and running of the program.

The advantages and disadvantages of BASIC are as follows:

■ *Advantage:* BASIC is very easy to use.

■ *Disadvantages:* (1) Processing is relatively slow, although compiler versions are faster than interpreter versions. (2) There is no one version of BASIC, although in 1987 ANSI adopted a new standard that eliminated portability problems.

One of the current evolutions of BASIC is Visual BASIC, covered shortly.

Without the complex computer system Dr. Stephen Hawking controls at the touch of a button, his genius would be silenced. The astrophysicist was struck in 1963 at the age of 21 with amyotrophic lateral sclerosis, an incurable nervous sytem affliction known as Lou Gehrig's disease. (Lou Gehrig was a famous old-time baseball player who gave a famous radio speech upon retiring from the game after he learned he had the disease.)

Pascal: The Simple Language

Named after the 17th-century French mathematician Blaise Pascal, **Pascal** is an alternative to BASIC as a language for teaching purposes and is relatively easy to learn. *(Refer back to Figure 10.12.)* A difference from BASIC is that Pascal uses structured programming.

A compiled language, Pascal offers these advantages and disadvantages:

■ *Advantages:* (1) Pascal is easy to learn. (2) It has extensive capabilities for graphics programming. (3) It is appropriate for scientific use.

■ *Disadvantages:* Pascal has limited input/output programming capabilities, which limits its business applications.

As described in Table 10.1, there are several other high-level languages that you may encounter. Some are special-purpose languages.

10.4 Object-Oriented and Visual Programming

KEY QUESTION How do object-oriented and visual programming compare?

Consider how it was for the computer pioneers, who had to program in machine language or assembly language. Novices putting together programs in BASIC can breathe a collective sigh of relief that they weren't around at the dawn of the Computer Age. Even some of the simpler third-generation languages represent a challenge, because they are *procedure oriented,* forcing the user (programmer) to follow a predetermined path from step A to step B, and so on. Fortunately, two new developments have made things easier—object-oriented programming and visual programming. These types of programming are *event driven*—that is, they respond to input from the user or other programs at unregulated times and thus are driven by user (programmer) choices.

Table 10.1	OTHER HIGH-LEVEL LANGUAGES

High-Level Language	Description
Ada	Ada is an extremely powerful structured programming language designed by the U.S. Department of Defense to ensure portability of programs from one application to another. Ada was named for Countess Ada Lovelace, considered the world's first programmer. Because Ada is a structured language, with a modular design, pieces of a large program can be written and tested separately. Another advantage is that features of the language permit the compiler to check for errors before the program is run, and so programmers are more apt to write error-free programs. However, Ada is complex and difficult. Moreover, longtime business users have so much invested in COBOL, FORTRAN, and C that they have little motivation to switch to this relatively new language.
LISP	LISP (for LISt Processor) is a third-generation language used principally to construct artificial intelligence programs. Developed at the Massachusetts Institute of Technology in 1958 by mathematician John McCarthy, LISP is used to write expert systems and natural language programs. Expert systems are programs that are imbued with knowledge by a human expert; the programs can walk you through a problem and help solve it.
PL/1	Introduced in 1964 by IBM, PL/1 (for Programming Language 1) is a high-level language designed for both business and scientific applications. It includes many of the best features of FORTRAN and COBOL and is quite flexible and easy to learn. However, it is also considered to have so many options as to diminish its usefulness. As a result, it has not given FORTRAN and COBOL much competition.
RPG	Also introduced in 1964 by IBM, RPG (for Report Program Generator) is a highly structured and relatively easy-to-learn high-level language designed to help generate business reports. The user fills out a special form specifying what information the report should include and in what format. In 1970, improvements were introduced in RPG II. A successor, RPG III, is an interactive fourth-generation language that uses menus to give programmers choices.
Logo	Logo was developed at MIT in 1967 by Seymour Papert, using a dialect of LISP. Logo is a third-generation language designed primarily to teach children problem-solving and programming skills. At the basis of Logo is a triangular pointer, called a turtle, which responds to a few simple commands such as forward, left, and right. The pointer produces similar movements on the screen, enabling users to draw geometric patterns and pictures on screen. Because of its highly interactive nature, Logo is also used to produce graphics for business reports.
APL	Designed in 1968 by Kenneth Iverson for use on IBM mainframes, APL (for A Programming Language) is a third-generation language that allows users to solve complex mathematical problems in a single step, by means of a special keyboard. The special keyboard is required because the APL symbols are not part of the familiar ASCII character set. Though hard to read, this mathematically oriented and scientific language is still found on a variety of computers.
FORTH	Created in 1971 by Charles Moore, FORTH (for FOuRTH-generation language) is actually a third-generation language designed for real-time control tasks, as well as business and graphics applications. Programs written in FORTH are used on all kinds of computers, from PCs to mainframes. They run very quickly, because they require less memory than other programs and consequently are ideal for applications where rapid data processing is essential—for instance, in processing data from sensors and instruments and also arcade games and robotics.
PROLOG	Invented in 1972 by Alan Colmerauer of France, PROLOG did not receive much attention until 1979, when a newer version appeared. PROLOG (for PROgramming LOGic) is used to develop artificial intelligence applications, such as natural language programs and expert systems.

Object-Oriented Programming: Block by Block

Imagine you're programming in a traditional third-generation language, such as BASIC, and creating your coded instructions one line at a time. As you work on some segment of the program (such as how to compute overtime pay), you may think, "I'll bet some other programmer has already written something like this. Wish I had it. It would save a lot of time."

Fortunately, a kind of recycling technique now exists. This is object-oriented programming (OOP), which is rapidly replacing structured programming.

> The popularity of OOP will continue to increase as the backlog of yet unwritten programs rises at large businesses and software houses. Today, applications are becoming larger and more complex. As the size and complexity of applications increase, so does the number of person-years required to complete a project. The result is that projects will be either stretched out over years and completed by the traditional small teams (impractical), or more programmers will be added to projects, along with the associated problems of coordination and integration. One of the few proven methodologies for handling this increase in complexity is object-oriented programming.[2]

The following four steps briefly describe OOP (pronounced "oop," as in "oops!"):

1. *What OOP is:* **Object-oriented programming (OOP)** is a programming method that combines data and instructions for processing that data into a self-sufficient "object" that can be used in other programs. The important thing here is the object.

2. *What an object is:* An **object** is a block of preassembled programming code that is a self-contained module. The module contains, or encapsulates, both (1) a chunk of data and (2) the processing instructions that may be performed on that data. In a banking system, some objects might be "ATM" and "account." In a flight simulation system, an aircraft is an object composed of subordinate objects like "rudder" and "engine."

3. *When an object's data is to be processed—sending the message:* Once the object becomes part of a program, the processing instructions may or may not be activated. That happens only when a *message* is sent. A message is an alert sent to the object when an operation involving that object needs to be performed.

4. *How the object's data is processed—the methods:* The message need only identify the operation. How it is actually to be performed is embedded within the processing instructions that are part of the object. These instructions about the operations to be performed on data within the object are called the *methods*.

Once you've written a block of program code (that computes overtime pay, for example), it can be reused in any number of programs. Thus, unlike with traditional programming, with OOP you don't have to start from scratch—that is, reinvent the wheel—each time. *(See Figure 10.13, next page.)*

Object-oriented programming takes longer to learn than traditional programming because it means training oneself to a new way of thinking. Once learned, however, OOP has definite advantages: An object can be used repeatedly in different applications and by different programmers, thereby speeding up development time and lowering costs.

Conventional Programs

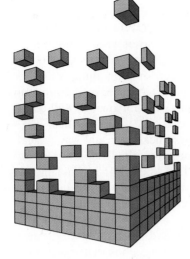

Object-Oriented Programs

Figure 10.13

Conventional versus object-oriented programs. *(Top)* When building conventional programs, programmers write every line of code from scratch. *(Bottom)* With object-oriented programs, programmers can use blocks, or "objects," of preassembled modules containing data and the associated processing instructions.

Three Important Concepts of OOP

Object-oriented programming involves three important concepts, which go under the jaw-breaking names of encapsulation, inheritance, and polymorphism. Actually, these terms are not as fearsome as they look:

■ *Encapsulation:* Encapsulation means an object contains (encapsulates) both (1) data and (2) the instructions for processing it, as we have seen. Once an object has been created, it can be reused in other programs. An object's uses can also be extended through concepts of class and inheritance.

■ *Inheritance:* Once you have created an object, you can use it as the foundation for similar objects that have the same behavior and characteristics. All objects that are derived from or related to one another are said to form a class. Each class contains specific instructions (methods) that are unique to that group.

Classes can be arranged in hierarchies—classes and subclasses. Inheritance is the method of passing down traits of an object from classes to subclasses in the hierarchy. Thus, new objects can be created by inheriting traits from existing classes.

Writer Alan Freedman gives this example: "The object MACINTOSH could be one instance of the class PERSONAL COMPUTER, which could inherit properties from the class COMPUTER SYSTEMS."[3] If you were to add a new computer, such as COMPAQ, you would need to enter only what makes it different from other computers. The general characteristics of personal computers could be inherited.

■ *Polymorphism:* Polymorphism means "many shapes." In object-oriented programming, polymorphism means that a message (generalized request) produces different results depending on the object that it is sent to. Polymorphism has important uses. It allows a programmer to create procedures for objects whose exact type is not known in advance but will be at the time the program is actually run on the computer. Freedman gives this example: "A screen cursor may change its shape from an arrow to a line depending on the program mode." The processing instructions "to move the cursor on screen in response to mouse movement would be written for 'cursor,' and polymorphism would allow that cursor to be whatever shape is required at runtime." It would also allow a new cursor shape to be easily integrated into the program.

Two Examples of OOP Languages

Two examples of object-oriented programming languages are Smalltalk and C++.

■ *Smalltalk—the first OOP language:* Smalltalk was invented by computer scientist Alan Kay in 1970 at Xerox Corporation's Palo Alto Research Center in California. Smalltalk, the first OOP language, uses a keyboard for entering text, but all other tasks are performed with a mouse.

■ *C++—more than C:* The plus signs in C++ stand for "more than C" because it combines the traditional C programming language with object-oriented capability. C++ was created by Bjarne Stroustrup. With C++, programmers can write standard code in C without the object-oriented features, use object-oriented features, or do a mixture of both.

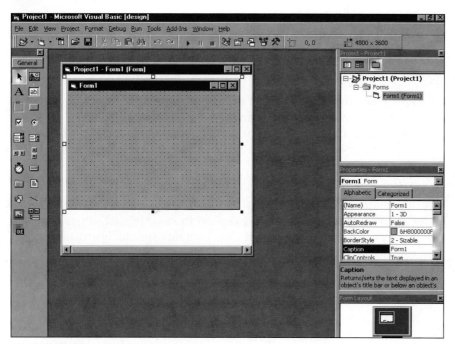

Visual BASIC screen

Visual Programming

Essentially, visual programming takes OOP to the next level. The goal of visual programming is to make programming easier for programmers and more accessible to nonprogrammers by borrowing OOP concepts but exercising them in a graphical or visual way. Visual programming enables users to think more about problem solving than about handling the programming language.

Visual programming is a method of creating programs by using icons that represent common programming routines. The programmer makes connections between objects by drawing, pointing, and clicking on diagrams and icons and by interacting with flowcharts. This type of programming became necessary to develop GUI-based (✔ p. 5.13) applications, for which earlier text-based languages are not efficient.

Visual BASIC, developed by Microsoft in the early 1990s, is the most popular visual programming language. It offers a visual environment for program construction, allowing users to build various application components using drag-and-drop tools, buttons, scroll bars, and menus. Visual BASIC, a fourth-generation OOP-based language, works with Microsoft Windows to create other Windows-compatible applications.

10.5 Internet Programming: HTML, XML, VRML, Java, & ActiveX

KEY QUESTION **What are the main characteristics of HTML, XML, VRML, Java, and ActiveX?**

Many of the thousands of Internet data and information sites around the world are text-based only; that is, the user sees no graphics, animation, or video and hears no sound. The World Wide Web, however, permits all of this.

One way to build such multimedia sites on the Web is to use some relatively recently developed markup languages and programming languages: HTML, XML, VRML, Java, and ActiveX.

■ *HTML—for creating 2-D Web documents and links:* **HTML (Hypertext Markup Language)** (✔ p. 8.10) is an authoring language for creating Web documents. HTML is a type of standard for embedding codes within standard ASCII (✔ p. 2.4) text documents to provide an integrated, two-dimensional display of text and graphics. *(Refer back to Figure 8.3.)* In other words, a document created with any word processor and stored in an ASCII format can become a Web page with the addition of HTML codes.

[handwritten note in margin:] * Not a programming language, it is a page descriptor language. Used with browser, word processor, translator, a set of standard codes.

One of the main features of HTML is its ability to insert hyperlinks (✔ p. 8.13) into a document. Hyperlinks enable you to display another Web document simply by clicking on a link area (usually underlined or highlighted) on the current screen. One document may contain links to many other related documents. The related documents may be on the same server (✔ p. 1.15) as the first document, or they may be on a computer halfway around the world. A link may be a word, a group of words, or a picture.

Most commercial applications software packages, such as Microsoft Word, can save documents in HTML format. In addition, if you don't want to learn everything about HTML, various HTML editors and filters—commercial HTML packages—will help you to create your own Web pages by choosing menu options and filling out templates; examples are Adobe's PageMill and Microsoft's FrontPage Editor. Recent releases of the Netscape and Microsoft Internet Explorer browsers also allow users to easily create their own Web pages. (Note that users generally need an Internet service provider, ✔ p. 8.3, to act as a server to store their Web pages.)

■ *XML—for making the Web work better:* The chief characteristics of HTML are its simplicity and ease when combining plain text and pictures. But HTML is unable to handle the business world's complex transactions.

Enter XML. Whereas HTML makes it easy for people to read Web sites, **XML (extensible markup language)** makes it easy for machines to read Web sites by enabling Web developers to add descriptive "tags" to a Web page. At present, when you use your browser to find a Web site, search engines can turn up too much, so that it's difficult to pinpoint the specific site you want, for example, one with a recipe for a low-fat Moroccan chicken dish for 12. XML makes Web sites smart enough to tell other machines whether they're looking at a recipe, an airline ticket, or a book for sale. XML lets Web site developers put tags on their Web pages that describe information in, for example, a food recipe as "ingredients," "calories," "cooking time," and "number of portions."

■ *VRML—for creating 3-D Web pages:* **VRML (Virtual Reality Markup Language)** is a type of programming language used to create three-dimensional Web pages. For example, Planet 9 Studios (*http://www.planet9.com*) has created a number of virtual cities one can tour. An architecture and landscaping firm in Philadelphia (*http://www.mrabsi.com/contents_top_nj.html*) uses VRML to market its products by developing interactive 3-D environments that prospective customers can walk through. The Geosphere Project (*http://www. infolane.com/geosphere*) offers a virtual control center for accessing a global library of earth-resource management visualizations (such as rain forest destruction or animal extinction patterns).

VRML (rhymes with "thermal") is not an extension of HTML. Thus, HTML Web browsers cannot interpret it, and users need a VRML browser plug-in—for example, Netscape's Live3D—to receive VRML Web pages. If they are not on a large computer system, they also need a high-end microcomputer such as a Power Macintosh or a Pentium-based PC. Like HTML, VRML is a document-centered ASCII language. Unlike HTML, it tells the computer how to create 3-D worlds. VRML pages can also be linked to other VRML pages.

Even though VRML's designers wanted to let nonprogrammers create their own virtual spaces quickly and painlessly, it's not as simple to describe a 3-D scene as it is to describe a page in HTML. However, many existing modeling and CAD (✔ p. 6.26) tools now offer VRML support, and new VRML-centered software tools are arriving.

■ *Java—for creating interactive Web pages:* Available from Sun Microsystems and derived from C++, Java is a major departure from the HTML coding that makes up most Web pages. Sitting atop markup languages such as HTML and XML, **Java** is an object-oriented, network-friendly high-level programming language that allows programmers to build applications that can run on almost any operating system. With Java, big applications programs can be broken into mini-applications, or "applets," that can be downloaded off the Internet and run on any computer. Moreover, Java enables a Web page to deliver, along with visual content, applets that when downloaded can make Web pages interactive.

Some microcomputers include special Java microprocessors designed to run Java software directly. However, Java is not compatible with many existing microprocessors, such as those from Intel and Motorola. For this reason, these users need to use a small "interpreter" program, called a Java Virtual Machine, that translates a Java program into a language that any computer or operating system can understand. They also need a Java-capable browser in order to view Java special effects on the Web.

Java development programs are available for programmers. In addition, Java software packages—such as ActionLine, Activator Pro, AppletAce, and Mojo—give nonprogrammers the ability to add multimedia effects to their Web pages, by producing applets that any Java-equipped browser can view. Such packages can be used by anyone who understands multimedia file formats and is willing to experiment with menu options.

■ *ActiveX—also for creating interactive Web pages:* ActiveX was developed by Microsoft as an alternative to Java for creating interactivity on Web pages. Indeed, Java and ActiveX are the two major contenders in the Web-applet war for transforming the Web into a complete interactive environment.

ActiveX is a set of controls, or reusable components, that enables programs or content of almost any type to be embedded within a Web page. Whereas a Java must be downloaded each time you visit a Web site, with ActiveX the component is downloaded only once, then stored on your hard disk for later, repeated use.

Thus, the chief characteristic of ActiveX is that it features *reusable* components—small modules of software code that perform specific tasks (such as a spelling checker), which may be plugged seamlessly into other applications. With ActiveX you can obtain from your hard disk any file that is suitable for the Web—such as a Java applet, animation, or pop-up menu—and insert it directly into an HTML document.

Programmers can create ActiveX controls or components in a variety of programming languages, including C, C++, Visual BASIC, and Java. Thousands of ready-made ActiveX components are commercially available from software development companies.

What do object-oriented, visual, and Internet programming imply for the future? Will tomorrow's programmer look less like a writer typing out words and more like an electrician wiring together circuit components? What does this mean for the five-step programming model we have described?

Some institutions are now teaching only object-oriented design techniques, which permit the ongoing improvement of working program models. Here programming stages overlap; the design process flows repeatedly through analysis, design, coding, and testing stages. Thus, users can test out new parts of programs and even entire programs as they go along. They need not wait until the end of the process to find out if what they said they wanted is what they really wanted.

Revolutionary new helmets allow firefighters to see *through* smoke in a burning building. By using infrared sensors and small digital video screens, the helmet—here worn by Gregory Brown of the Philadelphia Fire Department—locates the source of heat. The data is processed by a processing unit worn in a fireproof belt pouch.

Web Sites of Possible Interest

Overview of software engineering:
http://www.cio.com/archive/04/596_devenpor_content.html
http://rbse.jsc.nasa.gov/virt-lib/soft-eng.html

Software Engineering Institute:
http://www.sei.cmu.edu

Many programmers subscribe to *Dr. Dobb's Journal:*
http://www.ddj.com

Bugs and fixes:
http://www.bugnet.com/

Java:
http://www.javasoft.com

Flowcharting software:
http://www.zdnet.com/pcmag/features/flow/_open.htm

Job listings for programmers:
http://www.monster.com
http://www.hitechcareer.com

What is OOP?
http://www.soft-design.com/softinfo/objects.html
http://www.taligent.com/Technology/OTTerminology.html

Visual BASIC:
http://msdn.microsoft.com/vbasic
http://www.cgvb.com/

C++:
http://www.faqs.org/faqs/C-faq/toc

Music

The piano was invented 300 years ago and didn't change much over the last century. But for the last few years, digital pianos have been available in sizes not much larger than a keyboard, which you can plug into an amplifier. This has been a favorite of rock bands and people with not much room for a real piano; however, the sounds are recognizable as electronic.

Now, though, you can get the Disklavier GranTouch from Yamaha, which has been making pianos for more than a century, that is in the same form as an acoustic grand. The keyboard action is the same as that found in concert grands—but there are no strings and hence no heavy iron frame to support them.[a] The sounds themselves are drawn from a huge 30-megabyte database of digitized sounds. Because the sounds are synthesized, the instrument never needs tuning. In addition, it can summon the voices of more than 700 instruments, from harp to soprano sax.

You can also use the GranTouch to play actual performances by great composers of the past—Rachmaninoff, Paderewski, Gershwin, and the like—who long ago recorded on paper rolls for player pianos, now translated into digital formats. Finally, you can use the instrument to record and play back your own performances. And if you don't know how to play the piano, you can buy software (Teach Me Piano, Piano Suite) to teach yourself.

This is just one example of how information technology is changing the field of music. More importantly, it is also changing the financial underpinnings of the music industry. For example, Internet retailers such as CDNow and Amazon.com compete with brick-and-mortar record stores by providing easy online shopping for music CDs. Spinner Networks, owned by America Online, "broadcasts" about 2 million popular songs each day through the Net, reaching about 1.5 million listeners.[b]

But the World Wide Web is threatening to stand the system of music recording and distribution on its head. Not only are there now Web sites offering guitar chords and sheet music, there are also promotional sites featuring signed and unsigned artists, both garage bands and established professional musicians.[c] Some of these give away music to promote themselves. "The Internet gives you a way to reach your audience," says Peter Malik, who plays blues guitar. "It's a natural process and represents the future of how music will be marketed."[d]

Some musicians themselves want a revolution, believing that the Internet is a force that can democratize the market, bypassing record companies and radio stations and offering music directly to listeners. Many music lovers have become accustomed to using personal computers to download music in the form of MP3 files, which can be quickly copied for free—a mode of delivery that eliminates the need to package, manufacture, and distribute a CD.[e] Programs that play MP3 music include Winamp, Sonique, Audio Catalyst, MusicMatch, and Real Jukebox, which can be found at numerous Web sites.

There are legal MP3 sites on the Internet but also many illegal ones, which are operating in violation of copyright laws protecting ownership of music. Many of these will probably cease to exist as the recording industry develops new Web technologies that resist the free pirating of music and charge a fee.[f]

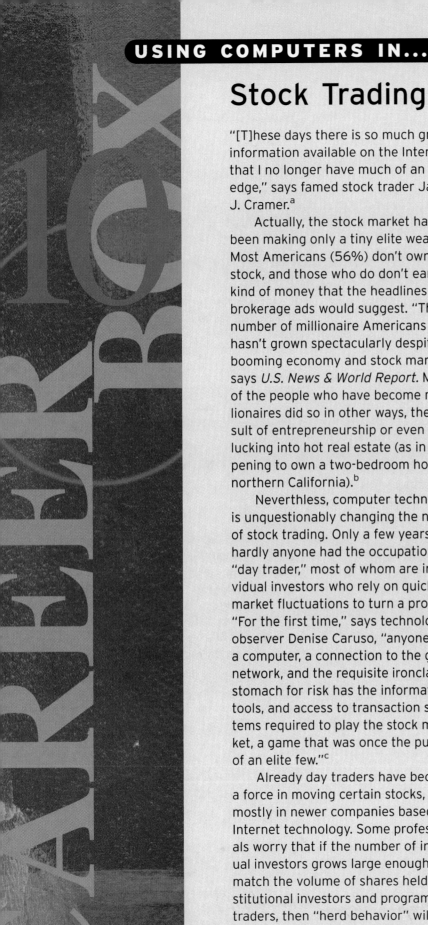

Stock Trading

"[T]hese days there is so much great information available on the Internet that I no longer have much of an edge," says famed stock trader James J. Cramer.[a]

Actually, the stock market has been making only a tiny elite wealthy. Most Americans (56%) don't own stock, and those who do don't earn the kind of money that the headlines and brokerage ads would suggest. "The number of millionaire Americans hasn't grown spectacularly despite the booming economy and stock market," says *U.S. News & World Report.* Many of the people who have become millionaires did so in other ways, the result of entrepreneurship or even in lucking into hot real estate (as in happening to own a two-bedroom house in northern California).[b]

Neverthless, computer technology is unquestionably changing the nature of stock trading. Only a few years ago, hardly anyone had the occupation of "day trader," most of whom are individual investors who rely on quick market fluctuations to turn a profit. "For the first time," says technology observer Denise Caruso, "anyone with a computer, a connection to the global network, and the requisite ironclad stomach for risk has the information, tools, and access to transaction systems required to play the stock market, a game that was once the purview of an elite few."[c]

Already day traders have become a force in moving certain stocks, mostly in newer companies based on Internet technology. Some professionals worry that if the number of individual investors grows large enough to match the volume of shares held by institutional investors and program traders, then "herd behavior" will move the larger markets in highly volatile ways.[d]

Online trading has also changed the nature of trading institutions themselves. For example, electronic rivals threaten the "open-outcry" trading pits such as the Chicago Board of Trade in which futures traders in garish jackets yell and gesture to one another.[e] The nation's two largest stock exchanges—the 207-year-old New York Stock Exchange (NYSE) and the 28-year-old Nasdaq—have felt the pressure from ECNs, or electronic trading networks, with names such as Island and Instinet.[f] ECNs "offer investors a way to trade for a fraction of what it costs to trade on the NYSE or Nasdaq," explains one report. "Their secret is that computers post, match, and execute all trades. No specialists or market makers serve as middlemen, as they do on the floor of the NYSE or in Nasdaq trading rooms."[g] Both exchanges began taking such steps as extending their trading day into the evening hours to accommodate investors on the West Coast.[h]

Full-service brokerage firms such as the 85-year-old Merrill Lynch & Co. began offering online trading, bowing to competition from such electronic discount brokerage firms as E*trade, Ameritrade, Schwab Online, and DLJ direct. As a *USA Today* editorial observed, "With the Internet, investors can quickly amass boatloads of company information, pick stocks, and execute trades on their own and on the cheap. Who needs brokers, particularly when their advice can easily cost 100 times as much."[i] But Allan Sloan, *Newsweek*'s Wall Street editor, begs to disagree: "The more information that's available online, the more valuable competent advisers and middlemen become . . . Someone has to filter the information—much of which may not be true—and do something useful with it."[j]

WHAT IT IS
WHAT IT DOES   WHY IT IS IMPORTANT

ActiveX (KQ 10.5, p. 10.28)   A set of controls, or reusable components, that enables programs or content of almost any type to be embedded within a Web page.

A rival of Java, ActiveX is intended as a means of transforming the Web into a complete interactive computing environment.

algorithm (KQ 10.1, p. 10.2)   Set of ordered steps for solving a problem.

Algorithms are fundamental to programming.

BASIC (Beginner's All-purpose Symbolic Instruction Code) (KQ 10.3, p. 10.21)   Developed in 1965, a popular microcomputer language that is easy to learn.

The interpreter form of BASIC is popular with first-time and casual users because it is interactive—user and computer can communicate during the writing and running of a program.

case control structure (KQ 10.1, p. 10.9)   The **case control structure** is a variation on the usual selection control structure that involves more than a single yes-or-no decision. The case structure allows several alternatives, or "cases," to be presented. ("IF Case 1 occurs, THEN do thus-and-so. IF Case 2 occurs, THEN follow an alternative course." And so on.)

The case control structure saves the programmer the trouble of having to indicate a lot of separate IF-THEN-ELSE conditions.

C (KQ 10.3, p. 10.21)   General-purpose, compiled language that works well for microcomputers and is portable among many computers.

C is widely used for writing operating systems and utilities and is also the programming language used most commonly in commercial software, including games, robotics, and graphics. It is now considered a necessary language for programmers to know.

COBOL (COmmon Business Oriented Language) (KQ 10.3, p. 10.19)   High-level programming language of business. First standardized in 1968, the language has been revised several times.

COBOL has been the most frequently used business language for large computers.

coding (KQ 10.1, p. 10.10)   Writing the program. Coding consists of translating the logic requirements from pseudocode, flowcharts, and the like into a programming language—letters, numbers, and symbols that make up the code.

Coding is what many people think of when they think of programming, although in fact it is only one of the five steps.

1, + 3 generation of programming languages (4th and 5th)

Compilers vs interpret x. assembler

syntax vs logic errors

compiler (KQ 10.2, p. 10.15)   Language translator that converts the entire program of a high-level language (called the *source code*) into machine language (called the *object code*) for execution later. Examples of compiler languages: C and COBOL.

Unlike other language translators (assemblers and interpreters), a compiler program allows the object code to be saved and executed later rather than run right away. The advantage of a compiler is that, once the object code has been obtained, the program executes more rapidly than when an interpreter is used.

control structure (KQ 10.1, p. 10.6)   Also called *logic structure;* in structured program design, an element controlling the logical sequence in which computer program instructions are executed. Four basic control structures are used to form the logic of a program: sequence, selection, case, and iteration (or loop).

Any control structures must have only one entry and one exit; that is, the control structure is entered at a single point and exited at another single point. This helps simplify the logic so that others following in a programmer's footsteps are better able to make sense of the program.

debugging (KQ 10.1, p. 10.11)   Form of program testing; the detection and removal of syntax and logic errors in a program.

Debugging may take several trials using different data before the programming team is satisfied the program can be released. Even then, some errors may remain, because removing them would be uneconomical.

desk-checking (KQ 10.1, p. 10.11)   Form of program testing; reading through the program to check for errors.

Desk-checking should be done before the program is actually run on a computer.

documentation (KQ 10.1, p. 10.11)   Written, graphic, and electronic descriptions of a program and how to use it. Documentation should be prepared during all programming steps.

Documentation is needed for everyone who will be involved with the program—users, operators, and programmers.

FORTRAN (FORmula TRANslator) (KQ 10.3, p. 10.19)   The first high-level programming language, developed in 1954 to express mathematical formulas.

The most widely used language for mathematical, scientific, and engineering problems, FORTRAN is also useful for complex business applications, such as forecasting and modeling. Because it cannot handle a large volume of input/output operations or file processing, it is not used for more typical business problems.

HTML (Hypertext Markup Language) (KQ 10.5, p. 10.26)   Type of standard for embedding codes within ASCII text documents to provide an integrated, two-dimensional display of text and graphics. Hypertext is used to link the displays.

HTML is used to create 2-D Web pages.

interpreter (KQ 10.2, p. 10.16)   Language translator that converts each high-level language statement into machine language and executes it immediately, statement by statement. Examples of high-level languages using an interpreter are BASIC and LISP.

When an interpreter is used, no object code is saved. The advantage of an interpreter is that programs are easier to develop.

iteration control structure (KQ 10.1, p. 10.9)   Also known as *loop structure;* one of the four control structures used in structured programming. A process is repeated as long as a certain condition remains true; the programmer can stop repeating the repetition at the *beginning* of the loop, using the DO WHILE iteration structure, or at the *end* of the loop, using the DO UNTIL iteration structure (which means the loop statements will be executed at least once.)

Iteration control structures help programmers write better-organized programs.

Java (KQ 10.5, p. 10.28)   Type of programming language used to create any conceivable type of software applications that will work on the Internet.

Java may be able to transform the Internet from just an information-delivering medium into a completely interactive computing environment.

language translator (KQ 10.2, p. 10.15)   Type of system software that translates a program written in a second- or higher-generation language into machine language. Language translators are of three types: (1) assemblers, (2) compilers, and (3) interpreters.

Because a computer can execute programs only in machine language, a translator is needed if the program is written in any other language.

logic errors (KQ 10.1, p. 10.11)   Programming errors caused by incorrect use of control structures.

If a program has logic errors, it will not run correctly or perhaps not run at all.

machine language (KQ 10.2, p. 10.14)   Lowest level of programming language; the language of the computer, representing data as 1s and 0s. Most machine language programs vary from computer to computer—they are machine dependent. All software programs must be translated into machine language by a compiler, an interpreter, or an assembler.

Machine language, which corresponds to the on and off electrical states of the computer, is not convenient for people to use. Assembly language and higher-level languages were developed to make programming easier.

natural languages (KQ 10.2, p. 10.17)   Fifth-generation programming languages that use human language to give people a more natural connection with computers.

Natural languages are part of the field of study known as artificial intelligence.

object (KQ 10.4, p. 10.24)   In object-oriented programming, block of preassembled programming code that is a self-contained module. The module contains (encapsulates) both (1) a chunk of data and (2) the processing instructions that may be performed on that data. Once the object becomes part of a program, the processing instructions may be activated only when a message is sent.

The object can be reused and interchanged among programs, thus making the programming process easier, more flexible and efficient, and faster.

object-oriented programming (OOP) (KQ 10.4, p. 10.24)   Programming method in which data and the instructions for processing that data are combined into a self-sufficient object—a piece of software that can be used in more than one program. Examples of OOP languages: Smalltalk, and C++.

Because objects can be reused and interchanged among programs, OOP is more flexible and efficient than are traditional programming methods.

Pascal (KQ 10.3, p. 10.22)   High-level programming language; an alternative to BASIC as a language for teaching purposes that is relatively easy to learn.

Pascal has extensive capabilities for graphics programming and is excellent for scientific use.

program (KQ 10.1, p. 10.2)   Also called *software;* list of instructions that the computer must follow in order to process data into information.

Without programs, computers could not process data into information.

program flowchart (KQ 10.1, p. 10.6)   Structured programming tool for designing a program in graphical (chart) form; it uses standard symbols called ANSI symbols.

The program flowchart graphically presents the detailed series of steps needed to solve a programming problem.

programming (KQ 10.1, p. 10.2)   Also called *software engineering;* five-step process for creating software instructions: (1) clarify the problem; (2) design a solution; (3) write (code) the program; (4) test the program; (5) document the program.

Programming is Phase 4.1 in the systems development life cycle.

programming language (KQ 10.1, p. 10.10)   Set of words and symbols that allow programmers to tell the computer what operations to follow. The five levels (generations) of programming languages are (1) machine language, (2) assembly language, (3) high-level (procedural) languages (FORTRAN, COBOL, C, BASIC, Pascal, etc.), (4) very-high-level (nonprocedural) languages (NOMAD, FOCUS, etc.), and (5) natural languages.

Not all programming languages are appropriate for all uses. Thus, a language must be chosen to suit the purpose of the program and to be compatible with other languages being used.

pseudocode (KQ 10.1, p. 10.6)   Structured programming tool for designing a program in narrative form using normal human-language statements to describe the logic and processing flow. Using pseudocode is like doing an outline or summary form of the program to be written.

By using such terms as IF, THEN, or ELSE, pseudocode follows the rules of control structures, an important aspect of structured programming.

selection control structure (KQ 10.1, p. 10.9)   Also known as an *IF-THEN-ELSE structure;* one of four basic control structures used in structured programming. It offers two paths to follow at points in the program where a decision must be made.

Selection control structures help programmers write better-organized programs.

sequence control structure (KQ 10.1, p. 10.9)   One of four basic control structures used in structured programming. In this case, each program statement follows another, in logical order; there are no decisions to make.

Sequence control structures help programmers write better-organized programs.

structured programming (KQ 10.1, p. 10.4)   Top-down approach to programming that breaks programs into modular forms and employs standard logic tools called *control structures* (sequence; selection; case; and iteration, or loop).

This approach helps programmers to write programs that are more efficient (with fewer lines of code) and better organized (more readable) and to use standard notations with clear, correct descriptions.

structured walkthrough (KQ 10.1, p. 10.10) Program review process in the design phase of the programming process; a programmer leads other development team members in reviewing a new segment of code.

The structured walkthrough helps programmers find errors, omissions, and duplications, which are easy to correct because the program is still on paper.

syntax (KQ 10.1, p. 10.10)   Rules of a programming language that specify how words and symbols are put together.

Each programming language has its own syntax, just as human languages do.

syntax errors (KQ 10.1, p. 10.11)   Programming errors caused by typographical errors and incorrect use of the programming language.

If a program has syntax errors, it will not run correctly or perhaps not run at all.

top-down program design (KQ 10.1, p. 10.4) Method of program design; a programmer identifies the top or principal processing step, or module, of a program and then breaks it down in hierarchical fashion into smaller processing steps. The design can be represented in a top-down hierarchy chart.

Top-down program design enables an entire program to be more easily developed because the parts can be developed and tested separately.

very-high-level languages (KQ 10.2, p. 10.17) Also known as *nonprocedural languages*, *fourth-generation languages (4GLs);* and *RAD (rapid applications development) tools;* more user-oriented than third-generation languages, 4GLs require fewer commands. 4GLs consist of report generators, query languages, and applications generators. Some 4GLs are tools for end-users, some are tools for programmers.

When using very-high-level languages, programmers need only tell the computer what they want done, without specifying all the procedures for doing it; this eliminates the time and labor of having to write many lines of code.

visual programming (KQ 10.4, p. 10.26)   Method of creating programs whereby the programmer makes connections between objects by drawing, pointing, and clicking on diagrams and icons. Programming is made easier because object-oriented programming concepts are used in a graphical or visual way.

Visual programming enables users to think more about problem solving than about handling the programming language.

VRML (Virtual Reality Markup Language) (KQ 10.5, p. 10.27)   Type of programming language used to create three-dimensional (3-D) Web pages.

VRML expands the information-delivering capabilities of the Web.

XML (extensible markup language) (KQ 10.5, p. 10.27)   Programming language that makes it easy for machines to read Web sites, by allowing Web developers to add descriptive tags.

XML is more powerful than HTML. It allows information on a Web site to be described by general tags—for example, one piece of information in a recipe may be identified as "cooking time" and others as "ingredients."

1. Fill in the blanks:

   a. Machine language is a _____-generation language.

   b. Fifth-generation languages are often called _____ languages.

   c. _____ programming takes a top-down approach that breaks programs into modular forms.

   d. In the _____ control structure, one program statement follows another in logical order.

   e. A _____ language is a language used to write instructions for the computer.

2. Label each of the following statements as either true or false.

   a. _____ The rules for using a programming language are called *syntax*.

   b. _____ Objects found in an object-oriented program can be reused in other programs.

   c. _____ The term *programming* means the same as the term *software engineering*.

   d. _____ A syntax error can be caused by a simple typographical error.

3. Describe each of the following:
   a. pseudocode
   b. program flowchart
   c. control structure

4. List four control structures:

   a. _____

   b. _____

   c. _____

   d. _____

5. Describe each of the following terms:
   a. debug
   b. syntax error
   c. logic error

6. Name the three types of tools of which fourth-generation languages consist.

   a. _____

   b. _____

   c. _____

7. What are the main characteristics of the following high-level programming languages?
   a. COBOL
   b. C
   c. BASIC
   d. FORTRAN

8. What are the main characteristics of the following Internet programming languages?
   a. HTML
   b. XML
   c. VRML

9. Object-oriented programming involves three important concepts, as listed below. Describe each in a few sentences.
   a. encapsulation
   b. inheritance
   c. polymorphism

10. What five steps are used for the development of programs using traditional programming languages?

   a. _____
   b. _____
   c. _____
   d. _____
   e. _____

IN YOUR OWN WORDS

1. Answer each of the Key Questions that appear at the beginning of this chapter.

2. How do third-generation languages differ from first- and second-generation languages?

3. What were the reasons for the development of high-level programming languages?

4. Why is documentation important during program development?

5. What advantage does a compiler have over an interpreter?

6. What does the term *desk-checking* mean?

7. What is user documentation? Provide several examples.

8. What is object-oriented programming (OOP)?

9. Describe visual programming.

10. What is ActiveX used for?

KNOWLEDGE IN ACTION

 1. **Downloading an HTML Primer.** Visit the NCSA site (*www.ncsa.uiuc.edu/General/ Internet/WWW/HTMLPrimer.html*) and print out the "Beginners Guide to HTML." This document is a primer for producing documents in HTML and provides many links to help you get started writing pages for the Web. Using this document, write at least ten lines of code that can be used on a Web page.

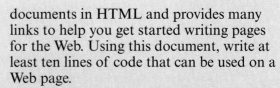 2. **Learning More About XML.** Visit the XML Web site at *www.xml.com* to learn more about this Internet programming language. What resources are available at this site? What have you learned about XML that you didn't know before?

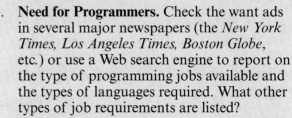 3. **Need for Programmers.** Check the want ads in several major newspapers (the *New York Times, Los Angeles Times, Boston Globe,* etc.) or use a Web search engine to report on the type of programming jobs available and the types of languages required. What other types of job requirements are listed?

4. **Working as a Programmer.** Can you imagine yourself becoming a programmer? If so, what types of problems would you like to work on? What programming languages would you like to use? Why?

Answers to Self-Test Exercises: 1a. first   1b. natural   1c. object-oriented   1d. sequence   1e. programming   2. T, T, T.   3a. Pseudocode is a tool for designing a program in narrative form using normal human-language statements to describe the logic and processing flow.   3b. Structured programming tool for designing a program in graphical (chart) form; it uses standard symbols called ANSI symbols.   3c. Also called logic structure; in structured program design, an element controlling the logical sequence in which computer program instructions are executed. Four basic control structures are used to form the logic of a program: sequence, selection, case, and iteration (or loop).   4. sequence, selection, case, iteration.   5a. Form of program testing; the detection and removal of syntax and logic errors in a program.   5b. Programming error caused by typographical errors and incorrect use of the programming language.   5c. Programming error caused by incorrect use of control structures.   6. report generators, query languages, application generators.   7a. High-level programming language of business. First standardized in 1968, the language has been revised several times.   7b. General-purpose, compiled language that works well for microcomputers and is portable among many computers.   7c. Developed in 1965, a popular microcomputer language that is easy to learn.   7d. The first high-level programming language, developed in 1954 to express mathematical formulas.   8a. Type of standard for embedding codes within ASCII text documents to provide an integrated, two-dimensional display of text and graphics. Hypertext is used to link the display.   8b. Programming language that makes it easy for machines to read Web sites, by allowing Web developers to add descriptive tags.   8c. Type of programming language used to create three-dimensional (3-D) Web pages.   9a. Encapsulation means an object contains (encapsulates) both (1) data and (2) the instructions for processing it, as we have seen. Once an object has been created, it can be reused in other programs. An object's uses can also be extended through concepts of class and inheritance.   9b. Once you have created an object, you can use it as the foundation for similar objects that have the same behavior and characteristics. All objects that are derived from or related to one another are said to form a class. Each class contains specific instructions (methods) that are unique to that group. Classes can be arranged in hierarchies—classes and subclasses. Inheritance is the method of passing down traits of an object from classes to subclasses in the hierarchy. Thus, new objects can be created by inheriting traits from existing classes.   9c. Polymorphism means "many shapes." In object-oriented programming, polymorphism means that a message (generalized request) produces different results depending on the object that it is sent to. Polymorphism has important uses. It allows a programmer to create procedures for objects whose exact type is not known in advance but will be at the time the program is actually run on the computer. Freedman gives this example: "A screen cursor may change its shape from an arrow to a line depending on the program mode." The processing instructions "to move the cursor on screen in response to mouse movement would be written for 'cursor,' and polymorphism would allow that cursor to be whatever shape is required at runtime." It would also allow a new cursor shape to be easily integrated into the program.   10. clarify the programming needs, design the program, code the program, test the program, document and maintain the program.

CHAPTER 11

INFORMATION MANAGEMENT

Who Needs to Know What, and When?

"We're experiencing the beginning of what is perhaps the most radical redefinition of the workplace since the Industrial Revolution, with some tremendous benefits involved," says a longtime proponent of flexible work arrangements. "Yet the early signs are that corporations are as likely as not to mess this up."

The speaker, a management consultant, was referring to the changes, a trickle now turning into a tidal wave, brought about by the mobile office—also called the virtual office (✔ p. 7.38).[1] Part of the redefinition of the workplace involves handing employees laptop computers with modems, portable phones, and beepers and telling them to work from their homes, cars, or customers' offices—virtually anywhere. Another part of it is to use a grab bag of electronic information organizers, personal communicators, personal digital assistants, and similar gadgets that help free people from a fixed office.

"Flex-time" shift hours and voluntary part-time telecommuting programs have been around for a few years. Unlike those slight alterations to traditional worklife, however, the virtual office and its high-tech tools are forcing some profound changes in the way people work. Many people, of course, like the flexibility of a mobile office. However, others resent having to work at home or being unable to limit their work hours. One computer-company vice president worries about getting her staff to stop sending faxes to each other in the middle of the night. Some employees may work 90 hours a week and still feel as if they are falling short. At some point, a constant-work lifestyle becomes counterproductive.

At Queen Eilzabeth Hospital in Hong Kong, nurse Law Wai Fong holds up a card that patients can carry in their wallets. The card can contain the equivalent of an entire filing cabinet—about 2000 pages—of a patient's medical history.

11.1 Trends Forcing Change in the Workplace

KEY QUESTION   **What trends are changing the way we work?**

The virtual office is only one of several trends that have had a profound effect on the way we work. Others include, but are not limited to, the following:

- Automation
- Downsizing and outsourcing
- Total quality management
- Employee empowerment
- Reengineering

The Virtual Office

As we mentioned earlier, the virtual office is essentially a mobile office. Using integrated computer and communications technologies, corporations will increasingly be defined not by concrete walls or physical space but by collaborative networks linking hundreds, thousands, even tens of thousands of people together. Widely scattered workers can operate as individuals or as if they were all at company headquarters. Such "road warriors" break the time and space barriers of the organization, operating anytime, anywhere.

Automation

When John Diebold wrote his prophetic book *Automation* in the 1950s, the computer was nearly new. Yet Diebold predicted that computers would make many changes. First, he suggested, they would change how we do our jobs. Second, he

At Case Western Reserve University, Dr. Michael Huff, an electrical engineering professor, holds on the tip of his finger a microprocessor complete with valves that can precisely administer intravenous (IV) drugs with a level of accuracy unparalleled by today's standards. The IV pump can be implanted in a patient.

thought, they would change the kind of work we do. He was right, of course, on both counts. In the 1950s and 1960s, computers changed how factory work, for instance, was done. In the 1970s and 1980s, factory work itself began to decline as Western nations went from manufacturing economies to information economies.

Diebold's third prediction was that the technologies would change the world in which we work. This is the next great development in computers and automation, he says, begun in the 1990s.

Downsizing and Outsourcing

The word *downsizing* has two meanings. First, it means the movement in the 1980s from mainframe-based computer systems to systems composed of smaller computers in networks. Second, downsizing means reducing the size of an organization by eliminating workers and consolidating and/or eliminating operations.

As a result of automation, economic considerations, and the drive for increased profitability, in recent years many companies have had to downsize their staffs—lay off employees. In the process, they have, in business jargon, "flattened the hierarchy," reducing the levels and numbers of middle managers. Of course, much of the company's work still remains, forcing the rest of the staff to take up the slack. For instance, the secretary may be gone, but the secretarial work remains. The lower-level and middle-level managers found that with personal computers they could accomplish much of this work.

Downsizing has also led to another development: outsourcing. *Outsourcing* means the contracting with outside businesses or services to perform the work once done by in-house departments. The outside specialized contractors, whether janitors or computer-system managers, can often do the work more cheaply and efficiently.

Total Quality Management

Total quality management (TQM) is managing with an organization-wide commitment to continuous work improvement and satisfaction of customer needs. The group that probably benefited most from TQM principles was the American automobile makers, who had been devastated by better-made foreign imports. However, much of the rest of U.S. industry would most likely also have been shut out of competition in the global economy without the quality strides made in the last few years.

Employee Empowerment

Empowerment means giving employees the authority to act and make decisions on their own—balanced against the appropriate amount of supervision. The old style of management was to give lower-level managers and employees only the information they "needed" to know, which minimized their power to make decisions. As a result, truly good work could not be achieved because of the attitude "If it's not part of my job, I don't do it." Today's philosophy is that information should be spread widely, not closely held by top managers, to enable employees lower down in the organization to do their jobs better. Indeed, the availability of networks and groupware (✔ p. 6.18) has enabled the development of task-oriented teams of workers who no longer depend on individual managers for all decisions in order to achieve company goals.

Reengineering

Trends such as the foregoing force—or should force—organizations to face basic realities. Sometimes the organization has to actually reengineer—rethink and redesign itself or key parts of it. *Reengineering* is the search for and implementation of radical change in business processes to achieve breakthrough results. Reengineering, also known as *process innovation* and *core process redesign,* is not just fixing up what already exists. Says one description:

> Reengineers start from the future and work backward, as if unconstrained by existing methods, people, or departments. In effect they ask, "If we were a new company, how would we run this place?" Then, with a meat ax and sandpaper, they conform the company to their vision.[2]

Reengineering works best with big processes that really matter, such as new-product development or customer service. Thus, candidates for this procedure include companies experiencing big shifts in their definition, markets, or competition. Examples are information technology companies—computer makers, cable-TV providers, local and long-distance phone companies, and publishers—which are wrestling with technological and regulatory change. Expensive software systems are available to help companies reengineer and standardize their information systems so as to give employees the data they need when they need it.

To understand how to bring about change in an organization, we need to understand how organizations work—how they need, organize, and use information.

11.2 Organizations: Departments, Tasks, Management Levels, and Types of Information

KEY QUESTION What are the traditional organizational departments, tasks, levels of managers, and types of information needed by managers and workers?

Consider any sizable organization you are familiar with. Its purpose is to perform a service or deliver a product. If it's nonprofit, for example, it may deliver the service of educating students or the product of food for famine victims. If it's profit-oriented, it may, for example, sell the service of fixing computers or the product of computers themselves.

Information—whether computer-based or not—has to flow within an organization in a way that will help managers, and the organization, achieve their goals. To this end, business organizations are often structured with five departments.

Departments: R&D, Production, Marketing, Accounting, Human Resources

Depending on the services or products they provide, most companies have five departments that perform different functions: research and development, production, marketing, accounting and finance, and human resources (personnel).

Figure 11.1 Examples of computer-based information systems in production

Computer-Aided Design
Create, simulate, and evaluate models of products and manufacturing processes.

Computer-Aided Manufacturing
Use computers and robots to fabricate, assemble, and package products.

Factory Management
Plan and control production runs, coordinate incoming orders and raw material requests, oversee cost, and operate quality assurance programs.

Quality Management
Evaluate product and process specifications, test incoming materials and outgoing products, test production processes in progress, and design quality assurance programs.

Logistics
Purchase and receive materials, control and distribute materials, and control inventory and shipping of products.

Maintenance
Monitor and adjust machinery and processes, perform diagnostics, and do corrective and preventive maintenance.

■ *Research and development:* The research and development (R&D) department does two things: (1) It conducts basic research, relating discoveries to the organization's current or new products. (2) It does product development and tests and modifies new products or services created by researchers. Special software programs are available to aid in these functions.

■ *Production/operations:* The production/operations department makes the product or provides the service. In a manufacturing company, it takes the raw materials and has people or machinery turn them into finished goods. In many cases, this department uses CAD/CAM software and workstations (✔ p. 1.14), as well as robotics. *(See Figure 11.1.)* Other production activities may include purchasing, handling the inventories, and controlling the flow of goods and services.

■ *Marketing:* The marketing department oversees advertising, promotion, and sales. *(See Figure 11.2.)* The people in this department plan, price, advertise, promote, package, and distribute the services or goods to customers or clients. The sales reps may use laptop computers, cell phones, wireless e-mail, and faxes in their work while on the road.

■ *Accounting and finance:* The accounting and finance department takes care of all financial matters. It handles cash management, pays bills, issues paychecks, records payments, makes investments, and compiles financial statements and reports. It also produces financial budgets and forecasts financial performance after receiving information from the other departments.

■ *Human resources:* This department finds and hires people and administers sick leave and retirement matters. It is also concerned with compensation levels, professional development, employee relations, and government regulations.

Whatever the organization—grocery store, computer maker, law firm, hospital, or university—it is likely to have departments corresponding to these. Each department has managers and employees. Although office automation brought about by computers, networks, and groupware has given employees more decision-making power than they used to have, managers in each of these departments still perform five basic functions, which we will now consider.

Figure 11.2 Examples of computer-based information systems in marketing

Sales Management
Plan, monitor, and support the performance of salespeople and sales of products and services.

Sales Force Automation
Automate the recording and reporting of sales activity by salespeople and the communications and sales support from sales management.

Product Management
Plan, monitor, and support the performance of products, product lines, and brands.

Advertising and Promotion
Help select media and promotional methods and control and evaluate advertising and promotion results.

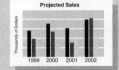

Sales Forecasting
Produce short- and long-range sales forecasts.

Market Research
Collect and analyze internal and external data on market variables, developments, and trends.

Marketing Management
Develop marketing strategies and plans based on corporate goals and market research and sales activity data, and monitor and support marketing activities.

Management Tasks: Five Functions

Management is about overseeing resources, including the tasks of planning, organizing, staffing, supervising, and controlling business activities. These five functions, considered the classic tasks of management, are defined as follows:

Essay:
5 functions
of Management.

- *Planning*—setting objectives, both long-term and short-term, and developing strategies for achieving them. Whatever you do in planning lays the groundwork for the other four tasks.

- *Organizing*—making orderly arrangements of resources, such as people and materials.

- *Staffing*—selecting, training, and developing people. In some cases, it may be done by specialists, such as those in the personnel department.

- *Supervising (leading)*—directing, guiding, and motivating employees to work toward achieving the organization's goals.

- *Controlling*—monitoring the organization's progress and adapting methods toward achieving its goals.

All managers perform all these tasks, to some degree, as part of their jobs. However, the level of responsibility regarding these tasks varies with the level of the manager, as we discuss next. A manager may also be responsible for maintaining an image within the company or within the community.

Management Levels: Three Levels, Three Kinds of Decisions

How do managers carry out the tasks just described? They do it by making decisions on the basis of the information available to them. A manager's daily job is to decide on the best course of action, based on the facts known at the time.

For each of the five departments there are three traditional levels of management—top, middle, and lower. These levels are reflected in the organization chart. An organization chart is a schematic drawing showing the hierarchy of formal relationships among an organization's employees. *(See Figure 11.3.)*

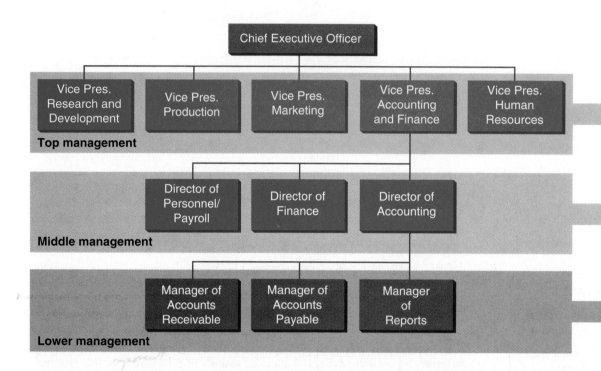

Top management

Middle management

Lower management

FOUR-YEAR SALES TREND BY PRODUCT($1000)					
PRODUCT	1997	1998	1999	2000	4-YEAR AVERAGE
SILVERS	4,201	4,575	5,210	5,976	4,991
GOLDS	5,889	6,123	6,780	7,105	6,474
REDS	2,675	3,106	3,699	4,520	3,500
BLUES	1,437	1,670	1,980	2,521	1,902
TOTALS	14,202	15,474	17,669	20,122	

CORPORATE SALES REGIONAL SUMMARY($1000)—1ST QUARTER					
REGION	SILVERS	GOLDS	REDS	BLUES	TOTAL
CALIFORNIA	422	399	350	450	1,621
NEVADA	560	601	609	576	2,346
OREGON	349	357	210	673	1,589
WASHINGTON	252	289	190	311	1,042
TOTALS	1,583	1,646	1,359	2,010	6,598

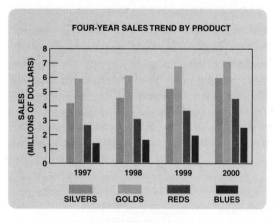

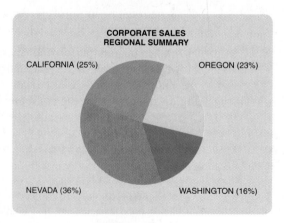

Strategic-Level Inquiry/Report

Tactical-Level Inquiry/Report

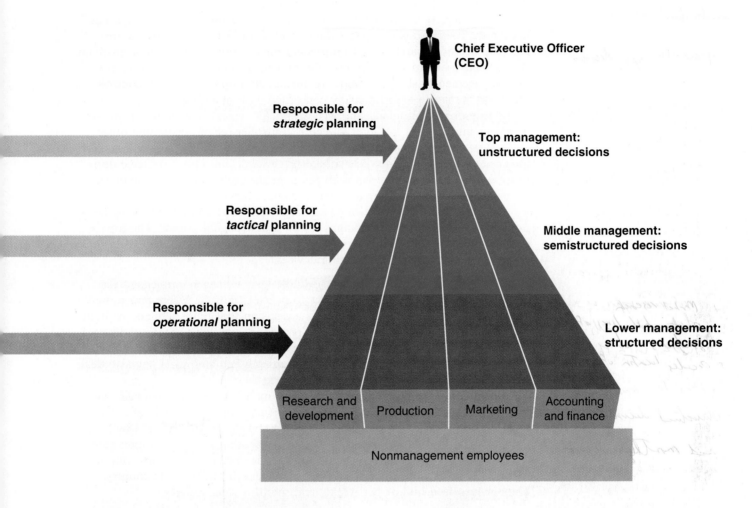

Chief Executive Officer (CEO)

Responsible for *strategic* planning

Top management: unstructured decisions

Responsible for *tactical* planning

Middle management: semistructured decisions

Responsible for *operational* planning

Lower management: structured decisions

| Research and development | Production | Marketing | Accounting and finance |

Nonmanagement employees

SALES DEPARTMENT — NEVADA SALES SUMMARY($1000) — 1ST QUARTER					
SALESPERSON	SILVERS	GOLDS	REDS	BLUES	TOTAL
VINE	70	10	14	65	159
WU	90	85	99	110	384
HERNANDEZ	95	126	111	115	447
WASHINGTON	120	98	103	28	349
LEE	60	225	219	180	684
OGG	93	33	35	68	229
WILLIAMS	32	24	28	10	94
TOTALS	560	601	609	576	2,346

SALES DEPARTMENT— NEVADA SALES SUMMARY($1000) —1ST QUARTER SALESPERSONS WITH SALES < $15,000 FOR ANY PRODUCT					
SALESPERSON	SILVERS	GOLDS	REDS	BLUES	TOTAL
VINE	70	10	14	65	159
WILLIAMS	32	24	28	10	94

Operational-Level Inquiry/Report

Figure 11.3 Management levels and responsibilities. (*Left*) An organization generally has five departments: research and development, production, marketing, accounting and finance, and human resources. This organization chart shows the management hierarchy for just one department, accounting and finance. Three levels of management are shown—top, middle, and lower. (*Right*) The entire organization can also be represented as a pyramid, with the five departments and three levels of management as shown. Top managers are responsible for strategic decisions, middle management for tactical decisions, and lower management for operational decisions. Office automation is changing the flow of information in many organizations, thus "flattening" the pyramid, because not all information continues to flow through traditional hierarchical channels. (*Bottom*) Examples of strategic, tactical, and operational information.

Managers on each of the three levels have different kinds of responsibility and are therefore required to make different kinds of decisions.

■ *Top managers—strategic decisions:* The chief executive officer (CEO) or president is the very top manager. "Top management" also includes the vice presidents, one of whom heads each of the departments.

Top managers are concerned with long-range planning and external market forces. Their job is to make strategic decisions. Strategic decisions are complex decisions rarely based on predetermined routine procedures, involving the subjective judgment of the decision maker. *Strategic* means that of the five management tasks (planning, organizing, staffing, supervising, controlling), top managers are principally concerned with planning.

Besides CEO, president, and vice president, typical titles found at the top management level are treasurer, director, controller (chief accounting officer), and senior partner. Examples of strategic decisions are how growth should be financed and what new markets should be tackled first. Other strategic decisions are deciding the company's five-year goals, evaluating future financial resources, and deciding how to react to competitors' actions.

An AT&T vice president of marketing might have to make strategic decisions about promotional campaigns to sell a new paging service. The top manager who runs an electronics store might have to make strategic decisions about stocking a new line of paging devices.

■ *Middle managers—tactical decisions:* Middle-level managers implement the goals of the organization. Their job is to oversee the supervisors and to make tactical decisions. A tactical decision is a decision that must be made without a base of clearly defined informational procedures, perhaps requiring detailed analysis and computations. *Tactical* means that of the five management tasks, middle managers deal principally with organizing and staffing. They also deal with shorter-term goals than top managers do.

Examples of middle managers are plant manager, division manager, sales manager, branch manager, and director of personnel. An example of a tactical decision is deciding how many units of a specific product should be kept in inventory. Another is whether or not to purchase a larger computer system.

The director of sales, who reports to the vice president of marketing for AT&T, sets sales goals for district sales managers throughout the country. They in turn feed him or her weekly and monthly sales reports.

■ *Lower or supervisory managers—operational decisions:* Lower-level managers, or supervisory managers, manage or monitor nonmanagement employees. Their job is to make operational decisions. An operational decision is a predictable decision that can be made by following a well-defined set of routine procedures. *Operational* means these managers focus principally on supervising (leading) and controlling. They monitor day-to-day events and, if necessary, take corrective action.

An example of a supervisory manager is a warehouse manager in charge of inventory restocking. An example of an operational decision is one in which the manager must choose whether or not to restock inventory. (The guideline on when to restock may be determined at the level above.)

A district sales manager for AT&T would monitor the promised sales and orders for pagers coming in from the sales representatives. When sales begin to drop off, the supervisor would need to take immediate action.

Decision Structure	Operational Management	Tactical Management	Strategic Management
Unstructured	Cash management	Work group reorganization	New business planning
		Work group performance analysis	Company reorganization
Semistructured	Credit management	Employee performance appraisal	Product planning
	Production scheduling	Capital budgeting	Mergers and aquisitions
	Daily work assignment	Program budgeting	Site location
Structured	Inventory control	Program control	

Figure 11.4 Examples of decisions by the type of decision structures and by level of management

Types of Information: Unstructured, Semistructured, and Structured

To make the appropriate decisions—strategic, tactical, operational—the different levels of managers need the right kind of information: unstructured, semistructured, and structured. *(See labels at right of Figure 11.3, and see Figure 11.4.)*

In general, all information to support intelligent decision making at all three levels must be correct—that is, accurate. It must also be complete, including *all* relevant data, yet concise, including *only* relevant data. It must be cost-effective, meaning efficiently obtained, yet understandable. It must be current, meaning timely, yet also time-sensitive, based on historical, current, or future information needs. This shows that information has three distinct properties:

    1. Level of summarization   2. Degree of accuracy   3. Timeliness

These properties may vary in the degree to which they are structured or unstructured, depending on the level of management and type of decision making required. **Structured information** is detailed, current, concerned with past events; requires highly accurate, nonsubjective data; records a narrow range of facts; and covers an organization's internal activities. **Unstructured information** is the opposite. Unstructured information is summarized, less current, concerned with future events; requires subjective data; records a broad range of facts; and covers activities outside as well as inside an organization. It also involves some degree of risk or uncertainty. **Semistructured information** includes some structured information and some unstructured information.

Consider, for example, what information the three levels of management might deal with in a food-supply business. *(See Figure 11.5.)*

Figure 11.5 Areas covered by the three management levels in a food-supply business

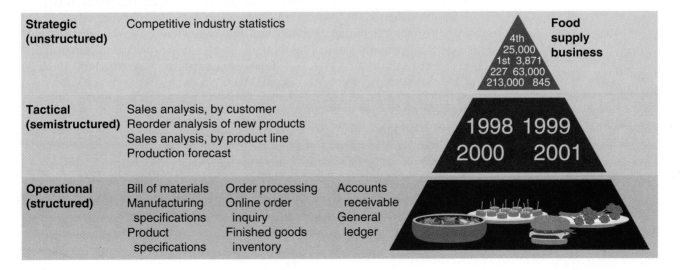

Strategic (unstructured)	Competitive industry statistics			Food supply business

Tactical (semistructured)	Sales analysis, by customer
	Reorder analysis of new products
	Sales analysis, by product line
	Production forecast

Operational (structured)	Bill of materials	Order processing	Accounts receivable
	Manufacturing specifications	Online order inquiry	General ledger
	Product specifications	Finished goods inventory	

Now that we've covered some basic concepts about how organizations are structured and what kinds of information are needed at different levels of management, we need to examine what types of management information systems provide the information.

11.3 Management Information Systems

KEY QUESTION Who are the intended users of the TPS, MIS, DSS, EIS, ES, and OAS management information systems?

Top managers (executives) make strategic decisions using unstructured information, as we have seen. Middle managers make tactical decisions using semistructured information. Lower-level managers make operational decisions using structured information. The purpose of a computer-based information system is to provide managers (and various categories of employees) with the appropriate kind of information to help them make decisions.

Here we describe the following types of computer-based information systems, corresponding to the three management layers and their requirements. Note that we are taking this material from the bottom up because the higher levels build on the lower levels. *(See Figure 11.6.)*

Different types of data and methods to deal with them

- For lower managers: Transaction processing systems (TPSs)

- For middle managers: Management information systems (MISs) and decision support systems (DSSs)

- For top managers: Decision support systems (DSSs) and executive information systems (EISs)

- For all levels including nonmanagement: Expert systems (ESs) and office automation systems (OASs)

Transaction Processing Systems: To Support Operational Decisions

In most organizations, particularly business organizations, most of what goes on takes the form of transactions. A **transaction** is a recorded event having to do with routine business activities. This includes everything concerning the product or service in which the organization is engaged: production, distribution, sales, orders. It also includes materials purchased, employees hired, taxes paid, and so on. Today in most organizations, the bulk of such transactions are recorded in a computer-based information system. These systems tend to have clearly defined inputs and outputs, and there is an emphasis on efficiency and accuracy. Transaction processing systems record data but do little in the way of converting data into information.

A **transaction processing system (TPS)** is a computer-based information system that keeps track of the transactions needed to conduct business.

Some features of a TPS are as follows:

- *Input and output:* The inputs to the system are transaction data: bills for amounts of money paid to the company, orders, inventory levels, and the like. The output consists of processed transactions: bills for amounts owed to the company, paychecks, and so on.

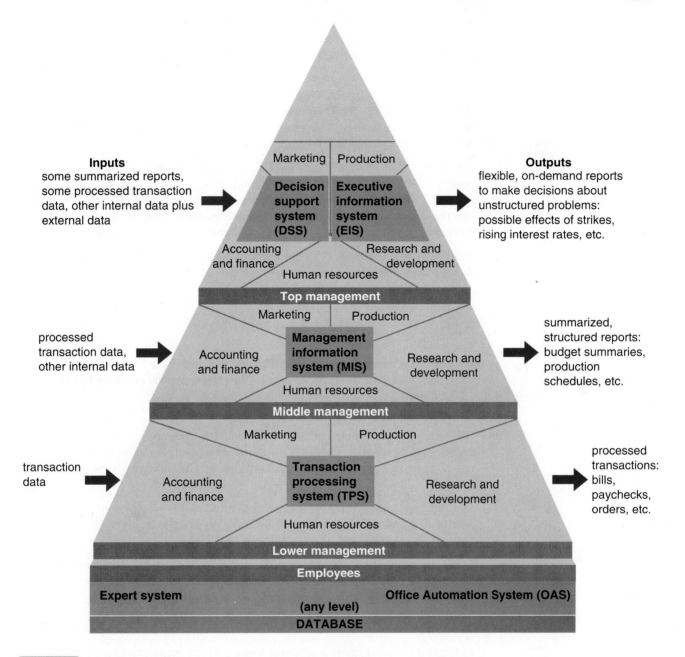

Inputs
some summarized reports, some processed transaction data, other internal data plus external data

Outputs
flexible, on-demand reports to make decisions about unstructured problems: possible effects of strikes, rising interest rates, etc.

Marketing | Production

Decision support system (DSS) | **Executive information system (EIS)**

Accounting and finance | Research and development

Human resources

Top management

processed transaction data, other internal data

summarized, structured reports: budget summaries, production schedules, etc.

Marketing | Production

Accounting and finance | **Management information system (MIS)** | Research and development

Human resources

Middle management

transaction data

processed transactions: bills, paychecks, orders, etc.

Marketing | Production

Accounting and finance | **Transaction processing system (TPS)** | Research and development

Human resources

Lower management

Employees

Expert system | **Office Automation System (OAS)**

(any level)

DATABASE

Figure 11.6 Six information systems for three levels of management. The pyramid shows the following: (1) The three levels of management: top, middle, and lower. (2) The five departments for each level: research and development, production, marketing, accounting and finance, and human resources. (3) The kinds of computer-based information systems corresponding to each management level. (4) The kind of data input for each level, and the kind of information output.

- *For lower managers:* Because the TPS deals with day-to-day matters, it is principally of use to supervisory managers. That is, the TPS helps in making operational decisions. Such systems are not usually helpful to middle or top managers.

- *Produces detail reports:* A lower-level manager typically will receive information in the form of detail reports. A detail report contains specific information about routine activities. An example might be the information needed to decide whether to restock inventory.

- *One TPS for each department:* Each department or functional area of an organization—Research and Development, Production, Marketing, Accounting and Finance, and Human Resources—usually has its own TPS. For example, the Accounting and Finance TPS handles order processing, accounts receivable, inventory and purchasing, accounts payable, and payroll.

- *Basis for MIS and DSS:* The database of transactions stored in a TPS is used to support management information systems and decision support systems.

Management Information Systems: To Support Tactical Decisions

A **management information system (MIS)** is a computer-based information system that uses data recorded by TPSs as input into programs that produce routine reports as output.

Features of an MIS are as follows:

- *Input and output:* Inputs consist of processed transaction data, such as bills, orders, and paychecks, plus other internal data. Outputs consist of summarized, structured reports: budget summaries, production schedules, and the like.

- *For middle managers:* A MIS is intended principally to assist middle managers. That is, it helps them with tactical decisions. It enables them to spot trends and get an overview of current business activities.

- *Draws from all departments:* The MIS draws from all five departments or functional areas, not just one.

- *Produces several kinds of reports:* Managers at this level usually receive information in the form of several kinds of reports: summary, exception, periodic, on-demand.
  —*Summary reports* show totals and trends. An example would be a report showing total sales by office, by product, by salesperson, or as total overall sales.
  —*Exception reports* show out-of-the-ordinary data. An example would be an inventory report that lists only those items that number fewer than 10 in stock.
  —*Periodic reports* are produced on a regular schedule. These may be daily, weekly, monthly, quarterly, or annually. They may contain sales figures, income statements, or balance sheets. Such reports are usually produced on paper, such as computer printouts.
  —*On-demand reports* produce information in response to an unscheduled demand. A director of finance might order an on-demand credit-background report on a new customer who wants to place a large order. On-demand reports are often produced on a terminal or microcomputer screen rather than on paper.

It's not just a kayak, it's also a high-tech, undercover U.S. Coast Guard surveillance vehicle. Captain Edward Page patrols close to the action in the waters off Long Beach, California. He charts his position with a handheld Global Positioning System (GPS) device. He reports to base via cell phone or radio.

Decision Support Systems: To Support Strategic Decisions

A **decision support system (DSS)** is an interactive, computer-based information system that provides a flexible tool for analysis and helps managers focus on the future. To reach the DSS level of sophistication in information technology, an organization must have established a transaction processing system and a management information system.

Some features of a DSS are as follows:

- *Input and output:* Inputs consist of some summarized reports, some processed transaction data, and other internal data. They also include data that is external to that produced by the organization. This external data may be produced by trade associations, marketing research firms, the U.S. Bureau of the Census, and other government agencies.

  The outputs are flexible, on-demand reports with which a top or middle manager can make decisions about unstructured problems.

- *Mainly for top and middle managers:* A DSS is intended principally to assist top managers, although it is now being used by other managers, too. Its purpose is to help them make strategic decisions—decisions about unstructured problems, often unexpected and nonrecurring. These problems may involve the effect of events and trends outside the organization. Examples are rising interest rates or a possible strike in an important materials-supplying industry. DSSs are also used for making tactical decisions.

- *Produces analytic models:* The key attribute of a DSS is that it uses models. A model is a mathematical representation of a real system. The models use a DSS database, which draws on the TPS and MIS files, as well as external data such as stock reports, government reports, national and international news. The system is accessed through DSS software.

  The model allows the manager to do a simulation—that is, produce an imitation of a process or an object—to reach decisions. Thus, the manager can simulate an aspect of the organization's environment in order to decide how to react to a change in conditions affecting it. By changing the hypothetical inputs to the model—number of workers available, distance to markets, or whatever—the manager can see how the model's outputs are affected.

Tomorrow's scientists track the wind's speed, direction, and temperature on a hillside in Wales. Their findings are then e-mailed to school children in other parts of Wales.

Components of a DSS

Figure 11.7 illustrates the components of a DSS:[3]

- *Hardware:* Personal workstations provide the primary resource for a DSS. They can be used on a stand-alone basis. However, they are typically connected by wide area or local area networks (✔ pp. 7.25, 7.27) to other computer systems for access to other DSS software and resources.

- *Software:* DSS software packages (DSS generators) contain software modules to manage DSS databases, decision modules, and interaction (dialogue) between user and system.

- *Data resources:* A DSS database contains data and information extracted from the database of the organization, external databases, and managers' personal databases. It includes summarized data and information most needed by managers.

- *Model resources:* The model base includes a library of mathematical models and analytical techniques stored as programs, subroutines, spreadsheets, and command files.

- *People resources:* A DSS can be used by managers or their staff specialists to explore decision alternatives. DSSs can also be developed by such end users. However, the development of large or complex DSSs is typically left to information systems specialists.

Figure 11.7 Components of a DSS

Interactive decision support

Model base management ⟷ Model base

Dialog generation and management

Database management ⟷ Database

Manager or staff specialists   Management workstation   DSS software

Examples of DSS Applications

Many DSSs are developed to support the types of decisions faced by specific industries, such as the airline and real estate industries. Here are three examples:[4]

■ *Airline DSS:* The American Analytical Information Management System (AAIMS) is a decision support system used in the airline industry. It was developed by American Airlines but is used by other airlines, aircraft manufacturers, airline financial analysts, consultants, and associations. AAIMS supports a variety of airline decisions by analyzing data collected on airline aircraft utilization, seating capacity and utilization, and traffic statistics. For example, it produces forecasts of airline market share, revenue, and profitability. Thus, AAIMS helps airline management make decisions on aircraft assignments, route requests, ticket classifications, pricing, and so on.

   Another successful DSS for American Airlines is its *yield management system.* This DSS helps managers and analysts decide how much to overbook and how to set prices for each seat so that a plane is filled and profits are maximized. American's yield management system deals with more than 250 decision variables. The system is estimated to generate up to 5% of American Airline's revenues.

■ *Real estate DSS:* RealPlan is a DSS used in the real estate industry to do complex analyses of investments in commercial real estate. For example, investing in commercial real estate properties typically involves highly detailed income, expense, and cash flow projections. RealPlan easily performs such analyses, even for properties with multiple units, lease terms, rents, and cost-of-living adjustments. Since RealPlan can also make forecasts of property values up to 40 years into the future, it helps decision makers not only with acquisition decisions but with real estate improvement and divestment decisions as well.

■ *Geographic DSS:* Geographic information systems (GISs) are a special category of DSS that integrate computer graphics and geographic databases with other DSS features. *(See Figure 11.8.)* A geographic information system is a

Figure 11.8 Geographic DSS (GIS) screen. Using Mapinfo technology, insurance underwriters can set rates and examine potential financial liability in the event of a natural disaster. Here, policyholders who live on earthquake fault lines are visualized and analyzed.

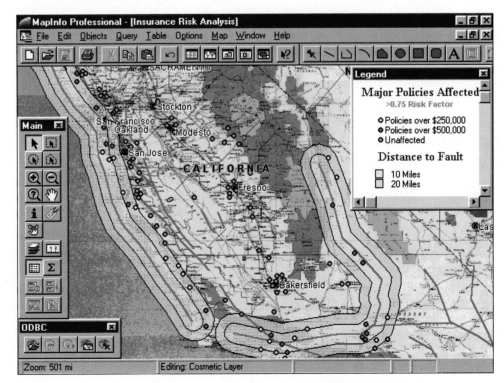

DSS that constructs and displays maps and other graphics that support decisions affecting the geographic distribution of people and other resources. Many companies use GIS technology to choose new store locations, optimize distribution routes, and analyze the demographics of target audiences. For example, companies like Levi Strauss, Arby's, Consolidated Rail, and FedEx use GISs to integrate maps, graphics, and other geographic data with business data from spreadsheets and statistical packages. GIS software is also available for microcomputers—for example, MapInfo and Atlas GIS. The use of GISs for decision support should accelerate the use of mapping capabilities that have been integrated in the latest versions of spreadsheet packages such as Lotus 1-2-3 and Microsoft Excel. DSSs are also used in generating environmental impact reports, in hospital patient cost management, and helicopter aircrew decision making.

As communications becomes a more important component of an information system, so does a kind of DSS called *group decision support systems.* A group decision support system (GDSS) enables teams of co-workers to use networks of microcomputers to share information and cooperate on projects. A group decision support system is also called *workgroup computing* and is facilitated by groupware. By sharing ideas, workers can build consensus and arrive at decisions collaboratively. GDSSs are being found in fields ranging from banking and insurance to architectural design and newspaper publishing.

Executive Information Systems

An **executive information system (EIS)** is an easy-to-use DSS made especially for top managers; it specifically supports strategic decision making. *(See Figure 11.9.)* An EIS is also called an *executive support system (ESS)*. It draws on data not only from systems internal to the organization but also from those outside. An EIS might allow senior executives to call up predefined reports from their personal computers, whether desktops or laptops. They might, for instance, call up sales figures in many forms—by region, by week, by fiscal year, by projected increases. The EIS includes capabilities for analyzing data and doing "what if" scenarios. EISs also have the capability to browse through summarized information on all aspects of the organization and then zero in on ("drill down" to) detailed areas the manager believes require attention.

Figure 11.9 Components of an EIS

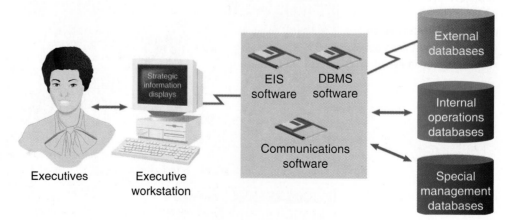

Expert Systems

An **expert system (ES)**, or *knowledge system,* is a set of interactive computer programs that helps users solve problems that would otherwise require the assistance of a human expert. Expert systems are used by both management and nonmanagement personnel to solve specific problems, such as how to reduce production costs, improve workers' productivity, or reduce environmental impact.

Expert systems simulate the reasoning process of human experts in certain well-defined areas. That is, professionals called *knowledge engineers* interview the expert or experts and determine the rules and knowledge that must go into the system. Programs incorporate not only surface knowledge ("textbook knowledge") but also deep knowledge ("tricks of the trade"). What, exactly, is this latter kind of knowledge? "An expert in some activity has by definition reduced the world's complexity by his or her specialization," say some authorities. One result is that "much of the knowledge lies outside direct conscious awareness."[5]

Expert systems exist in many areas. MYCIN helps diagnose infectious diseases. PROSPECTOR assesses geological data to locate mineral deposits. DENDRAL identifies chemical compounds. Home-Safe-Home evaluates the residential environment of an elderly person. Business Insight helps businesses find the best strategies for marketing a product. REBES (Residential Burglary Expert System) helps detectives investigate crime scenes. CARES (Computer Assisted Risk Evaluation System) helps social workers assess families for risk of child abuse. CLUES (Countryside Loan Underwriting System) evaluates home-mortgage-loan applications. Muckraker assists journalists with investigative reporting. Crush takes a body of expert advice and combines it with worksheets reflecting a user's business situation to come up with a customized strategy to beat out competitors. Environmental impact assessment (EIA) uses expert systems to examine how new development will affect the environment. And you can even use a Whale Watcher Expert System via a laptop and the Web to identify whales seen on a whale-watching trip.

Office Automation Systems

Office automation systems (OASs) are those that combine various technologies to reduce the manual labor required in operating an efficient office environment. These technologies include voice mail, e-mail, scheduling software, desktop publishing, word processing, and fax. OASs are used throughout all levels of an organization. The backbone of office automation is a network—perhaps a LAN (p. 7.27), an intranet over a LAN, or an extranet (p. 7.37). All office functions—including dictation, typing, filing, copying, fax, Telex, microfilm and records management, and telephone calls and telephone switchboard operations—are candidates for integration.

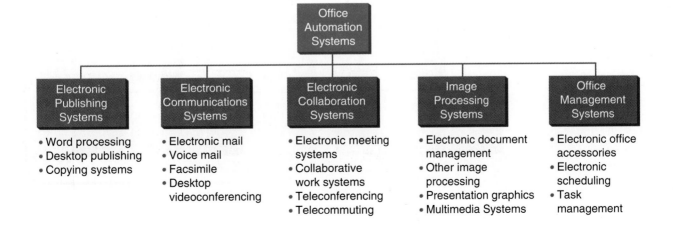

11.4 The Future: Going Sideways

KEY QUESTION What is the major future direction of information management?

As we described in the beginning of this chapter, things are changing rapidly in the business and organizational worlds. Networks and new technologies are flattening the traditional pyramid-shaped hierarchical structure of management levels and sending information of many types in a more lateral (horizontal) manner than was previously the case. *(See Figure 11.10.)*

Says Frances Hesselbein, president and chief executive officer of the Peter F. Drucker Foundation for Nonprofit Management, "I think today most organizations, whether public, private or nonprofit, are really trying to manage well. They're trying to reduce the rigidity of the old hierarchy." Hesselbein thinks organizations retain the old hierarchy of top-down management at their peril. She prefers "circular management," which places the leader in the center of the organizational chart and managers at various points along three concentric circles around that center. That way, she says, "People functions move easily across the organization." It gives all members of the organization the freedom to do their best work.

Figure 11.10 The traditional pyramid-shaped hierarchical structure of management levels is changing.

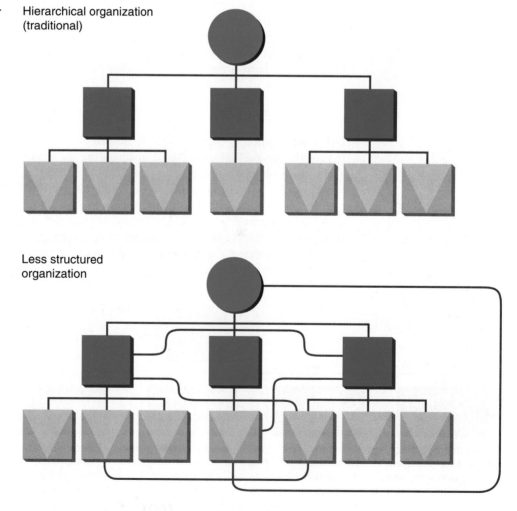

Hierarchical organization (traditional)

Less structured organization

"Almost every company inherited the old hierarchy where rank equaled responsibility, and it doesn't work in today's world," Hesselbein says. Instead people are trying to use new technologies to allow more fluid structures that release people to be more creative and productive. "When you have an energetic, highly motivated workforce, performance and morale just soar. You don't get magnificent performance from dispirited workers who feel they are not appreciated."

Web Sites of Possible Interest

Trends in business technology:
http://www.upside.com
www.techreview.com

Organizational charts:
web.miep.org/bus_plan/organ_chart.html

Office automation:
http://www.banking.com
http://www.dbcams.com

Transaction processing:
http://www.hursley.ibm.com/cics

DSS:
power.cba.uni.edu/isworld/dsshistory.html
http://www.uky.edu/BusinessEconomics/dssakba/periodcl.html

Expert systems:
http://www.ghgcorp.com/clips/ExpertSystems.html
http://www.exsys.com/info/whatisit.html

Sergeant Scott Decker tests high-tech equipment that the U.S. Army hopes to have in the field soon. It's easy to identify fellow soldiers via a helmet-mounted microphone and an earphone connected to a radio system. The lightweight computer in Decker's backpack features a GPS device that feeds data into the eyepice display over his right eye, showing his precise location. His rifle includes a digital compass and a digital video camera that can send images back to base.

Health

Viktor Yazykov, competing in the perilous Around Alone sailing competition, in which solo sailors race each other around the world, found himself in the stormy South Atlantic with a seriously infected arm that needed emergency surgery. So, with the help of step-by-step e-mail instructions sent from Boston-based Dr. Daniel Carlin to his solar-powered laptop computer, Yazykov operated on his own arm.[a]

Here we have a dramatic example of *telemedicine*—medical care delivered via telecommunications—one of the more exciting changes the computer is bringing to health care. For some time, physicians in rural areas lacking local access to radiologists have used "teleradiology" to exchange digital images such as X-rays via telephone-linked networks with expert physicians in metropolitan areas. Now telemedicine is moving to another level, using digital cameras and sound that, in effect, moves patients to doctors rather than the reverse. Already telemedicine is being embraced by administrators in the American prison system, where by law inmates are guaranteed medical treatment—and where the increase in prisoners of 8% every year has led to the need to control health costs.[b]

But it is not just physicians who are going online. So are patients and health consumers, who in growing numbers are seeking medical advice on the Internet—by tapping into health-care databases, e-mailing health professionals, or communicating with people with similar conditions in online chat rooms. For instance, hours after 10-year-old Robert Lord of San Diego fractured his spine in a fall from a tree, his father found an experimental drug on the Internet that saved the boy from lifetime paralysis.[c] Often patients arrive in the offices of health-care professionals already steeped in information about their conditions. "It's a fundamental shift of knowledge, and therefore power, from physicians to patients," says one consultant.[d] In addition, health-care consumers are able to share experiences and information with each other. Inquisitive moms-to-be, for example, can find a gathering spot at the Pregnancy Today Web site.[e]

The tools of medicine are also being radically changed. "All medical information—X-ray or lab test or blood pressure or pulse monitor—can now be digitized," says surgeon Rick Satava. "It can all be brought to the physician or surgeon in digital format."[f] Some digital breakthroughs are producing results that would have been science fiction only 10 years ago. Software is available that can compute a woman's breast cancer risk.[g] Mental-health researchers are using computers to screen troubled teen-agers in need of psychotherapy.[h] Online psychotherapy can provide short-term relief.[i] Epidemiologists are using the Web to improve public health in developing nations.[j] MIT has developed a "micropill," a pharmacy on a chip that can be implanted in the body to deliver tiny amounts of medicine on a controlled-release basis.[k] And a patient paralyzed by a stroke has received an implant that allows communication between his brain and a computer, enabling him to use his brainpower to move a cursor across a screen and convey simple messages—a la "Star Trek."[l]

The 10 most-sought-after health condition topics on the Web are depression, allergies or sinus, cancer, bipolar disorder, arthritis/rheumatism, high blood pressure/hypertension, migraine, anxiety disorder, heart disease, and sleep disorders.[m] Some health Web sites are Healthfinder (*www.healthfinder.gov*), Medscape (*www.medscape.com*), Medical World Search (*www.mwsearch.com*), and Mental Health Net (*www.cmhc.com*).

Journalism

The September 1998 report by independent prosecutor Kenneth Starr, which contained details of President Clinton's sex life, arrived at the U.S. Congress in several van loads of cartons. But perhaps the most important part of the delivery was the single 3½-inch floppy disk also carrying the report, which within hours was uploaded onto the World Wide Web.

"With dizzying speed, it turned into an information wildfire that sent the Starr report almost instantaneously onto millions of computer and TV screens," says one account. "And as it raced around the world, the Starr report made communications history just as dramatically as it was making political history."[a]

Old-media competitors to the Internet have found themselves in a changed game. "With tools proliferating on the Net that allow users to pick and choose sports scores, stock quotes, and stories of interest," says an article in the old-media *New York Times,* "the individual has greater control over news consumption—and particularly over the time when the consumption actually takes place."[b] Indeed, homes with Internet and online access are watching 15% less television than other homes.[c] A study found that 43% of people online said they watch less TV.[d]

To put this in perspective, however, it needs to be pointed out that only 27% of American homes boast an online connection, whereas TV sets are found in nearly every home. Before the Web can truly become a mass medium, suggests *Wall Street Journal* technology commentator Walter Mossberg, there will need to be more bandwidth to the home to provide faster connections, cheaper access, com-

pelling content, and perhaps a star performer who can popularize the Net. And the Web will have to be available through an "information appliance" or some other box that is less complex than the standard PC.[e]

Nevertheless, the Web is clearly already having an impact on journalism. Cyberspace is redefining the meaning of "scoops," as reporters find themselves following reports posted first on Web sites.[f] During the 1999 conflict in Kosovo, almost anyone with a phone line and a PC could become a "war correspondent." Ethnic Albanians, Macedonians, and Serbs sent their stories out into cyberspace.[g] For instance, 16-year-old Finnegan Hamill of Berkeley, California, received e-mail messages from an ethnic Albanian girl, which he in turn broadcast over Berkeley Youth Radio, available as audio files on a Web site.[h] As the Internet becomes more of an advertising medium, draining ads from other media, it also threatens the financial underpinnings to newspapers and magazines, which are supported more by advertising than by sales to readers.[i]

Of course, newspapers and TV news channels are fighting back. Most have already joined the Net fray and are offering Web news sites.[j]

Many newspapers and TV channels have their own Web sites, but some sites of general interest are the following: *American Journalism Review*'s Newslink (*ajr.newslink. org/searchn.html,* which lists 4,925 newspapers online), Newsdirectory. (*www.Newsdirectory.com,* which lists 7,500 newspapers and magazines with English-language content), and NewsWatch (*www.newswatch.org,* which offers media criticism).

WHAT IT IS
WHAT IT DOES

WHY IT IS IMPORTANT

decision support system (DSS) (KQ 11.3, p. 11.15)   An interactive, computer-based information system (integrated hardware and software) that provides a flexible tool for analysis and helps managers focus on the future.

To reach the DSS level of sophistication in information technology, an organization must have established a transaction processing system and a management information system.

executive information system (EIS) (KQ 11.3, p. 11.18)   Also called an *executive support system (ESS);* an easy-to-use DSS made especially for top managers; it specifically supports strategic decision making.

An EIS draws on data internal and external to the organization. It allows senior executives to call up predefined reports from their personal computers, such as sales figures by region, by week, by fiscal year, and by projected increases. The EIS includes capabilities for analyzing data and doing "what if" scenarios. With an EIS a manager can browse through information on all aspects of the organization and then zero in on areas requiring attention.

expert system (ES) (KQ 11.3, p. 11.19)   Also called a *knowledge system;* a set of interactive computer programs that helps users solve problems that would otherwise require the assistance of a human expert.

Expert systems are used by both management and nonmanagement personnel to solve specific problems, such as how to reduce production costs, improve workers' productivity, or reduce environmental impact.

management information system (MIS) (KQ 11.3, p. 11.14)   Computer-based information system that uses data recorded by TPSs as input into programs that produce routine reports as output.

An MIS principally assists middle managers, helping them make *tactical* decisions—spotting trends and getting an overview of current business activities.

office automation systems (OASs) (KQ 11.3, p. 11.19)   Systems that combine various technologies to reduce the manual labor required in operating an efficient office environment. These technologies include voice mail, e-mail, scheduling software, desktop publishing, word processing, and fax.

OASs are used throughout all levels of an organization.

semistructured information (KQ 11.2, p. 11.11)   Information that does not necessarily result from clearly defined, routine procedures. Middle managers need semistructured information that is detailed but more summarized than information for operating managers.

Semistructured information involves review, summarization, and analysis of data to help plan and control operations and implement policy formulated by upper managers.

★ TQM

structured information (KQ 11.2, p. 11.11)   Detailed, current information concerned with past events; it records a narrow range of facts and covers an organization's internal activities.

transaction (KQ 11.3, p. 11.12)   A recorded event having to do with routine business activities. This includes everything concerning the product or service in which the organization is engaged: production, distribution, sales, orders. It also includes materials purchased, employees hired, taxes paid, and so on.

transaction processing system (TPS) (KQ 11.3, p. 11.12)   Computer-based information system that keeps track of the transactions needed to conduct business. Inputs are transaction data (for example, bills, orders, inventory levels, production output). Outputs are processed transactions (for example, bills, paychecks). Each functional area of an organization—research and development, production, marketing, accounting and finance, and human resources—usually has its own TPS.

unstructured information (KQ 11.2, p. 11.11) Summarized, less current information concerned with future events; it records a broad range of facts and covers activities outside as well as inside an organization.

Lower-level managers need easily defined information that relates to the current status and activities within the basic business functions.

Today in most organizations, the bulk of such transactions are recorded in a computer-based information system. These systems tend to have clearly defined inputs and outputs, and there is an emphasis on efficiency and accuracy. TPSs record data but do little in the way of converting data into information.

The TPS helps supervisory managers in making *operational decisions.* The database of transactions stored in a TPS is used to support a management information system and a decision support system.

Top managers need information in the form of highly unstructured reports. The information should cover large time periods and survey activities.

1. Fill in the following blanks:

   a. Middle managers make _____ decisions.

   b. A(n) _____ _____ system is one that combines various technologies to reduce the manual labor required in operating an efficient office environment.

   c. _____ refers to the transition from mainframe-based computer systems to linking smaller computers in networks.

   d. Information has three properties that vary in importance depending on the decision and the decision maker. They are: (a) _____ , (b) _____ , and (c) _____ .

   e. A report that shows out-of-the-ordinary data is a(n) _____ report.

2. Label each of the following statements as either true or false.

   a. _____ A transaction processing system supports day-to-day business activities.

   b. _____ A management information system is a computer-based information system.

   c. _____ Decision support systems are used mainly by upper management.

   d. _____ The lowest level of management is strategic management.

   e. _____ Lower management deals with unstructured decisions.

IN YOUR OWN WORDS

1. Answer each of the Key Questions that appear at the beginning of this chapter.

2. Define each of the following:
   a. transaction processing system
   b. management information system
   c. decision support system
   d. executive information system

3. Respond to each of the following:
   a. What five departments exist in most companies?
   b. What is the difference between structured information and semistructured information, and which type of information is easier to manage using computers?
   c. What are the main components of a decision support system?

4. In your career, what can you imagine using an expert system for?

KNOWLEDGE IN ACTION

1. **Reengineering the Workplace.** In this chapter we describe six trends affecting the reengineering of the workplace. Profile an organization that has been forced to

reengineer some of its processes. Where did you find information about this organization? To date, what processes have been reengineered? Why? What additional processes, if any, does the organization plan to reengineer in the future? Which ones? Why? Do you think this organization will be more successful as a result of these reengineering efforts?

2. **Making a Decision.** Suppose you are the owner of a bakery in a medium-sized city. You have three full-time employees and two part-time employees. Customers choose from a variety of baked goods, a selection of gourmet coffees, and have the option of sitting at one of ten tables. The bakery is busiest in the morning hours.

   Because of the growing popularity of your restaurant, you are considering opening a second bakery in town. You would also like to add additional tables to the current bakery, but this would require some remodeling of the existing space. Unfortunately, for now, it is only feasible for you to pursue one of these efforts. What should you do? Open a second bakery or expand the existing one? What information will you need in order to make the best decision? What is your decision?

3. **Assessing Decision Support Systems.** Decision support systems often take years to develop. Given this long development period, some experts argue that the system will be obsolete by the time it is complete and that information needs will have changed. Other experts argue that no alternatives exist. By reviewing current computer publications that describe management information systems or performing research on the Internet, formulate an opinion about this issue.

4. **Obtaining Information about your School's Information Systems Department.** Does your university/college have an information systems department that is responsible for developing and supporting all the university information systems? If so, interview a management staff member about the services and functions of the department. Can this person identify the various levels of management within the department? What kinds of user input were requested when the department was being set up? Does it use any sophisticated decision support software? What kinds of services does the department offer to students?

Answers to Self-Test Exercises: 1a. tactical 1b. office automation 1c. downsizing 1d. level of summarization, degree of accuracy, timeliness 1e. exception 2. T, T, T, F, F

CHAPTER 12

FILES AND DATABASES

Organizing and Maintaining Digital Data

KEY QUESTIONS

You should be able to answer the following questions:

12.1 All Databases Great and Small *What is a database? a database administrator?*

12.2 The Data Storage Hierarchy and the Key Field *What are the parts of the data hierarchy, and what is the key field?*

12.3 File Handling: Basic Concepts *What are the characteristics of the various types of file handling and storage?*

12.4 File Management Systems *What is a file management system and what are its disadvantages?*

12.5 Database Management Systems *What advantages do database management systems have over file management systems?*

12.6 Types of Database Organization *What are the characteristics of the main database models?*

12.7 Features of a DBMS *What are the main features of a DBMS?*

12.8 New Approaches: Mining, Warehouses, and "Siftware" *What is a data warehouse?*

12.9 The Ethics of Using Databases: Concerns About Accuracy and Privacy *In what ways can database users invade people's privacy?*

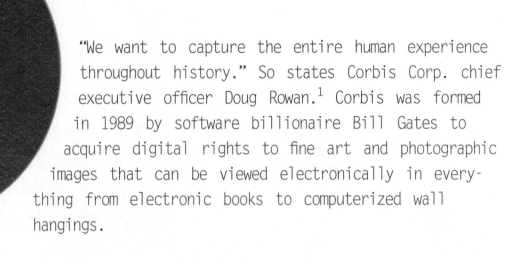

"We want to capture the entire human experience throughout history." So states Corbis Corp. chief executive officer Doug Rowan.[1] Corbis was formed in 1989 by software billionaire Bill Gates to acquire digital rights to fine art and photographic images that can be viewed electronically in everything from electronic books to computerized wall hangings.

In 1995 Corbis acquired the Bettmann Archive of 17 million photographs for scanning into its digital database. Its founder, Dr. Otto Bettmann, called his famous collection a "visual story of the world," and indeed many of the images are unique. They include tintypes of African-American soldiers in the Civil War, the 1937 crash of the *Hindenburg* dirigible, and John F. Kennedy, Jr. saluting the casket of his assassinated father in 1963.

However, when Rowan says Corbis wants to capture all of human experience, he means not just photos and art works from the likes of the National Gallery in London and the State Hermitage Museum in St. Petersburg, Russia, for which Corbis also owns digital imaging rights. "Film, video, audio," he says. "We are interested in those fields too."[2]

Are there any ethical problems with one company having in its database the exclusive digital rights to our visual and audio history? Like many museums and libraries (such as the Library of Congress), Corbis is democratizing art and scholarship by converting images and texts into digital form and making them available to people who could never travel to, say, London or St. Petersburg.

However, Bill Gates's acquisition of the Bettmann images, for example, put their future use "into the hands of an aggressive businessman who, unlike Dr. Bettmann, is planning his own publishing ventures," points out one reporter. "While Mr. Gates's initial plans will make Bettmann images more widely accessible, this savvy competitor now ultimately controls who can use them—and who can't."[3] Adds Paul Saffo, of the nonprofit Institute for the Future, "The cultural issue raised by the Bettmann purchase is whether we're seeing history sold to the highest bidder or we'll eventually see history made more accessible to the public as a result."[4] Curators of art museums and families of famous persons are afraid that the rights to art works will slip away for less than they are worth or that the images will be pirated or used in silly ways in advertising. (For example, one of Fred Astaire's children sent an angry letter to several publications after a well-known film clip of his dancing father was used in a vacuum cleaner ad on TV.)

All forms of information technology are affecting our social and business institutions in significant ways. However, as the Corbis example suggests, the arrival of databases promises to stand some of them on their heads.

12.1 All Databases Great & Small

KEY QUESTION What is a database? a database administrator?

Databases are collections of related files, which, as we shall see, makes them useful in ways that traditional filing systems (even computerized ones) are not. A database may be small, contained entirely within your own personal computer. Or it may be massive, like those of Corbis, available online through computer and telephone connections. *(See Figure 12.1.)* Such online databases are of special interest to us in this book because they offer phenomenal resources that until recently were unavailable to most ordinary computer users.

Microcomputer users can set up their personal databases using popular database management software like that we discussed earlier (✔ p. 6.16). Examples are Paradox, FileMaker Pro, Access, FoxPro, and dBASE. Such programs are used, for example, by graduate students to conduct research, by salespeople to keep track of clients, by purchasing agents to monitor orders, and by coaches to keep watch on other teams and players.

Some databases are so large that they cannot possibly be stored in a microcomputer. Some of these can be accessed by going online through a microcomputer or other computer. Such databases, sometimes called *information utilities,* represent enormous compilations of data, any part of which is available, for a fee, to the public.

Examples of well-known information utilities—more commonly known as *online services* (✔ p. 8.4)—are America Online, CompuServe, and Prodigy. As we described in Chapter 8, these offer access to news, weather, travel information, home shopping services, reference works, and a great deal more. Some public-access databases are specialized; for example, Lexis allows lawyers to search local, state, and federal laws.

Other public-access databases are online archives. For instance, "virtual art museums" have been created by institutions such as the Smithsonian's National Museum of American Art, which has put images from its collections online since 1993, and the National Gallery of Art in Washington, D.C. The Library of Congress also is involved in an ambitious plan to digitize some of its 104 million items—books, manuscripts, drawings, photographs—for access online.

Other types of databases are private collections of records shared or distributed throughout a company or other organization. Generally, the records are available only to employees or selected individuals and not to outsiders.

Figure 12.1 Examples of small (personal), medium-size, and large databases

Type	Example	Typical number of users	Typical size of database
Personal	Mary Richards House Painting	1	< 10 MB
Medium-size (workgroup)	Seaview Yacht Sales	25 or less	< 100 MB
Large organizational	Automobile Licensing and Registration	100s	> 1 trillion bytes

Figure 12.2 Building a library database. Father Patrick Creeden enters data into a computer at the Monastery of the Holy Cross in Chicago.

"CHICAGO–Father Thomas Baxter stands in his habit, holding a computer printout. Later today, he'll review the Scriptures in his cell here at the Monastery of the Holy Cross of Jerusalem, but this morning he's carefully proofreading a library's computerized records.

He and two other monks in this community of five are modern-day scribes, using computers to participate in an age-old monastic tradition: preserving knowledge. In this case, they're helping university and public libraries transform drawers of catalogue cards into electronic databases.

Father Baxter is pointing at a line of text highlighted in yellow, indicating a discrepancy between two data fields. One of his jobs as prior, or leader, of the monastery is to look for typographical errors, call them to the attention of the brother responsible for them, and remind him to concentrate more closely on his work.

This monastery is part of an effort to bring religious communities back into the information business. A company calling itself The Electronic Scriptorium—referring to the room where monks would use quills and ink to copy intricate manuscripts long ago—is matching up monastic communities with libraries and others in need of complex data-entry work. The partnerships benefit the monasteries and convents, which need flexible jobs to support themselves, and the libraries, which need their records entered accurately. "

–Jeffrey R. Young, "Modern-Day-Monastery, " *Chronicle of Higher Education*

For example, many university libraries have been transforming drawers of catalog cards into electronic databases for use by their students and faculty. Libraries at Yale, Johns Hopkins, and other universities have contracted with a Virginia company called The Electronic Scriptorium, which employs monks and nuns at six monasteries to convert card catalogs to an electronic system. *(See Figure 12.2.)*

A private database may be *shared* or *distributed*. A **shared database** is shared by users of one company or organization in one location. Shared databases can be found in local area networks ( p. 7.27). The company owns the database, which is often stored on a minicomputer or mainframe. Users are linked to the database through terminals or microcomputer workstations.

A **distributed database** is one that is stored on different computers in different locations connected by a client-server network ( p. 7.27). For example, sales figures for a chain of discount stores might be located in computers at the various stores, but they would also be available to executives in regional offices or at corporate headquarters. An employee using the database would not know where the data is coming from. However, all employees still use the same commands to access and use the database.

One thing that large databases have in common is that they must be professionally managed. This is done by database managers.

The Database Administrator

Technically, a single user's personal database must also be managed. Often personal database administration is informal. For example, each individual follows simple procedures for backing up his or her database and keeping minimal records for documentation. However, the information in a large database—such as a corporation's patents, formulas, advertising strategies, and sales information—is the organization's lifeblood and much more difficult to manage. Accordingly, professional *database administrators (DBAs)*, are employed to coordinate all activities related to an organization's database. Their responsibilities include:

■ *Database design, implementation, and operation:* At the beginning, the DBA helps determine the design of the database. Later he or she determines how space will be used on secondary storage devices, how files and records may be added and deleted, and how changes are documented. (Note that a change in the database structure may cause an error that is not revealed for months, and, without proper documentation of the change, diagnosing the problem may be next to impossible. Today, CASE (computer-aided systems engineering) tools (✔ p. 9.19) can be used to document database design.)

■ *Coordination with users:* The DBA determines user access privileges; sets standards, guidelines, and control procedures; assists in establishing priorities for requests; and adjudicates conflicting user needs.

■ *System security:* The DBA sets up and monitors a system for preventing unauthorized access to the database.

■ *Backup and recovery:* Because loss of data or a crash in the database could vitally affect the organization, the DBA needs to make sure the system is regularly backed up. He or she also needs to develop plans for recovering data or operations should a failure occur.

■ *Performance monitoring:* The database administrator compiles and analyzes statistics concerning the database's performance and identifies problem areas. The DBA monitors the system to make sure it is serving users appropriately. A standard complaint is that the system is too slow, usually because too many users are trying to access it.

For example, on a particular Super Bowl Sunday, the National Football League's Web site scored 6 million "hits"—a measure of the number of transmissions of text, video, graphics, or audio files. Expecting heavy traffic, managers of the site had used five servers, but network problems still affected visitors, and many reported long waits or just being turned away.[5] Although the Super Bowl is a once-a-year event, it will be the job of the database manager in charge of the site to make sure things run more smoothly next time.

A satellite news service transmits real-time weather reports and local farm prices to about 110,000 U.S. subscribers. Farmer Dave Mennenga of Urbana, Illinois, receives information on a dedicated Data Transmission Network (DTN) terminal.

12.2 The Data Storage Hierarchy & the Key Field

KEY QUESTION **What are the parts of the data hierarchy, and what is the key field?**

How does a database actually work? To understand this, first we need to consider how stored data is structured—the *data storage hierarchy* and the concept of the *key field.* We then need to discuss *file management systems,* and finally *database management systems.*

The Data Storage Hierarchy

Data can be grouped into a hierarchy of categories, each increasingly complex. The **data storage hierarchy** consists of the levels of data stored in a computer file: bits, bytes (characters), fields, records, files, and databases. *(See Figure 12.3.)*

   Computers, we have said, are based on the principle that electricity may be "on" or "off," or "high-voltage" or "low-voltage," or "present" or "absent," or organized in some similar two-state system. Thus, individual items of data are represented by 0 for off and 1 for on. A 0 or 1 is called a *bit.* A unit of 8 bits is called a *byte;* it may be used to represent a character, digit, or other value, such as A, ?, or 3. Bits and bytes are the building blocks for representing data, whether it is being processed, stored, or telecommunicated. While the computer hardware deals with bits and bytes, most users need not be concerned with them. They will, however, be dealing with characters, fields, records, files, and databases.

- *Character:* Whereas a byte is a unit of measure, a **character** is a singleton set of data such as a single letter, number, or special character such as ; or $ or %. In computers, a character is usually—but not necessarily—represented with a number of bits that equals one byte.

- *Field:* A **field** is a unit of data consisting of one or more characters. An individual field typically contains a fact about a person, place, thing, or event. An example of a field is your name, date of birth, or Social Security number.
   Note: One reason the Social Security number is often used in computing—for good or for ill—is that, perhaps unlike your name, it is a *distinctive* (unique) field. Thus, it can be used to easily locate information about you. Such a field is called a *key field.* More on this below.

- *Record:* A **record** is a collection of related fields. An example of a record would be your name *and* date of birth *and* Social Security number.

- *File:* A **file** is a collection of related records. An example of a file is collected data on everyone employed in the same department of a company, including all names, addresses, and Social Security numbers.

- *Database:* A **database** is a collection of interrelated files. A company database might include files on all past and current employees in all departments. There would be various files for each employee: payroll, retirement benefits, sales quotas and achievements (if in sales), and so on.

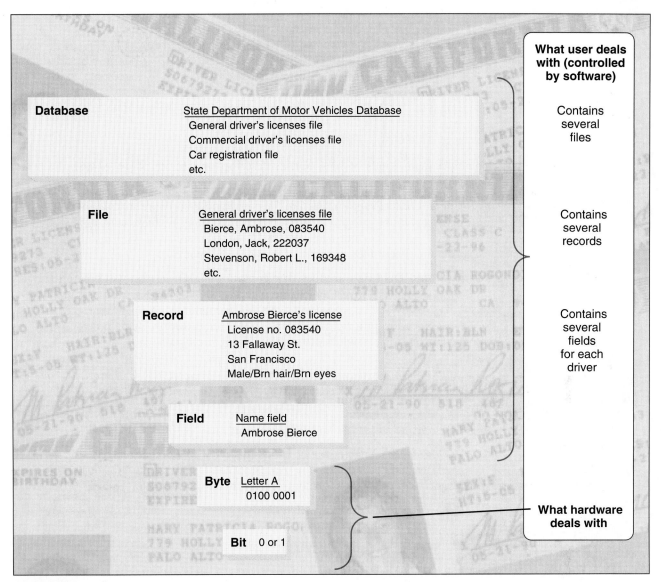

What user deals with (controlled by software)

Contains several files

Contains several records

Contains several fields for each driver

What hardware deals with

Database   State Department of Motor Vehicles Database
General driver's licenses file
Commercial driver's licenses file
Car registration file
etc.

File   General driver's licenses file
Bierce, Ambrose, 083540
London, Jack, 222037
Stevenson, Robert L., 169348
etc.

Record   Ambrose Bierce's license
License no. 083540
13 Fallaway St.
San Francisco
Male/Brn hair/Brn eyes

Field   Name field
Ambrose Bierce

Byte   Letter A
0100 0001

Bit   0 or 1

Figure 12.3 Data storage hierarchy: How data is organized. Bits are organized into bytes, bytes into fields, fields into records, records into files. Related files may be organized into a database.

The Key Field

An important concept in data organization is that of the *key field*. A **key field** contains unique data used to identify a record so that it can be easily retrieved and processed and not be confused with another record. The key field is also used for sorting database records into an alternate order. The key field is often an automatically generated identification number, Social Security number, customer account number, or the like. Because the primary characteristic of the key field is that it must be *unique,* the use of numbers rather than names as key fields is clearly preferable, otherwise, the records of people with common names like James Johnson, Susan Williams, Ann Wong, or Roberto Sanchez might be confused.

12.3 File Handling: Basic Concepts

KEY QUESTION **What are the characteristics of the various types of file handling and storage?**

Types of Files: Program and Data Files

There are many kinds of files, but, as described in Chapter 4 (✔ p. 4.6), the principal division is between program files and data files.

■ *Program files:* **Program files** are files containing software instructions. In a word processing program, for example, there may be files (with names such as SETUP.EXE) that perform specific functions associated with installing the program. These files are part of the software package.

■ *Data files:* **Data files** are files that contain data. Often you will create these files yourself and give them names such as DOCUMENT-1 or Psychology-Rpt. We advise that you don't type in a filename extension when naming files; the application program will then automatically supply its own extension. Such extensions provide information about the file's type.

Two Types of Data Files: Master and Transaction

Among the several types of data files two are commonly used to update data in large systems: a master file and a transaction file.

■ *Master file:* The **master file** contains relatively permanent records that are generally updated periodically. An example of a master file would be the address-label file for all students currently enrolled at your college.

■ *Transaction file:* The **transaction file** is a temporary holding file that holds all changes to be made to the master file: additions, deletions, revisions. For example, in the case of the address labels for your college, a transaction file would hold new names and addresses to be added (because over time new students enroll) and names and addresses to be deleted (because students leave). It would also hold revised names and addresses (because students change their names or move). Each month or so, the master file would be *updated* with the changes called for in the transaction file.

The New World Department Store in Shanghai, China, saves space by letting shoppers try on clothes right on the sales floor. After their video image is captured on screen, customers can see themselves in any outfit in any color, at the click of a mouse.

Batch Versus Online Processing

Data may be taken from secondary storage (✔ p. 4.2) and processed in either of two ways: (1) "later," via *batch processing,* or (2) "right now," via *online (real-time) processing.*

■ *Batch processing:* In **batch processing,** data is collected over several days or weeks and then processed all at once, as a "batch," to update a master file. Thus, if users need to make some request of the system, they must wait until the batch has been processed. Batch processing is less expensive than real-time processing and is suitable for work in which immediate answers to queries are not needed.

For example, banks use batch processing to balance checking accounts. When you deposit a check in the morning, the bank will make a record of it. However, it will not compute your account balance until the end of the day, after all checks have been processed in a batch.

■ *Online processing:* **Online processing,** also called *real-time processing,* means entering transactions into a computer system as they take place and updating the master files immediately, as the transactions occur. For example, when you withdraw cash from an automated teller machine, the system automatically computes your account balance then and there. Airline reservation systems also use online processing.

Offline Versus Online Storage

Whether it's on magnetic tape or on some form of disk, data may be stored either offline or online.

■ **Offline storage** means that data is not directly accessible for processing until the tape or disk has been loaded onto an input device. That is, the storage is not under the direct control of the central processing unit.

■ **Online storage** means that stored data is directly accessible for processing. That is, storage is under the direct control of the central processing unit. You need not wait for a tape or disk to be loaded onto an input device.

For processing to be online, the storage must be online and fast. Generally, this means storage on disk rather than magnetic tape. With tape, it is not possible to go instantly to the record on the tape you are looking for (✔ p. 4.8); instead, the read/write head has to search through all the records that precede it, which takes time. With disk storage, however, the system can go directly and quickly to the record—just as a CD player can go directly to a particular spot on a music CD.

File Organization: Three Methods

To quickly review some material from Chapter 4, tape storage falls in the category of sequential access storage. *Sequential access storage* means that information is stored in sequence, such as alphabetically. Thus, you would have to search a tape past all the information from A to J, say, before you got to K. This process may require running several inches or feet off a reel of tape, which, as we've said, takes time.

Disk storage, by contrast, generally falls into the category of direct access storage (although data *can* be stored sequentially). *Direct access storage* means that the system can go directly to the required information. Because you can directly access information, retrieving data is much faster with magnetic or optical disk than it is with magnetic tape.

In Hollywood, California, Scot Burklin helps oversee the dinosaur park ride at Universal Studios. Paleontologists, robotics engineers, animation experts, and $100 million helped Universal translate the illusion of the movies into a realistic 5½-minute ride.

From these two fundamental forms, computer scientists have devised three methods of organizing files for secondary storage: *sequential, direct,* and *indexed-sequential.*

■ *Sequential file organization:* Sequential file organization stores records in sequence, one after the other. Records can be retrieved only in the sequence in which they were stored. This is the only method that can be used with magnetic tape; it can also be used with disk.

For example, if you are looking for employee record 8888, the computer will have to start with record 0001, then go past 0002, 0003, and so on, until it finally comes to record 8888.

Sequential file organization is useful, for example, when a large portion of the records needs to be accessed, as when a mail-order house is sending out catalogs to all names on a mailing list. The method also is less expensive than other methods because magnetic tape is cheaper than magnetic or optical disk.

The disadvantage of sequential file organization is that records must be ordered in a particular way and so searching for data is slow.

■ *Direct file organization:* Instead of storing records in sequence, direct file organization, or *random file organization,* stores records in no particular sequence. A record is retrieved according to its key field, or unique element of data. This method of file organization is used with disk storage. It is ideal for applications such as airline reservations systems and computerized directory-assistance operations. In these cases, records need to be retrieved only one at a time, and there is no fixed pattern to the requests for records.

A mathematical formula, called a *hashing algorithm,* is used to produce a unique number that will identify the record's physical location on the disk. (For example, one hashing algorithm divides the record's key field number by the prime number closest to that of the total number of records stored.)

Direct file organization is much faster than sequential file organization for finding a specific record. However, because the method requires hard-disk or optical-disk storage, it is more expensive than magnetic tape. Moreover, it is not as efficient as sequential file organization for listing large numbers of records.

■ *Indexed-sequential file organization:* A compromise has been developed between the two preceding methods. Indexed-sequential file organization, or simply *indexed file organization,* stores records in sequential order. However, the file in which the records are stored contains an index that lists each record by its key field and identifies its physical location on the disk. The method requires magnetic or optical disk.

For example, a company could index certain ranges of employee identification numbers—0000 to 1000, 1001 to 2000, and so on. For the computer to find the record with the key field 8888, it would go first to the index, which would give the location of the range in which the key field appears (for example, 8001 to 9000). The computer would then search sequentially (from 8001) to find the key field 8888.

This method is slower than direct file organization because of the need to do an index search. The indexed-sequential method is best when large batches of transactions must be occasionally updated, yet users want frequent, rapid access to records. For example, bank customers and tellers want to have up-to-the-minute information about checking accounts, but every month the bank must update bank statements to send to customers.

An illustration of the three file organization methods was shown in Figure 4.1, page 4.4.

12.4 File Management Systems

KEY QUESTION   **What is a file management system and what are its disadvantages?**

In the 1950s, when commercial use of computers was just beginning, magnetic tape was the storage medium and records and files were stored sequentially. In order to work with these files, a user needed a file management system. A **file management system,** or *file manager,* is software for creating, retrieving, and manipulating files, one file at a time. Traditionally, a large organization such as a university would have different files for different purposes. For you as a student, for example, there might be one file for course grades, another for student records, and a third for tuition billing. Each file would be used independently to produce its own separate reports. *(See Figure 12.4.)* If you changed your address, someone had to make the change separately in each file.

Disadvantages of File Management Systems

File management systems worked well enough for the time, but they had several disadvantages:

Figure 12.4 File management system. In the traditional file management system, some of the same data elements, such as addresses, were repeated in different files. Information was not shared among files.

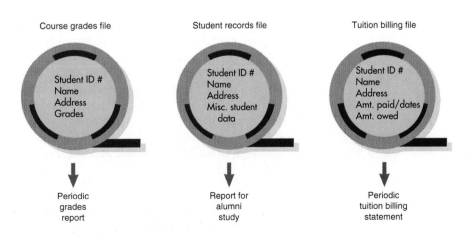

Course grades file
Student ID #
Name
Address
Grades

Student records file
Student ID #
Name
Address
Misc. student data

Tuition billing file
Student ID #
Name
Address
Amt. paid/dates
Amt. owed

Periodic grades report

Report for alumni study

Periodic tuition billing statement

■ *Data redundancy: Data redundancy* means that the same data fields appear in many different files and often in different formats. Thus, separate files tend to repeat some of the same data over and over. A student's course grades file and tuition billing file would both contain similar data (name, address, telephone number). When data fields are repeated in different files, they waste storage space and create headaches if a field that is common to all files must be updated.

■ *Lack of data integrity: Data integrity* means that data is accurate, consistent, and up to date. However, when the same data fields (a student's address and phone number, for example) must be changed in different files, some files may be missed or mistakes will be made. The result is that some reports will be produced with erroneous information.

■ *Lack of program independence:* With file management systems, different files were often written by different programmers using different file formats. Thus, the files were not *program independent.* This meant more time was required to maintain files. It also prevented a programmer from writing a single program that would access all the data in multiple files.

As computers grew more and more important in daily life, the frustrations of working with separate, redundant files lacking data integrity and program independence became overwhelming. Fortunately, magnetic disks and then optical disks began to supplant magnetic tape as the most popular medium of secondary storage, leading to new possibilities for managing data, which we discuss next.

12.5 Database Management Systems

KEY QUESTION What advantages do database management systems have over file management systems?

As disk replaced magnetic tape, direct access storage began to replace sequential access storage. The result was a new technology and new software: the database management system.

As mentioned, a *database* is a collection of many related files. More specifically, the files are usually *integrated,* meaning that the file records are logically related, or cross-referenced, to one another. Thus, even though all data elements on a topic are kept in records in different files, they can easily be organized and retrieved with simple requests.

The software for manipulating databases is a **database management system (DBMS),** or a *database manager,* a program that controls the structure of a database and access to the data. With a DBMS, then, a large organization such as a university might still have different files for different purposes. If you were a student, your files might be the same in a file management system (one for course grades, another for student records, and a third for tuition billing). However, in the database management system, data elements would be integrated (cross-referenced) and shared among different files. *(See Figure 12.5.)* Thus, if your address were to change, the address change would automatically be reflected in all the different files.

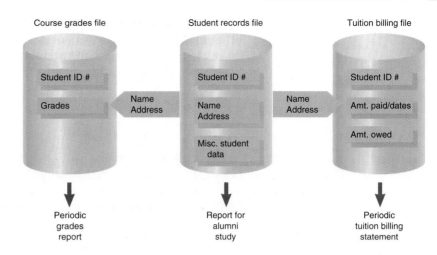

Figure 12.5 File management system. In the traditional file management system, some of the same data elements, such as addresses, were repeated in different files. Information was not shared among files.

Advantages and Disadvantages of a DBMS

The advantages of databases and DBMSs are as follows:

- *Reduced data redundancy:* In a file management system, some of the same data fields are repeated in different files; in a database, by contrast, the information appears just once. The single biggest advantage of a database is that the same information is available to different users. Moreover, reduced redundancy lowers the expense of storage media and hardware because the data is more concise.

- *Improved data integrity:* Reduced redundancy increases the chances of data integrity—data that is accurate, consistent, and up to date—because each updating change is made in only one place.

- *More program independence:* With a database management system, the program and the file formats are the same, so that one programmer or even several programmers can spend less time maintaining files.

- *Increased user productivity:* Database management systems are fairly easy to use, so that users can get their requests for information answered without having to resort to technical manipulations. In addition, users don't have to wait for a computer professional to provide what they need.

- *Increased security:* Although various departments may share data in common, access to specific information can be limited to selected users. Thus, through the use of passwords, a student's financial, medical, and grade information in a university database is made available only to those who have a legitimate need to know.

Although there are clear advantages to having databases, there are still some disadvantages:

- *Cost issues:* Installing and maintaining a database is expensive, particularly in a large organization. In addition, there are costs associated with training people to use it correctly.

- *Data vulnerability issues:* Although databases can be structured to restrict access, it's always possible unauthorized users will get past the safeguards. And when they do, they may have access to *all* the files, not just a few. In addition, if a database were destroyed by fire, earthquake, theft, or a hardware or software problem, it could be fatal to an organization's business activities—unless steps had been taken to regularly make backup copies of the files and store them elsewhere.

■ *Privacy issues:* Databases may hold unsanctioned information that may be used for unintended purposes; this poses a risk to people's privacy. Medical data, for instance, may be used inappropriately in evaluating an employee for a job promotion. (Privacy and other ethical issues are discussed later in this chapter.)

12.6 Types of Database Organization

KEY QUESTION What are the characteristics of the main database models?

Just as files can be organized in different ways (sequentially or directly, for example), so can databases. The four most common arrangements for database management systems are *hierarchical, network, relational,* and *object-oriented.* Except for personal microcomputer databases, the installation and maintenance of each of the four types of databases require a database administrator trained in its structure.

Hierarchical Database

In a **hierarchical database,** fields or records are arranged in related groups resembling a family tree; lower-level records are subordinate to higher-level records. *(See Figure 12.6.)* A lower-level record is called a *child,* and a higher-level record is called a *parent.* The parent record at the top of the database is called the *root record.*

Figure 12.6 Hierarchical database: example of a cruise ship reservation system. Records are arranged in related groups resembling a family tree, with "child" records subordinate to "parent" records. Cabin numbers (A-1, A-2, A-3) are children of the parent July 15. Sailing dates (April 15, May 30, July 15) are children of the parent The Love Boat. The parent at the top, Miami, is called the *root record.*

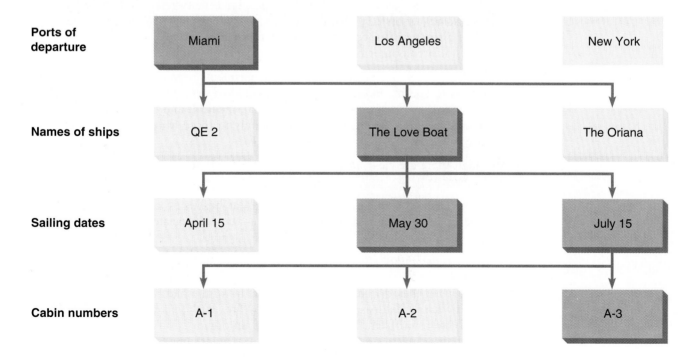

Unlike families in real life, a parent in a hierarchical database may have more than one child, but a child always has only *one* parent. This is called a *one-to-many relationship.* To find a particular record, you have to start at the top with a parent and trace down the chart to the child.

Hierarchical DBMSs are the oldest of the four forms of database organization and are still used in some reservations systems. Accessing or updating data is very fast because the relationships have been predefined. However, because the structure must be defined in advance, it is quite rigid. There may be only one parent per child and no relationships among the child records. Moreover, adding new fields to database records requires that the entire database be redefined.

Network Database

A **network database** is similar to a hierarchical DBMS, but each child record can have more than one parent record. *(See Figure 12.7.)* Thus, a child record, which in network database terminology is called a *member,* may be reached through more than one parent, called an *owner.*

This arrangement is more flexible than the hierarchical system because different relationships may be established between different branches of data. However, it still requires that the structure be defined in advance. Moreover, there are limits to the number of links that can be made among records.

Network and hierarchical databases are commonly used in large computer systems.

Figure 12.7 Network database: example of a college class scheduling system. This is similar to a hierarchical database, but each child, or "member," record can have more than one parent, or "owner." For example, Student B's owners are instructors D. Barry and R. DeNiro. Owner Broadcasting 210 has three members—D. Barry, R. DeNiro, and D. Rather.

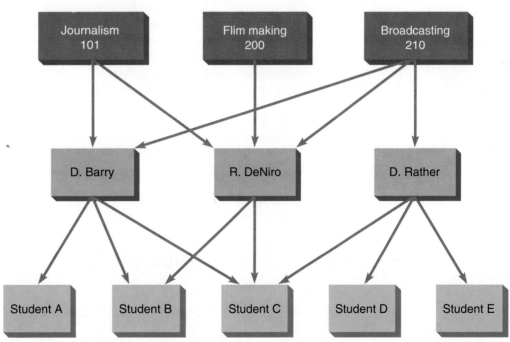

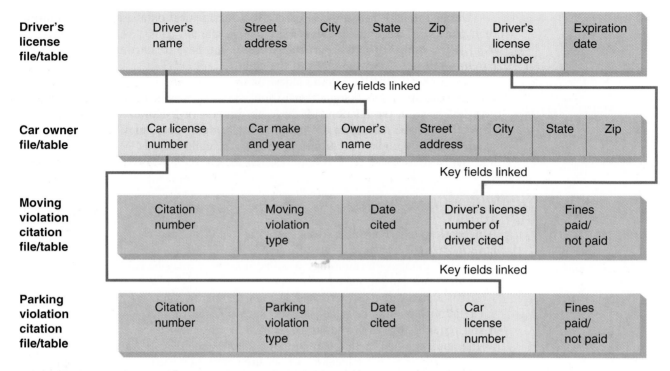

Figure 12.8   Relational database: example of a state department of motor vehicles database. This kind of database relates, or connects, data in different files through the use of a key field, or common data element. The relational database does not require predefined relationships.

Relational Database

More flexible than hierarchical and network database models, the **relational database** relates, or connects, data in different files through the use of a key field, or common data element. *(See Figure 12.8.)* In this arrangement there are no access paths down through a hierarchy. Instead, data elements are stored in different tables made up of rows and columns. In the technical terminology of database designers, the tables are called *relations* (files), the rows are called *tuples* (records), and the columns are called *attributes* (fields).

Within a table, a row resembles a record—for example, a car license-plate number, which is one field, and the car owner's name and address, which is another field. All related tables must have a key field that uniquely identifies each row. Thus, another table might have a row consisting of a driver's license number, the key field, and any traffic violations (such as speeding) attributed to the license holder. Another table would have the driver's license number and the bearer's name and address.

The advantage of relational databases is that the user does not have to be aware of any "structure." Thus, they can be used with little training. Moreover, entries can easily be added, deleted, or modified. A disadvantage is that some searches can be time-consuming. Nevertheless, the relational model has become popular for *microcomputer* DBMSs, such as Paradox and Access.

Object-Oriented Database (OODBMS)

Object-oriented databases can handle any type of data—not only numerical and text data but also graphics, audio, and video. Object-oriented databases, then, are important in the new world of video servers and businesses related to technological convergence and data storage in multimedia form, such as those that deliver multimedia information through the Web.

In the late 1980s, the graphical user interface (GUI, ✔ p. 5.13) for IBM-type microcomputers, with its support for windows, icons, mouse, and pointers, became increasingly common. Object-oriented programming languages (✔ p. 10.24) are invaluable to the development of GUIs, which further enhanced the popularity of object orientation. As these languages matured, object orientation found its way into the realm of database design.

An **object-oriented database management system (OODBMS)** uses objects (✔ p. 10.24) as elements within database files. An **object** consists of data in the form of (1) text, sound, video, and pictures and (2) instructions (algorithms) on the action to be taken on the data. A hierarchical or network database would contain only numerical and text data about a student—identification number, name, address, and so on. By contrast, an object-oriented database might also contain multimedia—the student's photograph, a "sound bite" of his or her voice, and even a short piece of video. Moreover, the object would store operations (called *methods*), programs that objects use to process themselves—for example, how to calculate the student's grade-point average and how to display or print the student's record. Objects interact by sending messages to one another.

In the data hierarchy discussed at the beginning of this chapter, an object would be approximately at the level of a record, but of course an object contains more types of data than a record, as well as some processing instructions, which a traditional record or tuple does not. (Some relational databases can handle sound, graphics, and video as well as alphanumeric text, but their components do not include processing instructions.)

Object-oriented databases are not yet commonly used in more traditional businesses. Such databases are very expensive to develop, and most organizations have millions or billions of bytes of data already stored in relational databases. Thus these companies are unwilling to bear the cost and risk of converting their databases to an OODBMS format. However, database experts predict greater use in some areas in which the multimedia capabilities of OODBMSs offer great benefits such as:[6]

■ *Medical information systems:* In addition to text-based data elements, databases could include images such as X-rays, CAT scans, and MRI (magnetic resonance imaging) scans, electrocardiogram recordings, and photographs.

■ *Engineering information systems:* Databases could contain blueprints, sketches, diagrams, photos, and illustrations.

■ *Geographic databases:* Maps of all kinds, as well as aerial and satellite photographs, could be stored, coordinated, and analyzed.

■ *Training and education:* These databases could include video clips demonstrating how thing work, how to repair things, how to assemble things, and how to perform certain operations.

12.7 Features of a DBMS

KEY QUESTION **What are the main features of a DBMS?**

A database management system may have a number of components, including the following. *(See Figure 12.9.)*

Figure 12.9 Some important features of a database management system

Component	Description
Data dictionary	Describes files and fields of data
Utilities	Help maintain the database by creating, editing, and monitoring data input
Query language	Enables users to make queries to a database and retrieve selected records
Report generator	Enables nonexperts to create readable, attractive on-screen or hardcopy reports of records
Access security	Specifies user access privileges
Data recover	Enables contents of database to be recovered after system failure

Data Dictionary

Some databases have a **data dictionary,** in itself a small database that stores the data definitions—descriptions of the structure of data used in the database. This includes the name, type, source, and authorization for access for each data element. The data dictionary may monitor the data being entered to make sure it conforms to the rules established during data definition, such as field name, field size, type of data (text, numeric, date, and so on). It also indicates which application programs use that data so that, when a change in data structure is planned, a list of affected programs can be generated.

Utilities

DBMS utilities are programs that allow you to maintain the database by creating, editing, and deleting data, records, and files. The utilities allow you to establish what is acceptable input data, to monitor the types of data being input, and to adjust display screens for data input.

Query Language

Also known as a *data manipulation language,* a **query language** is an easy-to-use computer language for making queries to a database and for retrieving selected records, on the basis of the particular criteria and format indicated. Query languages were developed to provide an interface to the database that does not require the user to type in traditional programming commands in a procedural language (✔ p. 10.17). Typically, the query is in the form of a sentence or near-English command, using such basic words as SELECT, DELETE, and MODIFY. There are several different query languages, each with its own vocabulary and procedures. One of the most popular is *Structured Query Language,* or *SQL* (pronounced "see quill").

Originally developed by IBM for its mainframes, SQL is a relational database search standard recognized by the American National Standards Institute. Software designers use this standard to design database query interfaces with which users conduct data searches. Thus SQL is the data access language used by many commercial DBMS products, including ORACLE, SYBASE, dBASE, Paradox, and Microsoft Access. Consider the following query:

```
SELECT   PRODUCT-NUMBER, PRODUCT-NAME
FROM     PRODUCT
WHERE    PRICE < 100.00
```

This query selects all records in the PRODUCT file for products that cost less than $100.00 and displays the selected records according to product number and name—for example, like this:

```
A-34    MIRROR
C-50    CHAIR
D-168   TABLE
```

Another popular query language is *query by example (QBE),* whereby a user will seek information in a database by describing a procedure for finding it. Specifically, the user asks for information in a database by using a sample record to define the qualifications he or she wants for selected records.

For example, a university's loan database, consisting of records of its students and the amounts they owe, might have the column headings (field names) NAME, ADDRESS, CITY, STATE, ZIP, AMOUNT OWED. In the QBE method, the database would display an empty record with these column headings. You would then type in the relevant search conditions in the appropriate columns.

Thus, if you wanted to find all Beverly Hills, California, students with a loan balance due of $3000 or more, you would type *BEVERLY HILLS* under the CITY column, *CA* under the STATE column, and *.>=3000* ("greater than or equal to $3000") in the AMOUNT OWED column.

Some newer DBMSs, such as Symantec's Q&A, use natural language (✔ p. 10.17) interfaces, which allow even more flexibility and convenience in conducting database searches. With this type of interface, users can make queries in the normal form of any spoken language—in this case, English. An example would be: "How many sales reps sold more than 1 million dollars of sniglets in South Dakota in January?" This query could be typed into the computer or, if a voice-recognition system has been installed, simply spoken.

Report Generator

A **report generator** is a program used to produce an on-screen or printed-out document from all or part of a database. You can specify the format of the report in advance—row headings, column headings, page headers, and so on. With a report generator, even nonexperts can create attractive, readable reports on short notice.

Access Security

At one point in the movie *Disclosure,* Michael Douglas's character, a beleaguered division head suddenly at odds with his company, types SHOW PRIVILEGES into his desktop computer, which is tied to the corporate network. To his consternation, the system responds by showing him downgraded from PRIOR USER LEVEL: 5 to CURRENT USER LEVEL: 0, shutting him out of files to which he formerly had access.

This is an example of the use of *access security,* a feature allowing database administrators to specify different access privileges for different users of a DBMS. For instance, one kind of user might be allowed only to retrieve (view) data, whereas another might have the right to update data and delete records. The purpose of this security feature, of course, is to protect the database from unauthorized access and sabotage.

Using computer simulation, Barbara Teixera peeks over the edge of the Golden Gate Bridge in San Francisco at the Pacific Ocean 250 feet below. Until recently, she wouldn't have dared look: She suffers from acrophobia, the terror of heights. Teixera vanquished her fear using the 3-D simulation environment created by the computer to work up her courage before stepping out onto the real bridge.

Physical security is also important. *Isolation* is a preventive strategy based on procedures to insulate the physical database from destruction. For example, one organization keeps backup copies of important databases on removable magnetic disks, stored in a guarded vault. To gain access to the vault, employees need a badge with an encoded personal voice print.[7] Many companies are building total backup computer centers, which contain duplicate databases and documentation.

System Recovery

Database management systems should have *system recovery* features that enable the DBA to recover contents of the database in the event of a hardware or software failure and allow business functions to continue. Performing a recovery may be very difficult. It is impossible to simply fix the problem and resume processing where it was interrupted. Even if no data is lost during a failure (which assumes that all types of memory are nonvolatile (✔ p. 1.11)—an unrealistic assumption), the timing and scheduling of computer processing are too complex to be accurately recreated. It is simply not possible to roll back the clock and put all the electrons in the same configuration they were in at the time of failure. Thus four approaches are possible: *mirroring, reprocessing, rollforward,* and *rollback.*

In database *mirroring,* frequent simultaneous copying of the database maintains two or more complete copies of the database online but in different locations. Mirroring is an expensive backup strategy but is necessary when recovery is needed very quickly—say in seconds or minutes—as with an airline reservation system's database.

In *reprocessing,* the DBA goes back to a known point of database activity (before the failure) and reprocesses the workload from there. To make reprocessing an available option, periodic database copies (called *database saves*) must be made and records kept of all the transactions made since each save. Then, when there is a failure, the database can be restored from the save, and all the transactions made since that save can be reentered and reprocessed. This type of recovery can be very time-consuming, and the processing of new transactions must be delayed until the database recovery is completed.

Like reprocessing, *rollforward,* also called *forward recovery,* involves recreating the current database using a previous database state—a recent copy of the database. However, in this case, transactions made since the last save are not completely reentered and reprocessed. Instead, the lost data is recovered using a more sophisticated transaction log that contains what are called *after-image records* and includes some processing information.

Rollback, or *backward recovery,* in contrast, is used to *undo* unwanted changes to the database—for example, when some failure interrupts a half-completed transaction.

12.8 New Approaches: Mining, Warehouses, & "Siftware"

KEY QUESTION **What is a data warehouse?**

Today, to manage databases that are almost unimaginably large-scale, involving records of millions of households and thousands of terabytes of data, new approaches are being adopted; some of these require so-called *massively parallel database computers* costing $1 million or more. "These machines gang together scores or even hundreds of the fastest microprocessors around," says one description, "giving them the oomph to respond in minutes to complex database queries."[8]

Such approaches go under the name *data mining,* which we'll consider next.

Data Mining: What It Is, What It's Used For

Data mining (DM), also called *knowledge discovery,* is the computer-assisted process of sifting through and analyzing vast amounts of data in order to extract meaning and discover new knowledge. The purpose of DM is to describe past trends and predict future trends. Although the definition seems simple enough, data mining has overwhelmed traditional query-and-report methods of organizing and analyzing data, such as those just described. The result has been the need for "data warehouses" and for new software tools, as we shall discuss.

Data mining has come about because, in today's fierce competitive business environment, companies need to turn the gazillions of bytes of raw data at their disposal to new uses for further profitability. Nonprofit institutions have also found DM methods useful, for example, in the pursuit of scientific and medical discoveries. Applications include:[9]

■ *Marketing:* Marketers uses DM tools (such as Spotlight) to mine the point-of-sale databases of retail stores, which contain facts (such as prices, quantities sold, dates of sale) for thousands of products in hundreds of geographic areas. By understanding customer preferences and buying patterns, marketers hope to target consumers' individual needs.

■ *Health:* A coach in the U.S. Gymnastics Federation is using a DM system (called IDIS) to discover what long-term factors contribute to an athlete's performance, so as to know what problems to treat early on. A Los Angeles hospital is using the same tool to see what subtle factors affect success and failure in back surgery. Another system helps health-care organizations pinpoint groups whose costs are likely to increase in the near future, so that medical interventions can be taken.

■ *Science:* DM techniques are being employed to find new patterns in genetic data, molecular structures, global climate changes, and more. For instance, one DM tool (called SKICAT) is being used to catalog more than 50 million galaxies, which will be reduced to a 3-terabyte galaxy catalog.

Clearly, short-term payoffs can be dramatic. One telephone company, for instance, mined its existing billing data to identify 10,000 supposedly "residential" customers who spent more than $1000 a month on their phone bills. When it looked more closely, the company found these customers were really small businesses trying to avoid paying the more expensive business rates for their telephone service.[10]

However, the payoffs in the long term could be truly astonishing. Sifting medical-research data or subatomic-particle information may reveal new treatments for diseases or new insights into the nature of the universe.

Preparing Data for the Data Warehouse

Data mining begins with acquiring data and preparing it for what is known as the "data warehouse, as follows." *(See Figure 12.10.)*

1. *Data sources:* Data may come from a number of sources: (1) point-of-sale transactions in files (flat files) managed by file management systems on mainframes, (2) databases of all kinds, and (3) other—for example, news articles transmitted over news wires or online sources such as the Internet. We may also add (4) data from existing data warehouses.

2. *Data fusion and cleansing:* Data from diverse sources, whether from inside the company (internal data) or purchased from outside the company (external data), must be fused together, then put through a process known as *data cleansing* or *scrubbing.*

   Even if the data comes from just one source, such as the company's mainframe, the data may be of poor quality, full of errors and inconsistencies. Therefore, for data mining to produce accurate results, the source data has to be *scrubbed*—that is, cleaned of errors and checked for consistency of formats.

3. *Data and meta-data:* The cleansing process yields both the cleaned-up data and a variation of it called *meta-data.* Meta-data shows the origins of the data, the transformations it has undergone, and summary information about it, which makes it more useful than the unintegrated, unsummarized data. The meta-data also describes the contents of the data warehouse.

4. *The data warehouse:* Both the data and the meta-data are sent to the data warehouse. A *data warehouse* is a special database of cleaned-up data and meta-data. It is a replica, or close reproduction, of a mainframe's data. The data warehouse is stored using disk storage technology such as RAID (redundant arrays of independent disks, ✔ p. 4.18). Small data warehouses may hold 100 gigabytes of data or less. Beyond 500 gigabytes, *massively parallel processing (MPP)* computers (✔ p. 2.11) are needed. Projections indicate that large data warehouses holding hundreds of terabytes will be required fairly soon. Data warehouses commonly serve organizations' decision support systems and executive information systems (✔ p. 11.18).

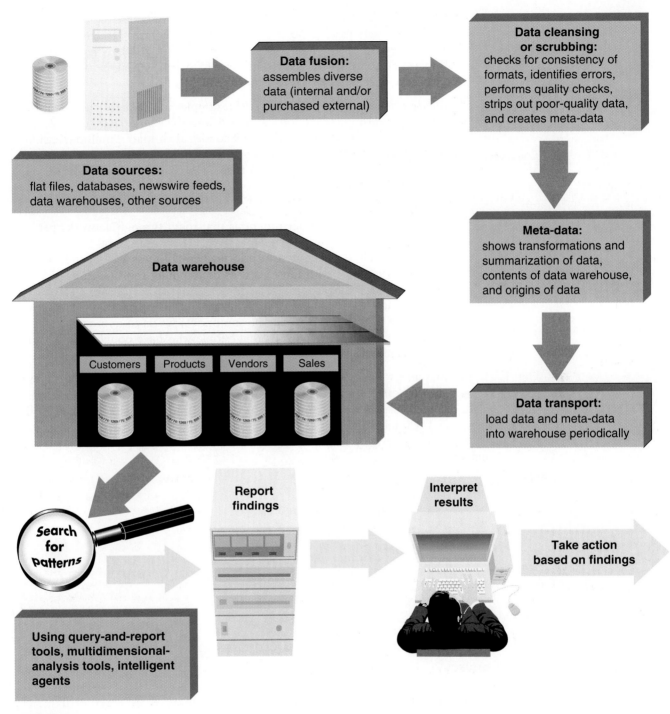

Figure 12.10 The data-mining process

"Siftware" for Finding and Analyzing

Three kinds of software, or "siftware," tools are used to perform data mining—that is, to do finding and analyzing tasks. They are *query-and-reporting tools, multidimensional-analysis (MDA) tools,* and *intelligent agents.*[11]

■ *Query-and-reporting tools* (examples are Focus Reporter and Esperant) require a database structure and work well with relational databases. They may have graphical interfaces. Their best use is for specific questions to verify hypotheses.

For example, if a company decides to mine its database in search of customers most likely to respond to a mail-order promotion, it might use a query-and-reporting tool and construct a query (using SQL): "How many credit-card customers who made purchases of over $100 on sporting goods in August have at least $2000 of available credit?"[12]

■ *Multidimensional-analysis (MDA) tools* (examples are Essbase and Lightship) can do "data surfing" to explore all dimensions of a particular subset of data. With MDA, according to one writer, "The idea is to load a multidimensional server with data that is likely to be combined. Imagine all the possible ways of analyzing clothing sales: by brand name, size, color, location, advertising, and so on."[13] Using MDA tools, you can analyze this multidimensional database from all points of view.

■ *Intelligent agents* are computer programs that roam through networks performing complex work tasks for people. While there are several kinds of intelligent agents, such as those used to prioritize e-mail messages for individuals, we are concerned here with those used as data-mining tools (such as DataEngine and Data/Logic).

Intelligent agents are best used for turning up unsuspected relationships and patterns. "These patterns may be so nonobvious as to appear almost nonsensical," says one writer, "such as that people who have bought scuba gear are good candidates for taking Australian vacations."[14]

Is data about you finding its way into data warehouses? No doubt it is. Gathering data isn't difficult. You participate in probably hundreds of transactions a year, recorded in point-of-sale terminals (✔ p. 3.33), teller machines, credit-card files, and 1-800 telemarketing responses. Sooner or later, some of the records of your past activities will be used—most likely by marketing companies—to try to influence you.

12.9 The Ethics of Using Databases: Concerns About Accuracy & Privacy

KEY QUESTION In what ways can database users invade people's privacy?

"The corrections move by bicycle while the stories move at the speed of light," complains Richard Lamm, a former governor of Colorado. Lamm was quoted out of context by a Denver newspaper in a speech he made in 1994. Yet even years afterward—long after the paper had run a correction—he still saw the error repeated in later newspaper articles.[15]

How do such mistakes get perpetuated? The answer, suggests journalist Christopher Feola, is the Misinformation Explosion. "Fueled by the growing popularity of both commercial and in-house computerized news databases," he says, "journalists have found it that much easier to repeat errors or rely on the same tired anecdotes and experts."[16]

MIT student Bradley Geilfuss prepares to swallow a radio transmitter that will send information about his metabolism via wireless modem to fellow students during his participation in a San Francisco Marathon.

If news reporters—who are supposed to be trained in careful handling of the facts—can continue to repeat inaccuracies found in databases, what about those without training who have access to computerized data? How can you be sure that databases with essential information about you—medical, credit, school, employment, and so on—are accurate and, equally important, are secure in guarding your privacy? We examine the topics of *accuracy and completeness* and of *privacy* in this section.

Accuracy and Completeness of Data

Databases—including public databases such as Nexis, Lexis, Dialog, and Dow Jones News/Retrieval—can provide you with *more* facts and *faster* facts but not always *better* facts. Penny Williams, professor of broadcast journalism at Buffalo State College in New York and formerly a television anchor and reporter, suggests there are five limitations to bear in mind when using databases for research:[17]

■ *You can't get the whole story:* For some purposes, databases are only a foot in the door. There may be many facts or aspects to the topic you are looking into that are not in a database. Reporters, for instance, find a database is a starting point, but it may take old-fashioned shoe leather to get the rest of the story.

■ *It's not the gospel:* Just because you see something on a computer screen doesn't mean it's accurate. Numbers, names, and facts may need to be verified in other ways.

■ *Know the boundaries:* One database service doesn't have it all. For example, you can find full text articles from the *New York Times* on Lexis/Nexis, from the *Wall Street Journal* on Dow Jones News/Retrieval, and from the *San Jose Mercury News* on America Online, but no service carries all three.

■ *Find the right words:* You have to know which key words (search words) to use when searching a database for a topic. As Lynn Davis, a professional researcher with ABC News, points out, in searching for stories on guns, the key word "can be guns, it can be firearms, it can be handguns, it can be pistols, it can be assault weapons. If you don't cover your bases, you might miss something."[18]

More than 22 million photos make up Time Inc.'s historic archive. Until 1996, they consisted of slides, negatives, and prints, kept in hundreds of file cabinets. Today, a team of archivists is scanning the images and entering them into a digital database that can be searched by numerous researchers simultaneously.

■ *History is limited:* Most public databases, Davis says, have information going back to 1980, and a few into the 1970s, but this poses problems if you're trying to research something earlier.

Privacy

Privacy is the right of people to not reveal information about themselves. Whom you vote for in a voting booth and what you say in a letter sent through the U.S. mail are private matters. However, the ease with which databases and communications lines may pull together and disseminate information has put privacy under extreme pressure.

As you've no doubt discovered, it's no trick at all to get your name on all kinds of mailing lists. Theo Theoklitas, for instance, has received applications for credit cards, invitations to join video clubs, and notification of his finalist status in Ed McMahon's $10 million sweepstakes. Theo is a 6-year-old black cat whose owner once sent in an application for a rebate on cat food.[19] A whole industry has grown up of professional information gatherers and sellers, who collect personal data and sell it to fund-raisers, direct marketers, and others.

How easy is it to find out about you or anyone else? Using his home computer, journalist Jeffrey Rothfeder once obtained former U.S. vice-president Dan Quayle's credit report. All Rothfeder had to do was pay an information seller $50 and type in Dan Quayle's name. He also found out from another data seller where TV anchorman Dan Rather shops. "This seller warmed to me quickly," Rothfeder said. "As a bonus, I was sent Vanna White's home phone number for free."[20] In an even worse case of invasion of privacy, a California man, obsessed with a woman he had once known, was able to hatch intricate schemes of harassment—from within a maximum-security prison. He filed post office change-of-address forms so her mail was forwarded to him in prison and obtained a credit report on her. He even sent the IRS forged power-of-attorney forms so he could get her tax returns.[21]

In the 1970s, the U.S. Department of Health, Education, and Welfare developed a set of five Fair Information Practices. These rules have since been adopted by a number of public and private organizations. The practices also led to the enactment of a number of laws to protect individuals from invasion of privacy. Perhaps the most important law is the Federal Privacy Act, or Privacy Act of 1974. The *Privacy Act of 1974* prohibits secret personnel files from being kept on individuals by government agencies or their contractors. It gives individuals the right to see their records, to see how the data is used, and to correct errors. Another significant piece of legislation was the *Freedom of Information Act,* passed in 1970, which allows ordinary citizens to have access to data gathered about them by federal agencies. Most privacy laws regulate only the behavior of government agencies or government contractors. For example, the *Computer Matching and Privacy Protection Act of 1988* prevents the government from comparing certain records to try to find a match. This law does not affect most private companies.

Of particular concern for privacy are the areas of finances, health, employment, commerce, and communications:

- *Finances:* The banking and credit industries are subject to federal privacy laws. The *Fair Credit Reporting Act of 1970* gives you the right to have access to and to challenge your credit records. If you have been denied credit, this access must be given to you free of charge. The *Right to Financial Privacy Act of 1978* sets restrictions on federal agencies that want to search customer records in banks.

  In the past, credit bureaus have been severely criticized for disseminating errors and for producing reports that were difficult to interpret. Although it may still not be easy to clear up a mistake, the industry has a dispute-resolution process that should help. The major credit bureaus are Experian, Equifax, and Trans Union.

- *Health:* No federal laws protect medical records in the United States (except those related to treatment for drug and alcohol abuse and psychiatric care, or records in the custody of the federal government). Of course, insurance companies can get a look at your medical data, but so can others that you might not suspect. Getting a divorce or suing an employer for wrongful dismissal? A lawyer might subpoena your medical records in hopes of using, say, a drinking problem or treatment for depression against you. When employers have information about personal health, they often use it in making employment-related decisions.

  Your best strategy is to decline to fill out medical questionnaires or histories unless there is a clear need for them. You should also not tell any business more than it needs to know about your health. You can ask your doctor to release only the minimum possible amount of information. Finally, ask for a copy of your medical records if you have doubts about the information they contain.

- *Employment:* Nongovernmental employers are the least regulated by privacy legislation. If you apply for a job, for instance, a background-checking service may verify your educational background and employment history. It may also take a look at your credit, driving violations, workers' compensation claims, and criminal record if any.

Stuffing an e-mailed prayer into the cracks of the Wailing Wall in Jerusalem, Israel, a messenger from Virtual Jerusalem helps far-flung Jews talk to God. About 200 e-mailed prayers a day reach the Wall, sacred to Jews who believe prayers delivered there reach God more quickly. The company's Web site offers live video of the Wall, as well as chat rooms.

Cellular phones, global positioning systems, and "active badges" (clip-on ID cards readable by infrared sensors throughout a building) can tell your employer where you are. Software that counts keystrokes or tracks sales can monitor your productivity. E-mail memos may be read not only by the recipient but perhaps by your boss, if company policy allows.

■ *Commerce:* As we've seen, marketers of all kinds would like to get to know you. For example, Virginia Sullivan, a retired school teacher, weighed the junk mail she received every month. She found after 11 months that she had received about 98 pounds' worth. Sullivan also noticed that the junk mail companies seemed to know personal details of her private life, such as her age, buying habits, and favorite charities.

"We constantly betray secrets about ourselves," says Erik Larson, author of *The Naked Consumer,* "and these secrets are systematically collected by the marketers' intelligence network."[22] Larson has a number of suggestions for staying off mailing lists in the first place.

With few exceptions, the law does not prohibit companies from gathering information about you for one purpose and using it without your permission for another. This information is culled from both public information sources, such as driver's license records, and commercial transactions, such as warranty cards. One exception is the *Video Privacy Protection Act*, enacted in 1988, which prevents retailers from disclosing a person's video rental records without that individual's consent or a court order.

"Somewhere along the way," Larson points out, "the data keepers made the arbitrary decision that everyone is automatically on their lists unless they ask to be taken off."[23] Why not have a law that keeps consumers off all lists unless they ask to be included? Congress has considered this approach, but lobbyists for direct marketing companies object that it would put them out of business.

■ *Communications:* Privacy concerns don't stop with the use or misuse of information in databases; they also extend to communications. Although the government is constrained by several laws on acquiring and disseminating information, and listening in on private conversations, privacy advocates still worry. In recent times, the government has tried to impose new technologies that would enable law-enforcement agents to gather a wealth of personal information. Proponents have urged that Americans must be willing to give up some personal privacy in exchange for safety and security. We discuss this matter in Chapter 14.

Education

Computers are pervasive on campus. More than a third of college courses require the use of e-mail, and many have their own dedicated Web pages.[a,b] College students spend an average of 5.6 hours a week on the Internet.[c] And as computer prices drop, more and more students have their own PCs. (For the rest, colleges often make public microcomputers available.)

The payoff of this computer literacy is not only increased productivity while in college but also the acquisition of tangible skills students can offer employers. "There are so many grads that play back to us that the computer skills they take with them give them a leg up over other candidates for the same position," says Tom Harris, of Drew University in Madison, New Jersey. "It has helped so many of them get that first job."[d]

Many students, however, have been exposed to computers since the lower grades. In 1997, for example, 75% of elementary schools (and 89% of secondary schools) were wired to the Internet, according to the U.S. Department of Education.[e] The results have not always been productive, especially in elementary schools. However, when used selectively by trained teachers in middle schools, according to research, computers can significantly enhance performance in math learning.[f] In art classes, computers can be used to encourage creativity without the mess, as children learn to make art digitally.[g] Thousands of schoolchildren have tapped into a Web site by a Wake Forest University biology researcher to explore data tracking albatrosses across the Pacific Ocean, giving them a chance to test their own hypotheses.[h] Students exposed to the Internet in high school say they think the Web has helped them improve the quality of their academic research and of their written work.[i] There is even software such as Intelligent Essay Assessor and E-Rater that grades essays, although its effectiveness is still debated.[j,k]

One of the greatest revolutions in education—before, during, and after the college years—is the advent of distance learning, or "cyberclasses," along with the explosion of Internet resources. The home-schooling movement, for example, has come of age, thanks to Internet resources.[l] Many colleges, both individually and in associations such as that of the Western Governors University (backed by 17 states and Guam) and the Community College Distance Learning Network, are offering a variety of Internet and/or video-based online courses.[m,n] Corporations are also offering training classes via the Internet or corporate intranet.[o]

Studying online has its advantages: you can log on from anywhere, at any time of day or night, and participate in discussions to whatever extent you choose. There are a number of trade-offs, however, among them the fact that with convenience also comes responsibility and accountability. "Online school is a venue for self-starters," says one writer, "which may be one reason that, though 10 people enrolled in the class I took, only half were ever heard from after the first few weeks."[p]

Here are some Web sites of interest to college students: Student Advantage (www.studentadvantage.com), which offers all kinds of discounts; Student Market (www.studentmkt.com) and CollegeDepot.com (www.collegedepot.com) offer all kinds of products for students. For financial aid and scholarships, log on to Free Application for Federal Student Aid (www.fafsa.ed.gov), Sallie Mae (scholarships.salliemae.com), and FastWEB.com (www.fastweb.com).

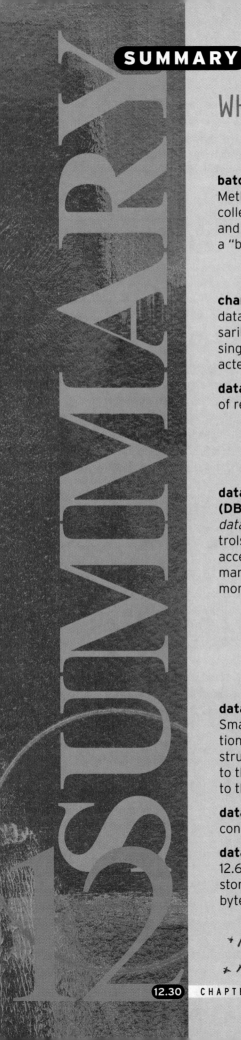

WHAT IT IS
WHAT IT DOES

batch processing (KQ 12.3, p. 12.9) Method of processing whereby data is collected over several days or weeks and then processed all at one time, as a "batch."

character (KQ 12.2, p. 12.6) Set of data that may be—but is not necessarily—the same as a byte (8 bits); a single letter, number, or special character such as ; or $, or %.

database (KQ 12.2, p. 12.6) Collection of related files in a computer system.

database management system (DBMS) (KQ 12.5, p. 12.12) Also called *database manager;* software that controls the structure of a database and access to the data. In contrast to a file manager, it allows users to manipulate more than one file at a time.

data dictionary (KQ 12.7, p. 12.18) Small database that stores data definitions and descriptions of database structure. It also monitors new entries to the database as well as user access to the database.

data file (KQ 12.3, p. 12.8) File that contains data.

data storage hierarchy (KQ 12.2, p. 12.6) The respective levels of data stored in a computer database; bits, bytes, fields, records, and files.

WHY IT IS IMPORTANT

With batch processing, if users need to make a request of the system, they must wait until the batch has been processed. Batch processing is less expensive than online processing and is suitable for work in which immediate answers to queries are not needed.

Characters (bytes) are at the lowest level of the data hierarchy.

Businesses and organizations build databases to help them keep track of and manage their affairs. In addition, online database services put enormous research resources at the user's disposal.

This software enables: sharing of data (the same information is available to different users); economy of files (several departments can use one file instead of each individually maintaining its own files, thus reducing data redundancy, which in turn reduces the expense of storage media and hardware); data integrity (files are automatically updated to include changes made in the files in other departments); security (access to specific information can be limited to selected users).

The data dictionary checks that the data being entered conforms to the rules established during data definition and may also help protect the security of the database by indicating who has the right to access it.

Contrast *program files.*

Bits and bytes are what the computer hardware deals with, so users need not be concerned with them. They will, however, deal with characters, fields, records, files, and databases.

+ physical vs. logical record

+ master file vs. transaction file

+ online and offline storage

+ 6.7 components of database system files

DBMS utilities (KQ 12.7, p. 12.18)   Programs that allow the maintenance of databases by creating, editing, and deleting data, records, and files.

DBMS utilities allow people to establish what is acceptable input data, to monitor the types of data being input, and to adjust display screens for data input.

distributed database (KQ 12.1, p. 12.4)   Database stored in more than one physical location, to which users are connected through a client-server network.

Data need not be centralized in one location.

field (KQ 12.2, p. 12.6)   Unit of data consisting of one or more characters (bytes). An example of a field is your name, your date of birth, or your Social Security number.

A collection of fields make up a record. Also see *key field.*

file (KQ 12.2, p. 12.6)   Collection of related records.

A collection of related files makes up a database.

file management system (KQ 12.4, p. 12.11)   Also called *file manager;* software for creating, retrieving, and manipulating files, one file at a time.

In the 1950s, magnetic tape was the storage medium, and records and files were stored sequentially. File managers were created to work with these files. Today, however, database managers are more common.

hierarchical database (KQ 12.6, p. 12.14)   Oldest of four common arrangements for database management systems; fields or records are arranged in related groups resembling a family tree, with "child" records subordinate to "parent" records. A parent may have more than one child, but a child always has only one parent. To find a particular record, start at the top with a parent and trace down the chart to the child.

Hierarchical DBMSs work well when the data elements have an intrinsic one-to-many relationship, as might happen with a reservations system. The difficulty, however, is that the structure must be defined in advance and is quite rigid.

key field (KQ 12.2, p. 12.7)   Field that contains unique data used to identify a record so that it can be easily retrieved and processed. The key field is often an identification number, Social Security number, customer account number, or the like. The primary characteristic of the key field is that it is *unique.*

Key fields are needed to identify and retrieve specific records in a database.

master file (KQ 12.3, p. 12.8)   Data file containing relatively permanent records that are generally updated periodically.

Master files contain relatively permanent information used for reference purposes. They are updated through the use of transaction files.

network database (KQ 12.6, p. 12.15)   One of four common arrangements for database management systems; it is similar to a hierarchical DBMS, but each child record can have more than one parent record. Thus, a child record may be reached through more than one parent.

Network DBMSs are more flexible than their hierarchical counterpart. However, the structure must still be defined in advance. Moreover, there are limits to the possible number of links that can be made among records.

object (KQ 12.6, p. 12.17)   In an OODBMS, an element consisting of data in the form of (1) text, sound, video, and pictures and (2) instructions (algorithms) on the action to be taken on the data.

See *object-oriented database management system.*

object-oriented database management system (OODBMS) (KQ 12.6, p. 12.17)   Most recent of the four common database structures; it uses objects as elements within database files.

In addition to textual data, an object-oriented database can store, for example, a person's photo, "sound bites" of his or her voice, and a video clip.

offline storage (KQ 12.3, p. 12.9)   System in which stored data is not directly accessible for processing until a tape or disk has been loaded onto an input device.

The storage medium and data are not under the immediate, direct control of the central processing unit.

online processing (KQ 12.3, p. 12.9)   Also called *real-time processing;* entering transactions into a computer system as they take place and updating the master files as the transactions occur. Online processing requires direct access storage.

Online processing gives users accurate information from an ATM machine or an airline reservations system, for example.

online storage (KQ 12.3, p. 12.9)   System in which stored data is directly accessible for processing.

Storage is under the immediate, direct control of the central processing unit; users need not wait for a tape or disk to be loaded onto an input device before they can access stored data.

program file (KQ 12.3, p. 12.8)   File containing software instructions.

Contrast *data files.*

query language (KQ 12.7, p. 12.18)   Also known as *data manipulation language;* easy-to-use computer language for making queries to a database and retrieving selected records.

Query languages make it easier for users to deal with databases.

record (KQ 12.2, p. 12.6)   Collection of related fields. An example of a record would be your name *and* date of birth *and* Social Security number.

Related records make up a file.

relational database (KQ 12.6, p. 12.16)   One of four common arrangements for database management systems; relates, or connects, data in different files through the use of a key field, or common data element. In this arrangement there are no access paths down through a hierarchy. Instead, data elements are stored in different tables made up of rows called *tuples* and columns called *attributes.* Within a table, a row resembles a record. All related tables must have a key field that uniquely identifies each row.

Relational databases are more flexible than hierarchical or network databases. Because the user does not have to be aware of any "structure," relational databases can be used with little training. Moreover, entries can easily be added, deleted, or modified. A disadvantage is that some searches can be time-consuming. Nevertheless, the relational model has become popular for microcomputer DBMSs.

report generator (KQ 12.7, p. 12.19)   DBMS program for producing on-screen or printed-out documents from all or part of a database.

Report generators allow users to produce finished-looking reports without much fuss.

shared database (KQ 12.1, p. 12.4)   Database in one location that is shared by users within one company or organization.

Shared databases give all users in one organization access to the same information.

transaction file (KQ 12.3, p. 12.8)   Temporary data file that holds all changes to be made to the master file: additions, deletions, revisions.

The transaction file is used to periodically update the master file.

1. Fill in the following blanks:

    a. According to the data storage hierarchy, databases are composed of

        _____ , _____ , _____ , and

        _____ .

    b. An individual piece of data within a record is called a _____ .

    c. A special file in the DBMS called the _____ _____
        maintains descriptions of the structure of data used in the database.

    d. A(n) _____ is a collection of multiple related files that are created

        and managed by a _____ management system.

    e. A(n) _____ _____ coordinates all activities related to
        an organization's database.

2. Label each of the following statements as either true or false.

    _____ Ensuring backup and recovery of a database is not one of the functions of
          a database administrator.

    _____ Old file-management methods provided the user with an easy way to estab-
          lish relationships among records in different files.

    _____ The use of key fields makes it easier to locate a record in a database.

    _____ A transaction file contains permanent records that are periodically up-
          dated.

    _____ The hierarchical database structure is the most flexible form of database
          organization.

3. Describe each of the following database organizations:
    a. hierarchical
    b. network
    c. relational
    d. object-oriented

4. List five responsibilities of a database administrator.

    a. _____

    b. _____

    c. _____

    d. _____

    e. _____

5. Define the following terms:

    a. sequential file organization

    b. direct file organization

    c. indexed-sequential file organization

6. List three disadvantages of file management systems:

    a. _____

    b. _____

    c. _____

1. Answer each of the Key Questions that appear at the beginning of this chapter.

2. What is the difference between master and transaction files?

3. What is the difference between batch and online processing?

4. What is a query language?

5. What is meant by the term *data mining*?

KNOWLEDGE IN ACTION

1. **Conducting an Interview.** Interview someone who works with or manages a company database. What types of records make up the database, and which departments use it? What types of transactions do these departments enact? Which database structure is used? What are the types and sizes of the storage devices? Was the software custom-written?

2. **Creating a Contact Database.** Networking may very well be the key to finding a job. Assuming you're in the process of looking for a job, what type of database would be helpful for keeping track of all the people you meet? What fields would you want to include in the database? Why?

3. **Conceptualizing an Object-Oriented Database.** Describe the characteristics of an object-oriented database that might be useful to a large number of people, including yourself. What type of objects would this database contain? How would this database be used? Who would typically access this database? Does this type of database exist already? Why? Why not?

4. **Selling Information.** Companies exist today that are in the business of selling information. For example, for a fee you can purchase a list of all the businesses in your area that sell sporting goods, use Windows-based computers, and have 10 or more employees. The more specific your information request, the more expensive the information is. What type of database do you think would be especially valuable? What kinds of information would this database contain? What would a record look like? (Give an example.) How big do you think the database would get? Is information of the type you are describing already being sold today? How would you find out?

Answers to Self-Test Exercises: 1a. characters, fields, records, files. 1b. field. 1c. data dictionary. 1d. database. 1e. database administrator. 2. F, F, T, F, F. 3a. Oldest of four common arrangements for database management systems; fields or records are arranged in related groups resembling a family tree, with "child" records subordinate to "parent" records. A parent may have more than one child, but a child always has only one parent. To find a particular record, start at the top with a parent and trace down the chart to the child. 3b. One of four common arrangements for database management systems; it is similar to a hierarchical DBMS, but each child record can have more than one parent record. Thus, a child record may be reached through more than one parent. 3c. One of four common arrangements for database management systems; relates, or connects, data in different files through the use of a key field, or common data element. In this arrangement there are no access paths down through a hierarchy. Instead, data elements are stored in different tables made up of rows called *tuples* and columns called *attributes*. Within a table, a row resembles a record. All related tables must have a key field that uniquely identifies each row. 3d. Most recent of the four common database structures; it uses objects as elements within database files. 4. Database design, implementation, and operation; Coordination with users; System security; Backup and recovery; Performance monitoring. 5a. Sequential file organization stores records in sequence, one after the other. Records can be retrieved only in the sequence in which they were stored. This is the only method that can be used with magnetic tape; it can also be used with disk. 5b. Instead of storing records in sequence, direct file organization, or *random file organization,* stores records in no particular sequence. A record is retrieved according to its key field, or unique element of data. This method of file organization is ideal for applications such as airline reservations systems and computerized directory-assistance operations. In these cases, records need to be retrieved only one at a time, and there is no fixed pattern to the requests for records. 5c. A compromise has been developed between the two preceding methods. Indexed-sequential file organization, or simply *indexed file organization,* stores records in sequential order. However, the file in which the records are stored contains an index that lists each record by its key field and identifies its physical location on the disk. The method requires magnetic or optical disk. 6. data redundancy, lack of data integrity, lack of program independence

13

ADVANCES IN COMPUTING

Multimedia, Artificial Intelligence, and Intelligent Agents

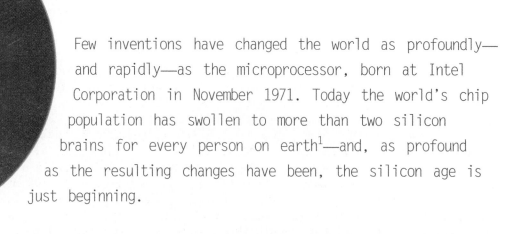

Few inventions have changed the world as profoundly—and rapidly—as the microprocessor, born at Intel Corporation in November 1971. Today the world's chip population has swollen to more than two silicon brains for every person on earth[1]—and, as profound as the resulting changes have been, the silicon age is just beginning.

Experts predict that by 2011, one chip will be crammed with the power of 250 Pentium Pros.[2] The implications of such power growth are staggering. Perhaps we will have autonomously intelligent machines: tell them what to do, and they'll figure out how to do it. Multimedia will be combined with virtual reality to create environments that *become* reality. These technologies represent a few of the cutting-edge aspects of computerization, the topic of this chapter. How do you think *you* will be using computers in 2011?

13.1 Multimedia as Part of Your World

Key Question **What are some applications for multimedia, and what are some of the jobs and activities involved in this field?**

In the chapters on processing, input, output, storage, and software, we discussed the system requirements for users wishing to take advantage of multimedia offerings. In the following sections we review some of that information and go into more detail about what people are using multimedia for, and how they create it.

Business and Industry

Kiosk

The increased use of multimedia technology by corporate America can be largely attributed to easy-to-use presentation software (✔ p. 6.15) like Microsoft PowerPoint, together with decreasing costs for the necessary hardware, such as LCD projection panels and notebook computers. Presentation software lets novice computer users design and build professional-looking on-screen presentations in less time than it would take to print overhead acetates. With more advanced multimedia authoring software, corporations are creating in-house advertising and promotional programs for display using kiosks at trade shows and during product demonstrations. (A **kiosk** is a small, self-contained structure such as a newsstand or a ticket booth, designed to serve a large number of people. Unattended multimedia kiosks dispense information via computer screens. Keyboards and touch screens are used for input.) Other common uses for multimedia in business include interactive product catalogs, annual reports, safety manuals, employee handbooks, and electronic performance support systems (EPSS).

Education and Training

The education and training industry is by far the most active area in multimedia. The benefits of multimedia technology in providing flexibility for students and in enhancing learning are well documented. Most people agree that "learners retain about 20% of what they hear; 40% of what they see and hear; and 75% of what they see, hear, and do."[3] For younger children, multimedia programs provide teachers with an exciting new tool for stimulating class discussions, conducting student research, and promoting teamwork. For older learners, the interactive nature of multimedia promotes active participation and affords user control over the pace and flow of delivery. Educational multimedia, also called *courseware,* allows adult learners to determine when and where they want to access training, whether at home, work, or school. Other multimedia resources related to education include multimedia reference material, electronic textbooks and course supplements, online lecture notes, interactive testing, and virtual simulations.

Entertainment and Games

Although educational courseware is the most established multimedia product, the entertainment and games industry has had the greatest commercial success. Software development companies such as Electronic Arts and Id Software have achieved huge financial returns and recognition for games like *Doom, 7th Guest,* and *Riven.* Multimedia CD-ROMs in glossy packaging are now commonplace on the shelves of your local software store. But aside from these video-arcade-like programs, several excellent educational/entertainment (edutainment) titles are available. The Random House/Brøderbund Living Book series produces such popular children's titles as *Arthur's Teacher Trouble, Just Grandma and Me,* and *The Tortoise and the Hare.* Not only do these titles help children learn to read, they promote computer literacy at a very young age.

Games are also used in training executives, such as for Bankers Trust. The games can range from simple card games and quizzes to high-speed extravaganzas based on Doom and Quake. For example, a version of solitaire might test employees on the topic of administering Windows. In Straight Shooter, players negotiate their way through a 3-D maze of streets and offices in different cities of the world, zapping villains and winning points by offering answers to typical problems that clients might face.

The Multimedia Computer

Shopping for a new computer is one of those enlightening experiences that you can complain about to your friends. In 1993, most multimedia computer systems were sold in pieces that you had to assemble yourself on the living room floor. Today, thankfully, almost every retail computer system that is sold is multimedia-capable. To help consumers identify a minimum system configuration for playing back multimedia on Intel-based and similar computers, the Multimedia PC Marketing Council publishes a set of minimum standards known as **MPC classifications.** The *minimum* MPC Level 3 standard, for example, recommends the following hardware:

1. Pentium (or equivalent) 75 MHz CPU

2. 8 MB of RAM (for optimum performance, 32–64 MB)

3. 540 MB hard disk, with at least 500 MB available

4. 3.5-inch, high-density floppy disk drive

5. 4X CD-ROM drive with 600 Kbps data transfer

6. 16-bit wavetable sound card with MIDI playback and speakers

7. VGA graphics card with 8-bit (256) colors

8. MPEG video playback

9. 101-key keyboard and two-button mouse

10. I/O ports for MIDI, serial, parallel, and joystick

The precise equipment that you need for multimedia will depend on your level of involvement. To experiment with the technology, you need only purchase a personal computer capable of playing back multimedia. Creating multimedia content requires a more advanced system configuration. You will require specialized input hardware devices, such as a flatbed scanner and video capture card, to create the individual media elements. To output a completed production to CD-ROM requires that you have access to a removable storage device (to send to a service bureau for mastering a CD) or your own CD-ROM recordable unit.

Creating Multimedia

Development of multimedia is a complex process, and not many of us will become deeply involved in it. However, to give you an idea of what that process is like, this section offers a brief overview.

The multimedia production process, similar to video and film production, consists of the following stages: pre-production, production, and post-production. In the *pre-production* stage, the program objectives, design, and details are worked out through audience analysis, script writing, and storyboarding (visually mapping out the sequence of, and links among, information on bulletin-type boards). *Production* entails gathering content, either by acquiring another's content through copyright and licensing arrangements or by creating your own media elements. *Post-production* is the process by which the media elements are combined to meet the overall design and program objectives.

Within these stages, there are nine specific steps that you should complete from start to finish.

In the Oregon Coast Aquarium, the orca Keiko's vocalizations are recorded and catalogued on a computer database. Keiko is helping scientists learn more about orca behavior.

1. *Develop the project specification,* which includes the statement of purpose, audience analysis, concept treatment, and content requirements.

2. *Plan and budget your production,* which results in a production calendar, resource schedule, financial budget, and summary of equipment and staff requirements.

3. *Prepare a treatment and storyboard,* which provides a written script and visual outline for the entire production.

4. *Design the user interface* to finalize the look and feel of the production.

5. *Prepare a prototype or working model,* which lets you test interface features, concept implementations, and audience assumptions.

6. *Acquire the content* by converting, purchasing, or producing media elements.

7. *Author and program* the title (the project being created) to assemble the media elements and build in interactivity.

8. *Test and evaluate* the title to ensure consistency, accuracy, and audience acceptance.

9. *Prepare the title for distribution,* which typically results in a CD-ROM master complete with an installation or setup program and user documentation.

Acquiring Content

Let's review our definition of multimedia: *multimedia* is any combination of text, images, illustrations, animation, sound, and video for the purpose of communicating information electronically. Therein lie the media elements to be considered when assembling a multimedia production. In the simplest terms, you have three choices for acquiring media: *convert, purchase,* or *produce.* Since multimedia titles are often derived from existing print materials or video programs, you can use a scanner, video capture card, or other hardware device to convert media to a digital form. Before doing so, however, ensure that you have written permission to manipulate and use the material that you want to convert. If you decide to purchase the content from a professional media service, you will spend most of your time browsing image catalogs and sound libraries, not to mention reading copyright and licensing statements. If you decide to produce original content, you must then determine whether to create it yourself or hire a writer, artist, animator, musician, or video producer. Although it can be expensive to hire a professional, creating your own media gives you complete control over the production quality, copyright, and deliverables.

In larger multimedia productions, the producer will establish a database management system to catalog and track the digitized media elements. This database will typically contain the following information for each element:

- File name and version control number

- Description of contents, usage, and location in the final production

- File format and specifications, such as color-depth, resolution, track length, or sampling rate (✔ p. 3.18)

- Copyright, licensing, and royalty information, if required

- Media service vendor's name and address, if required

- Author, developer, or person responsible for acquiring the media

This media database is an extremely important resource that is shared among all team members. It allows the producer (and peers) to manage the deadlines and deliverables for media content production. Because the database is centrally located on a networked file server, the entire library of media elements can be backed up regularly for safekeeping. Furthermore, the database provides an excellent reusable resource for new productions. (This database is likely to be an object-oriented database management system—OODBMS, ✔ p. 12.17.)

Text

Text is the primary media element for communicating information in a multimedia production. However, people do not enjoy reading from the computer screen. Therefore, you must make text more appealing by limiting passages to less than 40 words, selecting easy-to-read typefaces, and choosing a large-sized font (✔ p. 6.9). Also, ensure that you proofread your on-screen text very carefully to avoid grammatical and spelling mistakes. Most authoring software tools allow you to enter text directly, import text from an editor or word processor, or scan text using a scanner and optical character recognition (OCR) software (✔ p. 3.13).

Graphics

Two types of graphics are normally included in a multimedia production. *Draw,* or *vector-based, graphics* (✔ p. 6.28) are created using an illustration program, such as Adobe Illustrator or CorelDRAW. Vector graphics are stored as a set of instructions for drawing lines on an invisible screen grid. These files are much smaller than bit-mapped graphics, but they cannot reproduce the quality necessary for displaying photo-realistic images. *Bit-mapped, or raster-based, graphics* (✔ p. 6.28) are created by scanning images and using paint programs, such as Adobe Photoshop or Paint Shop Pro. A bit-mapped image can contain millions of pixels (✔ p. 3.27), which is the smallest unit a computer can display on a monitor. These pixels contain color information that must travel from the storage medium (hard disk or CD-ROM) through memory to the processor, back to memory, and finally to the video card. The larger or more colorful the bit-mapped image, the more storage space is required, and the longer it takes to display on the screen.

Sound

Audio is often the forgotten element in a multimedia production. We get so distracted with the appearance of the screens that we forget to set the ambience and tone using background music, sound effects, and voice narration. Used effectively, sound can enhance the audience's enjoyment of your production. Used ineffectively, sound can elicit reactions opposite to those desired and distract focus from other, more important content.

Using the sound card in a computer, you record sounds by a process called *sampling.* Sampling lets you determine how much information you want to digitize or capture, which also directly affects the file size once the recorded information is saved to a disk. The higher the rate of sampling, the more information must be stored, and the higher the quality of the recorded sound. (For example, a sampling rate of 44.1 kHz means that 44,100 samples are taken every second. If each sample contains 16 bits of information, a sound file can become very large very fast.)

Animation

Animation in a multimedia production can be as simple as an icon bouncing around the screen or as complex as a virtual walkthrough of ancient Greece. Most authoring tools let you animate drawn and text objects, but you will need animation software, such as Autodesk's Animator Pro or LightWave 3D, for more complex sequences. Animation software can produce either a digitized movie file or a series of bit-mapped images that you can later assemble like a *flipbook* (a book that contains a gradually changing image over a series of pages). You create animation similarly to creating a bit-mapped graphic, using a scanner and paint software. Because this is an extremely detail-oriented and time-consuming process, multimedia producers commonly hire a professional animator or contract out their requirements.

Video

Video is an exciting component of multimedia. To retain the attention of your audience, nothing seems to be more effective than sound and motion. In the past few years, digital video on the personal computer has exploded in popularity, in large part because of hardware improvements with accelerated graphics cards and video capture boards (✔ p. 3.18). In fact, many of the leading editing solutions for professional video producers are currently based on the personal computer platform. However, incorporating video into your multimedia production still requires compromises.

You digitize video using a video capture card or a professional media service. Depending on the original quality of the video and the equipment used during the digitizing process, you may create some very large files. Digital video requires more storage space and processing power than any other form of media. For example, a 10-second video clip that will play back using one-quarter of the screen requires about 68 MB of storage space. You can reduce the storage requirements using compression technologies (✔ p. 5.9) and by decreasing the frame output size, the color depth, or the frames per second (fps) display rate. You can also enhance your video clips with voice-overs, music and sound effects, animated titles, and scene transitions using video-editing software such as Adobe Premiere.

The Authoring Process

Today's popular authoring programs simplify the task of multimedia development by providing a user-friendly environment for placing and presenting digital media. Within the typical authoring environment, you will find design templates, pre-built component libraries, and media catalogs. The existence of these elements allows you to spend more time designing the user interface and flow of the multimedia title, rather than having to write and debug lines of code. To get the desired interactivity from your title, however, you will most likely attach some procedural code to objects like graphics, buttons, and menus.

Several multimedia authoring and presentation programs offer a click-and-drag model for creating multimedia titles. In reality, the development of a commercial multimedia title is much more intense, closely resembling the model for applications software development. Although the click-and-drag technique may be used for creating electronic slide presentations and for prototyping a production, most developers adopt sophisticated authoring and programming tools to get the performance and interactivity desired by end-users.

Selecting a multimedia authoring software is much more involved than determining which word processor or electronic spreadsheet to use. Unlike word processors that contain basically the same features, one authoring tool can differ dramatically from the next. One way to categorize authoring software is by the output that is created. Some authoring tools are geared toward developing *linear slide-based presentations,* while other tools are better for creating *interactive presentations* or *computer-based training (CBT) programs.* Not surprisingly, most of the authoring software currently available lets you develop and deliver content via the World Wide Web.

Multimedia Presentation Software

Presentation software allows you to create multimedia slide-shows, animated business presentations, and informational kiosk applications. Software in this category uses a slide-based, *timeline* metaphor for sequencing a multimedia presentation. This linear format is supplemented by outlining and sorting tools, which allow you to easily rearrange and navigate the slides in your presentation. You can also specify hyperlinks for jumping directly to a specific slide. Some of the more advanced multimedia features that you can incorporate include path animation, object and slide transitions, background music, and video clips. In addition to the program files, most presentation software packages also include clip art media, bit-mapped images, sound and video clips, and graphical elements such as buttons and icons. Products in this software category include Adobe Persuasion, Astound, Asymetrix Compel, Corel Click & Create, HyperCard, Lotus Freelance, and Microsoft PowerPoint.

This PowerPoint screen shows some layouts to choose from to prepare a presentation using a slide.

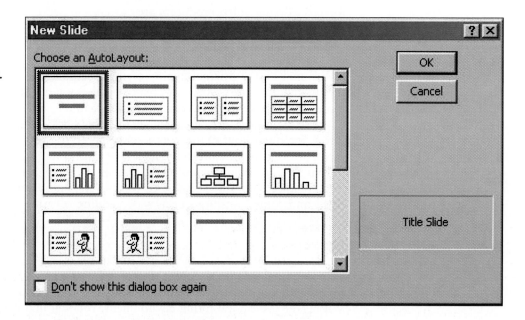

Multimedia Authoring Software

To move beyond creating simple business presentations, you can consider using a full-featured multimedia authoring tool like Macromedia Director. Tools in this category provide much greater control over media elements, synchronization, and interactivity. Although these features may not be critical for creating slide-based presentations to the board of directors or for organizing your lecture notes, they are extremely important for developing interactive titles that must capture and retain your audience's attention. Some products that can help in this category include Allen Communication's Quest, Macromedia Director, and QuarkImmedia.

Multimedia CBT Authoring Software

Approximately 80% of the authoring tools purchased today are used in the development of computer-based training. Aside from the development process, the features required for administering and managing computer-based instruction far exceed the capabilities of today's presentation software. Authoring software for computer-based training (CBT) must support high levels of interactivity and complex evaluation methods, along with exceptional media and device handling.

Therefore, computer-based authoring software is typically much more advanced, complex, and costly than presentation-oriented authoring software. Products in this software category include AimTech IconAuthor, Asymetrix Toolbook, and Macromedia Authorware.

Career Opportunities in Multimedia

Developing a multimedia production requires many skilled and talented people. Although you may be able to assemble content yourself using one of the previously mentioned authoring tools, few people have the expertise to create all the necessary media elements. To be successful working alone requires that you identify the people or companies to whom you can *outsource* work. Some roles and responsibilities that you may require in completing a multimedia production include:

■ *Producer/director:* The producer or director acts as the manager of a multimedia production. This role requires competence in planning and budgeting, cost control and analysis, resource scheduling, and personnel management. This person is also responsible for directing the content, focusing and motivating the team, and dealing with the client. Project management software (✔ p. 6.25) may come in handy here.

■ *Scriptwriter/content expert:* The scriptwriter or content expert researches the topic and prepares a written treatment for the multimedia production. This role requires excellent research, writing, and communication skills. In addition to being directly involved in storyboarding, this person works closely with the producer and media content developers throughout the production process.

■ *Editor/proofreader:* The editor and proofreader refines the script and ensures consistency among the storyboards and written treatment. In other words, this person is responsible for finalizing and polishing all the written material on-screen for interest, clarity, and accuracy. In many cases, the editor or proofreader also acts as a tester as the production nears completion.

■ *Interface designer:* The interface designer provides the "look and feel" of a production. This person prepares the initial storyboards from the written treatment, designs the flow and navigation controls, and establishes the program's physical and logical structure, also called a *map.* Working closely with the art director and producer, the interface designer selects the fonts, colors, illustrations, and images, and then determines the placement of all media elements.

■ *Artist/illustrator:* The graphic artist or illustrator helps develop the storyboards with the interface designer and prepares the final graphics for the production. This person is responsible for producing vector illustrations and other graphics, scanning images and photographs, and acquiring stock content from libraries and catalogs.

■ *Animator:* The animator is responsible for preparing the final animation clips used in a production. With smaller production teams, this person also acts as the artist or illustrator. The animator is responsible for specifying path animation used for text and graphic objects, producing two- and three-dimensional animated sequences for digital video playback, and creating models and rendered objects for backgrounds, buttons, and icons.

■ *Audio technician:* The audio technician is responsible for preparing, producing, and digitizing the background music, sound effects, and voice-over narration.

Until 50 years ago, the surface of the ocean was an impenetrable curtain. Now, however, modern technology has enabled people to explore the ocean to depths of about 1000 feet. The deepest of the deep sea is best explored by microprocessor-controlled robots, like those shown here, which can take photographs at 7000 feet. Here *National Geographic* inventor and photographer Emory Christof controls the robots from a boat on the surface.

This person must also research existing stock content from libraries and catalogs.

■ *Video technician:* The video technician is responsible for staging, filming, and digitizing the required video clips. The role also includes researching existing stock content from libraries and catalogs.

■ *Programmer:* The programmer writes the code that integrates all the media elements and builds interactivity into the production. This role typically requires several people with specific skills in a variety of authoring software and programming languages. For example, one programmer may combine the media and implement the navigational controls using an authoring tool, such as Macromedia Director. Another programmer may use the C (✔ p. 10.21) language to create special programs for improving the performance of the title and for adding functions not found in the authoring software. And yet another programmer may be responsible for producing an optimized Internet version of the multimedia production based on the Java language.

■ *Evaluator/tester:* The testing process for a multimedia production is often separated into an alpha and a beta stage. In the *alpha* stage, only internal testers review and provide feedback on the production. In the *beta* stage, the production is released to outside testers for their feedback.

The Internet allows multimedia producers to access talented content developers from around the world. Take, for example, Paul D. Hibbitts of Software Usability Design Associates (SUDA), a one-person multimedia development company used by some of Canada's largest universities and colleges. Working from his home-based studio in Vancouver, British Columbia, Paul works with talented artists, writers, and programmers from across Canada to create educational multimedia courseware.

13.2 Artificial Intelligence (AI)

Key Question **What is artificial intelligence, and what are the primary areas of research within AI?**

You're having trouble with your new software program. You call the "help desk" at the software maker. Do you get a busy signal or get put on hold to listen to music for several minutes? Technical support lines are often swamped, and waiting is commonplace. Or, to deal with your software difficulty, do you find yourself dealing with . . . other software?

This event is not unlikely. Programs that can walk you through a problem and help solve it are called *expert systems* (✔ p. 11.19). Expert systems are one of the most useful applications of an area known as *artificial intelligence.*

Artificial intelligence (AI) is a group of related technologies used in developing machines to emulate human-like qualities, such as learning, reasoning, communicating, seeing, and hearing. AI evolved from early attempts to write programs that would allow computers to compete with humans in games such as chess and to prove mathematical theorems.

What Is AI Supposed to Do?

The aim of AI is to produce a generation of systems that will be able to communicate with us by speech and hearing, use "vision" (scanning) that approximates the way people see, and be capable of intelligent problem solving. In other words, AI refers to computer-based systems that can mimic or simulate human thought processes and actions. Some of the primary areas of research within AI that are of particular interest to business users are robotics, natural language processing, fuzzy logic, expert systems, neural networks, and virtual reality.

Robots and Perception Systems

Robotics is a field devoted to developing machines that can perform work normally done by people. The machines themselves, of course, are called robots. According to *Webster's Tenth New Collegiate Dictionary,* a **robot** is an automatic device that performs functions ordinarily ascribed to human beings or that operates with what appears to be almost human intelligence. It derives from the Polish word *robotnik,* which means "slave."

All robots are preprogrammed. That is, they can only respond to situations for which they have been specifically programmed. *(See Figure 13.1, next page.)* The most extensive uses of robots so far have been in automobile manufacturing or in dangerous environments. Dante II, for instance, is an eight-legged, 10-foot-high, satellite-linked robot used by scientists to explore the inside of Mount Spurr, an active volcano in Alaska.

Robots that emulate the human capabilities of sight, hearing, touch, and smell and then respond based on the new information are called *intelligent robots,* or **perception systems.** One future application of intelligent robotics is a machine that is small enough to be swallowed. It will be able to scan intestinal walls with a miniature camera, searching for possible tumors, and send the images to a doctor watching a monitor. Then, under instructions from the doctor, it will take a tissue sample. Obviously, this robot is very sensitive to touch.

Robot vision has already been successfully implemented in many manufacturing systems. To "see," a computer measures varying intensities of light reflected

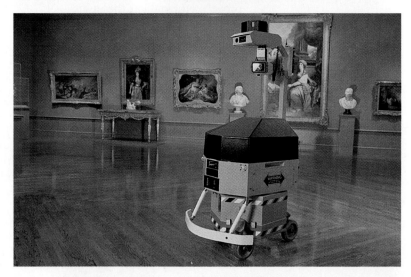

Figure 13.1

(*Top left*) The Human Extender Robot allows people to pick up very heavy packages. (*Top right*) NASA remote-controlled research robot. (*Middle left*) At Governor Hospital in New York City, 11-year-old Jamie Quinones strolls down the hall of the childrens' unit with SICO, the robot. Robots like SICO help children with emotional problems come out of their shells. (*Middle right*) Security robot on patrol at the Los Angeles Museum of Art. (*Lower right*) A police robot handles a live bomb via remote control.

Japanese robot technology: an artificial fish that looks and swims exactly like the real thing. The silicone sea bream created by Mitsubishi weighs 5 ½ pounds, is about 1 ½ feet long, and can swim for up to 38 minutes before it needs recharging.

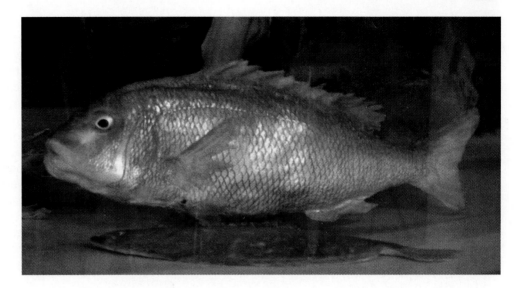

off a shape; each intensity has a numbered value that is compared to a template of intensity patterns stored in memory. One of the main reasons for the importance of vision is that production-line robots must be able to discriminate among parts. General Electric, for example, has Bin Vision Systems, which allows a robot to identify and pick up specific parts in an assembly-line format.

Another area of interest is the "personal" robot, familiar to us from science fiction. SRI International in Menlo Park, California, recently unveiled a robot that can do heart bypass operations that traditionally require a deep chest incision with no more than a small skin cut. Doctors will use the pencil-size robotics device to perform the complex operation. B.O.B. (Brains On Board) is a device sold by Visual Machines that can speak (using prerecorded phrases), follow people around using infrared sensors, and avoid obstacles by using ultrasonic sound. Software will allow the robot to bring its owner something to drink from the refrigerator. Another type of personal robot is the Spimaster, built by Cybermotion. This security robot patrols up to 15 miles per shift, collecting video images and recording data. If it senses a problem, it heads for the trouble zone and sounds alarms on-site and at security headquarters. Developers are working on a personal robot to act as a servant and a companion to the elderly.

The performance limitations of personal robots reflect the difficulties in designing and programming intelligent robots. In fact, we have just begun to appreciate how complicated such mundane tasks as recognizing a can of Pepsi in the refrigerator can be. Another concern is that if a robot does in fact become intelligent, what would stop it from deciding that work is something to avoid?

Natural Language Processing

Natural languages are ordinary human languages, such as English. (A second definition is that they are programming languages, called fifth-generation languages, that give people a more natural connection with computers; ✔ p. 10.17.) **Natural language processing** is the study of ways for computers to recognize and understand human language, whether in spoken or written form. The primary difficulty in implementing this kind of communication is the sheer complexity of everyday conversation. For example, we readily understand the sentence "The spirit is willing, but the flesh is weak." One natural language processing system, however, understood this sentence to mean "The wine is agreeable, but the meat has spoiled." It also understood the phrase "out of sight, out of mind" to mean "blind idiot." It turns out that the system must have access to a much larger body of knowledge than just a dictionary of terms. People use their world knowledge to help them understand what another person is saying. For example, we know the question "Coffee?" means "Do you want a cup of coffee?" But a computer would have difficulty understanding this one-word question.

Most existing natural language systems run on large computers; however, scaled-down versions are now available for microcomputers. For example, a commercial product called Intellect uses a limited English vocabulary to help users orally query databases on both mainframes and microcomputers. One of the most successful natural language systems is LUNAR, developed to help users analyze the rocks brought back from the moon. It has access to extensive detailed knowledge about geology in its knowledge database and answers users' questions. The U.S. Postal Service is currently using a language-processing system that was developed by Verbex to speed up the sorting and delivery of mail that doesn't include a zip code. After the human mail sorter reads the address into a microphone, the computer responds in an electronic voice with the correct zip code.

Fuzzy Logic

One relatively recent concept being used in the development of natural languages is fuzzy logic. Classical logic has been based on either/or propositions. For example, to evaluate the phrase "The cat is fat," classical logic requires a single cutoff point to determine when the cat is fat, such as a specific weight for a certain length. It is either in the set of fat cats or it is not. However, "fat" is a vague, or "gray," notion; it's more likely that the cat is "a little fat." **Fuzzy logic** is a method of dealing with imprecise data and vagueness, with problems that have many answers rather than one. Unlike traditional "crisp" digital logic, fuzzy logic is more like human reasoning: It deals with probability and credibility. That is, instead of being simply true or false, a proposition is *mostly* true or *mostly* false, or *more* true or *more* false.

A frequently given example of an application of fuzzy logic is in running elevators. How long will most people wait for an elevator before getting antsy? About a minute and a half, say researchers at the Otis Elevator Company. The Otis artificial intelligence division has done considerable research into how elevators may be programmed to reduce waiting time. Ordinarily when someone on a floor in the middle of a building pushes the call button, the system will send whichever elevator is closest. However, that car might be filled with passengers, who will be delayed by the new stop (perhaps making them antsy). Another car, however, might be empty. In a fuzzy logic system, the computer assesses not only which car is nearest but also how full the cars are before deciding which one to send.

Fuzzy logic circuitry is also used in autofocus cameras to enable the camera to focus properly.

Expert Systems: Human Expertise in a Computer

We described expert systems in Chapter 11 in relation to its uses by management and nonmanagement personnel to solve specific problems, such as how to reduce production costs or improve workers' productivity. In this section we describe expert systems in more detail. Recall from Chapter 11 that an *expert system* is a set of computer programs that performs a task at the level of a human expert. To expand on that definition, an **expert system** is an interactive computer program that can apply rules and data to input questions or problems in such a way as to generate conclusions. The program helps users solve problems that would otherwise require the assistance of a human expert. *It is important to emphasize that* *expert systems are designed to be users' assistants, not replacements. Also, their success depends on the quality of the data and rules obtained from the human experts.*

An expert system solves problems that require substantial expertise to understand. The system's performance depends on the body of facts (knowledge) and the heuristics (rules of thumb) that are fed into the computer. Knowledge engineers gather, largely through interviews, the expert knowledge and the heuristics from human experts in the relevant field, such as medicine, engineering, or geology. (For example, in medicine, an expert system might be asked whether one treatment is better for a patient than another.) The responses recorded during the interviews are codified and entered into a knowledge base that can be used by a computer. An expert system has the capacity to store the collection of knowledge and manipulate it in response to user inquiries; in some cases, it can even explain its responses to the user.

An expert system has three major program components *(see Figure 13.2):*

1. *Knowledge base:* A **knowledge base** is an expert system's database of knowledge about a particular subject. This includes relevant facts, information, beliefs, assumptions, and procedures for solving problems. One basic unit of knowledge is expressed as an IF-THEN-ELSE rule ("IF this happens, THEN do this, ELSE do that"). Programs can have as many as 10,000 rules (heuristics), which express the reasoning procedures of experts on the subject. A system called ExperTAX, for example, which helps accountants figure out a client's tax options, consists of more than 2000 rules.

2. *Inference engine:* The **inference engine** is the software that controls the search of the expert system's knowledge base and produces conclusions. It takes the problem posed by the user of the system and fits it into the rules in the knowledge base. It then derives a conclusion from the facts and rules contained in the knowledge base. *Reasoning* refers to the way the inference engine attacks problems. There are several types of reasoning processes, which are too technical to go into here. In any case, the system must be able to explain its reasoning process to the user, if requested.

3. *User interface:* The user interface is what appears on the display screen for the user to interact with. It gives the user the ability to ask questions and get answers.

Expert systems include stand-alone microcomputers, as well as workstations and terminals connected to servers and larger computer systems in local area networks and/or wide area networks (✔ p. 7.25).

Figure 13.2 Components of an expert system. The three components are the user interface, the inference engine, and the knowledge base.

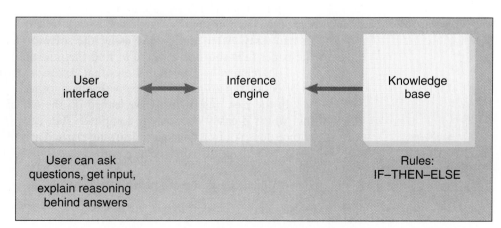

Expert Systems at Work

One of the most famous expert systems—although since replaced by updated ones—is MYCIN, which diagnoses infectious diseases and recommends appropriate drugs. For example, bacteremia (bacteria in the blood) can be fatal unless treated quickly. Whereas traditional tests require 24 to 48 hours to verify a diagnosis, MYCIN provides physicians with a diagnosis and recommended therapy within minutes. To use MYCIN, the physician enters data on a patient; as the data is being entered, MYCIN asks questions (for example, "Is patient a burn patient?"). On the basis of the answers, MYCIN's inference engine "reasons" out a diagnosis: "IF the infection is primary bacteria, AND the site of the culture is a gastrointestinal tract, THEN there is evidence (0.7) that the identity of the organism causing the disease is Bacteroides." The "0.7" means that MYCIN "thinks" there is a 7 out of 10 chance that this diagnosis is correct. This pattern closely follows that of human thought; much of our knowledge is inexact and incomplete, and we often reason using odds (for instance, "There's a 40% chance it's going to rain") when we don't have access to complete and accurate information.

The Residential Burglary Expert System (REBES) uses certain rules of thumb to help a detective investigate a crime scene. REBES, which acts like a partner to the detective, might ask "Did the intruder search the entire house? If so, an accomplice might be involved" or "Was valuable jewelry taken but cheaper jewelry left behind? If so, thieves may be professionals/repeaters."

Examples of other expert systems are XCON, which puts together the best arrangement of Digital Equipment Corporation (DEC) computer system components for a given company; DENDRAL, which identifies chemical compounds; PROSPECTOR, a system that evaluates potential geological sites of oil, natural gas, and so on; and DRILLING ADVISOR, which assists in diagnosing and resolving oil-rig problems. CLUES (Countrywide Loan Underwriting Expert System) evaluates home-mortgage-loan applications. CRUSH takes a body of expert advice and combines it with worksheets reflecting a user's business situation to come up with a customized strategy to "crush" competitors.

General users can also take advantage of expert systems on certain topics via the Web. Umagic's Web site offers consultations on fashion, dieting, stress management, and relationships.

Essay-Grading Technology: Expert Knowledge?

Peter Foltz, a professor of psycholinguistics at New Mexico State University in Las Cruces, has developed Intelligent Essay Assessor software, which uses a kind of artificial intelligence called *latent semantic analysis* to grade student essays.

Assessor first "learns" about a topic from an electronic encyclopedia or textbook. Then it "reads" pregraded essays to learn what constitutes a good or bad essay. After grading the essay, the software tells each student where the paper falls short and where to find the information to improve it.

Foltz claims his research shows that Assessor agrees with human graders as often as human graders agree with one another.

In the past, instructors have leaned on the use of multiple-choice testing, which is easily checked by computer. But, according to Foltz, multiple choice doesn't always measure learning particularly well. "Essay is a much better way to get at what people know," says Foltz. "It allows a much wider range of expression."

An Assessor demo is available at *www.knowledge-technologies.com.*

From *Online Learning News,* 12/22/98

Building an Expert System

Capturing human expertise for the computer is a time-consuming and difficult task. **Knowledge engineers** are trained to elicit knowledge (for example, by interview) from experts and build the expert system. The knowledge engineer may program the system in an artificial intelligence programming language, such as LISP or PROLOG, or may use system-building tools that provide a structure. Tools allow faster design but are less flexible than languages. An example of such a tool is EMYCIN, which is MYCIN without any of MYCIN's knowledge. A knowledge engineer can theoretically enter any knowledge (as long as it is describable in rules) into this empty shell and create a new system. The completed new system will solve problems as MYCIN does, but the subject matter in the knowledge base may be completely different (for example, car repair).

Expert systems are usually run on large computers—often dedicated artificial intelligence computers—because of these systems' gigantic appetites for memory; however, some scaled-down expert systems (such as the OS/2 [✔ p. 5.18] version of KBMS, Knowledge Base Management System) run on microcomputers. Negotiator Pro from Beacon Expert Systems for IBM and Apple Macintosh computers helps executives plan effective negotiations with other people by examining their personality types and recommending negotiating strategies. Scaled-down systems generally do not have all the capabilities of large expert systems, and most have limited reasoning abilities. LISP and PROLOG compilers (✔ p. 10.15) are available for microcomputers, as are some system-building tools such as EXPERT-EASE, NEXPERT, and VP-Expert, which allow relatively unsophisticated users to build their own expert system. Such software tools for building expert systems are called *shells*.

Using Computer Models to Study the Complexities of Human Society

The Anasazi Indians mysteriously abandoned Arizona's Long House Valley many centuries ago, but researchers have now brought them back—at least in a computer simulation.

In the computer model, hundreds of virtual people make decisions on whether to have children, to move to a new area of the valley, or to cultivate more land. The virtual people react to actual environmental conditions of the period from 400 to 1400 BCE, which have been programmed into the model.

The team of archeologists, anthropologists, and computer scientists who created the simulation can replay the history over and over again, changing the rules that govern the people's behavior and observing how small changes in rainfall and other factors might have affected settlement patterns long ago.

For more information about modeling, check *The Journal of Artificial Societies and Social Simulation* (*www.soc.surrey.ac.uk/JASSS/*).

From Jeffrey R. Young, "Using Computer Models to Study the Complexities of Human Society," *The Chronicle of Higher Education*

Implications for Business

Expert systems are becoming increasingly important to business and manufacturing firms. However, it is difficult to define what constitutes "expertise" in business. Unlike some other areas—notably math, medicine, and chemistry—business is not made up of a specific set of inflexible facts and rules. Some business activities, however, do lend themselves to expert system development. DEC has developed several in-house expert systems, including ILPRS (which assists in long-range planning) and IPPMS (which assists in project management).

Another difficulty is that businesses want systems that can be integrated into their existing computer systems, whereas expert systems are usually designed to run in a stand-alone mode. Furthermore, who will use the expert system? Who will be responsible for its maintenance? Who will have authority to add and/or delete knowledge in the expert system? What are the legal ramifications of decisions made by an expert system? These and other questions will have to be answered before expert systems are fully accepted in the business environment.

Cost is also a factor. Associated costs include purchasing hardware and software, hiring personnel, publishing and distribution costs (if the expert system is used at more than one location), and maintenance costs, which are usually more than the total of any costs already incurred. The costs can easily run into the many thousands of dollars. However, over the last few years, the number of implementations of expert systems has exploded from the hundreds to the thousands as businesses realize the benefits of better performance, reduced errors, and increased efficiency. In addition, less expensive micro-based tools are becoming increasingly powerful and available to businesses.

Neural Networks

Artificial intelligence and fuzzy logic principles are also being applied to the development of neural networks. **Neural networks** use physical electronic devices or software to mimic the neurological structure of the human brain. *(See Figure 13.3.)* Because they are structured to mimic the rudimentary circuitry of the cells in the human brain, they learn from example and don't require detailed instructions.

To understand how neural networks operate, let us compare them to the operation of the human brain.

■ *The human neural network:* The word *neural* comes from *neurons,* or nerve cells. The neurons are connected by a three-dimensional lattice called *axons.* Electrical connections between neurons are activated by synapses.

   The human brain is made up of about 100 billion neurons. However, these cells do not act as "computer memory" sites. You could eliminate any cell—or even a few million—in your brain and not alter your "mind." Where do memory and learning lie? In the electrical connections between cells, the synapses. Using electrical pulses, the neurons send "on/off" messages along the synapses.

■ *The computer neural network:* In a hardware neural network, the nerve cell is replaced by a transistor, which acts as a switch. Wires connect the cells (transistors) with one another. Synapses are replaced by electronic components called *resistors,* which determine whether cells should activate the electricity to other cells. A software neural network emulates a hardware neural network, although it doesn't work as fast.

   Computer-based neural networks use special AI software and complicated fuzzy-logic processor chips to take inputs and convert them to outputs with a kind of logic similar to human logic.

Ordinary computers mechanically obey instructions according to set rules. However, neural-network computers, like children, learn by example, problem solving, and memory by association. The network "learns" by fine-tuning its connections in response to each situation it encounters. (In the brain, learning takes place through changes in the synapses.) If you're teaching a neural network to

Figure 13.3 Neural networks are based on the brain's cell circuitry.

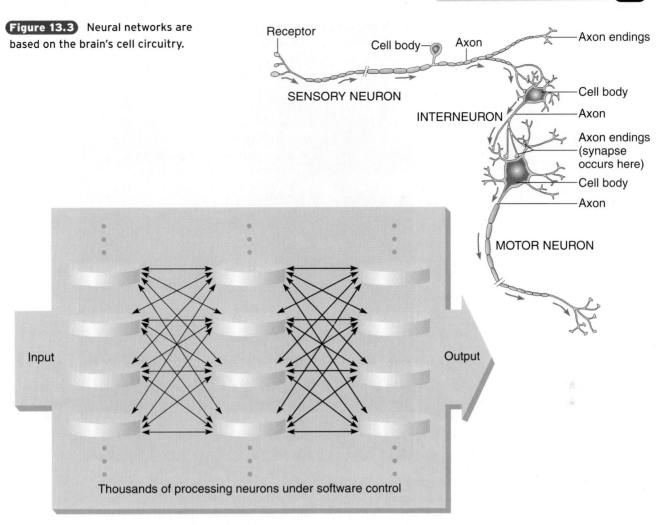

Thousands of processing neurons under software control

speak, for example, you train it by giving it sample words and sentences as well as the pronunciations. The connections between the electronic "neurons" gradually change, allowing more or less current to pass.

Using software from a neural-network producer, Intel has developed a neural-network chip that contains many more transistors than the Pentium. Other chip makers are also working on neural-network chips. Over the next few years, these chips will begin to bring the power of these silicon "brains" not only to your PC but also to such tasks as automatically balancing laundry loads in washing machines.

Neural networks are already being used in a variety of situations. One helped a mutual-fund manager to outperform the stock market by 2.3–5.6 percentage points over three years. At a San Diego hospital emergency room in which patients complained of chest pains, a neural-network program that was given all information available to the doctors correctly diagnosed patients with heart attacks 97% of the time, compared to 78% for the human physicians.[4] In Chicago, a neural-net system has also been used to evaluate patient X-rays to look for signs of breast cancer. It outperformed most doctors in distinguishing malignant tumors from benign ones.[5] Banks use neural-network software to spot irregularities in purchasing patterns associated with individual accounts, thus often noticing when a credit card is stolen before its owner does. Ford Motor Co. uses an advanced neural network program designed by NASA's Jet Propulsion Laboratory to diagnose engine trouble.

Robot arms are used to handle radioactive material.

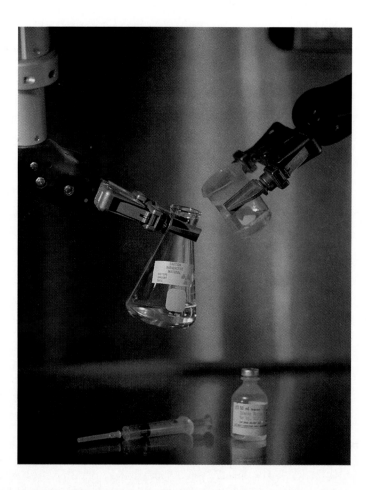

Another approach to combining the human system and a computer system is the "Soul Catcher" project, in which British researchers are attempting to develop a computer that can be implanted in the brain to complement human memory and computational skills. And in Santa Clara, California, engineers at Affymetrix are making computer chips containing DNA to diagnose genetic mutations.

Genetic Algorithms

A **genetic algorithm** is a program that uses Darwinian principles of random mutation to improve itself. The algorithms are lines of computer code that act like living organisms. Different sections of code haphazardly come together, producing programs. Like Darwin's rules of evolution, many chunks of code compete with one another to see which can best perform the desired solution—the aim of the program. Some chunks will even become extinct. Those that survive will combine with other survivors and will produce offspring programs.

Expert systems can capture and preserve the knowledge of expert specialists, but they may be slow to adapt to change. Neural networks can sift through mountains of data and discover obscure causal relationships, but if there is too much or too little data they may be ineffective—garbage in, garbage out. Genetic algorithms, by contrast, use endless trial and error to learn from experience—to discard unworkable approaches and grind away at promising approaches with the kind of tireless energy of which humans are incapable.

The awesome power of genetic algorithms has already found applications. LBS Capital Management Fund of Clearwater, Florida, uses it to help pick stocks for a pension fund. In something called the FacePrints project, witnesses have used a genetic algorithm to describe and identify criminal suspects. Drawing on the skills that salmon use to find spawning grounds, Texas Instruments is producing a genetic algorithm that shipping companies can use to let packages "seek" their own best routes to their destinations. A hybrid expert system–genetic algorithm called Engenous was used to boost performance in the Boeing 777 jet engine, a feat that involved billions of mind-boggling calculations.

Artificial Life, the Turing Test, and AI Ethics

Genetic algorithms would seem to lead us away from mechanistic ideas of artificial intelligence and into more fundamental questions: "What is life, and how can we replicate it out of silicon chips, networks, and software?" We are dealing now not with artificial intelligence but with artificial life. *Artificial life,* or *A-life,* is a field of study concerned with "creatures"—computer instructions or pure information—that are created, replicate, evolve, and die as if they were living organisms.

Of course, "silicon life" does not have two principal attributes associated with true living things—it is not water- and carbon-based. Yet in other respects such creatures mimic life: if they cannot learn or adapt, they perish.

How can we know when computers have achieved human intelligence? Can you always know, say, when you're on the phone, whether you're talking to a human being or to a computer? Clearly, with the strides made in artificial intelligence and artificial life, this question is no longer just academic.

Interestingly, this matter was addressed back in 1950 by Alan Turing, an English mathematician and computer pioneer. Turing predicted that by the end of the century computers would be able to mimic human thinking and to converse so naturally that their communications would be indistinguishable from a person's. Out of these observations came the Turing test. The **Turing test** is a test or game for determining whether a computer possesses "intelligence" or "self-awareness."

In the Turing test, a human judge converses by means of a computer terminal with two entities hidden in another location. One entity is a person typing on a keyboard. The other is a software program. As the judge types in and receives messages on the terminal, he or she must decide whether the entity is human. In this test, intelligence and the ability to think is demonstrated by the computer's success in fooling the judge. *(See Figure 13.4.)*

Judith Anne Gunther participated as one of eight judges in the third annual Loebner Prize Competition, which is based on Turing's ideas. (With support from the National Science Foundation and the Alfred P. Sloane Foundation, Hugh Loebner, a New York businessman has offered a $100,000 prize for the first computer system that can pass the Turing test by fooling the subject into thinking he or she is communicating with a person.) The "conversations" are restricted to predetermined topics, such as baseball. This is because today's best programs have neither the databases nor the syntactical ability to handle an unlimited number of subjects. Conversations with each entity are limited to 15 minutes. At the end of the contest, the program that fools the judges most is the one that wins.

Gunther found that she wasn't fooled by any of the computer programs. The winning program, for example, relied as much on deflection and wit as it did on responding logically and conversationally. (For example, to a judge trying to discuss a federally funded program, the computer said: "You want logic? I'll give you logic: shut up, shut up, shut up, shut up, shut up, now go away! How's that for logic?") However, Gunther *was* fooled by one of the five humans, a real person discussing abortion. "He was so uncommunicative," wrote Gunther, "that I pegged him for a computer."[6]

Figure 13.4 Turing test. In this test, a human judge converses via computer terminal with two entities in another location. One is a human being, the other a computer program. The task of the judge is to figure out whether the "intelligence" he or she is conversing with is human or not. Often the computer just gives itself away by being illogical, as in this "conversation."

"**Computer:** As a psychoanalyst, I am familiar with discussing such marital troubles with you as the patient on the couch. If you don't have a bad marriage just pretend that you do. Please start with 'My wife . . .' or 'My husband . . .'.
Judge: OK, I'll pretend I have a bad marriage. Let's say the reason is because he never picks up his dirty underwear. Is this marriage irreparable?
Computer: Well, if you think I'm hopeless, you can always just swear at me."
—Judith Anne Gunther, "An Encounter with A.I.," *Popular Science*

At the turn of the century, no machine has consistently passed the Turing test. And on those few occasions when interrogators have been fooled by computers, the transcripts reveal a less-than-penetrating interrogation. (Hence one problem with the Turing test: Is it measuring the thinking power of the machines or of the humans?)

Work with artificial intelligence and artificial life—like everything else that humans do—raises important ethical questions. Many users are not aware that computer software, such as expert systems, is often subtly shaped by the ethical judgments and assumptions of the people who create it. In his book *Ethics in Modeling,* William A. Wallace, professor of decision sciences at Rensselaer Polytechnic Institute, offers the example of a bank that had to modify its loan-evaluation software after discovering that the software rejected some applications because of an undue emphasis on old age as a negative factor.[7] Another expert system, used by health maintenance organizations (HMOs), instructs doctors on when they should opt for expensive medical procedures, such as magnetic resonance imaging tests (MRIs). HMOs like this system because it helps control expenses, but critics are concerned that doctors will have to base decisions not on the best medicine but simply on "satisfactory" medicine combined with cost cutting. Clearly, there is no such thing as completely "value-free" technology. Human beings build it, use it, and have to live with the results.

Also, some people think that AI is dangerous because it does not address the ethics of using machines to make decisions nor does it require machines to use ethics as part of the decision-making process. And certain commentators have expressed another concern: that, as machines take over more tasks once performed by humans, it becomes more plausible that humans are not so different from machines. Contrary to the lessons of religions and poetry, are we really just soulless automata?

According to philosopher David Chalmers, whose book *The Conscious Mind* deals with the enigma of human consciousness, "The more we think about computers, the more we realize how strange consciousness is."[8]

Virtual Reality (VR)

Want to take a trip to the moon? Be a race car driver? See the world through the eyes of an ocean-bottom creature or your cat? Without leaving your chair, you can experience almost anything you want through the form of AI called virtual reality (VR). **Virtual reality** is a kind of computer-generated artificial reality that projects a person into a sensation of three-dimensional space. *(See Figure 13.5, next page.)* In virtual reality, the user is inside a world instead of just observing an image on the screen. To put yourself into virtual reality, you need the following interactive sensory equipment:

■ *Headgear:* The headgear, or helmet—which is called a *head-mounted display (HMD)*—has two small video display screens, one for each eye, that create the sense of three-dimensionality. Headphones pipe in stereophonic sound or even three-dimensional sound, which makes you think you are hearing sounds not only near each ear but all around you.

■ *Glove:* The glove has sensors that collect data about your hand movements.

■ *Software:* Software gives the wearer of this special headgear and glove the interactive sensory experience that simulates real-world experiences.

You may have seen virtual reality used in arcade-type games, such as Atlantis, a computer simulation of The Lost Continent. You may even have tried playing golf on a virtual golf range or driven a virtual racing car. There are also a few virtual-reality home video games. However, a far more important application is in simulators for training.

Simulators are devices that represent the behavior of physical or abstract systems. Virtual-reality simulation technologies have been used, for instance, to instruct bus drivers by creating lifelike bus control panels and various scenarios such as icy road conditions. They are used to train pilots on various aircraft and to prepare air-traffic controllers for equipment failures. They also help children who prefer hands-on learning to explore subjects such as chemistry. In Virginia, a VR program allows divers-in-training to experience a 3-D underwater simulation of the Chesapeake Bay and its surrounding tributaries.

Of particular value are the uses of virtual reality in health and medicine. For instance, surgeons-in-training can rehearse their craft through simulation on "digital patients." Virtual-reality therapy has been used for autistic children and in the treatment of phobias, such as extreme fear of public speaking or high places. It has also been used to rally the spirits of quadriplegics and paraplegics by engaging them in plays and song-and-dance routines.

A recent development in VR is called CAVE, for Cave Automated Virtual Environment, created by the Electronic Visualization Laboratory at the University of Illinois in Chicago. A CAVE is about the size of a walk-in closet. Once inside, you put on 3-D glasses and immediately become part of a computer animation. Virtual reality is all around you, and you can interact with it using an electronic wand. There are more than 100 CAVEs at universities, government facilities, and companies, including General Motors and NASA. They help engineers see 3-D, full-size models of cars and enable scientists to walk inside models of single molecules. With older forms of VR, the experience was available only to the person wearing the helmet. With CAVE, however, several people can experience the virtual environment at the same time.

Perhaps the largest problem facing virtual-reality developers is how to keep users from getting sick. Although improvements in head tracking, force feedback, and tactile feedback have made virtual reality a better experience, users still

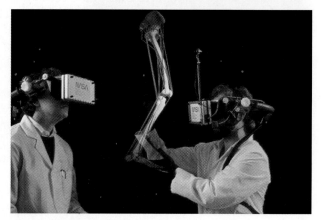

Figure 13.5 (*Top left*) Rotterdam, Netherlands. Seconds away from a disaster, a young captain at the helm tries to steer a container ship away from a collision course with an oil tanker in a virtual environment provided by a navigation simulator. (*Top right*) During a virtual reality experiment in Chapel Hill, North Carolina, a man uses a treadmill to walk through a virtual environment. (*Bottom left*) Using the Dismounted Infrared Combat Simulation Treadmill, Sergeant March Turchin practices using the latest combat equipment in a virtual city. (*Bottom right*) Two medical students study the leg bones of a "virtual cadaver."

sometimes get headaches, experience nausea, and are disoriented during total immersions. Because many virtual-reality systems have not achieved a high level of visual depth and a sophisticated method of anticipating head motion, the systems cause delays that confuse the brain. Any delays between the computer images and the user's movement increase the opportunity for simulator sickness.

Virtual Reality in the Real World

Cloning Buildings: In Dresden, in the former East Germany, there lie the ruins of a centuries-old cathedral called *die Frauenkirche*. Bombed out during the Allied air raids in World War II, this legendary European landmark has literally been a pile of rubble in the middle of the city for nearly 50 years. But now, thanks to German reunification and some IBM computers and software, Dresden is rebuilding the church with astonishing accuracy in a $177 million project. This project, which won't be completed until 2003, marks a turning point for virtual reality.

The Dresden project is arguably the most creative and useful application of virtual reality ever attempted. Using the original architectural plans and old photos, engineers have been able to recreate (simulate), on their computers, in impeccable detail the interior and exterior of the church exactly as it stood before its destruction.

Using 3-D models, the engineers can literally walk through the virtual church and examine its facades, ceilings, and metalwork up closely. In the process, they've managed to identify nearly a third of the original stones in the church and "place" them where they belong. Specialists in Eastern European Baroque interiors are using the same technology to recreate the church's vast, complex inner environments. Meanwhile, the real construction has begun, and there's a multimedia kiosk at the construction site where you can preview the reconstructed church.

Until now, landmarks destroyed by natural or human disaster stayed that way or were rebuilt as modern imitations. Now, with today's computer graphics and improving VR techniques, aging and ruined wonders can reappear before us and future generations. Can Rome rise again?

Digitized Battlefield: Bradley Fighting Vehicles turned their guns on the soldier as he ran to a tree line for cover. Comanche attack helicopters buzzed through the night air, accompanied by the sporadic pounding of bombs.

The soldier peered through his night-vision goggles to locate the source of the fire. He began moving toward higher ground, but 155-mm Howitzer shells turned him back. Debris from the shells fell all around, and the soldier retreated down the hill to the tree line, firing a Beretta pistol at the approaching enemy.

When it was over, no one had suffered so much as a scratch. In fact, no one had truly been in danger—or anywhere near a battlefield. The encounter had taken place in a new type of computerized combat simulator at Fort Belvoir, Virginia. The idea is to expose foot soldiers to the confusion, noise, and shock of battle without the cost and danger of live-fire exercises.

The trainee starts by putting on a virtual-reality helmet, in which tiny screens display images of a battlefield; the scene changes as the head is moved. The soldier walks on a stair-stepping exercise device, which offers more resistance when hills are climbed and less during a descent, to "move" around the simulated scene. An electronic pistol is the soldier's weapon.

Simulated Tours: In matters of tourism, art not only imitates life, it sometimes is better than life. Thus a new generation of attractions has sprung up on the coattails of established tourist destinations, appealing to those who want the travel experience without necessarily putting in much time or effort. Destination Cinema, Inc., runs IMAX theaters at the Grand Canyon, Honolulu, Seattle, Yellowstone Park, and Niagara Falls. Other types of synthetic destinations are also popping up at resort hotels, in malls, in major cities, and on cruise ships.

Driving these new attractions is technology such as virtual reality, big-screen projection, motion simulators, and computerized rides.

Grand Canyon IMAX attracts about 1 million visitors a year and offers viewers stunning views of the canyon that they otherwise would have to hike, fly, and raft to see. Some 650,000 visitors were attracted in 1995 to New York Skyride on the second floor of New York City's Empire State Building. The ride takes tourists on a simulated flight around the city. Ride Niagara offers a journey "over" the falls in a computerized motion simulator.

"Virtual War Can Be Mindgoggling," *San Francisco Chronicle;* Jeff Glasser, *Washington Post;* Susan Carey, "Unnatural Wonders: Simulated Tours Beat the Real Thing," *Wall Street Journal.*

13.3 Intelligent Agents, Information Filtering, & Avatars

Key Question **What are intelligent agents, avatars, and information filtering used for?**

What the online world really needs is a terrific librarian. What's in a library is standardized and well organized, and what's on the Web is unstandardized and chaotic. As a solution, scientists have been developing so-called *intelligent agents* to send out to computer networks to find and filter information. And to make them more friendly they have invented graphical on-screen personifications called *avatars.*

Intelligent Agents

An **intelligent agent** is a computer program that performs work tasks on your behalf, including roaming networks and compiling data. It acts as an electronic assistant that will filter messages, scan news services, and perform similar secretar-

In Linz, Austria, a visitor to a virtual reality center dives and flies effortlessly over cities and countryside, thanks to a computer-driven flight simulator.

ial chores for you. It will also travel over communications lines to nearly any kind of computer database, collecting files to add to your database. In this context, **filtering** means constructing, by means of a program, a custom-made electronic barrier through which only selected or desired data will pass.

Examples of agents are the following.

- *Electronic secretaries:* Wildfire is a voice recognition system (✔ p. 3.16), an electronic secretary that will answer the phone, take messages, track you down on your cell phone and announce the caller, place calls for you, handle e-mail and faxes, and remind you of appointments.

- *E-mail filters:* The ease of e-mail has resulted in a flood of unimportant messages, and people often express opinions they might otherwise have kept to themselves. Programs like BeyondMail will filter your e-mail, alerting you to urgent messages, telling you which require follow-up, and sorting everything according to priorities. For people whose e-mail threatens to overwhelm them with "cyberglut," such an agent is a great help.

- *Electronic clipping services:* Several companies offer customized electronic news services that will scan online news sources and publications looking for information that you have previously specified using keywords. Some will rank a selected article according to how closely it fits your request. Others will pull together articles in the form of a condensed electronic newspaper.

- *Internet agents—spiders, crawlers, and robots: Search engines,* as mentioned in Chapter 8 (✔ p. 8.15), are Web pages containing forms into which you type text regarding your search. The search engine then looks through its database and presents a list of Web sites matching your search criteria. Examples of search engines are AltaVista and Meta Crawler. Of particular interest here, however, are the intelligent agents used to assemble the database that a search engine searches. Most such databases are created by spiders. *Spiders,* also known as *crawlers* or *robots,* are software programs that roam the Web and look for new Web sites by following links from page to page. When a spider finds a new page, it adds information about it—its title, address, and perhaps a summary of the contents—to the search engine's database. (However, with the millions of pages on the Web and the constant changes being made to many of them, there's no way anyone can keep on top of it all, even with information filters and Internet agents.)

  Newer agents can be instructed in plain English to scour the Web for relevant information. For example, they can understand phrases such as "comparative prices and features of sport utility vehicles" and "best places to visit in Southeast Asia."

Avatars

Want to see yourself—or a stand-in for yourself—on your computer screen? Then try using a kind of cyberpersona called an *avatar.* An **avatar** is either (1) a graphical image of you or someone else on a computer screen or (2) a graphical personification of a computer or a process that's running on a computer.

- *Avatar as yourself or others:* The on-screen version of yourself could be "anything from a human form to a pair of cowboys boots with lips," wrote technology columnist Denise Caruso. "Users move them around while talking (via keyboard) with other avatars on the same screen."[9] On the Internet, users participating in online chat rooms furnished like cartoon sets can get together with other users, each of whom can construct an avatar from a variety of heads, clothing, shoes, and even animal identities.

■ *Avatars representing a process:* Avatars are promising as a means of creating an interface that's easier and more comfortable to use, especially for the millions of people who are still computerphobic. One difficulty with designing computer-controlled avatars—also called *agents, characters,* and *bots*—is making sure people don't react negatively to them. Thus, instead of faces or personifications, it may be better to use pictures of notepads, checkbooks, and similar objects.

Intelligent agents, information filtering, and avatars still need to be improved before they can really help us deal efficiently with information overload.

WABOT-2, a robot created in 1984 by Ichiro Kato of Waseda University, Japan, can read sheet music well enough to play simple tunes on an electric organ.

Science

Because science covers so much, here we can sketch only a couple of the ways scientists find information technology useful—looking to the future in space and to the past beneath the earth. We also show how even an amateur can use it to advance environmental science.

A new adventure among scientists is the idea of a "collaboratory," an Internet-based collaborative laboratory, in which researchers all over the world can work together easily even at a distance. An example is the Space Physics & Aeronomy Research Collaboratory, based at the University of Michigan at Ann Arbor. This arrangement allows space physicists to band together to measure the Earth's ionosphere from instruments on four satellites and in Massachusetts, Norway, Puerto Rico, and Peru, using a supercomputer to process the information; the results can be transmitted to scientists in many places at once.[a] The Puerto Rico observatory is also being used by astronomers in a program known as Serendip at the University of California at Berkeley, which is analyzing radio signals from the cosmos for evidence of intelligent life. Part of a project known as "SETI@home" (SETI stands for Search for Extraterrestrial Intelligence), Serendip is enlisting the help of thousands of home computer users to help crunch the numbers. "The plan is to give everybody a different chunk of the sky," said the director of the Berkeley program.[b,c]

On an entirely different scientific front, archaeologists are using ultrasensitive underwater sensors and satellite tracking to find the fabled Queen Cleopatra's Palace in the waters off the Egyptian city of Alexandria, which sank beneath the waves caused by an earthquake 1600 years ago.[d] Archaeologists are also using ground-penetrating radar and other remote-sensing tools coupled to software and high-powered computers to find underground objects and the remains of old buildings, thereby avoiding invasive excavations of prehistoric burial sites.[e] And they are using digital cameras and infrared cameras to take pictures of American Indian rock art in Wyoming and 32,000-year-old cave rock paintings in France, then store them in databases to create a permanent record of what may vanish because of erosion and vandalism.[f,g]

Whatever their feelings about the far-distant past or the unforeseeable future, even nonscientists should be concerned about environmental issues, since this is the world of the present in which we all live. A great deal of information about the environment, from global warming to guidelines on "socially responsible travel," is available on the World Wide Web.[h] The Environmental Defense Fund, for example, has developed a Web site called Scorecard that combines 150 government and university databases to allow users to locate polluters in their community, compile pollution rankings, or research the dangers of common household products.[i]

Some environmental-information Web sites include the following: The Environmental Defense Fund (*www.scorecard.org* and *www.edf.org*), the U.S. Environmental Protection Agency (*www.epa.gov*), the Natural Resources Defense Council (*www. nrdc.org/nrdc*), the Environmental Compliance Assistance Center (*www. hazmat.frcc.cccoes.edu*), and the National Wildlife Federation's Campus Ecology (*www.nwf.org/nwf/campus*).

Home-Based Work

Her job for a software firm—with its long hours and molasses commute—had destroyed her first marriage, and she sometimes wondered if it was destroying her, too. So Jan Jewell, 43, of Hollister, California, quit and started up her own one-woman home-based business—using an electronic knitting machine and software to produce custom-designed baby blankets. She does a half-dozen blankets a day, at $50 to $60 each, selling most of them to customers who come to her through her Web site.[a]

To be sure, there are some drawbacks. An outgoing type, Jewell finds that her work gives her little face-to-face interaction. Her contact with customers is by phone and computer. Her husband works outside the home. Her tasks are always there, all the time. On the other hand, she answers only to her customers. "There are no hidden agendas, no office politics," she says. Her business turned a profit after two and a half years.

Jewell is one of the 55% of Americans who would prefer to be their own boss, and one of the 19% who actually own their own firms, freelance, or are temporary workers.[b] Although the stereotype is that home-based businesses are female-owned enterprises, actually 59% of home-based workers are male, most of them performing traditional jobs such as sales and construction.[c] The average income for home-based business owners was $57,000 in 1999, compared with $41,600 for all households.[d]

Technology has made working at home far easier than ever before. "With such advances as voice mail, e-mail, and fax machines," says one freelance business writer, "it's possible to create a much more professional environment at home than was once possible."[e] Add computers, printers, and copiers, and it's clear that these are the glory days for many home workers.

One in eight U.S. households has at least one adult working full time from home—either self-employed or working for an employer—and this is expected to rise to one in five in 2002. The fastest-growing segment consists of full-time corporate telecommuters, expected to rise by 14% a year through 2020, according to Jack Nilles, an expert on "telework."[f] Already there are an estimated 8 million to 11 million people in the United States who telecommute, and most of them cite clear advantages to the alternative work arrangement. Nearly 75%, for example, say they get more work done at home or on the road than they would in a corporate office, and most estimated their productivity at 30% higher.[g]

Working at home isn't for everyone, though. "To be successful at it you must be highly disciplined," says Ken Scotch, 34, a technical support person with a Boston-based company who lives in New Orleans. "You have to be able to monitor yourself and set goals and limits. No one is going to do it for you."[h]

Some Web sites aimed at the self-employed, home-based businesspeople, "e-lancers," consultants, or telecommuters are the following:[i] Working Solo (www.workingsolo.com), Inc. magazine's Inc.Online (www.inc.com), Entrepreneur magazine (www.entrepreneurmag.com), Workz.com (www.workz.com), Onvia.com (www.onvia.com), and Webentrepreneurs.com (www.entrepreneurs.com).

WHAT IT IS
WHAT IT DOES

WHY IT IS IMPORTANT

✳ **artificial intelligence (AI)** (KQ 13.2, p. 13.11)   Group of related technologies used in developing machines to emulate human-like qualities, such as learning, reasoning, communicating, seeing, and hearing.

Thanks to AI, machines can do things formerly possible only with human effort.

avatar (KQ 13.3, p. 13.27)   Graphical image of you or someone else on a computer screen; (2) graphical personification of a computer or a process that's running on a computer.

It is hoped that avatars will make information technologies easier. The system's performance depends on the body of facts (knowledge) and the heuristics (rules of thumb) fed into the computer.

❀ **expert system** (KQ 13.2, p. 13.14)   Interactive computer program that can apply rules to input in such a way as to generate conclusions.

The program helps users solve problems that would otherwise require the assistance of a human expert.

filtering (KQ 13.3, p. 13.27)   Using a program to construct a custom-made electronic barrier through which only selected or desired data will pass.

Filtering helps limit and monitor the data and/or information the user receives.

⚓ **fuzzy logic** (KQ 13.2, p. 13.14)   Method of dealing with imprecise data and vagueness, with problems that have many answers rather than one.

Unlike traditional "crisp" digital logic, fuzzy logic is more like human reasoning: It deals with probability and credibility.

genetic algorithm (KQ 13.2, p. 13.20) Program that uses Darwinian principles of random mutation to improve itself.

Genetic algorithms use trial and error to learn from experience, thus constantly improving themselves.

inference engine (KQ 13.2, p. 13.15) Software that controls the search of the expert system's knowledge base and produces conclusions.

An inference engine fits the user's problem into the knowledge base and derives a conclusion from the rules and facts it contains.

intelligent agent (KQ 13.3, p. 13.26) Computer program that performs work tasks on your behalf, including roaming networks and compiling data.

Agents scan databases and electronic mail; clerical agents answer telephones and send faxes, user-interface agents learn individual work habits.

kiosk (KQ 13.1, p. 13.2)   Small, self-contained structure such as a newsstand or a ticket booth. Unattended multimedia kiosks dispense information via computer screens. Keyboards and touch screens are used for input.

Kiosks are designed to offer information to a large number of people. With more advanced multimedia authoring software, corporations are creating in-house advertising and promotional programs for display using kiosks at trade shows and during product demonstrations.

knowledge base (KQ 13.2, p. 13.15) Expert system's database of knowledge about a particular subject.

A knowledge base includes relevant facts, information, beliefs, assumptions, and procedures for solving problems.

knowledge engineers (KQ 13.2, p. 13.17) Persons who are trained to elicit knowledge (for example, by interview) from experts and build an expert system.

Capturing human expertise for the computer is a time-consuming and difficult task. The expert system is only as good as the quality of the data and rules obtained from the human experts.

MPC classifications (KQ 13.1, p. 13.3) The set of minimum hardware standards for personal computer multimedia use that are published by the Multimedia PC Marketing Council.

The Multimedia PC Marketing Council publishes the MPC classifications to help consumers identify a minimum system configuration for playing back multimedia on Intel-based and similar computers.

natural language processing (KQ 13.2, p. 13.13) Study of ways for computers to recognize and understand human language, whether in spoken or written form.

Natural language processing could further reduce the barriers to human/computer communications.

natural languages (KQ 13.2, p. 13.13) Programming languages, called fifth-generation languages, that give people a more natural connection with computers; ordinary human languages, such as English.

Natural languages make it easier for users to work with computers.

neural networks (KQ 13.2, p. 13.18) Artificial intelligence networks that use physical electronic devices or software to mimic the neurological structure of the human brain, with, for instance, transistors for nerve cells and resistors for synapses.

Neural networks are able to mimic human learning behavior and pattern recognition.

perception system (KQ 13.2, p. 13.11) Also called *intelligent robot;* robot that emulates the human capabilities of sight, hearing, touch, and smell and then responds to the new information.

Intelligent robots are used in factories for inspecting quality of products and in security patrols, among other things.

robot (KQ 13.2, p. 13.11) Automatic device that performs functions ordinarily ascribed to human beings or that operates with what appears to be almost human intelligence.

Robots are performing more and more functions in business and the professions, including situations that would be too dangerous for humans to work in.

robotics (KQ 13.2, p. 13.11) Field devoted to developing machines that can perform work normally done by people.

See *robot.*

simulators (KQ 13.2, p. 13.23) Devices that represent the behavior of physical or abstract systems.

Among much else, virtual-reality simulators are used to train pilots on various aircraft and to prepare air-traffic controllers for equipment failures.

Turing test (KQ 13.2, p. 13.21) A test or game for determining whether a computer possesses "intelligence" or "self-awareness." In the Turing test, a human judge converses by means of a computer terminal with two entities hidden in another location.

Some experts believe that once a computer has passed the Turing test, it will be judged to have achieved a level of human intelligence.

virtual reality (VR) (KQ 13.2, p. 13.23) Computer-generated artificial reality that projects a person into a sensation of three-dimensional space.

With virtual reality you can experience almost anything you want without ever leaving your chair. Virtual reality is employed in simulators for training programs of many types.

EXERCISES

13

1. Fill in the following blanks:

   a. A(n) _____ is an automatic device that performs functions ordinarily performed by a human being.

   b. A concept being used in the development of natural language processing is

      _____ _____ , which doesn't base decisions on either/or propositions.

   c. The goal of _____ _____ _____ is to enable the computer to communicate with the user in the user's native language.

   d. A robot that can hear, see, smell, and touch is referred to as a(n)

      _____ _____ .

   e. A(n) _____ _____ is a computer-based system that attempts to mimic the activities of the human brain.

2. Label each of the following statements as either true or false.

   a. _____ The hardware required to run multimedia software is the same as that required to create multimedia titles.

   b. _____ Text is the primary media element for communicating information in a multimedia production.

   c. _____ Software programs that roam the Web are commonly referred to as *spiders*.

   d. _____ Perception systems are more "intelligent" than robots.

   e. _____ The main limitation of expert systems is that they aren't interactive.

3. List five uses of multimedia.

   a. _____

   b. _____

   c. _____

   d. _____

   e. _____

4. How much RAM is needed for optimum multimedia performance?

5. What are the two types of graphics?

6. What are the three parts of an expert system?

7. What is a knowledge engineer?

8. What is a kiosk?

IN YOUR OWN WORDS

1. Answer each of the Key Questions that appear at the beginning of this chapter.

2. Define each of the following:
   a. intelligent agent
   b. information filtering
   c. avatar

3. Respond to each of the following:
   a. What is meant by the term *artificial intelligence*?
   b. What is an expert system?
   c. What do you need in order to experience virtual reality?
   d. Describe the relationship between the Turing test and research into artificial intelligence and natural language processing.

4. What are the minimum MPC requirements?

5. Do you think you would enjoy working in the multimedia industry? If so, what aspects would you specialize in?

6. Suppose you are going to design a robot. What kind would be most useful to society?

7. Do you really want computers to achieve the level of human intelligence? Why or why not?

KNOWLEDGE IN ACTION

1. **Learning with Multimedia.** What subjects are you studying now that you think would be easier to learn through the use of multimedia? How would multimedia aid the learning process? Be as specific as possible.

2. **Building an Expert System.** Do you have any expertise that would be useful to someone building an expert system? If so, what kind of system would it be? If you were the person building the system, what kinds of questions would you ask yourself to elicit the appropriate information?

3. **Artificial Intelligence Societies.** At professional societies, such as the American Association for Artificial Intelligence, provide a variety of published material as well as symposia, workshops, conferences, and related services and activities for those involved in various AI fields. These societies can be easily located with a Web browser, by searching for the phrase "artificial intelligence." Contact one or more societies and obtain information on activities, services, and fees.

Answers to Self-Test Exercises: 1a. robot 1b. fuzzy logic 1c. natural language processing 1d. intelligent robot/perception system 1e. neural network 2. F, T, T, T, F 3. *Answers will vary.* 4. 32–64 MB 5. vector-based; bit-mapped, or raster-based 6. knowledge base, inference engine, user interface 7. Knowledge engineers are trained to elicit knowledge (for example, by interview) from experts and build the expert system 8. Small, self-contained structure such as a newsstand or a ticket booth. Unattended multimedia kiosks dispense information via computer screens. Keyboards and touch screens are used for input.

CHAPTER 14

ETHICS, PRIVACY, SECURITY, AND SOCIAL QUESTIONS

Computing for Right Living

KEY QUESTIONS

You should be able to answer the following questions:

14.1 Computers & Privacy *How do computers affect our privacy?*

14.2 Intellectual Property Rights *How does information technology affect intellectual property rights?*

14.3 Truth in Art & Journalism *In art and journalism, how can computers be used to alter sounds, photos, videos, and facts?*

14.4 Free Speech, Civility, Pornography, Hate Speech, & Censorship *How does information technology affect such free-speech issues as civility, pornography, and censorship?*

14.5 Security: Threats to Computer & Communications Systems *What are some threats to computer systems?*

14.6 Security: Safeguarding Computers & Communications *What are some methods for securing computer systems?*

14.7 Social Questions: Will Information Technology Make Our Lives Better? *What effect does information technology have on the environment, health, workplace problems, employment rates, education, commerce, the entertainment industry, and government?*

The high-tech workplace is creating confusion about what constitutes ethical behavior on the job. One out of every six Americans feels that traditional standards of what's right and wrong at work are no longer relevant because of new technologies, according to a recent survey.[1] Not only do computers provide us with different ways of working, thinking, and playing; they also present some different moral choices: Which actions are right in the digital and online universe?

In this chapter we discuss several matters pertaining to right actions:

- Computers and privacy
- Intellectual property rights
- Truth in art and journalism
- Free speech, civility, pornography, and censorship
- The threats to computers and communications systems
- Security issues relating to computers and communications systems
- Social questions related to computers

The Visitors Forum touch screen at the Tech Museum

Questions of Ethics on Agenda at the Tech

Full of flashing neon, interactive exhibits, robots, and computer displays, the new Tech Museum of Innovation in San Jose, California, will undoubtedly impress visitors with its cutting-edge presentations of technology on the march. But the museum's designers are engaged in more than high-tech boosterism. They want visitors to leave the Tech with some important material to reflect on: the ethical implications and cost to society of technological change.

The Tech may be the first science museum to consciously build an ethical narrative through all its exhibits. Ethical discussions weave through dozens of displays on subjects as diverse as gene therapy, space exploration, and the V-chip. Visual and textual prompts are everywhere, nudging visitors to think about vital questions: Does genetic testing violate individual rights or enhance the common good? Would you welcome a robot at work? Do you think using technology to have a child is worth the cost and the risk involved to the child?

"Rather than saying, 'Hey it's a Brave New World and isn't technology amazing?' we say, 'Yeah the technology's amazing, *but*,'" explained Emily Routman, the Tech's vice president in charge of exhibits. "Technology's brought us to some scary new places where we have to make choices. So we're trying to explain the choice. We're not telling people *what* to think. We're telling them *to* think." Says Thomas Shanks, an ethicist at the Markkula Center for Applied Ethics, who is involved with the Tech: "Every kid who walks out of there should be able to make some choices *right now* about the way they're going to use technology."

From Richard Scheinin, "Questions of Ethics on Agenda at the Tech," *San Jose Mercury News.*

14.1 Computers & Privacy

Key Question **How do computers affect our privacy?**

As we mentioned in the chapter on databases, **privacy** is the right of people not to reveal information about themselves—the right to keep personal information, such as medical histories, personal e-mail messages, student records, and financial information from getting into the wrong hands. Information technology, however, puts constant pressure on this right.

Think your medical records are inviolable? Actually, private medical information is bought and sold freely by various companies since there is no federal law prohibiting it. (And they simply ignore the patchwork of varying state laws.)

Think the boss can't snoop on your e-mail at work? The law allows employers to "intercept" employee communications if one of the parties involved agrees to the "interception." The party "involved" is the employer. Indeed, employer snooping seems to be widespread. Thus a good rule of thumb is to think of an e-mail message not as a sealed letter but as a postcard that might well be read and copied in every post office it passes through, then kept on file for years afterward. Indeed, about 8 years' worth of Microsoft's e-mail, approximately 3.3 million messages, have been retrieved by the U.S government in its antitrust suit against Microsoft. (Using the little trash-can symbol on your display screen doesn't mean your e-mail is really deleted; most networks routinely store backups of all messages that pass through them.)

Think your student records are protected? Actually, attorneys, auditors, therapists, and some others can view them now anyway. But in addition, colleges are beginning to implement systems of transferring transcripts, disciplinary reports, and other student records by electronic means.

Think there are adequate controls on financial information collected about you? Then pray you're never the victim of identity theft, one of the fastest-growing forms of fraud. A relatively new crime, *identity theft* involves stealing identifying information about you—from loan documents, credit card offers, bank statements, utility bills, and the like—and then using it to establish new credit accounts. San Francisco couple Leonard and Olga Dudin, for instance, found themselves in a one-year nightmare, their credit ruined, after a co-worker obtained Leonard's Social Security number and used it to open several charge accounts, racking up more than $200,000 in bills. The Dudins didn't learn about it for a while because the fake Dudin put his own address on the new accounts.

A great many people are concerned about the loss of their right to privacy. Most computer-related privacy issues involve the use of large databases and electronic networks, particularly the Internet. Let us consider these.

Databases

Large organizations around the world are constantly compiling information about most of us. Worldwide, the number of online databases has skyrocketed—most are in the United States.

As explained earlier, related records are pulled together in databases by means of a *key field* (✔ p. 12.7). In the United States, the Social Security number is most frequently used as the key field. This number was intended principally to help collect taxes for the federally administered retirement system and disburse its payments to individuals. It was not designed as a kind of "universal identifier" for Americans, but that is what it has become, used by banks, insurance companies, loan companies, employers, and so on. Unfortunately, one's Social Security number can be obtained from a variety of sources. Indeed, for a while, the Social

Security Administration even offered a Web site that allowed anyone with enough information to access personal Social Security records.

Of course, there are other kinds of identifying numbers (key fields), and it's surprising how easy some of them are to find. For instance, computer columnist Gina Smith discovered that having an unlisted telephone number only meant that people couldn't find it in the phone book. Apparently, the online phone directories on the Web are good places to find unlisted phone numbers because these databases are assembled from mailing lists and warranty cards, not phone companies.

This illustrates just how sophisticated the building of databases has become. Professional data gatherers, or "information resellers," collect personal data and sell it to fund-raisers, direct marketers, and others. In the United States, even some motor-vehicle departments sell the car-registration data they store. From this database, companies have been able to collect names, addresses, and other information about the majority of American households. Some privacy experts estimate that the average person is on 100 mailing lists and in 50 databases at any one time. *(See Figure 14.1, next page.)*

One last point: Information volunteered for seemingly the most innocuous of reasons can end up being used in astonishing ways. For instance, when Texas resident Beverly Dennis filled out a written questionnaire about her buying habits in return for free product samples, she didn't realize that prison inmates were processing data from such questionnaires—until she got a disturbing letter from an imprisoned rapist.

Electronic Networks

People who surf the Internet think they're invisible, but that's not true. The illusion of anonymity on the Net is completely false.

Say you visit a cigarette company's Web site and give it your name or e-mail address in order to get discount coupons for cigarettes. The Web site deposits—on *your* computer—a so-called **cookie,** a special file that keeps track of your activities and visits. The cookie can connect your name or e-mail address to any future visit to that Web site. There's no requirement that you be notified that this information is being gathered. Moreover, there are practically no restrictions on how the information may be disseminated or otherwise used. Thus, for example, your health or life insurance company could eventually get hold of the information and decide to raise the premiums of people it believes are smokers. (You can set up your Web browser to notify you when a cookie is being sent, and you can delete cookies from your hard disk; look for a folder called "cookies.")

What about online services, such as AOL, CompuServe, MSN, and Prodigy? All of them can and do sell information about you to marketers, to be used for direct marketing purposes. Most (but not all) of the services allow you to specify that you don't want information about you disclosed in this way, but you have to take the initiative.

Most people using electronic networks rely on privacy by obscurity. In the case of the Internet, they hope that the huge volume of data that flows over the Net each day will keep browsing anonymous. Actually, tracing your travels on the Net is easier than you might think. For instance, Deja News, a site that catalogs and indexes Usenet news groups (✔ p. 8.31), provides a usage profile of each person who posts messages on Usenets. No one ever said that Usenet was a private way to exchange information, but it can still be disturbing to see one's own postings indexed and sorted by frequency and topic.

Figure 14.1 Junk mail: How your name gets on mailing lists. Lists are compiled from two principal sources about you: List brokers use public information sources, List compilers use commercial transactions in which you have been involved. Brokers and compilers then sell your name to each other and to various direct mailers.

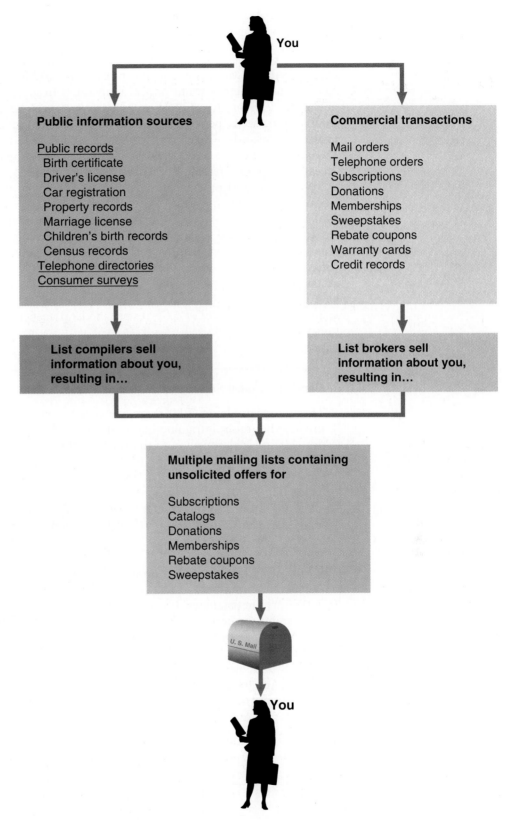

Rules and Laws on Privacy

As we noted in Chapter 12, a set of five Fair Information Practices developed in the 1970s by the U.S. Department of Health, Education, and Welfare has since been adopted by various public and private organizations and has prompted the enactment of federal laws to protect individuals from invasion of privacy. In particular, the *Privacy Act of 1974* prohibits government agencies or their contractors from keeping secret personnel files on individuals and gives individuals the right to see their records, to see how the data is used, and to correct errors while the *Freedom of Information Act,* passed in 1970, allows ordinary citizens to have access to data gathered about them by federal agencies.

Note that most privacy laws regulate only the behavior of government agencies or government contractors. For example, the *Computer Matching and Privacy Protection Act of 1988,* which prevents the government from comparing certain records to try to find a match, which does not affect most private companies. However, there are federal privacy laws relating to the banking and credit industries. According to the *Fair Credit Reporting Act of 1970,* you must be granted access to your credit record, and you have the right to challenge them. If you have been denied credit, access to your records must be free of charge. The *Right to Financial Privacy Act of 1978* restricts federal agencies' ability to search customer records in banks.

Could the United States Use a Dose of Europe's Privacy Medicine?

The European Union (EU) recently enacted a new law for the protection of privacy that raises intriguing questions about the relationship between property, liberty, government, and the rules of global trade. It also portends more conflict between the United States and its European trading partners, as their economies become ever more tightly linked. The EU's directive drastically limits the ability of companies to market data on consumers, something taken for granted in the United States. The EU's policy reflects what has long been a much tougher approach to consumer privacy throughout Europe. The directive requires member nations to enact conforming national laws.

Most of Europe already limits telemarketing. The new rules extend this to junk faxes and e-mail. They also create a general right for citizens to opt out of private databases. If a citizen requests it, data collected for one purpose cannot be bought and sold for other purposes. This provision is a direct assault on the now vast direct-marketing industry, and it affects anyone selling to a European consumer, including American companies.

U.S trade negotiators are fighting this directive on the grounds that it violates free trade. This is a battle they are likely to lose. Indeed, the Europeans do not simply want to protect European consumers, they also want the U.S government to increase privacy safeguards for American shoppers.

From Robert Kuttner, "The U.S. Could Use a Dose of Europe's Privacy Medicine," *Business Week.*

The Case for Limiting Privacy: Should We Really Fear "Data Rape"?

Employers read our e-mail and medical records. Strangers listen to our cellular-phone conversations. Is our privacy rapidly being stripped away? Should we seek even more laws to protect us from "data rape"?

Not so fast, says sociologist Amitai Etzioni. Restoring old-fashioned privacy is about as likely as vanquishing nuclear weapons, he says. "The genie is out of the bottle. We must either return to the Stone Age (pay cash, use carrier pigeons, and forget insurance) or learn to live with shrunken privacy."

Actually, Etzioni argues, "giving up some measure of privacy is exactly what the common good requires." After all, do we really want to let banks hide large amounts of money from drug transactions, to prohibit schools from screening out security personnel who have been child abusers, and to enable incompetent physicians who have caused patient deaths to cross state lines and continue practicing? Computer cross-checks would prevent all of these undesirable outcomes.

While we should tolerate new limitations on privacy *only* when there is a compelling need, says Etzioni, it must be accepted that privacy is not an absolute value.

For more information on privacy rights, call the Privacy Rights Clearinghouse at 619-298-3396, or check the following Web sites: *www.privacyrights.org, www.identitytheft.org, www.pirg.org/calpirg.*

14.2 Intellectual Property Rights

Key Question **How does information technology affect intellectual-property rights?**

Information technology has presented legislators and lawyers—and you—with some new ethical issues regarding rights to intellectual property. **Intellectual property** consists of the products of the human mind, tangible or intangible. There are three methods of protecting intellectual property: *patents* (as for an invention), *trade secrets* (as for a formula or method of doing business), and *copyrights*.

Copyright

Of principal interest to us is copyright protection. A **copyright** is a body of law that prohibits copying of intellectual property without the permission of the copyright holder. The law protects books, articles, pamphlets, music, art, drawings, movies, and other expressions of ideas. It also protects computer software.

A copyright protects the *expression* of an idea but not the idea itself. Thus, others may copy your idea for, say, a new shoot-'em-up video game but not your particular variant of it. Copyright protection is automatic and lasts a minimum of 50 years; you do not have to register your idea with the government (as you do with a patent) in order to receive protection.

These matters are important because the use of computers has made the act of copying far easier and more convenient than in the past. Copying a book on a photocopying machine might take hours and cost 20 dollars, so people felt they might as well buy the book. Copying a software program (✔ p. 6.32) might take just seconds and cost little or nothing. In addition, unlike a photocopied book, a copied program is identical to its original. Digitization threatens to compound the problem. For example, current copyright law doesn't specifically protect copyrighted material online.

We need to consider three copyright-related matters: software and network piracy, plagiarism, and ownership of images, sounds, and other media.

Software and Network Piracy

It may seem harmless to make a copy of some commercial software for a friend; however, that act falls within the definition of piracy and, ethically, speaking, is no different from shoplifting the product off a store shelf.

As we noted, in Chapter 6, *piracy* is theft or unauthorized distribution or use. An example would be the appropriation of a computer design or program. Thus, Apple Computer brought a piracy suit (since rejected) against Microsoft and Hewlett-Packard, alleging that items in its interface, such as icons and windows, had been copied. **Software piracy** is the unauthorized copying of copyrighted software—for instance, by copying a program from one diskette to another, by making a duplicate CD-ROM, or by downloading a program from a network and making a copy of it. **Network piracy** is using electronic networks to distribute unauthorized copyrighted materials in digitized form. Record companies, for example, would like to prevent computer users from sending unauthorized copies of digital recordings over the Internet.

You might say, "I'm just a poor student, and making this one copy isn't going to cause any harm." However, millions of such small acts of software piracy add up to the loss of billions of dollars for software publishers, who consequently have fewer resources for customer support and upgrading their products. Piracy also tends to increase prices.

Quite apart from ethics, self-interest suggests plenty of reasons for staying legal:

- *Staying up-to-date:* When you buy a software program and register your purchase with the manufacturer, you're generally entitled to discounts on new versions, so you can keep software up-to-date economically.

- *Ability to get help:* If you crash your computer or network with a pirated version of a software program, there's no one you can call for help. There's also usually no documentation to check.

- *Risk of getting a virus:* Every time you obtain illegal software, whether via diskette or off the Internet, you risk getting a software virus. As we explain in a few pages, a virus can corrupt or destroy your data or software.

- *Risk of getting caught:* If you, your company, or your college is caught using pirated software, the results can be unpleasant, to say the least. You or your organization could face civil fines of up to $100,000. The illegal software will be destroyed and you'll have to replace it with legal products at current retail prices. Finally, you may have to endure humiliating publicity and end up with a criminal record.

Software piracy is rampant according to the Business Software Alliance, a trade group charged with enforcing policies against piracy. In time, piracy may be curbed by the development of anticopying technology coupled with laws against disabling such technology. By some means, certainly, information providers—publishers, broadcasters, movie studios, and authors—must be assured of a reasonable financial return if they develop online and multimedia versions of their intellectual products. Otherwise, suggests one writer, the Information Superhighway will remain "empty of traffic because no one wants to put anything on the road."[2]

Who Counterfeits Software, and How Much?

Countries with the highest piracy rates in 1997:

Vietnam	98%
China	96%
Indonesia	93%

How we compare: United States	28%
Worldwide, estimate of business software on PCs that is counterfeit or otherwise illegal:	40%
What this cost the software industry last year:	$11.4 billion
What this cost the software industry in the United States last year:	$2.7 billion

From Martin J. Moylan, "Software in Gray and Black," *San Jose Mercury News*, data from Software Publishers Association.

Plagiarism

Plagiarism is the expropriation of another writer's text, findings, or interpretations and presentation of this material as one's own. Information technology offers plagiarists new opportunities for unauthorized copying but also provides new ways to catch people who steal other people's material.

Thus, the proliferation of low-budget electronic online journals, containing academic and scientific papers, may make it harder to detect plagiarism, since few readers will know if a similar paper has been published elsewhere. At the same time, the use of computers to search different documents for identical passages of text provides a tool for identifying plagiarism.

Ownership of Media

Scanners, digital cameras (still and video), and other multimedia equipment permit almost limitless manipulation of movies, images, and sounds. What does this mean for the original copyright holders? An unauthorized sample of singer James Brown's famous howl, for instance, can be electronically transformed to provide the background music for dozens of rap recordings. Images can be appropriated by scanning them into a computer system, then altered or placed in a new context. Universities have found themselves threatened with copyright-infringement lawsuits because their students have used the comic-strip characters of "Dilbert" and the "Playmates" of *Playboy* magazine in creating Web home pages without much thought as to who might own the copyrights. The Recording Industry Association of America (RIAA), which represents the U.S music industry, is challenging the many pirate Internet sites that post digital copies of music that users can listen to for free.

To avoid lawsuits for violating copyright, many artists who recycle material have taken steps to protect themselves, usually by paying flat fees or a percentage of their royalties to the original copyright holders.

MP3 Software, Free Songs Make Recording Industry Nervous

Homer, Hobbes, Dewey, and Earl Grey T are hardly household names. But thanks to a file-squishing technology called MP3 that has become a grass-roots movement on the Internet, their band, God Ate My Homework, is known by thousands of people. The group says 100,000 Web surfers have visited their site to download tunes like "Pirate This Song" and play them on a personal computer or on a portable, handheld MP3 player, the Diamond Rio PMP300, which can record MP3-compressed songs from the Internet or a CD and play them in high-quality stereo.

The growing popularity of MP3 has provided an instant Internet audience for weekend musicians like God Ate My Homework, a new promotional tool for known artists like Dionne Warwick and the Beastie Boys, and a major headache for the recording industry.

One measure of MP3's popularity is WinAmp, the leading MP3 software. According to WinAmp's creator, Justin "Bandino Tarantino" Frankel, copies are being downloaded at a rate of 60,000 per day.

The Recording Industry Association of America (RIAA) says that the Rio player, as well as MP3 itself, encourages illegal pirating of songs and thus cheats artists of their royalties. However, the RIAA recently failed to persuade a U.S federal judge to halt shipment of the Rio player.

There is a lot at stake. According to Jupiter Communications in New York City, online music sales in 1998 totaled $88 million, just a fraction of overall revenues. But by 2002, they say, online sales will hit nearly $1.4 billion or nearly 8% of the overall market. And there is no counting how many legitimate music sales are lost when fans copy songs from pirate MP3 sites.

The solution, some industry experts say, is for recording companies to agree on an encrypted digital musical standard that will keep songs from being illegally copied.

From Benny Evangelista, "Download That Tune—It's Web Music," *San Francisco Chronicle*.

14.3 Truth in Art & Journalism

Key Question In art and journalism, how can computers be used to alter sounds, photos, videos, and facts?

The ability to manipulate digitized images and sounds has brought a new tool to art but a big new problem to journalism. How can we now know that what we're seeing or hearing is the truth? Consider the following issues.

Manipulation of Sound

Frank Sinatra's 1994 album *Duets* pairs him through technological tricks with singers like Barbra Streisand. Sinatra recorded solos in a recording studio. His singing partners, while listening to his taped performances on earphones, dubbed in their own voices. These recordings were made not only at different times but often, through distortion-free phone lines, from different places. The illusion in the final recording is that the two singers are standing shoulder to shoulder.

Newspaper columnist William Safire called *Duets* "a series of artistic frauds." Said Safire, "The question raised is this: When a performer's voice and image can not only be edited, echoed, refined, spliced, corrected, and enhanced—but can be transported and combined with others not physically present—what is a performance?"[3] Another critic said that to call the disk *Duets* seemed a misnomer. "Sonic collage would be a more truthful description."[4]

Some listeners feel that new technology changes the character of a performance for the better—that the sour notes and clinkers can be edited out. Others, however, think the practice of assembling bits and pieces in a studio drains the music of its essential flow and unity.

Whatever the problems of misrepresentation in art, however, they pale beside those in journalism. What if a radio station edited a stream of digitized sound to achieve an effect entirely different from what actually happened?

Manipulation of Photos

Should a magazine that reports the news be taking such artistic license? Should *National Geographic* in 1982 have moved two Egyptian pyramids closer together, so that they would fit on a vertical cover? Was it right for *TV Guide* in 1989 to run a cover showing Oprah Winfrey's head placed on Ann-Margret's body?

The potential for abuse is clear. "For 150 years, the photographic image has been viewed as more persuasive than written accounts as a form of 'evidence,'" says one writer. "Now this authenticity is breaking down under the assault of technology."[5] Asks a former photo editor of the *New York Times Magazine*, "What would happen if the photograph appeared to be a straightforward recording of physical reality, but could no longer be relied upon to depict actual people and events?"[6]

Many editors try to distinguish between photos used for commercialism (advertising) versus journalism, or for feature stories versus news stories. However, this distinction implies that the integrity of photos applies only to some narrow definition of news. In the end, it can be argued, tampered photographs pollute the credibility of all of journalism. For this reason new types of digital film are becoming available that allow examiners to determine if any pixels have been manipulated.

Manipulation of Video

The technique of morphing, used in still photos, takes a quantum jump when used in movies, videos, and television commercials. In **morphing,** a film or video image is displayed on a computer screen and altered pixel by pixel, or dot by dot. *(See Figure 14.2, next page.)* The result is that the image metamorphoses into something else—a pair of lips into the front of a Toyota, for example.

Morphing and other techniques of digital image manipulation have had a tremendous impact on filmmaking. It can be used to erase jet contrails from the sky in a western and to make digital planes do impossible stunts. It can even be used to add and erase actors. In *Forrest Gump,* many scenes involved old film and TV footage that had been altered so that the Tom Hanks character was interacting with historical figures.

Films and videotapes are widely thought to be somewhat accurate versions of reality. Thus, the possibility of digital alterations raises some real problems. One is the possibility of doctoring videotapes supposed to represent actual events. Another concern is for film archives: Because videotapes suffer no loss in resolution, there are no "generations." Thus, it will be impossible for historians and archivists to tell whether the videotape they're viewing is the real thing or not.

Figure 14.2 Morphing

Information technology increasingly is blurring humans' ability to distinguish between natural and artificial experience, say Stanford University communication professors Byron Reeves and Clifford Nass.[7] For instance, they have found that showing a political candidate on a large screen (30 or 60 inches) makes a great difference in people's reactions. "We've found in the laboratory that big pictures automatically take more of a viewer's attention," said Reeves. "You will like someone more on the large screen and pay more attention to what he or she says but remember less." Our visual perception system, they find, is unable to discount information—to say that "this is artificial"—just because it is symbolic rather than real.

If our minds have this inclination anyway, how can we be expected to exercise our critical faculties when the "reality" is not merely artificial but actively doctored?

Manipulation of Facts

"Rumors have probably been around as long as humans have been able to speak," points out technology observer Tom Abate, "and social scientists say during crises, conflicts, or catastrophes people tend to spread stories that sound plausible but aren't true. . . . Now the Internet allows us to send messages around the world at the speed of light, exponentially increasing the power of rumormongers." There's one problem: Internet rumors shouldn't be accepted as being *news* in the true sense of the word.

Real news is the reporting of events by trained journalists who aren't involved directly in events or trends but have witnessed them or interviewed people involved.

What can you do to guard against being misled by online reports parading as "news"? The same thing you should do with stories reported elsewhere, as on TV or in newspapers: You should take advantage of a range of news sources, and you should exercise critical judgment in evaluating the report, for instance, by ascertaining the legitimacy of the source.

14.4 Free Speech, Civility, Pornography, Hate Speech, & Censorship

Key Question **How does information technology affect such free-speech issues as civility, pornography, and censorship?**

In Saudi Arabia and Iran, officials try to police taboo subjects (sex, religion, politics) on the Internet. In China, Net users must register with the government, which also blocks access to many Web sites. In Germany, prosecutors indicted the manager of CompuServe Deutschland on charges of trafficking in pornography—material its customers obtain from sites on the Internet—thus holding the online service responsible for carrying material it had no part in producing. In the United States, however, free speech is protected by the First Amendment to the Constitution.

But how free should free speech be in a cyberspace universe where children can access pornography and swindlers can fool the unsophisticated? Some people think federal regulators should curb "indecency" on the Internet and crack down on supposed consumer fraud. Others fear any regulation could reduce freedom of expression, and slow future growth and innovation of the Net and online services. No form of media in history has grown as fast as the Internet, and the Internet has grown precisely because it isn't regulated.

Let us consider some of the issues raised by the growth of the Internet.

Civility: Online Behavior and "Netiquette"

Civility is important, even online. The anonymity of the Internet allows for a wide range of behavior, some of it pretty obnoxious. Many online bulletin boards or chat forums have a set of "FAQs"—frequently asked questions—that newcomers, or "newbies," are expected to become familiar with before joining in any chat forums. Most FAQs offer **netiquette,** or "net etiquette," guides to appropriate behavior while online.

Examples of netiquette blunders are typing with the CAPS LOCK key on—the Net equivalent of yelling—discussing subjects not appropriate to the forum, repetition of points made earlier, sending "I agree" and "Me, too" messages, and improper use of the software. **Spamming,** or sending unsolicited mail, is especially irksome; a spam can take the form of chain letters, advertising, or similar junk mail. The U.S government is trying to develop some anti-spamming laws, but these laws need to be carefully worded in order to avoid violating free-speech rights.

One of the great things about the Internet is that it has gotten Americans to start writing again. However, writing shouldn't be sloppy. Most people who see poor spelling and poor grammar think the writer is dumb. Some writers just dash off an e-mail note and figure that it doesn't matter how it reads. That is a big mistake.

Pornography and Censorship

If a U.S. court decides *after* you have spoken that you have defamed or maliciously damaged someone, you may be sued for slander (spoken speech) or libel (written speech) or charged with harassment, but you cannot be stopped beforehand. However, "obscene" material is not constitutionally protected free speech. Obscenity is defined as sexually explicit material that is offensive as measured by "contemporary community standards"—a definition with considerable leeway, depending on localities.

In 1996, as part of its broad telecommunications law overhaul called the Communications Decency Act, Congress passed legislation that imposed heavy fines and prison sentences on people making "patently offensive," sexually explicit material available over the Internet in a manner such that children might be exposed to it. This part of the law was blocked by a federal judge as being constitutionally vague. In 1997, the U.S. Supreme Court ruled that it was indeed unconstitutional, and the law is being reworked.

Since computers are simply another way of communicating, there should be no surprise that a lot of people use them to communicate about sex. Yahoo, the Internet directory company, says that the word "sex" is the most popular search word on the Net.[8] All kinds of online X-rated Web sites, chat rooms, and Usenet newsgroups exist. A special problem is that children may participate in sexual conversations, download hard-core pictures, or encounter odious adults tempting them into a meeting. Indeed, people online are not always what they seem to be, and a message seemingly from a 12-year-old girl could really be from a 30-year-old man. Children should be warned never to give out personal information and to tell their parents if they encounter mail or messages that make them uncomfortable.

Not only are parents concerned about pornography in electronic form, so are employers. Many companies are concerned about the loss of productivity—and the risk of being sued for sexual harassment—as workers spend time online looking at sexually explicit material. What can be done about all this? Some possibilities:

- *Blocking software:* Some software developers have discovered a golden opportunity in making programs like SurfWatch, Net Nanny, and Cyber Patrol. These "blocking" programs, or filters, screen out objectionable matter—typically by identifying certain non-approved keywords in a user's request or comparing the user's request for information against a list of prohibited Web sites, newsgroups, e-mail, and chat rooms.

  In the case of children, some programs also prevent kids from giving out personal information such as addresses and credit card numbers.

  Some online services, including AOL, have built-in filters that users can turn on with a mouse click. Many ISPs also offer filters.

- *Browsers with ratings:* Another proposal in the works is browser software that contains built-in ratings for Internet, Usenet, and World Wide Web files. Parents could, for example, choose a browser that has been endorsed by the local school board or the online service provider. Special browsers include ChiBrow, KidDesk, and Surf Monkey.

- *The V-chip:* The 1996 Telecommunications Law officially launched the era of the V-chip, a device that may soon be required equipment in most new television sets. The V-chip allows parents to automatically block out programs that have been labeled as high in violence, sex, or other objectionable material. Who will do the ratings (of 600,000 hours of programming currently broadcast per year) and whether the system is really workable remain to be seen. However, as conventional television and the Internet converge, the V-chip could become a concern to Net users as well as TV watchers.

Hate Speech and Censorship

Hate speech and hate Web sites are also a focus of censorship movements. For example, a prominent nonprofit human rights organization, the Anti-Defamation League, has developed and will sell to the public an Internet filter blocking access to several hundred Web sites that allegedly advocate bigotry.[9]

14.5 Security: Threats to Computer & Communications Systems

Key Question **What are some threats to computer systems?**

There will probably always be a need for paper towels (or the equivalent), because there will always be household accidents and mistakes—spills, messes, leaky pipes. Similarly, accidents and other disasters will probably disable computer and communications systems from time to time, as they have in the past. What steps should we take to minimize them, and how should we deal with them when they do happen?

Here we discuss the following threats to computers and communications systems:

- Errors and accidents

- Natural and other hazards

- Crimes against information technology

- Crimes using information technology

- Worms and viruses

Errors and Accidents

ROBOT SENT TO DISARM BOMB GOES WILD IN SAN FRANCISCO, read the headline.[10] Evidently, a hazardous-duty police robot started spinning out of control when officers tried to get it to grasp a pipe bomb. Fortunately, it was shut off before any damage could be done. Most computer glitches are not so spectacular, although they can be almost as important.

In general, errors and accidents in computer systems may be classified as people errors, procedural errors, software errors, electromechanical problems, and "dirty data" problems.

People Errors

Recall that one part of a computer system is the people who manage it or run it. For instance, Brian McConnell of Roanoke, Virginia, found that he couldn't get past a bank's automated telephone system to talk to a real person. This was not the fault of the system so much as the people who programmed the system. McConnell, president of a software firm, thereupon wrote a program that automatically phoned eight different numbers at the bank. Employees picking up the phone heard the recording, "This is an automated customer complaint. To hear a live complaint, press. . . ." Quite often, what may seem to be "the computer's fault" is human indifference or bad management.

Procedural Errors

Some spectacular computer failures have occurred because someone didn't follow procedures. Consider the 2½-hour shutdown of NASDAQ, the nation's second largest stock market. NASDAQ is so automated that it likes to call itself "the stock market for the next 100 years." In July 1994, NASDAQ was shut down by an effort, ironically, to make the computer system more user-friendly. Technicians were phasing in new software, adding technical improvements a day at a time. A few days into this process, when the technicians tried to add more features, they inadvertently flooded the data-storage capability of the system. The resulting delay in opening the stock market shortened the trading day.

Software Errors

We are forever hearing about "software glitches" or "software bugs." A *software bug* is an error in a program that causes it not to work properly ($\checkmark$ p. 10.11). For example, consider what happened after a school employee in Newark, New Jersey, made a small error in coding the school system's master scheduling program: When 1000 students and 90 teachers showed up for the start of school at Central High School, half the students had incomplete or no schedules for classes. Some classrooms had no teachers while others had four instead of one.[11]

Especially with complex software, there are always bugs, even after the system has been thoroughly tested and "debugged." However, there comes a point in the software development process where debugging must end. That is, the probability of the bugs disrupting the system is considered to be so low that it is not worth searching further for them.

Electromechanical Problems

Mechanical systems, such as printers, and electrical systems, such as circuit boards, don't always work. They may be faultily constructed, get dirty or over-heated, wear out, or become damaged in some other way. Power failures (brownouts and blackouts) can shut a system down. Power surges can burn out equipment.

Whether electromechanical failure or another problem causes it, computer downtime is expensive. A survey of about 450 information system executives picked from Fortune 1000 companies found that companies on average suffer nine 4-hour computer-system failures a year. Each failure costs the company an average of $330,000. Because of such system failures, companies are unable to deliver a service, complete production, earn fees, or retrieve data. Moreover, employees lose productivity because of idle time.

"Dirty Data" Problems

When keyboarding a research paper, you undoubtedly make a few typing errors (which, hopefully, you clean up). Typos are also a fact of life for all the data-entry people around the world who feed a continual stream of raw data into computer systems. A lot of problems are caused by such "dirty data." **Dirty data** is data that is incomplete, outdated, or otherwise inaccurate.

A good reason for having a look at your records—credit, medical, school—is so you can make any corrections to them before they cause you complications.

Natural and Other Hazards

Some disasters do not merely lead to temporary system downtime, they can wreck the entire system. Examples are natural hazards, and civil strife and terrorism.

Natural Hazards

Whatever is harmful to property (and people) is harmful to computers and communications systems. This certainly includes natural disasters: fires, floods, earthquakes, tornadoes, hurricanes, blizzards, and the like. If they inflict damage over a wide area, as did 1998 hurricane Mitch in Central America, natural hazards can disable all the electronic systems we take for granted. Without power and communications connections, the automated teller machines, credit-card verifiers, and bank computers are useless.

Civil Strife and Terrorism

We may take comfort in the fact that wars and insurrections seem to take place in other parts of the world. Yet we are not immune to civil unrest, nor are we immune, apparently, to acts of terrorism, such as the 1995 truck-bombing of Oklahoma City's Federal Building. Following the 1993 bombing of New York's World Trade Center, companies found themselves frantically moving equipment to new offices and reestablishing their computer networks.

Crimes Against Computers and Communications

An **information technology crime** can be of two types. It can be an illegal act perpetrated *against* computers or telecommunications. Or it can be the *use* of computers or telecommunications to accomplish an illegal act. Here we discuss the first type.

Crimes against information technology include theft—of hardware, of software, of computer time, of cable or telephone services, of information—and also crimes of malice and destruction. Some examples are as follows.

Theft of Hardware

This can range from shoplifting an accessory in a computer store to removing a laptop or cellular phone from someone's car. Professional criminals may steal shipments of microprocessor chips off a loading dock or even pry cash machines out of shopping-center walls.

A particularly interesting case was the theft in December 1990 of a laptop computer from the car of a British officer right before the Gulf War. It happened to contain U.S. General Norman Schwarzkopf's preliminary military plans for the invasion of Iraq. Fortunately, the war plans were not compromised by the event.

Theft of computers has become a major problem on many campuses. Often the criminals, who may be professionals, don't take the peripheral devices, only the system unit. If the computers are bolted down, thieves often open the systems units and steal the RAM chips, drives, and processors.

Theft of Software

Stealing software can take the form of physically making off with someone's CD-ROMs, but it is more likely to be copying of programs. Software makers secretly prowl electronic bulletin boards in search of purloined products, then try to get a court order to shut down the bulletin boards. They also look for companies that "softlift"—buying one copy of a program and making copies for as many computers as they have. Many pirates are reported by co-workers or fellow students to the "software police," the Software Publishers Association. The SPA has a toll-free number (800-388-7478) on which anyone can report illegal copying.

Another type of software theft is copying or counterfeiting well-known software programs for commercial sale. These pirates often operate in Taiwan, Mexico, Russia, and various parts of Asia and Latin America. In some countries, more than 90% of U.S. microcomputer software in use is thought to be illegally copied.[12]

Theft of Time and Services

The theft of computer time is more common than you might think. Some people use their employer's computer time to play games; others run sideline businesses. The biggest abuse, however, is probably wasting time with electronic mail and the Internet. An analysis of e-mail logs of three companies (IBM, Apple, AT&T) found that employees visited *Penthouse* magazine's Web site 12,823 times in a single month. (Assuming an average visit of 13 minutes, that works out to 347 eight-hour days, a considerable loss of work time.)

Theft of telephone services has increased significantly. For instance, high-tech thieves use sophisticated radio scanners to pluck out of the air the phone numbers and electronic serial numbers broadcast by cellular phones. Once these numbers have been programmed into the microchips of other phones—a fraud called "cloning"—illegal users can make calls that are charged to innocent users. As a result, U.S. cellular phone companies lose an estimated $2 million every day.

Theft of Information

Not too long ago, "information thieves" were caught infiltrating the files of the U.S. Social Security Administration, stealing confidential personal records, and selling the information. Thieves have also broken into computers of the major credit bureaus and stolen credit information, which they have used to charge purchases or else resold to other people. On college campuses, thieves have snooped on or stolen private information such as grades.

Crimes of Malice and Destruction

Sometimes criminals are more interested in abusing or vandalizing computers and telecommunications systems than in profiting from them. For example, a student at a Wisconsin campus deliberately and repeatedly shut down a university computer system, destroying final projects for dozens of students. A judge sentenced him to a year's probation, and he left the campus.

Crimes Using Computers and Communications

Just as a car can be used to assist in a crime, so can a computer or communications system. For example, four college students on New York's Long Island who met via the Internet used a specialized computer program to steal credit-card numbers, then, according to police, went on a one-year, $100,000 shopping spree. When arrested, they were charged with grand larceny, forgery, and scheming to defraud.

In addition, investment fraud has come to cyberspace. Many people now use online services to manage their stock portfolios through brokerages hooked into the services. Scam artists have followed, offering nonexistent investment deals, phony solicitations, and manipulating stock prices.

Information technology has also been used simply to perpetrate mischief. For example, three students at a Wisconsin campus faced disciplinary measures after distributing bogus e-mail messages, one of which purported to be a message of resignation sent by the university's chancellor.

The "fake-buck" buster. This electronic device detects a counterfeit U.S. currency bill in 0.7 second.

Final

Worms and Viruses

Worms and viruses are forms of high-tech malice. A **worm** is a stand-alone program that copies itself repeatedly into memory or onto a disk drive until no more space is left. For example, a student at Cornell University unleashed a worm program that traveled through an e-mail network and shut down thousands of computers around the country.

A **virus** is a piece of computer code or program that is hidden within an existing program. When the infected application is run, the virus code is activated and copies itself onto other files in your computer (✔ p. 5.8). Some viruses just produce inane messages, such as "Happy birthday, Joshi," on your display screen. Some cause minor glitches, such as disabling a couple of keys on your keyboard. The worst, however, may erase all the contents of your hard drive, to the point where your computer won't even start again. Or a virus may evade your detection and spread its havoc elsewhere.

Viruses, then, are passed in two ways:

- *By diskette:* The first way is via an infected diskette, such as one you might get from a friend or a repair person. It's also possible to get a virus from a sales demo disk or even, in a very few cases, from a shrink-wrapped commercial disk.

- *By network:* The second way is via a network, as from e-mail, an electronic bulletin board, or the Internet. It is even possible to get a virus by simply opening an infected Web page, with virus code hidden in the HTML tags (✔ p. 8.10). This is why, despite all the freebie games and other software available online, you should use virus-scanning software to check downloaded files.

Viruses may take several forms. The three main traditional ones are *boot-sector viruses, file viruses,* and *multipartite viruses. (See Table 14.1, next page.)* A more recent one is the *macro virus,* which attaches to documents rather than programs. The Concept macro virus, for example, hitches rides on e-mail and attaches itself to documents created by Microsoft's popular word processing program, Microsoft Word 6.0 or higher. Another macro virus, Laroux, infects Microsoft Excel spreadsheets the same way.

Table 14.1

TYPES OF VIRUSES

- **Boot-sector virus:** The boot sector is that part of the system software containing most of the instructions for booting, or powering up, the system. The boot sector virus replaces these boot instructions with some of its own. Once the system is turned on, the virus is loaded into main memory before the operating system. From there it is in a position to infect other files. Any diskette that is used in the drive of the computer then becomes infected. When that diskette is moved to another computer, the contagion continues. Examples of boot-sector viruses: AntCMOS, AntiEXE, Form.A, NYB (New York Boot), Ripper, Stoned.Empire.Monkey.

- **File virus:** File viruses attach themselves to executable files—those that actually begin a program. (In DOS these files have the extensions .COM and .EXE.) When the program is run, the virus starts working, trying to get into main memory and infecting other files.

- **Multipartite virus:** A hybrid of the file and boot-sector types, the multipartite virus infects both files and boot sectors, which makes it better at spreading and more difficult to detect. Examples of multipartite viruses are Junkie and Parity Boot.

    A type of multipartite virus is the *polymorphic virus,* which can mutate and change form just as human viruses can. Such viruses are especially troublesome because they can change their profile, making existing antiviral technology ineffective.

    A particularly sneaky multipartite virus is the *stealth virus,* which can temporarily remove itself from memory to elude capture. An example of a multipartite, polymorphic stealth virus is One Half.

- **Macro virus:** Macro viruses take advantage of a procedure in which miniature programs, known as macros, are embedded inside common data files, such as those created by e-mail or spreadsheets, which are sent over computer networks. Until recently, such documents have typically been ignored by antivirus software. Examples of macro viruses are Concept, which attaches to Word documents and e-mail attachments, and Laroux, which attaches to Excel spreadsheet files. Fortunately, the latest versions of Word and Excel come with built-in macro virus protection.

- **Logic bomb:** Logic bombs, or simply *bombs,* differ from other viruses in that they are set to go off at a certain date and time. A disgruntled programmer for a defense contractor created a bomb in a program that was supposed to go off two months after he left. Designed to erase an inventory tracking system, the bomb was discovered only by chance.

- **Trojan horse:** The Trojan horse covertly places illegal, destructive instructions in the middle of a legitimate program, such as a computer game. Once you run the program, the Trojan horse goes to work, doing its damage while you are blissfully unaware. An example of a Trojan horse is FormatC.

A variety of virus-fighting programs are on the market, often available in the utility section in software stores. **Antivirus software** scans a computer's hard disk, diskettes, and main memory to detect viruses and, sometimes, to destroy them. Such virus watchdogs operate in two ways. First, they scan disk drives for "signatures," characteristic strings of 1s and 0s left by known viruses. Second, they look for suspicious virus-like behavior, such as attempts to erase or change areas on your disks. You can employ antivirus programs as constant sentries. Like metal detectors scanning people entering an airport, antivirus monitors can detect any viruses trying to enter your computer.

Among the antiviral programs available are Dr. Solomon's Anti-Virus Toolkit, F-PROT Professional, IBM AntiVirus, McAfee VirusScan, Norton AntiVirus, ThunderByte Anti-Virus Utilities, TouchStone PC-Cillin, and (for Macs) Disinfectant. IBM and Symantec are working on technologies that will automatically destroy viruses that haven't been analyzed by researchers. (A detailed list of antivirus software can be found on the World Wide Web at *http://www.icsa.net.*)

Computer Criminals

Know example

What kind of people are perpetrating most of the information-technology crime? More than 80% may be employees, and the rest are outside users, hackers and crackers, and professional criminals.

Employees

"Employees are the ones with the skill, the knowledge, and the access to do bad things," says Don Parker, an expert on computer security at SRI International in Menlo Park, California. Dishonest or disgruntled employees, he says, pose "a far greater problem than most people realize."[13]

Most common frauds involve credit cards, telecommunications, employees' personal use of computers, unauthorized access to confidential files, and unlawful copying of copyrighted or licensed software. In addition, the increasing use of laptops off the premises, away from the eyes of supervisors, concerns some security experts, who worry that dishonest employees or outsiders can more easily intercept communications or steal company trade secrets.

Workers may use information technology for personal profit or steal hardware or information to sell. They may also use it to seek revenge for real or imagined wrongs, such as being passed over for promotion. Sometimes they may use the technology simply to demonstrate to themselves that they have power over people. This may have been the case with a Georgia printing-company employee convicted of sabotaging the firm's computer system. As files mysteriously disappeared and the system randomly crashed, other workers became so frustrated and enraged that they quit.

Outside Users

Suppliers and clients may also gain access to a company's information technology and use it to commit crimes. Such opportunities increase as electronic connections such as Electronic Data Interchange systems (✔ p. 7.37) become more commonplace.

Hackers and Crackers

Hackers are people who gain unauthorized access to computer or telecommunications systems for the challenge or even the principle of it. For example, in 1996, Swedish hackers broke into the Web site of the CIA, the American Central Intelligence Agency, and posted a message declaring it the "Central Stupidity Agency."

(CIA officials said their home page is not linked to mainframe computers containing secrets.) In November of 1998, hackers in Sweden and Canada broke into several Stanford University systems and stole about 5000 passwords. However, there was no evidence that the hackers disturbed any research or caused any serious damage to the systems.

Eric Corley, publisher of a magazine called *2600: The Hackers' Quarterly,* believes that hackers are merely engaging in "healthy exploration." In fact, by breaking into corporate computer systems and revealing their flaws, he says, they are performing a favor and a public service. Such unauthorized entries show the corporations involved the leaks in their security systems. Indeed, at one point, Netscape launched a so-called Bugs Bounty program, offering a cash reward to the first hacker to identify a "significant" security flaw in its latest Web browser software.

Hacking seems to be taking a less-benign direction by combining its activities with political activism. For example, two New Yorkers, Ricardo Dominguez and Stefen Wray, have established the Electronic Disturbance Theater to recruit hackers to attack the Web sites of any person or company they deem responsible for oppression.

Crackers also gain unauthorized access to information technology but do so for malicious purposes. (Some observers think the term *hacker* covers malicious intent, also.) Crackers attempt to break into computers and deliberately obtain information for financial gain, shut down hardware, pirate software, or destroy data.

The tolerance for "benign explorers"—hackers—has waned. Most communications systems administrators view any kind of unauthorized access as a threat, and they pursue the offenders vigorously. Educators try to point out to students that universities can't provide an education for everybody if hacking continues. The most flagrant cases of hacking/cracking are met with federal prosecution. Two young Berkeley, California, men ages 20 and 21, who broke into a Tower Records security network and downloaded a file containing 1700 credit-card numbers, had no plans to exploit their find, only to show off their accomplishment at a hackers' convention. Contrary to the hacker myth that says if you don't actually use the numbers you cannot be prosecuted, the pair were sentenced to many months in federal prison.

Professional Criminals

Members of organized crime rings don't just steal information technology. They also use it the way that legal businesses do—as a business tool, but for illegal purposes. For instance, databases can be used to keep track of illegal gambling debts and stolen goods. Not surprisingly, the old-fashioned illegal booking operation has gone high-tech, with bookies using computers and fax machines in place of betting slips and paper tally sheets.

Drug dealers have used pagers as a link to customers. Microcomputers, scanners, and printers can be used to print counterfeit money and forge checks, immigration papers, passports, and driver's licenses. Telecommunications can be used to transfer funds illegally.

As information-technology crime has become more sophisticated, so have the people charged with preventing it and disciplining its outlaws. Campus administrators are no longer being quite as easy on offenders and are turning them over to police. Industry organizations such as the Software Publishers Association are going after software pirates large and small. (Commercial software piracy is now a felony, punishable by up to five years in prison and fines of up to $250,000 for anyone convicted of stealing at least ten copies of a program, or more than $2500 worth of software.) Police departments as far apart as Medford, Massachusetts, and San Jose, California, now have police patrolling a "cyber beat." That is, they cruise online bulletin boards looking for pirated software, stolen trade secrets, child molesters, and child pornography.

In 1988, after the last widespread Internet break-in, the U.S. Defense Department created the Computer Emergency Response Team (CERT), charged with addressing network security problems and Internet emergencies, including hacking and viruses. Although it has no power to arrest or prosecute, CERT provides round-the-clock international information and security-related support services to users of the Internet. Whenever it gets a report of an electronic snooper, whether on the Internet or on a corporate e-mail system, CERT stands ready to lend assistance. It counsels the party under attack, helps thwart the intruder, and evaluates the system afterward to protect against future break-ins. (Find out more at *www.cert.org.*)

14.6 Security: Safeguarding Computers & Communications

Key Question **What are some methods for securing computer systems?**

Does your Social Security number say anything about you? Indeed it does. The first three numbers, called area numbers, generally tell in which state you were born or, if you recently emigrated, where you lived when you received your working papers. The next six digits can tell government officials whether a Social Security Number is fraudulent.

It's usually nobody's business but your own where you came from, and you'd like to keep it that way. However, the ongoing dilemma of the Digital Age is balancing convenience against security. **Security** is a system of safeguards for protecting information technology against disasters, systems failure, and unauthorized access that can result in damage or loss. We consider four components of security:

- Identification and access
- Encryption
- Protection of software and data
- Disaster-recovery planning

Identification and Access

Are you who you say you are? The computer wants to know.

There are three ways a computer system can verify that you have legitimate right of access. Some security systems use a mix of these techniques. The systems try to authenticate your identity by determining (1) what you have, (2) what you know, or (3) who you are.

What You Have—Cards, Keys, Signatures, Badges

Credit cards, debit cards, and cash-machine cards all have magnetic strips or built-in computer chips that identify you to the machine. Many require you to display your signature, for verification purposes. Computer rooms are always kept locked, requiring a key. Many people also keep a lock on their personal computers. A

In 1986, after receiving a diagnosis of Lou Gehrig's disease, Intel physicist and engineer Mike Ward began drawing blueprints for a computer system that would allow him to continue working as the disease progressed. "Typing" an e-mail message using eye-gaze technology, Ward says, "I cannot move or speak, but I can still be productive."

computer room may also be guarded by security officers, who may need to see an authorized signature or a badge with your photograph before letting you in.

Of course, credit cards, keys, and badges can be lost or stolen. Signatures can be forged. Badges can be counterfeited.

What You Know—PINs, Passwords, and Digital Signatures

To gain access to your bank account through an automated teller machine (ATM), you key in your PIN. A *PIN,* or *personal identification number,* is the security number known only to you that is required to access the system. Telephone credit cards also use a PIN. If you carry either an ATM or a phone card, *never* carry the PIN written down elsewhere in your wallet (even disguised).

A *password* is a special word, code, or symbol that is required to access a computer system. Passwords are one of the weakest security links. Passwords can be guessed, forgotten, or stolen. Too many passwords, like your mother's maiden name, are easily guessed by outsiders. Some intruders are aided by password-guessing software. The most common password is the users' name; the second-place choice is the word "secret." To reduce a stranger's guessing, experts recommends never choosing a real word or variations of your name, birthdate, or those of your friends or family. Also, don't use any portion of your phone number, or 1111 or 0000. Instead you should mix letters, numbers, and punctuation marks in an oddball sequence of no fewer than nine characters, such as *2blorNOT2b%* or *Alfred!E!Newman7.*

The advice is sound, but the problem today is that many people have to remember several passwords. Now that every computer online service, voice-mail box, burglar-alarm system, and office computer network demands a unique password, we run the risk of password overload.

Skilled hackers may break into national computer networks and detect passwords as they are being used. Or they pose on the telephone as computer technicians to cajole passwords out of employees. They may even find access codes in discarded technical manuals in trash bins.

Some computer security systems have a "call-back" provision. In a *call-back system,* the user calls the computer system, punches in the password, and hangs up. The computer then calls back a certain preauthorized number. This measure will block anyone who has somehow gotten hold of a password but is calling from an unauthorized telephone.

Another technology is the digital signature, which security experts hope will lead to a world of paperless commerce. A *digital signature* is a string of characters and numbers that a user signs to an electronic document being sent by his or her computer. The receiving computer performs mathematical operations on the alphanumeric string to verify its validity. The system works by using a *public-private key system.* That is, the system involves a pair of numbers called a private key and a public key. One person creates the signature with a secret private key, and the recipient reads it with a second, public key. This process in effect certifies the document and ensures its integrity.

For example, when you write your boss an electronic note, you sign it with your secret private key. (This could be some bizarre string beginning 479XY283 and continuing on for 25 characters.) When your boss receives the note, he or she looks up your public key, which is available from a source such as an electronic bulletin board, the Postal Service, or a corporate computer department. If the document is altered in any way, it will no longer produce the same signature sequence.

Who You Are—Your Physical Traits

Some forms of identification can't be easily faked—such as your physical traits. Biometrics tries to use these in security devices. *Biometrics* is the science of measuring individual body characteristics.

Biological characteristics read by biometric devices include fingerprints, hand-prints, voices, the blood vessels in the back of the eyeball, the lips, and even one's entire face. For example, Who Vision Systems has developed TactileSense, an inexpensive fingerprint system. It costs about only $25 to embed the fingerprint reader in a monitor or a keyboard.

The sensor pad is a stamp-size sheet of special electro-sensitive plastic, which turns pressure into light. Put your finger on it, and it generates a glowing image of your fingerprint on the underside. This image is digitized and encrypted (we discuss encryption shortly) before being sent to a host computer for validation, so the fingerprint itself doesn't float around on a network, where it could be stolen.

This fingerprint check system can be mounted on a door or on a safe. Entry is granted only after one's fingerprints are verified.

This system verifies the identity of computer users by iris scans.

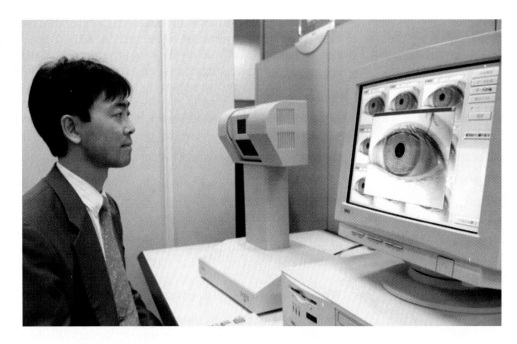

Iris Scan (*www.iriscan.com*) began developing ID devices based on the human iris in 1995. Sensor (*www.sensor.com*) has developed an iris scanning system for the financial services industry.

The U.S Immigration and Naturalization Service (INS) has instituted a biometric system that speeds up processing time for certain travelers arriving in the United States from overseas. Citizens of the United States, Canada, and Bermuda—as well as people who travel to the United States three or more times a year may enroll in the system, called Inspass. This system uses fingerprint and handprint recognition.

Other biometric systems can authenticate signatures written on a digital pad by remembering the shape, speed, and pen pressure used to create the original signature (Cyber-SIGN: *www.cybersign.com*). VeriVoice makes Internet Security Systems, Unix and Windows software to authenticate you by voice, either on the telephone or over the Internet (*www.verivoice.com*). Visionics offers FaceIt software that, in use with a video camera, analyzes your face shape for authentification.

Encryption

PGP is a computer program written for encrypting computer messages—putting them into secret code. **Encryption,** or enciphering, is the altering of data so that it is not usable unless the changes are undone. PGP (for *Pretty Good Privacy*) is so good that it is practically unbreakable. PGP can be used by organizations, companies, and individuals. It can be downloaded from *www.nai.com/products/security/freeware.asp* for noncommercial use. Otherwise it can be purchased from Network Associates, Inc. Other encryption programs are also available, such as SynCrypt. Microsoft and Netscape include S/MIME encryption options in their e-mail programs.

When you encrypt something, you scramble it. To decrypt, you unscramble it. Both activities require a key, somewhat like a password. If you're encrypting your own files and are the only person with access to them, you need only one key to both encrypt and decrypt. If you are sending files or messages to another computer, the person on that end needs a different key to decrypt.

Silicon Eyes Will Soon Be Everywhere

Chips that "see," a new kind of imaging chip, will soon be watching you and helping you, say many chipmakers.

Consumer photography Smart sensors will automatically correct exposure and allow images to be edited—for example, cropped, color adjusted—right on the camera.

Computers "Eyeball" digital cameras will be built into monitors for video mail or for verifying the user's identity. Keyboards with built-in fingerprint scanners will substitute for passwords.

Handheld gadgets Small digital cameras will soon become common accessories for cellular phones and PDAs.

Retailing Fingerprint and retinal scanners that can instantly verify someone's identity will be widely used by retail stores, banks, and government agencies.

Medicine Imaging chips may help blind people see and will be commonly used in surgery.

Cars Digital cameras will replace rearview mirrors, check tire pressure and monitor occupants as part of advanced safety systems.

Industry Among hundreds of possible applications, digital technology will sharply reduce the cost of sophisticated security systems and allow aircraft makers to monitor hard-to-reach places inside airplanes.

From Geoffrey Smith, "Silicon Eyes," *Business Week.*

Encryption is clearly useful for some organizations, especially those concerned with trade secrets, military matters, and other sensitive data. However, encryption also has a downside. For instance, police in Sacramento, California, found that PGP blocked them from reading the computer diary of a convicted child molester and finding links to a suspected child pornography ring. *Should* the government be allowed to read the coded e-mail of its citizens? What about its being blocked from surveillance of overseas terrorists, drug dealers, and other enemies?

Protection of Software and Data

Organizations go to tremendous lengths to protect their programs and data. As might be expected, this includes educating employees about making backup disks, protecting against viruses, and so on.

Other security procedures include the following:

- *Control of access:* Access to online files is restricted only to those who have a legitimate right to access—because they need them to do their jobs. Many organizations keep a transaction log that notes all accesses or attempted accesses to data. (Most LAN management software includes this function.)

- *Firewalls:* For security, organizations with their own internal networks often install guarded gateways known as firewalls. A **firewall** is software or hardware that prevents hackers and others from infiltrating a computer or internal network from an outside network, usually the rough-and-tumble Internet.

   A firewall admits only those outside communications you decide to select. If you want to close off your network to everyone except Sue at International, communicating by e-mail at certain hours of the day, you can do that. Everyone else will be kept away. Besides allowing those with need-to-access to access an Internet network, a firewall should log suspicious events and alert system administrators when attempts are made to breach security.

■ *Audit controls:* Many networks have *audit controls* to track which programs and servers were used, which files opened, and so on. This creates an *audit trail,* a record of how a transaction was handled from input through processing and output.

■ *People controls:* Because people are the greatest threat to a computer system, security precautions begin with the screening of job applicants. That is, resumes are checked to see if people did what they said they did. Another control is to separate employee functions, so that people are not allowed to wander freely into areas not essential to their jobs. Manual and automated controls—input controls, processing controls, and output controls—are used to check that data is handled accurately and completely during the processing cycle. Printouts, printer ribbons, and other waste that may yield passwords and trade secrets to outsiders are disposed of through shredders or locked trash barrels.

Disaster-Recovery Plans

A **disaster-recovery plan** is a method of restoring information-processing operations that have been halted by destruction or accident.

Mainframe computer systems are operated in separate departments by professionals, who tend to have disaster plans. Mainframes are regularly and frequently backed up. However, many personal computers, and even entire local area networks, are not backed up. The consequences of this lapse can be great. It has been reported that, on average, a company loses as much as 3% of its gross sales within eight days of a sustained computer outage. In addition, the average company struck by a computer outage lasting more than 10 days never fully recovers.[14]

A disaster-recovery plan is more than a big fire-drill. It has the following characteristics:

■ *Priorities of business functions:* It includes a list of all business functions, ranked in priority according to which functions must be back in operation first. Thus, most companies would consider it important for programs computing customer billing and accounts receivable to be up and running before the programs computing employee pension plans. A college would want its payroll programs in operation before its alumni contribution lists.

■ *Support resources needed:* The disaster-recovery plan includes a list of everything and everybody needed to support these business functions: the hardware, software, data, facilities, and people needed.

■ *Backup sites:* The disaster-recovery plan includes the ongoing process of backing up and storing programs and data in another location, either a hot site or a cold site. A *hot site* is a fully equipped computer center, with everything needed to resume business functions. A *cold site* is a building or other suitable environment in which a company can install its own computer system.

■ *Procedures for implementing plan:* The recovery plan describes ways of getting access to the support resources, procedures for alerting necessary personnel, and the steps to take to implement the plan. The action plan should describe how input and output data is to be handled at a different site.

■ *Training and practice:* The plan describes how the people involved should be trained and practice for disasters.

Sometimes organizations join together in a consortium or mutual-aid arrangement, so that even competitors, for example, will share resources until the emergency is over.

14.7 Social Questions: Will Information Technology Make Our Lives Better?

Key Question **What effect does information technology have on the environment, health, workplace problems, employment rates, education, commerce, the entertainment industry, and government?**

Much of our society is built on an abiding faith that technology is good, that innovation drives progress. Clearly, however, it is not that simple. Here let us examine information technology in relation to several key areas:

■ Environmental problems

■ Mental-health problems

■ Workplace problems

■ Economic issues and employment

■ Education and information

■ Commerce and electronic money

■ Government and electronic democracy

Environmental Problems

As the upgrade merry-go-round continues, as it has since the birth of the computer industry, more and more people are getting in on the Digital Revolution. Everyone hopes, of course, that the principal effects of this growth will be beneficial. But you need not be anti-technology to wonder just what negative impact computerization will have. How, for instance, will it affect the environment—in particular energy consumption and environmental pollution?

Energy Consumption and "Green PCs"

Running the computers and communications devices discussed in this book wastes a lot of electricity. Not only have computers themselves been built in ways that used power unnecessarily, but an office full of computers generates a lot of heat, so that additional power is consumed by air-conditioning systems to keep people comfortable. Finally, people leave their computer systems on even when they're not sitting in front of them—not just during the day but overnight and on weekends as well.

In recent years, the Environmental Protection Agency has launched Energy Star, a voluntary program to encourage the use of computers that consume a minimal amount of power. The goal of Energy Star is to reduce the amount of electricity microcomputers and monitors use from the typical 150 watts of power to more than 60 watts, which is about the power requirement for a moderately bright light bulb. (Half the wattage would be for the system unit, the other half for the monitor.) As a result, manufacturers are now producing Energy Star–compliant "green PCs."

"If you use your PC for 8 hours a day but always leave it on," says one writer, "a green PC could save about $70 a year. If everyone used only green PCs, $2 billion could be saved annually."[15]

Environmental Pollution

Communities like to see computer manufacturers move to their areas because they are viewed as nonpolluting. Is this true? Actually, in the past, chemicals used in manufacturing semiconductors polluted air, soil, and groundwater. Today, however, computer makers are literally cleaning up their act, although clusters of cancer and birth defects have been reported among workers in older semiconductor manufacturing plants in Scotland, California, and Asia.

Also, as people rush to buy the newest hardware, their discarded computers, printers, monitors, fax machines, and so on wind up as junk in landfills, although some are stripped by recyclers for valuable metals. More problematic is the disposal of batteries, as from portable computers. The cadmium in nickel-cadmium batteries is a toxic element and can leach from a landfill garbage dump into groundwater supplies. When their useful life is over, such batteries should be sent to local toxic-waste disposal programs. Newer battery technology, such as nickel-hydride and lithium cells, may eventually replace nickel-cadmium.

If you have an old-fashioned computer system, consider donating it to an organization that can make use of it. Don't abandon it in a closet. Don't dump it in the trash. Even if you regard it as horribly antiquated, someone else may be grateful for all it will do. Machines can also be taken apart and used for parts.

Several nonprofit groups will find a new home for your old computer equipment. For example, if you use your browser and the AltaVista search tool and type in "used computers," you'll find more than 8000 sites that deal with accepting, buying, donating, and selling used computers.

Software packaging also poses a problem. Estimates cited by the Software Manufacturer's Association state that about 40 million software boxes and other packaging materials are thrown away and that less than 30% of all packaged software is recycled. What's more, over 1 billion diskettes are thrown away each year, and it takes a diskette more than 450 years to decompose in a landfill. This information clearly demonstrates the advantages of downloading software from suppliers over the Internet.

Mental-Health Problems: Isolation, Gambling, Net Addiction, Stress

From a mental-health standpoint, will being wired together really set us free? Consider the following issues.

Isolation

Automation allows us to go days without actually speaking with or touching another person, from buying gas to playing games. Even the friendships we make online in cyberspace, some believe, "are likely to be trivial, short lived, and disposable—junk friends." Recently, in the first concentrated study of the social and psychological effects of Internet use at home, researchers at Carnegie Mellon University have found that people who spend even a few hours a week online experience higher levels of depression and loneliness than those who use the computer network less frequently.[16] Based on the data, the researchers hypothesize that relationships maintained over long distances without face-to-face contact ultimately do not provide the kind of support and reciprocity necessary for psychological security and happiness; they do not allow you, for instance, to babysit in a pinch for a friend or to grab a cup of coffee. The researchers also theorize that perhaps time spent on the Internet would otherwise be devoted to socializing with friends and family.

Gambling

Gambling is already widespread in North America, but information technology could make it almost unavoidable. Although gambling by wire has been illegal in the United States since the 1960s, all kinds of moves are afoot to get around this ban. For example, host computers for Internet casinos and sports books are being set up in Caribbean tax havens, while satellites, decoders, and remote-control devices allow TV viewers to engage in racetrack wagering from home. About 175 gambling Web sites were in operation in 1998.[17] In July 1998, the U.S Senate approved a broad ban on Internet gambling meant to strengthen previous laws. It remains to be seen if this effort will prove effective.

Net Addiction

Don't let this happen to you: A student e-mails friends, browses the World Wide Web, blows off homework, botches exams, flunks out of school. This is the downward spiral of the "Net addict," often a college student, though it can be anyone. Some become addicted (although some professionals feel "addiction" is too strong a word) to chat groups, some to online pornography, some simply to the escape from real life.

Stress

Surveys indicate that, for a wide range of users, personal computers increased job satisfaction and/or are a key to success and learning. However, many users find PCs stressful and get angry at them.

Workplace Problems

First the mainframe computer, then the desktop stand-alone PC, and now the networked computer were all brought into the workplace for one reason only: to improve productivity. How is it working out? Let's consider two aspects: the misuse of technology and information overload.

Misuse of Technology

"For all their power," says an economics writer, "computers may be costing U.S. companies tens of billions of dollars a year in downtime, maintenance and training costs, useless game playing, and information overload."[18]

Consider games. Employees may look busy, staring into their computer screens with crinkled brows. But often they're just playing games or surfing the Net.

All the fussing that employees do with hardware and software also wastes time. Says one editor, "Back in the old days, when I toiled on a typewriter, I never spent a whole morning installing a new ribbon . . . I did not scan the stores for the proper cables to affix to my typewriter or purchase books that instructed me on how to get more use from my liquid white-out."[19] One study estimated that microcomputer users waste 5 billion hours a year waiting for programs to run, checking computer output for accuracy, helping co-workers use their applications, organizing cluttered disk storage, and calling for technical support.[20]

A particularly interesting misuse is the continual upgrade. Ask yourself, "Do I really need that slick new product?" Ron Erickson, former chairman of the Egghead Software stores and now a technology consultant, advises consumers not to buy the new software version if the old one is working O.K. For many businesses, he says, the rule should be: "Stop buying new software, and train employees on what you have."

Information Overload

Information technology is definitely a two-edged sword. Cellular phones, pagers, portable computers, fax machines, and modems may free employees from the office, but those employees tend to work longer hours under more severe deadline pressure than do their counterparts who stay at the office. Moreover the gadgets that once promised to do away with irksome business travel by ushering in a new era of communications have done the opposite—created the office-in-a-bag that allows business travelers to continue to work from airplane seats and hotel desks. Many people feel overwhelmed by information. One more billboard, radio jingle, fax, spam e-mail, TV ad, or phone message, and we suspect we will fry like an overloaded circuit.

What does being overwhelmed with information do to you, besides inducing stress and burnout? One result is that, with so many choices to entice and confuse us, we become more averse to making decisions. Home buyers now take twice as long as a decade ago to sign a contract on a new house, organizations take months longer to hire top executives, and managers tend to consider worst-case scenarios rather than benefits when considering investment in a new venture.

"The volume of information available is so great that I think people generally are suffering from a lack of meaning in their lives," says Neil Postman, chair of the department of culture and communication at New York University. "People are just adrift in the sea of information, and they don't know what the information is about or why they need it."[21]

Economic Issues: Employment and the Haves/Have-Nots

People who don't like technology in general, and today's information technology in particular, have been called *neo-Luddites*. The original Luddites were a group of weavers in northern England who, while proclaiming their allegiance to a legendary King Ludd, in 1812–1814 went about smashing modern looms that moved cloth production out of the hands of peasant weavers and into inhumane factories. Some of today's neo-Luddites make the alarming case that technological progress is actually no progress at all—indeed, it is a curse. The two biggest charges (which are related) are, first, that information technology is killing jobs and, second, that it is widening the gap between the rich and the poor.

Technology, the Job Killer

Technological advances play a variety of roles, good and bad, in social progress. But is it true, as Jeremy Rifkin says in *The End of Work,* that intelligent machines are replacing humans in countless tasks, "forcing millions of blue-collar and white-collar workers into temporary, contingent, and part-time employment and, worse, unemployment"?[22]

This is too large a question to be fully considered in this book. Numerous factors are responsible for the downsizing of companies and the rise of unemployment among many sectors of society. The U.S. economy is undergoing powerful structural changes brought on not only by the widespread diffusion of technology but also by the growth of international trade, the shift from manufacturing to service employment, the weakening of labor unions, more rapid immigration, and other factors.

Many economists seem to agree that the economic boom that the United States enjoyed in the 1950s and 1960s won't return until there is more public investment and more personal saving instead of spending. Investment in recent years has been concentrated in computers. Surprisingly, however, as one economics writer points out, "so far computers have not yielded the rapid growth in production that came from investments in railroads, autos, highways, electric power, and aircraft—all huge outlays, involving government as well as the private sector, that changed the way Americans lived and worked."[23]

Gap Between Rich and Poor

"In the long run," says Stanford University economist Paul Krugman, "improvements in technology are good for almost everyone. . . . Unfortunately, what is true in the long run need not be true over shorter periods."[24] We are now, he believes, living through one of those difficult periods in which technology doesn't produce widely shared economic gains but instead widens the gap between those who have the right skills and those who don't.

A U.S. Department of Commerce survey of "information have-nots" reveals that about 20% of the poorest households in the U.S. do not have telephones. Moreover, only a fraction of those poor homes that do have phones will be able to afford the information technology that most economists agree is the key to a comfortable future. The richer the family, the more likely it is to have and use a computer.

Schooling—especially college—makes a great difference. Every year of formal schooling after high school adds 5 to 15% to annual earnings later in life.[25] Being well educated is only part of it, however; one should also be technologically literate. Employees who are skilled at technology "earn roughly 10 to 15% higher pay," according to the chief economist for the U.S. Labor Department.[26]

In the remote Australian outback, more then 200 miles away from the nearest bank in Alice Springs, 8-month-old Shanley Malbunka helps his mother Celina withdraw money from her bank account. Handheld ATM machines enable the 1000 aboriginal residents in the town of Yuendumu to conduct their banking electronically.

"If we could shrink the Earth's population to a village of precisely 100 people, with all the existing human ratios remaining the same, it would look something like the following. There would be 57 Asians . . . 21 Europeans . . . 14 from the Western Hemisphere, both north and south . . . 8 Africans . . . 52 would be female . . . 48 would be male . . . 70 would be non-white . . . 30 would be white . . . 70 would be non-Christian . . . 30 would be Christian . . . 89 would be heterosexual . . . 11 would be homosexual . . . 6 people would possess 59% of the entire world's wealth . . . 80 would live in substandard housing . . . 70 would be unable to read . . . 50 would suffer from malnutrition . . . 1 would be near death . . . 1 would be near birth . . . 1 (yes, only 1) would have a college education . . . **1 would own a computer.**"

Dr. Phillip M. Harter, Stanford University

Advocates of information access for all find hope in the promises of NII (National Information Infrastructure) proponents for "universal service" and the wiring of every school to the Net. But this won't happen automatically. Ultimately we must become concerned with the effects of growing economic disparities on our social and political health. "Computer technology is the most powerful and the most flexible technology ever developed," says Terry Bynum, chair of the American Philosophical Association's Committee on Philosophy and Computing. "Even though it's called a technical revolution, at heart it's a social and ethical revolution because it changes everything we value."[27]

Education and Information

The government is interested in reforming education, and technology can assist that effort. Presently the United States has more computers in its classrooms than other countries, but many machines are old and some teachers aren't completely computer-literate. Also, the poorer the school district, the less likely it is to have modems and online connections.

Of particular interest is distance learning, or the "virtual university." *Distance learning* is the use of computer and/or video networks to teach courses to students outside the conventional classroom. At present, distance learning is largely outside the mainstream of campus life. That is, it concentrates principally on part-time students, those who cannot easily travel to campus, those interested in non-credit classes, or those seeking special courses in business or engineering.

Computers can also be used to create "virtual" classrooms not limited by scheduled class time. Some institutions (Stanford, MIT) are replacing the lecture hall with forms of learning based on multimedia programs, workstations, and television courses at remote sites. The Information Superhighway could be used to enable students to take video field trips to distant places and to pull information from remote museums and libraries.

As we have seen, making information available—and having it make sense—is one of our greatest challenges. Can everything in the Library of Congress be made available online to citizens and companies? What about government records, patents, contracts, and other legal documents? Or satellite-generated geographical maps? Indeed, satellite imaging based on technology from Cold War spy satellites will soon be so good that companies, cities, and other buyers could use it to get views of land use, traffic patterns—and even of your back yard. (The technology also has some people worried about privacy invasion and a free-for-all expansion of espionage.)

Computers help blind children learn how to read by converting lessons into Braille printouts. Kent Cullers, a prominent astrophysicist who is blind, says, "I interact as many other people do nowadays, through their machines. And the wonder of the technology is that I can do the job just as well as many other people can."

Health

Another goal of the Information Superhighway is to improve health care. The government is calling for an expansion of "telemedicine." *Telemedicine* is the use of telecommunications to link health-care providers and researchers, enabling them to share medical images, patient records, and research. Of particular interest would be the use of networks for "teleradiology" (the exchange of X rays, CAT scans, and the like) so that specialists could easily confer. Telemedicine would also allow long-distance patient examinations, using video cameras and, perhaps, virtual-reality gloves that would transmit and receive tactile sensations.

Another application is technology for translating human anatomy into billions of bytes of computer memory. Such models would help medical students with their training, surgeons with preoperative planning, and furniture designers with building better chairs. Another important health goal is to bring interactive, multimedia materials to the public to promote health and outline healthcare options.

Still another health goal is to eliminate *repetitive stress injury (RSI)*, which can be caused by repetitive tasks, such as typing on a computer keyboard and using a mouse or touch pad. RSI symptoms are tightness, stiffness, tingling, numbness, pain in the hands, wrists, fingers, forearms, neck, or back. Keyboard manufacturers are developing new styles of keyboards to help alleviate this problem. Users can also help themselves by using good posture, taking breaks, and stretching. (For advice about choosing a keyboard and avoiding RSI, try these Web sites: *http://engr-www.unl.edu/ee/eeshop/rsi/html; http://ergo.human.cornell.edu; http://www.cs.princeton.edu/~dwallach/tifaq/keyboards.html; http://web.mit.edu:1962/ tiserve.mit.edu/9000/32823.html; http://www.agilecorp.com/ergonomics/AboutThisSite. html.*)

Commerce and Electronic Money

Businesses clearly see information technology as a way to enhance productivity and competitiveness. However, the changes will probably go well beyond this.

The thrust of the original Industrial Revolution was separation—to break work up into its component parts so as to permit mass production. The effect of computer networks in the Digital Revolution, however, is unification—to erase boundaries between company departments, suppliers, and customers.

Indeed, the parts of a company can now as easily be global as down the hall from one another. Thus, designs for a new product can be tested and exchanged with factories in remote locations. With information flowing faster, goods can be sent to market faster and inventories kept down. Says an officer of the Internet Society, "Increasingly you have people in a wide variety of professions collaborating in diverse ways in other places. The whole notion of 'the organization' becomes a blurry boundary around a set of people and information systems and enterprises."[28]

The electronic mall, in which people make purchases online, is already here. Record companies, for instance, are putting sound and videos of new albums on Web sites, where you can sample the album and then order it sent as a cassette or CD. Banks in cyberspace are allowing users to adopt avatars or personas of themselves and then meet in three-dimensional virtual space on the World Wide Web, where they can query bank tellers and officers and make transactions. Wal-Mart Stores and Microsoft have developed a joint online shopping venture that allows shoppers to browse online and buy merchandise.

Cybercash, or E-cash, will change the future of money. Whether it takes the form of smart cards or of electronic blips online, cybercash will probably begin to displace (though not completely supplant) checks and paper currency. This would change the nature of how money is regulated as well as the way we buy and sell.

Government and Electronic Democracy

Will information technology help the democratic process? There seem to be two parts to this. The first is its use as a campaign tool; the second is its use in governing and in delivering government services.

Santa Monica, California, established a computer system, called Public Electronic Network (PEN), which residents may hook into free of charge. PEN gives Santa Monica residents access to city council agendas, staff reports, public safety tips, and the public library's online catalog. Citizens may also enter into electronic conferences on topics both political and nonpolitical; this has been by far the most popular attraction.

PEN could be the basis for wider forms of electronic democracy. For example, electronic voting might raise the percentage of people who vote. Interactive local-government meetings could enable constituents and town council members to discuss proposals.

Information technology could also deliver federal services and benefits. In 1994, the government unveiled a program in which Social Security pensioners and other recipients of federal aid without bank accounts could walk up to any ATM and withdraw the funds due them, using a plastic card and PIN code.

Where will you be in all this? People pursuing careers find the rules are changing very rapidly. Up-to-date skills are becoming ever more crucial. Job descriptions of all kinds are metamorphosing, and even familiar jobs are becoming more demanding. Today, experts advise, you need to be prepared to continually upgrade your skills, to specialize, and to market yourself. In a world of breakneck change, you can still thrive. The most critical knowledge, however, may turn out to be self-knowledge.

Spies-R-Us! The pen in Robert Wendt's breast pocket is a sensor that detects hidden electronic devices; the watch is actually a digital camera; and the tie conceals a video camera capable of transmitting images to either the monitor in Wendt's left hand or to a remote receiver. Wendt's walkie-talkie scrambles communication, making eavesdropping impossible; a wireless receiver lodged in his ear, allows him to listen to instructions from afar; and his eyepiece provides him with perfect night vision.

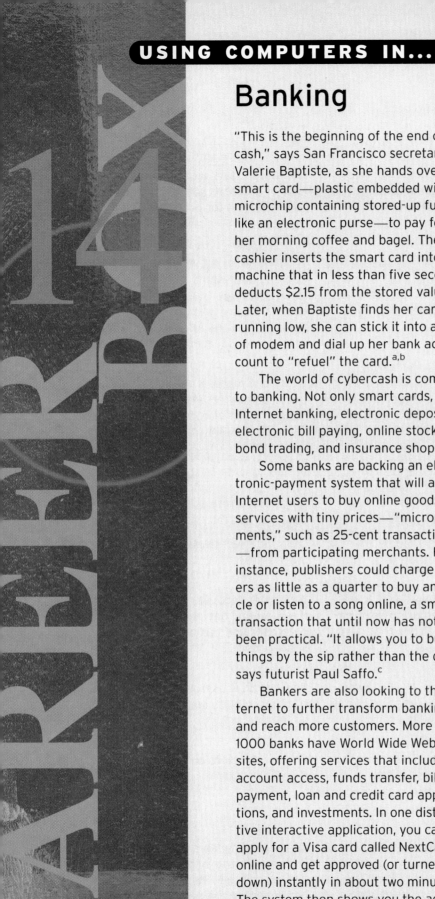

Banking

"This is the beginning of the end of cash," says San Francisco secretary Valerie Baptiste, as she hands over her smart card—plastic embedded with a microchip containing stored-up funds like an electronic purse—to pay for her morning coffee and bagel. The cashier inserts the smart card into a machine that in less than five seconds deducts $2.15 from the stored value. Later, when Baptiste finds her card running low, she can stick it into a kind of modem and dial up her bank account to "refuel" the card.[a,b]

The world of cybercash is coming to banking. Not only smart cards, but Internet banking, electronic deposits, electronic bill paying, online stock and bond trading, and insurance shopping.

Some banks are backing an electronic-payment system that will allow Internet users to buy online goods and services with tiny prices—"micropayments," such as 25-cent transactions —from participating merchants. For instance, publishers could charge buyers as little as a quarter to buy an article or listen to a song online, a small transaction that until now has not been practical. "It allows you to buy things by the sip rather than the gulp," says futurist Paul Saffo.[c]

Bankers are also looking to the Internet to further transform banking and reach more customers. More than 1000 banks have World Wide Web sites, offering services that include account access, funds transfer, bill payment, loan and credit card applications, and investments. In one distinctive interactive application, you can apply for a Visa card called NextCard online and get approved (or turned down) instantly in about two minutes. The system then shows you the account balances on your other credit cards—automatically, without asking you for the card numbers—so that, if you wish, you can transfer your balances to NextCard and benefit from a lower interest rate.[d]

Only about 46% of U.S. workers have their paychecks electronically deposited into their bank accounts (as opposed to 95% or more in Japan, Norway, and Germany, for example), but this is sure to change as Americans discover that direct deposit is actually safer and faster.[e] Getting them used to electronic bill paying will probably take longer, but that day too is arriving. For more than two decades, it has been possible to pay your bills online with special software and direct modem hookups to your bank, but only about 3% of U.S. households have tried it. The main delay has been that scarcely any bills are delivered online, but now banks have convinced corporations to electronically deliver bills to them, which will then be sent to customers via the Web.[f,g,h]

Banks are clamoring to get into the brokerage business, but some Internet brokerage firms are moving into banking. Companies such as E*Trade and Ameritrade Holding Corp. are building one-stop financial supermarkets offering a variety of money-related services, including home mortgage loans and insurance.[i,j] Insurance companies are also chasing consumers in cyberspace, marketing insurance policies through banks.[k]

Some Internet banks are Atlanta Internet Bank (*www.atlantabank.com*), Net.B@nk (*www.netbank.com*), Security First Network Bank (*www.fnb.com*), and Telebank (*www.telebankonline.com*). The NextCard is available at *www.nextcard.com*. Insurance information is available at *www.insweb.com* and *www.insuremarket.com*. If you're suspicious about an Internet bank's charter, you can check with the FDIC Suspicious Internet Banking site (*www.fdic.gov/consumer/suspicious*).

SUMMARY

WHAT IT IS
WHAT IT DOES   WHY IT IS IMPORTANT

antivirus software (KQ 14.5, p. 14.21) Program that scans a computer's hard disk, diskettes, CD-ROMs, and main memory to detect viruses and, sometimes, to destroy them.

Computer users must find out what kind of antivirus software to install in their systems for protection against damage or shutdown.

cookie (KQ 14.1, p. 14.4)   A special file that keeps track of your activities and visits on the Web. It's automatically created on your hard disk when you visit certain Web sites.

Without notifying you, cookies can connect your name or e-mail address to any Web site that you visit. Moreover, there are practically no restrictions on how the information obtained in this way may be disseminated or used.

copyright (KQ 14.2, p. 14.7)   A body of law that prohibits copying of intellectual property without the permission of the copyright holder.

Copyright matters are important because computers and networks have made the act of copying far easier and more convenient than in the past.

crackers (KQ 14.5, p. 14.22)   People who gain unauthorized access to information technology for malicious purposes.

Crackers attempt to break into computers so as to deliberately obtain information for financial gain, shut down hardware, pirate software, or destroy data.

dirty data (KQ 14.5, p. 14.16)   Data that is incomplete, outdated, or otherwise inaccurate.

Dirty data can cause information to be inaccurate.

disaster-recovery plan (KQ 14.6, p. 14.28)   Method of restoring information-processing operations that have been halted by destruction or accident.

A disaster-recovery plan is important if a company desires to resume its computer and business operations in short order.

encryption (KQ 14.6, p. 14.26) Also called *enciphering;* the altering of data so that it is not usable unless the changes are undone.

Encryption is useful when transmitting trade or military secrets or other sensitive data.

firewall (KQ 14.6, p. 14.27) Software or hardware that prevents hackers and others from infiltrating a computer or internal network from an outside network.

Firewalls protect an organization's data and systems.

hackers (KQ 14.5, p. 14.21) People who gain unauthorized access to computer or telecommunications systems for the challenge or even the principle of it.

The acts of hackers create problems not only for the institutions that are victims of break-ins but also for ordinary users of the systems.

information technology crime (KQ 14.5, p. 14.17) (1) An illegal act perpetrated *against* computers or telecommunications. (2) The *use* of computers or telecommunications to accomplish an illegal act.

Crimes against information technology include theft—of hardware, of software, of computer time, of cable or telephone services, of information—and also crimes of malice and destruction.

intellectual property (KQ 14.2, p. 14.7) Products of the human mind, tangible or intangible.

Information technology has presented legislators and lawyers—and you—with some new ethical issues regarding rights to intellectual property.

morphing (KQ 14.3, p 14.11) Altering a film or video image displayed on a computer screen pixel by pixel, or dot by dot.

Morphing and other techniques of digital image manipulation can produce images that misrepresent reality.

netiquette (KQ 14.4, p. 14.13) "Net etiquette"; guides to appropriate behavior while online.

Netiquette rules help users to avoid offending other users.

network piracy (KQ 14.2, p. 14.8) Using electronic networks to distribute unauthorized copyrighted materials in digitized form.

Computer users commit network piracy when they, for example, send unauthorized copies of digital recordings over the Internet. Network piracy is illegal.

plagiarism (KQ 14.2, p. 14.9) The expropriation of another writer's text, findings, or interpretations and presentation of this material as one's own.

Information technology offers plagiarists new opportunities for unauthorized copying but also provides new ways to catch plagiarism.

privacy (KQ 14.1, p. 14.3) The right of people not to reveal information about themselves—the right to keep personal information, such as medical histories, personal e-mail messages, student records, and financial information from getting into the wrong hands.

Information technology puts constant pressure on privacy.

security (KQ 14.6, p. 14.23) System of safeguards for protecting information technology against disasters, systems failure, and unauthorized access that can result in damage or loss.

With proper security, organizations and individuals can minimize information technology losses from disasters, system failures, and unauthorized access.

software piracy (KQ 14.2, p. 14.8) The unauthorized copying of copyrighted software.

One act of software piracy is to copy a program from one diskette to another. Another is to download a program from a network and make a copy of it. Software piracy is illegal.

spamming (KQ 14.4, p. 14.13) Sending unsolicited mail.

Examples of spam include chain letters, advertising, or similar junk mail, which take up server space and annoy e-mail recipients.

virus (KQ 14.5, p. 14.19) Deviant program that overwrites or attaches itself to programs and/or documents and destroys or corrupts data.

Viruses can cause users to lose data or files or can even shut down entire computer systems.

worm (KQ 14.5, p. 14.19) A program that copies itself repeatedly into memory or onto a disk drive until no more space is left.

Worms can shut down computers.

1. Fill in the following blanks:

   a. _____ is a set of moral values or principles that govern the conduct of an individual or group.

   b. Computer _____ are "deviant" programs that can cause destruction to computers that contract them.

   c. _____ is the expropriation of another writer's text, findings, or interpretations and presentation of this material as one's own.

   d. _____ _____ is using electronic networks to distribute unauthorized copyrighted materials in digitized form.

   e. _____, or enciphering, is the altering of data so that it is not usable unless the changes are undone.

2. Label each of the following statements as either true or false.

   a. _____ The Freedom of Information Act of 1970 gives citizens the right to look at data concerning themselves that is stored by the U.S. government.

   b. _____ Crackers gain unauthorized access to information technology for malicious reasons.

   c. _____ The V-chip is used primarily with the Internet to block out Web pages that have been labeled as high in violence.

   d. _____ Junk mail on the Internet is commonly referred to as *spam*.

   e. _____ Most computer-related privacy issues involve the use of large databases and electronic networks.

3. Define the following terms:
   a. copyright
   b. plagiarism

4. Errors and accidents in computer systems can be classified as
   a.
   b.
   c.
   d.
   e.

5. Define the following terms:
   a. worm
   b. virus
   c. antivirus software

6. Security is a system of safeguards for protecting information technology against

   (a) _____, (b) _____, and (c) _____ that can result in damange or loss.

7. Define the following terms:
   a. encryption
   b. firewall
   c. audit control

8. What are three characteristics of disaster recovery plans?

a. _____

b. _____

c. _____

IN YOUR OWN WORDS

1. Answer each of the Key Questions that appear at the beginning of this chapter.

2. What basic steps protect computer systems against viruses?

3. What is meant by the term *intellectual property*?

4. What is software piracy?

5. What is meant by the term *morphing* and how does this term relate to the topic of truth in art and journalism?

6. What is meant by the terms *netiquette* and *spamming*?

7. What is the difference between a hacker and a cracker?

8. What does the term *biometrics* mean?

9. What is a "green PC"?

10. What is meant by the term *dirty data*?

KNOWLEDGE IN ACTION

1. **Protecting Your Privacy.** Are you concerned about protecting your privacy? What online actions would you avoid to protect your privacy?

2. **Photo Manipulation.** Do you believe that photo manipulation is acceptable? Under what circumstances?

3. **Disadvantages to Using Computers.** What, in your opinion, are the most significant disadvantages of using computers? What do you think can be done about these problems?

4. **Speaking Freely.** What's your opinion about the issue of free speech on an electronic network? Research some recent legal decisions in various countries, as well as some articles on the topic, and then give a short report about what you think. Should the contents of messages be censored? If so, under what conditions?

5. **Behaving Ethically.** In your opinion, have people become less ethical with the invention and widespread use of computers and related technology, or is some unethical behavior just more obvious now because news can travel so much faster and farther? Explain your answer.

6. **Contacting the Electronic Privacy Information Center.** Contact the Electronic Privacy Information Center (EPIC), 666 Pennsylvania Avenue, SE, Suite 301, Washington, DC 20003 (202-544-9240, *www.epic.org*). Obtain a copy of a document that addresses "the A to Z's of privacy." Prepare a short report describing the major privacy issues identified in the document.

7. **Contacting the Software Publishers Association.** Contact the Software Publishers Association (*www.spa.org*). Obtain guidelines and literature on keeping software legal. Give a short report based on the information you receive.

Answers to Self-Test Exercises: 1a. ethics 1b. viruses 1c. plagiarism 1d. network piracy 1e. encryption 2. T, 3a. T, F, T 3b. A body of law that prohibits copying of intellectual property without the permission of the copyright holder. 3b. The expropriation of another writer's text, findings, or interpretations and presentation of this material as one's own. 4. people errors, procedural errors, software errors, electromechanical problems, "dirty data" problems 5a. A program that copies itself repeatedly into memory or onto a disk drive until no more space is left. 5b. Deviant program that overwrites or attaches itself to programs and/or documents and destroys or corrupts data. 5c. Program that scans a computer's hard disk, diskettes, CD-ROMs, and main memory to detect viruses and, sometimes, to destroy them. 6. disasters, systems failure, unauthorized access 7a. Also called *enciphering;* the altering of data so that it is not usable unless the changes are undone. 7b. Software or hardware that prevents hackers and others from infiltrating a computer or internal network from an outside network. 7c. Many networks have *audit controls* to track which programs and servers were used, which files opened, and so on. This creates an *audit trail,* a record of how a transaction was handled from input through processing and output. 8. priorities of business functions, support resources needed, backup sites, procedures for implementing a plan, training and practice

Now that your site is up and running, your job is over, right? Wrong. Aside from managing the day-to-day operations of your business, including taking and filling orders, you must take steps to ensure that customers will keep visiting your site. In this Episode, we explore some of these considerations in more detail.

On May 15, 1997, Amazon.com made headlines when it went public and became valued at $438 million. In 1999, Amazon.com's financial results for the first quarter alone showed net sales of $296 million, which is an increase of over 236% over the same quarter in 1998. During this same period in 1999, repeat customers accounted for over 66% of the orders. What brings customers back to Amazon.com?

PLANNING FOR THE FUTURE AT AMAZON.COM

The secret to Amazon.com's success can be found in its customer-centric approach. Amazon.com continues to build on its distribution infrastructure, providing customers with even faster delivery times, and to invest in technology and customer support functions. Amazon.com uses a team of customer support representatives to respond to customer inquiries about their orders. Many Amazon.com support services are currently automated including the process used to send customers an e-mail notice acknowledging the receipt of an order.

Beyond improving the efficiency of existing customer-support functions, Mr. Bezos plans to expand into a number of new product areas. In March of 1999, he announced plans to invest in drugstore.com (*www.drugstore.com*), an online source of health and beauty products, and pets.com (*www.pets.com/*), a leading supplier of pet supplies for all types of animals. Around the same time, he also announced plans to acquire Exchange.com, which specializes in locating hard-to-find books, recordings, and other memorabilia. In April of 1999, Amazon.com launched a new greeting card service that allows customers to select from a wide range of greeting cards and to customize their messages. Customers can access this service by simply clicking on the e-cards tab on the Amazon.com Home page. These and other ongoing efforts keep customers coming back and asking for more.

MANAGING YOUR WEB SITE

Aside from continually updating your site with fresh content and services, your Web business won't have any future at all if you don't develop a plan for managing your site and then sticking to the plan. Nothing will turn customers off more than if your site contains outdated information. Perform the following management tasks on a daily or weekly basis:

1. Keep the content fresh by adding new information.

2. Update existing information.

3. Verify that your site correctly references the file locations of your graphics files.

4. Verify that your site's navigation buttons work correctly and that other internal links are correct.

5. Verify that any links to external sites work correctly.

WHAT DO YOU THINK?

1. Describe the following elements of your online business in a 2–3 page report and then (optionally) present the report to your class:

- The name of your business

- Your product

- The features of your Home page

- Your online catalog

- Your plan for taking orders and collecting payment

- Steps you plan to take in order to establish a Web presence

- How you plan to gather, and then use, information about your customers

- What will be your competitive advantage? How will you survive competitive pressures from other Web-based businesses?

- Your hopes for the future expansion of your business

2. What tasks do you anticipate that you will perform to manage your site on an ongoing basis?

Vision Statement
AITP will be recognized as the professional organization of choice among
Information Technology professionals by providing industry leadership and opportunities
for professional development and personal growth.

Mission Statement
It is the mission of AITP to provide superior leadership and education in Information Technology.
AITP is dedicated to using the synergy of Information Technology partnerships to provide
education and benefits to our members and to working with the industry to assist in the overall
promotion and direction of Information Technology.

AITP <u>Code Of Ethics</u>
I acknowledge:

That I have an obligation to management, therefore, I shall promote the understanding of
information processing methods and procedures to management using every resource
at my command.

That I have an obligation to my fellow members, therefore, I shall uphold the high ideals of AITP as
outlined in its Association Bylaws. Further, I shall cooperate with my fellow members and shall
treat them with honesty and respect at all times.

That I have an obligation to society and will participate to the best of my ability in the
dissemination of knowledge pertaining to the general development and understanding of
information processing. Further, I shall not use knowledge of a confidential nature to further my
personal interest, nor shall I violate the privacy and confidentiality of information entrusted to me
or to which I may gain access.

That I have an obligation to my College or University, therefore, I shall uphold its ethical and moral
principles. That I have an obligation to my employer whose trust I hold, therefore, I shall endeavor
to discharge this obligation to the best of my ability, to guard my employer's interests, and to
advise him or her wisely and honestly.

That I have an obligation to my country, therefore, in my personal business and social contracts, I
shall uphold my nation and shall honor the chosen way of life of my fellow citizens.

I accept these obligations as a personal responsibility and as a member of this Association.
I shall actively discharge these obligations and I dedicate myself to that end.

If you have any questions, call our Membership Department at
800.224.9371, FAX 847.825.1693 or AITP_HQ@AITP.org

Association of INFORMATION TECHNOLOGY PROFESSIONALS
3155 Northwest Highway #200
Park Ridge, IL 60068-4272

NOTES

CHAPTER 1

1. Richard Bolles, cited in T. Minton, "Job-Hunting Requires Eyes and Ears of Friends, *San Francisco Chronicle,* January 25, 1991, p. D5.
2. Field Institute survey, reported in Jonathan Marshall, "High-Tech Often Equals Higher Pay," *San Francisco Chronicle,* September 3, 1996, p. A5.
3. Alan Krueger, Princeton University, cited in Marshall, 1996.
4. Adapted from Daniel Bell, *The Coming of Post-Industrial Society: A Venture in Social Forecasting,* New York, Basic Books, 1973.
5. Merritt Jones, quoted in "FYI," *Popular Science,* November 1995, pp. 88–89.
6. Kerry Pechter, "Office Memos: Some Predictions About the Workplace of the Future," *Wall Street Journal,* June 4, 1990, p. R5.

REAL ESTATE BOX

a. Michael Diamond, "Internet Makes Home Buying Easier," *USA Today,* June 16, 1998, p. 6E.
b. Barbara Whitaker, "House Hunting with Cursor and Click," *New York Times,* September 24, 1998, pp. D1, D5.
c. *Internet World,* December 1996, p. 47.
d. Susan N. Futterman, "Quick-Hit Research of a Potential Employer," *CompuServe Magazine,* September 1993, p. 36.
e. J. Peder Zane, "Now, the Magazines of 'Me,'" *New York Times,* May 14, 1995, sec. 4, p. 5.
f. R. U. Serius, "Virtual Banality," *San Francisco Examiner,* June 30, 1996, pp. C-5, C-6.

GOVERNMENT BOX

a. Dan Johnson, "Politics in Cyberspace," *The Futurist,* January 1999, p. 14.
b. *The State of "Electronically Enhanced Democracy": A Survey of the Internet* (New Brunswick, NJ: Rutgers University, Douglass Campus, Walt Whitman Center, Department of Political Science, 1998).
c. "Minus a Daily Paper, City Turns Online," *San Francisco Chronicle,* September 8, 1998, p. A22.
d. William A. Long, "For Neighborhoods in Many Cities, Virtual Community Centers," *New York Times,* March 4, 1999, p. D7.
e. Rick Lyman, "Got a Cause and a Computer? You Can Fight City Hall," *New York Times,* October 3, 1998, p. A12.
f. Associated Press, "Citizens Monitor Lawmakers Through Use of the Internet," *North Lake Tahoe Bonanza,* March 19, 1999, p. 12A.
g. Rebecca Fairley Raney, "Voting on the Web: Not Around the Corner, but on the Horizon," *New York Times,* September 17, 1998, p. D8.
h. Douglas Heller, "If We Can Shop Online, We Can Vote Online," *San Francisco Chronicle,* March 11, 1999, p. A25.
i. Laura Hamburg, "Touch-Screen Voting Wins Rave Reviews," *San Francisco Chronicle,* March 3, 1998, pp. A13, A15.
j. Michael Cornfield, quoted in Jon Swartz, "Electronic Engineering," *San Francisco Chronicle,* March 27, 1999, pp. D1, D3.
k. David Shribman, "www.SomeThingsNeverChange.gov," *Fortune,* May 10, 1999, p. 34.
l. Associated Press, "IRS Pushes for Online Tax Returns," *San Francisco Chronicle,* December 4, 1998, p. A9.
m. Lisa Carden, "Tips for Getting or Renewing a U.S. Passport," *San Francisco Examiner,* November 15, 1998, pp. T-8, T-9.
n. Steven Komarow, "Selective Service Goes On Line," *USA Today,* December 1, 1998, p. 11A.
o. Laura Casteneda, "Emergency Housing in a Hurry," *New York Times,* November 5, 1998, p. E9.

CHAPTER 2

1. Randy Pausch, quoted in John W. Verity and Paul C. Judge, "Making Computers Disappear," *Business Week,* June 24, 1996, pp. 118–119.
2. Michael S. Malone, "The Tiniest Transformer," *San Jose Mercury News,* September 10, 1995, pp. 1D–2D.
3. *Ibid.*
4. Martin Campbell-Kelly and William Aspray, *Computer: A History of the Information Machine* (New York, Basic Books, 1996), p. 105.

LAW BOX

a. Hindi Greenberg, "Lawyers Have Many Options," *San Francisco Examiner,* February 14, 1999, p. J5.
b. Steve Hamm, "A Database to Die For," *Business Week,* March 15, 1999, p. 40.
c. Cindy Cohn, quoted in Amy Harmon, "The Law Where There Is No Land," *New York Times,* March 16, 1998, pp. C1, C9.
d. Dan Rubin, "Swift Justice," *San Francisco Examiner,* January 17, 1999, p. D5.
e. Susan Adams and David Lipschultz, "Lawsuit.com," *Forbes,* December 1, 1997, pp. 47–48.
f. Allen G. Breed, "Software Helps Wrongly Accused Parents," *San Jose Mercury News,* May 3, 1998, p. 28A.
g. Daniel Fisher, "Arrest That Software!" *Forbes,* March 8, 1999, p. 94.

INFORMATION TECHNOLOGY BOX

a. Robert Greene, "Students Opting for Low-Tech Majors," *San Francisco Chronicle,* August 20, 1998, p. D3.
b. Del Jones, "Stereotype Turns Students Off of High-Paying Career," *USA Today,* February 16, 1998, pp. 1B, 2B.
c. Susan Gregory Thomas, "Capitalists on Campus: Students with Computer Skills Cash In," *U.S. News & World Report,* September 7, 1998, pp. 82–83.
d. Jones, 1998.
e. Marcia Stepanak, "Techies Keep Laughing All the Way to the Bank," *Business Week,* February 8, 1999, p. 110A.
f. 1999 Salary Survey Forecast/RHI Consulting, reported in Stepanek, 1999.
g. Thomas, 1998.
h. Stephan Baker, Ann Barrett, and Linda Himelstein, "Call All Nerds," *Business Week,* March 10, 1997, pp. 36–37.

CHAPTER 3

LAW ENFORCEMENT BOX

a. Catherine Greenman, "A Well-Equipped Patrol Officer: Gun, Flashlight, Computer," *New York Times,* January 21, 1999, p. D9.
b. Gordon Witkin, "Making Mean Streets Nice. Computer Maps That take the 'Random' Out of Violence," *U.S. News & World Report,* December 30, 1996/January 6, 1997, p. 63.
c. Verne G. Kopytoff, "High-Tech Help for Frequent Travelers Entering U.S.," *New York Times,* January 14, 1999, pp. D1, D5.
d. Seanna Browder, "Now, the Cops Are Strapping on Computers," *Business Week,* July 13, 1998, p. 126J.
e. Crime-Scene Analyzer," *Popular Science,* September 1998, p. 17.
f. Associated Press, "Tailing Suspects Much Easier Using Satellite Technology," *New York Times,* March 16, 1999, p. A20.
g. Sana Siwoloop, "Imagine Finding Your Picture on a Virtual Post Office Wall," *New York Times,* November 10, 1996, sec. 3, p.3.
h. Michelle Locke, "Wells Uses the Web to Catch Criminals," *San Francisco Chronicle,* November 30, 1996, pp. D1, D7.
i. Raoul V. Mowatt, "Cable TV Show Helps Uncover Fugitives," *San Jose Mercury News,* September 8, 1996, pp. 1B, 5B.

j.   Carolyn Zinko and Michael McCabe, "High-Tech Hunt Sped Rescue of Missing San Jose Bay," *San Francisco Chronicle*, December 7, 1996, pp. A1, A11.

GENEALOGY BOX

a.   Neal Templin, "More People Trace Their Family's Past Using PCs and Other High-Tech Tools," *Wall Street Journal*, April 10, 1996, p. B1.

b.   Ramon G. McLeod, "Finding Your Roots via Cyberspace," *San Francisco Chronicle*, February, 22, 1997, pp. A1, A13.

c.   Hilary Stout, "Historians-for-Hire Chronicle Lives of Ordinary Folks," *Wall Street Journal*, December 29, 1998, pp. B1, B4.

d.   Jefferson Graham, "Family Trees Blossom on Net's Branches," *USA Today*, August 12, 1998, p. 5D.

e.   Edward Harris, "The Web Finds Lost-Lost Ancestors," *Wall Street Journal*, March 4, 1999, p. B10.

f.   Merrill Goozner, "Help Nears for Those Searching at Ellis Island," *San Jose Mercury News*, December 28, 1997, p. 10A; reprinted from *Chicago Tribune*.

g.   Margaret Mannix, "Plugging In to Your Roots," *U.S. News & World Report*, December 23, 1996, pp. 73–76.

CHAPTER 4

AGRICULTURE BOX

a.   Dennis J. Strevelr, "Telemedicine: A Primer," *California Medicine*, May 1996, pp. 17–18.

b.   Los Angeles Times technology poll, reported in Greg Miller, "Southlanders Gaga Over Computers, Poll Says," *San Francisco Examiner*, October 6, 1996, p. C7; reprinted from the *Los Angeles Times*.

c.   Michael M. Phillips, "Greenspan Credits New Technology for Helping Farmers Weather Crisis," *Wall Street Journal*, March 17, 1999, p. A2.

d.   Kathleen Travers, quoted in 1996.

e.   Alan Freedman, *The Computer Desktop Encyclopedia* (New York: AMACOM, 1996), p. 547.

f.   Alan Greenspan, quoted in James Worsham, "The Flip Side of Downsizing," *Nation's Business*, October 1996, pp. 18–25.

g.   Barnaby J. Feder, "Amber Waves of Data in U.S. Farm Country," *New York Times*, May 4, 1998, pp. C1, C4.

CHAPTER 5

PHOTOGRAPHY BOX

a.   Vincent J. Alabiso, quoted in Otis Port, "Digital finds Its Photo Op," *Business Week*, April 15, 1996, pp. 71–72.

b.   *Ibid.*

c.   Stephen Manes, "Digital Photos as Fuzzy Snapshots," *New York Times*, March 19, 1996, p. B9.

d.   Doug Levy, "Kodak-Intel Deal Aims to Put Your Photos on Line," *USA Today*, September, 29, 1998, p. 3B.

e.   Chris O'Malley, "Film in the Round," *Popular Science*, December 1998, p. 38.

f.   Nichols Van den Berghe, quoted in Jon Swartz, "Battle Begins Over Web Photo Software," *San Francisco Chronicle*, September 12, 1996, pp. B1, B9.

CHAPTER 6

1.   Edward Rothstein, "Between the Dream and the Reality lies the Shadow. Or is it the Interface?" *New York Times*, December 11, 1995, p. C3.

2.   Stacey Richardson, quoted in Peter H. Lewis, "Pairing People Management with Project Management," *New York Times*, April 11, 1993, sec. p. 12.

3.   Barbara Kantrowitz, Andrew Cohen, and Melinda Lieu, "My Info Is NOT Your Info," *Newsweek*, July 18, 1994, p. 54.

MOTOR VEHICLES BOX

a.   Robert Shumacher, quoted in Arthur J. Cummins, "Industry Guidelines Are Considered for Vehicle Gadgets Distracting Drivers," *Wall Street Journal*, March 18, 1998, p. B4.

b.   Joshua Quittner, "Free Maps Online," *Time*, August 17, 1998, p. 80.

c.   Joseph Siano, "Exploring the Maze of New-Care Navigation Systems," *New York Times*, April 26, 1998, sec. C, p. 30.

d.   Deborah Solomon, "Roadcast Keeps Eye on Traffic," *San Francisco Chronicle*, November 19, 1998, p. B3.

e.   Richard Stepler, "Fill It Up, with RAM," *New York Times*, August 27, 1998, pp. D1, D5.

f.   Gregory L. White, "Smart Cars Sense Swerves," *Wall Street Journal*, March 5, 1999, pp. B1, B4.

g.   William J. Holstein, "Car 2004, Where Are You?" *U.S. News & World Report*, February 8, 1999, pp. 62–63.

h.   Dan McCosh, "Voice Control for Your Car," *Popular Science*, February 1999, p. 38.

i.   Gregory L. White, "Cars That Listen Promise a New Direction in Driving," *Wall Street Journal*, December 28, 1998, pp. B3, B4.

j.   "Computer on Board: Cars' Latest Add-On," *USA Today*, November 12, 1998, p. 4D.

k.   Sara Kehaulani Goo, "Steering Wheels Are Lap Desks in Scary Mobile Offices," *Wall Street Journal*, September 23, 1998, pp. B1, B4.

l.   Alex Taylor III, "A PC in Your Car? Why?" *Fortune*, September 7, 1998, pp. 112–115.

m.   Mike Snider, "Automakers Fueling Interest in Customized 'Road Theater,'" *USA Today*, January 20, 1999, p. 6D.

n.   Suzanne Kantra Kirschner, "Wired Wheels," *Popular Science*, March 1998, pp. 54–55.

SPORTS BOX

a.   Peter Teitelbaum, quoted in Gary Mihoces, "The Wide World of Future Sports," *USA Today*, May 19, 1999, pp. 1C, 2C.

b.   Steve Lohr, "Electronics Replacing Coaches' Clipboards'" *New York Times*, May 4, 1993, pp. C1, C3.

c.   Ron Kroichick, "Candid Camera," *San Francisco Chronicle*, December 11, 1996, pp. B1, B8.

d.   Matt Beer, "Sailing, Sailing Over Virtual Waves," *San Francisco Examiner*, October 18, 1998, pp. B1, B3.

e.   Andrew Ross Sorkin, "Microchips Are Latest Addition to Gear for London's Marathon," *New York Times*, March 19, 1998, p. D4.

f.   David Kushner, "Where All Lanes Are Fast Lanes: The High-Tech Bowling Alley," *New York Times*, January 7, 1999, p. D9.

g.   Sally McGrane, "Maybe an Electric Ski Would Help," *New York Times*, December 3, 1998, pp. D1, D6.

h.   Ronald Grover, "Online Sports: Cyber Fans Are Roaring," *Business Week*, June 1, 1998, p. 155.

i.   Matt Richtel, "For Fanatics, Sports Webcasts," *New York Times*, March 19, 1998, p. D9.

j.   Jon Swartz, "Cyber Sports Coverage Puts Fans in the Thick of It," *San Francisco Chronicle*, December 7, 1998, p. B3.

CHAPTER 7

1.   Thomas A. Stewart, "The Information Age in Charts," *Fortune*, April 4, 1994, pp. 75–79.

2.   Tom Mandel, in "Talking About Portables," *Wall Street Journal*, January 23, 1997, pp. B1, B6.

3.   Bart Ziegler, "IBM's Gerstner Vows Funds for Lotus in Microsoft Duel and Internet Battle," *Wall Street Journal*, January 23, 1996, p. B7.

RETAILING BOX

a.   Kevin Maney, "Will Technology Help Retail Industry Buy the Farm?" *USA Today*, May 19, 1999, p. 3B.

b.   Mary J. Cronin, "Business Secrets of the Billion-Dollar Website," *Fortune*, February 2, 1998, p. 142.

c.   Robert D. Hof, "Will Shoppers Take to Cyber Groceries?" *Business Week*, February 23, 1998, p. 110R.

d.   1998 Andersen Consulting study, cited in "Market for On-Line Supermarkets," *USA Today*, January 6, 1999, p. 1B.

e.   David Leonhardt, "The Meat and Potatoes of Online Shopping?" *Business Week*, December 7, 1998, p. 46.

f.   George Anders, "Co-Founder of Borders to Launch Online Megagrocer," *Wall Street Journal*, February 22, 1999, pp. B1, B4.

g.   Lorrie Grant, "Soon, On-Line Grocers Will Deliver the Goods to Your Door," *USA Today*, March 8, 1999, p. 1B.

h.   George Anders, "Amazon.com Buys 35% Stake of Seattle Online Grocery Firm," *Wall Street Journal*, May 18, 1999, p. B8.

CHAPTER 8

1. Michael J. Himowitz, "Web Phone Calls Made Easy," *Fortune,* November 10, 1997, p. 230.
2. David Einstein, "Tuning into the Dead via the Web," *San Francisco Chronicle,* February 10, 1998, p. C3.
3. David Einstein, "New Era Dawns as Radio Comes to the Internet," *San Francisco Chronicle,* May 18, 1995, pp. B1, B2.
4. Thomas E. Weber, "Will Video Be an Internet Start?" *Wall Street Journal,* July 17, 1997, p. B6.
5. Adapted from *The New Republic,* February 17, 1997, pp. 15–18.
6. "Where the Information Highway Is Taking Us," *San Francisco Chronicle,* March 14, 1996, p. A23.

AUCTION BOX

a. Lisa Napoli, "Taking the Fish Market into Cyberspace," *New York Times,* March 15, 1999, p. C5.
b. Martin Miller, "Sold! To the Highest Clicker," *Los Angeles Times,* November 30, 1998, pp. E1, E3.
c. Laura Bly, "Online Travel Auctions Can Be Treats but Watch Out—There Are Also Tricks," *San Jose Mercury News,* March 28, 1999, pp. 1H, 9H.
d. Robert Foff, "Independence Day," *Forbes,* February 22, 1999, pp. 166–167.
e. Mike Tucker, "Going, Going, Gone in Cyberspace," *USA Today,* June 16, 1998, p. 5E.
f. Jamie Beckett, "Rise of the Online Middlemen," *San Francisco Chronicle,* January 14, 1999, pp. B1, B4.
g. Bob Tedeschi, "As On-Line Auctions Move into Pricier Merchandise, Escrow Services Offer Those About to Be Scammed a Little Safety," *New York Times,* April 19, 1999, p. C4.
h. "Tip: Protect Yourself Before Paying for Items," *USA Today,* March 10, 1998, p. 2A.
i. Roberta Furger, "Going Once, Going Twice," *Parade Magazine,* November 29, 1998, p. 24.
j. Ken Bensinger, "The Perils of Online Auctions," *Wall Street Journal,* March 5, 1999, pp. W1, W12.

CHAPTER 9

1. Jeffrey L. Whitten and Lonnie Bentley, *Systems Analysis and Design Methods,* 4th ed. (Burr Ridge, IL: Irwin/McGraw-Hill, 1997), pp. 99, 100.
2. James O'Brien, *Introduction to Information Systems,* 8th ed. (Burr Ridge, IL: Irwin/McGraw-Hill, 1997), p. 385.
3. Penny A. Kendall, *Introduction to Systems Analysis and Design: A Structured Approach,* 3rd ed. (Burr Ridge, IL: Irwin/McGraw-Hill), p. 53.
4. Whitten/Bentley, 1997, p. 126.

MOVIES BOX

a. Peter Stack, "An Animated Future," *San Francisco Chronicle,* December 17, 1996, pp. E1, E3.
b. Peter Stack, "The Digital Divide," *San Francisco Chronicle,* May 19, 1999, p. E1.
c. Peter Stack, "Growing Demand for Computer Animators Spurs New Program at U. of Washington," *Chronicle of Higher Education,* August 7, 1998, pp. A2.
d. Iana DeBare, "New-Media Fast Track," *San Francisco Chronicle,* February 26, 1999, pp. C1, C3.
e. David Ansen and Ray Sawhill, "The New Jump Cut," *Newsweek,* September 2, 1996, pp. 64–66.
f. Eric Taub, "Riding to Rescue in the Last Scene: Saving Movies," *New York Times,* March 25, 1999, p. D11.
g. Bruce Haring, "Digitally Created Actors: Death Becomes Them," *USA Today,* June 24, 1998, p. 8D.
h. Verne G. Kopytoff, "For Actors and Agents, On-Line Links to Casting Directors," *New York Times,* December 31, 1998, p. D6.
i. Bonnie Rothman Morris, "Screenwriters Find a Toehold on Net," *New York Times,* January 14, 1999, p. D7.
j. David Hansen and Ray Sawhill, "Now at a Desktop Near You," *Newsweek,* March 15, 1999, pp. 80, 82.

CHAPTER 10

1. R. Wild, "Maximize Your Brain Power," *Men's Health,* April 1992, pp. 44–49.
2. Gene Wang, *The Programmer's Job Handbook* (New York: McGraw-Hill, 1996), p. 129.
3. Alan Freedman, *The Computer Glossary,* 6th ed. (New York: AMACOM, 1993, p. 370.

MUSIC BOX

a. Peter H. Lewis, "Play It Again, RAM," *New York Times,* November 12, 1998, pp. D1, D3.
b. Benny Evangelista, "AOL Trying to Catch Internet Music Wave," *San Francisco Chronicle,* June 2, 1999, pp. B1, B12.
c. Charles Bermant, "Musicians Tap Rich Lode of Sheet Music, Sold, and Shared," *New York Times,* April 23, 1998, p. D5.
d. Peter Malick, quoted in Charles Bermant, "Musicians and Listeners Find each Other on Web Pages," *New York Times,* August 6, 1998, p. D6.
e. Jon Pareles, "Musicians Want a Revolution Waged on the Internet," *New York Times,* March 8, 1999, pp. B1, B8.
f. Lee Gomes, "Free Tunes for Everyone!" *Wall Street Journal,* June 15, 1999, pp. B1, B4.

STOCK TRADING

a. James J. Cramer, "Yeah, Day Traders!" *Time,* May 31, 1999, p. 106.
b. Kim Clark and Margaret Mannix, "Show Me the Money!" *U.S. News & World Report,* May 24, 1999, pp. 53–57.
c. Denise Caruso, "On-Line Day Traders Are Starting to Have an Impact on a Few Big-Cap Internet Stocks in What Some Call a 'Feeding Frenzy,'" *New York Times,* December 14, 1998, p. C3.
d. Peter Schwartz, quoted in Caruso, 1998.
e. Terzah Ewing, "'Open-Outcry' Trading Faces Threats from Electronic Rivals," *Wall Street Journal,* pp. C1, C15.
f. Rebecca Buckman and Aaron Lucchetti, "Electronic Networks Threaten Trading Desks on Street," *Wall Street Journal,* December 23, 1998, pp. C1, C15.
g. Fred Vogelstein, "A Virtual Stock Market," *U.S. News & World Report,* April 26, 1999, pp. 47–48.
h. Eileen Glanton, "Will Extended Hours Benefit Small Investors?" *San Francisco Examiner,* June 6, 1999, p. B3.
i. "Net Catches Merrill Lynch, but On-Line Waters Remain Rough," editorial, *USA Today,* June 2, 1999, p. 14A.
j. Allan Sloan, "Long Live the Middleman," *Newsweek,* June 14, 1999, p. 46.

CHAPTER 11

1. Gil Gordon, cited in Sue Shellenberger, "Overwork, Low Morale Vex the Mobile Office," *Wall Street Journal,* August 17, 1994, pp. B1, B4.
2. David Greising, "Quality: How to Make It Pay," *Business Week,* August 8, 1994, pp. 54–59.
3. James O'Brien, *Management Information Systems* (Burr Ridge, IL: Irwin/McGraw-Hill, 1996, pp. 376–377.
4. *Ibid.* p. 375.
5. Robert Benfer, Jr., Louanna Furbee, and Edward Brent, Jr., quoted in Steve Weinberg, "Steve's Brain," *Columbia Journalism Review,* February 1991, pp. 50–53.

HEALTH BOX

a. April Lynch, "Bleeding Sailor Performs Self-Surgery Via E-Mail," *San Francisco Chronicle,* November 19, 1998.
b. Kate Murphy, "Telemedicine Getting a Test in Efforts to Cut Costs of Treating Prisoners," *New York Times,* June 8, 1998, p. C3.
c. Associated Press, "Dad Uses Internet to Find Wonder Drug for His Son," *San Francisco Chronicle,* May 29, 1998, p. A22.
d. Jim Hudak, quoted in Heather Green and Linda Himelstein, "A Cyber Revolt in Health Care," *Business Week*, October 19, 1998, pp. 154–156.
e. Tanya Schevitz, "Pregnant in Cyberspace," *San Francisco Chronicle,* July 19, 1998, pp. A13, A17.
f. Rick Satava, quoted in Gary Taubes, "Surgery in Cyberspace," *Discover,* December 1994, pp. 85–94.

g.   Denise Grady, "Software to Compute Women's Cancer Risk," *New York Times,* December 17, 1998, p. D9.

h.   Rita Beamish, "Computers Now Helping to Screen for Troubled Teenagers," *New York Times,* December 17, 1998, p. D9.

i.   Jamie Beckett, "Sorting Out Cybershrinks," *San Francisco Chronicle,* August 11, 1998, p. C3.

j.   Vincent Kiernan, "Using the Web, Epidemiologist Aims to Improve Public Health in Developing Nations," *Chronicle of Higher Education,* January 30, 1998, pp. A21–A22.

k.   John O'Neil, "Implanted Chip Offers Hope of Simplifying Drug Regimens," *New York Times,* February 2, 1999, p. D6.

l.   Associated Press, "Implant Transmits Brain Signals Directly to Computer," *New York Times,* October 22, 1998, p. G9.

JOURNALISM BOX

a.   Burt Ziegler, Thomas E. Weber, and Michael W. Miller, "Wildfire Transforms the Global Village," *Wall Street Journal,* September 11, 1998, pp. B1, B11.

b.   Lisa Napoli, "The Post-Lewinsky Winner Is the Web," *New York Times,* September 28, 1998, p. C7.

c.   Nielsen Media Research study, reported in Mike Snider, "Wired Homes Watch 15% Less Television," *USA Today,* August 13, 1998, p. 1A.

d.   America Online/Roper Starch Cyberstudy, reported in "Study Says Web Eats into TV Time," *San Francisco Chronicle,* December 7, 1998, p. B2; reprinted from *Hollywood Reporter.*

e.   Walter Mossberg, "To Be a Mass Medium, the Web Must Be Freed from the PC," *Wall Street Journal,* November 5, 1998, p. B1.

f.   Elizabeth Weise, "Net Pushes the Pace of News," *USA Today,* January 28, 1998, p. 6D.

g.   Ellen Goodman, "First Online War Hot-Links Irony to Disaster," *San Jose Mercury News,* April 11, 1999, p. 4c; reprinted from *Boston Globe.*

h.   Charles Burress, "Kosovo Teen E-Mails Her Diary to the World," *San Francisco Chronicle,* March 25, 1999, p. A14.

i.   Dan Gilmor, "Online Threat to Print Journalism Will Have Consequences," *San Jose Mercury News,* March 28, 1999, pp. 1E, 6E.

j.   Bruce Haring, "All the News That Fits," *USA Today,* October 21, 1998, p. 4D.

CHAPTER 12

1.   Doug Rowan, Quoted in Ronald B. Lieber, "Picture This: Bill Gates Dominating the Wide World of Digital Contents," *Fortune,* December 11, 1995, p. 38.

2.   *Ibid.*

3.   Wendy Bounds, "Bill Gates Owns Otto Bettman's Lifework," *Wall Street Journal,* January 17, 1996, pp. B1, B2.

4.   Paul Saffo, quoted in Steve Lohr, "Huge Photo Archive Bought by Software Billionaire Gates," *New York Times,* October 11, 1995, pp. A1, C5.

5.   Mike Snider and Kevin Maney, "Patience Is a Plus as System Keeps Evolving," *USA Today,* February 16, 1996, pp. 1D, 2D.

6.   James A. Larson, *Database Directories* (Upper Saddle River, NJ: Prentice Hall PTR, 1995).

7.   *Ibid.*

8.   Jonathan Berry, John Verity, Kathleen Kerwin, and Gail DeGeorge, "Database Marketing," *Business Week,* September 5, 1994, pp. 56–62.

9.   Sara Reese Hedberg, "The Data Gold Rush," *Byte,* October 1995, pp. 83–88.

10.   Cheryl D. Krivda, "Data-Mining Dynamite," *Byte,* October 1994, pp. 97–103.

11.   Karen Watterson, "A Data Miner's Tools," *Byte,* October 1995, pp. 91–96.

12.   *Ibid.*

13.   *Ibid.*

14.   *Ibid.*

15.   Richard Lamm, quoted in Christopher J. Feola, "The Nexis Nightmare," *American Journalism Review,* July/August, 1994, pp. 39–42.

16.   *Ibid.*

17.   Penny Williams, "Database Dangers," *Quill,* July/August 1994, pp. 37–38.

18.   Lynn Davis, quoted in Williams, 1994.

19.   Associated Press, "Many Companies Are Willing to Give a Cat a Little Credit," *San Francisco Chronicle,* January 8, 1994, p. C1.

20.   Jeffrey Rothfelder, "What Happened to Privacy?" *New York Times,* April 13, 1993, p. A15.

21.   Ken Hoover, "Prisoner's Long-Distance Victims," *San Francisco Chronicle,* June 1, 1993, pp. A1, A6.

22.   Erik Larson, quoted in Martin J. Smith, "Marketers Want to Know Your Secrets," *San Francisco Examiner,* November 21, 1993, pp. E3, E8.

23.   Erik Larson, quoted in Martin J. Smith, Tactics for Evading Nosy Marketers, *San Francisco Examiner,* November 21, 1993, p. E3.

EDUCATION BOX

a.   Campus Computing Project 1997 survey, reported in Lisa Guernsey, "E-Mail Is Now Used in a Third of College Courses, Survey Finds," *Chronicle of Higher Education,* October 17, 1997, p. A30.

b.   Edward C. Baig, "A Little High Tech Goes a Long Way," *Business Week,* November 10, 1997, p. 154E10.

c.   Student Monitor LLC, cited in Danielle Sessa, "For College Students, Web Offers a Lesson in Discounts," *Wall Street Journal,* January 21, 1999, p. B7.

d.   Tom Harris, quoted in Tina Kelley, "Campuses Are Turning to Laptops for Students," *New York Times,* April 16, 1998, p. D7.

e.   U.S. Department of Education, cited in Steve Rhodes, "Classrooms with Class—and Possibly Espresso Machines," *Newsweek,* December 14, 1998, p. 20.

f.   *Does It Compute?,* study by Harold Wenglinsky, reported in Ethan Bronner, "Computers Help Math Learning, Study Finds," *New York Times,* September 30, 1998, p. A16.

g.   Dulcie Leimbach, "Encouraging Creativity, Without the Mess," *New York Times,* November 12, 1998, p. D12.

h.   Kelly McCollum, "Web Site Lets Thousands of Schoolchildren Follow Research on Albatross," *Chronicle of Higher Education,* February 13, 1998, p. A32.

i.   Kelly McCollum, "High School Students Use Web Intelligently for Research, Study Finds," *Chronicle of Higher Education,* December 4, 1998, p. A25.

j.   Kelly McCollum, "How a Computer Learns to Grade Essays," *Chronicle of Higher Education,* September 4, 1998, pp. A37–A38.

k.   William H. Honan, "High Tech Comes to the Classroom," *New York Times,* January 27, 1999, p. A22.

l.   Nanette Asimov, "Home-Schoolers Plug into the Internet for Resources," *San Francisco Chronicle,* January 29, 1999, pp. A1, A15.

m.   Mary Beth Marklein, "Distance Learning Takes a Gigantic Leap Forward," *USA Today,* June 4, 1998, pp. 1D, 2D.

n.   Goldie Blumenstyk, "Leading Community Colleges Go National with New Distance-Learning Network," *Chronicle of Higher Education,* July 10, 1998, pp. A16–A17.

o.   Rebecca Quick, "Software Seeks to Breathe Life into Corporate Training Classes," *Wall Street Journal,* August 6, 1998, p. B8.

p.   Bruce Weber, "Notes from Cyberclass," *New York Times,* January 3, 1999, sec. 4A, pp. 15, 46.

CHAPTER 13

1.   *Business Week,* December 9, 1996, p. 148.

2.   *Ibid.*

3.   John Villanil-Casanova and Louis Molina, *An Introductive Guide to Multimedia* (Indianapolis: Que Education and Training, Macmillan, 1996), p. 8.

4.   Michael Waldholz, "Computer 'Brain' Outperforms Doctors Diagnosing Heart Attack Patients," *Wall Street Journal,* December 2, 1991, p. B78.

5.   Otis Port, "A Neural Net to Snag Cancer," *Business Week,* March 13, 1995, p. 95.

6. Judith Anne Gunther, "An Encounter with AI," *Popular Science,* June 1994, pp. 90–93.

7. William A. Wallace, *Ethics in Modeling* (New York: Elsevier Science, Inc.: 1994).

8. *Time,* 1996.

9. Denise Caruso, "Virtual-World Users Put Themselves in a Sort of Electronic Puppet Show," *New York Times,* July 10, 1995, p. C5.

SCIENCE BOX

a. Vincent Kiernan, "Intent-Based 'Collaboratories' Help Scientists Work Together," *Chronicle of Higher Education,* March 12, 1999, pp. A22–A23.

b. Dan Wertheimer, quoted in Henry Fountain, "Download Data, in Search of Intelligent Life," *New York Times,* December 8, 1998, p. D3.

c. Kelly McCollum, "Berkeley Astronomers Enlist Internet Users to Seek Alien Life," *Chronicle of Higher Education,* December 11, 1998, p. A40.

d. Frank Vizard, "In Search of Cleopatra's Palace," *Popular Science,* May 1999, pp. 78–81.

e. David L. Wheeler, "Archaeologists Use Technology to Avoid Invasive Excavations," *Chronicle of Higher Education,* November 30, 1998, pp. A13–A14.

f. Mindy Sink, "Fading Indian Rock Art Saved, at Least in Database," *New York Times,* October 1, 1998, p. D10.

g. Sharon Begly, "Secrets of the Vase's Art," *Newsweek,* May 24, 1999, pp. 64–66.

h. Sreenath Sreenivasan, "Environmental Issues Are Clarified," *New York Times,* October 27, 1997, p. C6.

i. Alex Barnum, "Finding Polluters Close to Home," *San Francisco Chronicle,* April 21, 1998, p. C3.

HOME-BASED WORK BOX

a. Larry Slonaker, "Entrepreneur Trades Software for Soft Blankets," *San Jose Mercury News,* October 27, 1996, pp. 1E, 3E.

b. U.S. News/Bozell poll, reported in Amy Saltzman, "You, Inc.," *U.S. News & World Report,* October 28, 1996, pp. 66–79.

c. Study by Kathryn Stafford, Barbara R, Rowe, and George W. Haynes, reported in Eleena de Lisser and Dan Morse, "More Men Work at Home Than Women, Study Shows," *Wall Street Journal,* May 18, 1999, p. B2.

d. Study by International Data Corp., reported in de Lisser and Morse, 1999.

e. Stuart Weiss, "Will Working at Home Work for You?" *Business Week,* August 19, 1996, p. 84E8.

f. Jack Niles, cited in Sue Shellenberger, "Telecommuters Might Change Neighborhoods," *San Francisco Sunday Examiner & Chronicle,* May 24, 1998, p. CL17.

g. Kensington Telecommuting Survey, reported in Bob Weinstein, "How One Man Made Shift to Telecommuting," *San Francisco Sunday Examiner & Chronicle,* June 28, 1998, p. CL27.

h. Ken Scotch, quoted in Weinstein, 1998.

i. Peter Sinton, "Good Sites for Tiny Firms," *San Francisco Chronicle,* June 23, 1999, p. D3.

CHAPTER 14

1. Ethics Officer Association and American Society of Chartered Life Underwriters and Chartered Financial Consultants, in Ilana De Bare, "Office Ethics Confusion," *San Francisco Chronicle.*

2. David Edelson, "What Price Superhighway Information?" (letter), *New York Times,* January 16, 1994, p. 16.

3. William Safire, "Art vs. Artifice," *New York Times,* January 3, 1994, p. A11.

4. Hans Fantel, "Sinatra's 'Duets': Music Recording or Wizardry?" *New York Times,* January 1, 1994, p. 13.

5. Jonathan Alter, "When Photographs Lie," *Newsweek,* July 30, 1990, pp. 44–45.

6. Fred Ritchlin, quoted in Alter, 1990.

7. Kathleen O'Toole, "High Tech TVs, Computers Blur Line Between Artificial, Real," *Stanford Observer,* November–December 1992, p. 8.

8. Yahoo!, cited in Del Jones, "Cyber-Porn Poses Workplace Threat," *USA Today,* November 27, 1995, p. 1B.

9. Pamela Mendels, "Filter Blocks Access to Hate Speech on Internet," *New York Times,* November 28, 1998, p. A2-A5.

10. Associated Press, "Robot Sent to Disarm Bomb Goes Wild in San Francisco," *New York Times,* August 28, 1993, p. 7.

11. Joseph F. Sullivan, "A Computer Glitch Causes Bumpy Starts in a Newark School," *New York Times,* September 19, 1991, p. A25.

12. Suzanne P. Weisband and Seymour E. Goodman, "Subduing Software Pirates," *Technology Review,* October 1993, pp. 31–33.

13. Donald Parker, quoted in William M. Carley, "Rigging Computers for Fraud or Malice Is Often an Inside Job," *Wall Street Journal,* August 27, 1992, pp. A1, A4.

14. The Enterprise Technology Center, cited in "Disaster Avoidance and Recovery Is Growing Business Priority," special advertising supplement in *LAN Magazine,* November 1992, p. SS3.

15. Brian Nadel, "Power to the PC," *PC Magazine,* April 26, 1994, pp. 114–183.

16. Amy Harmon, "Sad, Lonely World Discovered in Cyberspace," *New York Times,* April 1999.

17. David Rogers, "Senate Votes 90–10 to Support Broad Ban on Internet Gambling, Virtual Casinos," *New York Times,* July 24, 1998, p. B8.

18. Jonathan Marshall, "Some Say High-Tech Boom Is Actually a Bust," *San Francisco Chronicle,* July 10, 1995, pp. A1, A4.

19. Steven Levy, quoted in Marshall, 1995.

20. STB Accounting Systems 1992 survey, reported in Jones, 1995.

21. Neil Postman, quoted in Evenson, 1994.

22. Rifkin, 1995.

23. Louis Uchitelle, "It's a Slow-Growth Economy, Stupid," *New York Times,* March 17, 1996, sec. 4, pp. 1, 5.

24. Paul Krugman, "Long-Term Riches, Short-Term Pain," *New York Times,* September 25, 1994, sec. 3, p. 9.

25. Beth Belton, "Degree-Based Earnings Gap Grows Quickly," *USA Today,* February 16, 1996, p. 1B.

26. Alan Kreuger, quoted in LynNell Hancock, Pat Wingert, Patricia King, Debra Rosenberg, and Allison Samules, "The Haves and the Have Nots," *Newsweek,* February 27, 1995, pp. 50–52.

27. Terry Bynum, quoted in Lawrence Hardy, "Tapping into New Ethical Quandaries," *USA Today,* August 1, 1995, p. 6D.

28. Tony Ruthkowski, quoted in Schnaidt, 1993.

BANKING BOX

a. Brian Bremner, Joan Warner, and Jonathan Ford, "Hold It Right There, Citibank," *Business Week,* March 25, 1996, p. 176.

b. Adam Zagorin, "Cashless, Not Bankless," *Time,* September 23, 1996, p. 52.

c. Paul Saffo, quoted in Jared Sandberg, "CyberCash Lowers Barriers to Small Transactions at Internet Storefronts," *Wall Street Journal,* September 30, 1996, p. B6.

d. Stewart Alsop, "The First Powerhouse Bank of the Virtual World," *Fortune,* September 7, 1998, pp. 159–160.

e. Christine Dugas, "Direct Deposit Wins for Safety, Speed," *USA Today,* January 25, 1999, p. 5B.

f. Arthur M. Louis, "The Check's on the Net," *San Francisco Chronicle,* June 22, 1999, pp. C1, C3.

g. Christine Dugas, "Bank Deal Puts Stamp on Bill Delivery Online," *USA Today,* June 24, 1999, p. 1B.

h. Martha Brannigan, "Bill Payments Via the Internet Get a Big Boost," *Wall Street Journal,* January 28, 1999, pp. B1, B14.

i. Rebecca Buckman, "Internet Brokerage Firms Break into Banking," *Wall Street Journal,* July 2, 1998, pp. C1, C21.

j. William Gurley, "Banking in the New Millennium," *Fortune,* June 7, 1999, p. 194.

k. Andrew Osterland, "Click Here for Coverage," *Business Week,* June 1, 1998, p. 162.

CREDITS

PHOTOS

Page 1.3 Gerd Ludwig *1.4 (top)* PhotoEdit/Mark Richards *(bottom)* Kaluzny/Thatcher/Tony Stone Images *1.6 (left)* Wayne R. Bilenduke/Tony Stone Images/Wayne R. Bilenduke *(right)* PhotoEdit/David Young-Wolff *1.8* Courtesy of International Business Machines Corporation. Unauthorized use not permitted. *1.9 (top)* Courtesy of International Business Machines Corporation. Unauthorized use not permitted. *(bottom)* Hewlett-Packard *1.10 (bottom)* The Stock Market/Don Mason *1.11 (top left)* Epson *(bottom left)* © John S. Reid *(top and bottom right)* © Tom Pantages *1.12 (top)* PhotoEdit/© Tony Freeman *1.12 (bottom)* Courtesy of Microsoft Corporation *1.13* Tony O'Brien *1.14 (top left)* Photophile/© Tom Tracy *(top right)* Courtesy of Sun Microsystems *(bottom left)* © R. Ian Lloyd *(bottom right)* © Fujifotos/The Image Works *1.15 (top left)* Silicon Valley, Inc. *(middle left)* Sony *(bottom left)* Toshiba *(top right)* U.S. Robotics *(middle right)* Sharp Electronics *(bottom right)* Courtesy of International Business Machines Corporation. Unauthorized use not permitted. *1.16 (a–c, f)* Courtesy of International Business Machines Corporation. Unauthorized use not permitted. *(d–e)* Smithsonian Institution *1.17 (top)* AP/Wide World Photos, Inc./Christof Stacke *(bottom)* Unisys Archives *1.19* AP/Wide World Photos, Inc./Barry Sweet *1.20 (top)* AP/Wide World Photos, Inc./Seiko Instruments, Inc. *(bottom)* AP/Wide World Photos, Inc./Eric Draper *1.24* PhotoEdit/© Mark Richards *2.2* © Peter Menzel, for *One Digital Day* *2.3* Photo Researchers, Inc./© Science Photo Library *2.6* Network Aspen/© Jeffrey Aaronaon *2.9* Courtesy of International Business Machines Corporation. Unauthorized use not permitted. *2.10 (left)* © J. Kyle Keener *(top right)* Intel Corp. *2.14* Contact Press Images/© Dilip Mehta *2.17* © Munshi Ahmed *2.19 (top)* Will & Deni McIntyre/Photo Researchers, Inc. *(bottom)* © Tom Pantages *2.25 (left)* © John S. Reid *(right)* © Tom Pantages *2.26* Tony Stone Images/© Robert E. Daemmrich *3.6 (top)* AP/Wide World Photos, Inc. /Bill Sikes *(bottom left)* Stock Boston/© Bob Daemmrich *(bottom right)* Rainbow/© Coco McCoy *(lower right)* Stock Boston/ © Owen Franken *3.7 (top left)* Courtesy of International Business Machines Corporation. Unauthorized use not permitted. *(top middle)* Rainbow/© Coco McCoy *(top right)* © Tom Pantages *(bottom left)* The Image Works/© Esbin-Anderson *(bottom right)* © John S. Reid *3.8* © Kerry T. Givens/Bruce Coleman, Inc. *3.9* © Davis Barber/PhotoEdit *3.10 (top)* The Image Works/© L. Mulvehill *(bottom left)* PhotoEdit/ © Cindy Charles *(bottom left)* PhotoEdit/© Michael Newman *3.11 (left)* Courtesy of International Business Machines Corporation. Unauthorized use not permitted. *(right)* 3Com Corp. 3Com and the 3Com logo are registered trademarks. Palm III™ and the Palm III™ logo are trademarks of Palm Computing, Inc., 3Com Corporation or its subsidiaries *3.12 (top left)* Stock Boston/© Charles Gupton *(top right)* Photo Researchers, Inc./© St. Bartholomew's Hospital/SPL *(bottom left)* Stock Boston/Tim Barnwell *(bottom right)* © Melissa Farlow *3.13* Check-Mate Electronics *3.14 (top left)* Stock Market/© LWA-Stephen Weistead *(top right)* Hayes *(bottom left)* Rainbow/© Dan McCoy *(bottom right)* PhotoEdit/© Richard Lord *3.15 (top)* Wildlight Photo Agency/© Philip Quirk *(middle)* Tony Stone Images/© Chris Honeywell *(bottom)* © John S. Reid *3.18* Rainbow/© Dan McCoy *3.21* © Gary Braasch *3.24 (top and bottom)* PhotoEdit/© Michael Newman *3.26 (left)* Xerox ColorgrafX Systems *(right)* Rainbow/© Dan McCoy *3.27* Stock Market/© Don Mason *3.29 (top left and top right)* Planar Systems, Inc. *(bottom)* ViewSonic Corp. *3.33 (left)* Contact Press Images/© Greg Girgard *(right)* Stock Boston/© Rob Crandell *3.34* PhotoEdit/ © Young-Wolff *3.35* AP/Wide World Photos, Inc. /Michael Schmelling *3.36 (left)* AP/Wide World Photos, Inc. /John Rottet *(right)* PhotoEdit/© Myrleen Cate *4.3* Charles O'Rear *4.8* Courtesy of International Business Machines Corporation. Unauthorized use not permitted. *4.9 (left)* © Tom Pantages *(right)* Sun Images *4.12* Courtesy of International Business Machines Corporation. Unauthorized use not permitted. *4.15 (left and right)* © Charles O'Rear *4.16 (top left)* © John S. Reid *(right)* © Coco McCoy/Rainbow *(bottom left)* Rainbow/© Dan McCoy *4.17* Photo Researchers, Inc./© Jerry Mason/Science Photo Library *4.18* Courtesy of International Business Machines Corporation. Unauthorized use not permitted. *4.20 (left)* Toshiba *(right)* Courtesy of International Business Machines Corporation. Unauthorized use not permitted. *4.21* The Image Works/© Greenlar *4.22* Imation *4.26* Courtesy of International Business Machines Corporation. Unauthorized use not permitted. *5.7* © Leonard Lueras *5.15* © Lori Adamski-Peck *5.18 (all on left)* Waggener Erdstrom/Marti Lucich for Microsoft *(bottom right)* Courtesy of International Business Machines Corporation. Unauthorized use not permitted. *6.7* © Jay Dickman *6.16* Imation *6.19* © Torin Boyd *6.26 (left)* Autodesk *(right)* Courtesy of International Business Machines Corporation. Unauthorized use not permitted. *6.31* © Joel Sartore *6.33* © Nick Kelsh *7.3* © John S. Reid *7.5 (top)* Hayes *(bottom)* Multitech Systems *7.9 (top left, top right, bottom right)* AT&T *(bottom left)* U.S. Sprint *7.12 (top)* Rainbow/© Hank Morgan *(bottom)* PhotoEdit/© Mark Richards *7.15 (middle and bottom)* Nokia *7.21* Seaworld, Inc./© Bob Couey *7.33 (top)* Visum/© Rudi Meisal *(bottom)* Rainbow/© Larry Mulvehill *7.36 (top and bottom left)* Contact Press/© Lori Grinker *(bottom right)* © Rick Allen, Cindy Burnham/Nautilus Productions *7.38 (top)* PhotoEdit, © Amy C. Etra *(bottom)* Contact Press/© Dilip Mehta *8.6* © Héctor Mendez-Caratini *9.9, 9.11, 9.22, 9.23, 9.26* PhotoDisc, Inc. *9.20* © James Balog *10.9* © Shelly Katz *10.11* Naval Surface Warfare Center *10.22* © David Modell *10.29* © Nick Kelsh *11.2* Network Aspen/© Jeffrey Aaronson *11.3* © Lori Adamson-Peck *11.15* © Sarah Leen *11.16* © Jeffrey Morgan *11.21* Matrix/© Karen Kasmauski *12.4* AP/Wide World Photos, Inc. *12.5* © Joel Sartore *12.8* © Fritz Hoffmann *12.10* © Andy Levin *12.20* © Charles O'Rear *12.25* © Denise Rocco *12.26* © Misha Erwitt *12.28* © Ricki Rosen *13.2* © David Young-Wolff/PhotoEdit *13.4* © Gary Braasch *13.10* © Wes Skiles *13.12 (top left)* UC Berkeley/© Denise Rocco *(top right)* PhotoEdit/© Mark Richards *(middle left)* © Misha Erwitt *(middle right)* Rainbow/© Hank Morgan *(bottom right)* Stock Boston/© Spencer Grant *13.13* The Image Works/© Fujifotos *13.20* Photo Researchers, Inc./© Will and Deni McIntyre *13.22* PhotoDisc, Inc. *13.24 (top left)* Visum/© Rudi Meisel *(top right)* © Charles Gupton *(bottom left)* © Karen Kasmauski *(bottom right)* © Peter Menzel *13.26* © Lois Lammerhuber *13.28* © Kaku Karita *14.2* San Jose Mercury News/© Barry Gutierrez *14.12* Elastic Reality, Inc. *14.19* The Image Works/© Fujifotos *14.24* © J. Kyle Keener *14.25* The Image Works/© Hironori Miyata/Fujifotos *14.26* The Image Works/ © Yoshida-Fujifotos *14.33* Wildlight Photo Agency/© Philip Quirk *14.34* © Barry Lewis *14.36* © Theo Westenberger

ART

Page 2.22–2.23 Adapted from *Teach Yourself Computers and the Internet*, 1998, p. 76 *3.4–3.5* Adapted from *Teach Yourself Computers and the Internet*, 1998, pp. 28–29 *7.8* Adapted from "Downloading the Times . . . 10 Times," *New York Times*, April 28, 1999 *7.14* Adapted from Jared Schneidman, "How It Works," *Wall Street Journal*, Feb. 11, 1994, p. R5, and *Popular Science* *7.17* Adapted from *Byte*, Sept. 9, 1996, p. 69 *7.21* *San Jose Mercury News* *7.24* Adapted from Alan Freedman, *The Computer Desktop Encyclopedia*, New York, AMACOM, 1996, p. 617 *8.11* Adapted from Brenden P. Kehoe, *Zen and the Art of the Internet*, Englewood Cliffs, Prentice Hall–PTR, 1996, pp. 203-208 *8.16–8.19* Adapted from "A Field Guide to Web Searches," *New York Times,* September 3, 1998   *8.23* Adapted from Howard Bryany and Wes Killingbeck, "Net-phones Hit Sound Barriers," *San Jose Mercury News,* August 3, 1997, p. 1D   *9.6* Adapted from Penny A. Kendall, *Introduction to Systems Analysis and Design: A Structured Approach,* 3rd edition, Burr Ridge, IL: Irwin/McGraw-Hill, 1996, p. 8   *9.7* Adapted from Penny A. Kendall, *Introduction to Systems Analysis and Design: A Structured Approach,* 3rd edition, Burr Ridge, IL: Irwin/McGraw-Hill, 1996, p. 21   *9.8 (left)* Adapted from Penny A. Kendall, *Introduction to Systems Analysis and Design: A Structured Approach,* 3rd edition, Burr Ridge, IL: Irwin/McGraw-Hill, 1996, p. 30   *(right)* Whitten/Bentley, *Systems Analysis and Design Methods,* Burr Ridge, IL: Irwin/McGraw-Hill, 1997, p. 21   *9.17* Adapted from Penny A. Kendall, *Introduction to Systems Analysis and Design: A Structured Approach,* 3rd edition, Burr Ridge, IL: Irwin/McGraw-Hill, 1996, p. 171   *10.6* Adapted from Elizabeth A. Dickson, *Computer Programming Design,* Burr Ridge, IL: Irwin/McGraw-Hill, 1996, pp. 30–31   *11.6 Management Information Systems,* Burr Ridge, IL: Irwin/McGraw-Hill, 1996, p. 314   *11.7 Management Information Systems,* Burr Ridge, IL: Irwin/McGraw-Hill, 1996, p. 319   *12.23* Adapted from "Data Mining Process," illustrated by Victor Grad, p. 84, in Sara Reese Hedberg, "The Data Gold Rush," *Byte,* Oct. 1995, pp. 83–88   *12.25* Denise Rocco   *12.26* Misha Erwitt   *12.28* Ricki Rosen   *13.1* PhotoEdit/David Young-Wolff   *13.4* Gary Braasch

TEXT

Page 5.18 (box) Company Reports, "The Mother of All Software Projects," in *Business Week,* Feb. 22, 1999, 9.69   *7.41–7.42* Copyright, August 10, 1998, *U.S. News and World Report* (visit us at our Web site at www.usnews.com for additional information   *8.5* April Lynch © *San Francisco Chronicle,* reprinted with permission   *8.19 (bottom box)* Reprinted with permission of Wai-Tai Kwok, president, Dae Interactive Marketing, San Francisco   *13.16 (box)* From *Online Learning News,* Dec. 22, 1998, Vol. 1, No. 38, © Lakewood Publications, Inc. Distributed by MessageMedia, Inc. (www.messagemedia.com)   *13.17 (box)* From Jeffrey R. Young, "Using Computers to Study the Complexities of Human Society," *The Chronicle of Higher Education,* July 24, 1998, p. A17   *14.2 (box)* From Richard Scheinen, "Questions of Ethics on Agenda at the Tech," Oct. 11, 1998, *San Jose Mercury News,* p. 1A   *14.6 (box)* From Robert Kuttner, "The U.S. Could Use a Dose of Europe's Privacy Medicine," *Business Week,* Nov. 16, 1998, p. 22   *14.9 (box)* From Martin J. Moylan, "Software in Gray and Black," Nov. 11, 1998, *San Jose Mercury News,* p. F1, data from the Software Publishers Association   *14.10 (box)* From Benny Evangelista, "Download That Tune—It's Web Music," Dec. 3, 1998, *San Francisco Chronicle,* p. A1 *14.27 (box)* From Geoffrey Smith, "Silicon Eyes," Oct. 12, 1998, *Business Week,* p. 95

INDEX

Boldface numbers indicate pages on which key terms are defined.